MEDICAL STAFF SUPPORT

Hospital Telephone Directory 2004 Edition

MEDICAL STAFF SUPPORT

A national ready reference and index listing over 7,000 US Hospitals and Medical Centers. Alphabetical – Geographical.

HENRY A. ROSE, Editor

All information published herein is gathered from sources which are considered reliable by the editors. We have tried our best to record all the information correctly, any errors or omissions will be corrected in a subsequent edition.

In most cases, the hospitals have furnished or verified their own data, thus assuring a high degree of accuracy.

The publisher does not assume responsibility for errors, omissions, or interpretations.

Published by:

UNICOL, Inc.
655 N.W. 128th Street, P.O. Box 1690
Miami, Florida 33168
PHONE: (305) 769-1808
FAX: (305) 769-1817
WEB: unicol-publishing.com

Lincoln County Medical Center
1000 East Cherry St.
Troy, Missouri 63379

The hospital logo is a trademark of SIA.

Hospital Telephone Directory
2004 Edition

*A complete name and address book of
Hospitals in the U.S.A.*

Published by:

UNICOL, Inc.
655 N.W. 128th Street, P.O. Box 1690
Miami, Florida 33168
PHONE: (305) 769-1808
FAX: (305) 769-1817
WEB: unicol-publishing.com

ISBN 1-880973-34-0

© Copyright 2004 by UNICOL, Inc.

It is illegal under Federal Copyright Law (17 USC 101 et al) to reproduce this publication or any portion of its contents without the publisher's permission.

This publication may not be copied, in whole or in part, for use as a mailing list or for incorporation into a list available for rent, exchange, or sale to another. UNICOL, Inc. retains exclusive right to rent or exchange this list. All rights reserved. No part of this work covered by the copyright hereon may be reproduced, stored in a retrieval system or transmitted in any form or by any means electronic, mechanical, photocopying, recording or otherwise without permission of UNICOL, Inc.

UNICOL, Inc. will pay a reward of up to $1,000 for actionable evidence of illegal use, copying, or faxing. Contact our legal department to report abuses. Confidentiality assured.

*Printed in the U.S.A.
Manufactured in the U.S.A.*

Product Stock #200-7

Federal ID Number 65-0288668

Preface

The HOSPITAL TELEPHONE DIRECTORY is a quick reference, name, address and telephone number book with over 7,000 listings. Printed in large size BOLD PRINT for easy reading and use. The HOSPITAL TELEPHONE DIRECTORY is divided into two sections, alphabetical and geographical. The alphabetical index will be of great value when only the hospital name is known and not the exact location. The hospitals are arranged in alphabetical sequence in their respective cities.

Listed are the Hospitals and Medical Centers public, private, for profit, not for profit, federal, state, county, city, general, special, rehabilitation, psychiatric, children's, etc. Alabama thru Wyoming.

The publisher assumes no responsibility or liability for unintentional errors or omissions. The information contained in this phone book is believed to be from reliable sources, however, we do not guarantee nor warranty their accuracy.

The most current information available at the time of publication.

Published by:

UNICOL, Inc.
655 N.W. 128th Street, P.O. Box 1690
Miami, Florida 33168
PHONE: (305) 769-1808
FAX: (305) 769-1817
WEB: unicol-publishing.com

STATE HOSPITAL ASSOCIATIONS

Alabama
Alabama Hospital Association
http://www.alaha.org

Alaska
Alaska State Hospitals & Nursing Home Association
http://www.ashnha.com

Arizona
Arizona Hospital and Healthcare Association
http://www.azhha.org

Arkansas
Arkansas Hospital Association
http://www.arkhospitals.org

California
California Health Care Association
http://www.calhealth.org

Colorado
Colorado Hospital Association
http://www.cha.com

Connecticut
Connecticut Hospital Association
http://www.chime.org

Delaware
Association of Delaware Hospitals
http://www.deha.org

District of Columbia
District of Columbia Hospital Association
http://www.dcha.org

Florida
Florida Hospital Association
http://www.fha.org

Georgia
Georgia Hospital Association
http://www.gha.org

STATE HOSPITAL ASSOCIATIONS

Hawaii
Healthcare Association of Hawaii
http://www.hah.org

Idaho
Idaho Hospital Association
http://www.teamiha.org

Illinois
Illinois Hospital & Health Systems Association
http://www.ihatoday.org

Indiana
Indiana Hospital & Health Association
http://www.inhha.org

Iowa
Iowa Hospital Association Online
http://www.ihaonline.org

Kansas
Kansas Hospital Association
http://www.kha-net.org

Kentucky
Kentucky Hospital Association
http://www.kyha.com

Louisiana
Louisiana Hospital Association
http://www.lhaonline.org

Maine
Maine Hospital Association
http://www.themha.org

Maryland
The Association of Maryland Hospitals & Health Systems
http://www.mdhospitals.org

Massachusetts
Massachusetts Hospital Association
http://www.mhalink.org

STATE HOSPITAL ASSOCIATIONS

Michigan
Michigan Hospital Association
http://www.mha.org

Minnesota
Minnesota Hospital and Healthcare Partnership
http://www/mnhospitals.org

Mississippi
Mississippi Hospital Association
http://www.mhanet.org

Missouri
Missouri Hospital Association
http://web.mhanet.com

Montana
Montana Hospital Association
http://www.mtha.org

Nebraska
Nebraska Hospital Association
http://www.nahhsnet.org

Nevada
Nevada Hospital Association
http://www.nvha.net

New Hampshire
New Hampshire Hospital Association
http://www.nhha.org

New Jersey
New Jersey Hospital Association
http://www.njha.com

New Mexico
New Mexico Hospitals & Health Systems Association
http://www.nmhhsa.org

New York
Healthcare Association of New York State
http://www.hanys.org

STATE HOSPITAL ASSOCIATIONS

North Carolina
North Carolina Hospital Association
http://www.ncha.org

North Dakota
North Dakota Healthcare Association
http://www.ndha.org

Ohio
Ohio Hospital Association
http://www.ohanet.org

Oklahoma
Oklahoma Hospital Association
http://www.okoha.com

Oregon
Oregon Association of Hospitals and Health Systems
http://www.oahhs.org

Pennsylvania
Hospital & Healthsystem Association of Pennsylvania
http://www.HAP2000.org

Puerto Rico
Puerto Rico Hospital Association
http://www.asociacionhosppr.org

Rhode Island
Hospital Association of Rhode Island
http://www.hari.org

South Carolina
South Carolina Hospital Association
http://www.scha.org

South Dakota
South Dakota Association of Healthcare Organizations
http://www.sdaho.org

Tennessee
Tennessee Hospital Association
http://www.tha.com

STATE HOSPITAL ASSOCIATIONS

Texas
Texas Hospital Association
http://www.thaonline.org

Utah
Utah Hospitals & Health Systems Association
http://www.uha-utah.org

Vermont
Vermont Association of Hospitals and Health Systems
http://www.vahhs.org

Virginia
Virginia Hospital & Healthcare Association
http://www.vhha.com

Washington
Washington State Hospital Association
http://www.wsha.org

West Virginia
West Virginia Hospital Association
http://www.wvha.com

Wisconsin
Wisconsin Health and Hospital Association
http://www.wha.org

Wyoming
Wyoming Hospital Association
http://www.wyohospitals.com

Area Codes – Alphabetically by Location

205	Alabama	404	Georgia	763	Minnesota	610	Pennsylvania
251	Alabama	470	Georgia	952	Minnesota	717	Pennsylvania
256	Alabama	478	Georgia	228	Mississippi	724	Pennsylvania
334	Alabama	678	Georgia	601	Mississippi	814	Pennsylvania
907	Alaska	706	Georgia	662	Mississippi	835	Pennsylvania
403	Alberta	770	Georgia	314	Missouri	878	Pennsylvania
780	Alberta	912	Georgia	417	Missouri	787	Puerto Rico
684	American Samoa	473	Grenada	573	Missouri	939	Puerto Rico
264	Anguilla	671	Guam	636	Missouri	418	Quebec
268	Antigua and Barbuda	808	Hawaii	660	Missouri	438	Quebec
480	Arizona	208	Idaho	816	Missouri	450	Quebec
520	Arizona	217	Illinois	406	Montana	514	Quebec
602	Arizona	224	Illinois	664	Montserrat	819	Quebec
623	Arizona	309	Illinois	308	Nebraska	401	Rhode Island
928	Arizona	312	Illinois	402	Nebraska	306	Saskatchewan
479	Arkansas	331	Illinois	702	Nevada	803	South Carolina
501	Arkansas	464	Illinois	775	Nevada	843	South Carolina
870	Arkansas	618	Illinois	506	New Brunswick	864	South Carolina
242	Bahamas	630	Illinois	603	New Hampshire	605	South Dakota
246	Barbados	708	Illinois	201	New Jersey	869	St. Kitts & Nevis
441	Bermuda	773	Illinois	551	New Jersey	758	St. Lucia
250	British Columbia	815	Illinois	609	New Jersey	784	St. Vincent & Grenada
604	British Columbia	847	Illinois	732	New Jersey	423	Tennessee
778	British Columbia	872	Illinois	848	New Jersey	615	Tennessee
284	British Virgin Is.	219	Indiana	856	New Jersey	731	Tennessee
209	California	260	Indiana	862	New Jersey	865	Tennessee
213	California	317	Indiana	908	New Jersey	901	Tennessee
310	California	574	Indiana	973	New Jersey	931	Tennessee
323	California	765	Indiana	505	New Mexico	210	Texas
408	California	812	Indiana	212	New York	214	Texas
415	California	319	Iowa	315	New York	254	Texas
424	California	515	Iowa	347	New York	281	Texas
510	California	563	Iowa	516	New York	325	Texas
530	California	641	Iowa	518	New York	361	Texas
559	California	712	Iowa	585	New York	409	Texas
562	California	876	Jamaica	607	New York	430	Texas
619	California	316	Kansas	631	New York	432	Texas
626	California	620	Kansas	646	New York	469	Texas
650	California	785	Kansas	716	New York	512	Texas
661	California	913	Kansas	718	New York	682	Texas
707	California	270	Kentucky	845	New York	713	Texas
714	California	502	Kentucky	914	New York	806	Texas
760	California	606	Kentucky	917	New York	817	Texas
805	California	859	Kentucky	709	Newfoundland	830	Texas
818	California	225	Louisiana	252	North Carolina	832	Texas
831	California	318	Louisiana	336	North Carolina	903	Texas
858	California	337	Louisiana	704	North Carolina	915	Texas
909	California	504	Louisiana	828	North Carolina	936	Texas
916	California	985	Louisiana	910	North Carolina	940	Texas
925	California	207	Maine	919	North Carolina	956	Texas
949	California	204	Manitoba	980	North Carolina	972	Texas
345	Cayman Islands	227	Maryland	701	North Dakota	979	Texas
670	CNMI	240	Maryland	902	Nova Scotia	868	Trinidad and Tobago
303	Colorado	301	Maryland	216	Ohio	649	Turks & Caicos Islands
719	Colorado	410	Maryland	234	Ohio	340	US Virgin Islands
720	Colorado	443	Maryland	330	Ohio	385	Utah
970	Colorado	667	Maryland	419	Ohio	435	Utah
203	Connecticut	339	Massachusetts	440	Ohio	801	Utah
475	Connecticut	351	Massachusetts	513	Ohio	802	Vermont
860	Connecticut	413	Massachusetts	567	Ohio	276	Virginia
959	Connecticut	508	Massachusetts	614	Ohio	434	Virginia
302	Delaware	617	Massachusetts	740	Ohio	540	Virginia
202	District of Columbia	774	Massachusetts	937	Ohio	571	Virginia
809	Dominican Republic	781	Massachusetts	405	Oklahoma	703	Virginia
767	Dominica	857	Massachusetts	580	Oklahoma	757	Virginia
239	Florida	978	Massachusetts	918	Oklahoma	804	Virginia
305	Florida	231	Michigan	226	Ontario	206	Washington
321	Florida	248	Michigan	289	Ontario	253	Washington
352	Florida	269	Michigan	416	Ontario	360	Washington
386	Florida	313	Michigan	519	Ontario	425	Washington
407	Florida	517	Michigan	613	Ontario	509	Washington
561	Florida	586	Michigan	647	Ontario	304	West Virginia
727	Florida	616	Michigan	705	Ontario	262	Wisconsin
754	Florida	679	Michigan	807	Ontario	414	Wisconsin
772	Florida	734	Michigan	905	Ontario	608	Wisconsin
786	Florida	810	Michigan	503	Oregon	715	Wisconsin
813	Florida	906	Michigan	541	Oregon	920	Wisconsin
850	Florida	947	Michigan	971	Oregon	307	Wyoming
863	Florida	989	Michigan	215	Pennsylvania	867	Yukon, NW Terr., Nunavut
904	Florida	218	Minnesota	267	Pennsylvania		
941	Florida	320	Minnesota	412	Pennsylvania		
954	Florida	507	Minnesota	445	Pennsylvania		
229	Georgia	612	Minnesota	484	Pennsylvania		
		651	Minnesota	570	Pennsylvania		

Operator Information can be dialed direct.
First dial "0" or "1", then the area code as shown above, then 555-1212.

Toll-Free Prefixes – 800, 866, 877, and 888.

X

Area Codes – Numerically

201 New Jersey	386 Florida	609 New Jersey	809 Dominican Republic
202 District of Columbia	401 Rhode Island	610 Pennsylvania	810 Michigan
203 Connecticut	402 Nebraska	612 Minnesota	812 Indiana
204 Manitoba	403 Alberta	613 Ontario	813 Florida
205 Alabama	404 Georgia	614 Ohio	814 Pennsylvania
206 Washington	405 Oklahoma	615 Tennessee	815 Illinois
207 Maine	406 Montana	616 Michigan	816 Missouri
208 Idaho	407 Florida	617 Massachusetts	817 Texas
209 California	408 California	618 Illinois	818 California
210 Texas	409 Texas	619 California	819 Quebec
212 New York	410 Maryland	620 Kansas	828 North Carolina
213 California	412 Pennsylvania	623 Arizona	830 Texas
214 Texas	413 Massachusetts	626 California	831 California
215 Pennsylvania	414 Wisconsin	630 Illinois	832 Texas
216 Ohio	415 California	631 New York	835 Pennsylvania
217 Illinois	416 Ontario	636 Missouri	843 South Carolina
218 Minnesota	417 Missouri	641 Iowa	845 New York
219 Indiana	418 Quebec	646 New York	847 Illinois
224 Illinois	419 Ohio	647 Ontario	848 New Jersey
225 Louisiana	423 Tennessee	649 Turks & Caicos Islands	850 Florida
226 Ontario	424 California	650 California	856 New Jersey
227 Maryland	425 Washington	651 Minnesota	857 Massachusetts
228 Mississippi	430 Texas	660 Missouri	858 California
229 Georgia	432 Texas	661 California	859 Kentucky
231 Michigan	434 Virginia	662 Mississippi	860 Connecticut
234 Ohio	435 Utah	664 Montserrat	862 New Jersey
239 Florida	438 Quebec	667 Maryland	863 Florida
240 Maryland	440 Ohio	670 CNMI	864 South Carolina
242 Bahamas	441 Bermuda	671 Guam	865 Tennessee
246 Barbados	443 Maryland	678 Georgia	867 Yukon, NW Terr., Nunavut
248 Michigan	445 Pennsylvania	679 Michigan	868 Trinidad and Tobago
250 British Columbia	450 Quebec	682 Texas	869 St. Kitts & Nevis
251 Alabama	464 Illinois	684 American Samoa	870 Arkansas
252 North Carolina	469 Texas	701 North Dakota	872 Illinois
253 Washington	470 Georgia	702 Nevada	876 Jamaica
254 Texas	473 Grenada	703 Virginia	878 Pennsylvania
256 Alabama	475 Connecticut	704 North Carolina	901 Tennessee
260 Indiana	478 Georgia	705 Ontario	902 Nova Scotia
262 Wisconsin	479 Arkansas	706 Georgia	903 Texas
264 Anguilla	480 Arizona	707 California	904 Florida
267 Pennsylvania	484 Pennsylvania	708 Illinois	905 Ontario
268 Antigua and Barbuda	501 Arkansas	709 Newfoundland	906 Michigan
269 Michigan	502 Kentucky	712 Iowa	907 Alaska
270 Kentucky	503 Oregon	713 Texas	908 New Jersey
276 Virginia	504 Louisiana	714 California	909 California
281 Texas	505 New Mexico	715 Wisconsin	910 North Carolina
284 British Virgin Is.	506 New Brunswick	716 New York	912 Georgia
289 Ontario	507 Minnesota	717 Pennsylvania	913 Kansas
301 Maryland	508 Massachusetts	718 New York	914 New York
302 Delaware	509 Washington	719 Colorado	915 Texas
303 Colorado	510 California	720 Colorado	916 California
304 West Virginia	512 Texas	724 Pennsylvania	917 New York
305 Florida	513 Ohio	727 Florida	918 Oklahoma
306 Saskatchewan	514 Quebec	731 Tennessee	919 North Carolina
307 Wyoming	515 Iowa	732 New Jersey	920 Wisconsin
308 Nebraska	516 New York	734 Michigan	925 California
309 Illinois	517 Michigan	740 Ohio	928 Arizona
310 California	518 New York	754 Florida	931 Tennessee
312 Illinois	519 Ontario	757 Virginia	936 Texas
313 Michigan	520 Arizona	758 St. Lucia	937 Ohio
314 Missouri	530 California	760 California	939 Puerto Rico
315 New York	540 Virginia	763 Minnesota	940 Texas
316 Kansas	541 Oregon	765 Indiana	941 Florida
317 Indiana	551 New Jersey	767 Dominica	947 Michigan
318 Louisiana	559 California	770 Georgia	949 California
319 Iowa	561 Florida	772 Florida	952 Minnesota
320 Minnesota	562 California	773 Illinois	954 Florida
321 Florida	563 Iowa	774 Massachusetts	956 Texas
323 California	567 Ohio	775 Nevada	959 Connecticut
325 Texas	570 Pennsylvania	778 British Columbia	970 Colorado
330 Ohio	571 Virginia	780 Alberta	971 Oregon
331 Illinois	573 Missouri	781 Massachusetts	972 Texas
334 Alabama	574 Indiana	784 St. Vincent & Grenada	973 New Jersey
336 North Carolina	580 Oklahoma	785 Kansas	978 Massachusetts
337 Louisiana	585 New York	786 Florida	979 Texas
339 Massachusetts	586 Michigan	787 Puerto Rico	980 North Carolina
340 US Virgin Islands	601 Mississippi	801 Utah	985 Louisiana
345 Cayman Islands	602 Arizona	802 Vermont	989 Michigan
347 New York	603 New Hampshire	803 South Carolina	
351 Massachusetts	604 British Columbia	804 Virginia	
352 Florida	605 South Dakota	805 California	
360 Washington	606 Kentucky	806 Texas	
361 Texas	607 New York	807 Ontario	
385 Utah	608 Wisconsin	808 Hawaii	

Operator Information can be dialed direct.
First dial "0" or "1", then the area code as shown above, then 555-1212.

Toll-Free Prefixes – 800, 866, 877, and 888.

TABLE OF CONTENTS

Preface III
State Hospital Associations IV
Area Codes – Alphabetically by Location X
Area Codes - Numerically XI
Alabama 1
Alaska 4
Arizona 5
Arkansas 7
California 10
Colorado 23
Connecticut 25
Delaware 27
District of Columbia 27
Florida 28
Georgia 34
Hawaii 39
Idaho 40
Illinois 42
Indiana 48
Iowa 52
Kansas 55
Kentucky 60
Louisiana 63
Maine 68
Maryland 69
Massachusetts 71
Michigan 75
Minnesota 80
Mississippi 84
Missouri 88
Montana 91
Nebraska 93
Nevada 96
New Hampshire 97
New Jersey 98
New Mexico 101
New York 103
North Carolina 111
North Dakota 115
Ohio 116
Oklahoma 122
Oregon 126
Pennsylvania 128
Puerto Rico 135
Rhode Island 137
South Carolina 137
South Dakota 140
Tennessee 142
Texas 146
Utah 160
Vermont 161
Virginia 161
Washington 165
West Virginia 168
Wisconsin 169
Wyoming 173
U.S. Possessions 174
Alphabetical Index 175
Health Information Toll-Free Numbers 243

Hospital Telephone Directory

ALABAMA

ALABAMA

ALABASTER

SHELBY BAPTIST MEDICAL CENTER
1000 First Street North
Alabaster, AL 35007-8607
(205)620-8100

ALEXANDER CITY

RUSSELL HOSPITAL
PO Box 939 U S Highway 280 Bypass
Alexander City, AL 35011-0939
(256)329-7100

ANDALUSIA

ANDALUSIA REGIONAL HOSPITAL
849 South Three Notch St PO Box 760
Andalusia, AL 36420-1214
(334)222-8466

ANNISTON

NORTHEAST ALABAMA REGIONAL MEDICAL CENTER
400 East 10th Street PO Box 2208
Anniston, AL 36202-2208
(256)235-5121

STRINGFELLOW MEMORIAL HOSPITAL
301 East 18th St
Anniston, AL 36207-3999
(256)235-8900

ASHLAND

CLAY COUNTY HOSPITAL
544 East First Avenue
Ashland, AL 36251
(256)354-2131

ATHENS

ATHENS-LIMESTONE HOSPITAL
700 West Market Street
Athens, AL 35611-2457
(256)233-9292

ATMORE

ATMORE COMMUNITY HOSPITAL
401 Medical Park Drive, Medical Park Plaza
Atmore, AL 36502
(251)368-2500

BAY MINETTE

NORTH BALDWIN HOSPITAL
1815 Hand Avenue PO Box 1409
Bay Minette, AL 36507-1409
(251)937-5521

BESSEMER

UAB MEDICAL WEST
PO Box 847 995 9th Avenue
Bessemer, AL 35021-0847
(205)481-7000

BIRMINGHAM

ALABAMA CLINICAL SCHOOLS
1221 Alton Drive
Birmingham, AL 35210-4308
(205)836-9923

BAPTIST MONTCLAIR MEDICAL CENTER
800 Montclair Road
Birmingham, AL 35213-1908
(205)592-1000

BAPTIST MEDICAL CENTER PRINCETON
701 Princeton Avenue Sw
Birmingham, AL 35211-1318
(205)783-3000

BROOKWOOD MEDICAL CENTER
2010 Brookwood Medical Center Drive
Birmingham, AL 35209-6875
(205)877-1000

CALLAHAN EYE FOUNDATION HOSPITAL
1720 University Boulevard
Birmingham, AL 35233-1895
(205)325-8100

CARRAWAY METHODIST MEDICAL CENTER
1600 Carraway Boulevard
Birmingham, AL 35234-1990
(205)502-6000

CHILDRENS HOSPITAL OF ALABAMA
1600 Seventh Avenue South
Birmingham, AL 35233-1786
(205)939-9100

COOPER GREEN HOSPITAL
1515 6th Avenue South
Birmingham, AL 35233-1687
(205)930-3200

HEALTHSOUTH LAKESHORE REHAB HOSPITAL
3800 Ridgeway Drive
Birmingham, AL 35209-5506
(205)868-2000

HEALTHSOUTH MEDICAL CENTER
1201 Eleventh Avenue South
Birmingham, AL 35205-5299
(205)930-7000

HILL CREST BEHAVIORAL HEALTH SERVICES
6869 Fifth Avenue South
Birmingham, AL 35212-1866
(205)833-9000

MEDICAL CENTER EAST
50 Medical Park East Drive
Birmingham, AL 35235-3499
(205)838-3000

SAINT VINCENTS HOSPITAL
810 St Vincents Drive
Birmingham, AL 35205-1695
(205)939-7000

SELECT SPECIALTY HOSPITAL - BIRMINGHAM
800 Montclair Road
Birmingham, AL 35213-1908
(205)599-4600

SELECT SPECIALTY HOSPITAL - BIRMINGHAM PRINCETON
701 Princeton Avenue Southwest
Birmingham, AL 35211-1303
(205)686-3251

UNIVERSITY OF ALABAMA HOSPITAL
619 South 19th Street
Birmingham, AL 35249-0001
(205)934-4011

VA MEDICAL CENTER - BIRMINGHAM
700 South 19th Street
Birmingham, AL 35233-1996
(205)933-8101

BOAZ

MARSHALL MEDICAL CENTER SOUTH
2505 U S Highway 431 North, PO Box 758
Boaz, AL 35957-0758
(256)593-8310

BREWTON

D W MCMILLAN MEMORIAL HOSPITAL
1301 Belleville Avenue PO Box 908
Brewton, AL 36427-0908
(251)867-8061

CAMDEN

J PAUL JONES HOSPITAL
317 Mcwilliams Avenue
Camden, AL 36726-1623
(334)682-4131

CARROLLTON

PICKENS COUNTY MEDICAL CENTER
PO Box 360
Carrollton, AL 35447-0360
(205)367-8111

CENTRE

BAPTIST MEDICAL CENTER CHEROKEE
400 Northwood Drive
Centre, AL 35960-1023
(256)927-5531

CENTREVILLE

BIBB MEDICAL CENTER HOSPITAL
208 Pierson Avenue
Centreville, AL 35042-2918
(205)926-4881

CHATOM

WASHINGTON COUNTY INFIRMARY AND NURSING HOME
St Stephens Avenue PO Box 597
Chatom, AL 36518-0597
(251)847-2223

CLANTON

CHILTON MEDICAL CENTER
1010 Lay Dam Road
Clanton, AL 35045-2306
(205)755-2500

CULLMAN

CULLMAN REGIONAL MEDICAL CENTER
1912 Alabama Highway 157
Cullman, AL 35058-0609
(256)737-2000

WOODLAND COMMUNITY HOSPITAL
1910 Cherokee Avenue Sw
Cullman, AL 35055-5502
(256)739-3500

DADEVILLE

LAKE MARTIN COMMUNITY HOSPITAL
PO Box 629
Dadeville, AL 36853-0629
(256)825-7821

DAPHNE

MERCY MEDICAL
101 Villa Drive PO Box 1090
Daphne, AL 36526-1090
(251)621-4200

DECATUR

DECATUR GENERAL HOSPITAL
1201 7th Street Se
Decatur, AL 35601-3303
(256)341-2000

ALABAMA
Hospital Telephone Directory

DECATUR GENERAL HOSPITAL - WEST
2205 Beltline Road Southwest, PO Box 2240
Decatur, AL 35602-0224
(256)341-2000

NORTH ALABAMA REGIONAL HOSPITAL
Highway 31 South
Decatur, AL 35609
(256)560-2200

PARKWAY MEDICAL CENTER HOSPITAL
1874 Beltline Road Southwest
Decatur, AL 35601-5509
(256)350-2211

DEMOPOLIS

BRYAN W WHITFIELD MEMORIAL HOSPITAL
105 Highway 80 East PO Box 890
Demopolis, AL 36732-0890
(334)289-4000

DOTHAN

FLOWERS HOSPITAL
4370 West Main Street
Dothan, AL 36305-4000
(334)793-5000

HEALTHSOUTH REHABILITATION HOSPITAL
1736 East Main Street
Dothan, AL 36301-3025
(334)712-6333

RAMSAY YOUTH SERVICES
700 East Cottonwood Road
Dothan, AL 36301-3644
(334)794-7373

SOUTHEAST ALABAMA MEDICAL CENTER
1108 Ross Clark Circle PO Drawer 6987
Dothan, AL 36301-3024
(334)793-8111

ELBA

ELBA GENERAL HOSPITAL
987 Drayton Street PO Drawer G
Elba, AL 36323-1494
(334)897-2257

ENTERPRISE

MEDICAL CENTER ENTERPRISE
400 N Edwards Street
Enterprise, AL 36330-2584
(334)347-0584

EUFAULA

LAKEVIEW COMMUNITY HOSPITAL
820 West Washington Street
Eufaula, AL 36027-1899
(334)687-5761

EUTAW

GREENE COUNTY HOSPITAL AND NURSING HOME
509 Wilson Avenue
Eutaw, AL 35462-1099
(205)372-3388

EVERGREEN

EVERGREEN MEDICAL CENTER
101 Crestview Avenue
Evergreen, AL 36401-3396
(251)578-2480

FAIRFIELD

HEALTHSOUTH METRO WEST HOSPITAL
701 Richard M Scrushy Parkway
Fairfield, AL 35064-2699
(205)783-5121

FAIRHOPE

THOMAS HOSPITAL
PO Box 929 750 Morphy Avenue
Fairhope, AL 36533-0929
(251)928-2375

FAYETTE

FAYETTE MEDICAL CENTER AND LONG TERM CARE UNIT
1653 Temple Avenue North PO Drawer 878
Fayette, AL 35555-1314
(205)932-5966

FLORALA

FLORALA MEMORIAL HOSPITAL
PO Box 189
Florala, AL 36442-0189
(334)858-3287

FLORENCE

ELIZA COFFEE MEMORIAL HOSPITAL
205 Marengo St PO Box 818
Florence, AL 35631-0818
(256)768-9191

ELIZA COFFEE MEMORIAL HOSPITAL - EAST
2111 Cloyd Blvd
Florence, AL 35630-1503
(256)768-8140

FOLEY

SOUTH BALDWIN REGIONAL MEDICAL CENTER
1613 North Mckenzie Street
Foley, AL 36535-2247
(251)952-3400

FORT PAYNE

BAPTIST MEDICAL CENTER DEKALB
200 Medical Center Drive PO Box 778
Fort Payne, AL 35968
(256)845-3150

FORT RUCKER

LYSTER ARMY COMMUNITY HOSPITAL
700 Dustoff Street
Fort Rucker, AL 36362
(334)255-7337

U.S. ARMY AEROMEDICAL CENTER
Fort Rucker, AL 36362
(334)255-7359

GADSDEN

GADSDEN REGIONAL MEDICAL CENTER
1007 Goodyear Avenue
Gadsden, AL 35903-1195
(256)494-4000

HEALTHSOUTH REHABILITATION HOSPITAL
801 Goodyear Avenue
Gadsden, AL 35903-1133
(256)439-5000

MOUNTAIN VIEW HOSPITAL
3001 Scenic Highway
Gadsden, AL 35904-3047
(256)546-9265

RIVERVIEW REGIONAL MEDICAL CENTER
600 South Third Street PO Box 268
Gadsden, AL 35902-0268
(256)543-5200

GENEVA

WIREGRASS MEDICAL CENTER
1200 W Maple Avenue
Geneva, AL 36340-1694
(334)684-3655

GEORGIANA

GEORGIANA DOCTORS HOSPITAL
515 Miranda St
Georgiana, AL 36033-4520
(334)376-2205

GREENSBORO

HALE COUNTY HOSPITAL
First And Green Streets
Greensboro, AL 36744
(334)624-3024

GREENVILLE

L V STABLER MEMORIAL HOSPITAL
PO Box 1000
Greenville, AL 36037-1000
(334)382-2671

GROVE HILL

GROVE HILL MEMORIAL HOSPITAL
295 South Jackson PO Box 935
Grove Hill, AL 36451-0935
(251)275-3191

GUNTERSVILLE

MARSHALL MEDICAL CENTER NORTH
8000 Alabama Highway 69
Guntersville, AL 35976-7140
(256)753-8000

HALEYVILLE

LAKELAND COMMUNITY HOSPITAL
Highway 195
Haleyville, AL 35565
(205)486-5213

HAMILTON

NORTH MISSISSIPPI MEDICAL CENTER-HAMILTON
1256 Military Street South
Hamilton, AL 35570-5003
(205)921-6200

HARTSELLE

HARTSELLE MEDICAL CENTER
201 Pine Street Nw PO Box 969
Hartselle, AL 35640-0969
(256)773-6511

HUNTSVILLE

CRESTWOOD MEDICAL CENTER
One Hospital Drive
Huntsville, AL 35801-6455
(256)882-3100

HEALTHSOUTH REHAB HOSPITAL OF NORTH ALABAMA
107 Governors Drive Se
Huntsville, AL 35801-4322
(256)535-2300

HUNTSVILLE HOSPITAL
101 Sivley Road
Huntsville, AL 35801-4470
(256)517-8020

HUNTSVILLE HOSPITAL EAST
911 Big Cove Road
Huntsville, AL 35801-3784
(256)517-8020

Hospital Telephone Directory — ALABAMA

JACKSON
JACKSON MEDICAL CENTER
220 Hospital Drive
Jackson, AL 36545-2459
(251)246-9021

JACKSONVILLE
JACKSONVILLE HOSPITAL
1701 South Pelham Road PO Box 999
Jacksonville, AL 36265-0999
(256)435-4970

JASPER
WALKER BAPTIST MEDICAL CENTER
3400 Highway 78 East PO Box 3547
Jasper, AL 35502-3547
(205)387-4000

LUVERNE
CRENSHAW BAPTIST HOSPITAL
101 Baptist Lane
Luverne, AL 36049-7317
(334)335-3374

MADISON
BRADFORD HEALTH SERVICES
1600 Brown Ferry Road
Madison, AL 35758-9601
(256)461-7272

MOBILE
MOBILE INFIRMARY MEDICAL CENTER
PO Box 2144 5 Mobile Infirmary Circle
Mobile, AL 36652-2144
(251)435-2400

PROVIDENCE HOSPITAL
6801 Airport Boulevard
Mobile, AL 36608-3785
(251)633-1000

SPRINGHILL MEDICAL CENTER
3719 Dauphin Street
Mobile, AL 36608-1753
(251)344-9630

UNIVERSITY OF SOUTH ALABAMA CHILDREN'S AND WOMEN'S
1700 Center St Box 1708
Mobile, AL 36604-3301
(251)415-1000

UNIVERSITY OF SOUTH ALABAMA KNOLLWOOD PARK HOSPITAL
5600 Girby Road
Mobile, AL 36693-3320
(251)660-5120

UNIVERSITY OF SOUTH ALABAMA MEDICAL CENTER
2451 Fillingim Street
Mobile, AL 36617-2293
(251)471-7000

MONROEVILLE
MONROE COUNTY HOSPITAL
PO Box 886 1901 South Alabama Avenue
Monroeville, AL 36461-0886
(251)575-3111

MONTGOMERY
BAPTIST MEDICAL CENTER-EAST
400 Taylor Road Box 241267
Montgomery, AL 36117-3511
(334)244-8178

BAPTIST MEDICAL CENTER-SOUTH
2105 E South Boulevard
Montgomery, AL 36116-2498
(334)288-2100

GREIL MEMORIAL PSYCHIATRIC HOSPITAL
2140 Upper Wetumpka Road
Montgomery, AL 36107-1342
(334)262-0363

HEALTHSOUTH REHAB HOSPITAL OF MONTGOMERY
4465 Narrow Lane Road
Montgomery, AL 36116-2953
(334)284-7700

JACKSON HOSPITAL AND CLINIC
1725 Pine Street
Montgomery, AL 36106-1117
(334)293-8000

LONG TERM CARE HOSPITAL OF JACKSON
1725 Pine Street, 5th Floor North
Montgomery, AL 36106-1109
(334)240-0532

VA HEALTHCARE SYSTEM - CENTRAL ALABAMA WEST
215 Perry Hill Road
Montgomery, AL 36109-3725
(334)272-4670

MOULTON
LAWRENCE BAPTIST MEDICAL CENTER
202 Hospital Street PO Box 39
Moulton, AL 35650-0039
(256)974-2200

MOUNT VERNON
SEARCY HOSPITAL
PO Box 1090
Mount Vernon, AL 36560-1090
(251)662-6700

MUSCLE SHOALS
SHOALS HOSPITAL
201 West Avalon Avenue Box 3359
Muscle Shoals, AL 35661-2805
(256)386-1600

NORTHPORT
NORTHPORT MEDICAL CENTER
2700 Hospital Drive
Northport, AL 35476-3360
(205)333-4500

ONEONTA
MEDICAL CENTER BLOUNT
150 Gilbreath Drive PO Box 1000
Oneonta, AL 35121-0013
(205)274-3000

OPELIKA
EAST ALABAMA MEDICAL CENTER
2000 Pepperell Parkway
Opelika, AL 36801-5422
(334)749-3411

OPP
MIZELL MEMORIAL HOSPITAL
PO Box 1010
Opp, AL 36467-1010
(334)493-3541

OZARK
DALE MEDICAL CENTER
126 Hospital Ave
Ozark, AL 36360-2080
(334)774-2601

PELHAM
BRADFORD HEALTH SERVICES AT OAK MOUNTAIN
2280 Highway 35
Pelham, AL 35124-2189
(205)664-3480

PELL CITY
SAINT CLAIR REGIONAL HOSPITAL
2805 Hospital Drive
Pell City, AL 35125-1448
(205)338-3301

PRATTVILLE
PRATTVILLE BAPTIST MEDICAL CENTER
PO Box 681630
Prattville, AL 36068-1630
(334))365-0651

RED BAY
RED BAY HOSPITAL
211 Hospital Road PO Box 490
Red Bay, AL 35582-0490
(256)356-9532

ROANOKE
RANDOLPH COUNTY HOSPITAL
1000 Wadley Highway
Roanoke, AL 36274
(334)863-4111

RUSSELLVILLE
RUSSELLVILLE HOSPITAL
15155 Highway 43 Ne PO Box 1089
Russellville, AL 35653-1089
(256)332-1611

SCOTTSBORO
JACKSON COUNTY HOSPITAL AND NURSING HOME
380 Woods Cove Road PO Box 1050
Scottsboro, AL 35768-1050
(256)259-4444

SELMA
VAUGHAN REGIONAL MEDICAL CENTER
1015 Medical Center Parkway
Selma, AL 36701-6748
(334)418-4100

SHEFFIELD
HELEN KELLER MEMORIAL HOSPITAL
1300 South Montgomery Avenue PO Box 610
Sheffield, AL 35660-0610
(256)386-4196

SYLACAUGA
COOSA VALLEY BAPTIST MEDICAL CENTER
315 W Hickory St
Sylacauga, AL 35150-2996
(256)249-5000

TALLADEGA
CITIZENS BAPTIST MEDICAL CENTER
604 Stone Avenue
Talladega, AL 35160-2217
(256)362-8111

TALLASSEE
COMMUNITY HOSPITAL
PO Box 707 805 Friendship Road
Tallassee, AL 36078-0018
(334)283-6541

ALASKA · Hospital Telephone Directory

THOMASVILLE

THOMASVILLE INFIRMARY
33700 Highway 43
Thomasville, AL 36784-3351
(334)636-4431

TROY

TROY REGIONAL MEDICAL CENTER
1330 Highway 231 South
Troy, AL 36081-3067
(334)670-5000

TUSCALOOSA

BRYCE HOSPITAL
200 University Boulevard
Tuscaloosa, AL 35401-1294
(205)759-0799

DCH REGIONAL MEDICAL CENTER
809 University Boulevard East
Tuscaloosa, AL 35401-2071
(205)759-7111

MARY S HARPER GERIATRIC PSYCHIATRY
CENTER
200 University Boulevard
Tuscaloosa, AL 35401-1250
(205)759-0900

TAYLOR HARDIN SECURE MEDICAL
FACILITY
1301 River Road Northeast
Tuscaloosa, AL 35404
(205)556-7060

VA MEDICAL CENTER - TUSCALOOSA
3701 Loop Road
Tuscaloosa, AL 35404-5099
(205)554-2000

TUSKEGEE

VA HEALTHCARE SYSTEM - CENTRAL
ALABAMA EAST
2400 Hospital Road
Tuskegee, AL 36083-5001
(334)727-0550

UNION SPRINGS

BULLOCK COUNTY HOSPITAL
102 West Conecuh Avenue
Union Springs, AL 36089-1300
(334)738-2140

VALLEY

GEORGE H LANIER MEMORIAL HOSPITAL
PO Box 348
Valley, AL 36854-0348
(334)756-9180

WARRIOR

BRADFORD HEALTH SERVICES,
BIRMINGHAM LODGE
1189 Allbritton Road
Warrior, AL 35180-2663
(205)647-1945

WEDOWEE

WEDOWEE HOSPITAL
301 North Main Street
Wedowee, AL 36278-7101
(256)357-2111

WETUMPKA

ELMORE COMMUNITY HOSPITAL
500 Hospital Drive
Wetumpka, AL 36092-1600
(334)567-4311

WINFIELD

CARRAWAY NORTHWEST MEDICAL
CENTER
Highway 78 West PO Box 130
Winfield, AL 35594-0130
(205)487-7000

YORK

HILL HOSPITAL OF SUMTER COUNTY
751 Derby Drive
York, AL 36925-2194
(205)392-5263

ALASKA

ANCHORAGE

ALASKA PSYCHIATRIC INSTITUTE
2900 Providence Drive
Anchorage, AK 99508-4677
(907)269-7100

ALASKA REGIONAL HOSPITAL
2801 Debarr Road, PO Box 143889
Anchorage, AK 99514-3889
(907)276-1754

NORTH STAR BEHAVIORAL HEALTH
SYSTEM
1650 South Bragaw
Anchorage, AK 99508-3435
(907)258-7575

NORTH STAR HOSPITAL
2530 DeBarr Road
Anchorage, AK 99508-2996
(907)258-7575

PHS/IHS ALASKA NATIVE MEDICAL CENTER
4315 Diplomacy Drive
Anchorage, AK 99508-5999
(907)729-1994

PROVIDENCE ALASKA MEDICAL CENTER
3200 Providence Drive
Anchorage, AK 99508-4693
(907)562-2211

VA HEALTHCARE SYSTEM - ALASKA
2925 De Barr Road
Anchorage, AK 99508-2983
(907)257-4700

BARROW

PHS/IHS ARCTIC SLOPE NATIVE ASSOC.
AND SAMUEL SIMMONDS MEMORIAL
HOSPITAL
PO Box 1232
Barrow, AK 99723-1232
(907)852-4611

BETHEL

PHS/IHS YUKON KUSKOKWIM DELTA
REGIONAL HOSPITAL
Box 287
Bethel, AK 99559-0287
(907)543-6014

CORDOVA

CORDOVA COMMUNITY MEDICAL CENTER
PO Box 160
Cordova, AK 99574-0160
(907)424-8000

DILLINGHAM

PHS/IHS BRISTOL BAY AREA HEALTH -
KANAKANAK HOSPITAL
PO Box 130
Dillingham, AK 99576-0130
(907)842-5201

ELMENDORF AIR FORCE BASE

3RD MEDICAL GROUP
5955 Zermer Avenue
Elmendorf Air Force Base, AK 99506-3700
(907)580-3006

FAIRBANKS

FAIRBANKS MEMORIAL HOSPITAL
1650 Cowles Street
Fairbanks, AK 99701-5998
(907)452-8181

FORT WAINWRIGHT

BASSETT ARMY COMMUNITY HOSPITAL
1060 Gaffney Road #7400
Fort Wainwright, AK 99703-7401
(907)353-5172

HOMER

SOUTH PENINSULA HOSPITAL
4300 Bartlett St
Homer, AK 99603-7000
(907)235-8101

JUNEAU

BARTLETT REGIONAL HOSPITAL
3260 Hospital Drive (PO Box 3-3000)
Juneau, AK 99803-3000
(907)586-2611

JUNEAU RECOVERY HOSPITAL
3250 Hospital Drive
Juneau, AK 99801-7808
(907)586-9508

KETCHIKAN

KETCHIKAN GENERAL HOSPITAL
3100 Tongass Avenue
Ketchikan, AK 99901-5794
(907)225-5171

KODIAK

PROVIDENCE KODIAK ISLAND MEDICAL
CENTER
1915 East Rezanof Drive
Kodiak, AK 99615-6602
(907)486-3281

KOTZEBUE

MANIILAQ ASSOCIATION AND HEALTH
CENTER
PO Box 43
Kotzebue, AK 99752-0043
(907)442-3321

NOME

PHS/IHS NORTON SOUND REGIONAL
HOSPITAL
PO Box 966
Nome, AK 99762-0966
(907)443-3311

PALMER

VALLEY HOSPITAL
515 East Dahlia PO Box 1687
Palmer, AK 99645-1687
(907)748-8600

PETERSBURG

PETERSBURG MEDICAL CENTER
103 Fram St (Box 589)
Petersburg, AK 99833-0589
(907)772-4291

Hospital Telephone Directory — ARIZONA

SEWARD

PROVIDENCE SEWARD MEDICAL CENTER
417 First Avenue (PO Box 365)
Seward, AK 99664-0365
(907)224-5205

SITKA

PHS/IHS MOUNT EDGECUMBE HOSPITAL
222 Tongass Drive
Sitka, AK 99835-9416
(907)966-8310

SITKA COMMUNITY HOSPITAL
209 Moller PO Box 500
Sitka, AK 99835-0500
(907)747-3241

SOLDOTNA

CENTRAL PENINSULA GENERAL HOSPITAL
250 Hospital Place
Soldotna, AK 99669-6999
(907)262-4404

VALDEZ

VALDEZ COMMUNITY HOSPITAL
1000 Meals Avenue PO Box 550
Valdez, AK 99686-0550
(907)835-2249

WRANGELL

WRANGELL GENERAL HOSPITAL
310 Bennett
Wrangell, AK 99929
(907)874-7000

ARIZONA

BENSON

BENSON HOSPITAL
450 South Ocotillo
Benson, AZ 85602-6490
(520)586-2261

BISBEE

COPPER QUEEN COMMUNITY HOSPITAL
101 Cole Avenue
Bisbee, AZ 85603-1399
(520)432-5383

BULLHEAD CITY

WESTERN ARIZONA REGIONAL MEDICAL CENTER
2735 Silver Creek Road
Bullhead City, AZ 86442-8303
(928)763-2273

CASA GRANDE

CASA GRANDE REGIONAL MEDICAL CENTER
1800 East Florence Boulevard
Casa Grande, AZ 85222-5399
(520)426-6300

CHANDLER

CHANDLER REGIONAL HOSPITAL
475 South Dobson Road
Chandler, AZ 85224-5695
(480)963-4561

PARC PLACE
2190 North Grace Boulevard
Chandler, AZ 85225-3416
(480)917-9301

CHINLE

PHS/IHS CHINLE COMPREHENSIVE HEALTH CARE FACILITY
PO Box PH
Chinle, AZ 86503
(928)674-7011

COTTONWOOD

VERDE VALLEY MEDICAL CENTER
269 South Candy Lane
Cottonwood, AZ 86326-4170
(928)634-2251

DAVIS-MONTHAN AIR FORCE BASE

355TH MEDICAL GROUP
4175 South Alamo Avenue
Davis-Monthan Air Force Base, AZ 85707-6097
(520)228-2564

DOUGLAS

SOUTHEAST ARIZONA MEDICAL CENTER
Rural Route 1 PO Box 30
Douglas, AZ 85607
(520)364-7931

FLAGSTAFF

FLAGSTAFF MEDICAL CENTER
1200 North Beaver Street
Flagstaff, AZ 86001-3118
(928)779-3366

GUIDANCE CENTER, THE
2187 North Vickey Street
Flagstaff, AZ 86004-6106
(928)527-1899

FORT DEFIANCE

PHS INDIAN HOSPITAL - FORT DEFIANCE
PO Box 649
Fort Defiance, AZ 86504-0649
(928)729-5741

FORT HUACHUCA

RAYMOND W BLISS ARMY COMMUNITY HOSPITAL
Winrow Road Building 45001
Fort Huachuca, AZ 85613
(520)533-9026

GANADO

SAGE MEMORIAL HOSPITAL
Ganado Mission PO Box 457
Ganado, AZ 86505-0457
(928)755-3411

GLENDALE

ARROWHEAD COMMUNITY HOSPITAL
18701 North 67th Avenue
Glendale, AZ 85308-7101
(623)561-1000

HEALTHSOUTH VALLEY OF SUN REHAB
13460 North 67th Avenue
Glendale, AZ 85304-1000
(623)878-8800

THUNDERBIRD SAMARITAN HOSPITAL AND HEALTH CENTER
5555 West Thunderbird Road
Glendale, AZ 85306-4696
(602)588-5555

GLOBE

COBRE VALLEY COMMUNITY HOSPITAL
5880 S Hospital Dr
Globe, AZ 85501-9454
(928)425-3261

KINGMAN

KINGMAN REGIONAL MEDICAL CENTER
3269 Stockton Hill Road
Kingman, AZ 86401-3691
(928)757-2101

LAKE HAVASU CITY

HAVASU REGIONAL MEDICAL CENTER
101 Civic Center Lane
Lake Havasu City, AZ 86403-5683
(928)855-8185

LUKE AIR FORCE BASE

56TH MEDICAL GROUP
7219 North Litchfield Road
Luke Air Force Base, AZ 85309-1529
(623)856-7500

MESA

ARIZONA SPINE AND JOINT HOSPITAL
4620 East Baseline Road
Mesa, AZ 85206-4624
(480)832-4770

DESERT SAMARITAN MEDICAL CENTER
1400 South Dobson Road
Mesa, AZ 85202-4758
(480)464-4000

LUTHERAN HEART HOSPITAL
6750 East Baywood Avenue
Mesa, AZ 85206-1749
(480)854-5000

MESA GENERAL HOSPITAL
515 North Mesa Drive
Mesa, AZ 85201-5989
(480)969-9111

MESA LUTHERAN HOSPITAL
525 West Brown Road
Mesa, AZ 85201-3299
(480)834-1211

SELECT SPECIALTY HOSPITAL - MESA
525 West Brown Road
Mesa, AZ 85201-3202
(480)461-2706

VALLEY LUTHERAN HOSPITAL
6644 Baywood Avenue
Mesa, AZ 85206-1797
(480)981-2000

MORENCI

MORENCI HEALTH CARE CENTER
Coronado Boulevard Burro Alley
Morenci, AZ 85540
(928)865-4511

NOGALES

CARONDELET HOLY CROSS HOSPITAL
1171 West Target Range Road
Nogales, AZ 85621-2487
(520)285-3000

PAGE

PAGE HOSPITAL
North Navajo And Vista PO Box 1447
Page, AZ 86040-1447
(928)645-2424

ARIZONA

Hospital Telephone Directory

PARKER

LA PAZ REGIONAL HOSPITAL
1200 W Mohave Rd
Parker, AZ 85344-6349
(928)669-9201

PHS INDIAN HOSPITAL - PARKER
12033 Agency Road
Parker, AZ 85344-7718
(928)669-2137

PAYSON

PAYSON REGIONAL MEDICAL CENTER
807 South Ponderosa
Payson, AZ 85541-5599
(928)474-3222

PHOENIX

ARIZONA HEART HOSPITAL
1930 East Thomas Road
Phoenix, AZ 85016-7711
(602)532-1000

ARIZONA STATE HOSPITAL
2500 E Van Buren St
Phoenix, AZ 85008-6079
(602)244-1331

ARIZONA SURGICAL HOSPITAL
6501 North 19th Avenue
Phoenix, AZ 85015-1602
(602)795-6020

GOOD SAMARITAN REGIONAL MEDICAL
CENTER
1111 East McDowell Road
Phoenix, AZ 85006-2666
(602)239-2000

HACIENDA DE LOS NINOS
2303 East Thomas
Phoenix, AZ 85016-7827
(602)243-4231

JOHN C LINCOLN HOSPITAL AND HEALTH
CENTER
250 East Dunlap
Phoenix, AZ 85020-2871
(602)943-2381

JOHN C LINCOLN HOSPITAL-DEER VALLEY
19829 North 27th Avenue
Phoenix, AZ 85027-4002
(623)879-6100

KINDRED HOSPITAL PHOENIX
40 E Indianola Avenue
Phoenix, AZ 85012-2019
(602)280-7000

MARICOPA MEDICAL CENTER
2601 East Roosevelt Street
Phoenix, AZ 85008-4973
(602)344-5011

MARYVALE HOSPITAL MEDICAL CENTER
5102 West Campbell Avenue
Phoenix, AZ 85031-1799
(623)848-5000

MAYO CLINIC HOSPITAL
5777 East Mayo Blvd
Phoenix, AZ 85054-4502
(480)515-6296

PARADISE VALLEY HOSPITAL
3929 East Bell Road
Phoenix, AZ 85032-2196
(602)923-5000

PHOENIX BAPTIST HOSPITAL AND MEDICAL
CENTER
2000 W Bethany Home Road
Phoenix, AZ 85015-2467
(602)249-0212

PHOENIX CHILDRENS HOSPITAL
1919 East Thomas Road
Phoenix, AZ 85016-7710
(602)546-1000

PHOENIX MEMORIAL HOSPITAL
1201 South 7th Avenue
Phoenix, AZ 85007-3995
(602)258-5111

PHS/IHS PHOENIX INDIAN MEDICAL
CENTER
4212 N 16th Street
Phoenix, AZ 85016-5389
(602)263-1200

SAINT JOSEPHS HOSPITAL MEDICAL
CENTER
350 West Thomas Road
Phoenix, AZ 85013-4496
(602)406-3000

SAINT LUKES BEHAVIORAL HEALTH
CENTER
1800 East Van Buren
Phoenix, AZ 85006-3742
(602)251-8535

SAINT LUKES MEDICAL CENTER
1800 East Van Buren
Phoenix, AZ 85006-3742
(602)251-8100

SELECT SPECIALTY HOSPITAL - PHOENIX
350 West Thomas Rd 3rd Floor
Phoenix, AZ 85013-4409
(602)406-6800

VA MEDICAL CENTER - CARL T HAYDEN
650 E Indian School Road
Phoenix, AZ 85012-1892
(602)277-5551

POLACCA

PHS/IHS HOPI HEALTH CARE CENTER
PO Box 4000
Polacca, AZ 86042-4000
(928)737-6000

PRESCOTT

VA HEALTHCARE SYSTEM - NORTHERN
ARIZONA
580 N Hwy 89
Prescott, AZ 86313
(928)445-4860

YAVAPAI REGIONAL MEDICAL CENTER
1003 Willow Creek Road
Prescott, AZ 86301-1668
(928)445-2700

SACATON

PHS/IHS HU HU KAM MEMORIAL HOSPITAL
PO Box 38
Sacaton, AZ 85247-0038
(520)562-3321

SAFFORD

MOUNT GRAHAM COMMUNITY HOSPITAL
1600 20th Avenue
Safford, AZ 85546-4097
(928)348-4000

SAN CARLOS

PHS INDIAN HOSPITAL - SAN CARLOS
PO Box 208
San Carlos, AZ 85550-0208
(928)475-2371

SCOTTSDALE

HEALTHSOUTH SCOTTSDALE REHAB
HOSPITAL
9630 E Shea Blvd
Scottsdale, AZ 85260-6267
(480)860-0671

KINDRED HOSPITAL ARIZONA -
SCOTTSDALE
11250 North 92nd Street
Scottsdale, AZ 85260-6148
(480)391-4040

SAMARITAN BEHAVIORAL HEALTH
7575 E Earll Dr
Scottsdale, AZ 85251-6915
(480)941-7500

SAMARITAN BEHAVIORAL HEALTH CENTER
SCOTTSDALE
7575 East Earll Drive
Scottsdale, AZ 85251-6915
(480)941-7500

SCOTTSDALE HEALTH CARE-OSBORN
7400 East Osborn Road
Scottsdale, AZ 85251-6403
(480)675-4000

SCOTTSDALE HEALTHCARE
9003 East Shea Blvd
Scottsdale, AZ 85260-6709
(480)860-3000

SENIOR HORIZONS
7100 East Mescal St
Scottsdale, AZ 85254-6126
(480)443-5107

SELLS

PHS INDIAN HOSPITAL - SELLS
PO Box 548
Sells, AZ 85634-0548
(520)383-7251

SHOW LOW

NAVAPACHE HOSPITAL
2200 Show Low Lake Road
Show Low, AZ 85901-7831
(928)537-4375

SIERRA VISTA

SIERRA VISTA COMMUNITY HOSPITAL
300 El Camino Real
Sierra Vista, AZ 85635-2899
(520)458-4641

SPRINGERVILLE

WHITE MOUNTAIN COMMUNITY HOSPITAL
118 South Mountain Avenue
Springerville, AZ 85938-5104
(928)333-4368

SUN CITY

SUNHEALTH BOSWELL MEMORIAL
HOSPITAL
10401 Thunderbird Boulevard
Sun City, AZ 85351-3004
(623)977-7211

SUN CITY WEST

DEL E WEBB MEMORIAL HOSPITAL
14502 West Meeker Boulevard
Sun City West, AZ 85375-5299
(623)214-4000

TEMPE

TEMPE SAINT LUKES HOSPITAL
1500 South Mill Avenue
Tempe, AZ 85281-6699
(480)784-5510

TUBA CITY

PHS/IHS TUBA CITY INDIAN MEDICAL CENTER
PO Box 600
Tuba City, AZ 86045-0600
(928)283-2501

TUCSON

CARONDELET SAINT JOSEPHS HOSPITAL
350 North Wilmot Road
Tucson, AZ 85711-2678
(520)296-3211

CARONDELET SAINT MARYS HOSPITAL
1601 West Saint Mary's Road
Tucson, AZ 85745-2682
(520)622-5833

EL DORADO HOSPITAL
1400 North Wilmot Road, PO Box 13070
Tucson, AZ 85732-3070
(520)886-6361

HEALTHSOUTH REHAB INSTITUTE OF TUCSON
2650 North Wyatt Drive
Tucson, AZ 85712-6108
(520)325-1300

HEALTHSOUTH REHABILITATION HOSPITAL OF SOUTHERN ARIZONA
1921 West Hospital Drive
Tucson, AZ 85704-7890
(520)742-2800

KINDRED HOSPITAL TUCSON
355 North Wilmot Road
Tucson, AZ 85711-2601
(520)584-4500

KINO COMMUNITY HOSPITAL
2800 East Ajo Way
Tucson, AZ 85713-6289
(520)294-4471

NORTHWEST MEDICAL CENTER
6200 N La Cholla Boulevard
Tucson, AZ 85741-3599
(520)742-9000

PALO VERDE HOSPITAL
2695 North Craycroft Road, Box 40030
Tucson, AZ 85712-2244
(520)324-4340

SONORA BEHAVIORAL HEALTH
6050 North Corona Road
Tucson, AZ 85704-1096
(520)469-8700

SUMMIT HOSPITAL OF SOUTHEAST ARIZONA
7220 East Rosewood Drive
Tucson, AZ 85710-1350
(520)546-4595

TUCSON HEART HOSPITAL
4888 North Stone Avenue
Tucson, AZ 85704-5799
(520)696-2328

TUCSON MEDICAL CENTER
5301 East Grant Road
Tucson, AZ 85712-2874
(520)327-5461

UNIVERSITY MEDICAL CENTER
1501 N Campbell Avenue
Tucson, AZ 85724-0002
(520)694-6148

VA HEALTHCARE SYSTEM - SOUTHERN ARIZONA
3601 S 6th Avenue
Tucson, AZ 85723-0001
(520)792-1450

WHITERIVER

PHS INDIAN HOSPITAL - WHITERIVER
PO Box 860
Whiteriver, AZ 85941-0860
(928)338-4911

WICKENBURG

WICKENBURG REGIONAL HOSPITAL
520 Rose Lane
Wickenburg, AZ 85390-1447
(928)684-5421

WILLCOX

NORTHERN COCHISE COMMUNITY HOSPITAL
901 West Rex Allen Drive
Willcox, AZ 85643-1009
(520)384-3541

WINSLOW

WINSLOW MEMORIAL HOSPITAL
1501 Williamson Avenue
Winslow, AZ 86047-2797
(928)289-4691

YUMA

PHS INDIAN HOSPITAL - FORT YUMA
PO Box 1368
Yuma, AZ 85366-1368
(928)572-4100

YUMA REGIONAL MEDICAL CENTER
2400 Avenue A
Yuma, AZ 85364-7170
(928)344-2000

ARKANSAS

ARKADELPHIA

BAPTIST MEDICAL CENTER ARKADELPHIA
3050 Twin Rivers Drive
Arkadelphia, AR 71923-4299
(870)245-2622

ASHDOWN

LITTLE RIVER MEMORIAL HOSPITAL
451 W Locke St
Ashdown, AR 71822-3325
(870)898-5011

BATESVILLE

WHITE RIVER MEDICAL CENTER
1710 Harrison Street PO Box 2197
Batesville, AR 72503-2197
(501)793-1200

BENTON

RIVENDELL BEHAVIORAL HEALTH
100 Rivendell Drive
Benton, AR 72015-9188
(501)316-1255

SALINE MEMORIAL HOSPITAL
#1 Medical Park Drive
Benton, AR 72015-3354
(501)776-6000

TIMBER RIDGE RANCH
15000 Highway 298
Benton, AR 72015-9282
(501)594-5211

BENTONVILLE

BATES MEDICAL CENTER
602 N Walton Boulevard
Bentonville, AR 72712-4576
(479)273-2481

BERRYVILLE

CARROLL REGIONAL MEDICAL CENTER
214 Carter Street
Berryville, AR 72616-4303
(870)423-3355

BLYTHEVILLE

BAPTIST MEMORIAL HOSPITAL BLYTHEVILLE
1520 North Division Street PO Box 108
Blytheville, AR 72316-0108
(870)838-7300

BOONEVILLE

BOONEVILLE COMMUNITY HOSPITAL
PO Box 290
Booneville, AR 72927-0290
(479)675-2800

CALICO ROCK

COMMUNITY MEDICAL CENTER OF IZARD COUNTY
Grasse Street
Calico Rock, AR 72519
(870)297-3726

CAMDEN

OUACHITA COUNTY MEDICAL CENTER
638 California Avenue
Camden, AR 71701-4699
(870)836-1000

CHEROKEE VILLAGE

EASTERN OZARKS REGIONAL HEALTH SYSTEM
122 South Allegheny Drive
Cherokee Village, AR 72529
(870)257-4101

CLARKSVILLE

JOHNSON REGIONAL MEDICAL CENTER
1100 East Poplar Street
Clarksville, AR 72830-4419
(479)754-5454

CLINTON

OZARK HEALTH MEDICAL CENTER
Highway 65 South
Clinton, AR 72031
(501)745-7000

CONWAY

CONWAY REGIONAL MEDICAL CENTER
2302 College Avenue
Conway, AR 72034-6297
(501)329-3831

CROSSETT

ASHLEY COUNTY MEDICAL CENTER
1015 Unity Road
Crossett, AR 71635
(870)364-4111

ARKANSAS — Hospital Telephone Directory

DANVILLE
JOHN ED CHAMBERS MEMORIAL HOSPITAL
Highway 10 At Detroit St PO Box 639
Danville, AR 72833-0639
(479)495-2241

DARDANELLE
DARDANELLE HOSPITAL
PO Box 578
Dardanelle, AR 72834-0578
(479)229-4677

DE QUEEN
DE QUEEN REGIONAL MEDICAL CENTER
1306 West Collin Raye Drive
De Queen, AR 71832-2502
(870)584-4111

DE WITT
DEWITT HOSPITAL AND NURSING HOME
1641 Whitehead Drive
De Witt, AR 72042-2971
(870)946-3571

DUMAS
DELTA MEMORIAL HOSPITAL
PO Box 887
Dumas, AR 71639-0887
(870)382-4303

EL DORADO
MEDICAL CENTER OF SOUTH ARKANSAS
700 West Grove
El Dorado, AR 71730-4416
(870)864-3200

EUREKA SPRINGS
EUREKA SPRINGS HOSPITAL
24 Norris Street
Eureka Springs, AR 72632-3541
(479)253-7400

FAYETTEVILLE
FAYETTEVILLE CITY HOSPITAL AND GERIATRIC CENTER
221 S School St
Fayetteville, AR 72701-5997
(479)442-5100

HEALTHSOUTH REHABILITATION HOSPITAL
153 East Monte Painter Drive
Fayetteville, AR 72703-4002
(479)444-2200

VA MEDICAL CENTER - FAYETTEVILLE
1100 N College Avenue
Fayetteville, AR 72703-1999
(479)443-4301

VISTA HEALTH
4253 Crossover Road
Fayetteville, AR 72703-4593
(479)521-5731

WASHINGTON REGIONAL MEDICAL CENTER
1125 North College
Fayetteville, AR 72703-1994
(479)713-1000

FORDYCE
DALLAS COUNTY HOSPITAL
201 Clifton Street
Fordyce, AR 71742-3099
(870)352-3155

MILLCREEK HABILATION CENTER
Highway 79 North
Fordyce, AR 71742
(870)352-8203

FORREST CITY
BAPTIST MEMORIAL HOSPITAL FORREST CITY
1601 Newcastle Road
Forrest City, AR 72335
(870)261-0000

FORT SMITH
HARBOR VIEW MERCY HOSPITAL
10301 Mayo Road PO Box 17000
Fort Smith, AR 72917-7000
(479)484-5550

HEALTHSOUTH REHAB HOSPITAL OF FORT SMITH
1401 South J Street
Fort Smith, AR 72901-5158
(479)785-3300

SAINT EDWARD MERCY MEDICAL CENTER
7301 Rogers Avenue
Fort Smith, AR 72903-4100
(479)484-6000

SELECT SPECIALTY HOSPITAL - FORT SMITH
1131 South I Street
Fort Smith, AR 72901-4537
(479)441-5416

SPARKS REGIONAL MEDICAL CENTER
PO Box 17006
Fort Smith, AR 72917-7006
(479)441-4000

GRAVETTE
GRAVETTE MEDICAL CENTER HOSPITAL
PO Box 450
Gravette, AR 72736-0450
(479)787-5291

HARRISON
NORTH ARKANSAS REGIONAL MEDICAL CENTER
620 North Willow
Harrison, AR 72601-2994
(870)365-2000

HEBER SPRINGS
BAPTIST MEDICAL CENTER HEBER SPRINGS
Highway 110 West
Heber Springs, AR 72543
(501)206-3000

HELENA
HELENA REGIONAL MEDICAL CENTER
1801 Martin Luther King Jr Drive
Helena, AR 72342-8998
(870)338-5800

HOPE
MEDICAL PARK HOSPITAL
2001 South Main Street
Hope, AR 71801-8194
(870)777-2323

HOT SPRINGS
ADVANCE CARE HOSPITAL
300 Werner Street, Third Floor
Hot Springs, AR 71913-6406
(501)609-4300

HOT SPRINGS REHABILITATION CENTER
105 Reserve Avenue
Hot Springs, AR 71901-4195
(501)624-4411

HOT SPRINGS SURGICAL HOSPITAL
1636 Higdon Ferry Road
Hot Springs, AR 71913-6912
(501)520-2000

LEO N LEVI NATIONAL ARTHRITIS HOSPITAL
300 Prospect Avenue
Hot Springs, AR 71901-4003
(501)624-1281

NATIONAL PARK MEDICAL CENTER
1910 Malvern Avenue
Hot Springs, AR 71901-7752
(501)321-1000

SAINT JOSEPHS REGIONAL HEALTH CENTER
300 Werner Street
Hot Springs, AR 71913-6406
(501)622-1000

JACKSONVILLE
REBSAMEN REGIONAL MEDICAL CENTER
1400 Braden Street
Jacksonville, AR 72076-3788
(501)985-7000

JOHNSON
WILLOW CREEK WOMEN'S HOSPITAL
4301 Greathouse Springs Road, PO Box 544
Johnson, AR 72741-0544
(479)684-3000

JONESBORO
HEALTHSOUTH REHABILITATION HOSPITAL
1201 Fleming Avenue
Jonesboro, AR 72401-4311
(870)932-0440

REGIONAL MEDICAL CENTER OF NORTHEAST ARKANSAS
3024 Stadium Boulevard
Jonesboro, AR 72401-7415
(870)972-7000

SAINT BERNARDS BEHAVIORAL HEALTH
2712 East Johnson Avenue
Jonesboro, AR 72401-1874
(870)932-2800

SAINT BERNARDS REGIONAL MEDICAL CENTER
225 East Jackson Avenue
Jonesboro, AR 72401-3156
(870)972-4100

LAKE VILLAGE
CHICOT MEMORIAL HOSPITAL
2729 Highway 65 And 82 South
Lake Village, AR 71653
(870)265-5351

LITTLE ROCK
ARKANSAS CHILDRENS HOSPITAL
800 Marshall Street
Little Rock, AR 72202-3591
(501)320-1100

ARKANSAS HEART HOSPITAL
1701 South Shackleford Road
Little Rock, AR 72211-4335
(501)219-7000

ARKANSAS STATE HOSPITAL PSYCHIATRIC DIVISION
4313 West Markham Street
Little Rock, AR 72205-4023
(501)686-9000

Hospital Telephone Directory — ARKANSAS

BAPTIST MEDICAL CENTER
9601 Interstate 630 Exit 7
Little Rock, AR 72205-7299
(501)202-2000

BAPTIST REHAB INSTITUTE OF ARKANSAS
9601 Interstate 630 Exit 7
Little Rock, AR 72205-7202
(501)202-7000

PINNACLE POINTE HOSPITAL
11501 Financial Centre Parkway
Little Rock, AR 72211-3715
(501)223-3322

SAINT VINCENT DOCTORS HOSPITAL
6101 West Capitol
Little Rock, AR 72205-5340
(501)661-4000

SAINT VINCENT INFIRMARY MEDICAL CENTER
Two St Vincent Circle
Little Rock, AR 72205-5499
(501)660-3000

SELECT SPECIALTY HOSPITAL - LITTLE ROCK
Two Saint Vincent Circle, 6th Floor
Little Rock, AR 72205-5423
(501)661-4198

SEMPERCARE HOSPITAL OF LITTLE ROCK
9601 Interstate 630 Exit 7
Little Rock, AR 72205-7202
(501)202-1090

SOUTHWEST REGIONAL MEDICAL CENTER
11401 Interstate 30
Little Rock, AR 72209-7042
(501)455-7100

UNIVERSITY HOSPITAL OF ARKANSAS
4301 West Markham Street
Little Rock, AR 72205-7101
(501)686-7000

VA MEDICAL CENTER - JOHN L. MCCLELLAN MEMORIAL HOSPITAL
4300 W 7th St
Little Rock, AR 72205-5446
(501)257-1000

MAGNOLIA

MAGNOLIA HOSPITAL
101 Hospital Drive PO Box 629
Magnolia, AR 71754-0629
(870)235-3000

MALVERN

HOT SPRING COUNTY MEDICAL CENTER
1001 Schneider Drive
Malvern, AR 72104-4828
(501)337-4911

MAUMELLE

METHODIST BEHAVIORAL HOSPITAL
1601 Murphy Drive
Maumelle, AR 72113-6187
(501)803-3388

MCGEHEE

MCGEHEE DESHA COUNTY HOSPITAL
900 South Third St PO Box 351
McGehee, AR 71654-0351
(870)222-5600

MENA

MENA MEDICAL CENTER
311 North Morrow Street
Mena, AR 71953-2516
(479)394-6100

MONTICELLO

DREW MEMORIAL HOSPITAL
778 Scogin Drive
Monticello, AR 71655-5729
(870)367-2411

MORRILTON

SAINT ANTHONYS HOSPITAL
4 Hospital Drive
Morrilton, AR 72110-4510
(501)977-2300

MOUNTAIN HOME

BAXTER COUNTY REGIONAL HOSPITAL
624 Hospital Drive
Mountain Home, AR 72653-2955
(870)508-1000

MOUNTAIN VIEW

STONE COUNTY MEDICAL CENTER
Highway 14 East PO Box 510
Mountain View, AR 72560-0510
(870)269-4361

MURFREESBORO

PIKE COUNTY MEMORIAL HOSPITAL
315 East 13th Street, PO Box F
Murfreesboro, AR 71958-1005
(870)285-3182

NASHVILLE

HOWARD MEMORIAL HOSPITAL
800 West Leslie
Nashville, AR 71852-4015
(870)845-4400

NEWPORT

HARRIS HOSPITAL
1205 McLain Street
Newport, AR 72112-3533
(870)523-8911

NEWPORT HOSPITAL AND CLINIC
2000 McLain Street
Newport, AR 72112-3697
(870)523-6721

NORTH LITTLE ROCK

BAPTIST MEMORIAL MEDICAL CENTER
3333 Springhill Dr
North Little Rock, AR 72117-2922
(501)202-3000

BRIDGEWAY
#21 Bridgeway Road
North Little Rock, AR 72113-9516
(501)771-1500

VA HEALTHCARE CENTER - EUGENE J. TOWBIN
2200 Fort Roots Drive
North Little Rock, AR 72114-1709
(501)257-1000

OSCEOLA

BAPTIST MEMORIAL HOSPITAL OSCEOLA
611 West Lee, PO Box 607
Osceola, AR 72370-0607
(870)563-7000

OZARK

MERCY HOSPITAL TURNER MEMORIAL
801 W River Street
Ozark, AR 72949-3023
(479)667-4138

PARAGOULD

ARKANSAS METHODIST HOSPITAL
900 West Kings Highway
Paragould, AR 72450-5942
(870)239-7000

PARIS

NORTH LOGAN MERCY HOSPITAL
500 East Academy
Paris, AR 72855-4040
(479)963-6101

PIGGOTT

PIGGOTT COMMUNITY HOSPITAL
1206 Gordon Duckworth Drive
Piggott, AR 72454-1911
(870)598-3881

PINE BLUFF

JEFFERSON REGIONAL MEDICAL CENTER
1600 W 40th Ave
Pine Bluff, AR 71603-6301
(870)541-7100

POCAHONTAS

RANDOLPH COUNTY MEDICAL CENTER
2801 Medical Center Drive
Pocahontas, AR 72455-9497
(870)892-6000

ROGERS

SAINT MARY ROGERS MEMORIAL HOSPITAL
1200 West Walnut Street
Rogers, AR 72756-3546
(479)636-0200

RUSSELLVILLE

SAINT MARYS REGIONAL MEDICAL CENTER
1808 West Main Street
Russellville, AR 72801-2724
(479)968-2841

SALEM

FULTON COUNTY HOSPITAL
Highway 9 North PO Box 517
Salem, AR 72576-0517
(870)895-2691

SEARCY

CENTRAL ARKANSAS HOSPITAL
1200 South Main Street
Searcy, AR 72143-7321
(501)278-3131

WHITE COUNTY MEDICAL CENTER
3214 East Race Avenue
Searcy, AR 72143-4847
(501)268-6121

SHERWOOD

SAINT VINCENT MEDICAL CENTER - SHERWOOD
2215 Wildwood Avenue
Sherwood, AR 72120-5089
(501)835-0900

SAINT VINCENT NORTH REHABILITATION HOSPITAL
2201 Wildwood Avenue Box 6930
Sherwood, AR 72120-5074
(501)834-1800

CALIFORNIA   Hospital Telephone Directory

SILOAM SPRINGS

SILOAM SPRINGS MEMORIAL HOSPITAL
205 East Jefferson
Siloam Springs, AR 72761-3697
(479)524-4141

SPRINGDALE

NORTHWEST MEDICAL CENTER
607 West Maple PO Box 47
Springdale, AR 72765-0047
(479)751-5711

STUTTGART

STUTTGART REGIONAL MEDICAL CENTER
North Buerkle Road
Stuttgart, AR 72160
(870)673-3511

TEXARKANA

LIVING HOPE TEXARKANA
801 Arkansas Blvd
Texarkana, AR 71854-2107
(870)774-4673

VAN BUREN

CRAWFORD COUNTY MEMORIAL HOSPITAL
East Main And South 20th Street
Van Buren, AR 72956
(479)474-3401

WALDRON

MERCY HOSPITAL OF SCOTT COUNTY
895 W 6th Street
Waldron, AR 72958-7001
(479)637-4135

WALNUT RIDGE

LAWRENCE MEMORIAL HOSPITAL
1309 West Main PO Box 839
Walnut Ridge, AR 72476-0839
(870)886-1200

WARREN

BRADLEY COUNTY MEDICAL CENTER
404 South Bradley Street
Warren, AR 71671-3493
(870)226-3731

WEST MEMPHIS

CRITTENDEN MEMORIAL HOSPITAL
200 Tyler
West Memphis, AR 72301-4277
(870)735-1500

WYNNE

CROSSRIDGE COMMUNITY HOSPITAL
PO Box 590
Wynne, AR 72396-0590
(870)238-3300

CALIFORNIA

ALAMEDA

ALAMEDA HOSPITAL
2070 Clinton Avenue
Alameda, CA 94501-4397
(510)522-3700

ALHAMBRA

ALHAMBRA HOSPITAL
100 S Raymond Avenue
Alhambra, CA 91801-3199
(626)570-1606

ALTURAS

MODOC MEDICAL CENTER
228 Mcdowell St
Alturas, CA 96101-3981
(530)233-5131

ANAHEIM

ANAHEIM GENERAL HOSPITAL
3350 W Ball Road
Anaheim, CA 92804-3799
(714)827-6700

ANAHEIM MEMORIAL HOSPITAL
1111 W La Palma Avenue
Anaheim, CA 92801-2881
(714)774-1450

KAISER PERMANENTE ORANGE COUNTY
MEDICAL CENTER
441 N Lakeview Avenue
Anaheim, CA 92807-3028
(714)279-4000

PARK ANAHEIM HEALTHCARE CENTER
3435 W Ball Road
Anaheim, CA 92804-3708
(714)827-5880

PARKVIEW HEALTHCARE CENTER
1514 E Lincoln Avenue
Anaheim, CA 92805-2219
(714)774-2222

WEST ANAHEIM MEDICAL CENTER
3033 W Orange Avenue
Anaheim, CA 92804-3183
(714)827-3000

WESTERN MEDICAL CENTER HOSPITAL
ANAHEIM
1025 S Anaheim Boulevard
Anaheim, CA 92805-5806
(714)533-6220

ANTIOCH

ANTIOCH CONVALESCENT HOSPITAL
1210 A St
Antioch, CA 94509-2378
(925)757-8787

DELTA MEMORIAL HOSPITAL
3901 Lone Tree Way
Antioch, CA 94509-6253
(925)779-7200

APPLE VALLEY

SAINT MARY REGIONAL MEDICAL CENTER
18300 Highway 18
Apple Valley, CA 92307-2206
(760)242-2311

ARCADIA

METHODIST HOSPITAL OF SOUTHERN
CALIFORNIA
300 W Huntington Drive
Arcadia, CA 91007-3473
(626)445-4441

ARCATA

MAD RIVER COMMUNITY HOSPITAL
3800 James Road
Arcata, CA 95521-4742
(707)822-3621

ARROYO GRANDE

ARROYO GRANDE COMMUNITY HOSPITAL
345 S Halcyon Road
Arroyo Grande, CA 93420-3899
(805)489-4261

ATASCADERO

ATASCADERO STATE HOSPITAL
PO Box 7001
Atascadero, CA 93423-7001
(562)468-2000

AUBURN

SUTTER AUBURN FAITH HOSPITAL
11815 Education Street
Auburn, CA 95602-2410
(530)888-4500

AVALON

AVALON MUNICIPAL HOSPITAL
100 Falls Canyon Road PO Box 1563
Avalon, CA 90704-1563
(310)510-0700

BAKERSFIELD

BAKERSFIELD HEART HOSPITAL
3001 Sillect Avenue
Bakersfield, CA 93308-6337
(661)316-6000

BAKERSFIELD MEMORIAL HOSPITAL
420 34th St
Bakersfield, CA 93301-2298
(661)327-1792

GOOD SAMARITAN HOSPITAL
901 Olive Drive
Bakersfield, CA 93308-4144
(661)399-4461

HEALTHSOUTH BAKERSFIELD REHAB
HOSPITAL
5001 Commerce Drive
Bakersfield, CA 93309-0648
(661)323-5500

KERN MEDICAL CENTER
1830 Flower St
Bakersfield, CA 93305-4186
(661)326-2000

MEMORIAL CENTER
5201 White Lane
Bakersfield, CA 93309-6200
(661)398-1800

MERCY HOSPITAL
2215 Truxtun Avenue
Bakersfield, CA 93301-3698
(661)632-5000

MERCY SOUTHWEST HOSPITAL
400 Old River Road
Bakersfield, CA 93311-9781
(661)663-6000

SAN JOAQUIN COMMUNITY HOSPITAL
2615 Eye St
Bakersfield, CA 93301-2026
(661)395-3000

BALDWIN PARK

KAISER PERMANENTE
1011 Baldwin Park Boulevard
Baldwin Park, CA 91706-5881
(626)851-1011

BANNING

SAN GORGONIO MEMORIAL HOSPITAL
600 N Highland Springs Avenue
Banning, CA 92220-3090
(909)845-1121

Hospital Telephone Directory — CALIFORNIA

BARSTOW
BARSTOW COMMUNITY HOSPITAL
555 South Seventh Avenue
Barstow, CA 92311-3086
(760)256-1761

BEALE AIR FORCE BASE
9TH MEDICAL GROUP
15301 Warren Shingle Road
Beale Air Force Base, CA 95903-1907
(530)634-4831

BELLFLOWER
ALTA BELLWOOD GENERAL HOSPITAL INC
10250 E Artesia Boulevard
Bellflower, CA 90706-6781
(562)866-9028

BELLFLOWER MEDICAL CENTER
9542 E Artesia Boulevard
Bellflower, CA 90706-6589
(562)925-8355

KAISER PERMANENTE MEDICAL CENTER BELLFLOWER
9400 E Rosecrans Avenue
Bellflower, CA 90706-2200
(562)461-3000

BERKELEY
ALTA BATES MEDICAL CENTER-ASHBY CAMPUS
2450 Ashby Avenue
Berkeley, CA 94705-2066
(510)204-4444

UNIVERSITY HEALTH SERVICES, TANG CENTER
2222 Bancroft Way
Berkeley, CA 94720-4301
(415)642-2000

BIG BEAR LAKE
BEAR VALLEY COMMUNITY HOSPITAL
41870 Garstin Drive
Big Bear Lake, CA 92315
(909)866-6501

BISHOP
NORTHERN INYO HOSPITAL
150 Pioneer Lane
Bishop, CA 93514-2599
(760)873-5811

BLYTHE
PALO VERDE HOSPITAL
250 N First Street
Blythe, CA 92225-1702
(760)922-4115

BRAWLEY
PIONEERS MEMORIAL HOSPITAL
207 W Legion Road
Brawley, CA 92227-7799
(760)351-3333

BREA
BREA COMMUNITY HOSPITAL
380 W Central Avenue
Brea, CA 92821-3075
(714)529-0211

KINDRED HOSPITAL BREA
875 N Brea Boulevard
Brea, CA 92821-2606
(714)529-6842

BUENA PARK
ANAHEIM GENERAL HOSPITAL-BUENA PARK CAMPUS
5742 Beach Boulevard
Buena Park, CA 90621-2043
(714)521-4770

BURBANK
PROVIDENCE SAINT JOSEPH MEDICAL CENTER
501 South Buena Vista
Burbank, CA 91505-4866
(818)843-5111

BURLINGAME
PENISULA MEDICAL CENTER
1783 El Camino Real
Burlingame, CA 94010-3205
(650)696-5400

CALABASAS
PITTSBURGH SPECIALTY HOSPITAL
23975 Park Sorrento Ste 370
Calabasas, CA 91302-4022
(818)661-0814

CAMARILLO
SAINT JOHNS PLEASANT VALLEY HOSPITAL
2309 Antonio Avenue
Camarillo, CA 93010-1401
(805)389-5800

CAMP PENDLETON
NAVAL HOSPITAL CAMP PENDLETON
Box 555191 Marine Corps Base
Camp Pendleton, CA 92055-5191
(760)725-1304

CAMPBELL
CHILDREN'S RECOVERY CENTER OF NORTH CALIFORNIA
3777 South Bascom Avenue
Campbell, CA 95008-7320
(408)377-1301

CARMICHAEL
MERCY SAN JUAN HOSPITAL
6501 Coyle Avenue
Carmichael, CA 95608-0394
(916)537-5000

CARSON
KAISER FOUNDATION HOSPITAL - CARSON
23621 South Main St
Carson, CA 90745-5743
(310)513-6707

CASTRO VALLEY
EDEN MEDICAL CENTER
20103 Lake Chabot Road
Castro Valley, CA 94546-5341
(510)537-1234

CEDARVILLE
SURPRISE VALLEY COMMUNITY HOSPITAL
Main And Washington St
Cedarville, CA 96104
(530)279-6111

CERRITOS
COLLEGE HOSPITAL
10802 College Place
Cerritos, CA 90703-1579
(562)924-9500

CHESTER
SENECA DISTRICT HOSPITAL
PO Box 737
Chester, CA 96020-0737
(530)258-2151

CHICO
ENLOE MEDICAL CENTER-COHASSET
1531 Esplanade
Chico, CA 95926-3310
(530)332-7300

ENLOE MEDICAL CENTER-ESPLANADE
560 Cohasset Rd
Chico, CA 95926-3310
(530)332-7300

ENLOE REHABILITATION CENTER
340 W East Avenue
Chico, CA 95926-7238
(530)332-3203

CHINO
CANYON RIDGE HOSPITAL
5353 G Street
Chino, CA 91710-5250
(909)590-3700

CHINO VALLEY MEDICAL CENTER
5451 Walnut Avenue
Chino, CA 91710-2672
(909)464-8600

HOSPITAL OF THE CALIFORNIA INSTITUTE FOR MEN
14901 Central Avenue
Chino, CA 91710-9500
(909)597-1821

CHOWCHILLA
CHOWCHILLA DISTRICT MEMORIAL HOSPITAL
1104 Ventura Avenue
Chowchilla, CA 93610-2298
(559)665-3781

CHULA VISTA
BAYVIEW HOSPITAL AND MENTAL HEALTH SYSTEM
330 Moss St
Chula Vista, CA 91911-2005
(619)426-6310

SCRIPPS MEMORIAL HOSPITAL CHULA VISTA
435 H Street
Chula Vista, CA 91910-4383
(619)691-7000

SHARP CHULA VISTA MEDICAL CENTER
751 Medical Center Court
Chula Vista, CA 91911-6617
(619)482-5800

CLEARLAKE
ADVENTIST HEALTH - REDBUD COMMUNITY HOSPITAL
15630 18th Avenue Highway 53
Clearlake, CA 95422
(707)994-6486

CALIFORNIA
Hospital Telephone Directory

CLOVIS

CLOVIS COMMUNITY MEDICAL CENTER
2755 Herndon Avenue
Clovis, CA 93611-6801
(559)324-4000

COALINGA

COALINGA REGIONAL MEDICAL CENTER
1191 Phelps Avenue
Coalinga, CA 93210-9609
(559)935-6400

COLTON

ARROWHEAD REGIONAL MEDICAL CENTER
400 North Pepper Avenue
Colton, CA 92324-1819
(909)580-1000

COLUSA

COLUSA REGIONAL MEDICAL CENTER
199 E Webster Street
Colusa, CA 95932-2954
(530)458-5821

CONCORD

MOUNT DIABLO HOSPITAL MEDICAL
CENTER
2540 East St
Concord, CA 94520-1960
(925)682-8200

MOUNT DIABLO MEDICAL PAVILION
2740 Grant St
Concord, CA 94520-2265
(925)680-6500

CORCORAN

CORCORAN DISTRICT HOSPITAL
1310 Hanna Avenue
Corcoran, CA 93212-2314
(559)992-5051

CORONA

CORONA REGIONAL MEDICAL CENTER
800 South Main Street
Corona, CA 92882-3420
(909)737-4343

CORONA REGIONAL MEDICAL CENTER-
REHAB
730 Magnolia Avenue
Corona, CA 92879-3117
(909)736-7200

CORONADO

SHARP CORONADO HOSPITAL AND HEALTH
CENTER
250 Prospect Place
Coronado, CA 92118-1943
(619)522-3600

COSTA MESA

COLLEGE HOSPITAL COSTA MESA
301 Victoria Street
Costa Mesa, CA 92627-7131
(949)642-2734

FAIRVIEW DEVELOPMENTAL CENTER
2501 Harbor Boulevard
Costa Mesa, CA 92626-6179
(714)957-5000

COVINA

AURORA BEHAVIORAL HEALTH CARE -
CHARTER OAK
1161 E Covina Boulevard
Covina, CA 91724-1523
(626)966-1632

CITRUS VALLEY MEDICAL CENTER-IC
CAMPUS
PO Box 6108
Covina, CA 91722-5108
(626)331-7331

CRESCENT CITY

SUTTER COAST HOSPITAL
800 E Washington Boulevard
Crescent City, CA 95531-8359
(707)464-8511

CULVER CITY

BROTMAN MEDICAL CENTER
3828 Delmas Terrace
Culver City, CA 90232-6806
(310)836-7000

DALY CITY

SETON MEDICAL CENTER
1900 Sullivan Avenue
Daly City, CA 94015-2229
(650)992-4000

DAVIS

SUTTER DAVIS HOSPITAL
Roads 99 And 31
Davis, CA 95616
(530)756-6440

DEER PARK

SAINT HELENA HOSPITAL
Sanitarium And Woodland Streets
Deer Park, CA 94576
(707)963-3611

DELANO

DELANO REGIONAL MEDICAL CENTER
1401 Garces Highway
Delano, CA 93215-3690
(661)725-4800

DOS PALOS

DOS PALOS MEMORIAL HOSPITAL
2118 Marguerite St
Dos Palos, CA 93620-2397
(209)392-6106

DOWNEY

DOWNEY REGIONAL MEDICAL CENTER
11500 Brookshire Avenue
Downey, CA 90241-4917
(562)904-5000

RANCHO LOS AMIGOS MEDICAL CENTER
7601 East Imperial Highway
Downey, CA 90242-3496
(562)401-7111

DUARTE

CITY OF HOPE NATIONAL MEDICAL
CENTER
1500 E Duarte Road
Duarte, CA 91010-3000
(626)359-8111

SANTA TERESITA HOSPITAL
819 Buena Vista Street
Duarte, CA 91010-1703
(626)359-3243

EDWARDS AIR FORCE BASE

95TH MEDICAL GROUP
30 Hospital Road
Edwards Air Force Base, CA 93524-1700
(661)277-2010

EL CENTRO

EL CENTRO REGIONAL MEDICAL CENTER
1415 Ross Avenue
El Centro, CA 92243-4398
(760)339-7100

ELDRIDGE

SONOMA DEVELOPMENTAL CENTER
15000 Arnold Drive
Eldridge, CA 95431
(707)938-6000

ENCINITAS

SCRIPPS MEMORIAL HOSPITAL ENCINITAS
354 Santa Fe Drive
Encinitas, CA 92024-5182
(760)753-6501

ENCINO

ENCINO-TARZANA REGIONAL MEDICAL
CENTER
16237 Ventura Boulevard
Encino, CA 91436-2201
(818)995-5000

ESCONDIDO

PALOMAR MEDICAL CENTER
555 E Valley Parkway
Escondido, CA 92025-3048
(760)739-3000

EUREKA

GENERAL HOSPITAL
2200 Harrison Avenue
Eureka, CA 95501-3215
(707)445-5111

SAINT JOSEPH HOSPITAL
2700 Dolbeer St
Eureka, CA 95501-4799
(707)445-8121

SEMPERVIRENS
720 Wood St
Eureka, CA 95501-4413
(707)445-7710

FAIRFIELD

NORTHBAY MEDICAL CENTER
1200 B Gale Wilson Boulevard
Fairfield, CA 94533-3587
(707)429-3600

TELECARE/SOLANO PSYCHIATRIC HEALTH
FACILITY
2101 Courage Drive
Fairfield, CA 94533-6717
(707)337-7950

FALL RIVER MILLS

MAYERS MEMORIAL HOSPITAL
Highway 299 Box 459
Fall River Mills, CA 96028-0459
(530)336-5511

Hospital Telephone Directory CALIFORNIA

FALLBROOK

FALLBROOK HOSPITAL
624 E Elder St
Fallbrook, CA 92028-3099
(760)728-1191

FOLSOM

KINDRED HOSPITAL SACRAMENTO
223 Fargo Way
Folsom, CA 95630-2961
(916)351-9151

MERCY HOSPITAL OF FOLSOM
1650 Creekside Drive
Folsom, CA 95630-3405
(916)983-7400

FONTANA

KAISER FOUNDATION HOSPITAL FONTANA
9961 Sierra Avenue
Fontana, CA 92335-6720
(909)427-5000

FORT BRAGG

MENDOCINO COAST DISTRICT HOSPITAL
700 River Drive
Fort Bragg, CA 95437-5495
(707)961-1234

FORT IRWIN

WEED ARMY USA MEDDAC COMMUNITY
HOSPITAL
PO Box 105109
Fort Irwin, CA 92310-5109
(760)380-3108

FORTUNA

REDWOOD MEMORIAL HOSPITAL
3300 Renner Drive
Fortuna, CA 95540-3198
(707)725-3361

FOUNTAIN VALLEY

FOUNTAIN VALLEY REGIONAL HOSPITAL
17100 Euclid Street
Fountain Valley, CA 92708-4043
(714)966-7200

ORANGE COAST MEMORIAL MEDICAL
CENTER
9920 Talbert Avenue
Fountain Valley, CA 92708-5153
(714)378-7000

FREMONT

FREMONT HOSPITAL
39001 Sundale Drive
Fremont, CA 94538-2005
(510)796-1100

WASHINGTON HOSPITAL
2000 Mowry Avenue
Fremont, CA 94538-1746
(510)797-1111

FRENCH CAMP

SAN JOAQUIN GENERAL HOSPITAL
500 West Hospital Road
French Camp, CA 95231
(209)468-6000

FRESNO

CEDAR VISTA HOSPITAL
575 E Locust Ave Ste 311
Fresno, CA 93720-2928
(559)449-8000

COMMUNITY MEDICAL CENTER - FRESNO
2823 Fresno Street
Fresno, CA 93721-1365
(559)459-6000

FRESNO SURGERY CENTER
6125 North Fresno St
Fresno, CA 93710-5207
(559)431-8000

KAISER FOUNDATION HOSPITAL - FRESNO
7300 North Fresno St
Fresno, CA 93720-2941
(559)448-4500

SAINT AGNES MEDICAL CENTER
1303 E Herndon Avenue
Fresno, CA 93720-3309
(559)450-3000

SAN JOAQUIN VALLEY REHABILITATION
HOSPITAL
7173 N Sharon Avenue
Fresno, CA 93720-3329
(559)436-3600

UNIVERSITY MEDICAL CENTER
445 S Cedar Avenue
Fresno, CA 93702-2998
(559)459-4000

VA HEALTHCARE SYSTEM - CENTRAL
CALIFORNIA
2615 E Clinton Avenue
Fresno, CA 93703-2223
(559)225-6100

FULLERTON

SAINT JUDE MEDICAL CENTER
101 E Valencia Mesa Drive
Fullerton, CA 92835-3809
(714)992-3000

GARBERVILLE

JEROLD PHELPS COMMUNITY HOSPITAL
733 Cedar St
Garberville, CA 95542-3201
(707)923-3921

GARDEN GROVE

GARDEN GROVE HOSPITAL
12601 Garden Grove Boulevard
Garden Grove, CA 92843-1908
(714)537-5160

GARDENA

COMMUNITY HOSPITAL OF GARDENA
1246 W 155th St
Gardena, CA 90247-4062
(310)323-5330

MEMORIAL HOSPITAL OF GARDENA
1145 W Redondo Beach Boulevard
Gardena, CA 90247-3528
(310)532-4200

GILROY

SAINT LOUISE REGIONAL MEDICAL
CENTER
9400 No Name Uno
Gilroy, CA 95020-3531
(408)848-2000

GLENDALE

GLENDALE ADVENTIST MEDICAL CENTER
1509 Wilson Terrace
Glendale, CA 91206-4098
(818)409-8000

GLENDALE MEMORIAL HOSPITAL AND
HEALTH CENTER
1420 S Central Avenue
Glendale, CA 91204-2594
(818)502-1900

VERDUGO HILLS HOSPITAL
1812 Verdugo Boulevard
Glendale, CA 91208-1409
(818)790-7100

GLENDORA

EAST VALLEY HOSPITAL MEDICAL CENTER
150 West Route 66
Glendora, CA 91740-6207
(626)335-0231

FOOTHILL PRESBYTERIAN HOSPITAL
250 S Grand Avenue
Glendora, CA 91741-4218
(626)963-8411

GRANADA HILLS

GRANADA HILLS COMMUNITY HOSPITAL
10445 Balboa Boulevard
Granada Hills, CA 91344-7382
(818)360-1021

GRASS VALLEY

SIERRA NEVADA MEMORIAL HOSPITAL
Highway 20 And Glasson Way
Grass Valley, CA 95945
(530)274-6000

GREENVILLE

INDIAN VALLEY DISTRICT HOSPITAL
184 Hot Springs Road
Greenville, CA 95947-9747
(530)284-7191

GRIDLEY

BIGGS-GRIDLEY MEMORIAL HOSPITAL
240 Spruce St
Gridley, CA 95948-2216
(530)846-5671

HANFORD

CENTRAL VALLEY GENERAL HOSPITAL
1025 N Douty St
Hanford, CA 93230-3722
(559)583-2100

HANFORD COMMUNITY MEDICAL CENTER
450 Greenfield Avenue
Hanford, CA 93230-3510
(559)582-9000

HARBOR CITY

KAISER PERMANENTE MEDICAL CENTER
25825 South Vermont Avenue
Harbor City, CA 90710-3599
(310)325-5111

HAWAIIAN GARDENS

TRI CITY REGIONAL MEDICAL CENTER
PO Box 2200
Hawaiian Gardens, CA 90716-0200
(562)860-0401

HAWTHORNE

LOS ANGELES METROPOLITAN MEDICAL
CENTER - HAWTHORN
13300 South Hawthorn Blvd
Hawthorne, CA 90250-5805
(310)679-3321

CALIFORNIA
Hospital Telephone Directory

ROBERT F KENNEDY MEDICAL CENTER
4500 116th Street
Hawthorne, CA 90250-2296
(310)973-1711

HAYWARD

KAISER MEDICAL CENTER
27400 Hesperian Boulevard
Hayward, CA 94545-4297
(510)784-4000

MORTON BAKAR CENTER
494 Blossom Way
Hayward, CA 94541-1948
(510)582-7676

SAINT ROSE HOSPITAL
27200 Calaroga Avenue
Hayward, CA 94545-4383
(510)264-4000

HEALDSBURG

HEALDSBURG DISTRICT HOSPITAL
1375 University Avenue
Healdsburg, CA 95448-3382
(707)431-6500

HEMET

DEVONSHIRE CARE CENTER
1350 Devonshire Avenue
Hemet, CA 92544-8629
(909)925-2571

HEMET VALLEY MEDICAL CENTER
1117 E Devonshire
Hemet, CA 92543-3084
(909)652-2811

HOLLISTER

HAZEL HAWKINS MEMORIAL HOSPITAL
911 Sunset Drive
Hollister, CA 95023-5695
(831)637-5711

HOLLYWOOD

HOLLYWOOD COMMUNITY HOSPITAL
6245 Delongpre Avenue
Hollywood, CA 90028-9001
(323)462-2271

HUNTINGTON BEACH

HUNTINGTON BEACH HOSPITAL
17772 Beach Boulevard
Huntington Beach, CA 92647-6819
(714)842-1473

HUNTINGTON PARK

COMMUNITY HOSPITAL OF HUNTINGTON PARK
2623 E Slausen Avenue
Huntington Park, CA 90255-2900
(323)583-1931

MISSION HOSPITAL OF HUNTINGTON PARK
3111 E Florence Avenue
Huntington Park, CA 90255-5800
(323)582-8261

INDIO

JOHN F KENNEDY MEMORIAL HOSPITAL
47-111 Monroe St
Indio, CA 92201-6799
(760)347-6191

INGLEWOOD

CENTINELA HOSPITAL MEDICAL CENTER
555 East Hardy Street
Inglewood, CA 90301-4073
(310)673-4660

DANIEL FREEMAN MEMORIAL HOSPITAL
333 North Prairie Avenue
Inglewood, CA 90301-4514
(310)674-7050

IRVINE

IRVINE REGIONAL HOSPITAL
16200 Sand Canyon Avenue
Irvine, CA 92618-3714
(949)753-2000

JACKSON

SUTTER AMADOR HOSPITAL
200 Mission Blvd
Jackson, CA 95642-2564
(209)223-7500

JOSHUA TREE

HI-DESERT MEDICAL CENTER
6601 Whitefeather Road
Joshua Tree, CA 92252-6607
(760)366-3711

KENTFIELD

KENTFIELD MEDICAL HOSPITAL
1125 Sir Francis Drake Boulevard
Kentfield, CA 94904-1418
(415)456-9680

KING CITY

GEORGE L MEE MEMORIAL HOSPITAL
300 Canal St
King City, CA 93930-3457
(831)385-6000

KINGSBURG

KINGSBURG MEDICAL CENTER
1200 Smith St
Kingsburg, CA 93631-2297
(559)897-5841

LA JOLLA

SCRIPPS GREEN HOSPITAL
10666 North Torrey Pines Road
La Jolla, CA 92037-1027
(858)455-9100

SCRIPPS MEMORIAL HOSPITAL LA JOLLA
9888 Genesee Avenue
La Jolla, CA 92037-1276
(858)626-4123

UNIVERSITY OF CALIFORNIA - THORNTON HOSPITAL
9300 Campus Point Drive
La Jolla, CA 92037-1300
(858)657-7000

LA MESA

ALVARADO PARKWAY INSTITUTE - SAN DIEGO
7050 Parkway Drive
La Mesa, CA 91942-1562
(619)465-4411

GROSSMONT HOSPITAL
5555 Grossmont Center Drive Box 158
La Mesa, CA 91942-3077
(619)465-0711

LA MIRADA

KINDRED HOSPITAL OF LA MIRADA
14900 E Imperial Highway
La Mirada, CA 90638-2172
(562)944-1900

LA PALMA

LA PALMA INTERCOMMUNITY HOSPITAL
7901 Walker Street
La Palma, CA 90623-1764
(714)670-7400

LAGUNA BEACH

SOUTH COAST MEDICAL CENTER
31872 Coast Highway
Laguna Beach, CA 92651-6775
(949)499-1311

LAGUNA HILLS

SADDLEBACK MEMORIAL MEDICAL CENTER
24451 Health Center Drive
Laguna Hills, CA 92653-3689
(949)837-4500

LAKE ARROWHEAD

MOUNTAINS COMMUNITY HOSPITAL
North Shore Road And Highway 173 Box 70
Lake Arrowhead, CA 92352-0070
(909)336-3651

LAKE ISABELLA

KERN VALLEY HOSPITAL
6412 Laurel Avenue
Lake Isabella, CA 93240-9529
(760)379-2681

LAKEPORT

SUTTER LAKESIDE HOSPITAL
5176 Hill Road East
Lakeport, CA 95453-6357
(707)262-5000

LAKEWOOD

LAKEWOOD REGIONAL MEDICAL CENTER
3700 East South Street, PO Box 6070
Lakewood, CA 90714-6070
(310)531-2550

LANCASTER

ANTELOPE VALLEY HOSPITAL MEDICAL CENTER
1600 W Avenue J
Lancaster, CA 93534-2894
(661)949-5000

LAC HIGH DESERT HOSPITAL
44900 N 60th St W
Lancaster, CA 93536-7621
(661)945-8581

LANCASTER COMMUNITY HOSPITAL
43830 North 10th Street West
Lancaster, CA 93534-4895
(661)948-4781

LEMON GROVE

CRESTA LOMA MENTAL HEALTH CENTER
7922 Palm Street
Lemon Grove, CA 91945-2996
(619)464-3488

Hospital Telephone Directory — CALIFORNIA

LEMOORE
NAVAL HOSPITAL LEMOORE
930 Franklin Avenue
Lemoore, CA 93245
(559)998-4201

LIVERMORE
VA MEDICAL CENTER - LIVERMORE
4941 Arroyo Road
Livermore, CA 94550-9650
(925)447-2560

VALLEY MEMORIAL HOSPITAL
1111 East Stanley Boulevard
Livermore, CA 94550-4199
(925)447-7000

LODI
LODI MEMORIAL HOSPITAL
975 S Fairmont Avenue
Lodi, CA 95240-5179
(209)334-3411

LODI MEMORIAL HOSPITAL WEST
800 South Lower Sacramento Road
Lodi, CA 95242-3635
(209)333-0211

LOMA LINDA
LOMA LINDA UNIVERSITY COMMUNITY
MEDICAL CENTER
25333 Barton Road
Loma Linda, CA 92354-3171
(909)558-6000

LOMA LINDA UNIVERSITY MEDICAL
CENTER
11234 Anderson St
Loma Linda, CA 92354-2871
(909)558-4000

VA MEDICAL CENTER - JERRY L. PETTIS
11201 Benton St
Loma Linda, CA 92357-1000
(909)825-7084

LOMPOC
LOMPOC HOSPITAL DISTRICT
508 East Hickory Avenue
Lompoc, CA 93436-7331
(805)737-3300

LONE PINE
SOUTHERN INYO HOSPITAL
501 E Locust St
Lone Pine, CA 93545
(760)876-5501

LONG BEACH
COMMUNITY HOSPITAL OF LONG BEACH
1720 Termino Avenue
Long Beach, CA 90804-2104
(562)498-1000

LA CASA MENTAL HEALTH REHABILITATION
CENTER
6060 Paramount Boulevard
Long Beach, CA 90805-3711
(562)634-9534

LA CASA PSYCHIATRIC HEALTHCARE
FACILITY
6060 Paramount Boulevard
Long Beach, CA 90805-3711
(562)634-9534

LONG BEACH MEMORIAL HOSPITAL
2801 Atlantic Avenue
Long Beach, CA 90806-1799
(562)933-2000

MILLER CHILDREN'S HOSPITAL
2801 Atlantic Avenue
Long Beach, CA 90806-1737
(562)933-5437

PACIFIC HOSPITAL OF LONG BEACH
2776 Pacific Avenue
Long Beach, CA 90806-2699
(562)595-1911

REDGATE RECOVERY CENTER
1775 Chestnut Avenue
Long Beach, CA 90813-1674
(562)599-8444

SAINT MARY MEDICAL CENTER
1050 Linden Avenue
Long Beach, CA 90813-3393
(562)491-9000

VA MEDICAL CENTER - LONG BEACH
5901 East 7th Street
Long Beach, CA 90822-5201
(562)826-8000

LOS ALAMITOS
LOS ALAMITOS MEDICAL CENTER
3751 Katella Avenue
Los Alamitos, CA 90720-3164
(562)598-1311

LOS ANGELES
BARLOW RESPIRATORY HOSPITAL
2000 Stadium Way
Los Angeles, CA 90026-2696
(213)250-4200

CALIFORNIA HOSPITAL MEDICAL CENTER
LA
1401 South Grand Avenue
Los Angeles, CA 90015-3010
(213)748-2411

CEDARS-SINAI MEDICAL CENTER
8700 Beverly Boulevard
Los Angeles, CA 90048-1865
(323)423-5000

CENTURY CITY HOSPITAL
2070 Century Park East
Los Angeles, CA 90067-1907
(310)553-6211

CHILDRENS HOSPITAL OF LOS ANGELES
4650 Sunset Boulevard
Los Angeles, CA 90027-6062
(323)660-2450

CITY OF ANGELS MEDICAL CENTER
1711 West Temple Street
Los Angeles, CA 90026-5421
(213)989-6100

EAST LOS ANGELES DOCTORS HOSPITAL
4060 Whittier Boulevard
Los Angeles, CA 90023-2596
(323)268-5514

ELASTAR COMMUNITY HOSPITAL
319 N Humphreys Avenue
Los Angeles, CA 90022-1422
(323)266-6500

GATEWAYS HOSPITAL AND MENTAL
HEALTH CENTER
1891 Effie St
Los Angeles, CA 90026-1793
(323)644-2000

GOOD SAMARITAN HOSPITAL
1225 Wilshire Boulevard
Los Angeles, CA 90017-1901
(213)977-2121

KAISER FOUNDATION HOSPITAL MENTAL
HEALTH CENTER
765 West College St
Los Angeles, CA 90012-5923
(213)580-7200

KAISER PERMANENTE LOS ANGELES
MEDICAL CENTER
4867 Sunset Boulevard
Los Angeles, CA 90027-5969
(323)783-4011

KAISER PERMANENTE WEST LOS
ANGELES MEDICAL CENTER
6041 Cadillac Avenue
Los Angeles, CA 90034-1702
(310)857-2000

KEDREN COMMUNITY HEALTH CENTER
4211 South Avalon Boulevard
Los Angeles, CA 90011-5699
(323)233-0425

KINDRED HOSPITAL LOS ANGELES
7366 W Manchester Ave Apt F
Los Angeles, CA 90045-2345
(310)642-0325

LAC/KING - DREW MEDICAL CENTER
12021 S Wilmington Avenue
Los Angeles, CA 90059-3019
(323)668-4321

LINCOLN HOSPITAL MEDICAL CENTER
443 South Soto Street
Los Angeles, CA 90033-4398
(323)261-1181

LOS ANGELES COMMUNITY HOSPITAL
4081 E Olympic Boulevard
Los Angeles, CA 90023-3300
(323)267-0477

LOS ANGELES COMMUNITY HOSPITAL OF
NORWALK
13222 Bloomfield Avenue
Los Angeles, CA 90650-3249
(562)863-4763

LOS ANGELES COUNTY - UNIVERSITY OF
SOUTHERN CALIFORNIA
1200 N State St
Los Angeles, CA 90089-0123
(213)226-2622

LOS ANGELES METROPOLITAN MEDICAL
CENTER - LA CAMPUS
2231 S Western Avenue
Los Angeles, CA 90018-1302
(323)730-7300

LOS ANGELES SHERIFFS DEPARTMENT
MEDICAL
441 Bauchet St
Los Angeles, CA 90012-2906
(213)473-6100

MIDWAY HOSPITAL MEDICAL CENTER
5925 San Vicente Boulevard
Los Angeles, CA 90019-6696
(323)938-3161

ORTHOPEDIC HOSPITAL
2400 S Flower St
Los Angeles, CA 90007-2697
(213)742-1000

PACIFIC ALLIANCE MEDICAL CENTER
531 W College St
Los Angeles, CA 90012-2315
(213)624-8411

PSYCHIATRIC SERVICES - LAC & USC
MEDICAL CENTER
1937 Hospital Place
Los Angeles, CA 90033-1011
(323)226-5616

QUEEN OF ANGELS/HOLLYWOOD
PRESBYTERIAN MEDICAL CENTER
1300 N Vermont Avenue
Los Angeles, CA 90027-6005
(323)913-4800

CALIFORNIA
Hospital Telephone Directory

SAINT VINCENT MEDICAL CENTER
2131 W 3rd St
Los Angeles, CA 90057-1901
(213)484-7111

SAN VICENTE HOSPITAL
6000 San Vicente Boulevard
Los Angeles, CA 90036-4404
(323)937-2504

SHRINERS HOSPITAL FOR CHILDREN
3160 Geneva St
Los Angeles, CA 90020-1199
(213)388-3151

TEMPLE COMMUNITY HOSPITAL
235 N Hoover St
Los Angeles, CA 90004-3672
(213)382-7252

UNIVERSITY OF CALIFORNIA - LOS ANGELES MEDICAL CENTER
10833 Le Conte Avenue
Los Angeles, CA 90095-3075
(310)825-9111

UNIVERSITY OF CALIFORNIA LOS ANGELES (UCLA) NEUROPSYCHIATRIC HOSPITAL CLINIC
760 Westwood Plaza
Los Angeles, CA 90095-8353
(310)825-0511

UNIVERSITY OF SOUTHERN CALIFORNIA (USC) KENNETH NORRIS JR CANCER HOSPITAL
1441 Eastlake Avenue, PO Box 33804
Los Angeles, CA 90033-0804
(323)865-3000

UNIVERSITY OF SOUTHERN CALIFORNIA (USC) UNIVERSITY HOSPITAL
1500 San Pablo Street
Los Angeles, CA 90089-0113
(213)442-8500

VA HEALTHCARE SYSTEM - GREATER LOS ANGELES
11301 Wilshire Boulevard
Los Angeles, CA 90073-1003
(310)478-37112

WHITE MEMORIAL MEDICAL CENTER
1720 Cesar Chavez Avenue
Los Angeles, CA 90033
(323)268-5000

WOMEN'S AND CHILDREN'S HOSPITAL - LAC
1240 N Mission Road
Los Angeles, CA 90033-1019
(323)226-3427

LOS BANOS

MEMORIAL HOSPITAL LOS BANOS
520 West I St
Los Banos, CA 93635-3419
(209)826-0591

LOS GATOS

COMMUNITY HOSPITAL LOS GATOS
815 Pollard Road
Los Gatos, CA 95032-1438
(408)378-6131

LOYALTON

SIERRA VALLEY DISTRICT HOSPITAL
700 Third St PO Box 178
Loyalton, CA 96118-0178
(530)993-1225

LYNWOOD

SAINT FRANCIS MEDICAL CENTER
3630 East Imperial Highway
Lynwood, CA 90262-2636
(310)900-8900

MADERA

CHILDREN'S HOSPITAL CENTRAL CALIFORNIA
9300 Valley Childrens Pl
Madera, CA 93638-8762
(559)353-3000

MADERA COMMUNITY HOSPITAL
1250 E Almond Avenue
Madera, CA 93637-5696
(559)675-5555

MAMMOTH LAKES

MAMMOTH HOSPITAL
85 Sierra Park Road, PO Box 3399
Mammoth Lakes, CA 93546-3399
(760)934-3311

MANTECA

DOCTORS HOSPITAL OF MANTECA
1205 E North St
Manteca, CA 95336-4900
(209)823-3111

SAINT DOMINICS HOSPITAL
1777 West Yosemite Avenue
Manteca, CA 95337-5187
(209)825-3500

MARINA DEL REY

DANIEL FREEMAN MARINA HOSPITAL
4650 Lincoln Boulevard
Marina Del Rey, CA 90292-6360
(310)823-8911

MARIPOSA

JOHN C FREMONT MEDICAL CLINIC
5189 Hospital Road
Mariposa, CA 95338-9524
(209)966-3631

MARTINEZ

CONTRA COSTA REGIONAL MEDICAL CENTER
2500 Alhambra Avenue
Martinez, CA 94553-3156
(925)370-5000

KAISER MEDICAL CENTER
200 Muir Road
Martinez, CA 94553-4672
(925)372-1000

VA HEALTHCARE SYSTEM - NORTHERN CALIFORNIA
150 Muir Rd
Martinez, CA 94553-4668
(925)372-2000

VA REHABILITATION AND EXTENDED CARE - MARTINEZ
150 Muir Road
Martinez, CA 94553-4668
(925)372-2000

MARYSVILLE

RIDEOUT MEMORIAL HOSPITAL
726 4th St
Marysville, CA 95901-5600
(530)749-4300

MENLO PARK

MENLO PARK SURGICAL HOSPITAL
570 Willow Road
Menlo Park, CA 94025-2617
(650)324-8500

VA MEDICAL CENTER - MENLO PARK
795 Willow Road
Menlo Park, CA 94025-2539
(650)493-5000

MERCED

MERCY MEDICAL CENTER - DOMINICAN CAMPUS
2740 M Street
Merced, CA 95340-2813
(209)384-6444

MERCY MEDICAL CENTER - MERCED
301 E 13th St
Merced, CA 95340-6211
(209)385-7000

MISSION HILLS

PROVIDENCE HOLY CROSS MEDICAL CENTER
15031 Rinaldi St
Mission Hills, CA 91345-1285
(818)365-8051

MISSION VIEJO

CHILDRENS HOSPITAL AT MISSION
27700 Medical Center Road, 5th Floor
Mission Viejo, CA 92691-6426
(949)364-1400

MISSION HOSPITAL REGIONAL MEDICAL CENTER
27700 Medical Center Road
Mission Viejo, CA 92691-6426
(949)364-1400

MODESTO

DOCTORS MEDICAL CENTER
1441 Florida Avenue
Modesto, CA 95350-4418
(209)578-1211

MEMORIAL MEDICAL CENTER
1700 Coffee Road
Modesto, CA 95355-2803
(209)526-4500

MODESTO REHAB HOSPITAL
730 17th St
Modesto, CA 95354-1209
(209)523-9006

STANISLAUS SURGICAL HOSPITAL
1421 Oakdale Road
Modesto, CA 95355-3359
(209)572-2700

MONROVIA

MONROVIA COMMUNITY HOSPITAL
323 S Heliotrope Avenue
Monrovia, CA 91016-2900
(626)359-8341

MONTCLAIR

DOCTORS HOSPITAL
5000 San Bernardino St
Montclair, CA 91763-2326
(909)625-5411

MONTEBELLO

BEVERLY HOSPITAL
309 W Beverly Boulevard
Montebello, CA 90640-4308
(323)726-1222

Hospital Telephone Directory   **CALIFORNIA**

MONTEREY

COMMUNITY HOSPITAL OF MONTEREY PENINSULA
23625 W R Holman Highway
Monterey, CA 93940-5902
(831)624-5311

MONTEREY PARK

GARFIELD MEDICAL CENTER
525 N Garfield Avenue
Monterey Park, CA 91754-1205
(626)573-2222

MONTEREY PARK HOSPITAL
900 S Atlantic Boulevard
Monterey Park, CA 91754-4780
(626)570-9000

MORENO VALLEY

MORENO VALLEY MEDICAL CENTER
27300 Iris Avenue
Moreno Valley, CA 92555-4800
(909)243-0811

RIVERSIDE COUNTY REGIONAL MEDICAL CENTER
26520 Cactus Avenue
Moreno Valley, CA 92555-3911
(909)486-4000

MOSS BEACH

SETON MEDICAL CENTER COASTSIDE
600 Marine Boulevard
Moss Beach, CA 94038-9641
(650)563-7100

MOUNT SHASTA

MERCY MEDICAL CENTER MOUNT SHASTA
914 Pine St
Mount Shasta, CA 96067-2143
(530)926-6111

MOUNTAIN VIEW

EL CAMINO HOSPITAL
2500 Grant Road
Mountain View, CA 94040-4378
(650)940-7000

MURRIETA

RANCHO SPRINGS MEDICAL CENTER
25500 Medical Center Drive
Murrieta, CA 92562-5965
(909)696-6000

NAPA

NAPA STATE HOSPITAL
2100 Napa Vallejo Highway
Napa, CA 94558-6293
(707)253-5000

QUEEN OF THE VALLEY HOSPITAL
1000 Trancas St
Napa, CA 94558-2941
(707)252-4411

NATIONAL CITY

PARADISE VALLEY HOSPITAL
2400 East Fourth Street
National City, CA 91950-2098
(619)470-4321

NEEDLES

COLORADO RIVER MEDICAL CENTER
1401 Bailey Avenue
Needles, CA 92363-3103
(760)326-4531

NEWPORT BEACH

HOAG MEMORIAL HOSPITAL PRESBYTERIAN
One Hoag Drive
Newport Beach, CA 92663
(949)645-8600

NEWPORT BAY HOSPITAL
1501 E 16th St
Newport Beach, CA 92663-5924
(949)650-9750

NORTHRIDGE

NORTHRIDGE HOSPITAL MEDICAL CENTER
18300 Roscoe Boulevard
Northridge, CA 91325-4167
(818)885-8500

NORWALK

COAST PLAZA DOCTORS HOSPITAL
13100 S Studebaker Road
Norwalk, CA 90650-2500
(562)868-3751

METROPOLITAN STATE HOSPITAL
11400 S Norwalk Boulevard
Norwalk, CA 90650-2084
(562)863-7011

NOVATO

NOVATO COMMUNITY HOSPITAL
180 Rowland Way
Novato, CA 94945-5009
(415)209-1300

OAKDALE

OAK VALLEY DISTRICT HOSPITAL
350 South Oak St
Oakdale, CA 95361-3581
(209)847-3011

OAKLAND

ALAMEDA COUNTY MEDICAL CENTER
1411 E 31st St
Oakland, CA 94602-1018
(510)437-4800

CHILDRENS HOSPITAL MEDICAL CENTER
51 St And Grove Streets
Oakland, CA 94609
(510)428-3000

GARFIELD NEUROBEHAVIORAL CENTER
1451 28th Avenue
Oakland, CA 94601-1632
(510)261-9191

GLADMAN PSYCH HEALTH FACILITY
2633 E 27th St
Oakland, CA 94601-1912
(510)536-8111

KAISER PERMANENTE MEDICAL CENTER OAKLAND CAMPUS
280 W Mac Arthur Boulevard
Oakland, CA 94611-5667
(510)752-1000

MPI TREATMENT SERVICES - CHEMICAL DEPENDENCY RECOVERY HOSPITAL
3012 Summit St 5th Floor
Oakland, CA 94609-3480
(510)652-7000

SUMMIT MEDICAL CENTER
Hawthorne And Webster Streets
Oakland, CA 94609
(510)655-4000

THUNDER ROAD CHEMICAL DEPENDENCY RECOVERY HOSPITAL
390 40th St
Oakland, CA 94609-2633
(510)653-5040

OCEANSIDE

TRI CITY MEDICAL CENTER
4002 Vista Way
Oceanside, CA 92056-4506
(760)724-8411

OJAI

OJAI VALLEY COMMUNITY HOSPITAL
1306 Maricopa Highway
Ojai, CA 93023-3163
(805)646-1401

ONTARIO

KINDRED HOSPITAL ONTARIO
550 North Monterey
Ontario, CA 91764-3399
(909)391-0333

ORANGE

CHAPMAN MEDICAL CENTER
2601 E Chapman Avenue
Orange, CA 92869-3206
(714)633-0011

CHILDRENS HOSPITAL OF ORANGE COUNTY
455 South Main Street
Orange, CA 92868-3835
(714)997-3000

HEALTHBRIDGE CHILDREN'S REHAB HOSPITAL
393 South Tustin Street
Orange, CA 92866-2501
(714)289-2400

SAINT JOSEPH HOSPITAL
1100 W Stewart Drive
Orange, CA 92868-3891
(714)633-9111

UNIVERSITY OF CALIFORNIA IRVINE MEDICAL CENTER
101 The City Drive S
Orange, CA 92868-3201
(714)456-6011

OROVILLE

OROVILLE HOSPITAL
2767 Olive Highway
Oroville, CA 95966-6118
(530)533-8500

OXNARD

SAINT JOHNS REGIONAL MEDICAL CENTER
1600 N Rose Avenue
Oxnard, CA 93030-3723
(805)988-2500

PALM SPRINGS

DESERT REGIONAL MEDICAL CENTER
1150 North Indian Canyon Drive
Palm Springs, CA 92262-4872
(760)323-6511

PALO ALTO

LUCILLE SALTER PACKARD CHILDRENS HOSPITAL
725 Welch Road
Palo Alto, CA 94304-1601
(650)497-8000

CALIFORNIA — Hospital Telephone Directory

VA HEALTHCARE SYSTEM - PALO ALTO
3801 Miranda Avenue
Palo Alto, CA 94304-1207
(650)493-5000

PANORAMA CITY

KAISER FOUNDATION HOSPITAL
13652 Cantara St
Panorama City, CA 91402-5423
(818)375-2000

MISSION COMMUNITY HOSPITAL
14850 Roscoe Boulevard
Panorama City, CA 91402-4677
(818)787-2222

PARADISE

FEATHER RIVER HOSPITAL
5974 Pentz Road
Paradise, CA 95969-5593
(530)877-9361

PARAMOUNT

SUBURBAN MEDICAL CENTER
16453 South Colorado Avenue
Paramount, CA 90723-5000
(562)531-3110

PASADENA

HUNTINGTON MEMORIAL HOSPITAL
100 W California Boulevard
Pasadena, CA 91105-3097
(626)397-5000

IMPACT DRUG & ALCOHOL TREATMENT CENTER
1680 North Fair Oaks Avenue
Pasadena, CA 91103-1642
(323)681-2575

LAS ENCINAS HOSPITAL
2900 E Del Mar Boulevard
Pasadena, CA 91107-4399
(626)795-9901

PATTON

PATTON STATE HOSPITAL
3102 East Highland Avenue
Patton, CA 92369
(909)425-7000

PERRIS

VALLEY PLAZA DOCTORS HOSPITAL
2224 Medical Center Drive
Perris, CA 92571-2638
(909)943-7380

PETALUMA

PETALUMA VALLEY HOSPITAL
400 N Mcdowell Boulevard
Petaluma, CA 94954-2369
(707)778-1111

PINOLE

DOCTORS MEDICAL CENTER PINOLE CAMPUS
2151 Appian Way
Pinole, CA 94564-2514
(510)724-5000

PLACENTIA

PLACENTIA LINDA HOSPITAL
1301 N Rose Drive
Placentia, CA 92870-3899
(714)993-2000

PLACERVILLE

MARSHALL HOSPITAL
Marshall Way
Placerville, CA 95667
(530)622-1441

PLEASANTON

VALLEY CARE MEDICAL CENTER
5555 W Las Positas Boulevard
Pleasanton, CA 94588-4000
(925)847-3000

POMONA

CASA COLINA HOSPITAL FOR REHAB MEDICINE
255 E Bonita Avenue
Pomona, CA 91767-1923
(909)596-7733

LANDMARK MEDICAL CENTER
2030 N Garey Avenue
Pomona, CA 91767-2795
(909)593-2585

LANTERMAN DEVELOPMENTAL CENTER
3530 W Pomona Boulevard
Pomona, CA 91768-3238
(909)595-1221

POMONA VALLEY HOSPITAL MEDICAL CENTER
1798 N Garey Avenue
Pomona, CA 91767-2918
(909)865-9500

PORTERVILLE

PORTERVILLE DEVELOPMENTAL CENTER
26501 Avenue 140
Porterville, CA 93257-9109
(559)782-2222

SIERRA VIEW DISTRICT HOSPITAL
465 W Putnam Avenue
Porterville, CA 93257-3320
(559)784-1110

PORTOLA

EASTERN PLUMAS HEALTH CARE
500 First Avenue PO Box 1075
Portola, CA 96122-1075
(530)832-4277

POWAY

POMERADO HOSPITAL
15615 Pomerado Road
Poway, CA 92064-2460
(858)485-6511

QUINCY

PLUMAS DISTRICT HOSPITAL
1065 Bucks Lake Road
Quincy, CA 95971-9599
(530)283-2121

RAMONA

BROAD HORIZONS OF RAMONA
1236 H St
Ramona, CA 92065-2837
(760)789-7060

RANCHO MIRAGE

BETTY FORD CENTER
39000 Bob Hope Drive
Rancho Mirage, CA 92270-3297
(760)340-4100

EISENHOWER MEDICAL CENTER
39000 Bob Hope Drive
Rancho Mirage, CA 92270-3296
(760)340-3911

RANCHO MIRAGE CARDIOLOGY MEDICAL CENTER
39000 Bob Hope Drive
Rancho Mirage, CA 92270-3221
(760)324-3278

RED BLUFF

SAINT ELIZABETH COMMUNITY HOSPITAL
2550 Sister Mary Columba Drive
Red Bluff, CA 96080-4397
(530)529-8000

REDDING

MERCY MEDICAL CENTER REDDING
2175 Rosaline Avenue, Clairmont Hgts
Redding, CA 96001-2509
(530)225-6000

NORTHERN CALIFORNIA REHAB HOSPITAL
2801 Eureka Way
Redding, CA 96001-0222
(530)246-9000

PATIENTS HOSPITAL OF REDDING
2900 Eureka Way
Redding, CA 96001-0220
(530)225-8700

REDDING MEDICAL CENTER
1100 Butte Street
Redding, CA 96001-0853
(530)244-5400

SHASTA COUNTY IN-PATIENT MENTAL HEALTH SERVICES
2640 Breslauer Way
Redding, CA 96001-4246
(530)225-5200

REDLANDS

LOMA LINDA UNIVERSITY BEHAVIORAL MEDICINE CENTER
1710 Barton Road
Redlands, CA 92373-5304
(909)558-9200

REDLANDS COMMUNITY HOSPITAL
350 Terracina Boulevard
Redlands, CA 92373-4897
(909)335-5500

REDWOOD CITY

CORDILLERAS MENTAL HEALTH REHABILITATION CENTER
200 Edmonds Road
Redwood City, CA 94062-3813
(650)367-1890

KAISER FOUNDATION HOSPITAL
1150 Veterans Boulevard
Redwood City, CA 94063-2037
(650)299-2000

SEQUOIA HOSPITAL
170 Alameda De Las Plugas
Redwood City, CA 94062-2799
(650)369-5811

REEDLEY

SIERRA KINGS DISTRICT HOSPITAL
372 W Cypress Avenue
Reedley, CA 93654-2199
(559)638-8155

Hospital Telephone Directory — CALIFORNIA

RIDGECREST

RIDGECREST REGIONAL HOSPITAL
1081 N China Lake Boulevard
Ridgecrest, CA 93555-3130
(760)446-3551

RIVERSIDE

KAISER FOUNDATION HOSPITAL - RIVERSIDE
10800 Magnolia Avenue
Riverside, CA 92505-3000
(909)353-2000

KNOLLWOOD PSYCH AND CHEMICAL DEPENDENCY CENTER
5900 Brockton Avenue
Riverside, CA 92506-1862
(909)275-8400

PARKVIEW COMMUNITY HOSPITAL
3865 Jackson St
Riverside, CA 92503-3998
(909)688-2211

RIVERSIDE COMMUNITY HOSPITAL
4445 Magnolia Avenue
Riverside, CA 92501-4199
(909)788-3000

ROSEMEAD

ALHAMBRA HOSPITAL
PO Box 369
Rosemead, CA 91770-0369
(626)286-1191

INGLESIDE HOSPITAL
7500 E Hellman Avenue
Rosemead, CA 91770-2216
(626)288-1160

PSYCHIATRIC SERVICES - LAC AND USC MEDICAL CENTER
7500 East Hellman Avenue
Rosemead, CA 91770-2216
(626)572-2114

ROSEVILLE

SUTTER ROSEVILLE MEDICAL CENTER
1 Medical Plaza Dr
Roseville, CA 95661-3037
(916)781-1000

SACRAMENTO

HERITAGE OAKS HOSPITAL
4250 Auburn Boulevard
Sacramento, CA 95841-4164
(916)489-3336

KAISER FOUNDATION HOSPITAL - SACRAMENTO
6600 Bruceville Road
Sacramento, CA 95823-4671
(916)688-2000

KAISER PERMANENTE SACRAMENTO
2025 Morse Avenue
Sacramento, CA 95825-2100
(916)973-5000

MERCY GENERAL HOSPITAL
4001 J St
Sacramento, CA 95819-3600
(916)453-4545

METHODIST HOSPITAL
7500 Timberlake Way
Sacramento, CA 95823
(916)423-3000

SHRINERS HOSPITAL FOR CHILDREN
2425 Stockton Boulevard
Sacramento, CA 95817-2215
(916)453-2000

SIERRA VISTA HOSPITAL
8001 Bruceville Road
Sacramento, CA 95823-2329
(916)423-2000

SUTTER CENTER FOR PSYCHIATRY
7700 Folsom Boulevard
Sacramento, CA 95826-2608
(916)386-3000

SUTTER GENERAL HOSPITAL
2801 L Street
Sacramento, CA 95816-5680
(916)454-2222

SUTTER MEMORIAL HOSPITAL
5151 F St
Sacramento, CA 95819-3295
(916)454-3333

UNIVERSITY OF CALIFORNIA - DAVIS MEDICAL CENTER
2315 Stockton Boulevard
Sacramento, CA 95817-2282
(916)734-2011

VA MEDICAL CENTER - SACRAMENTO AT MATHER
10535 Hospital Way
Sacramento, CA 95655-4200
(916)366-5366

SALINAS

NATIVIDAD MEDICAL CENTER
1330 Natividad Road Box 1611
Salinas, CA 93906-3197
(831)755-4111

SALINAS VALLEY MEMORIAL HOSPITAL
450 East Romie Lane
Salinas, CA 93901-4098
(831)757-4333

SAN ANDREAS

MARK TWAIN SAINT JOSEPHS HOSPITAL
768 Mountain Ranch Road
San Andreas, CA 95249-9710
(209)754-3521

SAN BERNARDINO

COMMUNITY HOSPITAL OF SAN BERNARDINO
1500 W 17th Street
San Bernardino, CA 92411-1203
(909)887-6333

ROBERT H BALLARD REHAB HOSPITAL
1760 West 16th St
San Bernardino, CA 92411-1150
(909)473-1200

SAINT BERNARDINE MEDICAL CENTER
2101 N Waterman Avenue
San Bernardino, CA 92404-4855
(909)883-8711

SAN BERNARDINO COMMUNITY HOSPITAL
1805 Medical Center Drive
San Bernardino, CA 92411-1217
(909)887-6333

SAN CLEMENTE

SAN CLEMENTE HOSPITAL AND MEDICAL CENTER
654 Camino De Los Mares
San Clemente, CA 92673-2827
(949)496-1122

SAN DIEGO

ALVARADO HOSPITAL MEDICAL CENTER
6655 Alvarado Road
San Diego, CA 92120-5296
(619)287-3270

AURORA SAN DIEGO
11878 Avenue Of Industry
San Diego, CA 92128-3423
(858)487-3200

CHILDRENS HOSPITAL AND HEALTH CENTER
3020 Childrens Way
San Diego, CA 92123-4282
(858)576-1700

CONTINENTAL REHAB HOSPITAL OF SAN DIEGO
555 Washington St
San Diego, CA 92103-2294
(619)260-8300

KAISER PERMANENTE HOSPITAL
4647 Zion Avenue
San Diego, CA 92120-2507
(619)528-5000

KINDRED HOSPITAL SAN DIEGO
1940 El Cajon Boulevard
San Diego, CA 92104-1005
(619)543-4500

NAVAL MEDICAL CENTER SAN DIEGO
34800 Bob Wilson Drive
San Diego, CA 92134-1098
(619)532-6400

SAN DIEGO CHOICES
3853 Rosecrans Street
San Diego, CA 92110-3115
(619)692-8225

SAN DIEGO COUNTY PSYCHIATRIC HOSPITAL
3851 Rosecrans Street
San Diego, CA 92110-3115
(619)692-8232

SAN DIEGO HOSPICE ACUTE CARE CENTER
4311 Third Avenue
San Diego, CA 92103-7499
(619)688-1600

SAN DIEGO REHABILITATION INSTITUTE
6645 Alvarado Road
San Diego, CA 92120-5285
(619)286-7374

SCRIPPS MERCY HOSPITAL AND MEDICAL CENTER
4077 5th Avenue
San Diego, CA 92103-2105
(619)294-8111

SHARP MARY BIRCH HOSPITAL FOR WOMEN
3003 Health Center Drive
San Diego, CA 92123-2700
(858)541-3400

SHARP MEMORIAL HOSPITAL
7901 Frost St
San Diego, CA 92123-2786
(858)541-3400

SHARP-MESA VISTA HOSPITAL
7850 Vista Hill Avenue
San Diego, CA 92123-2790
(858)694-8300

UNIVERSITY COMMUNITY MEDICAL CENTER
5550 University Avenue
San Diego, CA 92105-2307
(619)582-3516

UNIVERSITY OF CALIFORNIA - SAN DIEGO MEDICAL CENTER
200 West Arbor Drive
San Diego, CA 92103-9000
(619)543-6222

CALIFORNIA

Hospital Telephone Directory

VA HEALTHCARE SYSTEM - SAN DIEGO
3350 La Jolla Village Drive
San Diego, CA 92161-0002
(858)552-8585

SAN DIMAS

SAN DIMAS COMMUNITY HOSPITAL
1350 W Covina Boulevard
San Dimas, CA 91773-3219
(909)599-6811

SAN FRANCISCO

CALIFORNIA PACIFIC MEDICAL CENTER
2333 Buchanan St
San Francisco, CA 94115-1995
(415)563-4321

CALIFORNIA PACIFIC MEDICAL CENTER - EAST
3698 California Street
San Francisco, CA 94118-1702
(415)600-6000

CALIFORNIA PACIFIC MEDICAL CENTER DAVIES CAMPUS
Castro and Duboce Streets
San Francisco, CA 94114
(415)565-6000

CALIFORNIA PACIFIC MEDICAL CENTER PACIFIC CAMPUS
3700 California Street
San Francisco, CA 94118-1697
(415)387-8700

CHINESE HOSPITAL
845 Jackson St
San Francisco, CA 94133-4899
(415)982-2400

HEBREW HOME FOR THE AGED DISABLED
302 Silver Avenue
San Francisco, CA 94112-1510
(415)334-2500

KAISER PERMANENTE HOSPITAL
2425 Geary Boulevard
San Francisco, CA 94115-3358
(415)833-2000

LAGUNA HONDA HOSPITAL
375 Laguna Honda Boulevard
San Francisco, CA 94116-1499
(415)759-2300

LANGLEY PORTER PSYCH INSTITUTE
401 Parnassus Avenue
San Francisco, CA 94143-2211
(415)476-7000

SAINT FRANCIS MEMORIAL HOSPITAL
900 Hyde St
San Francisco, CA 94109-4899
(415)353-6000

SAINT LUKES HOSPITAL
3555 Cesar Chavez Street
San Francisco, CA 94110-4490
(415)647-8600

SAINT MARYS HOSPITAL MEDICAL CENTER
450 Stanyan St
San Francisco, CA 94117-1079
(415)668-1000

SAN FRANCISCO GENERAL HOSPITAL
1001 Potrero Avenue
San Francisco, CA 94110-3594
(415)206-8000

UNIVERSITY OF CALIFORNIA MEDICAL CENTER - SAN FRANCISCO
505 Parnassus Avenue
San Francisco, CA 94122-2722
(415)476-1000

VA MEDICAL CENTER - SAN FRANCISCO
4150 Clement St
San Francisco, CA 94121-1593
(415)221-4810

SAN GABRIEL

SAN GABRIEL VALLEY MEDICAL CENTER
438 West Las Tunas Drive
San Gabriel, CA 91776-1216
(626)289-5454

SAN JOSE

AGNEWS STATE HOSPITAL
3500 Zanker Road
San Jose, CA 95134-2299
(408)451-6000

GOOD SAMARITAN AND MISSION OAKS HOSPITAL
PO Box 240004
San Jose, CA 95154-2404
(408)356-4111

GOOD SAMARITAN HOSPITAL
2425 Samaritan Drive
San Jose, CA 95124-3985
(408)559-2011

O'CONNOR HOSPITAL
2105 Forest Avenue
San Jose, CA 95128-1471
(408)947-2500

REGIONAL MEDICAL CENTER OF SAN JOSE
225 N Jackson Avenue
San Jose, CA 95116-1603
(408)259-5000

SAN JOSE MEDICAL CENTER
675 E Santa Clara Street
San Jose, CA 95112-1982
(408)998-3212

SANTA CLARA VALLEY MEDICAL CENTER
751 S Bascom Avenue
San Jose, CA 95128-2699
(408)885-5000

SANTA TERESA COMMUNITY HOSPITAL
250 Hospital Parkway
San Jose, CA 95119-1199
(408)972-7000

SAN LEANDRO

ALAMEDA COUNTY MEDICAL CENTER
15400 Foothill Blvd
San Leandro, CA 94578-1015
(510)437-4800

KINDRED HOSPITAL SAN FRANCISCO BAY AREA
2800 Benedict Drive
San Leandro, CA 94577-6840
(510)357-8300

SAN LEANDRO HOSPITAL
13855 E 14th Street
San Leandro, CA 94578-2600
(510)357-6500

VILLA FAIRMONT MENTAL HEALTH REHABILITATION CENTER
15200 Foothill Boulevard
San Leandro, CA 94578-1013
(510)352-9690

SAN LUIS OBISPO

CALIFORNIA MENS COLONY
PO Box 8101
San Luis Obispo, CA 93403-8101
(805)547-7913

FRENCH HOSPITAL
1911 Johnson Avenue
San Luis Obispo, CA 93401-4197
(805)543-5353

SIERRA VISTA REGIONAL MEDICAL CENTER
1010 Murray St
San Luis Obispo, CA 93405-8801
(805)546-7600

SAN MATEO

MILLS HOSPITAL
100 South San mateo Drive
San Mateo, CA 94401-3867
(650)696-5400

SAN MATEO COUNTY GENERAL HOSPITAL
222 W 39th Avenue
San Mateo, CA 94403-4398
(650)573-2222

SAN PABLO

DOCTORS MEDICAL CENTER SAN PABLO CAMPUS
2000 Vale Road
San Pablo, CA 94806-3808
(510)970-5000

SAN PEDRO

SAN PEDRO HOSPITAL
1300 W 7th St
San Pedro, CA 90732-3505
(310)832-3311

SAN RAFAEL

KAISER FOUNDATION HOSPITAL
99 Monticello Road
San Rafael, CA 94903-3397
(415)444-2000

MARIN GENERAL HOSPITAL
PO Box 8010
San Rafael, CA 94912-8010
(415)925-7000

SAN RAMON

SAN RAMON REGIONAL MEDICAL CENTER
6001 Norris Canyon Road
San Ramon, CA 94583-5400
(925)275-9200

SANTA ANA

COASTAL COMMUNITIES HOSPITAL
2701 S Bristol St
Santa Ana, CA 92704-6278
(714)754-5454

KINDRED HOSPITAL AT SANTA ANA
1901 North College Avenue
Santa Ana, CA 92706-2334
(714)564-7800

SAINT LUKE MEDICAL CENTER
3 Imperial Promenade Ste 600
Santa Ana, CA 92707-5902
(714)797-1141

WESTERN MEDICAL CENTER
1001 N Tustin Avenue
Santa Ana, CA 92705-3577
(714)835-3555

SANTA BARBARA

GOLETA VALLEY COTTAGE HOSPITAL
351 S Patterson Avenue
Santa Barbara, CA 93111-2496
(805)967-3411

Hospital Telephone Directory — CALIFORNIA

SANTA BARBARA COTTAGE HOSPITAL
Pueblo At Bath Street
Santa Barbara, CA 93105
(805)682-7111

SANTA BARBARA COUNTY MENTAL HEALTH
315 Camino Del Remedio
Santa Barbara, CA 93110-1332
(805)681-5450

SANTA CLARA

KAISER FOUNDATION HOSPITAL
900 Kiely Boulevard
Santa Clara, CA 95051-5383
(408)236-6400

SANTA CRUZ

DOMINICAN HOSPITAL
1555 Soquel Drive
Santa Cruz, CA 95065-1794
(831)462-7700

SUTTER MATERNITY AND SURGERY CENTER
2900 Chanticleer Avenue
Santa Cruz, CA 95065-1816
(831)477-2200

SANTA MARIA

MARIAN MEDICAL CENTER
1400 E Church St
Santa Maria, CA 93454-5906
(805)739-3000

SANTA MONICA

SAINT JOHNS HOSPITAL HEALTH CENTER
1328 22nd St
Santa Monica, CA 90404-2091
(310)829-5511

SANTA MONICA - UCLA MEDICAL CENTER
1250 16th Street
Santa Monica, CA 90404-1200
(310)319-4000

SANTA PAULA

SANTA PAULA MEMORIAL HOSPITAL
PO Box 270
Santa Paula, CA 93061-0270
(805)525-7171

SANTA ROSA

KAISER FOUNDATION HOSPITAL-SANTA ROSA
401 Bicentennial Way
Santa Rosa, CA 95403-2149
(707)571-4000

NORTH COAST HEALTH CARE CENTERS
1287 Fulton Road
Santa Rosa, CA 95401-4923
(707)543-2400

SANTA ROSA MEMORIAL HOSPITAL
1165 Montgomery Drive
Santa Rosa, CA 95405-4897
(707)546-3210

SUTTER MEDICAL CENTER OF SANTA ROSA
3325 Chanate Road
Santa Rosa, CA 95404-1707
(707)576-4000

SUTTER WARRACK HOSPITAL
2449 Summerfield Road
Santa Rosa, CA 95405-7880
(707)576-4200

SEBASTOPOL

PALM DRIVE HOSPITAL
501 Petaluma Avenue
Sebastopol, CA 95472-4281
(707)823-8511

SELMA

SELMA DISTRICT HOSPITAL
1141 Rose Avenue
Selma, CA 93662-3293
(559)891-1000

SHERMAN OAKS

SHERMAN OAKS HOSPITAL AND HEALTH CENTER
4929 Van Nuys Boulevard
Sherman Oaks, CA 91403-1702
(818)981-7111

SIMI VALLEY

SIMI VALLEY HOSPITAL - SOUTH
1850 Heywood St
Simi Valley, CA 93065-3430
(805)955-7000

SIMI VALLEY HOSPITAL AND HEALTH CARE SERVICES
2975 North Sycamore Drive
Simi Valley, CA 93065-1277
(805)955-6000

SOLVANG

SANTA YNEZ VALLEY COTTAGE HOSPITAL
700 Alamo Pintado Road
Solvang, CA 93463-2295
(805)688-6431

SONOMA

SONOMA VALLEY HOSPITAL
347 Andrieux St
Sonoma, CA 95476-6863
(707)935-5000

SONORA

SONORA COMMUNITY HOSPITAL
1 South Forest Road
Sonora, CA 95370-4819
(209)532-3161

TUOLUMNE GENERAL HOSPITAL
101 Hospital Road
Sonora, CA 95370-5297
(209)533-7100

SOUTH EL MONTE

GREATER EL MONTE COMMUNITY HOSPITAL
1701 Santa Anita Avenue
South El Monte, CA 91733-3482
(626)579-7777

SOUTH LAKE TAHOE

BARTON MEMORIAL HOSPITAL
2170 South Avenue
South Lake Tahoe, CA 96150-7008
(530)541-3420

SOUTH SAN FRANCISCO

KAISER FOUNDATION HOSPITAL
1200 El Camino Real
South San Francisco, CA 94080-3208
(650)742-2000

STANFORD

STANFORD UNIVERSITY HOSPITAL
300 Pasteur Drive
Stanford, CA 94304-2299
(650)723-4000

STOCKTON

DAMERON HOSPITAL ASSOCIATION
525 West Acacia Street
Stockton, CA 95203-2484
(209)944-5550

SAINT JOSEPHS BEHAVIORAL HEALTH CENTER
2510 N California St
Stockton, CA 95204-5502
(209)461-2000

SAINT JOSEPHS MEDICAL CENTER OF STOCKTON
1800 N California St
Stockton, CA 95204-6019
(209)943-2000

SUN CITY

MENIFEE VALLEY MEDICAL CENTER
28400 Mccall Boulevard
Sun City, CA 92585-9537
(909)679-8888

SUN VALLEY

PACIFICA HOSPITAL OF THE VALLEY
9449 San Fernando Road
Sun Valley, CA 91352-1421
(818)767-3310

SUSANVILLE

BANNER LASSEN MEDICAL CENTER
1800 Spring Ridge Drive
Susanville, CA 96130-6100
(530)252-2000

SYLMAR

LAC/OLIVE VIEW - UCLA
14445 Olive View Drive
Sylmar, CA 91342-1437
(818)364-1555

TAFT

MERCY WEST SIDE DISTRICT HOSPITAL
110 East North Street
Taft, CA 93268-3909
(661)763-4211

TARZANA

ENCINO-TARZANA REGIONAL MEDICAL CENTER
18321 Clark St
Tarzana, CA 91356-3521
(818)881-0800

TEHACHAPI

TEHACHAPI HOSPITAL
115 West E Street
Tehachapi, CA 93561-1669
(661)822-3241

TEMPLETON

TWIN CITIES COMMUNITY HOSPITAL
1100 Las Tablas Road
Templeton, CA 93465-9704
(805)434-3500

CALIFORNIA
Hospital Telephone Directory

THOUSAND OAKS

LOS ROBLES REGIONAL MEDICAL CENTER
215 West Janss Road
Thousand Oaks, CA 91360-1847
(805)497-2727

TORRANCE

DEL AMO HOSPITAL
23700 Camino Del Sol
Torrance, CA 90505-5000
(310)530-1151

LAC/ HARBOR-UCLA MEDICAL CENTER
1000 W Carson St
Torrance, CA 90502-2004
(310)222-2345

LITTLE COMPANY OF MARY HOSPITAL
4101 Torrance Boulevard
Torrance, CA 90503-4664
(310)540-7676

TORRANCE MEMORIAL MEDICAL CENTER
3330 Lomita Boulevard
Torrance, CA 90505-5073
(310)325-9110

TRACY

TRACY COMMUNITY MEMORIAL HOSPITAL
1420 N Tracy Boulevard
Tracy, CA 95376-3497
(209)835-1500

TRAVIS AIR FORCE BASE

60TH MEDICAL GROUP - DAVID GRANT
MEDICAL CENTER
101 Bodin Circle
Travis Air Force Base, CA 94535-1802
(707)423-7300

TRUCKEE

TAHOE FOREST HOSPITAL
10120 Pine Street
Truckee, CA 96161-4833
(530)587-6011

TULARE

TULARE DISTRICT HOSPITAL
869 Cherry Avenue
Tulare, CA 93274-2287
(559)688-0821

TURLOCK

EMANUEL MEDICAL CENTER
825 Delbon Avenue
Turlock, CA 95382-2016
(209)667-4200

TUSTIN

HEALTHSOUTH TUSTIN REHABILITATION
HOSPITAL
14851 Yorba St
Tustin, CA 92780-2925
(714)832-9200

TUSTIN HOSPITAL AND MEDICAL CENTER
14662 Newport Avenue
Tustin, CA 92780-6064
(714)838-9600

TWENTY-NINE PALMS

ROBERT E. BUSH NAVAL HOSPITAL
Box 788250 Mgagcc
Twenty-Nine Palms, CA 92278-8250
(760)830-2190

UKIAH

UKIAH VALLEY MEDICAL CENTER/HOSPITAL
275 Hospital Drive
Ukiah, CA 95482-4564
(707)462-3111

UPLAND

SAN ANTONIO COMMUNITY HOSPITAL
999 San Bernardino Road
Upland, CA 91786-4992
(909)985-2811

VACAVILLE

CALIFORNIA MEDICAL FACILITY
1600 California Drive
Vacaville, CA 95696
(707)448-6841

VACA VALLEY HOSPITAL
1000 Nut Tree Road
Vacaville, CA 95687-4100
(707)446-4000

VALENCIA

HENRY MAYO NEWHALL MEMORIAL
HOSPITAL
23845 W Mcbean Parkway
Valencia, CA 91355-2083
(661)253-8000

VALLEJO

CALIFORNIA SPECIALITY HOSPITAL
525 Oregon St
Vallejo, CA 94590-3201
(707)648-2200

KAISER FOUNDATION HOSPITAL VALLEJO
975 Sereno Drive
Vallejo, CA 94589-2441
(707)651-1000

SUTTER SOLANO MEDICAL CENTER
300 Hospital Drive
Vallejo, CA 94589-2594
(707)554-4444

VAN NUYS

HOLLYWOOD COMMUNITY HOSPITAL-VAN
NUYS
14433 Emelita St
Van Nuys, CA 91401-4213
(818)787-1511

NORTHRIDGE HOSPITAL MEDICAL CENTER,
SHERMAN
14500 Sherman Circle
Van Nuys, CA 91405-3098
(818)997-0101

VALLEY PRESBYTERIAN HOSPITAL
15107 Vanowen St
Van Nuys, CA 91405-4597
(818)782-6600

VANDENBERG AIR FORCE BASE

30TH MEDICAL GROUP
338 South Dakota St Bldg 13580
Vandenberg Air Force Base, CA 93437-6307
(805)606-6726

VENTURA

COMMUNITY MEMORIAL HOSPITAL OF SAN
BUENAVENTURA
Loma Vista At Brent Street
Ventura, CA 93003
(805)652-5011

VENTURA COUNTY MEDICAL CENTER
3291 Loma Vista Road
Ventura, CA 93003-3099
(805)652-6000

VISTA DEL MAR HOSPITAL
801 Seneca St
Ventura, CA 93001-1411
(805)653-6434

VICTORVILLE

DESERT VALLEY HOSPITAL
16850 Bear Valley Road
Victorville, CA 92392-5795
(760)241-8000

VICTOR VALLEY COMMUNITY HOSPITAL
15248 11th St
Victorville, CA 92392-3787
(760)245-8691

VISALIA

KAWEAH DELTA AND VISALIA HOSPITAL
400 W Mineral King Avenue
Visalia, CA 93291-6263
(559)624-2000

WALNUT CREEK

JOHN MUIR MEDICAL CENTER
1601 Ygnacio Valley Road
Walnut Creek, CA 94598-3198
(925)939-3000

KAISER FOUNDATION HOSPITAL
1425 S Main St
Walnut Creek, CA 94596-5300
(925)295-4000

WATSONVILLE

WATSONVILLE COMMUNITY HOSPITAL
75 Neilson St
Watsonville, CA 95076-2468
(831)724-4741

WEAVERVILLE

TRINITY GENERAL HOSPITAL
410 N Taylor St
Weaverville, CA 96093
(530)623-5541

WEST COVINA

CITRUS VALLEY MEDICAL CENTER
1115 S Sunset Avenue
West Covina, CA 91790-3940
(626)962-4011

DOCTORS HOSPITAL OF WEST COVINA
725 S Orange Avenue
West Covina, CA 91790-2614
(626)338-8481

KINDRED HOSPITAL OF SOUTHERN
CALIFORNIA
845 N Lark Ellen Avenue
West Covina, CA 91791-1069
(626)339-5451

WEST HILLS

WEST HILLS HOSPITAL & MEDICAL CENTER
7300 Medical Center Drive
West Hills, CA 91307-1902
(818)676-4000

WESTMINSTER

KINDRED HOSPITAL WESTMINSTER
200 Hospital Circle
Westminster, CA 92683-3910
(714)893-4541

Hospital Telephone Directory — COLORADO

WHITTIER

PRESBYTERIAN INTERCOMMUNITY HOSPITAL
12401 E Washington Boulevard
Whittier, CA 90602-1099
(562)698-0811

WHITTIER HOSPITAL MEDICAL CENTER
9080 Colima Road
Whittier, CA 90605-1600
(562)945-3561

WILDOMAR

INLAND VALLEY REGIONAL MEDICAL CENTER
36485 Inland Valley Way
Wildomar, CA 92595-9700
(909)677-1111

WILLITS

FRANK R HOWARD MEMORIAL HOSPITAL
1 Madrone St
Willits, CA 95490-4298
(707)459-6801

WILLOWS

GLENN GENERAL HOSPITAL AND MEDICAL CENTER
1133 W Sycamore
Willows, CA 95988-2601
(530)934-1800

WINTERHAVEN

PHS INDIAN HEALTH SERVICE HOSPITAL
Winterhaven, CA 92283
(760)572-0217

WOODLAND

WOODLAND HEALTH CARE
1325 Cottonwood Street
Woodland, CA 95695-5199
(530)662-3961

WOODLAND HILLS

KAISER PERMANENTE HOSPITAL
5601 De Soto
Woodland Hills, CA 91367-6798
(818)719-2000

MOTION PICTURE AND TELEVISION HOSPITAL
23388 Mulholland Drive
Woodland Hills, CA 91364-2792
(818)876-1888

YOUNTVILLE

NELSON HOLDERMAN HOSPITAL
California Veterans Home
Yountville, CA 94599
(707)944-4500

YREKA

FAIRCHILD MEDICAL CENTER
444 Bruce Street
Yreka, CA 96097-3450
(530)842-4121

YUBA CITY

FREMONT MEDICAL CENTER
970 Plumas St
Yuba City, CA 95991-4087
(530)751-4000

COLORADO

ALAMOSA

SAN LUIS VALLEY REGIONAL MEDICAL CENTER
106 Blanca Avenue
Alamosa, CO 81101-2340
(719)589-2511

ASPEN

ASPEN VALLEY HOSPITAL
0401 Castle Creek Road
Aspen, CO 81611-1159
(970)925-1120

AURORA

MEDICAL CENTER OF AURORA - NORTH CAMPUS
1501 S Potomac St
Aurora, CO 80012-5411
(303)363-7200

MEDICAL CENTER OF AURORA - SOUTH CAMPUS
1501 South Potomac St
Aurora, CO 80012-5411
(303)695-2600

SCCI HOSPITAL - AURORA
700 Potomac Street
Aurora, CO 80011-6701
(720)857-8333

SCCI HOSPITAL AT CITY PARK CENTER
700 Potomac Street
Aurora, CO 80011-6701
(303)316-4121

SPALDING REHABILITATION HOSPITAL
900 Potomac St
Aurora, CO 80011-6716
(303)367-1166

BOULDER

BOULDER COMMUNITY HOSPITAL
1100 Balsam Avenue
Boulder, CO 80304-3496
(303)440-2273

BRIGHTON

PLATTE VALLEY MEDICAL CENTER
1850 Egbert St
Brighton, CO 80601-2404
(303)659-1531

BROOMFIELD

CLEO WALLACE CENTERS
8405 Church Ranch Boulevard
Broomfield, CO 80021-3918
(303)466-7391

BRUSH

EAST MORGAN COUNTY HOSPITAL
2400 W Edison
Brush, CO 80723-1642
(970)842-5151

BURLINGTON

KIT CARSON COUNTY MEMORIAL HOSPITAL
286 16th St
Burlington, CO 80807-1697
(719)346-5311

CANON CITY

SAINT THOMAS MORE HOSPITAL
1338 Phay Avenue
Canon City, CO 81212-2399
(719)269-2000

CHEYENNE WELLS

KEEFE MEMORIAL HOSPITAL
602 N 6th West Street - PO Box 578
Cheyenne Wells, CO 80810-0578
(719)767-5661

COLORADO SPRINGS

CEDAR SPRINGS HOSPITAL
2135 Southgate Road PO Box 640
Colorado Springs, CO 80901-0640
(303)633-4114

HEALTHSOUTH REHABILITATION HOSPITAL OF COLORADO SPRINGS
325 Parkside Drive
Colorado Springs, CO 80910-3134
(719)630-8000

MEMORIAL HOSPITAL
1400 East Boulder St
Colorado Springs, CO 80909-5599
(719)365-5000

PENROSE COMMUNITY HOSPITAL
3205 N Academy Boulevard
Colorado Springs, CO 80917-5198
(719)776-3000

PENROSE SAINT FRANCIS HEALTH SYSTEM
2215 North Cascade Avenue
Colorado Springs, CO 80907-6736
(719)776-5000

SAINT FRANCIS HEALTH CENTER
825 East Pikes Peak Avenue
Colorado Springs, CO 80903-3624
(719)776-8800

SEMPERCARE HOSPITALS - COLORADO SPRINGS
825 Pikes Peak Avenue
Colorado Springs, CO 80903-3624
(719)667-1009

CORTEZ

SOUTHWEST HEALTH SYSTEM
1311 North Mildred Road
Cortez, CO 81321-2231
(970)565-6666

CRAIG

MEMORIAL HOSPITAL
785 Russell St
Craig, CO 81625-2097
(970)824-9411

DEL NORTE

RIO GRANDE HOSPITAL
1280 Grande Avenue
Del Norte, CO 81132-3220
(719)657-2510

DELTA

DELTA COUNTY MEMORIAL HOSPITAL
100 Stafford Lane
Delta, CO 81416-2297
(970)874-7681

DENVER

CHILDRENS HOSPITAL
1056 E 19th Avenue
Denver, CO 80218-1088
(303)861-8888

COLORADO

Hospital Telephone Directory

COLORADO MENTAL HEALTH CENTER AT FORT LOGAN
3520 W Oxford Avenue
Denver, CO 80236-3108
(303)761-0220

DENVER HEALTH MEDICAL CENTER
777 Bannock St
Denver, CO 80204-4597
(303)436-6000

EXEMPLA HEALTHCARE SAINT JOSEPH HOSPITAL
1835 Franklin St
Denver, CO 80218-1126
(303)837-7111

KINDRED HOSPITAL DENVER
1920 High St
Denver, CO 80218-1213
(303)320-5871

LIFECARE HOSPITAL OF DENVER
1601 Lowell Blvd
Denver, CO 80204-1545
(303)899-5170

NATIONAL JEWISH MEDICAL CENTER
1400 Jackson St
Denver, CO 80206-2762
(303)388-4461

PORTER ADVENTIST HOSPITAL
2525 S Downing St
Denver, CO 80210-5817
(303)778-1955

PRESBYTERIAN - SAINT LUKE'S MEDICAL CENTER
1719 E 19th Avenue
Denver, CO 80218-1281
(303)839-6000

PRESBYTERIAN-DENVER HOSPITAL
1719 East 19th Avenue
Denver, CO 80218-1281
(303)839-6100

ROSE MEDICAL CENTER
4567 E 9th Avenue
Denver, CO 80220-3941
(303)320-2121

SAINT ANTHONY CENTRAL HOSPITAL
4231 W 16th Avenue
Denver, CO 80204-1335
(303)629-3511

SELECT SPECIALTY HOSPITAL - DENVER
1719 East 19th Avenue
Denver, CO 80218-1235
(303)563-3700

SELECT SPECIALTY HOSPITAL - DENVER SOUTH
2525 South Downing Street, Third Floor
Denver, CO 80210-5817
(303)715-7373

UNIVERSITY OF COLORADO HOSPITAL AND HEALTH SCIENCE
4200 E 9th Avenue
Denver, CO 80220-3706
(303)372-0000

VA MEDICAL CENTER - DENVER
1055 Clermont St
Denver, CO 80220-3808
(303)399-8020

DURANGO

MERCY MEDICAL CENTER OF DURANGO
375 E Park Avenue
Durango, CO 81301-5089
(970)247-4311

EADS

WEISBROD MEMORIAL COUNTY HOSPITAL
1208 Luther St
Eads, CO 81036
(719)438-5401

ENGLEWOOD

CRAIG HOSPITAL
3425 South Clarkson
Englewood, CO 80113-2899
(303)789-8000

SWEDISH MEDICAL CENTER
501 E Hampden Avenue
Englewood, CO 80113-2795
(303)788-5000

ESTES PARK

ESTES PARK MEDICAL CENTER
555 Prospect
Estes Park, CO 80517-6312
(970)586-2317

FORT CARSON

EVANS ARMY COMMUNITY HOSPITAL
7500 Cochrane Circle
Fort Carson, CO 80913
(719)526-7500

FORT COLLINS

MOUNTAIN CREST HOSPITAL
4601 Corbett Drive
Fort Collins, CO 80528-9579
(970)270-4800

POUDRE VALLEY HOSPITAL
1024 S Lemay Avenue
Fort Collins, CO 80524-3998
(970)495-7000

FORT MORGAN

COLORADO PLAINS MEDICAL CENTER
1000 Lincoln St
Fort Morgan, CO 80701-3210
(970)867-3391

FRUITA

FAMILY HEALTH WEST - RPCH
228 North Cherry Street PO Box 130
Fruita, CO 81521-0130
(970)858-9871

GLENWOOD SPRINGS

VALLEY VIEW HOSPITAL
1906 Blake Avenue
Glenwood Springs, CO 81601-4259
(970)945-6535

GRAND JUNCTION

COMMUNITY HOSPITAL
2021 N 12th St
Grand Junction, CO 81501-2999
(970)242-0920

SAINT MARYS HOSPITAL AND MEDICAL CENTER
2635 North 7th Street Box 1628
Grand Junction, CO 81501-8209
(970)244-2273

VA MEDICAL CENTER - GRAND JUNCTION
2121 North Avenue
Grand Junction, CO 81501-6428
(970)242-0731

GREELEY

NORTH COLORADO MEDICAL CENTER
1801 16th Street
Greeley, CO 80631-5199
(970)352-4121

GUNNISON

GUNNISON VALLEY HOSPITAL
711 N Taylor St
Gunnison, CO 81230-2296
(970)641-1456

HAXTUN

HAXTUN HOSPITAL/HERITAGE LIV CENTER
235 W Fletcher Street PO Box 308
Haxtun, CO 80731-0308
(970)774-6123

HOLYOKE

MELISSA MEMORIAL HOSPITAL
505 South Baxter
Holyoke, CO 80734-1496
(970)854-2241

HUGO

LINCOLN COMMUNITY HOSPITAL
PO Box 248
Hugo, CO 80821-0248
(719)743-2421

JULESBURG

SEDGWICK COUNTY MEMORIAL HOSPITAL
900 Cedar St
Julesburg, CO 80737-1199
(970)474-3323

KREMMLING

KREMMLING MEMORIAL HOSPITAL
212 S 4th St
Kremmling, CO 80459
(970)724-3442

LA JARA

CONEJOS COUNTY HOSPITAL
PO Box 639
La Jara, CO 81140-0639
(719)274-5121

LA JUNTA

ARKANSAS VALLEY REGIONAL MEDICAL CENTER
1100 Carson Avenue
La Junta, CO 81050-2799
(719)383-6000

LAMAR

PROWERS MEDICAL CENTER
401 Kendall Drive
Lamar, CO 81052-3993
(719)336-4343

LEADVILLE

SAINT VINCENT GENERAL HOSPITAL DISTRICT
822 W 4th St
Leadville, CO 80461-3897
(719)486-0230

LITTLETON

LITTLETON ADVENTIST HOSPITAL
7700 South Broadway St
Littleton, CO 80122-2628
(303)730-8900

LONE TREE

SKY RIDGE MEDICAL CENTER
10101 Ridge Gate Parkway
Lone Tree, CO 80124-5522
(303)225-1000

LONGMONT

LONGMONT UNITED HOSPITAL
1950 Mountain View Avenue
Longmont, CO 80501-9865
(303)651-5111

LOUISVILLE

AVISTA ADVENTIST HOSPITAL
100 Health Park Drive
Louisville, CO 80027-9583
(303)673-1000

CENTENNIAL PEAKS HOSPITAL
2255 South 88th St
Louisville, CO 80027-9728
(303)673-9990

LOVELAND

MCKEE MEDICAL CENTER
2000 Boise Avenue
Loveland, CO 80538-4281
(970)669-4640

MEEKER

PIONEERS HOSPITAL OF RIO BLANCO
345 Cleveland
Meeker, CO 81641-3237
(970)878-5047

MONTROSE

MONTROSE MEMORIAL HOSPITAL
800 S 3rd St
Montrose, CO 81401-4291
(970)249-2211

PUEBLO

COLORADO MENTAL HEALTH INSTITUTE AT PUEBLO
1600 West 24th Street
Pueblo, CO 81003-1411
(719)546-4000

PARKVIEW EPISCOPAL MEDICAL CENTER
400 W 16th St
Pueblo, CO 81003-2745
(719)584-4000

SAINT MARY CORWIN MEDICAL CENTER
1008 Minnequa Avenue
Pueblo, CO 81004-3798
(719)560-4000

RANGELY

RANGELY DISTRICT HOSPITAL
511 South White Avenue
Rangely, CO 81648-2104
(970)675-5011

RIFLE

GRAND RIVER HOSPITAL
501 Airport Road, PO Box 912
Rifle, CO 81650-0912
(970)625-1510

SALIDA

HEART OF THE ROCKIES REGIONAL MEDICAL CENTER
PO Box 429
Salida, CO 81201-0429
(719)539-6661

SPRINGFIELD

SOUTHEAST COLORADO HOSPITAL
373 E 10th Avenue
Springfield, CO 81073-1699
(719)523-4501

STEAMBOAT SPRINGS

YAMPA VALLEY MEDICAL CENTER
1024 Central Park Drive
Steamboat Springs, CO 80487-8813
(970)879-1322

STERLING

STERLING REGIONAL MEDICAL CENTER
615 Fairhurst St
Sterling, CO 80751-4564
(970)522-0122

THORNTON

NORTH SUBURBAN MEDICAL CENTER
9191 Grant St
Thornton, CO 80229-4341
(303)451-7800

NORTH VALLEY REHAB CENTER
8451 Pearl St
Thornton, CO 80229
(303)288-3000

TRINIDAD

MOUNT SAN RAFAEL HOSPITAL
410 Benedicta Avenue
Trinidad, CO 81082-2093
(719)846-9213

US AIR FORCE ACADEMY

10TH MEDICAL GROUP - USAF ACADEMY HOSPITAL
4102 Pinion Drive Suite 100
US Air Force Academy, CO 80840-2502
(719)333-5102

VAIL

VAIL VALLEY MEDICAL CENTER
181 W Meadow Dr Ste 100
Vail, CO 81657-5058
(970)476-2451

WALSENBURG

SPANISH PEAKS REGIONAL HEALTH CENTER
23500 Us Highway 160
Walsenburg, CO 81089-9524
(719)738-5100

WESTMINSTER

CLEO WALLACE CENTER HOSPITAL
8405 Church Ranch Blvd
Westminster, CO 80021-3918
(303)639-1700

SAINT ANTHONY NORTH HOSPITAL
2551 W 84th Avenue
Westminster, CO 80031-3887
(303)426-2151

WHEAT RIDGE

EXEMPLA LUTHERAN MEDICAL CENTER
8300 West 38th Avenue
Wheat Ridge, CO 80033-6099
(303)425-4500

EXEMPLA WEST PINES AT LUTHERAN MEDICAL CENTER
3400 Lutheran Parkway
Wheat Ridge, CO 80033-6035
(303)467-4000

WIDE HORIZON
8900 West 38th Avenue
Wheat Ridge, CO 80033-4204
(303)424-4445

WRAY

WRAY COMMUNITY DISTRICT HOSPITAL
1017 West 7th Street
Wray, CO 80758-1420
(970)332-4811

YUMA

YUMA DISTRICT HOSPITAL
910 S Main St
Yuma, CO 80759-3021
(970)848-5405

CONNECTICUT

BETHLEHEM

WELLSPRING FOUNDATION
PO Box 370
Bethlehem, CT 06751-0370
(203)266-7235

BRANFORD

CONNECTICUT HOSPICE
61 Burban Drive
Branford, CT 06405-4003
(203)481-6231

BRIDGEPORT

BRIDGEPORT HOSPITAL
267 Grant Street
Bridgeport, CT 06610-2870
(203)384-3000

SAINT VINCENTS MEDICAL CENTER
2800 Main St
Bridgeport, CT 06606-4292
(203)576-6000

SOUTHWEST CONNECTICUT MENTAL HEALTH SYSTEM
1635 Central Avenue
Bridgeport, CT 06610-2717
(203)551-7400

BRISTOL

BRISTOL HOSPITAL
Brewster Road
Bristol, CT 06010
(860)585-3000

DANBURY

DANBURY HOSPITAL
24 Hospital Avenue
Danbury, CT 06810-6077
(203)797-7000

DERBY

GRIFFIN HOSPITAL
130 Division St
Derby, CT 06418-1326
(203)735-7421

CONNECTICUT — Hospital Telephone Directory

FARMINGTON

UNIVERSITY OF CONNECTICUT HEALTH CENTER AND JOHN DEMPSEY HOSPITAL
263 Farmington Avenue
Farmington, CT 06032-1941
(860)679-2000

GREENWICH

GREENWICH HOSPITAL
5 Perryridge Road
Greenwich, CT 06830-4697
(203)863-3000

GROTON

NAVAL HOSPITAL
Box 600
Groton, CT 06340-0600
(860)694-4123

HARTFORD

CONNECTICUT CHILDRENS MEDICAL CENTER
282 Washington Street
Hartford, CT 06106-3322
(860)545-9000

HARTFORD HOSPITAL
80 Seymour St
Hartford, CT 06115-2700
(860)545-5000

INSTITUTE OF LIVING
400 Washington St
Hartford, CT 06106-3392
(860)545-7000

REHABILITATION HOSPITAL OF CONNECTICUT
490 Blue Hills Avenue
Hartford, CT 06112-1513
(860)714-3500

SAINT FRANCIS HEALTH CARE SYSTEM - MT. SINAI CAMPUS
500 Blue Hills Avenue
Hartford, CT 06112-1500
(860)714-4000

SAINT FRANCIS HOSPITAL AND MEDICAL CENTER
114 Woodland Street
Hartford, CT 06105-1208
(860)714-4000

MANCHESTER

MANCHESTER MEMORIAL HOSPITAL
71 Haynes St
Manchester, CT 06040-4188
(860)646-1222

MANSFIELD CENTER

NATCHAUG HOSPITAL
PO Box 260
Mansfield Center, CT 06250-0260
(860)456-1311

MERIDEN

MIDSTATE MEDICAL CENTER
435 Lewis Avenue
Meriden, CT 06451-2101
(203)694-8200

MIDSTATE MEDICAL CENTER - EAST
883 Paddock Avenue
Meriden, CT 06450-7044
(203)694-8200

MIDDLETOWN

CONNECTICUT VALLEY HOSPITAL
PO Box 351, Silver Street
Middletown, CT 06457-7023
(860)262-5000

MIDDLESEX HOSPITAL
28 Crescent St
Middletown, CT 06457-3650
(860)344-6000

RIVERVIEW HOSPITAL FOR CHILDREN
PO Box 2797
Middletown, CT 06457-9297
(860)704-4000

WHITING FORENSIC DIVISION-VALLEY HOSPITAL
PO Box 70
Middletown, CT 06457-0070
(860)344-2541

MILFORD

MILFORD HOSPITAL
300 Seaside Avenue
Milford, CT 06460-4600
(203)876-4000

NEW BRITAIN

HOSPITAL FOR SPECIAL CARE
2150 Corbin Avenue
New Britain, CT 06053-2298
(860)827-4758

NEW BRITAIN GENERAL HOSPITAL
100 Grand Street
New Britain, CT 06052-2017
(860)224-5011

NEW CANAAN

SILVER HILL HOSPITAL
208 Valley Road
New Canaan, CT 06840-3899
(203)966-3561

NEW HAVEN

CONNECTICUT MENTAL HEALTH CENTER
34 Park St
New Haven, CT 06519-1187
(203)974-7144

HOSPITAL OF SAINT RAPHAEL
1450 Chapel St
New Haven, CT 06511-4440
(203)789-3000

YALE PSYCHIATRIC INSTITUTE
184 Liberty St, PO Box 208038
New Haven, CT 06520-8038
(203)785-7200

YALE-NEW HAVEN HOSPITAL
20 York St
New Haven, CT 06504-8900
(203)688-4242

NEW LONDON

LAWRENCE AND MEMORIAL HOSPITAL
365 Montauk Avenue
New London, CT 06320-4700
(860)442-0711

U.S. COAST GUARD ACADEMY CLINIC
15 Mohegan Avenue
New London, CT 06320-8131
(860)444-8400

NEW MILFORD

NEW MILFORD HOSPITAL
21 Elm St
New Milford, CT 06776-2993
(860)355-2611

NEWINGTON

CEDARCREST REGIONAL HOSPITAL
525 Russell Road
Newington, CT 06111-1595
(860)666-4613

VA HEALTHCARE SYSTEM - CONNECTICUT AT NEWINGTON
555 Willard Avenue
Newington, CT 06111-2631
(860)666-6951

NORWALK

NORWALK HOSPITAL
34 Maple St
Norwalk, CT 06850-3894
(203)852-2000

NORWICH

WILLIAM W BACKUS HOSPITAL
326 Washington St
Norwich, CT 06360-2714
(860)889-8331

PORTLAND

SAINT FRANCIS BEHAVIORAL HEALTH CARE
25 Marlborough Street
Portland, CT 06480-1829
(860)342-0480

PUTNAM

DAY KIMBALL HOSPITAL
320 Pomfret Street
Putnam, CT 06260-1869
(860)928-6541

ROCKY HILL

VA DEPARTMENT OF VETERANS AFFAIRS
287 West St
Rocky Hill, CT 06067-3501
(860)529-2571

SHARON

SHARON HOSPITAL
PO Box 789
Sharon, CT 06069-0789
(860)364-4141

SOMERS

CONNECTICUT DEPARTMENT OF CORRECTIONS HOSPITAL
100 Bilton Road, PO Box 100
Somers, CT 06071-0100
(860)749-8391

SOUTHINGTON

BRADLEY MEMORIAL HOSPITAL AND HEALTH CENTER
81 Meriden Avenue
Southington, CT 06489-3297
(860)276-5000

STAFFORD SPRINGS

JOHNSON MEMORIAL HOSPITAL
201 Chestnut Hill Road
Stafford Springs, CT 06076-4005
(860)684-4251

Hospital Telephone Directory — DELAWARE/DC

STAMFORD
STAMFORD HOSPITAL
Shelburne Road And West Broad St
Stamford, CT 06904
(203)325-7000

TORRINGTON
CHARLOTTE HUNGERFORD HOSPITAL
540 Litchfield St
Torrington, CT 06790-6600
(860)496-6666

VERNON
ROCKVILLE GENERAL HOSPITAL
31 Union St
Vernon, CT 06066-3160
(860)872-0501

WALLINGFORD
GAYLORD HOSPITAL
PO Box 400, Gaylord Farm Road
Wallingford, CT 06492-7048
(203)284-2800

MASONIC GERIATRIC HEALTH CARE CENTER
22 Masonic Avenue PO Box 70
Wallingford, CT 06492-7001
(203)679-5900

WATERBURY
SAINT MARYS HOSPITAL
56 Franklin St
Waterbury, CT 06706-1281
(203)574-6000

WATERBURY HOSPITAL HEALTH CENTER
64 Robbins St
Waterbury, CT 06708-2600
(203)573-6000

WEST HARTFORD
HEBREW HOME AND HOSPITAL
1 Abrahms Boulevard
West Hartford, CT 06117-1525
(860)523-3800

WEST HAVEN
VA HEALTHCARE SYSTEM - CONNECTICUT AT WEST HAVEN
950 Campbell Avenue
West Haven, CT 06516-2770
(203)932-5711

WESTPORT
HALL-BROOKE HOSPITAL
47 Long Lots Road Box 31
Westport, CT 06880-3828
(203)221-8802

WILLIMANTIC
WINDHAM COMMUNITY MEMORIAL HOSPITAL AND HATCH HOSPITAL
112 Mansfield Avenue
Willimantic, CT 06226-2041
(860)456-9116

DELAWARE

DOVER
BAY HEALTH MEDICAL CENTER AT KENT GENERAL HOSPITAL
640 S State Street
Dover, DE 19901-3530
(302)674-4700

GEORGETOWN
SUSSEX CORRECTIONAL INSTITUTION
PO Box 500
Georgetown, DE 19947-0500
(302)856-5280

LEWES
BEEBE MEDICAL CENTER
424 Savannah Road
Lewes, DE 19958-1490
(302)645-3300

MILFORD
BAY HEALTH MEDICAL CENTER AT MILFORD MEMORIAL HOSPITAL
21 W Clarke Avenue
Milford, DE 19963-1840
(302)430-5613

NEW CASTLE
DELAWARE PSYCHIATRIC CENTER
1901 N Dupont Highway
New Castle, DE 19720-1100
(302)577-4000

MEADOW WOOD HOSPITAL
575 South Dupont Highway
New Castle, DE 19720-4600
(302)328-3330

NEWARK
CHRISTIANA HOSPITAL
4755 Ogletown Station Road
Newark, DE 19718-0001
(302)428-2570

ROCKFORD CENTER
100 Rockford Drive
Newark, DE 19713-2121
(302)996-5480

SEAFORD
NANTICOKE MEMORIAL HOSPITAL
801 Middleford Road
Seaford, DE 19973-3636
(302)629-6611

SMYRNA
DELAWARE HOSPITAL-CHRONICALLY ILL
100 Sunnyside Road
Smyrna, DE 19977-1752
(302)739-3884

WILMINGTON
ALFRED I DUPONT INSTITUTE FOR CHILDREN
1600 Rockland Road PO Box 269
Wilmington, DE 19899-0269
(302)651-4000

EUGENE DUPONT MEMORIAL DIVISION HOSPITAL
3506 Kennett Pike
Wilmington, DE 19807-3019
(302)428-2003

SAINT FRANCIS HOSPITAL
7th And Clayton Streets PO Box 2500
Wilmington, DE 19805-0500
(302)421-4100

SELECT SPECIALTY HOSPITAL - WILMINGTON
7th & Clayton Streets
Wilmington, DE 19801
(302)421-4590

VA MEDICAL CENTER - WILMINGTON
1601 Kirkwood Highway
Wilmington, DE 19805-4917
(302)633-5201

WILMINGTON HOSPITAL
PO Box 1668
Wilmington, DE 19899-1668
(302)733-1000

DISTRICT OF COLUMBIA

WASHINGTON
CHILDREN'S NATIONAL MEDICAL CENTER
111 Michigan Avenue Nw
Washington, DC 20010-2978
(202)884-5000

DISTRICT OF COLUMBIA GENERAL HOSPITAL
19th And E Streets Se
Washington, DC 20003
(202)698-5000

GEORGE WASHINGTON UNIVERSITY HOSPITAL
901 23rd St Nw
Washington, DC 20037-2377
(202)715-4000

GEORGETOWN UNIVERSITY HOSPITAL
3800 Reservior Road
Washington, DC 20007-2196
(202)784-3000

GREATER SOUTHEAST HOSPITAL
1310 Southern Avenue Se
Washington, DC 20032-4699
(202)574-6000

HADLEY MEMORIAL HOSPITAL
4601 Martin Luther King Jr Avenue, Sw
Washington, DC 20032-1199
(202)574-5700

HOSPITAL FOR SICK CHILDREN
1731 Bunker Hill Road Ne
Washington, DC 20017-3096
(202)832-4400

HOWARD UNIVERSITY HOSPITAL
2041 Georgia Avenue Nw
Washington, DC 20060-0002
(202)865-6100

MEDLINK HOSPITAL OF CAPITOL HILL
700 Constitution Avenue N E
Washington, DC 20002-6058
(202)546-5700

NATIONAL REHAB HOSPITAL
102 Irving St Nw
Washington, DC 20010-2949
(202)877-1000

PROVIDENCE HOSPITAL
1150 Varnum St Ne
Washington, DC 20017-2180
(202)269-7000

PSYCHIATRIC INSTITUTE OF WASHINGTON
4228 Wisconsin Avenue, Nw
Washington, DC 20016-2138
(202)965-8550

RIVERSIDE HOSPITAL
4460 McArthur Boulevard N W
Washington, DC 20007-2516
(202)333-9355

SAINT ELIZABETHS HOSPITAL
2700 Martin Luther King Jr Avenue Se
Washington, DC 20032-2698
(202)562-4000

SIBLEY MEMORIAL HOSPITAL
5255 Loughboro Road Nw
Washington, DC 20016-2695
(202)537-4000

FLORIDA — Hospital Telephone Directory

VA MEDICAL CENTER - WASHINGTON DC
50 Irving St Nw
Washington, DC 20422-0001
(202)745-8100

WALTER REED ARMY MEDICAL CENTER
6900 Georgia Avenue Nw
Washington, DC 20307-0004
(202)782-3501

WASHINGTON HOSPITAL CENTER
110 Irving St Nw
Washington, DC 20010-2975
(202)877-7000

FLORIDA

ALTAMONTE SPRINGS

FLORIDA HOSPITAL ALTAMONTE
601 E Altamonte Drive
Altamonte Springs, FL 32701-4898
(407)830-4321

APALACHICOLA

GEORGE E WEEMS MEMORIAL HOSPITAL
One Washington Square
Apalachicola, FL 32320
(850)653-8853

APOPKA

FLORIDA HOSPITAL APOPKA
201 North Park Avenue
Apopka, FL 32703-4198
(407)889-2566

SUMMIT
700 E Welch Road
Apopka, FL 32712-2921
(407)880-8700

ARCADIA

DESOTO MEMORIAL HOSPITAL
900 N Roberts Avenue
Arcadia, FL 34266-8765
(863)494-3535

ATLANTIS

JFK MEDICAL CENTER
5301 S Congress Avenue
Atlantis, FL 33462-1197
(561)965-7300

AVENTURA

AVENTURA HOSPITAL AND MEDICAL CENTER
20900 Biscayne Boulevard
Aventura, FL 33180-1495
(305)682-7000

BARTOW

BARTOW MEMORIAL HOSPITAL
PO Box 1050
Bartow, FL 33831-1050
(863)533-8111

BAY PINES

VA MEDICAL CENTER - BAY PINES
10000 Bay Pines Boulevard N
Bay Pines, FL 33708
(727)398-6661

BELLE GLADE

GLADES GENERAL HOSPITAL
1201 S Main St
Belle Glade, FL 33430-4911
(561)996-6571

BLOUNTSTOWN

CALHOUN LIBERTY HOSPITAL
PO Box 419
Blountstown, FL 32424-0419
(850)674-5411

BOCA RATON

BOCA RATON COMMUNITY HOSPITAL
800 Meadows Road
Boca Raton, FL 33486-2368
(561)395-7100

WEST BOCA MEDICAL CENTER
21644 State Road 7
Boca Raton, FL 33428-1899
(561)488-8000

BONIFAY

DOCTORS MEMORIAL HOSPITAL
401 E Byrd Avenue
Bonifay, FL 32425-3007
(850)547-1120

BOYNTON BEACH

BETHESDA MEMORIAL HOSPITAL
2815 South Seacrest Boulevard
Boynton Beach, FL 33435-7995
(561)737-7733

BRADENTON

BLAKE MEDICAL CENTER
2020 59th St W
Bradenton, FL 34209-4669
(941)792-6611

MANATEE GLEN HOSPITAL
2020 2nd Street East
Bradenton, FL 34208-1508
(941)741-3805

MANATEE MEMORIAL HOSPITAL
206 2 St E
Bradenton, FL 34208-1000
(941)746-5111

MANATEE PALMS YOUTH SERVICES
4480 51st Street West
Bradenton, FL 34210-2857
(941)792-2222

BRANDON

BRANDON REGIONAL HOSPITAL
119 Oakfield Drive
Brandon, FL 33511-5779
(813)681-5551

BROOKSVILLE

BROOKSVILLE REGIONAL HOSPITAL
55 Ponce De Leon Boulevard Box 37
Brooksville, FL 34601-3200
(352)796-5111

SPRINGBROOK HOSPITAL
7007 Grove Road
Brooksville, FL 34609-8610
(352)596-4306

CAPE CORAL

CAPE CORAL HOSPITAL
636 Del Prado Boulevard
Cape Coral, FL 33990-2695
(239)574-2323

CELEBRATION

FLORIDA HOSPITAL CELEBRATION HEALTH
400 Celebration Place
Celebration, FL 34747-4970
(407)303-4000

CHATTAHOOCHEE

FLORIDA STATE HOSPITAL
Unit 31 Building 243 Box 1000
Chattahoochee, FL 32324-1000
(850)663-7001

CHIPLEY

NORTHWEST FLORIDA COMMUNITY HOSPITAL
PO Box 889
Chipley, FL 32428-0889
(850)638-1610

CLEARWATER

MORTON PLANT HOSPITAL
300 Pinellas Street
Clearwater, FL 33756-3892
(727)462-7000

WINDMOOR HEALTHCARE OF CLEARWATER
11300 Us 19 North
Clearwater, FL 33764-7451
(727)541-2646

CLERMONT

SOUTH LAKE MEMORIAL HOSPITAL
1099 Citrus Tower Blvd
Clermont, FL 34711-2787
(352)394-4071

CLEWISTON

HENDRY REGIONAL MEDICAL CENTER
500 West Surgarland Highway
Clewiston, FL 33440-3094
(863)983-9121

COCOA BEACH

CAPE CANAVERAL HOSPITAL
701 W Cocoa Beach Causeway
Cocoa Beach, FL 32931-5595
(321)799-7111

CORAL GABLES

CORAL GABLES HOSPITAL
3100 Douglas Road
Coral Gables, FL 33134-6923
(305)445-8461

HEALTHSOUTH DOCTORS HOSPITAL
5000 University Drive
Coral Gables, FL 33146-2094
(305)666-2111

KINDRED HOSPITAL CORAL GABLES
5190 SW 8th Street
Coral Gables, FL 33134-2476
(305)448-1585

CORAL SPRINGS

CORAL SPRINGS MEDICAL CENTER
3000 Coral Hill Drive
Coral Springs, FL 33065-4125
(954)344-3000

CRESTVIEW

NORTH OKALOOSA MEDICAL CENTER
151 Redstone Avenue Se
Crestview, FL 32539-5352
(850)689-8100

CRYSTAL RIVER

SEVEN RIVERS COMMUNITY HOSPITAL
6201 N Suncoast Boulevard
Crystal River, FL 34428-6712
(352)795-6560

Hospital Telephone Directory — FLORIDA

DADE CITY

PASCO COMMUNITY HOSPITAL
13100 Fort King Road
Dade City, FL 33525-5294
(352)521-1100

DAVENPORT

HEART OF FLORIDA REGIONAL MEDICAL CENTER
40100 Hwy 27
Davenport, FL 33837-5900
(863)422-4971

DAYTONA BEACH

HALIFAX BEHAVIORAL SERVICES
841 Jimmy Ann Drive
Daytona Beach, FL 32117-4599
(386)274-5333

HALIFAX MEDICAL CENTER
303 N Clyde Morris Boulevard
Daytona Beach, FL 32114-2700
(386)254-4000

DEFUNIAK SPRINGS

HEALTHMARK REGIONAL MEDICAL CENTER
4413 Us Hwy 331 South
Defuniak Springs, FL 32435-6307
(850)892-5171

DELAND

FLORIDA HOSPITAL DELAND
701 W Plymouth Avenue
Deland, FL 32720-3236
(386)734-3320

DELRAY BEACH

DELRAY MEDICAL HOSPITAL
5352 Linton Boulevard
Delray Beach, FL 33484-6514
(561)498-4440

FAIR OAKS HOSPITAL
5440 Linton Boulevard
Delray Beach, FL 33484-6512
(561)495-1000

PINECREST REHABILITATION HOSPITAL
5360 Linton Boulevard
Delray Beach, FL 33484-6538
(561)495-0400

DUNEDIN

MEASE HOSPITAL DUNEDIN
601 Main Street
Dunedin, FL 34698-5848
(727)733-1111

EGLIN AIR FORCE BASE

96TH MEDICAL GROUP
307 Boatner Road Suite 114
Eglin Air Force Base, FL 32542-1391
(850)883-8221

ENGLEWOOD

ENGLEWOOD COMMUNITY HOSPITAL
700 Medical Boulevard
Englewood, FL 34223-3978
(941)475-6571

EUSTIS

FLORIDA HOSPITAL WATERMAN
201 N Eustis St
Eustis, FL 32726-3488
(352)589-3333

FERNANDINA BEACH

BAPTIST MEDICAL CENTER NASSAU
1250 S 18th St
Fernandina Beach, FL 32034-1902
(904)321-3500

FORT LAUDERDALE

ATLANTIC SHORES HOSPITAL
4545 N Federal Highway
Fort Lauderdale, FL 33308-5203
(954)771-2711

BROWARD GENERAL MEDICAL CENTER
1600 S Andrews Avenue
Fort Lauderdale, FL 33316-2589
(954)355-4400

DAYSTAR
3800 Flamingo Road
Fort Lauderdale, FL 33330-1699
(954)473-0167

DICKENSON COUNTY MEDICAL CENTER
888 E Las Olas Blvd Ste 210
Fort Lauderdale, FL 33301-2239
(954)926-0300

FLORIDA MEDICAL CENTER
5000 W Oakland Park Boulevard
Fort Lauderdale, FL 33313-1585
(954)735-6000

FORT LAUDERDALE HOSPITAL
1601 East Las Olas Boulevard
Fort Lauderdale, FL 33301-2393
(954)463-4321

HOLY CROSS HOSPITAL
4725 N Federal Highway
Fort Lauderdale, FL 33308-4668
(954)771-8000

IMPERIAL POINT MEDICAL CENTER
6401 North Federal Highway
Fort Lauderdale, FL 33308-1495
(954)776-8500

KINDRED HOSPITAL FORT LAUDERDALE
1516 E Las Olas Boulevard
Fort Lauderdale, FL 33301-2346
(954)764-8900

NORTH RIDGE MEDICAL CENTER
5757 N Dixie Highway
Fort Lauderdale, FL 33334-4182
(954)776-6000

FORT MYERS

GULF COAST HOSPITAL
13681 Doctors Way
Fort Myers, FL 33912-4309
(239)768-5000

LEE MEMORIAL HEALTH SYSTEM
2776 Cleveland Avenue
Fort Myers, FL 33901-5855
(239)332-1111

SOUTHWEST FLORIDA REGIONAL MEDICAL CENTER
2727 Winkler Avenue
Fort Myers, FL 33901-9340
(239)939-1147

FORT PIERCE

LAWNWOOD PAVILION
1860 N Lawnwood Circle
Fort Pierce, FL 34950-4828
(772)466-1500

LAWNWOOD REGIONAL MEDICAL CENTER
1700 S 23rd St
Fort Pierce, FL 34950-4899
(772)461-4000

FORT WALTON BEACH

FORT WALTON BEACH MEDICAL CENTER
1000 Mar Walt Drive
Fort Walton Beach, FL 32547-6795
(850)862-1111

GULF COAST TREATMENT CENTER
1015 Mar Walt Drive
Fort Walton Beach, FL 32547-6612
(850)863-4171

GAINESVILLE

NORTH FLORIDA REGIONAL MEDICAL CENTER
6500 Newberry Road
Gainesville, FL 32605-4392
(352)333-4000

SHANDS AGH HOSPITAL
801 Sw Second Avenue
Gainesville, FL 32601-6289
(352)372-4321

SHANDS HOSPITAL AT THE UNIVERSITY OF FLORIDA
1600 Sw Archer Road
Gainesville, FL 32610
(352)265-0111

SHANDS REHAB HOSPITAL
4101 NW 89th Boulevard
Gainesville, FL 32606-3813
(352)265-5491

TACACHALE DAHLIA HOSPITAL UNIT
1621 Ne Waldo Road
Gainesville, FL 32609-3918
(352)955-5000

VA MEDICAL CENTER - GAINESVILLE
1601 Sw Archer Road
Gainesville, FL 32608-1197
(352)376-1611

GRACEVILLE

CAMPBELLTON GRACEVILLE HOSPITAL
1305 College Drive
Graceville, FL 32440
(850)263-4431

GREEN COVE SPRINGS

KINDRED HOSPITAL NORTH FLORIDA
801 Oak Street
Green Cove Springs, FL 32043-4317
(904)284-9230

GULF BREEZE

FRIARY OF BAPTIST HEALTH CENTER
4400 Hickory Shores Blvd
Gulf Breeze, FL 32563-9111
(850)932-9375

GULF BREEZE HOSPITAL
1110 Gulf Breeze Parkway
Gulf Breeze, FL 32561-4897
(850)934-2000

HIALEAH

HIALEAH HOSPITAL
651 E 25 St
Hialeah, FL 33013-3878
(305)693-6100

PALM SPRINGS GENERAL HOSPITAL
1475 W 49 St
Hialeah, FL 33012-3275
(305)558-2500

PALMETTO GENERAL HOSPITAL
2001 W 68th St
Hialeah, FL 33016-1898
(305)823-5000

FLORIDA
Hospital Telephone Directory

SOUTHERN WINDS HOSPITAL-
WESTCHESTER
4225 W 20 Avenue
Hialeah, FL 33012-5835
(305)558-9700

HOLLYWOOD

HOLLYWOOD MEDICAL CENTER
3600 Washington St
Hollywood, FL 33021-8216
(954)966-4500

HOLLYWOOD PAVILION HOSPITAL
1201 N 37 Avenue
Hollywood, FL 33021-5498
(954)962-1355

JOE DIMAGGIO CHILDREN'S HOSPITAL
3501 Johnson Street
Hollywood, FL 33021-5487
(954)987-2000

KINDRED HOSPITAL HOLLYWOOD
1859 Van Buren Street
Hollywood, FL 33020-5127
(954)920-9000

MEMORIAL REGIONAL HOSPITAL
3501 Johnson St
Hollywood, FL 33021-5487
(954)987-2000

HOMESTEAD

HOMESTEAD HOSPITAL
160 Nw 13th Street
Homestead, FL 33030-4228
(305)248-3232

HUDSON

REGIONAL MEDICAL CENTER - BAYONET
POINT
14000 Fivay Road
Hudson, FL 34667-7103
(727)863-2411

INVERNESS

CITRUS MEMORIAL HOSPITAL
502 Highland Boulevard
Inverness, FL 34452-4754
(352)748-0374

JACKSONVILLE

BAPTIST MEDICAL CENTER
800 Prudential Drive
Jacksonville, FL 32207-8211
(904)202-2000

BROOKS REHABILITATION HOSPITAL
3599 University Boulevard, South
Jacksonville, FL 32216-4252
(904)858-7200

MEMORIAL HOSPITAL JACKSONVILLE
3625 University Boulevard South
Jacksonville, FL 32216-4222
(904)399-6111

NAVAL HOSPITAL JACKSONVILLE
2080 Child St
Jacksonville, FL 32214-5005
(904)542-7300

SAINT LUKES HOSPITAL
4201 Belford Road
Jacksonville, FL 32216-5898
(904)296-3700

SAINT VINCENTS MEDICAL CENTER
1800 Barrs St
Jacksonville, FL 32204-4799
(904)308-7300

SHANDS JACKSONVILLE MEDICAL CENTER
580 W 8th St
Jacksonville, FL 32209-6599
(904)244-0411

SHANDS JACKSONVILLE MEDICAL CENTER
655 W 8th St
Jacksonville, FL 32209-6596
(904)244-0411

SPECIALITY HOSPITAL OF JACKSONVILLE
4901 Richard Street
Jacksonville, FL 32207-7381
(904)737-3120

TEN BROECK RIVER HOSPITAL
6300 Beach Blvd
Jacksonville, FL 32216-2782
(904)724-9202

JACKSONVILLE BEACH

BAPTIST MEDICAL CENTER BEACHES
1350 13th Avenue South
Jacksonville Beach, FL 32250-3205
(904)247-2900

JASPER

TRINITY COMMUNITY HOSPITAL
506 Nw 4th St
Jasper, FL 32052-6698
(386)792-7200

JAY

JAY HOSPITAL
14114 Alabama St
Jay, FL 32565-1219
(850)675-8000

JUPITER

JUPITER MEDICAL CENTER
1210 S Old Dixie Highway
Jupiter, FL 33458-7205
(561)747-2234

KEY WEST

DE POO HOSPITAL
1200 Kennedy Drive
Key West, FL 33040-4023
(305)294-5531

LOWER FLORIDA KEYS HEALTH SYSTEMS
5900 Junior College
Key West, FL 33040-4342
(305)294-5531

KISSIMMEE

FLORIDA HOSPITAL KISSIMEE
2450 N Orange Blossom Trl
Kissimmee, FL 34744-2316
(407)846-4343

OSCEOLA REGIONAL MEDICAL CENTER
700 West Oak Street
Kissimmee, FL 34741-4900
(407)846-2266

LAKE BUTLER

LAKE BUTLER HOSPITAL - HAND SURGERY
CENTER
850 E Main St
Lake Butler, FL 32054-1353
(386)496-2323

NORTH FLORIDA RECEPTION CENTER
HOSPITAL
State Road 231 South, PO Box 628
Lake Butler, FL 32054-0628
(386)496-6000

LAKE CITY

LAKE CITY MEDICAL CENTER
340 North Commerce Blvd
Lake City, FL 32055-4709
(386)719-9000

SHANDS AT LAKE SHORE HOSPITAL
368 Ne Franklin St
Lake City, FL 32055-3047
(386)754-8000

VA MEDICAL CENTER - LAKE CITY
801 S Marion St
Lake City, FL 32025-5827
(386)755-3016

LAKE PLACID

FLORIDA HOSPITAL LAKE PLACID
1210 US Hwy 27 North
Lake Placid, FL 33852-7948
(863)465-3777

LAKE WALES

LAKE WALES MEDICAL CENTER
410 South 11th Street
Lake Wales, FL 33853-4256
(863)676-1433

LAKELAND

LAKELAND REGIONAL MEDICAL CENTER
1400 Lakeland Hills Boulevard
Lakeland, FL 33805-3202
(863)687-1100

LANTANA

A G HOLLEY STATE HOSPITAL
1199 W Lantana Road
Lantana, FL 33462-1514
(561)582-5666

LARGO

HEALTHSOUTH REHABILITATION CENTER
901 Clearwater Largo Road
Largo, FL 33770-4121
(727)586-2999

LARGO MEDICAL CENTER
201 14th St Sw
Largo, FL 33770-3199
(727)588-5200

SUN COAST HOSPITAL
2025 Indian Rocks Road S
Largo, FL 33774-1096
(727)581-9474

LAUDERDALE LAKES

SAINT JOHNS REHABILITATION HOSPITAL
3075 Nw 35th Avenue
Lauderdale Lakes, FL 33311-1107
(954)739-6233

LEESBURG

LEESBURG REGIONAL MEDICAL CENTER
600 E Dixie Avenue
Leesburg, FL 34748-5999
(352)323-5762

LIFESTREAM BEHAVIORAL CENTER
PO Box 491000
Leesburg, FL 34749-1000
(352)315-7500

LEHIGH ACRES

LEHIGH REGIONAL MEDICAL CENTER
1500 Lee Boulevard
Lehigh Acres, FL 33936-4835
(239)369-2101

Hospital Telephone Directory — FLORIDA

LIVE OAK

SHANDS AT LIVE OAK
1100s W 11th
Live Oak, FL 32060
(386)362-1413

LONGWOOD

SOUTH SEMINOLE COMMUNITY HOSPITAL
555 West State Road 434
Longwood, FL 32750-4999
(407)767-1200

LOXAHATCHEE

PALMS WEST HOSPITAL
13001 Southern Boulevard
Loxahatchee, FL 33470-9277
(561)798-3300

MAC DILL AIR FORCE BASE

6TH MEDICAL GROUP
8415 Bayshore Boulevard
Mac Dill Air Force Base, FL 33621-1607
(813)828-5258

MACCLENNY

ED FRASER MEMORIAL HOSPITAL AND BAKER COMMUNITY HEALTH CENTER
159 N 3rd St
MacClenny, FL 32063-2103
(904)259-3151

NORTHEAST FLORIDA STATE HOSPITAL
Highway 121 South
MacClenny, FL 32063
(904)259-6211

MADISON

MADISON COUNTY MEMORIAL HOSPITAL
201 E Marion St
Madison, FL 32340-2561
(850)973-2271

MAITLAND

LA AMISTAD BEHAVIORAL HEALTH SERVICES
1650 Park Avenue North
Maitland, FL 32751-6570
(407)647-0660

MARATHON

FISHERMENS HOSPITAL
3301 Overseas Highway Box 500068
Marathon, FL 33050-2398
(305)743-5533

MARGATE

NORTHWEST MEDICAL CENTER
2801 N State Road 7
Margate, FL 33063
(954)974-0400

MARIANNA

JACKSON COUNTY HOSPITAL
4250 Hospital Drive
Marianna, FL 32446-1917
(850)526-2200

MELBOURNE

CIRCLES OF CARE
400 E Sheridan Road
Melbourne, FL 32901-3184
(321)722-5200

HEALTHSOUTH SEA PINES HOSPITAL
101 East Florida Avenue
Melbourne, FL 32901-8301
(321)984-4600

HOLMES REGIONAL MEDICAL CENTER
1350 S Hickory St
Melbourne, FL 32901-3278
(321)434-7000

MIAMI

BAPTIST HOSPITAL OF MIAMI
8900 N Kendall Drive
Miami, FL 33176-2197
(305)596-1960

BASCOM PALMER EYE INSTITUTE - ANNE BATES LEACH EYE HOSPITAL
900 NW 17th St
Miami, FL 33136-1119
(305)326-6000

CEDARS MEDICAL CENTER
1400 Nw 12th Avenue
Miami, FL 33136-1087
(305)325-5511

HEALTHSOUTH REHABILITATION HOSPITAL
20601 Old Cutler Road
Miami, FL 33189-2441
(305)251-3800

HIGHLAND PARK PAVILION
1660 Nw 7th Court
Miami, FL 33136-1492
(305)324-8111

JACKSON MEMORIAL HOSPITAL
1611 Nw 12 Avenue
Miami, FL 33136-1096
(305)585-1111

JACKSON SOUTH COMMUNITY HOSPITAL
9333 Sw 152 St
Miami, FL 33157-1778
(305)251-2500

KENDALL MEDICAL CENTER
11750 Bird Drive
Miami, FL 33175-3530
(305)223-3000

MEADOWBROOK REHAB HOSPITAL OF WEST GABLES
2525 Sw 75th Avenue
Miami, FL 33155-2800
(305)262-6800

MERCY HOSPITAL
3663 S Miami Avenue
Miami, FL 33133-4237
(305)854-4400

MIAMI CHILDRENS HOSPITAL
6125 Sw 31st St
Miami, FL 33155-3098
(305)666-6511

MIAMI HEART INSTITUTE & MEDICAL CENTER - SOUTH CAMPUS
250 63rd St
Miami, FL 33141-5801
(305)672-1111

MIAMI JEWISH HOME AND HOSPITAL - DOUGLAS GARDENS
5200 Ne 2nd Avenue
Miami, FL 33137-2706
(305)751-8626

NORTH SHORE MEDICAL CENTER
1100 Nw 95th St
Miami, FL 33150-2098
(305)835-6000

PAN AMERICAN HOSPITAL
5959 Nw 7th St
Miami, FL 33126-3198
(305)264-1000

SELECT SPECIALTY HOSPITAL - MIAMI
935 Northwest 3rd Street
Miami, FL 33128-1213
(305)416-5700

SOUTH FLORIDA EVALUATION & TREATMENT CENTER
2200 Nw 7th Avenue
Miami, FL 33127-4291
(305)637-2500

SOUTH MIAMI HOSPITAL
6200 Sw 73 St
Miami, FL 33143-4679
(786)662-4000

SUNRISE REGIONAL
PO Box 430740
Miami, FL 33243-0740
(305)370-0200

UNICOL HOSPITAL SERVICES
PO Box 1690
Miami, FL 33168
(305)769-1808

UNIVERSITY OF MIAMI HOSPITAL AND CLINICS
1475 Nw 12 Avenue
Miami, FL 33136-1002
(305)243-1000

VA MEDICAL CENTER - MIAMI
1201 N W 16th St
Miami, FL 33125-1624
(305)324-4455

WEST GABLES REHABILITATION HOSPITAL
2525 Southwest 75th Avenue
Miami, FL 33155-2800
(305)262-6800

WESTCHESTER GENERAL HOSPITAL
2500 Sw 75 Avenue
Miami, FL 33155-2895
(305)264-5252

MIAMI BEACH

MIAMI HEART INSTITUTE AND MEDICAL CENTER SOUTH
4701 Meridan Avenue
Miami Beach, FL 33140-2997
(305)674-3114

MOUNT SINAI HOSPITAL
4300 Alton Road
Miami Beach, FL 33140-2800
(305)674-2121

SOUTH SHORE HOSPITAL AND MEDICAL CENTER
630 Alton Road
Miami Beach, FL 33139-5502
(305)672-2100

MILTON

SANTA ROSA MEDICAL CENTER
6002 Berryhill Rd
Milton, FL 32570-5062
(850)626-7762

WEST FLORIDA COMMUNITY CARE CENTER
400 Stewart St Ne
Milton, FL 32570
(850)983-5500

NAPLES

CLEVELAND CLINIC FLORIDA HOSPITAL
6101 Pine Ridge Road
Naples, FL 34119-3900
(239)348-4000

NAPLES COMMUNITY HOSPITAL
350 Seventh St North
Naples, FL 34102-5730
(239)436-5000

FLORIDA

Hospital Telephone Directory

WILLOUGHS HEALTHCARE SYSTEM AT
NAPLES
9001 Tamiami Trail East
Naples, FL 34113-3397
(239)775-4500

NEW PORT RICHEY

COMMUNITY HOSPITAL OF NEW PORT
RICHEY
5637 Marine Parkway
New Port Richey, FL 34652-4316
(727)848-1733

NORTH BAY MEDICAL CENTER
6600 Madison Street
New Port Richey, FL 34652-1900
(727)842-8468

NEW SMYRNA BEACH

BERT FISH MEDICAL CENTER
401 Palmetto St
New Smyrna Beach, FL 32168-7399
(386)424-5000

NICEVILLE

TWIN CITIES HOSPITAL
2190 Highway 85 North
Niceville, FL 32578-1045
(850)678-4131

NORTH MIAMI

SAINT CATHERINE'S REHABILITATION
HOSPITAL
1050 NE 125th St
North Miami, FL 33161-5805
(305)357-1735

UNICOL HOSPITAL SERVICES
655 NW 128th St
North Miami, FL 33168-2735
(305)769-1808

NORTH MIAMI BEACH

PARKWAY REGIONAL MEDICAL CENTER
160 NW 170th St
North Miami Beach, FL 33169-5576
(305)651-1100

OCALA

MUNROE REGIONAL MEDICAL CENTER
131 Sw 15th St
Ocala, FL 34474-4029
(352)351-7200

OCALA REGIONAL MEDICAL CENTER
1431 SW First Street
Ocala, FL 34474-4058
(352)401-1000

WEST MARION COMMUNITY HOSPITAL
4600 Southwest 46th Court
Ocala, FL 34474-5752
(352)291-3000

OCOEE

HEALTH CENTRAL
1000 W Colonial Drive
Ocoee, FL 34761
(407)296-1000

OKEECHOBEE

RAULERSON HOSPITAL
1796 Highway 441 N
Okeechobee, FL 34972-1918
(863)763-2151

ORANGE CITY

FLORIDA HOSPITAL FISH MEMORIAL
1055 Saxon Boulevard
Orange City, FL 32763-8468
(386)917-5000

ORANGE PARK

ORANGE PARK MEDICAL CENTER
2001 Kingsley Avenue
Orange Park, FL 32073-5156
(904)276-8500

ORLANDO

ARNOLD PALMER HOSPITAL FOR
CHILDREN & WOMEN
92 W Miller St
Orlando, FL 32806-2036
(407)841-5111

FLORIDA HOSPITAL EAST ORLANDO
7727 Lake Underhill Road
Orlando, FL 32822-8299
(407)303-8110

FLORIDA HOSPITAL ORLANDO
601 E Rollins Avenue
Orlando, FL 32803-1273
(407)303-6611

LAKESIDE ALTERNATIVES HOSPITAL
434 Kennedy Blvd Ste A
Orlando, FL 32810-6228
(407)875-3700

LUCERNE MEDICAL CENTER
818 S Main Lane
Orlando, FL 32801-3797
(407)649-6111

ORLANDO REGIONAL MEDICAL CENTER
1414 S Kuhl Avenue
Orlando, FL 32806-2093
(407)841-5111

SAND LAKE HOSPITAL
9400 Turkey Lake Road
Orlando, FL 32819-8014
(407)351-8500

UNIVERSITY BEHAVIORAL CENTER
CROSSROADS HOSPITAL
2500 Discovery Drive
Orlando, FL 32826-3711
(407)281-7000

ORMOND BEACH

FLORIDA HOSPITAL OCEANSIDE
264 S Atlantic Avenue
Ormond Beach, FL 32176-8149
(386)672-4161

FLORIDA HOSPITAL ORMOND BEACH
875 Sterthaus Avenue
Ormond Beach, FL 32174-5131
(386)676-6000

PALATKA

PUTNAM MEDICAL CENTER
Highway 20 W Drawer 778
Palatka, FL 32178-0778
(386)328-5711

PALM BEACH GARDENS

PALM BEACH GARDENS MEDICAL CENTER
3360 Burns Road
Palm Beach Gardens, FL 33410-4384
(561)622-1411

PALM COAST

FLORIDA HOSPTIAL FLAGLER
60 Memorial Medical Parkway
Palm Coast, FL 32164
(386)586-2000

PANAMA CITY

BAY MEDICAL CENTER
615 N Bonita Avenue
Panama City, FL 32401-3600
(850)769-1511

GULF COAST MEDICAL CENTER
449 W 23rd St
Panama City, FL 32405-4593
(850)769-8341

HEALTHSOUTH EMERALD COAST REHAB
HOSPITAL
1847 Florida Avenue
Panama City, FL 32405-4640
(850)784-2000

MEDICAL BEHAVIORAL CENTER
1940 Harrison Avenue
Panama City, FL 32405-4542
(850)763-0017

PEMBROKE PINES

MEMORIAL HOSPITAL PEMBROKE
7800 Sheridan St
Pembroke Pines, FL 33024-2536
(954)962-9650

MEMORIAL HOSPITAL WEST
703 N Flamingo Road
Pembroke Pines, FL 33028-1014
(954)436-5000

SOUTH FLORIDA STATE HOSPITAL
800 E Cypress Drive
Pembroke Pines, FL 33025-4543
(954)392-3000

UNICOL HOSPITAL SERVICES
11590 SW 9th Court
Pembroke Pines, FL 33025-4324
(954)769-1808

PENSACOLA

BAPTIST HOSPITAL
1000 West Moreno Street
Pensacola, FL 32501-2393
(850)434-4011

NAVAL HOSPITAL PENSACOLA
6000 W Highway 98
Pensacola, FL 32512-0002
(850)505-6601

PAVILION, THE
8383 North Davis Highway
Pensacola, FL 32514-6039
(850)494-5000

REHABILITATION INSTITUTE OF WEST
FLORIDA
8383 North Davis Highway
Pensacola, FL 32514-6039
(850)494-6000

SACRED HEART HOSPITAL
5151 N 9 Avenue
Pensacola, FL 32504-8795
(850)416-7000

WEST FLORIDA REGIONAL MEDICAL
CENTER
8383 N Davis Highway
Pensacola, FL 32514-6088
(850)494-4000

Hospital Telephone Directory — FLORIDA

PERRY
DOCTORS MEMORIAL HOSPITAL
333 N Byron Butler Pkwy
Perry, FL 32347-2300
(850)584-0800

PLANT CITY
SOUTH FLORIDA BAPTIST HOSPITAL
301 Alexander St
Plant City, FL 33566
(813)757-1200

PLANTATION
PLANTATION GENERAL HOSPITAL
401 Nw 42 Avenue
Plantation, FL 33317-2882
(954)587-5010

WESTSIDE REGIONAL MEDICAL CENTER
8201 W Broward Boulevard
Plantation, FL 33324-2798
(954)473-6600

POMPANO BEACH
NORTH BROWARD MEDICAL CENTER
201 E Sample Road
Pompano Beach, FL 33064-3596
(954)941-8300

PORT CHARLOTTE
BON SECOURS - SAINT JOSEPH HOSPITAL PORT CHARLOTTE
2500 Harbor Boulevard
Port Charlotte, FL 33952-5000
(941)766-4122

FAWCETT MEMORIAL HOSPITAL
101 Nw Olean Boulevard
Port Charlotte, FL 33952
(941)629-1181

PORT SAINT JOE
GULF PINES HOSPITAL
PO Box 70
Port Saint Joe, FL 32457-0070
(850)227-1121

PORT SAINT LUCIE
SAINT LUCIE MEDICAL CENTER
1800 Se Tiffany Avenue
Port Saint Lucie, FL 34952-7521
(772)335-4000

SAVANNAS HOSPITAL
2550 Se Walton Road
Port Saint Lucie, FL 34952-7197
(772)335-0400

PUNTA GORDA
CHARLOTTE REGIONAL MEDICAL CENTER
809 E Marion Avenue
Punta Gorda, FL 33950-3819
(941)639-3131

QUINCY
GADSDEN COMMUNITY HOSPITAL
PO Box 1979
Quincy, FL 32353-1979
(850)875-1100

ROCKLEDGE
WUESTHOFF MEMORIAL HOSPITAL
110 Longwood Avenue
Rockledge, FL 32955-2887
(321)636-2211

SAFETY HARBOR
MEASE COUNTRYSIDE HOSPITAL
3231 Mcmullen Booth Road
Safety Harbor, FL 34695
(727)725-6111

SAINT AUGUSTINE
FLAGLER HOSPITAL WEST
400 Health Park Boulevard
Saint Augustine, FL 32086-5790
(904)829-5155

FLAGLER PSYCHIATRIC CENTER
400 Health Park Blvd
Saint Augustine, FL 32086-5784
(904)819-4560

SAINT CLOUD
ORLANDO REGIONAL - SAINT CLOUD HOSPITAL
2906 17th St
Saint Cloud, FL 34769-6099
(407)892-2135

SAINT PETERSBURG
ALL CHILDRENS HOSPITAL
801 Sixth St S
Saint Petersburg, FL 33701-4899
(727)898-7451

BAYFRONT MEDICAL CENTER
701 Sixth St S
Saint Petersburg, FL 33701-4891
(727)823-1234

EDWARD WHITE HOSPITAL
2323 Ninth Avenue N
Saint Petersburg, FL 33713-6898
(727)323-1111

KINDRED HOSPITAL SAINT PETERSBURG
3030 Sixth St South
Saint Petersburg, FL 33705-3720
(727)894-8719

NORTHSIDE HOSPITAL
6000 49th Street N
Saint Petersburg, FL 33709-2145
(727)521-4411

PALMS OF PASADENA HOSPITAL
1501 Pasadena Avenue South
Saint Petersburg, FL 33707-3798
(727)381-1000

SAINT ANTHONYS HOSPITAL
1200 7th Avenue North
Saint Petersburg, FL 33705-1388
(727)825-1100

SAINT PETERSBURG GENERAL HOSPITAL
6500 38th Avenue North
Saint Petersburg, FL 33710-1629
(727)384-1414

SANFORD
CENTRAL FLORIDA REGIONAL HOSPITAL
1401 W Seminole Boulevard
Sanford, FL 32771-6764
(407)321-4500

SARASOTA
DOCTORS HOSPITAL OF SARASOTA
5731 Bee Ridge Road
Sarasota, FL 34241-9705
(941)342-1100

HEALTHSOUTH REHAB HOSPITAL OF SARASOTA
3251 Proctor Road
Sarasota, FL 34231-8538
(941)921-8600

SARASOTA MEMORIAL BAYSIDE CENTER
1650 S Osprey Avenue
Sarasota, FL 34239-2928
(941)917-7760

SARASOTA MEMORIAL HOSPITAL
1700 S Tamiami Trail
Sarasota, FL 34239-3555
(941)917-9000

SEBASTIAN
SEBASTIAN RIVER MEDICAL CENTER
13695 U S Highway 1
Sebastian, FL 32958-3230
(772)589-3186

SEBRING
FLORIDA HOSPITAL HEARTLAND MEDICAL CENTER
4200 Sun N Lake Boulevard, PO Box 9400
Sebring, FL 33871-9400
(863)314-4466

HIGHLANDS REGIONAL MEDICAL CENTER
3600 S Highlands Avenue Drawer 2066
Sebring, FL 33870-5495
(863)385-6101

SOUTH MIAMI
LARKIN COMMUNITY HOSPITAL
7031 Sw 62 Avenue
South Miami, FL 33143-4781
(305)284-7500

SPRING HILL
OAK HILL HOSPITAL
11375 Cortez Boulevard Box 5300
Spring Hill, FL 34613-5409
(352)596-6632

SPRING HILL REGIONAL HOSPITAL
10461 Quality Drive
Spring Hill, FL 34609-9634
(352)688-8200

STARKE
SHANDS AT STARKE
922 East Call Street
Starke, FL 32091-3616
(904)368-2300

STUART
MARTIN MEMORIAL HOSPITAL - SOUTH
2100 Southwest Salerno Road
Stuart, FL 34997
(772)223-2300

MARTIN MEMORIAL MEDICAL CENTER
Box 9010
Stuart, FL 34995-9010
(772)287-5200

SUN CITY CENTER
SOUTH BAY HOSPITAL
4016 State Road 674
Sun City Center, FL 33573
(813)634-3301

SUNRISE
HEALTHSOUTH SUNRISE REHAB HOSPITAL
4399 Nob Hill Road
Sunrise, FL 33351-5813
(954)749-0300

FLORIDA
Hospital Telephone Directory

TALLAHASSEE

CAPITOL REGIONAL MEDICAL CENTER
2626 Capital Medical Boulevard
Tallahassee, FL 32308-4499
(850)656-5000

EASTSIDE PSYCHIATRIC HOSPITAL
2634 Capital Cir Ne
Tallahassee, FL 32308-4106
(850)487-0300

HEALTHSOUTH REHAB HOSPITAL OF
TALLAHASSEE
1675 Riggins Road
Tallahassee, FL 32308-5351
(850)656-4800

TALLAHASSEE MEMORIAL REGIONAL
MEDICAL CENTER
Magnolia Drive And Miccosukee Road
Tallahassee, FL 32304
(850)431-1155

TAMARAC

UNIVERSITY HOSPITAL AND MEDICAL
CENTER
7201 N University Drive
Tamarac, FL 33321-2996
(954)721-2200

UNIVERSITY PAVILION HOSPITAL
7425 N University Drive
Tamarac, FL 33321-2955
(954)722-9933

TAMPA

KINDRED HOSPITAL CENTRAL TAMPA
4801 N Howard Avenue
Tampa, FL 33603-1411
(813)874-7575

KINDRED HOSPITAL TAMPA
4555 S Manhattan Avenue
Tampa, FL 33611-2305
(813)839-6341

LEE MOFFITT CANCER CENTER AND
RESEARCH INSTITUTE
12902 Magnolia Drive
Tampa, FL 33612-9416
(813)972-4673

MEMORIAL HOSPITAL OF TAMPA
2901 Swann Avenue
Tampa, FL 33609-4057
(813)873-6400

SAINT JOSEPHS HOSPITAL
3001 W Martin Luther King Jr Boulevard
Tampa, FL 33607
(813)870-4000

SAINT JOSEPHS WOMENS HOSPITAL
3001 W Martin Luther King Blvd
Tampa, FL 33607
(813)879-4730

SHRINERS HOSPITAL FOR CHILDREN
12502 Pine Drive
Tampa, FL 33612-9499
(813)972-2250

TAMPA GENERAL HOSPITAL
Davis Island PO Box 1289
Tampa, FL 33601-1289
(813)844-7000

TOWN AND COUNTRY HOSPITAL
6001 Webb Road
Tampa, FL 33615-3291
(813)888-7060

UNIVERSITY COMMUNITY HOSPITAL
3100 E Fletcher Avenue
Tampa, FL 33613-4688
(813)971-6000

UNIVERSITY COMMUNITY HOSPITAL AT
CARROLLWOOD
7171 N Dale Mabry Highway
Tampa, FL 33614-2630
(813)932-2222

VA MEDICAL CENTER - JAMES A HALEY
13000 Bruce B Downs Boulevard
Tampa, FL 33612-4745
(813)972-2000

TARPON SPRINGS

HELEN ELLIS MEMORIAL HOSPITAL
1395 S Pinellas Avenue
Tarpon Springs, FL 34689-3790
(727)942-5000

TAVERNIER

MARINERS HOSPITAL
50 High Point Road
Tavernier, FL 33070-2006
(305)852-4418

TEQUESTA

SANDYPINES
11301 Se Tequesta Ter
Tequesta, FL 33469-8146
(561)744-0211

THE VILLAGES

THE VILLAGES REGIONAL HOSPITAL
1451 El Camino Real
The Villages, FL 32159-0041
(352)751-8000

TITUSVILLE

PARRISH MEDICAL CENTER
951 North Washington Avenue
Titusville, FL 32796-2163
(321)268-6111

TYNDALL AIR FORCE BASE

325TH MEDICAL GROUP
340 Magnolia Avenue
Tyndall Air Force Base, FL 32403-5612
(850)283-7621

VENICE

BON SECOURS VENICE HOSPITAL
540 The Rialto
Venice, FL 34285-2900
(941)485-7711

VERO BEACH

HEALTHSOUTH TREASURE COAST REHAB
HOSPITAL
1600 37th St
Vero Beach, FL 32960-6590
(772)778-2100

INDIAN RIVER MEMORIAL HOSPITAL
1000 36th St
Vero Beach, FL 32960-6592
(772)567-4311

VIERA

DEVEREUX HOSPITAL AND CHILDREN
CENTER
8000 Devereux Drive
Viera, FL 32940-7907
(321)242-9100

WAUCHULA

FLORIDA HOSPITAL WAUCHULA
533 W Carlton Street
Wauchula, FL 33873-3407
(863)773-3101

WEST PALM BEACH

COLUMBIA HOSPITAL
2201 45th Street
West Palm Beach, FL 33407-2095
(561)842-6141

GOOD SAMARITAN MEDICAL CENTER
1309 North Flagler Drive
West Palm Beach, FL 33401-3499
(561)655-5511

HOSPICE OF PALM BEACH COUNTY
5300 East Avenue
West Palm Beach, FL 33407-2387
(561)848-5200

OAKWOOD CENTER OF PALM BEACH
1041 45th St
West Palm Beach, FL 33407-2415
(561)383-7075

SAINT MARYS MEDICAL CENTER
901 45th St
West Palm Beach, FL 33407-2413
(561)844-6300

VA MEDICAL CENTER - WEST PALM BEACH
7305 N Military Trail
West Palm Beach, FL 33410-6400
(561)882-8262

WELLINGTON REGIONAL MEDICAL CENTER
10101 Forest Hill Boulevard
West Palm Beach, FL 33414-6199
(561)798-8500

WESTON

CLEVELAND CLINIC HOSPITAL
3100 Weston Road
Weston, FL 33331-3602
(954)689-5000

WILLISTON

NATURE COAST REGIONAL HOSPITAL
125 Sw 7th St
Williston, FL 32696-2403
(352)528-2801

WINTER HAVEN

WINTER HAVEN HOSPITAL
200 Avenue F Ne
Winter Haven, FL 33881-4193
(863)293-1121

WINTER PARK

WINTER PARK MEMORIAL HOSPITAL
200 N Lakemont Avenue
Winter Park, FL 32792-3273
(407)646-7000

ZEPHYRHILLS

EAST PASCO MEDICAL CENTER
7050 Gall Boulevard
Zephyrhills, FL 33541-1399
(813)788-0411

GEORGIA

ADEL

MEMORIAL HOSPITAL OF ADEL
706 N Parrish Avenue Box 677
Adel, GA 31620-1511
(229)896-8000

Hospital Telephone Directory — GEORGIA

ALBANY

PALMYRA MEDICAL CENTERS
2000 Palmyra Road Box 1908
Albany, GA 31701-1528
(229)434-2000

PHOEBE PUTNEY MEMORIAL HOSPITAL
417 Third Avenue
Albany, GA 31701-1960
(229)312-1000

ALMA

BACON COUNTY HOSPITAL
302 S Wayne St Box 745
Alma, GA 31510-2922
(912)632-8961

AMERICUS

SUMTER REGIONAL HOSPITAL
100 Wheatley Drive
Americus, GA 31709-3788
(229)924-6011

ARLINGTON

CALHOUN MEMORIAL HOSPITAL
209 Academy Avenue Se
Arlington, GA 31713
(229)725-4272

ATHENS

ATHENS REGIONAL MEDICAL CENTER
1199 Prince Avenue
Athens, GA 30606-2767
(706)475-7000

SAINT MARYS HOSPITAL OF ATHENS
1230 Baxter St
Athens, GA 30606-3791
(706)548-7581

ATLANTA

ANCHOR HOSPITAL
5454 Yorktowne Drive
Atlanta, GA 30349-5317
(770)991-6044

ASHTON WOODS REHAB
3535 Ashton Woods Drive
Atlanta, GA 30319-2201
(770)451-0236

ATLANTA MEDICAL CENTER
303 Parkway Drive Ne
Atlanta, GA 30312-1239
(404)265-4000

CHILDREN'S HEALTHCARE OF ATLANTA AT EGLESTON
1600 Tullie Circle
Atlanta, GA 30329-2303
(404)325-6000

CHILDRENS HEALTHCARE ATLANTA
1405 Clifton Road Ne
Atlanta, GA 30322-1062
(404)325-6000

CRAWFORD LONG HOSPITAL
550 Peachtree St Ne
Atlanta, GA 30308-2225
(404)686-4411

EMORY DUNWOODY MEDICAL CENTER
4575 N Shallowford Road
Atlanta, GA 30338-6445
(770)454-2000

EMORY UNIVERSITY HOSPITAL
1364 Clifton Road Ne
Atlanta, GA 30322-1061
(404)712-2000

GRADY MEMORIAL HOSPITAL
80 Butler St SE
Atlanta, GA 30303-3050
(404)616-4307

HALLMARK YOUTH CARE OF ATLANTA
300 Galleria Pkwy Se Ste 650
Atlanta, GA 30339-5926
(770)474-8888

HILLSIDE HOSPITAL
690 Courtenay Drive Ne
Atlanta, GA 30306-3421
(404)875-4551

HUGHES SPALDING CHILDREN'S HOSPITAL
3500 Jessie Hill Jr Drive Southwest
Atlanta, GA 30335
(404)616-6402

KINDRED HOSPITAL
705 Juniper Street
Atlanta, GA 30308-1307
(404)873-2871

LAUREL HEIGHTS HOSPITAL
934 Briarcliff Road Ne
Atlanta, GA 30306-2655
(404)888-7860

NORTHSIDE HOSPITAL
1000 Johnson Ferry Road Ne
Atlanta, GA 30342-1611
(404)851-8000

PARKWAY MEDICAL CENTER
4575 N Shallowford Rd
Atlanta, GA 30338-6445
(770)944-4141

PEACHFORD BEHAVIORAL HEALTH SYSTEM
2151 Peachford Road Ne
Atlanta, GA 30338-6599
(770)455-3200

PIEDMONT HOSPITAL
1968 Peachtree Road Nw
Atlanta, GA 30309-1285
(404)605-5000

SAINT JOSEPHS HOSPITAL OF ATLANTA
5665 Peachtree Dunwoody Road
Atlanta, GA 30342-1766
(404)851-7001

SCOTTISH RITE CHILDRENS MEDICAL CENTER
1001 Johnson Ferry Road
Atlanta, GA 30342-1600
(404)256-5252

SELECT SPECIALTY HOSPITAL - ATLANTA
615 Peachtree St Ne Ste 950
Atlanta, GA 30308-2332
(404)686-2270

SHEPHERD SPINAL CENTER
2020 Peachtree Road Nw
Atlanta, GA 30309-1465
(404)352-2020

SOUTHWEST HOSPITAL AND MEDICAL CENTER
501 Fairburn Road Sw
Atlanta, GA 30331-2099
(404)699-1111

WESLEY WOODS GERIATRIC HOSPITAL
1821 Clifton Road
Atlanta, GA 30329-4021
(404)728-6200

AUGUSTA

DOCTORS HOSPITAL
3651 Wheeler Road
Augusta, GA 30909-6426
(706)651-3232

EAST CENTRAL REGIONAL HOSPITAL
3405 Old Savannah Road
Augusta, GA 30906-3897
(706)792-7000

MEDICAL COLLEGE OF GEORGIA
1120 15th St
Augusta, GA 30912-0006
(706)721-0211

SAINT JOSEPH HOSPITAL
2260 Wrightsboro Road
Augusta, GA 30904-4726
(706)481-7000

SELECT SPECIALTY HOSPITAL - AUGUSTA
3651 Wheeler Road, 4th Floor
Augusta, GA 30909-6521
(706)651-3501

UNIVERSITY HOSPITAL
1350 Walton Way
Augusta, GA 30901-2629
(706)722-9011

VA MEDICAL CENTER - AUGUSTA
1 Freedom Way
Augusta, GA 30904-6258
(706)733-0188

WALTON REHABILITATION HOSPITAL
PO Box 2223
Augusta, GA 30903-2223
(706)724-7746

AUSTELL

WELLSTAR COBB HOSPITAL
3950 Austell Road
Austell, GA 30106-1121
(770)732-4000

BAINBRIDGE

MEMORIAL HOSPITAL
1500 E Shotwell St
Bainbridge, GA 39819-4294
(229)246-3500

BAXLEY

APPLING HEALTH CARE SYSTEMS
PO Box 2070
Baxley, GA 31515-2070
(912)367-9841

BLAIRSVILLE

UNION GENERAL HOSPITAL
214 Hospital Circle
Blairsville, GA 30512-3102
(706)745-2111

BLAKELY

EARLY MEMORIAL HOSPITAL
638 Columbia Road
Blakely, GA 39823-9604
(229)723-4241

BLUE RIDGE

FANNIN REGIONAL HOSPITAL
2855 Old Highway 5
Blue Ridge, GA 30513-6248
(706)632-3711

BREMEN

HIGGINS GENERAL HOSPITAL
200 Allen Memorial Drive
Bremen, GA 30110-2012
(770)537-5851

GEORGIA

Hospital Telephone Directory

BRUNSWICK

SOUTHEAST GEORGIA REGIONAL MEDICAL
CENTER
2415 Parkwood Drive Box 1518
Brunswick, GA 31520-4766
(912)466-7000

CAIRO

GRADY GENERAL HOSPITAL
1155 5th St Se
Cairo, GA 39828-3162
(229)377-1150

CALHOUN

GORDON HOSPITAL
PO Box 12938
Calhoun, GA 30703-7013
(706)629-2895

CAMILLA

MITCHELL COUNTY HOSPITAL
90 East Stephens Street
Camilla, GA 31730-1899
(229)336-5284

CANTON

NORTHSIDE HOSPITAL CHEROKEE
201 Hospital Road
Canton, GA 30114-2408
(770)720-5100

CARROLLTON

TANNER MEMORIAL CENTER
705 Dixie St
Carrollton, GA 30117-3818
(770)836-9666

CARTERSVILLE

EMORY CARTERSVILLE MEDICAL CENTER
960 Joe Frank Harris Pkwy PO Box 200008
Cartersville, GA 30120-9000
(770)382-1530

CEDARTOWN

POLK MEDICAL CENTER
424 N Main St
Cedartown, GA 30125-2644
(770)748-2500

CHATSWORTH

MURRAY MEDICAL CENTER
707 Old Dalton Ellijay Road PO Box 1406
Chatsworth, GA 30705-1406
(706)695-4564

CLAXTON

EVANS MEMORIAL HOSPITAL
200 N River St Box 518
Claxton, GA 30417-1659
(912)739-5000

CLAYTON

RABUN COUNTY MEMORIAL HOSPITAL
196 Ridgecrest Circle
Clayton, GA 30525-4111
(706)782-4233

COCHRAN

BLECKLEY MEMORIAL HOSPITAL
408 Peacock St
Cochran, GA 31014-1542
(478)934-6211

COLQUITT

MILLER COUNTY HOSPITAL
209 N Cuthbert St
Colquitt, GA 39837-3518
(229)758-3385

COLUMBUS

BRADLEY CENTER OF SAINT FRANCIS
2000 16th Avenue
Columbus, GA 31901-1665
(706)320-3700

COLUMBUS SPECIALTY HOSPITAL
710 Center Street, Ninth Floor
Columbus, GA 31901-1527
(706)321-6617

DOCTORS HOSPITAL
616 W 19 St
Columbus, GA 31901-1506
(706)494-4262

HUGHSTON SPORTS MEDICINE HOSPITAL
100 Frist Court PO Box 7188
Columbus, GA 31908-7188
(706)576-2100

MEDICAL CENTER
710 Center St Box 951
Columbus, GA 31901-1547
(706)571-1000

PHENIX REGIONAL HOSPITAL
PO Box 790
Columbus, GA 31902-0790
(706)291-8000

SAINT FRANCIS HOSPITAL
2122 Manchester Expressway Box 7000
Columbus, GA 31904-6804
(706)596-4000

WEST CENTRAL GEORGIA REGIONAL
HOSPITAL
3000 Schatulga Road Box 12435
Columbus, GA 31907-3117
(706)568-5000

COMMERCE

BANKS-JACKSON-COMMERCE HOSPITAL
70 Medical Center Drive
Commerce, GA 30529-1078
(706)335-1000

CONYERS

ROCKDALE HOSPITAL
1412 Milstead Avenue Ne
Conyers, GA 30012-3899
(770)918-3000

CORDELE

CRISP REGIONAL HOSPITAL
902 7th Street North
Cordele, GA 31015-3270
(229)276-3100

COVINGTON

NEWTON GENERAL HOSPITAL
5126 Hospital Drive Ne
Covington, GA 30014-2567
(770)786-7053

CUMMING

NORTHSIDE HOSPITAL FORSYTHE
1200 Baptist Medical Center Dr
Cumming, GA 30041
(770)844-3200

CUTHBERT

SOUTHWEST GEORGIA REGIONAL
MEDICAL CENTER
109 Randolph St
Cuthbert, GA 39840-1338
(229)732-2181

DAHLONEGA

CHESTATEE REGIONAL HOSPITAL
227 Mountain Dr
Dahlonega, GA 30533-1606
(706)864-6136

DALLAS

WELLSTAR PAULDING HOSPITAL
600 W Memorial Drive
Dallas, GA 30132-4117
(770)445-4411

DALTON

HAMILTON MEDICAL CENTER
1200 Memorial Drive
Dalton, GA 30720-2529
(706)272-6000

DECATUR

DECATUR HOSPITAL
450 North Candler Street
Decatur, GA 30030-2671
(404)501-6700

DEKALB MEDICAL CENTER
2701 N Decatur Road
Decatur, GA 30033-5918
(404)501-1000

GEORGIA REGIONAL HOSPITAL ATLANTA
3073 Panthersville Road
Decatur, GA 30034-3800
(404)243-2100

VA MEDICAL CENTER - ATLANTA
1670 Clairmont Road
Decatur, GA 30033-4098
(404)321-6111

DEMOREST

HABERSHAM COUNTY MEDICAL CENTER
Highway 441 Box 37
Demorest, GA 30535-0037
(706)754-2161

DONALSONVILLE

DONALSONVILLE HOSPITAL
102 Hospital Circle Box 677
Donalsonville, GA 39845-1199
(229)524-5217

DOUGLAS

COFFEE REGIONAL MEDICAL CENTER
1101 Ocilla Road PO Box 1248
Douglas, GA 31534-1248
(912)384-1900

DOUGLASVILLE

INNER HARBOUR HOSPITALS
4685 Dorsett Shoals Road
Douglasville, GA 30135-4999
(770)942-2391

WELLSTAR DOUGLAS HOSPITAL
8954 Hospital Drive
Douglasville, GA 30134-2272
(770)949-1500

Hospital Telephone Directory — GEORGIA

DUBLIN

FAIRVIEW PARK HOSPITAL
PO Box 1408
Dublin, GA 31040-1408
(478)275-2000

VA MEDICAL CENTER - CARL VINSON
1826 Veterans Boulevard
Dublin, GA 31021-3699
(478)272-1210

DULUTH

JOAN GLANCY MEMORIAL HOSPITAL
Mc Clure Bridge Road
Duluth, GA 30136
(770)497-4800

EAST POINT

SOUTH FULTON MEDICAL CENTER
1170 Cleveland Avenue
East Point, GA 30344-3665
(404)305-3500

EASTMAN

DODGE COUNTY HOSPITAL
715 Griffin St Box 706
Eastman, GA 31023-6716
(478)374-4000

EATONTON

PUTNAM GENERAL HOSPITAL
101 Greensboro Highway Box 32
Eatonton, GA 31024-6054
(706)485-2711

ELBERTON

ELBERT MEMORIAL HOSPITAL
4 Medical Drive
Elberton, GA 30635-1897
(706)283-3151

ELLIJAY

NORTH GEORGIA MEDICAL CENTER
1362 South Main Box 2239
Ellijay, GA 30540-5410
(706)276-4741

FAYETTEVILLE

FAYETTE COMMUNITY HOSPITAL
1255 Highway 54 West
Fayetteville, GA 30214-4526
(770)719-7000

FITZGERALD

DORMINY MEDICAL CENTER
182 Perry House Road Box 989
Fitzgerald, GA 31750-8838
(229)424-7100

FOLKSTON

CHARLTON MEMORIAL HOSPITAL
1203 N 3rd St
Folkston, GA 31537-1303
(912)496-2531

FORSYTH

MONROE COUNTY HOSPITAL
88 Martin Luther King Drive Box 1068
Forsyth, GA 31029-1682
(478)994-2521

FORT BENNING

MARTIN ARMY COMMUNITY HOSPITAL
9200 Marne Road
Fort Benning, GA 31905-5515
(706)544-2516

FORT GORDON

DWIGHT DAVID EISENHOWER ARMY MEDICAL CENTER
Building 300
Fort Gordon, GA 30905
(706)787-5811

FORT OGLETHORPE

HUTCHESON MEDICAL CENTER
100 Gross Crescent
Fort Oglethorpe, GA 30742-3669
(706)858-2000

FORT STEWART

WINN ARMY COMMUNITY HOSPITAL
1061 Harmon Avenue
Fort Stewart, GA 31314-5604
(912)370-6965

FORT VALLEY

PEACH REGIONAL MEDICAL CENTER
601 N Camellia Boulevard
Fort Valley, GA 31030-4599
(478)825-8691

GAINESVILLE

LANIER PARK HOSPITAL
675 White Sulphur Road
Gainesville, GA 30501-8921
(770)503-3000

NORTHEAST GEORGIA MEDICAL CENTER
743 Spring St
Gainesville, GA 30501-3741
(770)535-3553

GLENWOOD

WHEELER COUNTY HOSPITAL
111 North 3rd Street Box 398
Glenwood, GA 30428-2301
(912)523-5113

GRACEWOOD

GRACEWOOD STATE SCHOOL AND HOSPITAL
100 Myrtle Blvd
Gracewood, GA 30812
(706)790-2011

GREENSBORO

MINNIE G BOSWELL MEMORIAL HOSPITAL
1201 Siloam Rd
Greensboro, GA 30642-2811
(706)453-7331

GRIFFIN

SPALDING REGIONAL HOSPITAL
601 South 8th St Box 136
Griffin, GA 30224-4213
(770)228-2721

HARTWELL

HART COUNTY HOSPITAL
138 W Gibson St PO Box 280
Hartwell, GA 30643-0280
(706)856-6100

HAWKINSVILLE

TAYLOR REGIONAL HOSPITAL
Macon Road
Hawkinsville, GA 31036
(478)783-0200

HAZLEHURST

JEFF DAVIS HOSPITAL
PO Box 1200
Hazlehurst, GA 31539-1200
(912)375-7781

HIAWASSEE

CHATUGE REGIONAL HOSPITAL
110 East Main St
Hiawassee, GA 30546
(706)896-2222

HINESVILLE

LIBERTY REGIONAL MEDICAL CENTER
462 EG Miles Pkwy
Hinesville, GA 31313-4000
(912)369-9400

HOMERVILLE

CLINCH MEMORIAL HOSPITAL
PO Box 516
Homerville, GA 31634-0516
(912)487-5211

JACKSON

SYLVAN GROVE HOSPITAL
1050 Mcdonough Road
Jackson, GA 30233-1599
(770)775-7861

JASPER

MOUNTAINSIDE MEDICAL CENTER HOSPITAL
1266 Church St
Jasper, GA 30143
(706)692-2441

JESUP

WAYNE MEMORIAL HOSPITAL
865 S 1st St
Jesup, GA 31545-0210
(912)427-6811

KENNESAW

DEVEREUX GEORGIA TREATMENT NETWORK
1291 Stanley Road Nw
Kennesaw, GA 30152-4359
(770)422-2135

LA GRANGE

WEST GEORGIA MEDICAL CENTER
1514 Vernon Road Box 1567
La Grange, GA 30240-4198
(706)882-1411

LAKELAND

LOUIS SMITH MEMORIAL HOSPITAL
852 W Thigpen Avenue Box 306
Lakeland, GA 31635-1099
(229)482-3110

LAWRENCEVILLE

GWINNETT MEDICAL CENTER
1000 Medical Center Boulevard
Lawrenceville, GA 30045-7694
(678)442-4321

GEORGIA — Hospital Telephone Directory

LOUISVILLE

JEFFERSON HOSPITAL
PO Box 528
Louisville, GA 30434-0528
(478)625-7000

MACON

COLISEUM MEDICAL CENTERS
350 Hospital Drive
Macon, GA 31217-3871
(478)765-7000

COLISEUM PSYCHIATRIC HOSPITAL
340 Hospital Drive Box 9366
Macon, GA 31217-8002
(478)741-1355

HEALTHSOUTH CENTRAL GEORGIA
REHABILITATION HOSPITAL
3351 Northside Drive
Macon, GA 31210-2587
(478)471-3500

MACON NORTHSIDE HOSPITAL
400 Charter Box 4627
Macon, GA 31210-4853
(478)757-8200

MEDICAL CENTER OF CENTRAL GEORGIA
777 Hemlock St Box 6000
Macon, GA 31201-2155
(478)633-1000

MADISON

MORGAN MEMORIAL HOSPITAL
1077 S Main St
Madison, GA 30650-2073
(706)342-1667

MARIETTA

WELLSTAR KENNESTONE HOSPITAL
677 Church St
Marietta, GA 30060-1148
(770)793-5000

WELLSTAR WINDY HILL HOSPITAL
2540 Windy Hill Road
Marietta, GA 30067-8632
(770)644-1000

MC RAE

TAYLOR TELFAIR REGIONAL HOSPITAL
Route 1 Highway 341 South PO Box 150
Mc Rae, GA 31055-9745
(229)868-5621

METTER

CANDLER COUNTY HOSPITAL
Cedar Road Box 597
Metter, GA 30439-0597
(912)685-5741

MILLEDGEVILLE

CENTRAL STATE HOSPITAL
620 Broad Street
Milledgeville, GA 31062-7525
(478)445-4128

MEDICAL SURGICAL HOSPITAL
Vinson Highway
Milledgeville, GA 31062-0001
(478)445-5562

OCONEE REGIONAL MEDICAL CENTER
821 North Cobb St
Milledgeville, GA 31061
(478)454-3500

MILLEN

JENKINS COUNTY HOSPITAL
931 E Winthrope Ave
Millen, GA 30442-1839
(478)982-4221

MONROE

WALTON MEDICAL CENTER
330 Alcova St
Monroe, GA 30655-2140
(770)267-8461

MONTEZUMA

FLINT RIVER COMMUNITY HOSPITAL
509 Sumter St Box 574
Montezuma, GA 31063-1756
(478)472-3100

MONTICELLO

JASPER MEMORIAL HOSPITAL
898 College St
Monticello, GA 31064-1261
(706)468-6411

MOODY AIR FORCE BASE

347TH MEDICAL GROUP
3278 Mitchell Boulevard
Moody Air Force Base, GA 31699-1500
(229)257-3232

MOULTRIE

COLQUITT REGIONAL MEDICAL CENTER
PO Box 3548
Moultrie, GA 31776-3548
(229)985-3420

TURNING POINT HOSPITAL
PO Box 24
Moultrie, GA 31776-0024
(229)985-4815

NASHVILLE

BERRIEN COUNTY HOSPITAL
PO Box 665
Nashville, GA 31639-0665
(229)543-7100

NEWNAN

NEWNAN HOSPITAL
60 Hospital Road
Newnan, GA 30263-1210
(770)253-1912

OCILLA

IRWIN COUNTY HOSPITAL
710 N Irwin Avenue
Ocilla, GA 31774-5098
(229)468-3800

PERRY

PERRY GENERAL HOSPITAL
1120 Morningside Drive
Perry, GA 31069-2953
(478)987-3600

QUITMAN

BROOKS COUNTY HOSPITAL
903 N Court St Box 865
Quitman, GA 31643-1315
(229)263-4171

RICHLAND

STEWART WEBSTER HOSPITAL
300 Alston St
Richland, GA 31825-1406
(229)887-3366

RIVERDALE

SOUTHERN REGIONAL MEDICAL CENTER
11 Upper Riverdale Road Sw
Riverdale, GA 30274-2600
(770)991-8000

ROBINS AIR FORCE BASE

78TH MEDICAL GROUP
655 Seventh St
Robins Air Force Base, GA 31098-2227
(478)327-7995

ROME

FLOYD MEDICAL CENTER
304 Turner McCall Boulevard
Rome, GA 30165-5621
(706)802-2000

NORTHWEST GEORGIA REGIONAL
HOSPITAL
1305 Redmond Circle
Rome, GA 30165-1393
(706)295-6011

REDMOND REGIONAL MEDICAL CENTER
501 Redmond Road
Rome, GA 30165-1415
(706)291-0291

SPECIALTY HOSPITAL OF ROME
304 Turner McCall Blvd, 4th Floor
Rome, GA 30165-5621
(706)802-4165

WINDWOOD HOSPITAL
306 Shorter Avenue
Rome, GA 30165-4268
(706)802-2870

ROSWELL

NORTH FULTON REGIONAL HOSPITAL
11585 Alpharetta St
Roswell, GA 30076-3865
(770)751-2500

ROYSTON

COBB MEMORIAL HOSPITAL
577 Franklin Springs St
Royston, GA 30662-3934
(706)245-5071

SAINT MARYS

CAMDEN MEDICAL CENTER
2000 Dan Proctor Dr
Saint Marys, GA 31558-3810
(912)576-6200

SAINT SIMONS ISLAND

FOCUS BY-THE-SEA
2927 Demere Road
Saint Simons Island, GA 31522-1620
(912)638-1999

SANDERSVILLE

WASHINGTON COUNTY REGIONAL
MEDICAL CENTER
610 Sparta Highway
Sandersville, GA 31082-1893
(478)240-2000

SAVANNAH

CANDLER HOSPITAL
5353 Reynolds St
Savannah, GA 31405-6015
(912)692-6000

COASTAL HARBOR TREATMENT CENTER
1150 Cornell Avenue
Savannah, GA 31406-2702
(912)354-3911

GEORGIA REGIONAL HOSPITAL SAVANNAH
1915 Eisenhower Drive
Savannah, GA 31406-5098
(912)356-2011

MEMORIAL MEDICAL CENTER
4700 Waters Avenue Box 23089
Savannah, GA 31404-6283
(912)350-8000

SAINT JOSEPHS HOSPITAL
11705 Mercy Boulevard
Savannah, GA 31419-1791
(912)925-4100

SMYRNA

EMORY-ADVENTIST HOSPITAL
3949 South Cobb Drive
Smyrna, GA 30080-6342
(770)434-0710

RIDGEVIEW INSTITUTE
3995 S Cobb Drive
Smyrna, GA 30080-6397
(770)434-4567

SNELLVILLE

EMORY EASTSIDE MEDICAL CENTER
1700 Medical Way
Snellville, GA 30078-2195
(770)979-0200

SPRINGFIELD

EFFINGHAM COUNTY HOSPITAL
Highway 119 Box 386
Springfield, GA 31329-3083
(912)754-6451

STATESBORO

EAST GEORGIA REGIONAL HOSPITAL
1499 Fair Road
Statesboro, GA 30458-0803
(912)486-1000

WILLINGWAY HOSPITAL
311 Jones Mill Road
Statesboro, GA 30458-4765
(912)764-6236

STOCKBRIDGE

HENRY GENERAL HOSPITAL
1133 Eagles Landing Pkwy
Stockbridge, GA 30281-5099
(770)389-2200

SWAINSBORO

EMANUEL COUNTY HOSPITAL
117 Kite Road Box 7
Swainsboro, GA 30401-3231
(478)237-9911

SYLVANIA

SCREVEN COUNTY HOSPITAL
215 Mims Road
Sylvania, GA 30467-2097
(912)564-7426

SYLVESTER

PHOEBE WORTH MEDICAL CENTER
PO Box 545
Sylvester, GA 31791-0545
(229)776-6961

THOMASTON

UPSON REGIONAL MEDICAL CENTER
PO Box 1059
Thomaston, GA 30286-0027
(706)647-8111

THOMASVILLE

JOHN D ARCHBOLD MEMORIAL HOSPITAL
915 Gordon Avenue And Mimosa Drive
Thomasville, GA 31792-6699
(229)228-2000

SOUTHWESTERN STATE HOSPITAL
400 S Pinetree Boulevard Box 1378
Thomasville, GA 31792-7128
(229)227-2700

THOMSON

MCDUFFIE REGIONAL MEDICAL CENTER
521 Hill St Sw
Thomson, GA 30824-2199
(706)595-1411

TIFTON

TIFT REGIONAL HOSPITAL
901 E 18th St
Tifton, GA 31794-3699
(229)382-7120

TOCCOA

STEPHENS COUNTY HOSPITAL
Falls Road Box 947
Toccoa, GA 30577-1416
(706)282-4200

TUCKER

EMORY NORTHLAKE REGIONAL MEDICAL CENTER
1455 Montreal Road
Tucker, GA 30084-8229
(770)270-3000

VALDOSTA

GREENLEAF CENTER
2209 Pineview Drive
Valdosta, GA 31602-7316
(229)247-4357

SMITH NORTHVIEW HOSPITAL
4280 North Valdosta Rd
Valdosta, GA 31602
(229)671-2000

SOUTH GEORGIA MEDICAL CENTER
Pendleton Park Box 1727
Valdosta, GA 31603-1727
(229)333-1000

VIDALIA

MEADOWS REGIONAL MEDICAL CENTER
1703 Meadows Land Box 1048
Vidalia, GA 30474-8915
(912)537-8921

VILLA RICA

TANNER MEDICAL CENTER VILLA RICA
601 Dallas Highway
Villa Rica, GA 30180-1202
(770)456-3100

WARM SPRINGS

GEORGIA BAPTIST MERIWETHER HOSPITAL
5995 Spring St
Warm Springs, GA 31830-2149
(706)655-3331

ROOSEVELT WARM SPRINGS INSTITUTE FOR REHAB
PO Box 1000
Warm Springs, GA 31830-1000
(706)655-5000

WARNER ROBINS

HOUSTON MEDICAL CENTER
1601 Watson Boulevard
Warner Robins, GA 31093-3452
(478)922-4281

WASHINGTON

WILLS MEMORIAL HOSPITAL
120 Gordon St Box 370
Washington, GA 30673-1602
(706)678-2151

WAYCROSS

SATILLA REGIONAL MEDICAL CENTER
410 Darlington Avenue
Waycross, GA 31501-5200
(912)283-3030

WAYNESBORO

BURKE COUNTY HOSPITAL
351 Liberty St
Waynesboro, GA 30830-9686
(706)554-4435

WILDWOOD

WILDWOOD LIFESTYLE CENTER AND HOSPITAL
PO Box 129
Wildwood, GA 30757-0129
(706)820-1493

WINDER

BARROW MEDICAL CENTER
316 North Broad Street
Winder, GA 30680-2187
(770)867-3400

HAWAII

AIEA

KAPIOLANI MEDICAL CENTER AT PALI MOMI
98-1079 Moanalua Road
Aiea, HI 96701-4713
(808)486-6000

EWA BEACH

KAHI MOHALA
91-2301 Fort Weaver Road
Ewa Beach, HI 96706-3699
(808)671-8511

SAINT FRANCIS MEDICAL CENTER-WEST
91-2141 Fort Weaver Road
Ewa Beach, HI 96706-3606
(808)678-7000

HANA

HANA MEDICAL CENTER
4590 Hana Highway Box 807
Hana, HI 96713-0807
(808)248-8294

IDAHO　　　　　　　　　　　　　Hospital Telephone Directory

HILO

HILO MEDICAL CENTER
1190 Waianuenue Avenue
Hilo, HI 96720-2094
(808)974-4743

HONOKAA

HALE HOOLA HAMAKUA
45-547 Plumeria Street
Honokaa, HI 96727-6902
(808)775-7211

HONOLULU

HALE MOHALU HOSPITAL
3650 Maunalei Avenue
Honolulu, HI 96816-2396
(808)733-8080

KAISER PERMANENTE FOUNDATION HOSPITAL
3288 Moanalua Road
Honolulu, HI 96819-1495
(808)432-0000

KAPIOLANI WOMENS AND CHILDRENS MEDICAL CENTER
1319 Punahou Street
Honolulu, HI 96826-1080
(808)983-6000

KUAKINI MEDICAL CENTER
347 N Kuakini Street
Honolulu, HI 96817-2381
(808)536-2236

LEAHI HOSPITAL
3675 Kilauea Avenue
Honolulu, HI 96816-2398
(808)733-8000

QUEENS MEDICAL CENTER
1301 Punchbowl St
Honolulu, HI 96813-2499
(808)538-9011

REHABILITATION HOSPITAL OF THE PACIFIC
226 N Kuakini Street
Honolulu, HI 96817-2498
(808)531-3511

SAINT FRANCIS MEDICAL CENTER
2230 Liliha Street
Honolulu, HI 96817-1699
(808)547-6484

SHRINERS HOSPITAL FOR CHILDREN
1310 Punahou St
Honolulu, HI 96826-1099
(808)941-4466

STRAUB HOSPITAL
888 South King Street
Honolulu, HI 96813-3083
(808)522-4000

TRIPLER ARMY MEDICAL CENTER
1 Jarrett White Road
Honolulu, HI 96859-5000
(808)433-6661

VA MEDICAL CENTER - SPARK MATSUNAGA
459 Patterson Road
Honolulu, HI 96819-1522
(808)433-0600

KAHUKU

KAHUKU HOSPITAL
56-117 Pualalea Street
Kahuku, HI 96731-2052
(808)293-9221

KAILUA

CASTLE MEDICAL CENTER
640 Ulukahiki St
Kailua, HI 96734-4498
(808)263-5500

KAMUELA

NORTH HAWAII COMMUNITY HOSPITAL
67-1125 Mamalahoa Highway
Kamuela, HI 96743-8496
(808)885-4400

KANEOHE

HAWAII STATE HOSPITAL
45-710 Keaahala Road
Kaneohe, HI 96744-3597
(808)236-8237

KAPAA

SAMUEL MAHELONA MEMORIAL HOSPITAL
4800 Kawaihau Road
Kapaa, HI 96746-1964
(808)822-4961

KAPAAU

KOHALA HOSPITAL
PO Box 10
Kapaau, HI 96755-0010
(808)889-6211

KAUNAKAKAI

MOLOKAI GENERAL HOSPITAL
PO Box 408
Kaunakakai, HI 96748-0408
(808)553-5331

KEALAKEKUA

KONA COMMUNITY HOSPITAL
79-1019 Haukapila St
Kealakekua, HI 96750-7920
(808)322-4429

KULA

KULA HOSPITAL
204 Kula Highway
Kula, HI 96790-9471
(808)878-1221

LANAI CITY

LANAI COMMUNITY HOSPITAL
PO Box 630650
Lanai City, HI 96763-0650
(808)565-6411

LIHUE

WILCOX MEMORIAL HOSPITAL
3420 Kuhio Highway
Lihue, HI 96766-1099
(808)245-1100

PAHALA

KAU HOSPITAL
PO Box 40
Pahala, HI 96777-0040
(808)928-8331

WAHIAWA

WAHIAWA GENERAL HOSPITAL
128 Lehua Street
Wahiawa, HI 96786-2099
(808)621-8411

WAILUKU

MAUI MEMORIAL HOSPITAL
221 Mahalani Street
Wailuku, HI 96793-2581
(808)244-9056

WAIMEA

KAUAI VETERANS MEMORIAL HOSPITAL
PO Box 337
Waimea, HI 96796-0337
(808)338-9431

IDAHO

AMERICAN FALLS

HARMS MEMORIAL HOSPITAL
510 Roosevelt PO Box 420
American Falls, ID 83211-0420
(208)226-3200

ARCO

LOST RIVERS DISTRICT HOSPITAL
551 Highland Drive PO Box 145
Arco, ID 83213-0145
(208)527-8206

BLACKFOOT

BINGHAM MEMORIAL HOSPITAL
98 Poplar St Box 751
Blackfoot, ID 83221-1799
(208)785-4100

IDAHO STATE HOSPITAL SOUTH
700 East Alice (Box 400)
Blackfoot, ID 83221-0400
(208)785-1200

BOISE

HEALTHSOUTH TREASURE VALLEY HOSPITAL
8800 West Emerald Street
Boise, ID 83704-8205
(208)373-5000

IDAHO ELKS REHABILITATION HOSPITAL
204 Fort Place (Box 1100)
Boise, ID 83702-4527
(208)489-4444

INTERMOUNTAIN HOSPITAL
303 N Allumbaugh St
Boise, ID 83704-9208
(208)377-8400

SAINT ALPHONSUS REGIONAL MEDICAL CENTER
1055 North Curtis Road
Boise, ID 83706-1370
(208)367-2121

SAINT LUKES REGIONAL MEDICAL CENTER
190 East Bannock
Boise, ID 83712-6241
(208)381-2222

SUNHEALTH BEHAVIORAL HEALTH SYSTEM
8050 Northview Street
Boise, ID 83704-7126
(208)327-0504

VA MEDICAL CENTER - BOISE
500 W Fort St
Boise, ID 83702-4599
(208)422-1100

BONNERS FERRY

BOUNDARY COUNTY COMMUNITY HOSPITAL
6640 Kaniksu St
Bonners Ferry, ID 83805-7532
(208)267-3141

Hospital Telephone Directory — IDAHO

BURLEY
CASSIA REGIONAL MEDICAL CENTER
1501 Hiland Avenue
Burley, ID 83318-2682
(208)678-4444

CALDWELL
WEST VALLEY MEDICAL CENTER
1717 Arlington
Caldwell, ID 83605-4800
(208)459-4641

CASCADE
CASCADE MEDICAL CENTER
PO Box 1330
Cascade, ID 83611-1330
(208)382-4242

COEUR D'ALENE
KOOTENAI MEDICAL CENTER
2003 Lincoln Way
Coeur D'alene, ID 83814-2677
(208)666-2000

NORTH IDAHO BEHAVIORAL HEALTH INSTITUTE
2301 North Ironwood Place
Coeur D'alene, ID 83814-2696
(208)765-4800

COTTONWOOD
SAINT MARYS HOSPITAL
701 Lewiston Street PO Box 137
Cottonwood, ID 83522-0137
(208)962-3251

COUNCIL
COUNCIL COMMUNITY HOSPITAL
205 N Berkley Box 428
Council, ID 83612-0428
(208)253-4242

DRIGGS
TETON VALLEY HOSPITAL
120 East Howard
Driggs, ID 83422-5112
(208)354-2383

EMMETT
WALTER KNOX MEMORIAL HOSPITAL
1202 East Locust
Emmett, ID 83617-2715
(208)365-3561

GOODING
GOODING COUNTY MEMORIAL HOSPITAL
PO Box 418
Gooding, ID 83330-0418
(208)934-4433

GRANGEVILLE
SYRINGA GENERAL HOSPITAL
607 West Main
Grangeville, ID 83530-1396
(208)983-1700

IDAHO FALLS
EASTERN IDAHO REGIONAL MEDICAL CENTER
3100 Channing Way, Box 2077
Idaho Falls, ID 83404-7533
(208)529-6111

IDAHO FALLS RECOVERY CENTER
1957 17th Street
Idaho Falls, ID 83404-6429
(208)529-5285

JEROME
SAINT BENEDICTS FAMILY MEDICAL CENTER
709 North Lincoln
Jerome, ID 83338-1851
(208)324-4301

KELLOGG
SHOSHONE MEDICAL CENTER
Jacobs Gulch
Kellogg, ID 83837
(208)784-1221

KETCHUM
SAINT LUKE'S MEDICAL CENTER - WOOD RIVER
100 Hospital Drive, PO Box 100
Ketchum, ID 83340-0100
(208)727-8800

LEWISTON
SAINT JOSEPH REGIONAL MEDICAL CENTER
415 Sixth St
Lewiston, ID 83501-2434
(208)743-2511

MALAD
ONEIDA COUNTY HOSPITAL
PO Box 126 150 North 200 West
Malad, ID 83252-0126
(208)766-2231

MC CALL
MCCALL MEMORIAL HOSPITAL
Box 906 1000 State Street
Mc Call, ID 83638-3704
(208)634-2221

MONTPELIER
BEAR LAKE MEMORIAL HOSPITAL
164 South Fifth
Montpelier, ID 83254-1597
(208)847-1630

MOSCOW
GRITMAN MEMORIAL HOSPITAL
700 South Main
Moscow, ID 83843-3046
(208)882-4511

MOUNTAIN HOME
ELMORE MEMORIAL HOSPITAL
895 N Sixth E PO Box 1270
Mountain Home, ID 83647-1270
(208)587-8401

MOUNTAIN HOME AIR FORCE BASE
366TH MEDICAL GROUP
90 Hope Drive
Mountain Home Air Force Base, ID 83648-1062
(208)828-7600

NAMPA
MERCY MEDICAL CENTER
1512 Twelfth Avenue Road
Nampa, ID 83686-6008
(208)467-1171

OROFINO
CLEARWATER VALLEY HOSPITAL
301 Cedar
Orofino, ID 83544-9029
(208)476-4555

STATE HOSPITAL NORTH IDAHO
300 Hospital Drive
Orofino, ID 83544-9034
(208)476-4511

POCATELLO
PORTNEUF MEDICAL CENTER - EAST
777 Hospital Way
Pocatello, ID 83201-4004
(208)239-1000

PORTNEUF MEDICAL CENTER - WEST
651 Memorial Drive
Pocatello, ID 83201-4004
(208)239-1000

POST FALLS
NORTHWEST SPECIALTY HOSPITAL
1593 East Polston Avenue
Post Falls, ID 83854-5326
(208)457-9205

PRESTON
FRANKLIN COUNTY MEDICAL CENTER
44 North First East
Preston, ID 83263-1399
(208)852-0137

REXBURG
MADISON MEMORIAL HOSPITAL
450 East Main PO Box 310
Rexburg, ID 83440-0310
(208)356-3691

RUPERT
MINIDOKA MEMORIAL HOSPITAL
1224 Eighth St
Rupert, ID 83350-1599
(208)436-0481

SAINT MARIES
BENEWAH COMMUNITY HOSPITAL
229 Seventh St
Saint Maries, ID 83861-1894
(208)245-5551

SALMON
STEELE MEMORIAL HOSPITAL
810 Main (Box 700)
Salmon, ID 83467-4315
(208)756-4291

SANDPOINT
BONNER GENERAL HOSPITAL
520 North Third Street Box 1448
Sandpoint, ID 83864-1507
(208)263-1441

SODA SPRINGS
CARIBOU MEMORIAL HOSPITAL
300 South Third West
Soda Springs, ID 83276-1598
(208)547-3341

TWIN FALLS
CANYON VIEW HOSPITAL
228 Shoup Avenue W
Twin Falls, ID 83301-5078
(208)734-6760

ILLINOIS   Hospital Telephone Directory

MAGIC VALLEY REGIONAL MEDICAL
CENTER
650 Addison Avenue W Box 409
Twin Falls, ID 83301-5444
(208)737-2000

TWIN FALLS CLINIC HOSPITAL
666 Shoshone Street East
Twin Falls, ID 83301-6110
(208)733-3700

WEISER

WEISER MEMORIAL HOSPITAL
PO Box 550
Weiser, ID 83672-0550
(208)549-0370

ILLINOIS

ALEDO

MERCER COUNTY HOSPITAL
409 Nw Ninth Avenue
Aledo, IL 61231-1296
(309)582-5301

ALTON

ALTON MEMORIAL HOSPITAL
One Memorial Drive
Alton, IL 62002-6755
(618)463-7311

ALTON MENTAL HEALTH CENTER
4500 College Avenue
Alton, IL 62002-5099
(618)474-3800

SAINT ANTHONY HEALTH CENTER
St Anthonys Way
Alton, IL 62002
(618)465-2571

SAINT CLARES HOSPITAL
PO Box 340
Alton, IL 62002-0340
(618)463-5151

ANNA

CHOATE MENTAL HEALTH & DEVELOPMENT
CENTER
1000 N Main St
Anna, IL 62906-1699
(618)833-5161

UNION COUNTY HOSPITAL
517 N Main Street
Anna, IL 62906-1663
(618)833-4511

ARLINGTON HEIGHTS

NORTHWEST COMMUNITY HOSPITAL
800 W Central Road
Arlington Heights, IL 60005-2392
(847)618-1000

AURORA

PROVENA MERCY CENTER
1325 N Highland Avenue
Aurora, IL 60506-1458
(630)859-2222

RUSH-COPLEY MEMORIAL HOSPITAL
2000 Ogden Avenue
Aurora, IL 60504-7222
(630)978-6200

BARRINGTON

GOOD SHEPHERD HOSPITAL
450 West Highway 22
Barrington, IL 60010-7509
(847)381-9600

BELLEVILLE

MEMORIAL HOSPITAL
4500 Memorial Drive
Belleville, IL 62226-5399
(618)233-7750

SAINT ELIZABETH HOSPITAL
211 South 3rd Street
Belleville, IL 62220-1998
(618)234-2120

BELVIDERE

NORTHWEST SUBURBAN COMMUNITY
HOSPITAL
1625 South State Street
Belvidere, IL 61008-5907
(815)547-5441

BENTON

FRANKLIN HOSPITAL
201 Bailey Lane
Benton, IL 62812-1999
(618)439-3161

BERWYN

MAC NEAL MEMORIAL HOSPITAL
3249 South Oak Park Avenue
Berwyn, IL 60402-0715
(708)783-9100

BLOOMINGTON

SAINT JOSEPH MEDICAL CENTER
2200 E Washington
Bloomington, IL 61701-4364
(309)662-3311

BLUE ISLAND

SAINT FRANCIS HOSPITAL AND HEALTH
CENTER
12935 S Gregory
Blue Island, IL 60406-2470
(708)597-2000

BREESE

SAINT JOSEPHS HOSPITAL
Jamestown Road
Breese, IL 62230
(618)526-4511

CANTON

GRAHAM HOSPITAL ASSOCIATION
210 West Walnut Street
Canton, IL 61520-2497
(309)647-5240

CARBONDALE

MEMORIAL HOSPITAL
404 W Main
Carbondale, IL 62901-2904
(618)549-0721

CARLINVILLE

CARLINVILLE AREA HOSPITAL
1001 E Morgan St
Carlinville, IL 62626-1499
(217)854-3141

CARMI

WHITE COUNTY MEDICAL CENTER
400 Plum Street
Carmi, IL 62821-1751
(618)382-4171

CARROLLTON

THOMAS H BOYD MEMORIAL HOSPITAL
800 School Street
Carrollton, IL 62016-1498
(217)942-6946

CARTHAGE

MEMORIAL HOSPITAL
402 South Adams Street
Carthage, IL 62321-1600
(217)357-3131

CENTRALIA

SAINT MARYS HOSPITAL
400 North Pleasant
Centralia, IL 62801-3098
(618)532-6731

CENTREVILLE

TOUCHETTE REGIONAL HOSPITAL
5900 Bond Avenue
Centreville, IL 62207-2397
(618)332-3060

CHAMPAIGN

PAVILION FOUNDATION
809 W Church St
Champaign, IL 61820-3320
(217)373-1700

CHESTER

CHESTER MENTAL HEALTH CENTER
PO Box 31
Chester, IL 62233-0031
(618)826-4571

MEMORIAL HOSPITAL
1900 State Street PO Box 609
Chester, IL 62233-0609
(618)826-4581

CHICAGO

BETHANY HOSPITAL
3435 W Van Buren
Chicago, IL 60624-3308
(773)265-7700

CHICAGO LAKESHORE HOSPITAL
4840 N Marine Drive
Chicago, IL 60640-4296
(773)878-9700

CHICAGO-READ MENTAL HEALTH CENTER
4200 N Oak Park Avenue
Chicago, IL 60634-1417
(773)794-4000

CHILDRENS MEMORIAL HOSPITAL
2300 Childrens Plaza
Chicago, IL 60614-3363
(773)880-4000

COLUMBUS HOSPITAL
2875 W 19th St
Chicago, IL 60623-3501
(773)388-7300

COOK COUNTY HOSPITAL
1825 W Harrison St
Chicago, IL 60612-3701
(312)633-6000

GRANT HOSPITAL OF CHICAGO
550 W Webster Avenue
Chicago, IL 60614-3787
(773)883-2000

HARTGROVE HOSPITAL
520 N Ridgeway
Chicago, IL 60624-1299
(773)722-3113

HOLY CROSS HOSPITAL
2701 W 68th Street
Chicago, IL 60629-1882
(773)471-8000

ILLINOIS MASONIC MEDICAL CENTER
836 W Wellington
Chicago, IL 60657-5192
(773)975-1600

JACKSON PARK HOSPITAL FOUNDATION
7531 S Stoney Island Avenue
Chicago, IL 60649-3954
(773)947-7500

JOHNSTON R. BOWMAN HEALTH CENTER
710 South Paulina Street
Chicago, IL 60612-3814
(312)942-7000

KINDRED HOSPITAL CHICAGO - LAKE SHORE
6130 North Sheridan Road
Chicago, IL 60660-2830
(773)381-1222

KINDRED HOSPITAL CHICAGO CENTRAL
4058 W Melrose
Chicago, IL 60641-4794
(773)736-7000

KINDRED HOSPITAL CHICAGO NORTH
2544 W Montrose Avenue
Chicago, IL 60618-1530
(773)267-2622

LARABIDA CHILDRENS HOSPITAL
E 65th St At Lake Michigan
Chicago, IL 60649
(773)363-6700

LORETTO HOSPITAL
645 South Central Avenue
Chicago, IL 60644-5016
(773)626-4300

LOUIS A WEISS MEMORIAL HOSPITAL
4646 N Marine Drive
Chicago, IL 60640-5759
(773)878-8700

MERCY HOSPITAL AND MEDICAL CENTER
2525 South Michigan
Chicago, IL 60616-2332
(312)567-2000

METHODIST HOSPITAL OF CHICAGO
5025 N Paulina Street
Chicago, IL 60640-2772
(773)271-9040

MICHAEL REESE HOSPITAL AND MEDICAL CENTER
2929 S Ellis
Chicago, IL 60616-3376
(312)791-2000

MOUNT SINAI HOSPITAL MEDICAL CENTER
15th Street At California
Chicago, IL 60608
(773)542-2000

NORTHWESTERN MEMORIAL HOSPITAL
251 East Huron Street
Chicago, IL 60611-3232
(312)926-2000

NORWEGIAN-AMERICAN HOSPITAL
1044 N Francisco Avenue
Chicago, IL 60622-2794
(773)292-8200

OUR LADY OF THE RESURRECTION MEDICAL CENTER
5645 W Addison
Chicago, IL 60634-4403
(773)282-7000

PRENTICE WOMEN'S HOSPITAL
333 East Superior St
Chicago, IL 60611-2654
(312)926-2000

PROVIDENT HOSPITAL OF CHICAGO
500 E 51st St
Chicago, IL 60615-2400
(773)572-2000

RAVENSWOOD HOSPITAL AND MEDICAL CENTER
836 W Wellington Ave
Chicago, IL 60657-5147
(773)878-4300

REHABILITATION INSTITUTE OF CHICAGO
345 East Superior
Chicago, IL 60611-4805
(312)238-1000

RESURRECTION MEDICAL CENTER
7435 W Talcott
Chicago, IL 60631-3746
(773)774-8000

ROSELAND COMMUNITY HOSPITAL
45 W 111th Street
Chicago, IL 60628-4294
(773)995-3000

RUSH-PRESBYTERIAN-SAINT LUKES MEDICAL CENTER
1653 West Congress Parkway
Chicago, IL 60612-3839
(312)942-5000

SACRED HEART HOSPITAL
3240 W Franklin Boulevard
Chicago, IL 60624-1599
(773)722-3020

SAINT ANTHONYS HOSPITAL
2875 West 19th Street
Chicago, IL 60623-3596
(773)484-1000

SAINT BERNARD HOSPITAL
326 W 64th St
Chicago, IL 60621-3146
(773)962-3900

SAINT ELIZABETH HOSPITAL OF CHICAGO
1431 N Claremont Avenue
Chicago, IL 60622-1791
(773)278-2000

SAINT JOSEPH HOSPITAL AND HEALTH CARE CENTER
2900 North Lake Shore Drive
Chicago, IL 60657-5640
(773)665-3000

SAINT MARY OF NAZARETH HOSPITAL CENTER
2233 W Division St
Chicago, IL 60622-3086
(773)770-2000

SCHWAB REHABILITATION CENTER
1401 S California
Chicago, IL 60608-1694
(773)522-2010

SHRINERS HOSPITAL
2211 N Oak Park Avenue
Chicago, IL 60707-3392
(708)622-5400

SOUTH SHORE HOSPITAL
8012 South Crandon Avenue
Chicago, IL 60617-1175
(773)768-0810

STONE PAVILION
320 East Huron St
Chicago, IL 60611-3043
(312)926-2000

SWEDISH COVENANT HOSPITAL
5145 N California Avenue
Chicago, IL 60625-3687
(773)878-8200

THOREK HOSPITAL AND MEDICAL CENTER
850 W Irving Park Road
Chicago, IL 60613-3077
(773)525-6780

TRINITY HOSPITAL
2320 E 93rd St
Chicago, IL 60617-3982
(773)967-2000

UNIVERSITY OF CHICAGO HOSPITALS
5841 South Maryland
Chicago, IL 60637-1463
(773)702-1000

UNIVERSITY OF ILLINOIS HOSPITAL
1740 West Taylor St
Chicago, IL 60612-7232
(773)996-7000

VA HEALTHCARE SYSTEM - CHICAGO AT LAKESIDE
333 E Huron St
Chicago, IL 60611-4541
(312)640-2100

VA HEALTHCARE SYSTEM - CHICAGO AT WESTSIDE
820 S Damen Avenue
Chicago, IL 60612-3728
(773)943-6600

CHICAGO HEIGHTS

SAINT JAMES HOSPITAL AND HEALTH CENTERS
1423 Chicago Road
Chicago Heights, IL 60411-3483
(708)756-1000

CLINTON

DR JOHN WARNER HOSPITAL
422 W White Street
Clinton, IL 61727-2273
(217)935-9571

DANVILLE

UNITED SAMARITANS MEDICAL CENTER - LOGAN
812 North Logan
Danville, IL 61832-3752
(217)443-5000

UNITED SAMARITANS MEDICAL CENTER- SAGER
600 Sager
Danville, IL 61832-6346
(217)442-6300

VA HEALTHCARE SYSTEM - DANVILLE
1900 E Main St
Danville, IL 61832-5100
(217)442-8000

DE KALB

KISHWAUKEE COMMUNITY HOSPITAL
Route 23 Bethany Road
De Kalb, IL 60115
(815)756-1521

DECATUR

DECATUR MEMORIAL HOSPITAL
2300 North Edward Street
Decatur, IL 62526-4192
(217)876-8121

HERITAGE BEHAVIORAL HEALTH CENTER
PO Box 710
Decatur, IL 62525-0710
(217)877-8613

SAINT MARYS HOSPITAL
1800 E Lake Shore Drive
Decatur, IL 62521-3883
(217)464-2966

ILLINOIS
Hospital Telephone Directory

DES PLAINES

HOLY FAMILY MEDICAL CENTER
100 N River Road
Des Plaines, IL 60016-1255
(847)297-1800

DIXON

KATHERINE SHAW BETHEA HOSPITAL
403 E 1st St
Dixon, IL 61021-3187
(815)288-5531

DOWNERS GROVE

GOOD SAMARITAN HOSPITAL-ADVOCATE
3815 Highland Avenue
Downers Grove, IL 60515-1500
(630)275-5900

DU QUOIN

MARSHALL BROWNING HOSPITAL
PO Box 192
Du Quoin, IL 62832-0192
(618)542-2146

EAST SAINT LOUIS

SAINT MARYS HOSPITAL OF EAST SAINT
LOUIS
129 N 8th St
East Saint Louis, IL 62201-2999
(618)274-1900

EFFINGHAM

SAINT ANTHONYS MEMORIAL HOSPITAL
503 N Maple Street
Effingham, IL 62401-2099
(217)342-2121

ELDORADO

FERRELL HOSPITAL
1201 Pine Street
Eldorado, IL 62930-1634
(618)273-3361

ELGIN

ELGIN MENTAL HEALTH CENTER
750 S State St
Elgin, IL 60123-7692
(847)742-1040

SAINT JOSEPH HOSPITAL
77 N Airlite St
Elgin, IL 60123-4998
(847)695-3200

SHERMAN HOSPITAL
934 Center Street
Elgin, IL 60120-2198
(847)742-9800

ELK GROVE VILLAGE

ALEXIAN BROTHERS MEDICAL CENTER
800 W Biesterfield Road
Elk Grove Village, IL 60007-3397
(847)437-5500

ELMHURST

ELMHURST MEMORIAL HOSPITAL
200 Berteau Avenue
Elmhurst, IL 60126-2989
(630)833-1400

EUREKA

EUREKA COMMUNITY HOSPITAL
101 S Major Street
Eureka, IL 61530-1278
(309)467-2371

EVANSTON

EVANSTON HOSPITAL
2650 Ridge Avenue
Evanston, IL 60201-1781
(847)570-2000

SAINT FRANCIS HOSPITAL OF EVANSTON
355 Ridge Avenue
Evanston, IL 60202-3399
(847)316-4000

EVERGREEN PARK

LITTLE COMPANY OF MARY HOSPITAL
2800 W 95th St
Evergreen Park, IL 60805-2795
(708)422-6200

FAIRFIELD

FAIRFIELD MEMORIAL HOSPITAL
303 N W 11th St
Fairfield, IL 62837-1206
(618)842-2611

FLORA

CLAY COUNTY HOSPITAL
PO Box 280
Flora, IL 62839-0280
(618)662-2131

FOREST PARK

RIVEREDGE HOSPITAL
8311 West Roosevelt Road
Forest Park, IL 60130-2500
(708)771-7000

FREEPORT

FREEPORT MEMORIAL HOSPITAL
1045 West Stephenson Street
Freeport, IL 61032-4899
(815)599-6000

GALENA

GALENA-STAUSS HOSPITAL
215 Summitt St
Galena, IL 61036-1697
(815)777-1340

GALESBURG

GALESBURG COTTAGE HOSPITAL
695 N Kellogg St
Galesburg, IL 61401-2885
(309)343-8131

SAINT MARY MEDICAL CENTER
3333 North Seminary
Galesburg, IL 61401-1299
(309)344-3161

GENESEO

HAMMOND-HENRY HOSPITAL
600 N College Ave
Geneseo, IL 61254-1099
(309)944-6431

GENEVA

DELNOR COMMUNITY HOSPITAL
300 Randall Road
Geneva, IL 60134-4202
(630)208-3000

GIBSON CITY

GIBSON COMMUNITY HOSPITAL
1120 North Melvin
Gibson City, IL 60936-1066
(217)784-4251

GLENDALE HEIGHTS

GLENOAKS HOSPITAL AND MEDICAL
CENTER
701 Winthrop Avenue
Glendale Heights, IL 60139-1403
(630)545-8000

GLENVIEW

EVANSTON NORTHWESTERN HEALTH
CARE AND GLENBROOK HOSPITAL
2100 Pfingsten Road
Glenview, IL 60025-1301
(847)657-5800

GRANITE CITY

GATEWAY REGIONAL MEDICAL CENTER
2100 Madison Avenue
Granite City, IL 62040-4701
(618)798-3000

GREAT LAKES

NAVAL HOSPITAL GREAT LAKES
3001-a 6th Street
Great Lakes, IL 60088-3210
(847)688-4560

GREENVILLE

EDWARD A UTLAUT MEMORIAL HOSPITAL
100 Healthcare Drive
Greenville, IL 62246-1161
(618)664-1230

HARRISBURG

HARRISBURG MEDICAL CENTER
PO Box 428
Harrisburg, IL 62946-0428
(618)253-7671

HARVARD

HARVARD COMMUNITY MEMORIAL
HOSPITAL
901 Grant St
Harvard, IL 60033-1898
(815)943-5431

HARVEY

INGALLS MEMORIAL HOSPITAL
One Ingalls Drive
Harvey, IL 60426-3591
(708)333-2300

HAVANA

MASON DISTRICT HOSPITAL
520 East Franklin Street
Havana, IL 62644-1238
(309)543-4431

HAZEL CREST

SOUTH SUBURBAN HOSPITAL
17800 S Kedzie Avenue
Hazel Crest, IL 60429-0989
(708)799-8000

Hospital Telephone Directory — ILLINOIS

HERRIN
HERRIN HOSPITAL
201 S 14th St
Herrin, IL 62948-3631
(618)942-2171

HIGHLAND
SAINT JOSEPHS HOSPITAL
1515 Main Street
Highland, IL 62249-1698
(618)654-7421

HIGHLAND PARK
HIGHLAND PARK HOSPITAL
718 Glenview Avenue
Highland Park, IL 60035-2497
(847)432-8000

HILLSBORO
HILLSBORO AREA HOSPITAL
1200 Tremont St
Hillsboro, IL 62049-1900
(217)532-6111

HINES
JOHN J MADDEN MENTAL HEALTH CENTER
1200 S First Avenue
Hines, IL 60141
(708)338-7202

VA MEDICAL CENTER - EDWARD HINES JR.
5th Avenue And Roosevelt Road
Hines, IL 60141
(708)202-8387

HINSDALE
HINSDALE HOSPITAL
120 North Oak St
Hinsdale, IL 60521-3890
(630)856-9000

RML SPECIALTY HOSPITAL
5601 S County Line Road
Hinsdale, IL 60521-4875
(630)286-4000

HOFFMAN ESTATES
ALEXIAN BROTHERS BEHAVIORAL HEALTH HOSPITAL
1650 Moon Lake Boulevard
Hoffman Estates, IL 60194-1010
(847)882-1600

SAINT ALEXIUS MEDICAL CENTER
1555 N Barrington Road
Hoffman Estates, IL 60194-1018
(847)843-2000

HOOPESTON
HOOPESTON COMMUNITY MEMORIAL HOSPITAL
701 East Orange St
Hoopeston, IL 60942-1801
(217)283-5531

HOPEDALE
HOPEDALE HOSPITAL
107 Tremont Street
Hopedale, IL 61747
(309)449-3321

JACKSONVILLE
PASSAVANT AREA HOSPITAL
1600 W Walnut St
Jacksonville, IL 62650-1199
(217)245-9541

JERSEYVILLE
JERSEY COMMUNITY HOSPITAL
400 Maple Summit Road
Jerseyville, IL 62052-2028
(618)498-6402

JOLIET
PROVENA SAINT JOSEPH MEDICAL CENTER
2121 Oneida St Ste 102
Joliet, IL 60435-6571
(815)725-7133

SILVER CROSS HOSPITAL
1200 Maple Road
Joliet, IL 60432-1497
(815)740-1100

STATEVILLE CORRECTIONAL CENTER
PO Box 112
Joliet, IL 60434-0112
(708)727-3607

KANKAKEE
PROVENA SAINT MARYS HOSPITAL
500 W Court St
Kankakee, IL 60901-3691
(815)937-2180

RIVERSIDE MEDICAL CENTER HOSPITAL
350 N Wall St
Kankakee, IL 60901-2901
(815)933-1671

KEWANEE
KEWANEE HOSPITAL
PO Box 747
Kewanee, IL 61443-0747
(309)853-3361

LA GRANGE
LA GRANGE MEMORIAL HOSPITAL
5101 Willow Springs Road
La Grange, IL 60525-2600
(708)352-1200

LAKE FOREST
LAKE FOREST HOSPITAL
660 N Westmoreland Road
Lake Forest, IL 60045-1696
(847)234-5600

LAWRENCEVILLE
LAWRENCE COUNTY MEMORIAL HOSPITAL
2200 West State St
Lawrenceville, IL 62439-1899
(618)943-1000

LEMONT
ROCK CREEK CENTER
PO Box 728
Lemont, IL 60439-7028
(630)257-3636

LIBERTYVILLE
CONDELL MEDICAL CENTER
900 Garfield
Libertyville, IL 60048-3199
(847)362-2900

LINCOLN
ABRAHAM LINCOLN MEMORIAL HOSPITAL
315 8th St
Lincoln, IL 62656-2698
(217)732-2161

LITCHFIELD
SAINT FRANCIS HOSPITAL
1215 East Union Avenue
Litchfield, IL 62056-1700
(217)324-2191

MACOMB
MC DONOUGH DISTRICT HOSPITAL
525 East Grant Street
Macomb, IL 61455-3318
(309)833-4101

MARION
MARION MEMORIAL HOSPITAL
3333 W Deyoung St
Marion, IL 62959-5884
(618)997-5341

VA MEDICAL CENTER - MARION
2401 W Main St
Marion, IL 62959-1188
(618)997-5311

MARYVILLE
ANDERSON HOSPITAL
Ill Route 162 Old Edwardsville Road
Maryville, IL 62062
(618)288-5711

MATTOON
SARAH BUSH LINCOLN HEALTH CENTER
Route 16 PO Box 372
Mattoon, IL 61938-0372
(217)258-2525

MAYWOOD
LOYOLA UNIVERSITY CENTER AND RONALD MCDONALD CHILDRENS HOSPITAL
2160 S 1st Avenue
Maywood, IL 60153-5500
(708)216-9000

MC HENRY
NORTHERN ILLINOIS MEDICAL CENTER
4201 Medical Center Drive
Mc Henry, IL 60050-8499
(815)344-5000

MCLEANSBORO
HAMILTON MEMORIAL HOSPITAL
611 S Marshall
Mcleansboro, IL 62859-1297
(618)643-2361

MELROSE PARK
GOTTLIEB MEMORIAL HOSPITAL
701 West North Avenue
Melrose Park, IL 60160-1612
(708)681-3200

WESTLAKE COMMUNITY HOSPITAL
1225 Superior St
Melrose Park, IL 60160
(708)681-3000

MENDOTA
MENDOTA COMMUNITY HOSPITAL
Memorial Drive
Mendota, IL 61342
(815)539-7461

ILLINOIS

Hospital Telephone Directory

METROPOLIS

MASSAC MEMORIAL HOSPITAL
Memorial Heights
Metropolis, IL 62960
(618)524-2176

MOLINE

TRINITY MEDICAL CENTER - SEVENTH
STREET CAMPUS
500 John Deere St
Moline, IL 61265-6892
(309)779-5000

MONMOUTH

COMMUNITY MEDICAL CENTER
1000 W Harlem Avenue
Monmouth, IL 61462-1060
(309)734-3141

MONTICELLO

JOHN AND MARY KIRBY HOSPITAL
1111 North State Street
Monticello, IL 61856-1151
(217)762-2115

MORRIS

MORRIS HOSPITAL
150 W High St
Morris, IL 60450-1497
(815)942-2932

MORRISON

MORRISON COMMUNITY HOSPITAL
303 N Jackson Street
Morrison, IL 61270-3099
(815)772-4003

MOUNT CARMEL

WABASH GENERAL HOSPITAL DISTRICT
1418 College Drive
Mount Carmel, IL 62863-2638
(618)262-8621

MOUNT VERNON

CROSSROADS COMMUNITY HOSPITAL
8 Doctors Park Road
Mount Vernon, IL 62864-6224
(618)244-5500

GOOD SAMARITAN REGIONAL HEALTH
CENTER
605 N 12th Street
Mount Vernon, IL 62864-2899
(618)242-4600

MURPHYSBORO

SAINT JOSEPH MEMORIAL HOSPITAL
800 N 2nd St
Murphysboro, IL 62966-3337
(618)684-3156

NAPERVILLE

EDWARD HOSPITAL
801 South Washington
Naperville, IL 60540-7499
(630)527-3000

LINDEN OAKS HOSPITAL
852 West St
Naperville, IL 60540-6400
(630)305-5500

NASHVILLE

WASHINGTON COUNTY HOSPITAL
705 S Grand St
Nashville, IL 62263-1534
(618)327-8236

NORMAL

BROMENN HEALTHCARE
Virginia At Franklin
Normal, IL 61761
(309)454-1400

NORTH CHICAGO

VA MEDICAL CENTER - NORTH CHICAGO
3001 Green Bay Road
North Chicago, IL 60064-3049
(847)688-1900

NORTHLAKE

KINDRED HOSPITAL NORTHLAKE
365 E North Avenue
Northlake, IL 60164-2628
(708)345-8100

OAK FOREST

OAK FOREST HOSPITAL
159th And Cicero Avenue
Oak Forest, IL 60452
(708)687-7200

OAK LAWN

ADVOCATE CHRIST MEDICAL CENTER AND
HOPE CHILDREN'S HOSPITAL
4440 W 95th Street
Oak Lawn, IL 60453-2600
(708)425-8000

OAK PARK

OAK PARK HOSPITAL
520 S Maple Avenue
Oak Park, IL 60304-1097
(708)383-9300

WEST SUBURBAN HOSPITAL MEDICAL
CENTER
Erie At Austin Boulevard
Oak Park, IL 60302
(708)383-6200

OLNEY

RICHLAND MEMORIAL HOSPITAL
800 East Locust
Olney, IL 62450-2598
(618)395-2131

OLYMPIA FIELDS

SAINT JAMES OF OLYMPIA FIELDS
MEDICAL CENTER
20201 South Crawford Avenue
Olympia Fields, IL 60461-1010
(708)747-4000

OTTAWA

COMMUNITY HOSPITAL OF OTTAWA
1100 East Norris Drive
Ottawa, IL 61350-1604
(815)433-3100

PALOS HEIGHTS

PALOS COMMUNITY HOSPITAL
12251 South 80th Avenue
Palos Heights, IL 60463-0930
(708)923-4000

PANA

PANA COMMUNITY HOSPITAL
101 E Ninth Street
Pana, IL 62557-1785
(217)562-2131

PARIS

PARIS COMMUNITY HOSPITAL
East Court Street
Paris, IL 61944
(217)465-4141

PARK RIDGE

LUTHERAN GENERAL HOSPITAL
1775 Dempster St
Park Ridge, IL 60068-1173
(847)723-2210

PEKIN

PEKIN MEMORIAL HOSPITAL
Court And 14th Street
Pekin, IL 61554
(309)347-1151

PEORIA

GEORGE A ZELLER MENTAL HEALTH
CENTER
5407 North University Avenue
Peoria, IL 61614-4785
(309)693-5228

METHODIST MEDICAL CENTER OF ILLINOIS
221 N E Glen Oak Avenue
Peoria, IL 61636-0002
(309)672-5522

PROCTOR COMMUNITY HOSPITAL
5409 N Knoxville Avenue
Peoria, IL 61614-5016
(309)691-1000

SAINT FRANCIS MEDICAL CENTER
530 N E Glen Oak
Peoria, IL 61637-0001
(309)655-2000

PERU

ILLINOIS VALLEY COMMUNITY HOSPITAL
925 West St
Peru, IL 61354-2799
(815)223-3300

PINCKNEYVILLE

PINCKNEYVILLE COMMUNITY HOSPITAL
101 North Walnut Street
Pinckneyville, IL 62274-1099
(618)357-2187

PITTSFIELD

ILLINI COMMUNITY HOSPITAL
640 West Washington St
Pittsfield, IL 62363-1397
(217)285-2113

PONTIAC

PONTIAC CORRECTIONAL CENTER
PO Box 99
Pontiac, IL 61764-0099
(815)842-2816

SAINT JAMES HOSPITAL
610 E Water St
Pontiac, IL 61764-2143
(815)842-2828

Hospital Telephone Directory — ILLINOIS

PRINCETON
PERRY MEMORIAL HOSPITAL
530 Park Avenue E
Princeton, IL 61356-3901
(815)875-2811

QUINCY
BLESSING HOSPITAL
Broadway At 11th St
Quincy, IL 62301
(217)223-1200

RED BUD
RED BUD REGIONAL HOSPITAL
325 Spring St
Red Bud, IL 62278-1105
(618)282-3831

ROBINSON
CRAWFORD MEMORIAL HOSPITAL
1000 N Allen St
Robinson, IL 62454-1167
(618)546-1234

ROCHELLE
ROCHELLE COMMUNITY HOSPITAL
900 N 2nd St
Rochelle, IL 61068-1717
(815)562-2181

ROCK ISLAND
TRINITY MEDICAL CENTER WEST
2701 17th St
Rock Island, IL 61201-5393
(309)779-5000

ROCKFORD
H DOUGLAS SINGER MENTAL HEALTH CENTER
4402 N Main St
Rockford, IL 61103-1278
(815)987-7096

ROCKFORD MEMORIAL HOSPITAL
2400 North Rockton Avenue
Rockford, IL 61103-3681
(815)971-5000

SAINT ANTHONY MEDICAL CENTER
5666 East State Street
Rockford, IL 61108-2472
(815)226-2000

SWEDISH AMERICAN HOSPITAL
1401 E State St
Rockford, IL 61104-2298
(815)489-4000

VAN MATER HEALTHSOUTH
950 S Mulford Road
Rockford, IL 61108-4274
(815)381-8500

ROSICLARE
HARDIN COUNTY GENERAL HOSPITAL
Ferrell Road
Rosiclare, IL 62982
(618)285-6634

RUSHVILLE
SARAH D CULBERTSON MEMORIAL HOSPITAL
238 S Congress St
Rushville, IL 62681-1465
(217)322-4321

SALEM
SALEM TOWNSHIP HOSPITAL
1201 Ricker Drive
Salem, IL 62881-4263
(618)548-3194

SANDWICH
VALLEY WEST COMMUNITY HOSPITAL
11 East Pleasant Avenue
Sandwich, IL 60548-1100
(815)786-8484

SCOTT AIR FORCE BASE
375TH MEDICAL GROUP
310 West Losey St Stop 1
Scott Air Force Base, IL 62225-5250
(618)256-7456

SHELBYVILLE
SHELBY MEMORIAL HOSPITAL
200 S Cedar St
Shelbyville, IL 62565-1800
(217)774-3961

SILVIS
ILLINI HOSPITAL
801 Hospital Road
Silvis, IL 61282-1893
(309)792-9363

SKOKIE
RUSH NORTH SHORE MEDICAL CENTER
9600 Gross Point Road
Skokie, IL 60076-1257
(847)677-9600

SPARTA
SPARTA COMMUNITY HOSPITAL DISTRICT
PO Box 297
Sparta, IL 62286-0297
(618)443-2177

SPRING VALLEY
SAINT MARGARETS HOSPITAL
600 E 1st St
Spring Valley, IL 61362-1599
(815)664-5311

SPRINGFIELD
ANDREW MCFARLAND MENTAL HEALTH CENTER
901 Southwind Road
Springfield, IL 62703-5125
(217)786-6994

DOCTORS HOSPITAL
5230 South 6th Street
Springfield, IL 62703-5194
(217)529-7151

LINCOLN DEVELOPMENTAL CENTER
5020 Industrial Dr # B
Springfield, IL 62703-5324
(217)735-2361

MEMORIAL MEDICAL CENTER
800 N Rutledge
Springfield, IL 62781-0002
(217)788-3000

SAINT JOHNS HOSPITAL
800 E Carpenter St
Springfield, IL 62769-0002
(217)544-6464

STAUNTON
COMMUNITY MEMORIAL HOSPITAL
400 Caldwell
Staunton, IL 62088-1499
(618)635-2200

STERLING
CGH MEDICAL CENTER
100 East Lefevre Road
Sterling, IL 61081-1279
(815)625-0400

STREAMWOOD
STREAMWOOD HOSPITAL
1400 E Irving Park Road
Streamwood, IL 60107-3203
(630)837-9000

STREATOR
SAINT MARYS HOSPITAL
111 E Spring
Streator, IL 61364-3399
(815)673-2311

SYCAMORE
KINDRED HOSPITAL SYCAMORE
225 Edward Street
Sycamore, IL 60178-2137
(815)895-2144

TAYLORVILLE
SAINT VINCENT MEMORIAL HOSPITAL
201 East Pleasant St
Taylorville, IL 62568-1597
(217)824-3331

TINLEY PARK
TINLEY PARK MENTAL HEALTH CENTER
7400 W 183rd St
Tinley Park, IL 60477-3695
(708)614-4000

URBANA
CARLE FOUNDATION HOSPITAL
611 West Park Street
Urbana, IL 61801-2529
(217)383-3311

PROVENA COVENANT MEDICAL CENTER CHAMPAIGN-URBANA
1400 West Park Avenue
Urbana, IL 61801-2334
(217)337-2000

VANDALIA
FAYETTE COUNTY HOSPITAL
7th And Taylor
Vandalia, IL 62471
(618)283-1231

WATSEKA
IROQUOIS MEMORIAL HOSPITAL
200 Fairman Street
Watseka, IL 60970-1644
(815)432-5841

WAUKEGAN
VISTA HEALTH SAINT THERESE MEDICAL CENTER
2615 Washington St
Waukegan, IL 60085-4980
(847)249-3900

INDIANA — Hospital Telephone Directory

VISTA HEALTH VICTORY MEMORIAL HOSPITAL
1324 North Sheridan Road
Waukegan, IL 60085-2199
(847)360-4000

WHEATON

MARIANJOY REHABILITATION CENTER
26 W171 Roosevelt Road PO Box 795
Wheaton, IL 60189-0795
(309)462-4000

WINFIELD

BEHAVIORAL HEALTH SERVICES
27 West 350 High Lake Road
Winfield, IL 60190
(630)653-4000

CENTRAL DUPAGE HOSPITAL
25 North Winfield Road
Winfield, IL 60190-1295
(630)682-1600

WOODSTOCK

MEMORIAL MEDICAL CENTER
527 West South Street
Woodstock, IL 60098-3756
(815)338-2500

ZION

MIDWESTERN REGION MEDICAL CENTER
2520 Elisha Avenue
Zion, IL 60099-2587
(847)872-4561

INDIANA

ANDERSON

COMMUNITY HOSPITAL OF ANDERSON
1515 N Madison Avenue
Anderson, IN 46011-3457
(765)642-8011

SAINT JOHN'S HEALTH SYSTEM
2015 Jackson Street
Anderson, IN 46016-4337
(765)649-2511

ANGOLA

CAMERON HOSPITAL AND HOME HEALTH CARE
416 East Maumee Street
Angola, IN 46703-2001
(260)665-2141

AUBURN

DEKALB MEMORIAL HOSPITAL
1316 East Seventh Street PO Box 542
Auburn, IN 46706-0542
(260)925-4600

BATESVILLE

MARGARET MARY COMMUNITY HOSPITAL
321 Mitchel Avenue PO Box 226
Batesville, IN 47006-0226
(812)934-6624

BEDFORD

BEDFORD REGIONAL MEDICAL CENTER
2900 West 16th Street
Bedford, IN 47421-3583
(812)275-1200

DUNN MEMORIAL HOSPITAL
1600 23rd Street
Bedford, IN 47421-4791
(812)275-3331

BEECH GROVE

SAINT FRANCIS HOSPITAL CENTER
1600 Albany Street
Beech Grove, IN 46107-1593
(317)787-3311

SELECT SPECIALTY HOSPITAL
1600 Albany Street Suite 200
Beech Grove, IN 46107-1541
(317)783-8913

BLOOMINGTON

BLOOMINGTON HOSPITAL
601 W Second Street
Bloomington, IN 47403-2317
(812)336-6821

MEADOWS HOSPITAL
3600 N Prow Road
Bloomington, IN 47404-1616
(812)331-8000

SELECT SPECIALTY HOSPITAL - BLOOMINGTON
601 West Second Street
Bloomington, IN 47403-2317
(812)353-2000

BLUFFTON

BLUFFTON REGIONAL MEDICAL CENTER
303 South Main Street
Bluffton, IN 46714-2503
(260)824-3500

CAYLOR-NICKEL MEDICAL CENTER
One Caylor-nickel Square
Bluffton, IN 46714-2529
(260)824-3500

WELLS COMMUNITY HOSPITAL
1100 South Main Street
Bluffton, IN 46714-3615
(260)824-3210

BOONVILLE

SAINT MARYS WARRICK
1116 Millis Avenue PO Box 629
Boonville, IN 47601-0629
(812)897-4800

BRAZIL

SAINT VINCENT CLAY HOSPITAL
1206 East National Avenue
Brazil, IN 47834-2718
(812)448-2675

BREMEN

COMMUNITY HOSPITAL OF BREMEN
411 South Whitlock Street
Bremen, IN 46506-1699
(574)546-2211

CARMEL

SAINT ELIZABETH ANN SETON SPECIALTY CARE
13500 N Meridian, 2nd Floor
Carmel, IN 46032-1456
(317)582-8500

SAINT VINCENT CARMEL HOSPITAL
13500 N Meridian St
Carmel, IN 46032-1456
(317)582-7000

CHARLESTOWN

MEDICAL CENTER OF SOUTHERN INDIANA
2200 Market St, PO Box 69
Charlestown, IN 47111-0069
(812)256-3301

CLINTON

WEST CENTRAL COMMUNITY HOSPITAL
801 South Main Street
Clinton, IN 47842-2261
(765)832-2451

COLUMBIA CITY

PARKVIEW WHITLEY HOSPITAL
353 N Oak St
Columbia City, IN 46725-1697
(260)248-9000

COLUMBUS

BEHAVIORAL HEALTHCARE - COLUMBUS
2223 Poshard Drive PO Box 1549
Columbus, IN 47202-1549
(317)376-1711

COLUMBUS REGIONAL HOSPITAL
2400 East 17th Street
Columbus, IN 47201-5360
(812)379-4441

CONNERSVILLE

FAYETTE MEMORIAL HOSPITAL ASSOCIATION
1941 Virginia Avenue
Connersville, IN 47331-2893
(765)825-5131

CORYDON

HARRISON COUNTY HOSPITAL
245 Atwood Street
Corydon, IN 47112-1738
(812)738-4251

CRAWFORDSVILLE

SAINT CLARE MEDICAL CENTER
1710 Lafayette Road
Crawfordsville, IN 47933-1033
(765)362-2800

CROWN POINT

SAINT ANTHONY MEDICAL CENTER
1201 South Main Street
Crown Point, IN 46307-8483
(219)738-2100

DANVILLE

HENDRICKS COMMUNITY HOSPITAL
1000 East Main Street
Danville, IN 46122-1991
(317)745-4451

DECATUR

ADAMS COUNTY MEMORIAL HOSPITAL
PO Box 151
Decatur, IN 46733-0151
(260)724-2145

DYER

SAINT MARGARET MERCY HEALTHCARE CENTERS - SOUTH
24 Joliet Street
Dyer, IN 46311-1799
(219)865-2141

EAST CHICAGO

SAINT CATHERINE HOSPITAL
4321 Fir St
East Chicago, IN 46312-3097
(219)392-70000

48

Hospital Telephone Directory — INDIANA

ELKHART

ELKHART GENERAL HOSPITAL
600 East Boulevard PO Box 1329
Elkhart, IN 46515-1329
(574)294-2621

ELWOOD

SAINT VINCENT MERCY HOSPITAL
1331 South A Street
Elwood, IN 46036-1942
(765)552-4600

EVANSVILLE

DEACONESS CROSS POINTE CENTER
7200 E Indiana
Evansville, IN 47715-2753
(812)476-7200

DEACONESS HOSPITAL
600 Mary Street
Evansville, IN 47710-1674
(812)450-5000

EVANSVILLE STATE HOSPITAL
3400 Lincoln Avenue
Evansville, IN 47714-0146
(812)473-2100

HEALTHSOUTH TRI STATE REHAB HOSPITAL
4100 Covert Avenue PO Box 5349
Evansville, IN 47716-5349
(812)476-9983

SAINT ELIZABETH ANN SETON HOSPITAL
3700 Washington Avenue
Evansville, IN 47750-0001
(812)485-7450

SAINT MARYS MEDICAL CENTER OF EVANSVILLE
3700 Washington Avenue PO Box 5107
Evansville, IN 47750-0001
(812)485-4000

SELECT SPECIALTY HOSPITAL - EVANSVILLE
600 Mary St, Suite 3325
Evansville, IN 47747-0001
(812)450-5270

FORT WAYNE

DUPONT HOSPITAL
2520 East Dupont Road
Fort Wayne, IN 46825-1675
(260)416-3000

LUTHERAN HOSPITAL
7950 West Jefferson
Fort Wayne, IN 46804-4160
(260)435-7001

PARKVIEW BEHAVIORAL HEALTH
1720 Beacon Street
Fort Wayne, IN 46805-4749
(260)423-3651

PARKVIEW HOSPITAL
2200 Randalia Drive
Fort Wayne, IN 46805-4699
(260)373-4000

REHABILITATION HOSPITAL OF FORT WAYNE
7970 W Jefferson Boulevard
Fort Wayne, IN 46804-4140
(260)436-2644

SAINT JOSEPH MEDICAL CENTER OF FORT WAYNE
700 Broadway
Fort Wayne, IN 46802-1402
(260)425-3000

SELECT SPECIALTY HOSPITAL - FORT WAYNE
700 Broadway
Fort Wayne, IN 46802-1402
(260)425-3810

VA HEALTHCARE SYSTEM - FORT WAYNE
2121 Lake Avenue
Fort Wayne, IN 46805-5100
(260)460-1310

FRANKFORT

SAINT VINCENT FRANKFORT HOSPITAL
1300 S Jackson St
Frankfort, IN 46041-3313
(765)656-3000

FRANKLIN

JOHNSON MEMORIAL HOSPITAL
1125 West Jefferson St PO Box 549
Franklin, IN 46131-0549
(317)736-3300

GARY

METHODIST HOSPITALS NORTH LAKE
600 Grant St
Gary, IN 46402-6099
(219)886-4000

GOSHEN

GOSHEN GENERAL HOSPITAL
200 High Park Avenue
Goshen, IN 46526-4899
(574)533-2141

OAKLAWN PSYCHIATRIC CENTER
330 Lakeview Drive PO Box 809
Goshen, IN 46527-0809
(219)533-1234

GREENCASTLE

PUTNAM COUNTY HOSPITAL
1542 Bloomington St
Greencastle, IN 46135-2297
(765)653-5121

GREENFIELD

HANCOCK MEMORIAL HOSPITAL AND HEALTH SERVICES
801 North State Street, PO Box 827
Greenfield, IN 46140-0827
(317)462-5544

GREENSBURG

DECATUR COUNTY MEMORIAL HOSPITAL
720 North Lincoln Street
Greensburg, IN 47240-1398
(812)663-4331

GREENWOOD

KINDRED HOSPITAL INDIANAPOLIS SOUTH
898 E Main St
Greenwood, IN 46143-1407
(317)888-8155

VALLE VISTA HOSPITAL
898 East Main Street
Greenwood, IN 46143-1400
(317)887-1348

HAMMOND

SAINT MARGARET MERCY HEALTHCARE CENTERS - NORTH
5454 Hohman Avenue
Hammond, IN 46320-1931
(219)932-2300

SELECT SPECIALTY HOSPITAL - NORTHWEST INDIANA
5454 Hohman Avenue, 5th Floor
Hammond, IN 46320-1931
(219)937-9900

HARTFORD CITY

BLACKFORD COUNTY HOSPITAL
503 East Van Cleve Street
Hartford City, IN 47348-1897
(765)348-0300

HOBART

SAINT MARY MEDICAL CENTER
1500 S Lake Park Avenue
Hobart, IN 46342-6699
(219)942-0551

HUNTINGBURG

SAINT JOSEPHS HOSPITAL
1900 Medical Arts Drive
Huntingburg, IN 47542-9190
(812)683-2121

HUNTINGTON

PARKVIEW HUNTINGTON HOSPITAL
2001 Stults Rd
Huntington, IN 46750-1291
(260)356-3000

INDIANAPOLIS

CLARIAN HEALTH PARTNERS
PO Box 1367
Indianapolis, IN 46206-1367
(317)962-2000

COMMUNITY HOSPITAL INDIANAPOLIS
1500 N Ritter Avenue
Indianapolis, IN 46219-3095
(317)355-1411

COMMUNITY HOSPITAL NORTH
7150 Clearvista Drive
Indianapolis, IN 46256-4699
(317)849-6262

COMMUNITY HOSPITAL SOUTH
1402 E South County Line Road
Indianapolis, IN 46227
(317)887-7000

FAIRBANKS HOSPITAL
8102 Clearvista Parkway
Indianapolis, IN 46256-4698
(317)849-8222

INDIANA UNIVERSITY MEDICAL CENTER
550 University Boulevard
Indianapolis, IN 46202-5149
(317)274-5000

KINDRED HOSPITAL INDIANAPOLIS
1700 W 10th St
Indianapolis, IN 46222-3802
(317)636-4400

LARUE D CARTER MEMORIAL HOSPITAL
2601 Cole Spring Road
Indianapolis, IN 46222-2273
(317)941-4000

METHODIST HOSPITAL OF INDIANA
I-65 And 21st St PO Box 1367
Indianapolis, IN 46206-1367
(317)962-2000

REHABILITATION HOSPITAL OF INDIANA
4141 Shore Drive
Indianapolis, IN 46254-2607
(317)329-2000

INDIANA
Hospital Telephone Directory

RILEY HOSPITAL FOR CHILDREN
702 Barnhill Drive
Indianapolis, IN 46202-5200
(317)274-5000

SAINT FRANCIS HOSPITAL CENTER - SOUTH
8111 South Emerson Avenue
Indianapolis, IN 46237-8586
(317)865-5000

SAINT VINCENT CHILDREN'S SPECIALTY HOSPITAL
1707 West 86th Street, PO Box 40407
Indianapolis, IN 46240-0407
(317)415-5500

SAINT VINCENT HOSPITAL AND HEALTH CARE CENTER
2001 West 86th Street
Indianapolis, IN 46260-1902
(317)338-2345

SAINT VINCENT STRESS CENTER
8401 Harcourt Road
Indianapolis, IN 46260-2073
(317)338-4600

SELECT SPECIALTY HOSPITAL - INDIANAPOLIS
I-65 At 21st Street
Indianapolis, IN 46206
(317)931-1676

VA MEDICAL CENTER - RICHARD L. ROUDEBUSH
1481 W 10th St
Indianapolis, IN 46202-2803
(317)554-0000

WESTVIEW HOSPITAL
3630 Guion Road
Indianapolis, IN 46222-1699
(317)924-6661

WILLIAM N WISHARD MEMORIAL HOSPITAL
1001 West 10th Street
Indianapolis, IN 46202-2859
(317)639-6671

WINONA MEMORIAL HOSPITAL
3232 North Meridian Street
Indianapolis, IN 46208-4693
(317)924-3392

WOMENS HOSPITAL-INDIANAPOLIS
8111 Township Line Road
Indianapolis, IN 46260-5898
(317)875-5994

JASPER

MEMORIAL HOSPITAL AND HEALTH CARE CENTER
800 W 9th St
Jasper, IN 47546-2516
(812)482-2345

JEFFERSONVILLE

CLARK COUNTY MEMORIAL HOSPITAL
1220 Missouri Avenue
Jeffersonville, IN 47130-3743
(812)282-6631

KENDALLVILLE

PARKVIEW NOBLE HOSPITAL
PO Box 728
Kendallville, IN 46755-0728
(260)347-8700

KNOX

STARKE MEMORIAL HOSPITAL
PO Box 339
Knox, IN 46534-0339
(574)772-6231

KOKOMO

HEALTHSOUTH REHAB HOSPITAL
829 N Dixon Road
Kokomo, IN 46901-1795
(765)452-6700

HOWARD COMMUNITY HOSPITAL
3500 S La Fountain St
Kokomo, IN 46902-3800
(765)453-0702

SAINT JOSEPH HOSPITAL AND HEALTH CENTER
1907 West Sycamore Street
Kokomo, IN 46901-4113
(765)452-5611

LA PORTE

LA PORTE HOSPITAL
1007 Lincolnway
La Porte, IN 46350-3290
(219)326-1234

LAFAYETTE

LAFAYETTE HOME HOSPITAL
PO Box 7518
Lafayette, IN 47903-7518
(765)447-6811

SAINT ELIZABETH MEDICAL CENTER
1501 Hartford Street
Lafayette, IN 47904-2126
(765)423-6011

LAGRANGE

LAGRANGE COMMUNITY HOSPITAL
207 North Townline Road
Lagrange, IN 46761-1325
(260)463-2143

LAWRENCEBURG

COMMUNITY MENTAL HEALTH CENTER
285 Bielby Road
Lawrenceburg, IN 47025-1096
(812)537-1302

DEARBORN COUNTY HOSPITAL
600 Wilson Creek Road
Lawrenceburg, IN 47025-2751
(812)537-1010

LEBANON

WITHAM MEMORIAL HOSPITAL
1124 North Lebanon Street PO Box 1200
Lebanon, IN 46052-3005
(765)482-2700

LINTON

GREENE COUNTY GENERAL HOSPITAL
Rr 1 Box 555
Linton, IN 47441-9587
(812)847-2281

LOGANSPORT

FOUR COUNTY COUNSELING CENTER
1015 Michigan Avenue
Logansport, IN 46947-1526
(574)722-5151

LOGANSPORT STATE HOSPITAL
1098 South State Road 25
Logansport, IN 46947-6510
(574)722-4141

MEMORIAL HOSPITAL
1101 Michigan Avenue PO Box 7013
Logansport, IN 46947-7013
(574)753-7541

MADISON

KINGS DAUGHTERS HOSPITAL
One King's Daughters Drive
Madison, IN 47250-3357
(812)265-5211

MADISON STATE HOSPITAL
711 Green Road
Madison, IN 47250-2199
(812)265-2611

MARION

CORNERSTONE-GRANT-BLACKFORD MENTAL HEALTH
505 Wabash Avenue
Marion, IN 46952-2608
(765)662-3971

MARION GENERAL HOSPITAL
411 North Wabash Avenue
Marion, IN 46952-2612
(765)662-1441

VA HEALTHCARE SYSTEM - MARION
1700 E 38th St
Marion, IN 46953-4568
(765)674-3321

MARTINSVILLE

MORGAN COUNTY MEMORIAL HOSPITAL
2209 John R Wooden Drive PO Box 1717
Martinsville, IN 46151-0717
(765)342-8441

MERRILLVILLE

METHODIST HOSPITALS SOUTHLAKE
8701 Broadway
Merrillville, IN 46410-7035
(219)738-5500

SOUTHLAKE CENTER FOR MENTAL HEALTH
8555 Taft Street
Merrillville, IN 46410-6199
(219)769-4005

MICHIGAN CITY

SAINT ANTHONY MEMORIAL HEALTH CENTERS
301 W Homer St
Michigan City, IN 46360-4358
(219)879-8511

MISHAWAKA

SAINT JOSEPH COMMUNITY HOSPITAL
215 W 4th St
Mishawaka, IN 46544-1999
(574)259-2431

MONTICELLO

WHITE COUNTY MEMORIAL HOSPITAL
1101 Oconnor Boulevard
Monticello, IN 47960-1698
(574)583-7111

MOORESVILLE

SAINT FRANCIS HOSPITAL AND HEALTH CENTER
1201 Hadley Road
Mooresville, IN 46158-1737
(317)831-1160

MUNCIE

BALL MEMORIAL HOSPITAL
2401 University Avenue
Muncie, IN 47303-3499
(765)747-3111

Hospital Telephone Directory — INDIANA

MUNSTER

COMMUNITY HOSPITAL OF MUNSTER
901 Macartur Boulevard
Munster, IN 46321-2959
(219)836-1600

ILLIANA SURGERY AND MEDICAL CENTER
701 Superior Avenue
Munster, IN 46321-4037
(219)924-1300

NEW ALBANY

FLOYD MEMORIAL HOSPITAL AND HEALTH SERVICES
1850 State Street
New Albany, IN 47150-4997
(812)949-5500

SOUTHERN INDIANA REHABILITATION HOSPITAL
3104 Blackiston Boulevard
New Albany, IN 47150-9579
(812)941-8300

NEW CASTLE

HENRY COUNTY MEMORIAL HOSPITAL
1000 North 16th Street
New Castle, IN 47362-4395
(765)521-0890

NEWBURGH

WOMEN'S HOSPITAL
4199 Gateway Boulevard
Newburgh, IN 47630-8940
(812)842-4200

NOBLESVILLE

RIVERVIEW HOSPITAL
395 Westfield Road
Noblesville, IN 46060-1434
(317)773-0760

NORTH VERNON

SAINT VINCENT JENNINGS COMMUNITY HOSPITAL
301 Henry Street
North Vernon, IN 47265-1063
(812)352-4200

OAKLAND CITY

WIRTH REGIONAL HOSPITAL
Highway 64-west Rr3 Box 14a
Oakland City, IN 47660-9379
(812)749-6111

PAOLI

BLOOMINGTON HOSPITAL
642 W Hospital Road PO Box 499
Paoli, IN 47454-0499
(812)723-2811

PERU

DUKES MEMORIAL HOSPITAL
Grant And Boulevard
Peru, IN 46970
(765)472-8000

PLYMOUTH

BEHAVIORAL HEALTHCARE OF NORTHERN INDIANA
1800 N Oak Road
Plymouth, IN 46563-3406
(574)936-3784

SAINT JOSEPHS REGIONAL MEDICAL CENTER
1915 Lake Avenue PO Box 670
Plymouth, IN 46563-0670
(574)936-3181

PORTLAND

JAY COUNTY HOSPITAL
500 W Votaw St
Portland, IN 47371-1399
(260)726-7131

PRINCETON

GIBSON GENERAL HOSPITAL
2808 Sherman Drive
Princeton, IN 47670
(812)385-3401

RENSSELAER

JASPER COUNTY HOSPITAL
1104 East Grace Street
Rensselaer, IN 47978-3296
(219)866-5141

RICHMOND

REID HOSPITAL AND HEALTH CARE SERVICES
1401 Chester Boulevard
Richmond, IN 47374-1908
(765)983-3000

RICHMOND STATE HOSPITAL
498 North West 18th Street
Richmond, IN 47374-2898
(765)966-0511

ROCHESTER

WOODLAWN HOSPITAL
1400 East 9th St
Rochester, IN 46975-8937
(574)224-1173

RUSHVILLE

RUSH MEMORIAL HOSPITAL
PO Box 608
Rushville, IN 46173-0608
(765)932-4111

SALEM

WASHINGTON COUNTY MEMORIAL HOSPITAL
911 N Shelby St PO Box 171
Salem, IN 47167-0171
(812)883-5881

SCOTTSBURG

SCOTT MEMORIAL HOSPITAL
1451 N Gardner St PO Box 456
Scottsburg, IN 47170-0456
(812)752-8500

SEYMOUR

MEMORIAL HOSPITAL
411 West Tipton
Seymour, IN 47274-2363
(812)522-2349

SHELBYVILLE

MAJOR HOSPITAL
150 West Washington Street
Shelbyville, IN 46176-1265
(317)392-3211

SOUTH BEND

MADISON HOSPITAL
403 E Madison St
South Bend, IN 46617-2395
(574)234-0061

MEMORIAL HOSPITAL OF SOUTH BEND
615 N Michigan St
South Bend, IN 46601-1087
(574)234-9041

OUR LADY OF PEACE HOSPITAL
801 East La Salle Avenue, 4ht Floor
South Bend, IN 46617-2814
(574)280-5822

RIVERSIDE HOSPITAL
533 N Niles Avenue
South Bend, IN 46617-1919
(574)283-1104

SAINT JOSEPHS REGIONAL MEDICAL CENTER
801 E Lasalle PO Box 1935
South Bend, IN 46634-1935
(260)237-7111

SULLIVAN

SULLIVAN COUNTY COMMUNITY HOSPITAL
2200 North Section Street PO Box 10
Sullivan, IN 47882-0010
(812)268-4311

TELL CITY

PERRY COUNTY MEMORIAL HOSPITAL
1701 Hospital Rd
Tell City, IN 47586-8497
(812)547-7011

TERRE HAUTE

HAMILTON CENTER
620 8th Avenue PO Box 4323
Terre Haute, IN 47804-0323
(812)231-8323

HEALTHSOUTH REHABILITATION HOSPITAL
501 St Anthony's Drive
Terre Haute, IN 47802-9135
(812)235-5656

TERRE HAUTE REGIONAL HOSPITAL
3901 S 7th St
Terre Haute, IN 47802-4299
(812)232-0021

UNION HOSPITAL
1606 North 7th Street
Terre Haute, IN 47804-2780
(812)238-7000

TIPTON

TIPTON COUNTY MEMORIAL HOSPITAL
1000 South Main Street
Tipton, IN 46072-9799
(765)675-8500

VALPARAISO

PORTER MEMORIAL HOSPITAL
814 Laporte Avenue
Valparaiso, IN 46383-5898
(219)465-4600

VINCENNES

GOOD SAMARITAN HOSPITAL
520 South 7th Street
Vincennes, IN 47591-1098
(812)882-5220

IOWA — Hospital Telephone Directory

WABASH
WABASH COUNTY HOSPITAL
710 Ne Street
Wabash, IN 46992-1924
(260)563-3131

WARSAW
KOSCIUSKO COMMUNITY HOSPITAL
2101 East Dubois Drive
Warsaw, IN 46580-3288
(574)267-3200

OTIS R BOWEN CENTER FOR HUMAN SERVICES
850 N Harrison St
Warsaw, IN 46580-3163
(574)267-7169

WASHINGTON
DAVIESS COUNTY HOSPITAL
1314 Grand Avenue PO Box 760
Washington, IN 47501-0760
(812)254-2760

WEST LAFAYETTE
WABASH VALLEY HOSPITAL MENTAL HEALTH
2900 North River Road
West Lafayette, IN 47906-3766
(765)463-2555

WILLIAMSPORT
SAINT VINCENT WILLIAMSPORT HOSPITAL
412 N Monroe St
Williamsport, IN 47993-1097
(765)762-4000

WINAMAC
PULASKI MEMORIAL HOSPITAL
PO Box 279
Winamac, IN 46996-0279
(574)946-2100

WINCHESTER
SAINT VINCENT RANDOLPH COUNTY HOSPITAL
473 Greenville Avenue
Winchester, IN 47394-2242
(765)584-9001

IOWA

ALBIA
MONROE COUNTY HOSPITAL
Avery Road Box G-310
Albia, IA 52531
(641)932-2134

ALGONA
KOSSUTH COUNTY HOSPITAL
1515 S Phillips St
Algona, IA 50511-3694
(515)295-2451

AMES
MARY GREELEY MEDICAL CENTER
1111 Duff Avenue
Ames, IA 50010-5792
(515)239-2011

ANAMOSA
JONES REGIONAL MEDICAL CENTER
104 Broadway Place
Anamosa, IA 52205-1132
(319)462-6131

ATLANTIC
CASS COUNTY MEMORIAL HOSPITAL
1501 East Tenth Street
Atlantic, IA 50022-1997
(712)243-3250

AUDUBON
AUDUBON COUNTY MEMORIAL HOSPITAL
515 Pacific
Audubon, IA 50025-1052
(712)563-2611

BELMOND
BELMOND COMMUNITY HOSPITAL
403 First Street Se
Belmond, IA 50421-1201
(641)444-3223

BLOOMFIELD
DAVIS COUNTY HOSPITAL
507-509 North Madison
Bloomfield, IA 52537-1271
(641)664-2145

BOONE
BOONE COUNTY HOSPITAL
1015 Union Street
Boone, IA 50036-4898
(515)432-3140

BRITT
HANCOCK COUNTY MEMORIAL HOSPITAL
532 1st St Nw
Britt, IA 50423-1227
(641)843-3801

CARROLL
SAINT ANTHONY REGIONAL HOSPITAL
South Clark Street
Carroll, IA 51401
(712)792-8231

CEDAR FALLS
SARTORI MEMORIAL HOSPITAL
515 College Street
Cedar Falls, IA 50613-2599
(319)268-3000

CEDAR RAPIDS
MERCY MEDICAL CENTER
701 10th St Se
Cedar Rapids, IA 52403-1292
(319)398-6011

SAINT LUKES HOSPITAL
1026 A Avenue Ne
Cedar Rapids, IA 52402-5098
(319)369-7211

CENTERVILLE
SAINT JOSEPHS MERCY HOSPITAL
1 St Josephs Drive
Centerville, IA 52544-9017
(641)437-4111

CHARITON
LUCAS COUNTY HEALTH CENTER
1200 N 7th St
Chariton, IA 50049-1258
(641)774-3000

CHARLES CITY
FLOYD COUNTY MEMORIAL HOSPITAL
11th And South Main Street
Charles City, IA 50616
(641)228-6830

CHEROKEE
MENTAL HEALTH INSTITUTE
1200 North Cedar Street
Cherokee, IA 51012
(712)225-2594

SIOUX VALLEY MEMORIAL HOSPITAL
300 Sioux Valley Drive
Cherokee, IA 51012-1205
(712)225-5101

CLARINDA
CLARINDA MENTAL HEALTH INSTITUTE
1800 North 16th Street
Clarinda, IA 51632-1165
(712)542-2161

CLARINDA REGIONAL HEALTH CENTER
17th And Wells PO Box 217
Clarinda, IA 51632-0217
(712)542-2176

CLARION
WRIGHT MEDICAL CENTER
1316 South Main
Clarion, IA 50525-2019
(515)532-2811

CLINTON
MERCY MEDICAL CENTER
1410 N 4th Street
Clinton, IA 52732-2999
(563)244-5555

MERCY MEDICAL CENTER - SOUTH
638 S Bluff Boulevard
Clinton, IA 52732-4742
(563)244-5555

CORNING
MERCY HOSPITAL
Rosary Drive Box 368
Corning, IA 50841-0368
(641)322-3121

CORYDON
WAYNE COUNTY HOSPITAL
417 S East St
Corydon, IA 50060-1860
(641)872-2260

COUNCIL BLUFFS
JENNIE EDMUNDSON HOSPITAL
933 East Pierce Street
Council Bluffs, IA 51503-4652
(712)396-6000

MERCY HOSPITAL
800 Mercy Drive Box 1-c
Council Bluffs, IA 51503-3192
(712)328-5000

Hospital Telephone Directory — IOWA

CRESCO
REGIONAL HEALTH SERVICES OF HOWARD COUNTY
235 Eighth Avenue West
Cresco, IA 52136-1062
(563)547-2101

CRESTON
GREATER COMMUNITY HOSPITAL
1700 West Townline Road
Creston, IA 50801-1054
(641)782-7091

DAVENPORT
GENESIS MEDICAL CENTER
1227 E Rusholme Street
Davenport, IA 52803-2498
(563)421-1000

GENESIS MEDICAL CENTER-WEST
1401 W Central Park Avenue
Davenport, IA 52804-1707
(563)421-1000

TRINITY MEDICAL CENTER
1111 West Kimberly Road
Davenport, IA 52806-5781
(563)445-4020

DE WITT
DEWITT COMMUNITY HOSPITAL
1118 West 11th Street
De Witt, IA 52742-1235
(563)659-4200

DECORAH
WINNESHIEK COUNTY MEMORIAL HOSPITAL
901 Montgomery Street
Decorah, IA 52101-2399
(563)382-2911

DENISON
CRAWFORD COUNTY MEMORIAL HOSPITAL
2020 First Avenue South
Denison, IA 51442-2299
(712)263-5021

DES MOINES
BROADLAWNS MEDICAL CENTER
1801 Hickman Road
Des Moines, IA 50314-1597
(515)282-2200

IOWA LUTHERAN HOSPITAL
700 East University
Des Moines, IA 50316-2392
(515)263-5612

IOWA METHODIST MEDICAL CENTER
1200 Pleasant St
Des Moines, IA 50309-1453
(515)241-6212

MERCY CAPITAL
603 East 12th Street
Des Moines, IA 50309-5595
(515)643-1000

MERCY FRANKLIN CENTER
1818 48th St
Des Moines, IA 50310-1993
(515)271-6000

MERCY HOSPITAL MEDICAL CENTER
400 University
Des Moines, IA 50314-2611
(515)247-3121

RAYMOND BLANK MEMORIAL HOSPITAL FOR CHILDREN
1200 Pleasant Street
Des Moines, IA 50309-1406
(515)241-6212

VA MEDICAL CENTER - DES MOINES
3600 30th St
Des Moines, IA 50310-5774
(515)699-5999

DUBUQUE
FINLEY HOSPITAL
350 North Grandview
Dubuque, IA 52001-6392
(563)582-1881

MERCY HEALTH CENTER
250 Mercy Drive
Dubuque, IA 52001-7398
(563)589-8000

DYERSVILLE
MERCY HEALTH CENTER-SAINT MARYS
1111 3rd St Sw
Dyersville, IA 52040-1725
(563)875-7101

ELKADER
CENTRAL COMMUNITY HOSPITAL
901 Davidson Street
Elkader, IA 52043-9015
(563)245-7000

EMMETSBURG
PALO ALTO COUNTY HOSPITAL
3201 First Street
Emmetsburg, IA 50536-2599
(712)852-5500

ESTHERVILLE
HOLY FAMILY HOSPITAL
326 North Eighth Street
Estherville, IA 51334-1925
(712)362-2631

FAIRFIELD
JEFFERSON COUNTY HOSPITAL
400 Highland
Fairfield, IA 52556-3713
(641)472-4111

FORT DODGE
TRINITY REGIONAL HOSPITAL
South Kenyon Road
Fort Dodge, IA 50501
(515)573-3101

FORT MADISON
FORT MADISON COMMUNITY HOSPITAL
Hifhway 61 West Box 174
Fort Madison, IA 52627-0174
(319)372-6530

GLENWOOD
GLENWOOD RESOURCE CENTER
711 S Vine St
Glenwood, IA 51534-1927
(712)527-4811

GREENFIELD
ADAIR COUNTY MEMORIAL HOSPITAL
609 Se Kent Rr #2 Box 100
Greenfield, IA 50849-9454
(641)743-2123

GRINNELL
GRINNELL REGIONAL MEDICAL CENTER
210 Fourth Avenue
Grinnell, IA 50112-1886
(641)236-7511

GRUNDY CENTER
GRUNDY COUNTY MEMORIAL HOSPITAL
201 East J Avenue PO Box 97
Grundy Center, IA 50638-0097
(319)824-5421

GUTHRIE CENTER
GUTHRIE COUNTY HOSPITAL
710 North 12th Street
Guthrie Center, IA 50115-1544
(641)747-2201

GUTTENBERG
GUTTENBERG MUNICIPAL HOSPITAL
Second And Main Streets
Guttenberg, IA 52052
(563)252-1121

HAMBURG
GRAPE COMMUNITY HOSPITAL
2959 Us Highway 275
Hamburg, IA 51640-5067
(712)382-1515

HAMPTON
FRANKLIN GENERAL HOSPITAL
1720 Central Avenue East
Hampton, IA 50441-1859
(641)456-5000

HARLAN
SHELBY COUNTY MYRTUE MEMORIAL HOSPITAL
1213 Garfield Avenue
Harlan, IA 51537-2071
(712)755-5161

HAWARDEN
HAWARDEN COMMUNITY HOSPITAL
1111 11th Street
Hawarden, IA 51023-1999
(712)551-3100

HUMBOLDT
HUMBOLDT COUNTY MEMORIAL HOSPITAL
1000 15th North Box 587
Humboldt, IA 50548-1008
(515)332-4200

IDA GROVE
HORN MEMORIAL HOSPITAL
East Second Street
Ida Grove, IA 51445
(712)364-3311

INDEPENDENCE
MENTAL HEALTH INSTITUTE
PO Box 111
Independence, IA 50644-0111
(319)334-2583

PEOPLES MEMORIAL HOSPITAL
1600 1st Street East
Independence, IA 50644-3155
(319)334-6071

IOWA
Hospital Telephone Directory

IOWA CITY

MERCY HOSPITAL
500 Market Street
Iowa City, IA 52245-2689
(319)339-0300

STATE PSYCHIATRIC HOSPITAL
200 Hawkins Drive
Iowa City, IA 52242-1009
(319)356-4658

UNIVERSITY OF IOWA HOSPITAL AND
CLINIC
200 Hawkins Drive
Iowa City, IA 52242-1009
(319)356-1616

VA MEDICAL CENTER - IOWA CITY
Highway 6 West
Iowa City, IA 52246
(319)338-0581

IOWA FALLS

ELLSWORTH MUNICIPAL HOSPITAL
110 Rocksylvania Avenue
Iowa Falls, IA 50126-2400
(641)648-4631

JEFFERSON

GREENE COUNTY MEDICAL CENTER
1000 W Lincoln Way
Jefferson, IA 50129-1645
(515)386-2114

KEOKUK

KEOKUK AREA HOSPITAL
1600 Morgan St
Keokuk, IA 52632-3497
(319)524-7150

KEOSAUQUA

VAN BUREN COUNTY MEMORIAL HOSPITAL
Highway 1 North Box 70
Keosauqua, IA 52565-0070
(319)293-3171

KNOXVILLE

KNOXVILLE AREA COMMUNITY HOSPITAL
1002 South Lincoln
Knoxville, IA 50138-3155
(641)842-2151

VA HEALTHCARE SYSTEM - KNOXVILLE
1515 W Pleasant St
Knoxville, IA 50138-3354
(641)842-3101

LAKE CITY

STEWART MEMORIAL COMMUNITY
HOSPITAL
1301 West Main
Lake City, IA 51449-1586
(712)464-3171

LE MARS

FLOYD VALLEY HOSPITAL
Highway Three East
Le Mars, IA 51031
(712)546-3398

LEON

DECATUR COUNTY HOSPITAL
1405 Nw Church Street
Leon, IA 50144-1299
(641)446-4871

MANCHESTER

REGIONAL MEDICAL CENTER OF
NORTHEAST IOWA
709 West Main Street
Manchester, IA 52057-1526
(563)927-3232

MANNING

MANNING REGIONAL HEALTHCARE
CENTER
410 Main Street
Manning, IA 51455-1033
(712)655-2072

MAQUOKETA

JACKSON COUNTY PUBLIC HOSPITAL
700 W Grove St
Maquoketa, IA 52060-2163
(563)652-2474

MARENGO

MARENGO MEMORIAL HOSPITAL
300 West May Street
Marengo, IA 52301-1261
(319)642-5543

MARSHALLTOWN

MARSHALLTOWN MEDICAL AND SURGICAL
CENTER
3 South Fourth Avenue
Marshalltown, IA 50158-2998
(641)754-5151

MASON CITY

MERCY HEALTH CENTER - NORTH IOWA
1000 Fourth Street Sw
Mason City, IA 50401-2800
(641)422-7000

MISSOURI VALLEY

COMMUNITY MEMORIAL HOSPITAL
631 North Eighth Street
Missouri Valley, IA 51555-1199
(712)642-2784

MOUNT AYR

RINGGOLD COUNTY HOSPITAL
211 Shellway Drive
Mount Ayr, IA 50854-1299
(641)464-3226

MOUNT PLEASANT

HENRY COUNTY HEALTH CENTER
Saunders Park
Mount Pleasant, IA 52641
(319)385-3141

MOUNT PLEASANT MENTAL HEALTH
INSTITUTE
1200 East Washington Street
Mount Pleasant, IA 52641-1898
(319)385-7231

MUSCATINE

UNITY HOSPITAL
1518 Mulberry Avenue
Muscatine, IA 52761-3499
(563)264-9100

NEVADA

STORY COUNTY HOSPITAL
630 Sixth Street
Nevada, IA 50201-2289
(515)382-2111

NEW HAMPTON

MERCY MEDICAL CENTER - NEW HAMPTON
308 North Maple Avenue
New Hampton, IA 50659-1142
(641)394-4121

NEWTON

SKIFF MEDICAL CENTER
204 North Fourth Avenue East
Newton, IA 50208-3100
(641)792-1273

OAKDALE

IOWA MEDICAL & CLASSIFICATION CENTER
Highway 965 Box A
Oakdale, IA 52319-0001
(319)626-2391

OELWEIN

MERCY HOSPITAL OF FRANCISCAN
SISTERS
201 Eighth Avenue Se
Oelwein, IA 50662-2453
(319)283-6000

ONAWA

BURGESS MEMORIAL HOSPITAL
1600 Diamond Avenue
Onawa, IA 51040-1598
(712)423-2311

ORANGE CITY

ORANGE CITY MUNICIPAL HOSPITAL
400 Central Avenue
Orange City, IA 51041-1302
(712)737-4984

OSAGE

MITCHELL COUNTY MEMORIAL HOSPITAL
616 North Eighth Street
Osage, IA 50461-1498
(641)732-6000

OSCEOLA

CLARKE COUNTY PUBLIC HOSPITAL
800 South Fillmore Street
Osceola, IA 50213-1619
(641)342-2184

OSKALOOSA

MAHASKA COUNTY HOSPITAL
1229 C Avenue East
Oskaloosa, IA 52577-4298
(641)672-3100

OTTUMWA

OTTUMWA REGIONAL HEALTH CENTER
1001 E Pennsylvania
Ottumwa, IA 52501-6427
(641)684-2300

PELLA

PELLA REGIONAL HEALTH CENTER
404 Jefferson St
Pella, IA 50219-1299
(641)628-3150

PERRY

DALLAS COUNTY HOSPITAL
610 Tenth Street
Perry, IA 50220-2249
(515)465-3547

POCAHONTAS

POCAHONTAS COMMUNITY HOSPITAL
606 Nw Seventh Street
Pocahontas, IA 50574-1099
(712)335-3501

PRIMGHAR

BAUM HARMON MEMORIAL HOSPITAL
PO Box 528
Primghar, IA 51245-0528
(712)757-2300

RED OAK

MONTGOMERY COUNTY MEMORIAL HOSPITAL
PO Box 498
Red Oak, IA 51566-0498
(712)623-7000

ROCK RAPIDS

MERRILL PIONEER COMMUNITY HOSPITAL
801 South Greene Street
Rock Rapids, IA 51246-1998
(712)472-2591

ROCK VALLEY

HEGG MEMORIAL HEALTH CENTER
1202 21st Avenue
Rock Valley, IA 51247-1497
(712)476-8000

SAC CITY

LORING HOSPITAL
211 Highland Avenue Box 217
Sac City, IA 50583-2416
(712)662-7105

SHELDON

NORTHWEST IOWA HEALTH CENTER
118 North 7th Avenue
Sheldon, IA 51201-1235
(712)324-5041

SHENANDOAH

SHENANDOAH MEMORIAL HOSPITAL
300 Pershing Avenue
Shenandoah, IA 51601-2397
(712)246-1230

SIBLEY

OSCEOLA COMMUNITY HOSPITAL
600 North Ninth Avenue North
Sibley, IA 51249-1012
(712)754-2574

SIGOURNEY

KEOKUK COUNTY HEALTH CENTER
Rr3 Box 286 1312 South Stuart St
Sigourney, IA 52591-1154
(641)622-2720

SIOUX CENTER

COMMUNITY HOSPITAL AND HEALTH CENTER
605 S Main St
Sioux Center, IA 51250-1347
(712)722-1271

SIOUX CITY

MERCY BEHAVIORAL HEALTH CENTER
4301 Sergeant Road
Sioux City, IA 51106-4710
(712)279-2446

MERCY HEALTH CENTER
801 5th St Box #316B
Sioux City, IA 51101-1326
(712)279-2010

SAINT LUKES REGIONAL MEDICAL CENTER
2720 Stone Park Boulevard
Sioux City, IA 51104-3795
(712)279-3500

SPENCER

SPENCER MUNICIPAL HOSPITAL
1200 First Avenue East
Spencer, IA 51301-4342
(712)264-6111

SPIRIT LAKE

LAKES REGIONAL HEALTHCARE
Highway 71 South Box AB
Spirit Lake, IA 51360-0159
(712)336-1230

STORM LAKE

BUENA VISTA COUNTY HOSPITAL
1525 West Fifth Street
Storm Lake, IA 50588-3027
(712)732-4030

SUMNER

COMMUNITY MEMORIAL HOSPITAL
909 W 1st St
Sumner, IA 50674-1203
(563)578-3275

VINTON

VIRGINIA GAY HOSPITAL
502 North Ninth Avenue
Vinton, IA 52349-2299
(319)472-6200

WASHINGTON

WASHINGTON COUNTY HOSPITAL
400 East Polk Street
Washington, IA 52353-1254
(319)653-5481

WATERLOO

ALLEN MEMORIAL HOSPITAL
1825 Logan Avenue
Waterloo, IA 50703-1999
(319)235-3941

COVENANT MEDICAL CENTER
3421 West Ninth Street
Waterloo, IA 50702-5499
(319)272-8000

KIMBALL - RIDGE CENTER
2101 Kimball Avenue
Waterloo, IA 50702-5048
(319)272-8000

WAUKON

VETERANS MEMORIAL HOSPITAL
40 First Street Se
Waukon, IA 52172-2099
(563)568-3411

WAVERLY

WAVERLY MUNICIPAL HOSPITAL
312 9th St Sw
Waverly, IA 50677-2999
(319)352-4120

WEBSTER CITY

HAMILTON COUNTY PUBLIC HOSPITAL
800 Ohio Street Box 430
Webster City, IA 50595-2824
(515)832-9400

WEST BURLINGTON

GREAT RIVER MEDICAL CENTER
1221 South Gear Ave
West Burlington, IA 52655-1681
(319)768-1000

WEST UNION

PALMER LUTHERAN HEALTH CENTER
112 Jefferson Street
West Union, IA 52175-1022
(563)422-3811

WINTERSET

MADISON COUNTY MEMORIAL HOSPITAL
300 Hutchings
Winterset, IA 50273-2104
(515)462-2373

WOODWARD

WOODWARD RESOURCE CENTER
1251 334th St
Woodward, IA 50276-7509
(515)438-2600

KANSAS

ABILENE

MEMORIAL HOSPITAL
511 Ne 10th St
Abilene, KS 67410-2100
(785)263-2100

ANTHONY

HOSPITAL DISTRICT #6 OF HARPER COUNTY
1101 E Spring St
Anthony, KS 67003-2122
(620)842-5111

ARKANSAS CITY

SOUTH CENTRAL KANSAS REGIONAL MEDICAL CENTER
216 W Birch St
Arkansas City, KS 67005-1563
(620)442-2500

ASHLAND

ASHLAND DISTRICT HOSPITAL
709 Oak St
Ashland, KS 67831
(620)635-2241

ATCHISON

ATCHISON HOSPITAL
1301 N 2nd St
Atchison, KS 66002-1202
(913)367-2131

ATTICA

ATTICA DISTRICT HOSPITAL
302 N Botkin St
Attica, KS 67009-9032
(620)254-7253

KANSAS — Hospital Telephone Directory

ATWOOD
RAWLINS COUNTY HOSPITAL AND HEALTH CENTER
707 Grant St Box 47
Atwood, KS 67730-1598
(785)626-3211

AUGUSTA
AUGUSTA MEDICAL COMPLEX
2101 Dearborn
Augusta, KS 67010-2193
(316)775-5421

BELLEVILLE
REPUBLIC COUNTY HOSPITAL
2420 G St
Belleville, KS 66935-2400
(785)527-2254

BELOIT
MITCHELL COUNTY HOSPITAL
400 W 8th St
Beloit, KS 67420-1605
(785)738-2266

BURLINGTON
COFFEY COUNTY HOSPITAL
801 N 4th St PO Box 189
Burlington, KS 66839-0189
(620)364-2121

CALDWELL
SUMNER COUNTY HOSPITAL DISTRICT #1
601 S Osage St
Caldwell, KS 67022-1698
(620)845-6492

CEDAR VALE
CEDAR VALE COMMUNITY HOSPITAL
501 Cedar St
Cedar Vale, KS 67024
(620)758-2266

CHANUTE
NEOSHO MEMORIAL HOSPITAL
629 S Plummer
Chanute, KS 66720-1928
(620)431-4000

CLAY CENTER
CLAY COUNTY HOSPITAL AND MEDICAL CENTER
617 Liberty St
Clay Center, KS 67432-1599
(785)632-2144

COFFEYVILLE
COFFEYVILLE REGIONAL MEDICAL CENTER
1400 W 4th St
Coffeyville, KS 67337-3306
(620)251-1200

COLBY
CITIZENS MEDICAL CENTER
100 E College Drive
Colby, KS 67701-3799
(785)462-7511

COLDWATER
COMANCHE COUNTY HOSPITAL
2nd And Frisco Streets
Coldwater, KS 67029
(620)582-2144

COLUMBUS
MAUDE NORTON MEMORIAL CITY HOSPITAL
220 N Pennsylvania Avenue
Columbus, KS 66725-1197
(620)429-2545

CONCORDIA
CLOUD COUNTY HEALTH CENTER
1100 Highland Drive
Concordia, KS 66901-3923
(785)243-1234

COUNCIL GROVE
MORRIS COUNTY HOSPITAL
600 N Washington St Kpob 275
Council Grove, KS 66846-1499
(620)767-6811

DIGHTON
LANE COUNTY HOSPITAL
243 S Second St PO Box 969
Dighton, KS 67839-0969
(620)397-5321

DODGE CITY
WESTERN PLAINS REGIONAL HOSPITAL
3001 Avenue A
Dodge City, KS 67801-6508
(620)225-8400

EL DORADO
SUSAN B ALLEN MEMORIAL HOSPITAL
720 W Central St
El Dorado, KS 67042-2144
(316)321-3300

ELKHART
MORTON COUNTY HOSPITAL
445 N Hilltop
Elkhart, KS 67950
(620)697-2141

ELLINWOOD
ELLINWOOD DISTRICT HOSPITAL
605 N Main St
Ellinwood, KS 67526-1440
(620)564-2548

ELLSWORTH
ELLSWORTH COUNTY HOSPITAL
1604 Aylward Street PO Box 87
Ellsworth, KS 67439-0087
(785)472-3111

SAINT FRANCIS AT ELLSWORTH
PO Box 127
Ellsworth, KS 67439-0127
(785)472-4453

EMPORIA
EMPORIA SURGICAL HOSPITAL
PO Box 1509
Emporia, KS 66801-1509
(620)342-8822

NEWMAN MEMORIAL COUNTY HOSPITAL
1201 W 12th Avenue
Emporia, KS 66801-2597
(620)343-6800

EUREKA
GREENWOOD COUNTY HOSPITAL
100 W 16th St
Eureka, KS 67045-1096
(620)583-7451

FORT RILEY
IRWIN ARMY COMMUNITY HOSPITAL
600 Caisson Hill Road
Fort Riley, KS 66442-7037
(785)239-7555

FORT SCOTT
MERCY HOSPITAL
821 Burke St
Fort Scott, KS 66701-2409
(620)223-2200

FREDONIA
FREDONIA REGIONAL HOSPITAL
1527 Madison PO Box 579
Fredonia, KS 66736-0579
(620)378-2121

GARDEN CITY
SAINT CATHERINE HOSPITAL
401 East Spruce Street
Garden City, KS 67846-5679
(620)272-2222

GARDNER
MEADOWBROOK HOSPITAL
427 W Main
Gardner, KS 66030-1197
(913)856-8747

GARNETT
ANDERSON COUNTY HOSPITAL
421 S Maple
Garnett, KS 66032-1334
(785)448-3131

GIRARD
HOSPITAL DISTRICT 1 CRAWFORD COUNTY
302 N Hospital Drive
Girard, KS 66743-2000
(620)724-8291

GOODLAND
GOODLAND REGIONAL MEDICAL CENTER
220 W Second
Goodland, KS 67735-1602
(785)899-3625

GREAT BEND
CENTRAL KANSAS MEDICAL CENTER
3515 Broadway St
Great Bend, KS 67530-3691
(620)792-2511

SURGICAL AND DIAGNOSTIC CENTER OF GREAT BEND
514 Cleveland Street
Great Bend, KS 67530-3562
(620)792-8833

Hospital Telephone Directory   **KANSAS**

GREENSBURG
GREAT PLAINS OF KIOWA COUNTY
501 S Walnut St
Greensburg, KS 67054-1951
(620)723-3341

HANOVER
HANOVER HOSPITAL
205 S Hanover
Hanover, KS 66945-8924
(785)337-2214

HARPER
HARPER HOSPITAL
12th And Maple
Harper, KS 67058
(620)896-7324

HAYS
HAYS MEDICAL CENTER
2220 Canterbury Road
Hays, KS 67601-2370
(785)623-5000

HERINGTON
HERINGTON MUNICIPAL HOSPITAL
100 E Helen St
Herington, KS 67449-1697
(785)258-2207

HIAWATHA
HIAWATHA COMMUNITY HOSPITAL
300 Utah St
Hiawatha, KS 66434-2399
(785)742-2131

HILL CITY
GRAHAM COUNTY HOSPITAL
304 W Prout St
Hill City, KS 67642-1435
(785)421-2121

HILLSBORO
HILLSBORO COMMUNITY MEDICAL CENTER
701 S Main St
Hillsboro, KS 67063-1500
(620)947-3114

HOISINGTON
CLARA BARTON HOSPITAL
250 W 9th St
Hoisington, KS 67544-1799
(620)653-2114

HOLTON
HOLTON CITY HOSPITAL
510 Kansas Avenue
Holton, KS 66436-1545
(785)364-2116

HORTON
NORTHEAST KANSAS CENTER FOR HEALTH
240 W 18th St
Horton, KS 66439-1245
(785)486-2642

HOXIE
SHERIDAN COUNTY HEALTH COMPLEX
826 18th St PO Box 167
Hoxie, KS 67740-0167
(785)675-3281

HUGOTON
STEVENS COUNTY HOSPITAL
PO Box 10
Hugoton, KS 67951-0010
(620)544-8511

HUTCHINSON
HUTCHINSON HOSPITAL
1701 E 23rd St
Hutchinson, KS 67502-1191
(620)665-2000

INDEPENDENCE
MERCY HOSPITAL INDEPENDENCE
800 W Myrtle St PO Box 388
Independence, KS 67301-0388
(620)331-2200

IOLA
ALLEN COUNTY HOSPITAL
101 S 1st St
Iola, KS 66749-3505
(620)365-1000

JETMORE
HODGEMAN COUNTY HEALTH CENTER
PO Box 310
Jetmore, KS 67854-0310
(620)357-8361

JOHNSON
STANTON COUNTY HOSPITAL
404 N Chestnut
Johnson, KS 67855
(620)492-6250

JUNCTION CITY
GEARY COMMUNITY HOSPITAL
1102 St Marys Road
Junction City, KS 66441-4196
(785)238-4131

KANSAS CITY
PROVIDENCE MEDICAL CENTER
8929 Parallel Parkway
Kansas City, KS 66112-3607
(913)281-8400

RAINBOW MENTAL HEALTH FACILITY
Pox 3208
Kansas City, KS 66103
(913)384-1880

UNIVERSITY OF KANSAS MEDICAL CENTER
3901 Rainbow Boulevard
Kansas City, KS 66160-0003
(913)588-5000

KINGMAN
KINGMAN COMMUNITY HOSPITAL
750 Avenue D West
Kingman, KS 67068
(620)532-3147

KINSLEY
EDWARDS COUNTY HOSPITAL
620 W 8th St PO Box 99
Kinsley, KS 67547-0099
(620)659-3621

KIOWA
KIOWA DISTRICT HOSPITAL
810 Drumm St
Kiowa, KS 67070-1699
(620)825-4131

LA CROSSE
RUSH COUNTY HEALTHCARE CENTER
700 W 8th St
La Crosse, KS 67548
(785)222-2545

LAKIN
KEARNY COUNTY HOSPITAL
500 Thorpe St
Lakin, KS 67860
(620)355-7111

LARNED
CENTRAL KANSAS MEDICAL CENTER - SAINT JOSEPH CAMPUS
923 Carroll Avenue
Larned, KS 67550-2429
(620)285-3161

LARNED STATE HOSPITAL
Route #3 Box 89
Larned, KS 67550-9365
(620)285-2131

LAWRENCE
LAWRENCE MEMORIAL HOSPITAL
325 Maine St
Lawrence, KS 66044-1360
(785)749-6100

LEAVENWORTH
CUSHING MEMORIAL HOSPITAL
711 Marshall St
Leavenworth, KS 66048-3235
(913)684-1100

SAINT JOHN HOSPITAL
3500 S 4th St
Leavenworth, KS 66048-5044
(913)680-6000

VA MEDICAL CENTER - DWIGHT D. EISENHOWER
4101 S 4th St
Leavenworth, KS 66048-5014
(913)682-2000

LEAWOOD
DOCTORS SPECIALTY HOSPITAL
4901 College Boulevard
Leawood, KS 66211-1602
(913)529-1801

KANSAS CITY ORTHOPEDIC INSTITUTE
3651 College Blvd
Leawood, KS 66211-1904
(913)338-4100

LEOTI
WICHITA COUNTY HOSPITAL
211 E Earl
Leoti, KS 67861
(620)375-2233

WICHITA COUNTY HOSPITAL LONG TERM CARE
PO Box 968
Leoti, KS 67861-0968
(620)375-2233

LIBERAL
SOUTHWEST MEDICAL CENTER
315 W 15th St PO Box 1340
Liberal, KS 67905-1340
(580)624-1651

KANSAS — Hospital Telephone Directory

LINCOLN
LINCOLN COUNTY HOSPITAL
PO Box 406
Lincoln, KS 67455-0406
(785)524-4403

LINDSBORG
LINDSBORG COMMUNITY HOSPITAL
605 W Lincoln St
Lindsborg, KS 67456-2399
(785)227-3308

LYONS
HOSPITAL DISTRICT #1 OF RICE COUNTY
619 S Clark St
Lyons, KS 67554-3003
(620)257-5173

MANHATTAN
MANHATTAN SURGICAL HOSPITAL
1829 College Avenue
Manhattan, KS 66502-3381
(785)776-5100

MERCY HEALTH CENTER
1823 College Avenue
Manhattan, KS 66502-3381
(785)776-3322

MERCY MEMORIAL HOSPITAL
1105 Sunset Avenue PO Box 1289
Manhattan, KS 66505-1289
(785)776-3300

MANKATO
JEWELL COUNTY HOSPITAL
PO Box 327
Mankato, KS 66956-0327
(785)378-3137

MARION
SAINT LUKE HOSPITAL
1014 E Melvin
Marion, KS 66861-1299
(620)382-2179

MARYSVILLE
COMMUNITY MEMORIAL HEALTH CARE
708 N 18th St
Marysville, KS 66508-1399
(785)562-2311

MCPHERSON
MEMORIAL HOSPITAL
1000 Hospital Drive
McPherson, KS 67460-2321
(620)241-2250

MEADE
MEADE DISTRICT HOSPITAL
510 E Carthage
Meade, KS 67864
(620)873-2141

MEDICINE LODGE
MEDICINE LODGE MEMORIAL HOSPITAL
710 N Walnut St
Medicine Lodge, KS 67104-1019
(620)886-3771

MINNEAPOLIS
OTTAWA COUNTY HOSPITAL
215 E 8th
Minneapolis, KS 67467-1999
(785)392-2122

MINNEOLA
MINNEOLA DISTRICT HOSPITAL
212 Main St
Minneola, KS 67865-8511
(620)885-4264

MOUNDRIDGE
MERCY HOSPITAL
218 E Pack St PO Box 180
Moundridge, KS 67107-0180
(620)345-6391

NEODESHA
WILSON COUNTY HOSPITAL
PO Box 360
Neodesha, KS 66757-0360
(620)325-2611

NESS CITY
NESS COUNTY HOSPITAL
312 E Custer St
Ness City, KS 67560-1654
(785)798-2291

NEWTON
NEWTON MEDICAL CENTER
600 Medical Center Drive PO Box 308
Newton, KS 67114-0308
(316)283-2700

PRAIRIE VIEW MENTAL HEALTH CENTER
1901 East First St PO Box 467
Newton, KS 67114-0467
(316)283-2400

NORTON
NORTON COUNTY HOSPITAL
PO Box 250
Norton, KS 67654-0250
(785)877-3351

OAKLEY
LOGAN COUNTY HOSPITAL
211 Cherry St
Oakley, KS 67748-1201
(785)672-3211

OBERLIN
DECATUR COUNTY HOSPITAL
810 W Columbia
Oberlin, KS 67749-2450
(785)475-2208

OLATHE
OLATHE MEDICAL CENTER
20333 W 151st St
Olathe, KS 66061-7211
(913)791-4200

ONAGA
COMMUNITY HOSPITAL ONAGA
120 W 8th St
Onaga, KS 66521-9574
(785)889-4272

OSAWATOMIE
OSAWATOMIE STATE HOSPITAL PSYCHIATRIC
PO Box 500
Osawatomie, KS 66064-0500
(913)755-7000

OSBORNE
OSBORNE COUNTY MEMORIAL HOSPITAL
PO Box 70
Osborne, KS 67473-0070
(785)346-2121

OSWEGO
OSWEGO MEDICAL CENTER
800 Barker Drive
Oswego, KS 67356-9033
(620)795-2921

OTTAWA
RANSOM MEMORIAL HOSPITAL
1301 S Main St
Ottawa, KS 66067-3598
(785)229-8200

OVERLAND PARK
CHILDRENS MERCY HOSPITAL SOUTH
5808 W 110th Street
Overland Park, KS 66211-2504
(913)696-8000

MENORAH MEDICAL CENTER
5721 W 119th St
Overland Park, KS 66209-3753
(913)498-6000

MID AMERICA REHABILITATION HOSPITAL
5701 W 110th St
Overland Park, KS 66211-2503
(913)491-2400

OVERLAND PARK REGIONAL MEDICAL CENTER
10500 Quivira Road
Overland Park, KS 66215-2373
(913)541-5000

SAINT LUKE'S SOUTH HOSPITAL
12300 Metcalf
Overland Park, KS 66213-1324
(913)317-7000

SPECIALTY HOSPITAL OF MID AMERICA
6509 W 103rd St
Overland Park, KS 66212-1728
(913)649-3701

PAOLA
MIAMI COUNTY MEDICAL CENTER
2100 Baptiste Drive
Paola, KS 66071-1314
(913)294-2327

PARSONS
LABETTE COUNTY MEDICAL CENTER
South Highway 59 PO Box 956
Parsons, KS 67357-0956
(620)421-4880

PARSONS STATE HOSPITAL AND TRAINING
PO Box 738
Parsons, KS 67357-0738
(620)421-6550

PHILLIPSBURG
PHILLIPS COUNTY HOSPITAL
1150 State St
Phillipsburg, KS 67661-1743
(785)543-5226

PITTSBURG
MOUNT CARMEL MEDICAL CENTER
Centennial And Rouse Streets
Pittsburg, KS 66762
(620)231-6100

Hospital Telephone Directory — KANSAS

PLAINVILLE
PLAINVILLE RURAL HOSPITAL
304 S Colorado St
Plainville, KS 67663-2505
(785)434-4553

PRATT
PRATT REGIONAL MEDICAL CENTER
200 Commodore St
Pratt, KS 67124-3099
(620)672-7451

QUINTER
GOVE COUNTY MEDICAL CENTER
5th And Garfield
Quinter, KS 67752
(785)754-3341

RANSOM
GRISELL MEMORIAL HOSPITAL DISTRICT #1
210 S Vermont Ave
Ransom, KS 67572-9525
(785)731-2231

RUSSELL
RUSSELL REGIONAL HOSPITAL
200 S Main
Russell, KS 67665-2937
(785)483-3131

SABETHA
SABETHA COMMUNITY HOSPITAL
14th And Oregon
Sabetha, KS 66534
(785)284-2121

SAINT FRANCIS
CHEYENNE COUNTY HOSPITAL
210 W First St PO Box 547
Saint Francis, KS 67756-0547
(785)332-2104

SALINA
SAINT FRANCIS AT SALINA
5097 W Cloud St
Salina, KS 67401-9743
(785)825-0563

SALINA REGIONAL HEALTH CARE CENTER - PENN CAMPUS
139 North Penn St
Salina, KS 67401-3044
(785)452-7000

SALINA REGIONAL MEDICAL CENTER
400 S Santa Fe
Salina, KS 67401-4198
(785)452-7000

SALINA SURGICAL HOSPITAL
401 South Santa Fe
Salina, KS 67401-4143
(785)827-0610

SATANTA
SATANTA DISTRICT HOSPITAL
Cheyenne And Apache Streets PO Box 159
Satanta, KS 67870-0159
(620)649-2761

SCOTT CITY
SCOTT COUNTY HOSPITAL
310 East Third
Scott City, KS 67871-1203
(620)872-5811

SEDAN
SEDAN CITY HOSPITAL
300 W North St
Sedan, KS 67361-1051
(620)725-3115

SENECA
NEMAHA VALLEY COMMUNITY HOSPITAL
1600 Community Drive
Seneca, KS 66538-9758
(785)336-6181

SHAWNEE MISSION
SELECT SPECIALTY HOSPITAL - KANSAS CITY
10550 Quivira Rd # 450
Shawnee Mission, KS 66215-2306
(913)279-5100

SHAWNEE MISSION MEDICAL CENTER
9100 W 74th St
Shawnee Mission, KS 66204-4019
(913)676-2000

SMITH CENTER
SMITH COUNTY MEMORIAL HOSPITAL
614 S Main St
Smith Center, KS 66967-3000
(785)282-6845

STAFFORD
STAFFORD DISTRICT HOSPITAL #4
602 S Buckeye
Stafford, KS 67578-2002
(620)234-5221

SYRACUSE
HAMILTON COUNTY HOSPITAL
PO Box 948
Syracuse, KS 67878-0948
(620)384-7461

TOPEKA
KANSAS NEUROLOGICAL INSTITUTE
3107 West 21st St
Topeka, KS 66604-3298
(785)296-5301

KANSAS REHABILITATION HOSPITAL
1504 SW 8th Avenue
Topeka, KS 66606-2714
(785)235-6600

MENNINGER CF MEMORIAL HOSPITAL
5800 Sw 6th Avenue Box 829
Topeka, KS 66606-9604
(785)350-5000

SAINT FRANCIS HOSPITAL AND MEDICAL CENTER
1700 W 7th St
Topeka, KS 66606-1690
(785)295-8000

SELECT SPECIALTY HOSPITAL - TOPEKA
1700 W 7th Street, Suite 840
Topeka, KS 66606-1674
(785)295-5551

STORMONT VAIL HEALTH CARE
1500 Sw 10th St
Topeka, KS 66604-1353
(785)354-6000

VA MEDICAL CENTER - COLMERY O'NEIL
2200 Gage Boulevard
Topeka, KS 66622-0001
(785)350-3111

TRIBUNE
GREAT PLAINS OF GREELEY COUNTY
506 Third
Tribune, KS 67879
(620)376-4221

ULYSSES
BOB WILSON MEMORIAL GRANT COUNTY HOSPITAL
415 N Main St
Ulysses, KS 67880-2196
(620)356-1266

WAKEENEY
TREGO COUNTY-LEMKE MEMORIAL HOSPITAL
320 N 13th St
Wakeeney, KS 67672-2099
(785)743-2182

WAMEGO
WAMEGO CITY HOSPITAL
711 Genn Drive
Wamego, KS 66547-1199
(785)456-2295

WASHINGTON
WASHINGTON COUNTY HOSPITAL
304 E 3rd St
Washington, KS 66968-2098
(785)325-2211

WELLINGTON
SUMNER REGIONAL MEDICAL CENTER
1323 North A Street
Wellington, KS 67152-4319
(620)326-7451

WICHITA
GALICHIA HEART HOSPITAL
2610 North Woodlawn
Wichita, KS 67220-2729
(316)858-2610

KANSAS HEART HOSPITAL
3601 North Webb Road
Wichita, KS 67226-8129
(316)630-5000

KANSAS SURGERY AND RECOVERY CENTER LP
2770 N Webb Road
Wichita, KS 67226-8112
(316)634-0090

SELECT SPECIALTY HOSPITAL - WICHITA
550 North Hillside Street
Wichita, KS 67214-4910
(316)688-3900

VA MEDICAL CENTER - WICHITA
5500 E Kellogg
Wichita, KS 67218-1607
(316)685-2221

VIA CHRISTI REGION MEDICAL-SAINT JOSEPH
3600 E Harry St
Wichita, KS 67218-3784
(316)685-1111

VIA CHRISTI REGIONAL MEDICAL-SAINT FRANCIS
929 N St Francis St
Wichita, KS 67214-3882
(316)268-7000

VIA CHRISTI REHABILITATION CENTER
1151 North Rock Road
Wichita, KS 67206-1262
(316)634-3400

KENTUCKY — Hospital Telephone Directory

VIA CHRISTI RIVERSIDE MEDICAL CENTER
2622 W Central St
Wichita, KS 67203-4999
(316)946-5000

WESLEY MEDICAL CENTER
550 N Hillside St
Wichita, KS 67214-4976
(316)688-2000

WESLEY REHABILITATION HOSPITAL
8338 W 13th St
Wichita, KS 67212-2984
(316)729-9999

WICHITA SPECIALTY HOSPITAL
8080 E Pawnee
Wichita, KS 67207-5475
(316)682-0004

WINCHESTER

JEFFERSON COUNTY MEMORIAL HOSPITAL
408 Delaware Street
Winchester, KS 66097-4003
(913)774-4340

WINFIELD

WILLIAM NEWTON MEMORIAL HOSPITAL
1300 E Fifth Avenue
Winfield, KS 67156-2495
(620)221-2300

KENTUCKY

ALBANY

CLINTON COUNTY HOSPITAL
723 Burkesville Road
Albany, KY 42602-1654
(606)387-6421

ASHLAND

KINGS DAUGHTERS MEDICAL CENTER
2201 Lexington Avenue
Ashland, KY 41101-2874
(606)327-4000

OUR LADY OF BELLEFONTE HOSPITAL
St Christopher Drive
Ashland, KY 41101
(606)833-3333

BARBOURVILLE

KNOX COUNTY HOSPITAL
321 E High St
Barbourville, KY 40906-1317
(606)546-4175

BARDSTOWN

FLAGET MEMORIAL HOSPITAL
201 Cathedral Manor
Bardstown, KY 40004-1299
(502)348-3923

BENTON

MARSHALL COUNTY HOSPITAL
503 George Mcclain Drive
Benton, KY 42025-1399
(270)527-4800

BEREA

BEREA HOSPITAL
305 Estill St
Berea, KY 40403-1909
(859)986-3151

BOWLING GREEN

GREENVIEW REGIONAL HOSPITAL
1801 Ashley Circle
Bowling Green, KY 42104-3384
(270)793-1000

MEDICAL CENTER
250 Park St Box 90010
Bowling Green, KY 42101-1795
(270)745-1000

MEDIPLEX REHAB BOWLING GREEN
1300 Campbell Lane
Bowling Green, KY 42104-4162
(270)782-6900

RIVENDELL BEHAVIORAL HEALTH SERVICES
1035 Porter Pike
Bowling Green, KY 42103-9581
(270)843-1199

BURKESVILLE

CUMBERLAND COUNTY HOSPITAL
PO Box 280
Burkesville, KY 42717-0280
(270)864-2511

CADIZ

TRIGG COUNTY HOSPITAL
254 Main St
Cadiz, KY 42211-9153
(270)522-3215

CAMPBELLSVILLE

TAYLOR COUNTY HOSPITAL
1700 Old Lebanon Road
Campbellsville, KY 42718-9600
(270)465-3561

CARLISLE

NICHOLAS COUNTY HOSPITAL
2323 Concrete Road
Carlisle, KY 40311-9721
(859)289-7181

CARROLLTON

CARROLL COUNTY MEMORIAL HOSPITAL
309 Eleventh St
Carrollton, KY 41008-1400
(502)732-4321

COLUMBIA

WESTLAKE REGIONAL HOSPITAL
100 Westlake Drive PO Box 468
Columbia, KY 42728-0468
(270)384-4753

CORBIN

BAPTIST REGIONAL MEDICAL CENTER
1 Trillium Way
Corbin, KY 40701-8420
(606)528-1212

COVINGTON

NORTHKEY COMMUNITY CARE - CHILDREN'S INTENSIVE SERVICES
502 Farrell Drive
Covington, KY 41011-3717
(859)578-3200

SAINT ELIZABETH MEDICAL CENTER - NORTH
401 East 20th Street
Covington, KY 41014-1585
(859)292-4000

CYNTHIANA

HARRISON MEMORIAL HOSPITAL
1210 Ky Highway 36 E
Cynthiana, KY 41031-7490
(859)234-2300

DANVILLE

EPHRAIM MCDOWELL REGIONAL MEDICAL CENTER
217 S Third St
Danville, KY 40422-1823
(859)239-1000

EDDYVILLE

KENTUCKY STATE PENITENTIARY MEDICAL CLINIC
Box 128
Eddyville, KY 42038-0128
(270)388-2211

EDGEWOOD

HEALTHSOUTH NORTHERN KENTUCKY REHABILITATION HOSPITAL
201 Medical Village Drive
Edgewood, KY 41017-3407
(859)341-2044

SAINT ELIZABETH MEDICAL CENTER-SOUTH
1 Medical Village Drive
Edgewood, KY 41017-3403
(859)344-2000

ELIZABETHTOWN

HARDIN MEMORIAL HOSPITAL
913 North Dixie Avenue
Elizabethtown, KY 42701-2599
(270)737-1212

HEALTHSOUTH REHABILITATION HOSPITAL OF CENTRAL KENTUCKY
134 Heartland Drive
Elizabethtown, KY 42701-2778
(270)769-3100

FLEMINGSBURG

FLEMING COUNTY HOSPITAL
920 Elizaville Road
Flemingsburg, KY 41041-9209
(606)849-5000

FLORENCE

GATEWAY REHABILITATION HOSPITAL
5940 Merchants Street
Florence, KY 41042-1158
(859)426-2400

SAINT LUKE HOSPITAL WEST
7380 Turfway Road
Florence, KY 41042-1337
(859)962-5200

FORT CAMPBELL

COLONEL FLORENCE A BLANCHFIELD ARMY COMMUNITY HOSPITAL
650 Joel Drive
Fort Campbell, KY 42223-5318
(270)798-8040

FORT KNOX

IRELAND ARMY COMMUNITY HOSPITAL
851 Ireland Loop
Fort Knox, KY 40121-2713
(502)624-9020

Hospital Telephone Directory — KENTUCKY

FORT THOMAS
SAINT LUKE HOSPITAL EAST
85 N Grand Avenue
Fort Thomas, KY 41075-1796
(859)572-3100

FRANKFORT
FRANKFORT REGIONAL MEDICAL CENTER
299 Kings Daughters Drive
Frankfort, KY 40601-4186
(502)875-5240

FRANKLIN
MEDICAL CENTER AT FRANKLIN
1100 Brookhaven Road
Franklin, KY 42134-2746
(270)586-3253

FULTON
PARKWAY REGIONAL HOSPITAL
2000 Holiday Lane
Fulton, KY 42041-8401
(270)472-2522

GEORGETOWN
GEORGETOWN COMMUNITY HOSPITAL
1140 Lexington Road
Georgetown, KY 40324-9330
(502)868-1100

GLASGOW
T J SAMSON COMMUNITY HOSPITAL
1301 N Race St
Glasgow, KY 42141-3483
(270)651-4444

GREENSBURG
JANE TODD CRAWFORD MEMORIAL HOSPITAL
202 Milby St
Greensburg, KY 42743-1100
(270)932-4211

GREENVILLE
MUHLENBERG COMMUNITY HOSPITAL
440 Hopkinsville St Box 387
Greenville, KY 42345-1172
(270)338-8000

HARDINSBURG
BRECKINRIDGE MEMORIAL HOSPITAL
1011 Old Highway 60
Hardinsburg, KY 40143-2597
(270)756-7000

HARLAN
HARLAN ARH HOSPITAL
81 Ball Park Road
Harlan, KY 40831-1792
(606)573-8201

HARRODSBURG
JAMES B HAGGIN MEMORIAL HOSPITAL
464 Linden Avenue
Harrodsburg, KY 40330-1862
(859)734-5441

HARTFORD
OHIO COUNTY HOSPITAL
1211 Main St
Hartford, KY 42347-1619
(270)298-7411

HAZARD
HAZARD ARH REGIONAL MEDICAL CENTER
100 Medical Center Drive
Hazard, KY 41701-9429
(606)439-6600

HENDERSON
METHODIST HOSPITAL
1305 N Elm St
Henderson, KY 42420-2775
(270)827-7700

HOPKINSVILLE
FHC CUMBERLAND HALL
210 West 17th Street
Hopkinsville, KY 42240-1999
(270)886-1919

JENNIE STUART MEDICAL CENTER
PO Box 2400
Hopkinsville, KY 42241-2400
(270)887-0100

WESTERN STATE HOSPITAL
2400 Russellville Road
Hopkinsville, KY 42240-8942
(270)886-4431

HORSE CAVE
CAVERNA MEMORIAL HOSPITAL
1501 S Dixie St PO Box 120
Horse Cave, KY 42749-0120
(270)786-2191

HYDEN
MARY BRECKINRIDGE HOSPITAL
Hospital Drive
Hyden, KY 41749
(606)672-2901

IRVINE
MARCUM AND WALLACE MEMORIAL HOSPITAL
60 Mercy Ct
Irvine, KY 40336-1331
(606)723-2115

JACKSON
KENTUCKY RIVER MEDICAL CENTER
540 Jett Drive
Jackson, KY 41339-9622
(606)666-6305

JENKINS
JENKINS COMMUNITY HOSPITAL
Main St
Jenkins, KY 41537
(606)832-2171

LA GRANGE
KENTUCKY CORRECTIONAL PSYCH CENTER
PO Box 67
La Grange, KY 40031-0067
(502)222-7161

TRI COUNTY BAPTIST HOSPITAL
1025 New Moody Lane
La Grange, KY 40031-9154
(502)222-5388

LANCASTER
GARRARD COUNTY MEMORIAL HOSPITAL
308 W Maple Avenue
Lancaster, KY 40444-1098
(859)792-6844

LEBANON
NORTON SPRING VIEW HOSPITAL
320 Loretto Road
Lebanon, KY 40033-1323
(270)692-3161

LEITCHFIELD
TWINS LAKES REGIONAL MEDICAL CENTER
910 Wallace Avenue
Leitchfield, KY 42754-1499
(270)259-9400

LEXINGTON
CARDINAL HILL REHABILITATION HOSPITAL
2050 Versailles Road
Lexington, KY 40504-1499
(859)254-5701

CENTRAL BAPTIST HOSPITAL
1740 Nicholasville Road
Lexington, KY 40503-1499
(859)260-6100

CONTINUING CARE HOSPITAL AT SAINT JOSEPH EAST
150 North Eagle Creek Drive, Fourth Floor
Lexington, KY 40509-1805
(859)268-4800

EASTERN STATE HOSPITAL
627 W 4th St
Lexington, KY 40508-1294
(859)246-7000

FEDERAL MEDICAL CENTER - LEXINGTON
3301 Leestown Road
Lexington, KY 40511-8799
(859)255-6812

RIDGE BEHAVIORAL HEALTH SYSTEM
3050 Rio Dosa Drive
Lexington, KY 40509-1540
(859)269-2325

SAINT JOSEPH EAST
150 N Eagle Creek Drive
Lexington, KY 40509-1805
(859)268-4800

SAINT JOSEPH HOSPITAL
One St Joseph Drive
Lexington, KY 40504-3754
(859)278-3436

SAMARITAN HOSPITAL LEXINGTON
310 S Limestone St
Lexington, KY 40508-3059
(859)226-7000

SELECT SPECIALTY HOSPITAL - LEXINGTON
310 South Limestone Street
Lexington, KY 40508-3008
(859)226-7321

SHRINERS HOSPITAL
1900 Richmond Road
Lexington, KY 40502-1298
(859)266-2101

UNIVERSITY OF KENTUCKY - CHANDLER HOSPITAL
800 Rose St
Lexington, KY 40536-0001
(859)323-5000

VA MEDICAL CENTER - LEXINGTON
Leestown Road
Lexington, KY 40511
(859)233-4511

LIBERTY
CASEY COUNTY HOSPITAL
Wolford Street Route 2 Box 569a
Liberty, KY 42539-9802
(606)787-6275

KENTUCKY
Hospital Telephone Directory

LONDON

MARYMOUNT MEDICAL CENTER
310 East Ninth St
London, KY 40741-1299
(606)878-6520

LOUISA

THREE RIVERS MEDICAL CENTER
Highway 644 PO Box 769
Louisa, KY 41230-0769
(606)638-9451

LOUISVILLE

BAPTIST HOSPITAL EAST
4000 Kresge Way
Louisville, KY 40207-4676
(502)897-8100

CARITAS MEDICAL CENTER
1850 Bluegrass Avenue
Louisville, KY 40215-1161
(502)361-6000

CENTRAL STATE HOSPITAL
10510 Lagrange Road
Louisville, KY 40223-1228
(502)253-7000

FRAZIER REHAB CENTER
220 Abraham Flexner Way
Louisville, KY 40202-1887
(502)582-7400

GATEWAY REHABILITATION HOSPITAL
315 East Broadway
Louisville, KY 40202-1703
(502)315-8300

JEWISH HOSPITAL
200 Abraham Flexner Way
Louisville, KY 40202-1818
(502)587-4011

KINDRED HOSPITAL LOUISVILLE
1313 St Anthony Place
Louisville, KY 40204-1765
(502)587-7001

NORTON AUDUBON HOSPITAL
One Audubon Plaza Drive
Louisville, KY 40217-1397
(502)636-7111

NORTON HEALTH CARE PAVILION
315 E Broadway
Louisville, KY 40202-1703
(502)629-2000

NORTON HOSPITAL
200 East Chestnut Street
Louisville, KY 40202-1800
(502)629-8000

NORTON SOUTHWEST HOSPITAL
9820 Third St Road
Louisville, KY 40272-2802
(502)933-8100

NORTON SUBURBAN HOSPITAL
4001 Dutchmans Lane
Louisville, KY 40207-4714
(502)893-1000

NORTON-KOSAIR CHILDRENS HOSPITAL
200 E Chestnut St PO Box 35070
Louisville, KY 40232-5070
(502)629-6000

TEN BROECK DUPONT
1405 Browns Lane
Louisville, KY 40207-4608
(502)896-0495

TEN BROECK HOSPITAL
8521 Lagrange Road
Louisville, KY 40242-3800
(502)426-6380

UNIVERSITY OF LOUISVILLE HOSPITAL
530 S Jackson St
Louisville, KY 40202-3611
(502)562-3000

VA MEDICAL CENTER - LOUISVILLE
800 Zorn Avenue
Louisville, KY 40206-1499
(502)895-3401

MADISONVILLE

REGIONAL MEDICAL CENTER OF HOPKINS
COUNTY
900 Hospital Drive
Madisonville, KY 42431-1653
(270)825-5100

MANCHESTER

MEMORIAL HOSPITAL
11 Manchester Square
Manchester, KY 40962-8700
(606)598-5104

MARION

CRITTENDEN COUNTY HOSPITAL
Highway 60 S Box 386
Marion, KY 42064-0386
(270)965-5281

MARTIN

OUR LADY OF THE WAY HOSPITAL
Main St Box 910
Martin, KY 41649-0910
(606)285-5181

MAYFIELD

JACKSON PURCHASE MEDICAL CENTER
1099 Medical Center Circle
Mayfield, KY 42066-1143
(270)251-4100

MAYSVILLE

MEADOWVIEW REGIONAL MEDICAL
CENTER
989 Medical Park Drive
Maysville, KY 41056-8750
(606)759-5311

MC DOWELL

MCDOWELL APPALACHIAN REGIONAL
HOSPITAL
PO Box 247 Route 122
Mc Dowell, KY 41647-0247
(606)377-3400

MIDDLESBORO

MIDDLESBORO APPALACHIAN REGIONAL
HOSPITAL
3600 W Cumberland Avenue
Middlesboro, KY 40965-2614
(606)242-1300

MONTICELLO

WAYNE COUNTY HOSPITAL
166 Hospital St
Monticello, KY 42633-2430
(606)348-9343

MOREHEAD

SAINT CLAIRE MEDICAL CENTER
222 Medical Circle
Morehead, KY 40351-1180
(606)783-6500

MORGANFIELD

METHODIST HOSPITAL
4604 U S Highway 60 West
Morganfield, KY 42437-6515
(270)389-5000

MOUNT STERLING

MARY CHILES HOSPITAL
50 Sterling Avenue
Mount Sterling, KY 40353-1158
(859)497-6000

MOUNT VERNON

ROCKCASTLE HOSPITAL
145 Newcomb Avenue PO Box 1310
Mount Vernon, KY 40456-1310
(606)256-2195

MURRAY

MURRAY-CALLOWAY COUNTY HOSPITAL
803 Poplar St
Murray, KY 42071-2467
(270)762-1100

OWENSBORO

HEALTHPARK
1006 Ford Avenue
Owensboro, KY 42301-4677
(270)686-6100

OWENSBORO MEDICAL HEALTH SYSTEM
811 E Parrish Avenue PO Box 2799
Owensboro, KY 42303-3258
(270)688-2000

RIVER VALLEY BEHAVIORAL HEALTH
1000 Industrial Drive
Owensboro, KY 42301-8715
(270)689-6500

OWENTON

NEW HORIZONS HEALTH SYSTEMS
330 Roland Avenue
Owenton, KY 40359-1502
(502)484-3663

PADUCAH

LOURDES HOSPITAL
1530 Lone Oak Road
Paducah, KY 42003-7900
(270)444-2444

WESTERN BAPTIST HOSPITAL
2501 Kentucky Avenue
Paducah, KY 42003-3200
(270)575-2100

PAINTSVILLE

PAUL B HALL REGIONAL MEDICAL CENTER
625 W James S Trimble Boulevard Box 1487
Paintsville, KY 41240-1055
(606)789-3511

PARIS

BOURBON COMMUNITY HOSPITAL
9 Linville Drive
Paris, KY 40361-2129
(859)987-3600

PIKEVILLE

PIKEVILLE METHODIST HOSPITAL
911 S Bypass
Pikeville, KY 41501-1503
(606)218-3500

Hospital Telephone Directory — LOUISIANA

PINEVILLE

PINEVILLE COMMUNITY HOSPITAL
850 Riverview Avenue
Pineville, KY 40977-1400
(606)337-3051

PRESTONSBURG

HIGHLANDS REGIONAL MEDICAL CENTER
US 23 N Box 668
Prestonsburg, KY 41653-0668
(606)886-8511

PRINCETON

CALDWELL COUNTY HOSPITAL
101 Hospital Drive Box 410
Princeton, KY 42445-2300
(270)365-0300

RADCLIFF

LINCOLN TRAIL BEHAVIORAL HEALTH SYSTEM
3909 S Wilson Road PO Box 369
Radcliff, KY 40159-0369
(270)351-9444

RICHMOND

PATTIE A CLAY HOSPITAL
Eastern Bypass
Richmond, KY 40475
(859)623-3131

RUSSELL SPRINGS

RUSSELL COUNTY HOSPITAL
Dowell Road Box 1610
Russell Springs, KY 42642-1610
(270)866-4141

RUSSELLVILLE

LOGAN MEMORIAL HOSPITAL
1625 S Nashville Road
Russellville, KY 42276-8834
(270)726-4011

SALEM

LIVINGSTON HOSPITAL AND HEALTHCARE SERVICE
PO Box 138
Salem, KY 42078-0138
(270)988-2299

SCOTTSVILLE

MEDICAL CENTER AT SCOTTSVILLE
456 Burnley Road
Scottsville, KY 42164-6355
(270)622-2800

SHELBYVILLE

JEWISH HOSPITAL SHELBYVILLE
727 Hospital Drive
Shelbyville, KY 40065-1699
(502)647-4000

SOMERSET

LAKE CUMBERLAND REGIONAL HOSPITAL
305 Langdon St PO Box 620
Somerset, KY 42502-0620
(606)679-7441

SOUTH WILLIAMSON

WILLIAMSON APPALACHIAN REGIONAL HOSPITAL
2000 Central Avenue
South Williamson, KY 41503-4003
(606)237-1710

STANFORD

FORT LOGAN HOSPITAL
124 Portman Avenue
Stanford, KY 40484-1230
(606)365-2187

TOMPKINSVILLE

MONROE COUNTY MEDICAL CENTER
529 Capp Harlan Road
Tompkinsville, KY 42167-1840
(270)487-9231

VERSAILLES

BLUE GRASS COMMUNITY HOSPITAL
360 Amsden Avenue
Versailles, KY 40383-1851
(859)873-3111

WEST LIBERTY

MORGAN COUNTY APPALACHIAN REGIONAL HOSPITAL
Wells Hill Road Box 579
West Liberty, KY 41472-0579
(606)743-3186

WHITESBURG

WHITESBURG APPALACHIAN REGIONAL HOSPITAL
550 Jenkins Road
Whitesburg, KY 41858-7606
(606)633-3600

WILLIAMSTOWN

SAINT ELIZABETH MEDICAL CENTER GRANT COUNTY
238 Barnes Road
Williamstown, KY 41097-9482
(859)824-8240

WINCHESTER

CLARK REGIONAL MEDICAL CENTER
1107 W Lexington Avenue
Winchester, KY 40391-1169
(859)745-3500

LOUISIANA

ABBEVILLE

ABBEVILLE GENERAL HOSPITAL
118 N Hospital Drive
Abbeville, LA 70510-4077
(337)893-5466

VERMILION REHAB HOSPITAL
118 N Hospital Drive, 3rd Floor South
Abbeville, LA 70510-4039
(337)898-6116

ALEXANDRIA

CHRISTUS SAINT FRANCES CABRINI HOSPITAL
3330 Masonic Drive
Alexandria, LA 71301-3841
(318)487-1122

CROSSROAD REGIONAL HOSPITAL
110 John Eskew Drive
Alexandria, LA 71315
(318)445-5111

DUBUIS HOSPITAL FOR CONTINUING CARE
3330 Masonic Drive
Alexandria, LA 71301-3841
(318)448-6505

HEALTHSOUTH REHAB HOSPITAL OF ALEXANDRIA
104 N 3rd St
Alexandria, LA 71301-8581
(318)449-1370

PHYSICIANS HOSPITAL OF NEW ORLEANS
PO Box 11786
Alexandria, LA 71315-1786
(318)822-8222

RAPIDES REGIONAL MEDICAL CENTER
211 4th St
Alexandria, LA 71301-8454
(318)473-3000

AMITE

HOOD MEMORIAL HOSPITAL
301 Walnut St
Amite, LA 70422-2098
(985)748-9485

ARCADIA

LOUISIANA EXTENDED CARE HOSPITAL
1175 Pine St
Arcadia, LA 71001-3113
(318)263-2044

BARKSDALE AIR FORCE BASE

2ND MEDICAL GROUP
243 Curtiss Road Suite 100
Barksdale Air Force Base, LA 71110-2425
(318)456-6572

BASTROP

BASTROP REHAB HOSPITAL
323 W Walnut Street
Bastrop, LA 71220-4521
(318)556-1191

MOREHOUSE GENERAL HOSPITAL
423 W Walnut
Bastrop, LA 71220
(318)283-3600

BATON ROUGE

BATON ROUGE GENERAL MEDICAL CENTER - BLUEBONNET
8585 Picardy Avenue
Baton Rouge, LA 70809-3679
(225)763-4000

BATON ROUGE GENERAL MEDICAL CENTER - MID-CITY
3600 Florida Blvd
Baton Rouge, LA 70806-3889
(225)387-7000

BENTON REHABILITATION HOSPITAL
4660 Convention Street
Baton Rouge, LA 70806-4001
(225)336-1000

EARL K LONG MEDICAL CENTER
5825 Airline Highway
Baton Rouge, LA 70805-2498
(225)358-1000

HEALTHSOUTH REHAB HOSPITAL OF BATON ROUGE
8595 United Plaza Boulevard
Baton Rouge, LA 70809-2251
(225)927-0567

OUR LADY OF THE LAKE REGIONAL MEDICAL CENTER
5000 Hennessy Boulevard
Baton Rouge, LA 70808-4367
(225)765-6565

LOUISIANA
Hospital Telephone Directory

PREFERRED REHAB HOSPITAL
2325 Weymouth Dr Ste A
Baton Rouge, LA 70809-1481
(225)241-9774

SAGE REHAB INSTITUTE
8225 Summa Avenue
Baton Rouge, LA 70809-3422
(225)819-0703

SUMMIT HOSPITAL
17000 Medical Center Drive
Baton Rouge, LA 70816-3224
(225)752-2470

WOMANS HOSPITAL
9050 Airline Highway
Baton Rouge, LA 70815-4192
(225)927-1300

BERNICE

TRI WARD GENERAL HOSPITAL
409 1st St
Bernice, LA 71222-4001
(318)285-9066

BOGALUSA

BOGALUSA COMMUNITY MEDICAL CENTER
433 Plaza
Bogalusa, LA 70427-3793
(985)732-7122

BOGALUSA COMMUNITY REHAB HOSPITAL
433 Plaza
Bogalusa, LA 70427-3793
(985)732-1186

WASHINGTON SAINT TAMMANY REGIONAL MEDICAL CENTER
PO Box 459
Bogalusa, LA 70429-0459
(985)735-1322

BOSSIER CITY

BOSSIER MEDICAL CENTER
2105 Airline Drive
Bossier City, LA 71111-3190
(318)741-6000

SUMMIT HOSPITAL OF NORTHWEST LOUISIANA
4900 Medical Drive
Bossier City, LA 71112-4521
(318)747-9500

WILLIS KNIGHTON BOSSIER HEALTH CENTER
2400 Hospital Drive
Bossier City, LA 71111-2385
(318)752-7000

BREAUX BRIDGE

SAINT MARTIN HOSPITAL
210 Champagne Boulevard PO Box 357
Breaux Bridge, LA 70517-0357
(337)332-2178

BUNKIE

BUNKIE GENERAL HOSPITAL
427 Evergreen Street
Bunkie, LA 71322-3901
(318)346-6681

CAMERON

SOUTH CAMERON MEMORIAL HOSPITAL
5360 West Creole Highway
Cameron, LA 70631-5127
(337)542-4111

CHALMETTE

CHALMETTE MEDICAL CENTER
9001 Patricia St
Chalmette, LA 70043-1769
(504)620-6000

LIFECARE HOSPITAL OF NEW ORLEANS - CHALMETTE
801 Virtue Street
Chalmette, LA 70043-1253
(504)620-7061

VIRTUE STREET MEDICAL PAVILION
801 Virtue Street
Chalmette, LA 70043-1253
(504)620-6000

CHURCH POINT

ACADIA SAINT LANDRY PARISH HOSPITAL
810 S Broadway
Church Point, LA 70525-4402
(337)684-5435

CLINTON

CLINTON REHABILITATION HOSPITAL
9725 Grace Lane
Clinton, LA 70722-4925
(225)683-1600

COLUMBIA

CALDWELL MEMORIAL HOSPITAL
410 Main Street PO Box 899
Columbia, LA 71418-0899
(318)649-6111

CITIZENS MEDICAL CENTER
Highway 165 South PO Box 1079
Columbia, LA 71418-1079
(318)649-6106

RIVERBEND REHAB HOSPITAL
410 Main Street, PO Box 1618
Columbia, LA 71418-1618
(318)649-8774

COUSHATTA

CHRISTUS COUSHATTA HEALTH CARE
1635 Marvelle Street PO Box 589
Coushatta, LA 71019-0589
(318)932-2000

COMMUNITY REHABILITATION HOSPITAL OF COUSHATTA
1110 Ringgold Avenue
Coushatta, LA 71019-9073
(318)932-1770

COVINGTON

DIXON MEDICAL CENTER
20050 Crestwood Blvd
Covington, LA 70433-5207
(985)875-9398

GREENBRIER HOSPITAL
201 Greenbrier Boulevard Box 1836
Covington, LA 70433-7236
(985)893-2970

LAKEVIEW REGIONAL MEDICAL CENTER
95 East Fairway Drive
Covington, LA 70433-7500
(985)867-3800

SAINT TAMMANY PARISH HOSPITAL
1202 S Tyler
Covington, LA 70433-2394
(985)898-4000

CROWLEY

ACADIA REHABILITATION HOSPITAL
1305 Crowley Rayne Highway
Crowley, LA 70526-8202
(337)785-2111

AMERICAN LEGION HOSPITAL
1305 Crowley Rayne Highway
Crowley, LA 70526-8202
(337)783-3222

CUT OFF

LADY OF THE SEA GENERAL HOSPITAL
200 W 134th Pl
Cut Off, LA 70345-4145
(985)632-6401

DELHI

RICHLAND PARISH HOSPITAL DELHI
507 Cincinnati
Delhi, LA 71232-3009
(318)878-5171

DENHAM SPRINGS

DIXON MEDICAL CENTER
8375 Florida Boulevard
Denham Springs, LA 70726-7806
(225)665-8211

DEQUINCY

DEQUINCY MEMORIAL HOSPITAL
PO Box 1166
Dequincy, LA 70633-1166
(337)786-1200

DERIDDER

BEAUREGARD MEMORIAL HOSPITAL
PO Box 730
Deridder, LA 70634-0730
(337)462-7100

DONALDSONVILLE

PREVOST MEMORIAL HOSPITAL
301 Memorial Drive
Donaldsonville, LA 70346-4376
(225)473-7931

EUNICE

EUNICE COMMUNITY MEDICAL CENTER
400 Moosa Boulevard
Eunice, LA 70535-3628
(337)457-5244

FARMERVILLE

UNION GENERAL HOSPITAL
901 James Avenue
Farmerville, LA 71241-2234
(318)368-9751

FERRIDAY

PROFESSIONAL REHAB HOSPITAL
6818 A Highway St
Ferriday, LA 71334
(318)757-7575

RIVERLAND MEDICAL CENTER
1700 Wallace Boulevard
Ferriday, LA 71334-2239
(318)757-6551

Hospital Telephone Directory — LOUISIANA

FORT POLK

BAYNE JONES ARMY COMMUNITY HOSPITAL
Building 285
Fort Polk, LA 71459
(337)531-3928

FRANKLIN

FRANKLIN FOUNDATION HOSPITAL
1501 Hospital Avenue
Franklin, LA 70538-3724
(337)828-0760

FRANKLINTON

RIVERSIDE MEDICAL CENTER
1900 Main St
Franklinton, LA 70438-3688
(985)839-4431

GONZALES

ASCENSION HOSPITAL
615 E Worthy Road Box 1029
Gonzales, LA 70737-4240
(225)621-1248

SAINT ELIZABETH HOSPITAL
1125 Highway 30 West
Gonzales, LA 70737-5004
(225)647-5000

GREENSBURG

SAINT HELENA PARISH HOSPITAL
PO Box 337
Greensburg, LA 70441-0337
(225)222-6111

GREENWELL SPRINGS

GREENWELL SPRINGS HOSPITAL
PO Box 549
Greenwell Springs, LA 70739-0549
(225)261-2730

GRETNA

HEALTHWEST REHABILITATION HOSPITAL
3201 Wall Boulevard
Gretna, LA 70056-7755
(504)433-5551

MEADOWCREST HOSPITAL
2500 Belle Chasse Highway
Gretna, LA 70056-7196
(504)392-3131

HAMMOND

HAMMOND REHABILITATION HOSPITAL
15719 Belle Drive
Hammond, LA 70403-1439
(985)902-8148

NORTH OAKS MEDICAL CENTER
15790 Medical Center Drive
Hammond, LA 70403
(985)345-2700

NORTH OAKS REHAB HOSPITAL
PO Box 2668
Hammond, LA 70404-2668
(225)542-7777

HARAHAN

RIVER OAKS CHILD AND ADOLESCENT HOSPITAL
1525 River Oaks Road West
Harahan, LA 70123-2162
(504)733-2273

RIVER OAKS HOSPITAL
1525 River Oaks Road West
Harahan, LA 70123-2199
(504)734-1740

SAINT JOHN'S REHABILITATION HOSPITAL
405 Folse Street
Harahan, LA 70123-3671
(504)738-3339

HOMER

HOMER MEMORIAL HOSPITAL
620 East College Street
Homer, LA 71040-3202
(318)927-2024

HOUMA

LEONARD J CHAUBERT MEDICAL CENTER
1978 Industrial Boulevard
Houma, LA 70363-7094
(985)873-2200

PHYSICIANS SURGICAL SPECIALTY HOSPITAL
218 Corporate Drive
Houma, LA 70360-2768
(985)853-1390

TERREBONNE GENERAL MEDICAL CENTER
8166 Main Street
Houma, LA 70360-3498
(985)873-4141

INDEPENDENCE

LALLIE KEMP REGIONAL MEDICAL CENTER
900 Highway 51 South
Independence, LA 70443
(985)878-9421

JACKSON

EAST LOUISIANA MENTAL HEALTH SYSTEM
Highway 10 E Feliciana Parish
Jackson, LA 70748
(225)634-0100

VILLA FELICIANA MEDICAL COMPLEX
PO Box 438
Jackson, LA 70748-0438
(225)634-4000

JENA

LASALLE GENERAL HOSPITAL
PO 1388
Jena, LA 71342-1388
(318)992-9200

JENNINGS

JENNINGS AMERICAN LEGION HOSPITAL
1634 Elton Road
Jennings, LA 70546-3614
(337)616-7000

JONESBORO

JACKSON PARISH HOSPITAL
600 Beech Spring Road
Jonesboro, LA 71251-2064
(318)259-4435

KAPLAN

ABRAM KAPLAN MEMORIAL HOSPITAL
1310 W 7th St
Kaplan, LA 70548-2910
(337)643-8300

KAPLAN REHAB HOSPITAL
1310 W 7th Street
Kaplan, LA 70548-2910
(337)643-6009

KENNER

KENNER REGIONAL MEDICAL CENTER
180 W Esplanade Avenue
Kenner, LA 70065-6001
(504)468-8600

LIFECARE HOSPITAL OF NEW ORLEANS - KENNER
180 Esplanade
Kenner, LA 70065-2467
(504)464-8590

KENTWOOD

SOUTHEAST REGIONAL MEDICAL CENTER
719 Avenue G
Kentwood, LA 70444-2601
(985)229-9193

KINDER

ALLEN PARISH HOSPITAL
PO Box 1670
Kinder, LA 70648-1670
(337)738-2527

LA PLACE

LA PLACE REHABILITATION HOSPITAL
508 West 5th Street
La Place, LA 70068-3940
(985)653-8447

RIVER PARISHES HOSPITAL
500 Rue De Sante
La Place, LA 70068-5418
(985)652-7000

LACOMB

LOUISIANA HEART HOSPITAL
64030 Highway 434
Lacomb, LA 70445-3456
(985)690-7500

LAFAYETTE

COMMUNITY REHABILITATION OF LAFAYETTE
811 Martin Luther King Drive
Lafayette, LA 70501-1845
(337)234-4031

LAFAYETTE GENERAL MEDICAL CENTER
1214 Coolidge Avenue
Lafayette, LA 70503-2696
(337)289-7991

MEADOWBROOK REHAB HOSPITAL
204 Energy Parkway
Lafayette, LA 70508-3816
(337)232-1905

MEDICAL CENTER OF SOUTHWEST LOUISIANA
2810 Ambassador Caffery Parkway
Lafayette, LA 70506-5900
(337)981-2949

OUR LADY OF LOURDES REGIONAL MEDICAL CENTER
611 St Landry
Lafayette, LA 70506-4697
(337)289-2000

REHAB HOSPITAL OF ACADIANA
310 Youngsville Hwy
Lafayette, LA 70508-4524
(337)839-9880

UNIVERSITY MEDICAL CENTER
2390 W Congress
Lafayette, LA 70506-4298
(337)261-6000

LOUISIANA — Hospital Telephone Directory

VERMILION HOSPITAL
2520 N University Avenue
Lafayette, LA 70507-5306
(337)234-5614

WOMENS AND CHILDRENS HOSPITAL
4600 Ambassador Caffery Parkway
Lafayette, LA 70508-6923
(337)981-9100

LAKE CHARLES

CALCASIEU OAKS
2837 Ernest Street, Building A
Lake Charles, LA 70601-8408
(337)439-8111

DUBUIS CONTINUING CARE - LAKE CHARLES
524 South Ryan Street
Lake Charles, LA 70601-5725
(337)491-7752

EXTENDED CARE OF SOUTHWEST LOUISIANA
2837 Ernest Building B
Lake Charles, LA 70601-8408
(337)436-6111

LAKE CHARLES MEMORIAL HOSPITAL
1701 Oak Park Boulevard
Lake Charles, LA 70601-8911
(337)494-3000

MOSS REGIONAL MEDICAL CENTER
1000 Walters St
Lake Charles, LA 70607-4699
(337)475-8100

SAINT PATRICK HOSPITAL
524 S Ryan
Lake Charles, LA 70601-5799
(337)436-2511

WOMEN AND CHILDRENS HOSPITAL
4200 Nelson Road
Lake Charles, LA 70605-4118
(337)474-6370

LAKE PROVIDENCE

EAST CARROLL PARISH HOSPITAL
336 N Hood St
Lake Providence, LA 71254-2140
(318)559-2441

LEESVILLE

BYRD REGIONAL HOSPITAL
1020 Fertitta Boulevard
Leesville, LA 71446-4649
(337)239-9041

TRI PARISH REHAB HOSPITAL
8088 Hawks Road
Leesville, LA 71446-6649
(337)462-8880

LULING

LULING REHAB HOSPITAL
1125 Paul Maillard
Luling, LA 70070-4351
(985)331-2281

SAINT CHARLES PARISH HOSPITAL
PO Box 87
Luling, LA 70070-0087
(985)785-6242

LUTCHER

SAINT JAMES PARISH HOSPITAL
2471 Louisiana Avenue
Lutcher, LA 70071-5413
(225)869-5512

SAINT JAMES PSYCHIATRIC HOSPITAL
2471 Louisiana Ave
Lutcher, LA 70071-5413
(225)869-3344

MAMOU

SAVOY MEDICAL CENTER
801 Poinciana Avenue
Mamou, LA 70554-2298
(337)468-5261

MANDEVILLE

SOUTHEAST LOUISIANA HOSPITAL
PO Box 3850
Mandeville, LA 70470-3850
(504)626-6300

MANSFIELD

DESOTO REGIONAL HEALTH SYSTEM
207 Jefferson St
Mansfield, LA 71052-2603
(318)871-3100

MANY

RIVER NORTH HOSPITAL & TRANSITIONAL HEALTH SERVICE
240 Highland Dr
Many, LA 71449-3718
(318)473-8700

SABINE MEDICAL CENTER
240 Highland Drive
Many, LA 71449-3767
(318)256-5691

MARKSVILLE

AVOYELLES HOSPITAL
Highway 1192 Blue Town Road
Marksville, LA 71351
(318)253-8611

MARRERO

ADVANCE CARE HOSPITAL
1101 Medical Center Boulevard
Marrero, LA 70072-3147
(504)349-2470

WEST JEFFERSON MEDICAL CENTER
1101 Medical Center Boulevard
Marrero, LA 70072-3191
(504)347-5511

METAIRIE

DOCTORS HOSPITAL OF JEFFERSON
4320 Houma Boulevard
Metairie, LA 70006-2973
(504)849-4000

EAST JEFFERSON GENERAL HOSPITAL
4200 Houma Boulevard
Metairie, LA 70006-2996
(504)454-4000

LAKESIDE HOSPITAL
4700 I-10 Service Road West
Metairie, LA 70001-1290
(504)780-8282

SELECT SPECIALTY HOSPITAL - NEW ORLEANS
4200 Houma Boulevard
Metairie, LA 70006-2970
(504)454-4000

MINDEN

BERNICE COMMUNITY REHAB HOSPITAL
108 Meadowbrook Drive
Minden, LA 71055-6090
(318)285-0999

MINDEN MEDICAL CENTER
One Medical Plaza
Minden, LA 71055-3330
(318)377-2321

MONROE

LSU - E.A. CONWAY MEDICAL CENTER
4864 Jackson Street
Monroe, LA 71202-6400
(318)330-7000

MONROE SURGICAL HOSPITAL
2408 Broadmore Boulevard
Monroe, LA 71201-2963
(318)410-0002

NORTH MONROE HOSPITAL
3421 Medical Park Drive
Monroe, LA 71203-2399
(318)388-1946

SAINT FRANCIS MEDICAL CENTER
309 Jackson St
Monroe, LA 71201-7407
(318)327-4000

SAINT FRANCIS SPECIALTY HOSPITAL
309 Jackson Street
Monroe, LA 71201-7407
(318)327-4267

SAINT PATRICK'S PSYCHIATRIC HOSPITAL
309 Jackson Street
Monroe, LA 71201-7407
(318)327-4686

MORGAN CITY

TECHE REGIONAL MEDICAL CENTER
1125 Marguerite Street
Morgan City, LA 70380-1855
(985)384-2200

NAPOLEONVILLE

ASSUMPTION COMMUNITY HOSPITAL
135 Highway 402
Napoleonville, LA 70390-2217
(985)369-3600

NATCHITOCHES

LOUISIANA HEALTH CARE SPECIALTY HOSPITAL
501 Keyser Avenue, Third Floor
Natchitoches, LA 71457-6018
(318)354-2044

NATCHITOCHES PARISH HOSPITAL
501 Keyser Avenue
Natchitoches, LA 71457-6036
(318)214-4200

NEW IBERIA

DAUTERIVE HOSPITAL
600 N Lewis St
New Iberia, LA 70563-2043
(337)365-7311

IBERIA MEDICAL CENTER
2315 E Main St PO Box 13338
New Iberia, LA 70562-3338
(337)364-0441

NEW ORLEANS

CHILDRENS HOSPITAL
200 Henry Clay Avenue
New Orleans, LA 70118-5798
(504)899-9511

COMMUNITY CARE HOSPITAL
1421 General Taylor
New Orleans, LA 70115-3717
(504)899-2500

Hospital Telephone Directory — LOUISIANA

DE PAUL TULANE BEHAVIORAL HEALTH CENTER
1040 Calhoun St
New Orleans, LA 70118-5914
(504)899-8282

GENESIS SPECIALTY HOSPITAL
301 North Jefferson Davis Parkway, Fourth Floor
New Orleans, LA 70119-5311
(504)483-5548

KINDRED HOSPITAL NEW ORLEANS
3601 Coliseum
New Orleans, LA 70115-3606
(504)899-1555

LAKELAND MEDICAL CENTER
6000 Bullard Avenue
New Orleans, LA 70128-2898
(504)241-6335

LIFECARE HOSPITAL OF NEW ORLEANS
2700 Napolean Avenue
New Orleans, LA 70115-6914
(504)277-5433

MEDICAL CENTER OF LOUISIANA - CHARITY HOSPITAL
1532 Tulane Avenue
New Orleans, LA 70112-2860
(504)903-3000

MEDICAL CENTER OF LOUISIANA AT NEW ORLEANS
2021 Perdido St
New Orleans, LA 70112-1352
(504)903-3000

MEMORIAL MEDICAL CENTER - BAPTIST
2700 Napoleon Avenue
New Orleans, LA 70115-6996
(504)899-9311

MEMORIAL MEDICAL CENTER - MERCY
301 N Jefferson Davis Parkway
New Orleans, LA 70119-5311
(504)483-5000

METHODIST BEHAVIORAL RESOURCES
5610 Read Boulevard
New Orleans, LA 70127-3106
(504)244-5661

NEW ORLEANS ADOLESCENT HOSPITAL
210 State St
New Orleans, LA 70118-5797
(504)897-3400

OASIS REHAB HOSPITAL
1601 Perdido Street, 10th Floor
New Orleans, LA 70112-1262
(504)585-2956

OASIS REHAB HOSPITAL OF LAFAYETTE
1601 Perdido St # 10g
New Orleans, LA 70112-1262
(504)984-8878

OCHSNER FOUNDATION HOSPITAL
1516 Jefferson Highway
New Orleans, LA 70121-2484
(504)842-3000

PENDLETON MEMORIAL METHODIST HOSPITAL
5620 Read Boulevard
New Orleans, LA 70127-3154
(504)244-5100

SAINT CHARLES GENERAL HOSPITAL
3700 St Charles Avenue
New Orleans, LA 70115-4680
(504)899-7441

SAINT CLAUDE MEDICAL CENTER
3419 St Claude Avenue
New Orleans, LA 70117-6144
(504)948-8200

SPECIALTY HOSPITAL OF NEW ORLEANS
1401 Foucher Street
New Orleans, LA 70115-3515
(504)897-8942

TOURO INFIRMARY
1401 Foucher St
New Orleans, LA 70115-3593
(504)897-7011

TOURO REHAB CENTER
1401 Foucher St
New Orleans, LA 70115-3515
(504)897-8560

TULANE MEDICAL CENTER
1415 Tulane Avenue
New Orleans, LA 70112-2600
(504)588-5263

VA MEDICAL CENTER - NEW ORLEANS
1601 Perdido St
New Orleans, LA 70112-1262
(504)568-0811

NEW ROADS

POINTE COUPEE GENERAL HOSPITAL
2202 False River Road
New Roads, LA 70760-2614
(225)638-6331

OAK GROVE

WEST CARROLL MEMORIAL HOSPITAL
522 Ross Street
Oak Grove, LA 71263-9706
(318)428-3237

OAKDALE

OAKDALE COMMUNITY HOSPITAL
130 N Hospital Drive
Oakdale, LA 71463-3035
(318)335-3700

OLLA

HARDTNER MEDICAL CENTER
1102 N Pine St
Olla, LA 71465-4804
(318)495-3131

OPELOUSAS

DOCTORS HOSPITAL OF OPELOUSAS
3983 I-49 South Service Road
Opelousas, LA 70570-0758
(337)948-2100

OPELOUSAS GENERAL HOSPITAL
520 Prudhomme Lane
Opelousas, LA 70570-6498
(337)948-3011

SAINT LANDRY EXTENDED CARE HOSPITAL
539 East Prudhomme Lane
Opelousas, LA 70570-6499
(337)948-5184

PINEVILLE

CENTRAL LOUISIANA STATE HOSPITAL
242 W Shamrock St Box 5031
Pineville, LA 71360-6439
(318)484-6200

HUEY P LONG MEMORIAL CENTER
352 Hospital Boulevard
Pineville, LA 71360
(318)448-0811

VA MEDICAL CENTER - ALEXANDRIA
2495 Shreveport Hwy 71 North
Pineville, LA 71360-4044
(318)473-0010

PLAQUEMINE

RIVER WEST MEDICAL CENTER
PO Box 737
Plaquemine, LA 70765-0737
(225)687-9222

RACELAND

SAINT ANNE GENERAL HOSPITAL
4608 Highway 1
Raceland, LA 70394-2623
(985)537-6841

SAINT ANNE REHAB HOSPITAL
4608 Highway 1
Raceland, LA 70394-2623
(985)537-7736

RAYVILLE

RICHARDSON MEDICAL CENTER
PO Box 388 Greer Road
Rayville, LA 71269-0388
(318)728-4181

RICHLAND PARISH REHABILITATION HOSPITAL
307 Hayes Street
Rayville, LA 71269-2531
(318)728-4410

ROSEPINE

TRI-PARISH REHAB HOSPITAL
PO Box 1049
Rosepine, LA 70659-1049
(337)825-9971

RUSTON

HEALTH PARADIGM MEDICAL CENTER
PO Box 844
Ruston, LA 71273-0844
(225)254-8433

HEALTHSOUTH NORTH LOUISIANA REHAB HOSPITAL
1401 Ezell Box 490
Ruston, LA 71270-7218
(318)251-53546

LINCOLN GENERAL HOSPITAL
401 East Vaughn Street
Ruston, LA 71270-5978
(318)254-2100

SAINT FRANCISVILLE

WEST FELICIANA PARISH HOSPITAL
548 Commerce St Box 368
Saint Francisville, LA 70775-0368
(225)635-3811

SHREVEPORT

BRENTWOOD BEHAVIORAL HEALTHCARE
1006 Highland Avenue
Shreveport, LA 71101-4103
(318)221-1436

DOCTORS HOSPITAL OF SHREVEPORT
1130 Louisiana Avenue
Shreveport, LA 71101-3998
(318)227-1211

DUBUIS HOSPITAL - CONTINUING CARE
One Saint Mary Place, 5th & 6th Floors
Shreveport, LA 71101-4343
(318)678-1000

HIGHLAND HILLS HOSPITAL
453 Jordan St
Shreveport, LA 71101-4860
(318)424-6699

MAINE

Hospital Telephone Directory

HIGHLAND HOSPITAL
1453 E Bert Kouns Industrial Loop
Shreveport, LA 71105-6050
(318)798-4300

LAGNIAPPE HOSPITAL
1800 Irving Place Suite 100
Shreveport, LA 71101-4608
(318)425-4096

LIFECARE HOSPITAL - DOCTORS
1128 Louisiana Avenue Suite E
Shreveport, LA 71101-3976
(318)222-2273

LIFECARE HOSPITAL - MAIN
9320 Linwood Avenue
Shreveport, LA 71106-7003
(318)688-8504

LIFECARE HOSPITAL - PIERREMONT
8001 Youree Drive
Shreveport, LA 71115-2302
(318)212-3200

LOUISIANA STATE UNIVERSITY MEDICAL
CENTER
1541 Kings Highway
Shreveport, LA 71103-4228
(318)675-5000

SCHUMPERT MEDICAL CENTER
One St Mary Place
Shreveport, LA 71101-4399
(318)681-4500

SHRINERS HOSPITAL
3100 Samford Avenue
Shreveport, LA 71103-4289
(318)222-5704

VA MEDICAL CENTER - OVERTON BROOKS
510 E Stoner Avenue
Shreveport, LA 71101-4295
(318)221-8411

WILLIS KNIGHTON MEDICAL CENTER
2600 Greenwood Road
Shreveport, LA 71103-3971
(318)632-4600

SLIDELL

NORTHSHORE PSYCHIATRIC HOSPITAL
104 Medical Center Drive
Slidell, LA 70461-5575
(985)646-5500

NORTHSHORE REGIONAL MEDICAL
CENTER
100 Medical Center Drive
Slidell, LA 70461-8399
(985)646-5025

SLIDELL MEMORIAL HOSPITAL
1001 Gause Boulevard
Slidell, LA 70458-2987
(985)643-2200

SPRINGHILL

SPRINGHILL MEDICAL CENTER
2001 Doctors Drive Box 920
Springhill, LA 71075-4526
(318)539-1000

STERLINGTON

STERLINGTON REHAB HOSPITAL
111 Highway 2 PO Box 627
Sterlington, LA 71280-0627
(318)665-9950

STONEWALL

GREEN HILL HOSPITAL
960 Hwy 171 South
Stonewall, LA 71078-9594
(318)925-5565

SULPHUR

SUMMIT HOSPITAL OF SOUTHWEST
LOUISIANA
703 E Cypress St
Sulphur, LA 70663-5053
(337)527-1102

WEST CALCASIEU CAMERON HOSPITAL
701 East Cypress Street
Sulphur, LA 70663-5053
(337)527-4240

TALLULAH

MADISON PARISH HOSPITAL
900 Johnson St
Tallulah, LA 71282-4537
(318)574-2374

THIBODAUX

THIBODAUX REGIONAL HEALTH CENTERS
PO Box 1118
Thibodaux, LA 70302-1118
(225)447-5500

VILLE PLATTE

VILLE PLATTE MEDICAL CENTER
800 E Main
Ville Platte, LA 70586-4618
(337)363-5684

VIVIAN

NORTH CADDO MEDICAL CENTER
1000 S Spuce St
Vivian, LA 71082-3232
(318)375-3235

WEST MONROE

CORNERSTONE HOSPITAL OF NORTH
LOUISIANA
6198 Cypress Street
West Monroe, LA 71291-9010
(318)396-5600

GLENWOOD REGIONAL MEDICAL CENTER
PO Box 35805
West Monroe, LA 71294-5805
(318)329-4200

WINNFIELD

WINN PARISH MEDICAL CENTER
301 W Boundary
Winnfield, LA 71483-3427
(318)648-3000

WINNSBORO

FRANKLIN PARISH MEDICAL CENTER
2106 Loop Road
Winnsboro, LA 71295-3398
(318)435-9411

ZACHARY

LANE MEMORIAL HOSPITAL
6300 Main St
Zachary, LA 70791-4099
(225)658-4000

MAINE

AUGUSTA

AUGUSTA MENTAL HEALTH INSTITUTE
Arsenal St PO Box 724
Augusta, ME 04332-0724
(207)287-7200

MAINE GENERAL MEDICAL CENTER -
AUGUSTA CAMPUS
6 East Chestnut St
Augusta, ME 04330-5797
(207)626-1000

BANGOR

ACADIA HOSPITAL
268 Stillwater Avenue
Bangor, ME 04401-3980
(207)973-6100

BANGOR MENTAL HEALTH INSTITUTE
656 State St
Bangor, ME 04401-5609
(207)941-4000

EASTERN MAINE MEDICAL CENTER
489 State St
Bangor, ME 04401-6674
(207)973-7000

SAINT JOSEPH HOSPITAL
360 Broadway
Bangor, ME 04401-3900
(207)262-1000

BAR HARBOR

MOUNT DESERT ISLAND HOSPITAL
Wayman Lane
Bar Harbor, ME 04609
(207)288-5081

BELFAST

WALDO COUNTY GENERAL HOSPITAL
56 Northport Avenue
Belfast, ME 04915-6105
(207)338-2500

BIDDEFORD

SOUTHERN MAINE MEDICAL CENTER
1 Medical Center Drive
Biddeford, ME 04005-9496
(207)283-7000

BLUE HILL

BLUE HILL MEMORIAL HOSPITAL
Water St
Blue Hill, ME 04614
(207)374-2836

BOOTHBAY HBR

SAINT ANDREWS HOSPITAL
PO Box 417
Boothbay Hbr, ME 04538-0417
(207)633-2121

BRIDGTON

BRIDGTON HOSPITAL
S High St PO Box 230
Bridgton, ME 04009-0230
(207)647-8841

BRUNSWICK

MID COAST HOSPITAL
123 Medical Center Drive
Brunswick, ME 04011-2652
(207)729-0181

PARKVIEW HOSPITAL
329 Main Street
Brunswick, ME 04011-3398
(207)373-2000

CALAIS

CALAIS REGIONAL HOSPITAL
50 Franklin St
Calais, ME 04619
(207)454-7521

CARIBOU

CARY MEDICAL CENTER
163 Van Buren Road Mra Box 37
Caribou, ME 04736-3567
(207)498-3111

DAMARISCOTTA

MILES MEMORIAL HOSPITAL
Bristol Road
Damariscotta, ME 04543
(207)563-1234

DOVER FOXCROFT

MAYO REGIONAL HOSPITAL
75 West Main St
Dover Foxcroft, ME 04426
(207)564-8401

ELLSWORTH

MAINE COAST MEMORIAL HOSPITAL
50 Union St
Ellsworth, ME 04605-1586
(207)664-5311

FARMINGTON

FRANKLIN MEMORIAL HOSPITAL
129 Hospital Dr
Farmington, ME 04938-6151
(207)778-6031

FORT FAIRFIELD

COMMUNITY GENERAL HOSPITAL
3 Green St
Fort Fairfield, ME 04742-1010
(207)768-4700

FORT KENT

NORTHERN MAINE MEDICAL CENTER
143 E Main St
Fort Kent, ME 04743-1433
(207)834-3155

GREENVILLE

CHARLES A DEAN MEMORIAL HOSPITAL
Pritham Avenue
Greenville, ME 04441
(207)695-5200

HOULTON

HOULTON REGIONAL HOSPITAL
20 Hartford St
Houlton, ME 04730-1891
(207)532-9471

LEWISTON

CENTRAL MAINE MEDICAL CENTER
300 Main Street PO Box 1001
Lewiston, ME 04243-1001
(207)795-0111

SAINT MARYS REGIONAL MEDICAL CENTER
Campus Avenue
Lewiston, ME 04240
(207)777-8100

LINCOLN

PENOBSCOT VALLEY HOSPITAL
Transalpine Road, Box 368
Lincoln, ME 04457-0368
(207)794-3321

MACHIAS

DOWN EAST COMMUNITY HOSPITAL
Upper Court St
Machias, ME 04654
(207)255-3356

MARS HILL

AROOSTOOK HEALTH CENTER
15 Highland Avenue
Mars Hill, ME 04758
(207)768-4900

MILLINOCKET

MILLINOCKET REGIONAL HOSPITAL
200 Somerset St
Millinocket, ME 04462-1298
(207)723-5161

NORWAY

STEPHENS MEMORIAL HOSPITAL
80 Main St
Norway, ME 04268-5503
(207)743-5933

PITTSFIELD

SEBASTICOOK VALLEY HOSPITAL
99 Grove Street
Pittsfield, ME 04967-1199
(207)487-5141

PORTLAND

MAINE MEDICAL CENTER
22 Bramhall St
Portland, ME 04102-3175
(207)871-0111

MERCY HOSPITAL
144 State St
Portland, ME 04101-3795
(207)879-3000

NEW ENGLAND REHAB HOSPITAL OF PORTLAND
335 Brighton Avenue
Portland, ME 04102-2314
(207)775-4000

PRESQUE ISLE

AROOSTOOK MEDICAL CENTER
140 Academy St
Presque Isle, ME 04769-3171
(207)768-4000

ARTHUR R. GOULD MEMORIAL HOSPITAL
140 Academy Street
Presque Isle, ME 04769-3180
(207)768-4000

ROCKPORT

PENOBSCOT BAY MEDICAL CENTER
6 Glen Cove Drive
Rockport, ME 04856-4240
(207)596-8000

RUMFORD

RUMFORD COMMUNITY HOSPITAL
420 Franklin St
Rumford, ME 04276-2145
(207)369-1000

SANFORD

HENRIETTA D GOODALL HOSPITAL
25 June St
Sanford, ME 04073-2621
(207)324-4310

SKOWHEGAN

REDINGTON FAIRVIEW GENERAL HOSPITAL
Fairview Avenue
Skowhegan, ME 04976
(207)474-5121

SOUTH PORTLAND

SPRING HARBOR HOSPITAL
175 Running Hill Road
South Portland, ME 04106-3272
(207)761-2200

TOGUS

VA MEDICAL CENTER - TOGUS
1 VA Center
Togus, ME 04330-6796
(207)623-8411

WATERVILLE

INLAND HOSPITAL
200 Kennedy Memorial Drive
Waterville, ME 04901-4595
(207)861-3000

MAINE GENERAL MEDICAL CENTER
149 North Street
Waterville, ME 04901-4995
(207)872-1000

YORK

YORK HOSPITAL
15 Hospital Drive
York, ME 03909-1099
(207)363-4321

MARYLAND

ANDREWS AIR FORCE BASE

89TH MEDICAL GROUP, MALCOLM GROW U.S. AIR FORCE MEDICAL CENTER
1050 West Perimeter, Suite A-1-11
Andrews Air Force Base, MD 20762-6601
(240)857-3000

ANNAPOLIS

ANNE ARUNDEL MEDICAL CENTER
Franklin And Cathedral Streets
Annapolis, MD 21401
(410)481-1000

BALTIMORE

BON SECOURS HOSPITAL
2000 West Baltimore St
Baltimore, MD 21223-1558
(410)362-3000

FRANKLIN SQUARE HOSPITAL
9000 Franklin Square Drive
Baltimore, MD 21237-3997
(410)777-7000

GOOD SAMARITAN HOSPITAL
5601 Loch Raven Boulevard
Baltimore, MD 21239-2991
(410)532-8000

GREATER BALTIMORE MEDICAL CENTER
6701 N Charles St
Baltimore, MD 21204-6881
(410)849-2000

MARYLAND — Hospital Telephone Directory

HARBOR HOSPITAL CENTER
3001 S Hanover Street
Baltimore, MD 21225-1290
(410)350-3200

JAMES LAWRENCE KERNAN HOSPITAL
2200 Kernan Drive
Baltimore, MD 21207-6665
(410)448-2500

JOHNS HOPKINS BAYVIEW MEDICAL CENTER
4940 Eastern Avenue
Baltimore, MD 21224-2780
(410)550-0100

JOHNS HOPKINS HOSPITAL
600 N Wolfe St
Baltimore, MD 21287-0005
(410)955-5000

KENNEDY KRIEGER CHILDREN'S HOSPITAL
707 N Broadway
Baltimore, MD 21205-1888
(410)923-9200

LEVINDALE HEBREW GERIATRIC CENTER
Greenspring And Belvedere Aves
Baltimore, MD 21215
(410)466-8700

MARYLAND GENERAL HOSPITAL
827 Linden Avenue
Baltimore, MD 21201-4606
(410)225-8000

MARYLAND PENITENTIARY HOSPITAL
954 Forrest St
Baltimore, MD 21202-4294
(410)837-2135

MERCY MEDICAL CENTER
301 St Paul Place
Baltimore, MD 21202-2165
(410)332-9000

MOUNT WASHINGTON PEDIATRIC HOSPITAL
1708 W Rogers Avenue
Baltimore, MD 21209-4596
(410)578-8600

SAINT AGNES HOSPITAL
Wilkens And Caton Avenues
Baltimore, MD 21229
(410)368-6000

SINAI HOSPITAL
2401 West Belvedere Avenue
Baltimore, MD 21215-5270
(410)601-9000

UNION MEMORIAL HOSPITAL
201 E University Pkwy
Baltimore, MD 21218-2891
(410)554-2000

UNIVERSITY OF MARYLAND MEDICAL SYSTEM
22 S Greene St
Baltimore, MD 21201-1590
(410)328-8667

UNIVERSITY SPECIALTY HOSPITAL
601 S Charles St
Baltimore, MD 21230-3801
(410)547-8500

VA MEDICAL CENTER - BALTIMORE
10 N Green St
Baltimore, MD 21201-1524
(410)605-7000

VA REHABILITATION AND EXTENDED CARE CENTER
3900 Loch Raven Boulevard
Baltimore, MD 21218-2108
(410)605-7000

WALTER P CARTER CENTER
630 W Fayette Street
Baltimore, MD 21201-1585
(410)209-6000

BEL AIR

UPPER CHESAPEAKE MEDICAL CENTER
520 Upper Chesapeake Drive
Bel Air, MD 21014-4339
(443)643-1000

BERLIN

ATLANTIC GENERAL HOSPITAL
9733 Healthway Drive
Berlin, MD 21811-1156
(410)641-1100

BETHESDA

NATIONAL NAVAL MEDICAL CENTER
8901 Wisconsin Avenue
Bethesda, MD 20889-0001
(202)295-5800

SUBURBAN HOSPITAL ASSOCIATION
8600 Old Georgetown Road
Bethesda, MD 20814-1497
(301)896-3100

WARREN G. MAGNUSON CLINICAL CENTER
9000 Rockville Pike
Bethesda, MD 20892-0001
(301)496-4114

CAMBRIDGE

DORCHESTER GENERAL HOSPITAL
300 Byrn St Box 439
Cambridge, MD 21613-1941
(410)228-5511

EASTERN SHORE HOSPITAL CENTER
Route 2 PO Box 800
Cambridge, MD 21613-0800
(410)221-2525

CATONSVILLE

SPRING GROVE HOSPITAL CENTER
60 Wade Avenue
Catonsville, MD 21228-4614
(410)402-6000

CHESTERTOWN

KENT AND QUEEN ANNES HOSPITAL
Brown St
Chestertown, MD 21620
(410)778-3300

UPPER SHORE COMMUNITY MENTAL HEALTH CENTER
Scheeler Road PO Box 229
Chestertown, MD 21620-0229
(410)778-6800

CHEVERLY

PRINCE GEORGES HOSPITAL CENTER
3001 Hospital Drive
Cheverly, MD 20785-1189
(301)618-2000

CLINTON

SOUTHERN MARYLAND HOSPITAL
7503 Surratts Road
Clinton, MD 20735-3395
(301)868-8000

COLUMBIA

HOWARD COUNTY GENERAL HOSPITAL
Little Patuxent Parkway And Cedar Lane
Columbia, MD 21044
(410)740-7890

CRISFIELD

EDWARD MCCREADY MEMORIAL HOSPITAL
201 Hall Highway
Crisfield, MD 21817-1237
(410)968-1200

CROWNSVILLE

CROWNSVILLE HOSPITAL CENTER
Crownsville Anne Arundel County
Crownsville, MD 21032
(410)729-6000

CUMBERLAND

MEMORIAL HOSPITAL AND MEDICAL CENTER CUMBERLAND
600 Memorial Avenue
Cumberland, MD 21502-3795
(301)723-4000

SACRED HEART HOSPITAL
900 Seton Drive
Cumberland, MD 21502-1850
(301)723-4200

THOMAS B FINAN CENTER
Country Club Road PO Box 1722
Cumberland, MD 21501-1722
(301)777-2240

EAST NEW MARKET

WARWICK BEHAVIORAL HEALTH
3680 Warwick Road
East New Market, MD 21631-1420
(410)943-8108

EASTON

MEMORIAL HOSPITAL AT EASTON
219 S Washington St
Easton, MD 21601-2996
(410)822-1000

ELKTON

UNION HOSPITAL-CECIL COUNTY
106 Singerly Avenue
Elkton, MD 21921-5539
(410)398-4000

ELLICOTT CITY

TAYLOR MANOR HOSPITAL
4100 College Avenue PO Box 396
Ellicott City, MD 21041-0396
(301)465-3322

EMMITSBURG

MOUNTAIN MANOR TREATMENT CENTER
9701 Keysville Road
Emmitsburg, MD 21727-8619
(301)447-0136

FORT WASHINGTON

FORT WASHINGTON MEDICAL CENTER
11711 Livingston Road
Fort Washington, MD 20744-5151
(301)292-7000

FREDERICK

FREDERICK MEMORIAL HOSPITAL
West Seventh St
Frederick, MD 21701
(301)698-3300

GAITHERSBURG

COLUMBIA HOSPITAL FOR WOMEN
PO Box 130
Gaithersburg, MD 20884-0130
(301)293-6500

GLEN BURNIE

NORTH ARUNDEL HOSPITAL
301 Hospital Drive
Glen Burnie, MD 21061-5899
(410)787-4000

HAGERSTOWN

BROOK LANE PSYCHIATRIC CENTER
PO Box 1945
Hagerstown, MD 21742-1945
(301)733-0330

WASHINGTON COUNTY HOSPITAL
King And Antietam Streets
Hagerstown, MD 21740
(301)790-8000

WESTERN MARYLAND HOSPITAL CENTER
1500 Pennsylvania Avenue
Hagerstown, MD 21742-3194
(301)791-4400

HAVRE DE GRACE

HARFORD MEMORIAL HOSPITAL
501 S Union Avenue
Havre De Grace, MD 21078-3493
(410)843-5000

HYATTSVILLE

GLADYS SPELLMAN SPECIALTY HOSPITAL
& NURSING CENTER
2900 Mercy Lane
Hyattsville, MD 20785-1157
(301)618-2010

JESSUP

CLIFTON T PERKINS CENTER
8450 Dorsey Run Road
Jessup, MD 20794-9486
(410)724-3000

LA PLATA

CIVISTA MEDICAL CENTER
701 E Charles Street PO Box 1070
La Plata, MD 20646-1070
(301)609-4000

LANHAM

DOCTORS COMMUNITY HOSPITAL
8118 Good Luck Road
Lanham, MD 20706-3596
(301)552-8118

LAUREL

LAUREL REGIONAL HOSPITAL
7300 Van Dusen Road
Laurel, MD 20707-9266
(301)725-4300

LEONARDTOWN

SAINT MARY'S HOSPITAL
25500 Point Lookout Road, PO Box 527
Leonardtown, MD 20650-0527
(301)475-8981

OAKLAND

GARRETT COUNTY MEMORIAL HOSPITAL
251 N Fourth St
Oakland, MD 21550-1375
(301)533-4000

OLNEY

MONTGOMERY GENERAL HOSPITAL
18101 Prince Philip Drive
Olney, MD 20832-1512
(301)774-8882

PATUXENT RIVER

NAVAL MEDICAL CENTER PATUXENT RIVER
47149 Buse Road Bldg 1370
Patuxent River, MD 20670-1540
(301)342-1458

PERRY POINT

VA MEDICAL CENTER - PERRY POINT
Perry Point, MD 21902
(410)642-2411

PRINCE FREDERICK

CALVERT MEMORIAL HOSPITAL
100 Hospital Road
Prince Frederick, MD 20678-4016
(410)535-4000

RANDALLSTOWN

NORTHWEST HOSPITAL CENTER
5401 Old Court Road
Randallstown, MD 21133-5185
(410)521-2200

ROCKVILLE

EASTERN NEURO REHABILITATION
HOSPITAL
9909 Medical Center Dr
Rockville, MD 20850-6361
(301)989-2000

KESSLER ADVENTIST REHAB HOSPITAL
9909 Medical Center Drive
Rockville, MD 20850-6361
(240)864-6000

POTOMAC RIDGE BEHAVIORAL HEALTH
SYSTEM
14901 Broschart Road
Rockville, MD 20850-3318
(301)251-4500

SHADY GROVE ADVENTIST HOSPITAL
9901 Medical Center Drive
Rockville, MD 20850-3395
(301)279-6000

SALISBURY

DEERS HEAD CENTER
Emerson Avenue PO Box 2018
Salisbury, MD 21802-2018
(410)543-4000

HEALTHSOUTH CHESAPEAKE REHAB
HOSPITAL
220 Tilghman Road
Salisbury, MD 21804-1921
(410)546-4600

PENINSULA REGIONAL MEDICAL CENTER
100 E Carroll Avenue
Salisbury, MD 21801-5493
(410)546-6400

SILVER SPRING

HOLY CROSS HOSPITAL
1500 Forest Glen Road
Silver Spring, MD 20910-1484
(301)754-7000

SAINT LUKE INSTITUTE
8901 New Hampshire Avenue
Silver Spring, MD 20903-3611
(301)445-7970

SYKESVILLE

SPRINGFIELD HOSPITAL CENTER
6655 Sykesville Road
Sykesville, MD 21784-7966
(410)795-2100

TAKOMA PARK

WASHINGTON ADVENTIST HOSPITAL
7600 Carroll Avenue
Takoma Park, MD 20912-6392
(301)891-7600

TOWSON

SAINT JOSEPH MEDICAL CENTER
7620 York Road
Towson, MD 21204-7508
(410)337-1000

SHEPPARD ENOCH PRATT HOSPITAL
6501 N Charles Street PO Box 6815
Towson, MD 21204-6893
(410)938-3000

WESTMINSTER

CARROLL COUNTY GENERAL HOSPITAL
Memorial Avenue
Westminster, MD 21157
(410)871-6900

MASSACHUSETTS

AMHERST

UNIVERSITY HEALTH SERVICES
University Of Massachusetts
Amherst, MA 01002
(413)577-5000

ANDOVER

ISHAM HEALTH CENTER
Phillips Academy
Andover, MA 01810
(978)749-4455

ATHOL

ATHOL MEMORIAL HOSPITAL
2033 Main Street
Athol, MA 01331-3598
(978)249-3511

ATTLEBORO

STURDY MEMORIAL HOSPITAL
211 Park Street
Attleboro, MA 02703-3137
(508)222-5200

AYER

DEACONESS - NASHOBA HOSPITAL
200 Groton Avenue
Ayer, MA 01432-3300
(978)784-9000

MASSACHUSETTS
Hospital Telephone Directory

BARNSTABLE

BARNSTABLE COUNTY HOSPITAL
PO Box 427
Barnstable, MA 02630-0427
(508)563-5941

BEDFORD

VA HOSPITAL - EDITH NOURSE ROGERS
200 Springs Road
Bedford, MA 01730-1114
(781)687-2000

BELMONT

MCLEAN HOSPITAL
115 Mill St
Belmont, MA 02478-1048
(617)855-2000

BEVERLY

BEVERLY HOSPITAL
85 Herrick Streets
Beverly, MA 01915-1777
(978)922-3000

BOSTON

BETH ISRAEL DEACONESS MEDICAL
CENTER
330 Brookline Avenue
Boston, MA 02215-5400
(617)667-7000

BETH ISRAEL DEACONESS MEDICAL
CENTER - WEST CAMPUS
One Deaconess Road
Boston, MA 02215-5321
(617)632-7000

BOSTON MEDICAL CENTER - HAC
818 Harrison Avenue
Boston, MA 02118-2370
(617)638-8000

BOSTON UNIVERSITY MEDICAL CENTER
1 Boston Medical Center Pl
Boston, MA 02118-2908
(617)638-8000

BRIGHAM AND WOMENS HOSPITAL
75 Francis St
Boston, MA 02115-6110
(617)732-5500

CARITAS SAINT ELIZABETHS MEDICAL
CENTER
736 Cambridge St
Boston, MA 02135-2907
(617)789-3000

CARNEY HOSPITAL
2100 Dorchester Avenue
Boston, MA 02124-5666
(617)296-4000

CHILDRENS HOSPITAL
300 Longwood Avenue
Boston, MA 02115-5737
(617)355-6000

DANA-FARBER CANCER INSTITUTE
44 Binney St
Boston, MA 02115-6084
(617)632-3000

DR SOLOMON CARTER FULLER M H
CENTER
85 East Newton Street
Boston, MA 02118-2389
(617)626-8700

ERICH LINDEMANN MENTAL HEALTH
CENTER
25 Staniford Street
Boston, MA 02114-2575
(617)626-8500

FAULKNER HOSPITAL
1153 Centre St
Boston, MA 02130-3446
(617)983-7000

FRANCISCAN CHILDRENS HOSPITAL
30 Warren St
Boston, MA 02135-3602
(617)254-3800

HEBREW REHABILITATION CENTER FOR
THE AGED
1200 Centre Street
Boston, MA 02131-1011
(617)325-8000

JEWISH MEMORIAL HOSPITAL
59 Townsend St
Boston, MA 02119-1399
(617)442-8760

KINDRED HOSPITAL BOSTON
1515 Commonwealth Avenue
Boston, MA 02135-3617
(617)254-1100

LEMUEL SHATTUCK HOSPITAL
170 Morton St
Boston, MA 02130-3735
(617)522-8110

MASSACHUSETTS EYE AND EAR
INFIRMARY
243 Charles St
Boston, MA 02114-3002
(617)523-7900

MASSACHUSETTS GENERAL HOSPITAL
Fruit St
Boston, MA 02114
(617)726-2000

NEW ENGLAND BAPTIST HOSPITAL
125 Parker Hill Avenue
Boston, MA 02120-2847
(617)754-5800

SHRINERS HOSPITALS FOR CHILDREN -
SHRINERS BURNS HOSPITAL
51 Blossom St
Boston, MA 02114-2601
(617)722-3000

SPAULDING REHAB HOSPITAL
125 Nashua St
Boston, MA 02114-1198
(617)573-7000

TUFFS-NEW ENGLAND MEDICAL CENTER
750 Washington Street
Boston, MA 02111-1533
(617)636-5000

VA MEDICAL CENTER AT JAMAICA PLAIN
150 S Huntington Avenue
Boston, MA 02130-4817
(617)232-9500

BRAINTREE

HEALTHSOUTH BRAINTREE REHAB
HOSPITAL
250 Pond St
Braintree, MA 02184-5351
(718)848-5353

NORTHEAST SPECIALTY HOSPITAL
2001 Washington St
Braintree, MA 02184-8664
(781)848-2600

BRIDGEWATER

BRIDGEWATER STATE HOSPITAL
20 Administration Road
Bridgewater, MA 02324-3201
(508)279-4521

BRIGHTON

SAINT ELIZABETHS HOSPITAL
736 Cambridge St
Brighton, MA 02135-2997
(617)789-3000

BROCKTON

BROCKTON HOSPITAL
680 Center Street
Brockton, MA 02302-3395
(508)941-7000

GOOD SAMARITAN MEDICAL CENTER
235 North Pearl St
Brockton, MA 02301-1700
(508)427-3000

VA MEDICAL CENTER - BOSTON AT
BROCKTON
940 Belmont St
Brockton, MA 02301-5568
(508)583-4500

BROOKLINE

ARBOUR HUMAN RESOURCE INSTITUTE OF
BOSTON
227 Babcock Street
Brookline, MA 02446-6799
(617)731-3200

BOURNEWOOD HOSPITAL
300 South Street
Brookline, MA 02467-3694
(617)469-0300

BURLINGTON

LAHEY CLINIC
41 Mall Road
Burlington, MA 01803-4521
(781)744-5100

CAMBRIDGE

CAMBRIDGE HOSPITAL
1493 Cambridge St
Cambridge, MA 02139-1099
(617)665-1000

MIT MEDICAL DEPARTMENT
77 Massachusetts Avenue
Cambridge, MA 02139-4301
(617)253-4481

MOUNT AUBURN HOSPITAL
330 Mt Auburn St
Cambridge, MA 02138-5597
(617)492-3500

STILLMAN INFIRMARY-HARVARD
UNIVERSITY
75 Mount Auburn Street
Cambridge, MA 02138-4960
(617)495-2034

YOUVILLE HOSPITAL
1575 Cambridge St
Cambridge, MA 02138-4398
(617)876-4344

CANTON

MASSACHUSETTS HOSPITAL SCHOOL
3 Randolph Street
Canton, MA 02021-2351
(781)828-2440

CHELSEA

LAWRENCE F. QUIGLEY MEMORIAL
HOSPITAL
91 Crest Avenue
Chelsea, MA 02150-2154
(617)884-5660

Hospital Telephone Directory — MASSACHUSETTS

CHESTNUT HILL
BOURNEWOOD HOSPITAL
300 South St
Chestnut Hill, MA 02467-3694
(617)469-0300

CLINTON
CLINTON HOSPITAL ASSOCIATION
201 Highland St
Clinton, MA 01510-1096
(978)368-3000

CONCORD
EMERSON HOSPITAL
Old Road To 9 Acre Corner
Concord, MA 01742
(978)369-1400

DEVENS
FEDERAL MEDICAL CENTER - DEVENS
42 Patton Road
Devens, MA 01432-3801
(978)796-1000

EAST SANDWICH
REHAB HOSPITAL OF THE CAPE AND ISLANDS
311 Service Road
East Sandwich, MA 02537-1371
(508)833-4000

EVERETT
WHIDDEN MEMORIAL HOSPITAL
103 Garland St
Everett, MA 02149-5095
(617)389-6270

FALL RIVER
CHARLTON MEMORIAL HOSPITAL
363 Highland Avenue
Fall River, MA 02720-3700
(508)679-3131

DR JOHN C CORRIGAN MENTAL HEALTH CENTER
49 Hillside St
Fall River, MA 02720-5266
(508)235-7200

SAINT ANNES HOSPITAL
795 Middle St
Fall River, MA 02721-1798
(508)674-5741

FALMOUTH
FALMOUTH HOSPITAL
67&100 Ter Heun Drive
Falmouth, MA 02540
(508)548-5300

FITCHBURG
HEALTH ALLIANCE BURBANK HOSPITAL
275 Nichols Road
Fitchburg, MA 01420-1931
(978)343-5000

FRAMINGHAM
BETHANY HEALTHCARE CENTER
97 Bethany Road
Framingham, MA 01702-7237
(508)872-6750

METROWEST MEDICAL CENTER - FRAMINGHAM UNION HOSPITAL
115 Lincoln St
Framingham, MA 01702-6342
(508)383-1000

GARDNER
HEYWOOD HOSPITAL
242 Green Street
Gardner, MA 01440-1373
(978)632-3420

GEORGETOWN
BALDPATE HOSPITAL
Baldpate Road
Georgetown, MA 01833
(978)352-2131

GLOUCESTER
ADDISON GILBERT HOSPITAL
298 Washington St
Gloucester, MA 01930-4889
(978)283-4000

GREAT BARRINGTON
FAIRVIEW HOSPITAL
29 Lewis Avenue
Great Barrington, MA 01230-1796
(413)528-0790

GREENFIELD
FRANKLIN MEDICAL CENTER
164 High St
Greenfield, MA 01301-2613
(413)773-0211

HAVERHILL
MERRIMACK VALLEY HOSPITAL
140 Lincoln Avenue
Haverhill, MA 01830-6798
(978)374-2000

WHITTIER REHABILITATION HOSPITAL
76 Summer St
Haverhill, MA 01830-5896
(978)372-8000

HOLYOKE
HOLYOKE HOSPITAL INC
575 Beech St
Holyoke, MA 01040-2296
(413)534-2500

PROVIDENCE HOSPITAL
1233 Main St
Holyoke, MA 01040-5394
(413)536-5111

SOLDIERS HOME OF HOLYOKE
Cherry St
Holyoke, MA 01040
(413)532-9475

HYANNIS
CAPE COD HOSPITAL
27 Park St
Hyannis, MA 02601-5203
(508)771-1800

JAMAICA PLAIN
ARBOUR HOSPITAL
49 Robinwood Ave
Jamaica Plain, MA 02130-2156
(617)522-4400

LAWRENCE
LAWRENCE GENERAL HOSPITAL
One General Street
Lawrence, MA 01841-2997
(978)683-4000

LEEDS
VA MEDICAL CENTER - NORTHAMPTON
421 N Main St
Leeds, MA 01053-9700
(413)584-4040

LEOMINSTER
HEALTH ALLIANCE LEOMINSTER HOSPITAL
60 Hospital Road
Leominster, MA 01453-2242
(978)466-2000

LOWELL
DR HARRY SOLOMON MHC
391 Varnum Avenue
Lowell, MA 01854-2119
(978)322-5000

HEALTHSOUTH SAINT JOSEPH HEALTHCARE CENTER
220 Pawtucket Street
Lowell, MA 01854-3573
(978)453-1761

LOWELL GENERAL HOSPITAL
295 Varnum Avenue
Lowell, MA 01854-2193
(978)937-6000

SAINTS MEMORIAL MEDICAL CENTER
One Hospital Drive
Lowell, MA 01852-1389
(978)458-1411

LUDLOW
HEALTHSOUTH HOSPITAL OF WESTERN MASSACHUSETTS
14 Chestnut Place
Ludlow, MA 01056-3476
(413)589-7581

LYNN
BAY RIDGE HOSPITAL
60 Granite St
Lynn, MA 01904-2915
(781)598-5100

UNION HOSPITAL
500 Lynfield St
Lynn, MA 01904-1424
(781)581-9200

MALDEN
HALLMARK HEALTH - MALDEN MEDICAL CENTER
100 Hospital Road
Malden, MA 02148-3591
(781)322-7560

MARLBOROUGH
MARLBOROUGH HOSPITAL
57 Union St
Marlborough, MA 01752-1208
(508)481-5000

MEDFORD
LAWRENCE MEMORIAL HOSPITAL OF MEDFORD
170 Governors Avenue
Medford, MA 02155-1643
(781)306-6000

MASSACHUSETTS
Hospital Telephone Directory

MELROSE

MELROSE-WAKEFIELD HOSPITAL
585 Lebanon St
Melrose, MA 02176-3298
(781)979-3000

METHUEN

HOLY FAMILY HOSPITAL AND MEDICAL CENTER
70 East St
Methuen, MA 01844-4597
(978)687-0151

MILFORD

MILFORD WHITINSVILLE REGIONAL HOSPITAL
14 Prospect Street
Milford, MA 01757-3090
(508)473-1190

MILTON

MILTON MEDICAL CENTER
92 Highland St
Milton, MA 02186-3800
(617)696-4600

NAHANT

CHARLES RIVER HOSPITAL
8 Summer St
Nahant, MA 01908-1415
(781)235-8400

NANTUCKET

NANTUCKET COTTAGE HOSPITAL
S Prospect St
Nantucket, MA 02554
(508)228-1200

NATICK

METROWEST MEDICAL CENTER - LEONARD MORSE HOSPITAL
67 Union Street
Natick, MA 01760-6089
(508)650-7000

NEEDHAM

DEACONESS-GLOVER HOSPITAL
148 Chestnut St
Needham, MA 02492-2505
(781)453-3000

NEW BEDFORD

NEW BEDFORD REHAB HOSPITAL
4499 Acushnet Avenue
New Bedford, MA 02745-4707
(508)995-6900

SAINT LUKES HOSPITAL
101 Page St
New Bedford, MA 02740-3400
(508)997-1515

NEWBURYPORT

ANNA JAQUES HOSPITAL
25 Highland Avenue
Newburyport, MA 01950-3894
(978)463-1000

NEWTON LOWER FALLS

NEWTON-WELLESLEY HOSPITAL
2014 Washington St
Newton Lower Falls, MA 02462-1699
(617)243-6000

NORFOLK

MASSACHUSETTS CORRECTIONAL INSTITUTION
PO Box 43
Norfolk, MA 02056-0043
(508)668-0800

NORTH ADAMS

NORTH ADAMS REGIONAL HOSPITAL
Hospital Avenue
North Adams, MA 01247
(413)663-3701

NORTHAMPTON

COOLEY DICKINSON HOSPITAL
30 Locust St
Northampton, MA 01060-2093
(413)582-2000

NORWOOD

CARITAS NORWOOD HOSPITAL
800 Washington St
Norwood, MA 02062-3487
(781)769-4000

OAK BLUFFS

MARTHAS VINEYARD HOSPITAL
75 Linton Lane
Oak Bluffs, MA 02557
(508)693-0410

PALMER

WING MEMORIAL HOSPITAL
Wright St
Palmer, MA 01069-1187
(413)283-7651

PEABODY

KINDRED HOSPITAL BOSTON NORTH SHORE HOSPITAL
15 King St
Peabody, MA 01960-4379
(978)531-2900

PEMBROKE

PEMBROKE HOSPITAL
199 Oak St
Pembroke, MA 02359-1953
(781)826-8161

PITTSFIELD

BERKSHIRE MEDICAL CENTER
725 North Street
Pittsfield, MA 01201-4124
(413)447-2000

HILLCREST HOSPITAL
165 Tor Court
Pittsfield, MA 01201-3001
(413)443-4761

PLYMOUTH

JORDAN HOSPITAL
275 Sandwich Street
Plymouth, MA 02360-2196
(508)746-2000

POCASSET

CAPE COD AND ISLANDS COMMUNITY MENTAL HEALTH CENTER
830 County Road
Pocasset, MA 02559-2110
(508)564-9600

QUINCY

QUINCY AND SOUTH SHORE MENTAL HEALTH CENTER
460 Quincy Avenue
Quincy, MA 02169-8130
(617)626-9000

QUINCY HOSPITAL
114 Whitewell Street
Quincy, MA 02169-1870
(617)773-6100

SALEM

NORTH SHORE CHILDREN'S HOSPITAL
57 Highland Avenue
Salem, MA 01970-2197
(978)745-2100

SALEM HOSPITAL
81 Highland Avenue
Salem, MA 01970-2768
(978)741-1200

SHAUGHNESSY-KAPLAN REHAB HOSPITAL HOSPITAL
Dove Avenue
Salem, MA 01970
(978)745-9000

SOMERVILLE

SOMERVILLE HOSPITAL
230 Highland Avenue
Somerville, MA 02143-1491
(617)666-4400

SOUTH ATTLEBORO

ARBOUR-FULLER HOSPITAL
200 May St
South Attleboro, MA 02703-5520
(508)761-8500

SOUTH WEYMOUTH

SOUTH SHORE HOSPITAL
55 Fogg Road
South Weymouth, MA 02190-2455
(781)340-8000

SOUTHBRIDGE

HARRINGTON MEMORIAL HOSPITAL
100 South St
Southbridge, MA 01550-4051
(508)765-9771

SPRINGFIELD

BAYSTATE MEDICAL CENTER
759 Chestnut St
Springfield, MA 01199-0001
(413)794-0000

MERCY HOSPITAL
271 Carew Street
Springfield, MA 01104-2398
(413)748-9000

PARK VIEW SPECIALTY HOSPITAL SPRINGFIELD
1400 State St
Springfield, MA 01109-2550
(413)787-6700

SHRINERS HOSPITAL
516 Carew St
Springfield, MA 01104-2396
(413)787-2000

STOCKBRIDGE

AUSTEN RIGGS CENTER
PO Box 962
Stockbridge, MA 01262-0962
(413)298-5511

STOUGHTON

NEW ENGLAND SINAI HOSPITAL AND REHAB CENTER
150 York St
Stoughton, MA 02072-1881
(781)344-0600

TAUNTON

MORTON HOSPITAL AND MEDICAL CENTER
88 Washington St
Taunton, MA 02780-2499
(508)828-7000

TAUNTON STATE HOSPITAL
60 Hodges Avenue, PO Box 4007
Taunton, MA 02780-0997
(508)977-3000

TEWKSBURY

TEWKSBURY HOSPITAL
365 East Street
Tewksbury, MA 01876-1998
(978)851-7321

WALTHAM

STERLING MEDICAL CENTER
9 Hope Avenue
Waltham, MA 02453
(781)647-6000

WARE

MARY LANE HOSPITAL
85 South St
Ware, MA 01082-1667
(413)967-6211

WAREHAM

SOUTH COAST HOSPITAL GROUP/TOBEY HOSPITAL
43 High St
Wareham, MA 02571-2097
(508)295-0880

WEBSTER

HUBBARD REGIONAL HOSPITAL
340 Thompson Road
Webster, MA 01570-1512
(508)943-2600

WEST ROXBURY

VA MEDICAL CENTER - WEST ROXBURY
1400 Vfw Parkway
West Roxbury, MA 02132-4927
(617)323-7700

WESTBOROUGH

MEDFIELD STATE HOSPITAL
PO Box 288
Westborough, MA 01581-0288
(508)242-8000

WESTBOROUGH STATE HOSPITAL DANIELS BUILDING
Lyman St PO Box 288
Westborough, MA 01581-0288
(508)616-2100

WHITTIER REHAB HOSPITAL - WESTBOROUGH
150 Flanders Road
Westborough, MA 01581-1017
(508)871-2000

WESTFIELD

NOBLE HOSPITAL
115 W Silver St
Westfield, MA 01085-3693
(413)568-2811

WESTERN MASSACHUSETTS HOSPITAL
91 East Mountain Road
Westfield, MA 01085-1889
(413)562-4131

WESTWOOD

WESTWOOD LODGE HOSPITAL
45 Clapboardtree St
Westwood, MA 02090-2903
(781)762-7764

WINCHESTER

WINCHESTER HOSPITAL
41 Highland Avenue
Winchester, MA 01890-1496
(781)729-9000

WOBURN

HEALTHSOUTH NEW ENGLAND REHAB HOSPITAL
2 Rehabilitation Way
Woburn, MA 01801-6099
(781)935-5050

WORCESTER

ADCARE HOSPITAL OF WORCESTER
107 Lincoln St
Worcester, MA 01605-2499
(508)799-9000

FAIRLAWN REHABILITATION HOSPITAL
189 May St
Worcester, MA 01602-4399
(508)791-6351

SAINT VINCENT HOSPITAL AT WORCESTER MEDICAL CENTER
20 Worcester Center Road
Worcester, MA 01608-1309
(508)363-5000

UNIVERSITY OF MASSACHUSETTS MEMORIAL HEALTH CARE CENTER - UNIVERSITY CAMPUS
55 Lake Avenue North
Worcester, MA 01655-0002
(508)334-1000

UNIVERSITY OF MASSACHUSETTS MEMORIAL HEALTH CARE
119 Belmont St
Worcester, MA 01605-2903
(508)334-1000

UNIVERSITY OF MASSACHUSETTS MEMORIAL MEDICAL CENTER - HAHNEMANN CAMPUS
281 Lincoln Street
Worcester, MA 01605-2138
(508)334-1000

WORCESTER STATE HOSPITAL
305 Belmont Street
Worcester, MA 01604-1695
(508)368-3300

MICHIGAN

ADRIAN

BIXBY MEDICAL CENTER
818 Riverside Avenue
Adrian, MI 49221-1488
(517)263-0711

ALLEGAN

ALLEGAN GENERAL HOSPITAL
555 Linn St
Allegan, MI 49010-1594
(269)673-8424

ALLEN PARK

OAKWOOD HEALTHCARE CENTER-ALLEN PARK
15915 Southfield Road
Allen Park, MI 48101-2512
(313)294-1000

ALMA

GRATIOT COMMUNITY HOSPITAL
300 Warwick Drive
Alma, MI 48801-1096
(989)463-1101

ALPENA

ALPENA GENERAL HOSPITAL
1501-1511 W Chisholm St
Alpena, MI 49707-1498
(989)356-7245

ANN ARBOR

C S MOTT CHILDREN'S HOSPITAL
1500 E Medical Center Drive
Ann Arbor, MI 48109-0999
(734)936-4000

SAINT JOSEPH MERCY HOSPITAL
5301 E Huron River Drive
Ann Arbor, MI 48106
(517)712-3456

SELECT SPECIALTY HOSPITAL - ANN ARBOR
5301 East Huron River Drive, 6th Floor
Ann Arbor, MI 48106
(517)712-0500

UNIVERSITY OF MICHIGAN HEALTH SYSTEM
1500 E Medical Center Drive
Ann Arbor, MI 48109-0001
(734)936-4000

VA HEALTHCARE SYSTEM - ANN ARBOR
2215 Fuller Road
Ann Arbor, MI 48105-2303
(734)769-7100

AUBURN HILLS

HAVENWYCK HOSPITAL
1525 University Drive
Auburn Hills, MI 48326-2675
(248)373-9200

BAD AXE

HURON MEMORIAL HOSPITAL
1100 South Van Dyke Road
Bad Axe, MI 48413-9799
(989)269-8933

BATTLE CREEK

BATTLE CREEK HEALTH SYSTEM
300 North Avenue
Battle Creek, MI 49017-3307
(269)966-8000

FIELDSTONE CENTER
165 Washington Avenue N
Battle Creek, MI 49017-2929
(269)966-8000

MICHIGAN — Hospital Telephone Directory

SELECT SPECIALTY HOSPITAL - BATTLE CREEK
300 North Avenue, 6th Floor
Battle Creek, MI 49017-3307
(269)565-8900

SOUTHWESTERN MICHIGAN REHABILITATION HOSPITAL
183 West Street
Battle Creek, MI 49017-3424
(269)965-3206

VA MEDICAL CENTER - BATTLE CREEK
5500 Armstrong Road
Battle Creek, MI 49015-1014
(269)966-5600

BAY CITY

BAY MEDICAL CENTER
1900 Columbus Avenue
Bay City, MI 48708-6880
(989)894-3000

BAY MEDICAL CENTER - SAMARITAN
713 Ninth Street
Bay City, MI 48708-6403
(989)894-3799

BAY SPECIAL CARE CENTER
3250 E Midland Road, Suite 1
Bay City, MI 48706-2835
(989)667-6750

BERRIEN CENTER

LAKELAND SPECIALTY HOSPITAL - BERRIEN
6418 Deans Hill Road
Berrien Center, MI 49102-9750
(269)471-7761

BIG RAPIDS

MECOSTA COUNTY GENERAL HOSPITAL
405 Winter
Big Rapids, MI 49307-2099
(231)796-8691

BRIGHTON

BRIGHTON HOSPITAL
12851 E Grand River
Brighton, MI 48116-8596
(810)227-1211

CADILLAC

MERCY HOSPITAL-CADILLAC
400 Hobart
Cadillac, MI 49601-2389
(231)876-7200

CARO

CARO COMMUNITY HOSPITAL
PO Box 435
Caro, MI 48723-0435
(989)673-3141

CARO REGIONAL MENTAL HEALTH CENTER
2000 Chambers Rd
Caro, MI 48723-9293
(989)673-3191

CARSON CITY

CARSON CITY HOSPITAL
Elm At 3rd St
Carson City, MI 48811
(989)584-0053

CASS CITY

HILLS AND DALES GENERAL HOSPITAL
4675 Hill St
Cass City, MI 48726-1099
(989)872-2121

CHARLEVOIX

CHARLEVOIX AREA HOSPITAL
Lake Shore Drive
Charlevoix, MI 49720
(231)547-4024

CHARLOTTE

HAYES GREEN BEACH MEMORIAL HOSPITAL
321 Harris Street
Charlotte, MI 48813-1697
(517)543-1050

CHEBOYGAN

CHEBOYGAN MEMORIAL HOSPITAL
748 S Main
Cheboygan, MI 49721-2299
(231)627-5601

CHELSEA

CHELSEA COMMUNITY HOSPITAL
775 S Main St
Chelsea, MI 48118-1370
(734)475-1311

CLARE

MIDMICHIGAN REGIONAL MEDICAL CENTER-CLARE
703 N Mcewan St
Clare, MI 48617-1440
(989)802-5000

CLINTON TOWNSHIP

SAINT JOSEPH'S MERCY HOSPITAL - WEST
15855 19 Mile Road
Clinton Township, MI 48038-6324
(586)263-2300

COLDWATER

COMMUNITY HEALTH CENTER OF BRANCH COUNTY
274 E Chicago St
Coldwater, MI 49036-2088
(517)279-5400

COMMERCE

HURON VALLEY-SINAI HOSPITAL
1 William Carls Drive
Commerce, MI 48382-2201
(248)937-3300

DEARBORN

OAKWOOD HOSPITAL AND MEDICAL CENTER
18101 Oakwood Boulevard
Dearborn, MI 48124-4095
(313)593-7000

DECKERVILLE

DECKERVILLE COMMUNITY HOSPITAL
3559 Pine St
Deckerville, MI 48427
(810)376-2835

DETROIT

CHILDRENS HOSPITAL OF MICHIGAN
3901 Beaubien
Detroit, MI 48201-2196
(313)966-5110

DETROIT RECEIVING HOSPITAL AND UNIVERSITY HEALTH CENTER
4201 St Antoine
Detroit, MI 48201-2194
(313)745-3603

HARPER HOSPITAL
3990 John R Street
Detroit, MI 48201-2097
(313)745-8040

HENRY FORD HOSPITAL
2799 W Grand Boulevard
Detroit, MI 48202-2689
(313)916-2600

HENRY FORD MEDICAL CENTER
7800 West Outer Drive
Detroit, MI 48235-3461
(313)653-2000

HUTZEL HOSPITAL
4707 St Antoine Boulevard
Detroit, MI 48201-1498
(313)745-7555

KINDRED HOSPITAL METRO DETROIT
2700 Martin Luther King Jr Boulevard
Detroit, MI 48208-2576
(313)361-8000

REHABILITATION INSTITUTE
261 Mack Boulevard
Detroit, MI 48201-2495
(313)745-1203

RENAISSANCE HOSPITAL AND MEDICAL CENTERS
801 Virginia Park
Detroit, MI 48202-1925
(313)874-5660

SAINT JOHN HOSPITAL AND MEDICAL CENTER
22101 Moross Road
Detroit, MI 48236-2172
(313)343-4000

SAINT JOHN NORTHEAST COMMUNITY HOSPITAL
4777 E Outer Dr
Detroit, MI 48234-3241
(313)369-9100

SAINT JOHNS DETROIT RIVERVIEW HOSPITAL
7733 E Jefferson
Detroit, MI 48214-2598
(313)499-4000

SCCI HOSPITAL - DETROIT
15000 Gratiot Avenue
Detroit, MI 48205-1973
(313)372-2200

SELECT SPECIALTY HOSPITAL - NORTHWEST DETROIT
6071 West Outer Drive
Detroit, MI 48235-2624
(313)966-3939

SELECT SPECIALTY HOSPITAL OF NORTHWEST DETROIT
6071 West Outer Drive
Detroit, MI 48235-2624
(313)966-6740

SINAI-GRACE HOSPITAL
6071 W Outer Drive
Detroit, MI 48235-2679
(313)966-3300

Hospital Telephone Directory — **MICHIGAN**

VA MEDICAL CENTER - JOHN D. DINGELL
4646 John R Detroit
Detroit, MI 48201-1916
(313)576-1000

DOWAGIAC

BORGESS-LEE MEMORIAL HOSPITAL
420 West High Street
Dowagiac, MI 49047-1996
(269)782-8681

EAST CHINA

SAINT JOHN RIVER DISTRICT HOSPITAL
4100 River Road
East China, MI 48054-2914
(810)329-7111

EATON RAPIDS

EATON RAPIDS COMMUNITY HOSPITAL
1500 South Main Street
Eaton Rapids, MI 48827-1999
(517)663-2671

ESCANABA

SAINT FRANCIS HOSPITAL
3401 Ludington St
Escanaba, MI 49829-1377
(906)786-3311

FARMINGTON

BOTSFORD GENERAL HOSPITAL
28050 Grand St
Farmington, MI 48336-5933
(248)471-8000

FERNDALE

HENRY FORD-KINGSWOOD HOSPITAL
10300 W Eight Mile Road
Ferndale, MI 48220-2198
(248)398-3200

FLINT

HURLEY MEDICAL CENTER
1 Hurley Plaza
Flint, MI 48503-5902
(810)257-9000

MCLAREN REGIONAL MEDICAL CENTER
401 Ballenger Highway
Flint, MI 48532-3685
(810)342-2000

SELECT SPECIALTY HOSPITAL - FLINT
One Hurley Plaza
Flint, MI 48503-5902
(810)762-7200

FRANKFORT

PAUL OLIVER MEMORIAL HOSPITAL
224 Park Avenue
Frankfort, MI 49635-9658
(231)352-9621

FREMONT

GERBER MEMORIAL HOSPITAL
212 S Sullivan St
Fremont, MI 49412-1585
(231)924-3300

GARDEN CITY

GARDEN CITY OSTEOPATHIC HOSPITAL
6245 North Inkster Road
Garden City, MI 48135-4001
(734)421-3300

GAYLORD

OTSEGO MEMORIAL HOSPITAL
825 N Center St
Gaylord, MI 49735-1560
(989)731-2100

GLADWIN

MIDMICHIGAN REGIONAL MEDICAL
CENTER-GLADWIN
455 Quarter Street
Gladwin, MI 48624-1918
(989)426-9286

GRAND BLANC

GENESYS REGIONAL MEDICAL CENTER
One Genesys Parkway
Grand Blanc, MI 48439-8066
(810)606-5000

GRAND HAVEN

NORTH OTTAWA COMMUNITY HOSPITAL
1309 Sheldon Road
Grand Haven, MI 49417-2488
(616)842-3600

GRAND RAPIDS

FOREST VIEW HOSPITAL
1055 Medical Park Se
Grand Rapids, MI 49546-8323
(616)942-9610

MARY FREE BED HOSPITAL AND REHAB
235 Wealthy Se
Grand Rapids, MI 49503-5247
(616)242-0300

METROPOLITIAN HOSPITAL
1919 Boston S E
Grand Rapids, MI 49506-4199
(616)252-7200

PINE REST CHRISTIAN HOSPITAL
300 - 68th Street, Se
Grand Rapids, MI 49548-6927
(616)455-5000

SAINT MARYS HEALTH SERVICES
200 Jefferson St Se
Grand Rapids, MI 49503-4598
(616)752-6090

SPECTRUM HEALTH - BLODGETT CAMPUS
1840 Wealthy St S E
Grand Rapids, MI 49506-2968
(616)774-7444

SPECTRUM HEALTH - KENT COMMUNITY
750 Fuller Avenue, Ne
Grand Rapids, MI 49503-1918
(616)336-3300

SPECTRUM HEALTH CARE - DOWNTOWN
100 Michigan N E
Grand Rapids, MI 49503-2560
(616)391-1774

GRAYLING

MERCY HOSPITAL
1100 Michigan Avenue
Grayling, MI 49738-1398
(989)348-5461

GREENVILLE

UNITED MEMORIAL HOSPITAL
615 S Bower Street
Greenville, MI 48838-2628
(616)754-4691

GROSSE POINTE

BON SECOURS HOSPITAL
468 Cadieux Road
Grosse Pointe, MI 48230-1592
(313)343-1000

GROSSE POINTE FARMS

BON SECOURS COTTAGE HOSPITAL
159 Kercheval Avenue
Grosse Pointe Farms, MI 48236-3692
(313)640-1000

HANCOCK

PORTAGE HEALTH SYSTEM
500 Campus Drive
Hancock, MI 49930-1569
(906)483-1000

HARBOR BEACH

HARBOR BEACH COMMUNITY HOSPITAL
210 South First Street
Harbor Beach, MI 48441-1236
(989)479-3201

HARRISON TOWNSHIP

SAINT JOHN NORTH SHORE HOSPITAL
26755 Ballard Road
Harrison Township, MI 48045-2419
(586)465-5501

HASTINGS

PENNOCK HOSPITAL
1009 W Green St
Hastings, MI 49058-1790
(269)945-3451

HILLSDALE

HILLSDALE COMMUNITY HEALTH CENTER
168 S Howell Street
Hillsdale, MI 49242-2040
(517)437-4451

HOLLAND

HOLLAND COMMUNITY HOSPITAL
602 Michigan Avenue
Holland, MI 49423-4999
(616)392-5141

HOWELL

SAINT JOSEPH MERCY LIVINGSTON
HOSPITAL
620 Byron Road
Howell, MI 48843-1002
(517)545-6000

IONIA

IONIA COUNTY MEMORIAL HOSPITAL
479 Lafayette St
Ionia, MI 48846-1899
(616)527-4200

IRON MOUNTAIN

DICKINSON COUNTY MEMORIAL HOSPITAL
1721 S Stephenson Avenue
Iron Mountain, MI 49801-3637
(906)774-1313

VA MEDICAL CENTER - IRON MOUNTAIN
325 East H Street
Iron Mountain, MI 49801-4792
(906)774-3300

MICHIGAN
Hospital Telephone Directory

IRON RIVER

IRON COUNTY GENERAL HOSPITAL
1400 W Ice Lake Road
Iron River, MI 49935-9594
(906)265-6121

IRONWOOD

GRAND VIEW HOSPITAL
N10561 Grand View Lane
Ironwood, MI 49938-9359
(906)932-2525

ISHPEMING

BELL MEMORIAL HOSPITAL
101 S 4th St
Ishpeming, MI 49849-2151
(906)486-4431

JACKSON

DOCTORS HOSPITAL OF JACKSON
110 N Elm Avenue
Jackson, MI 49202-3595
(517)787-1440

DUANE L WATERS HOSPITAL
3857 Cooper St
Jackson, MI 49201-7521
(517)780-5600

FOOTE HEALTH SYSTEM
205 N East Avenue
Jackson, MI 49201-1753
(517)788-4800

TRILLIUM HOSPITAL
205 N East Ave
Jackson, MI 49201-1753
(517)629-2191

KALAMAZOO

BORGESS MEDICAL CENTER
1521 Gull Road
Kalamazoo, MI 49048-1666
(269)226-4800

BRONSON METHODIST HOSPITAL
252 East Lovell Street
Kalamazoo, MI 49007-5363
(269)341-7654

KALAMAZOO PSYCHIATRIC HOSPITAL
1312 Oakland Drive
Kalamazoo, MI 49008-1205
(269)337-3000

KALKASKA

KALKASKA MEMORIAL HEALTH CENTER
419 South Coral, Box 249
Kalkaska, MI 49646-2500
(231)258-7500

L'ANSE

BARAGA COUNTY MEMORIAL HOSPITAL
770 North Main Street
L'anse, MI 49946-1195
(906)524-3300

LAKEVIEW

KELSEY MEMORIAL HOSPITAL
418 Washington Avenue
Lakeview, MI 48850
(989)352-7211

LANSING

EDWARD W SPARROW HOSPITAL
1215 E Michigan Avenue
Lansing, MI 48912-1896
(517)483-2700

INGHAM REGIONAL MEDICAL CENTER
2727 S Pennsylvania Avenue
Lansing, MI 48910-3494
(517)372-8220

INGHAM REGIONAL MEDICAL CENTER - GREENLAWN CAMPUS
401 W Greenlawn Avenue
Lansing, MI 48910-0899
(517)334-2121

SPARROW HEALTH SYSTEM - SAINT LAWRENCE HOSPITAL
1210 W Saginaw St
Lansing, MI 48915-1927
(517)372-3610

LAPEER

LAPEER REGIONAL HOSPITAL
1375 N Main St
Lapeer, MI 48446-1376
(810)667-5500

LAURIUM

KEWEENAW MEMORIAL MEDICAL CENTER
205 Osceola Street
Laurium, MI 49913-2199
(906)337-6500

LINCOLN PARK

KINDRED HOSPITAL DETROIT
26400 W Outer Drive
Lincoln Park, MI 48146-2088
(313)386-2000

LIVONIA

SAINT MARY MERCY HOSPITAL
36475 Five Mile Road
Livonia, MI 48154-1971
(734)655-4800

LUDINGTON

MEMORIAL MEDICAL CENTER OF WEST MICHIGAN
1 Atkinson Drive
Ludington, MI 49431-1906
(231)843-2591

MADISON HEIGHTS

SAINT JOHN HEALTH SYSTEM OAKLAND GENERAL
27351 Dequindre
Madison Heights, MI 48071-3499
(248)967-7000

MADISON HTS

MADISON COMMUNITY HOSPITAL
30773 Stephenson Hwy
Madison Hts, MI 48071-1618
(248)588-8000

MANISTEE

WEST SHORE HOSPITAL
1465 E Parkdale Avenue
Manistee, MI 49660-9785
(231)398-1000

MANISTIQUE

SCHOOLCRAFT MEMORIAL HOSPITAL
500 Main St
Manistique, MI 49854-1599
(906)341-3200

MARLETTE

MARLETTE COMMUNITY HOSPITAL
2770 Main Street
Marlette, MI 48453-1195
(989)635-4000

MARQUETTE

MARQUETTE GENERAL HOSPITAL
420 West Magnetic Street
Marquette, MI 49855-2794
(906)228-9440

MARSHALL

OAKLAWN HOSPITAL
200 N Madison
Marshall, MI 49068-1199
(269)781-4271

MIDLAND

MIDMICHIGAN REGIONAL MEDICAL CENTER
4005 Orchard Drive
Midland, MI 48670-0001
(989)839-3000

MONROE

MERCY-MEMORIAL HOSPITAL
740 N Macomb Street, PO Box 67
Monroe, MI 48161-0067
(734)241-1700

MOUNT CLEMENS

MOUNT CLEMENS GENERAL HOSPITAL
1000 Harrington Boulevard
Mount Clemens, MI 48043-2992
(586)493-8000

SAINT JOSEPH'S MERCY HOSPITAL - EAST
215 North Avenue
Mount Clemens, MI 48043-1700
(586)466-9300

SELECT SPECIALTY HOSPITAL - MACOMB COUNTY
215 North Avenue, Suite 200
Mount Clemens, MI 48043-1716
(586)307-9000

MOUNT PLEASANT

CENTRAL MICHIGAN COMMUNITY HOSPITAL
1221 South Drive
Mount Pleasant, MI 48858-3234
(989)772-6700

MUNISING

MUNISING MEMORIAL HOSPITAL
1500 Sand Point Road
Munising, MI 49862-1497
(906)387-4110

MUSKEGON

HACKLEY HOSPITAL
1700 Clinton Street
Muskegon, MI 49442-5591
(231)726-3511

LIFECARE HOSPITAL
1700 Oak Avenue
Muskegon, MI 49442-2407
(231)777-6452

MERCY GENERAL HEALTH PARTNERS
1700 Oak Avenue
Muskegon, MI 49442-2407
(231)773-3311

MERCY GENERAL HOSPITAL
1500 E Sherman Boulevard
Muskegon, MI 49444-1889
(231)739-9341

SELECT SPECIALTY HOSPITAL - WESTERN MICHIGAN
1700 Clinton St, South 2
Muskegon, MI 49442-5502
(231)728-5800

NEW BALTIMORE

HARBOR OAKS HOSPITAL
35031 23 Mile Road
New Baltimore, MI 48047-3649
(586)725-5777

NEWBERRY

HELEN NEWBERRY JOY HOSPITAL
502 W Harrie Street
Newberry, MI 49868-1209
(906)293-9200

NILES

LAKELAND HOSPITAL - NILES
31 N Saint Joseph Avenue
Niles, MI 49120-2207
(269)683-5510

NORTHPORT

LEELANAU MEMORIAL HEALTH CENTER
215 S High Street
Northport, MI 49670-9755
(231)386-0000

NORTHVILLE

HAWTHORN CENTER
18471 Haggerty Road
Northville, MI 48167-9575
(248)735-6790

NORTHVILLE PSYCHIATRIC HOSPITAL
41001 Seven Mile Road
Northville, MI 48167-2655
(248)349-1800

ONTONAGON

ONTONAGON MEMORIAL HOSPITAL
601 7th St
Ontonagon, MI 49953-1496
(906)884-4134

OWOSSO

MEMORIAL HEALTHCARE CENTER
826 West King Street
Owosso, MI 48867-2120
(989)723-5211

PAW PAW

LAKEVIEW COMMUNITY HOSPITAL
408 Hazen St Box 209
Paw Paw, MI 49079-1019
(269)657-3141

PETOSKEY

NORTHERN MICHIGAN HOSPITAL
416 Connable Avenue
Petoskey, MI 49770-2297
(231)487-4000

PIGEON

SCHEURER HOSPITAL
170 North Caseville Road
Pigeon, MI 48755-9781
(989)453-3223

PLAINWELL

BORGESS PIPP HEALTH CENTER
411 Naomi St
Plainwell, MI 49080-1222
(269)685-6811

PONTIAC

NORTH OAKLAND MEDICAL CENTERS
461 W Huron St
Pontiac, MI 48341-1651
(248)857-7200

PONTIAC OSTEOPATHIC HOSPITAL
50 North Perry
Pontiac, MI 48342-2253
(248)338-5000

SAINT JOSEPH MERCY HOSPITAL
44405 Woodward Ave
Pontiac, MI 48341-5023
(248)858-3000

SELECT SPECIALTY HOSPITAL - PONTIAC
44405 Woodward Ave
Pontiac, MI 48341-5023
(248)858-3146

PORT HURON

MERCY HOSPITAL
2601 Electric Avenue
Port Huron, MI 48060-6518
(810)985-1500

PORT HURON HOSPITAL
1221 Pine Grove Avenue, PO Box 5011
Port Huron, MI 48061-5011
(248)987-5000

REED CITY

SPECTRUM HEALTH - REED CITY CAMPUS
PO Box 75
Reed City, MI 49677-0075
(231)832-3271

ROCHESTER

CRITTENTON HOSPITAL
1101 W University Drive
Rochester, MI 48307-1831
(248)652-5000

ROGERS CITY

ROGERS CITY REHABILITATION HOSPITAL
555 N Bradley Hwy Ste C
Rogers City, MI 49779-1539
(989)734-7545

ROMEO

SAINT JOSEPHS MERCY NORTH
80650 Van Dyke Road
Romeo, MI 48065-1333
(810)798-3551

ROYAL OAK

WILLIAM BEAUMONT HOSPITAL
3601 W 13 Mile Road
Royal Oak, MI 48073-6769
(248)551-5000

SAGINAW

COVENANT HEALTH CARE SYSTEM
1447 N Harrison Street
Saginaw, MI 48602-4785
(989)583-0000

COVENANT MEDICAL CENTER - MICHIGAN
515 N Michigan
Saginaw, MI 48602-4316
(989)583-2701

HEALTHSOURCE SAGINAW
3340 Hospital Road
Saginaw, MI 48603-9623
(989)790-7700

SAINT MARYS MEDICAL CENTER
800 S Washington Ave
Saginaw, MI 48601-2594
(989)776-8000

SELECT SPECIALTY HOSPITAL - SAGINAW
1447 North Harrison Street
Saginaw, MI 48602-4727
(989)583-4850

VA MEDICAL CENTER - ALEDA E. LUTZ
1500 Weiss St
Saginaw, MI 48602-5251
(989)497-2500

SAINT IGNACE

MACKINAC STRAITS HOSPITAL AND HEALTH CENTER
220 Burdette St
Saint Ignace, MI 49781-1712
(906)643-8585

SAINT JOHNS

CLINTON MEMORIAL HOSPITAL
805 S Oakland
Saint Johns, MI 48879-2253
(989)224-6881

SAINT JOSEPH

LAKELAND HOSPITAL - SAINT JOSEPH
1234 Napier Avenue
Saint Joseph, MI 49085-2112
(269)983-8300

SALINE

SALINE COMMUNITY HOSPITAL
400 Russell St
Saline, MI 48176-1192
(734)429-1500

SANDUSKY

MCKENZIE MEMORIAL HOSPITAL
120 Delaware Street
Sandusky, MI 48471-1087
(810)648-3770

SAULT SAINTE MARIE

CHIPPEWA COUNTY WAR MEMORIAL HOSPITAL
500 Osborn Boulevard
Sault Sainte Marie, MI 49783-1884
(906)635-4460

SHELBY

LAKESHORE COMMUNITY HOSPITAL
72 S State St
Shelby, MI 49455-1299
(231)861-2156

SHERIDAN

SHERIDAN COMMUNITY HOSPITAL
301 N Main Street
Sheridan, MI 48884-9235
(989)291-3261

SOUTH HAVEN

SOUTH HAVEN COMMUNITY HOSPITAL
955 S Bailey Avenue
South Haven, MI 49090-9797
(269)637-5271

MINNESOTA

Hospital Telephone Directory

SOUTHFIELD

GREAT LAKES REGIONAL REHAB HOSPITAL
22401 Foster Winter Drive
Southfield, MI 48075-3724
(248)483-5545

PROVIDENCE HOSPITAL
16001 W Nine Mile Road
Southfield, MI 48075-4803
(248)424-3000

STRAITH HOSPITAL FOR SPECIAL
SURGERY
23901 Lahser
Southfield, MI 48034-6035
(248)357-3360

STANDISH

STANDISH COMMUNITY HOSPITAL
Box 579 805 W Cedar Street
Standish, MI 48658-9526
(989)846-3400

STURGIS

STURGIS HOSPITAL
916 Myrtle Avenue
Sturgis, MI 49091-2391
(269)651-7824

TAWAS CITY

TAWAS SAINT JOSEPH HOSPITAL
200 Hemlock
Tawas City, MI 48763-9360
(989)362-3411

TAYLOR

OAKWOOD HEALTH CARE SYSTEMS
HERITAGE
10000 Telegraph Road
Taylor, MI 48180-3330
(313)295-5000

TECUMSEH

HERRICK MEMORIAL HOSPITAL
500 E Pottawatamie St
Tecumseh, MI 49286-2097
(517)424-3000

THREE RIVERS

THREE RIVERS AREA HOSPITAL
701 S Health Parkway Pkwy
Three Rivers, MI 49093-8352
(269)278-1145

TRAVERSE CITY

MUNSON HEALTH CARE
1105 Sixth Street
Traverse City, MI 49684-2349
(231)935-5000

TRENTON

OAKWOOD SOUTHSHORE MEDICAL
CENTER
5450 Fort Street
Trenton, MI 48183-4601
(734)671-3800

RIVERSIDE HOSPITAL
PO Box 1168
Trenton, MI 48183-6168
(734)676-4200

TROY

WILLIAM BEAUMONT HOSPITAL - TROY
44201 Dequindre
Troy, MI 48085-1198
(248)828-5100

VICKSBURG

BRONSON VICKSBURG HOSPITAL
13326 North Boulevard
Vicksburg, MI 49097-1099
(269)649-2321

WARREN

BI-COUNTY COMMUNITY HOSPITAL
13355 E Ten Mile Road
Warren, MI 48089-2065
(586)759-7300

KERN HOSPITAL AND MEDICAL CENTER
21230 Dequindre Road
Warren, MI 48091-2287
(586)427-1000

SAINT JOHN MACOMB HOSPITAL CENTER
11800 East Twelve Mile Road
Warren, MI 48093-3494
(586)573-5000

WATERVLIET

COMMUNITY HOSPITAL
Medical Park Drive
Watervliet, MI 49098
(269)463-3111

WAYNE

OAKWOOD HOSPITAL ANNAPOLIS CENTER
33155 Annapolis Avenue
Wayne, MI 48184-2493
(734)467-4000

WEST BRANCH

WEST BRANCH REGIONAL MEDICAL
CENTER
2463 South M-30
West Branch, MI 48661-9312
(989)345-3660

WESTLAND

OAKWOOD HOSPITAL MERRIMAN CENTER -
WESTLAND
2345 Merriman Road
Westland, MI 48186-5306
(734)467-2300

WALTER REUTHER HOSPITAL
30901 Palmer Road
Westland, MI 48186-5389
(734)367-8400

WYANDOTTE

HENRY FORD WYANDOTTE HOSPITAL
2333 Biddle Avenue
Wyandotte, MI 48192-4668
(734)246-6000

SELECT SPECIALTY HOSPITAL -
WYANDOTTE
2333 Biddle Avenue
Wyandotte, MI 48192-4668
(734)324-3636

YPSILANTI

FOREST HEALTH MEDICAL CENTER
135 South Prospect Street
Ypsilanti, MI 48198-7914
(734)547-4700

ZEELAND

ZEELAND COMMUNITY HOSPITAL
100 S Pine St
Zeeland, MI 49464-1600
(616)772-4644

MINNESOTA

ADA

BRIDGES MEDICAL SERVICES
201 9th St W
Ada, MN 56510-1243
(218)784-5000

ADRIAN

ARNOLD MEMORIAL HOSPITAL
601 Louisiana Avenue
Adrian, MN 56110-1051
(507)483-2668

AITKIN

RIVERWOOD HEALTH CARE CENTER
301 Minnesota Avenue South
Aitkin, MN 56431-1626
(218)927-2121

ALBANY

ALBANY AREA HOSPITAL
300 Third Avenue, Box 370
Albany, MN 56307-9363
(320)845-2121

ALBERT LEA

ALBERT LEA MEDICAL CENTER
404 Fountain Street
Albert Lea, MN 56007-2437
(507)373-2384

ALEXANDRIA

DOUGLAS COUNTY HOSPITAL
111 17th Avenue East
Alexandria, MN 56308-3798
(320)762-1511

ANOKA

ANOKA-METRO REGIONAL TREATMENT
CENTER
3301 7th Ave
Anoka, MN 55303-4516
(763)712-4000

APPLETON

APPLETON MUNICIPAL HOSPITAL
30 South Behl Street
Appleton, MN 56208-1699
(320)289-2422

ARLINGTON

SIBLEY MEDICAL CENTER
601 West Chandler
Arlington, MN 55307-2127
(507)964-2271

AURORA

WHITE COMMUNITY HOSPITAL
5211 Highway 110
Aurora, MN 55705-1599
(218)229-2211

Hospital Telephone Directory — **MINNESOTA**

AUSTIN
AUSTIN MEDICAL CENTER
1000 First Drive Northwest
Austin, MN 55912-2904
(507)437-4551

BAGLEY
CLEARWATER COUNTY MEMORIAL HOSPITAL
203 4th Street Northwest
Bagley, MN 56621-8307
(218)694-6501

BAUDETTE
LAKEWOOD HEALTH CENTER
600 South Main Avenue, Route 1, Box 2120
Baudette, MN 56623-2855
(218)634-2120

BEMIDJI
NORTH COUNTRY REGIONAL HOSPITAL
1100 W 38th St
Bemidji, MN 56601-5117
(218)751-5430

BENSON
SWIFT COUNTY-BENSON HOSPITAL
1815 Wisconsin Avenue
Benson, MN 56215-1653
(320)843-4232

BIGFORK
NORTHERN ITASCA HOSPITAL
258 Pine Tree Drive
Bigfork, MN 56628
(218)743-3177

BLUE EARTH
UNITED HOSPITAL DISTRICT
515 S Moore St
Blue Earth, MN 56013-2158
(507)526-3273

BRAINERD
BRAINERD REGIONAL HUMAN SERVICES CENTER
11615 State Ave
Brainerd, MN 56401-7388
(218)828-2201

MINNESOTA NEURO REHABILITATION HOSPITAL
11800 Hwy 18 East
Brainerd, MN 56401-7388
(218)828-2201

SAINT JOSEPHS MEDICAL CENTER
523 North 3rd Street
Brainerd, MN 56401-3098
(218)829-2861

BRECKENRIDGE
SAINT FRANCIS MEDICAL CENTER
415 Oak Street
Breckenridge, MN 56520-1298
(218)643-3000

BUFFALO
BUFFALO HOSPITAL
303 Catlin St
Buffalo, MN 55313-1947
(763)682-7180

BURNSVILLE
FAIRVIEW RIDGES HOSPITAL
201 East Nicollet Boulevard
Burnsville, MN 55337-5799
(952)892-2000

CAMBRIDGE
CAMBRIDGE MEDICAL CENTER
701 South Dellwood
Cambridge, MN 55008-1923
(763)689-7700

CANBY
SIOUX VALLEY HEALTH SERVICES-CANBY CAMPUS
112 St Olaf Avenue
Canby, MN 56220
(507)223-7277

CANNON FALLS
CANNON FALLS COMMUNITY HOSPITAL
1116 West Mill Street
Cannon Falls, MN 55009-1898
(507)263-4221

CASS LAKE
PHS INDIAN HOSPITAL - CASS LAKE
425 7th St Nw
Cass Lake, MN 56633-3360
(218)335-3200

CHISAGO CITY
FAIRVIEW LAKE REGIONAL MEDICAL CENTER
11725 Stinson Avenue
Chisago City, MN 55013-9542
(651)257-8400

CLOQUET
COMMUNITY MEMORIAL HOSPITAL
512 Skyline Boulevard
Cloquet, MN 55720-1139
(218)879-4641

COOK
COOK COMMUNITY HOSPITAL
10 Fifth Street Southeast
Cook, MN 55723-9745
(218)666-5945

COON RAPIDS
MERCY HOSPITAL
4050 Coon Rapids Boulevard
Coon Rapids, MN 55433-2522
(763)236-6000

CROOKSTON
RIVERVIEW HOSPITAL
323 South Minnesota
Crookston, MN 56716-1600
(218)281-9200

CROSBY
CUYUNA REGIONAL MEDICAL CENTER
320 East Main Street
Crosby, MN 56441-1645
(218)546-7000

DAWSON
JOHNSON MEMORIAL HOSPITAL
1282 Walnut Street
Dawson, MN 56232-2333
(320)769-4323

DEER RIVER
DEER RIVER HEALTHCARE CENTER
1002 Comstock Drive
Deer River, MN 56636-9700
(218)246-2900

DETROIT LAKES
SAINT MARYS REGIONAL HEALTH CENTER
1027 Washington Avenue
Detroit Lakes, MN 56501-3416
(218)847-5611

DULUTH
MILLER DWAN MEDICAL CENTER
502 E Second St
Duluth, MN 55805-1982
(218)727-8762

SAINT LUKES HOSPITAL OF DULUTH
915 E 1st St
Duluth, MN 55805-2193
(218)726-5555

SAINT MARYS MEDICAL CENTER
407 E 3rd St
Duluth, MN 55805-1984
(218)786-4000

EDINA
FAIRVIEW SOUTHDALE HOSPITAL
6401 France Avenue South
Edina, MN 55435-2199
(952)924-5000

ELBOW LAKE
ELEAH MEDICAL CENTER
930 First Street Northeast
Elbow Lake, MN 56531-4611
(218)685-4461

ELY
ELY BLOOMENSON COMMUNITY HOSPITAL
328 W Conan Street
Ely, MN 55731-1198
(218)365-3271

EVELETH
EVELETH HEALTH SERVICES
227 McKinley Avenue
Eveleth, MN 55734-1606
(218)744-1950

FAIRMONT
FAIRMONT COMMUNITY HOSPITAL
PO Box 835
Fairmont, MN 56031-0835
(507)238-8011

FARIBAULT
RICE COUNTY DISTRICT ONE HOSPITAL
631 1st St Se
Faribault, MN 55021-6398
(507)334-6451

FERGUS FALLS
FERGUS FALLS REGIONAL TREATMENT CENTER
North Union Avenue, Box 157
Fergus Falls, MN 56538-0157
(218)739-7200

LAKE REGION HOSPITAL
712 South Cascade
Fergus Falls, MN 56537-2900
(218)736-8000

81

MINNESOTA — Hospital Telephone Directory

FOSSTON
FIRST CARE MEDICAL SERVICES
900 South Hilligoss Boulevard East
Fosston, MN 56542-1599
(218)435-1133

FRIDLEY
UNITY HOSPITAL
550 Osborne Road
Fridley, MN 55432-2799
(763)236-5000

GLENCOE
GLENCOE AREA HEALTH CENTER
705 E 18th St
Glencoe, MN 55336-1432
(320)864-3121

GLENWOOD
GLACIAL RIDGE HOSPITAL
10 Fourth Avenue Southeast
Glenwood, MN 56334-1898
(320)634-4521

GRACEVILLE
GRACEVILLE HEALTH CENTER
115 West Second Street, Box 157
Graceville, MN 56240-0157
(320)748-7223

GRAND MARAIS
COOK COUNTY NORTH SHORE HOSPITAL
515 5th Ave W
Grand Marais, MN 55604-3017
(218)387-3040

GRAND RAPIDS
ITASCA MEDICAL CENTER
126 1st Avenue S E
Grand Rapids, MN 55744-3698
(218)326-3401

GRANITE FALLS
GRANITE FALLS MUNICIPAL HOSPITAL
345 10th Avenue
Granite Falls, MN 56241-1499
(320)564-3111

HALLOCK
KITTSON MEMORIAL HEALTH CARE CENTER
1010 South Birch
Hallock, MN 56728-4208
(218)843-3612

HASTINGS
REGINA MEDICAL CENTER
1175 Nininger Road
Hastings, MN 55033-1098
(651)480-4100

HENDRICKS
HENDRICKS COMMUNITY HOSPITAL
503 E Lincoln St
Hendricks, MN 56136-9598
(507)275-3134

HIBBING
FAIRVIEW UNIVERSITY MEDICAL CENTER-MESABI
750 East 34th St
Hibbing, MN 55746-2341
(218)262-4881

HUTCHINSON
HUTCHINSON COMMUNITY HOSPITAL
1095 Highway 15 South
Hutchinson, MN 55350-3182
(320)234-5000

INTERNATIONAL FALLS
FALLS MEMORIAL HOSPITAL
1400 Highway 71
International Falls, MN 56649-2189
(218)283-4481

IVANHOE
DIVINE PROVIDENCE HEALTH CENTER
PO Box G, 312 East George Street
Ivanhoe, MN 56142-9707
(507)694-1414

JACKSON
JACKSON MUNICIPAL HOSPITAL
1430 North Highway
Jackson, MN 56143-1093
(507)847-2420

LAKE CITY
LAKE CITY MEDICAL CENTER
500 W Grant Street
Lake City, MN 55041-1143
(651)345-3321

LE SUEUR
MINNESOTA VALLEY MEMORIAL HOSPITAL
621 South Fourth Street
Le Sueur, MN 56058-2298
(507)665-8661

LITCHFIELD
MEEKER COUNTY MEMORIAL HOSPITAL
612 South Sibley Avenue
Litchfield, MN 55355-3398
(320)693-3242

LITTLE FALLS
SAINT GABRIELS HOSPITAL
815 Southeast Second Street
Little Falls, MN 56345-3596
(320)632-5441

LONG PRAIRIE
LONG PRAIRIE MEMORIAL HOSPITAL
20 9th Street S E
Long Prairie, MN 56347-1404
(320)732-2141

LUVERNE
LUVERNE COMMUNITY HOSPITAL
PO Box 1019
Luverne, MN 56156-2519
(507)283-2321

MADELIA
MADELIA COMMUNITY HOSPITAL
121 Drew Avenue Se
Madelia, MN 56062-1841
(507)642-3255

MADISON
MADISON HOSPITAL
820 Third Avenue
Madison, MN 56256-1014
(320)598-7556

MAHNOMEN
MAHNOMEN HEALTH CENTER
414 West Jefferson Avenue, Box 396
Mahnomen, MN 56557-4912
(218)935-2511

MANKATO
IMMANUEL-SAINT JOSEPHS-MAYO HEALTH SYSTEMS
1025 Marsh Street, PO Box 8673
Mankato, MN 56002-8673
(507)625-4031

MAPLEWOOD
SAINT JOHNS NORTHEAST COMMUNITY HOSPITAL
1575 Beam Avenue
Maplewood, MN 55109-1169
(651)232-7000

MARSHALL
WEINER MEMORIAL MEDICAL CENTER
300 South Bruce Street
Marshall, MN 56258-1934
(507)532-9661

MELROSE
MELROSE AREA HOSPITAL - CENTRACARE
11 N 5th Avenue W
Melrose, MN 56352-1071
(320)256-4231

MINNEAPOLIS

ABBOTT - NORTHWESTERN HOSPITAL
800 East 28th Street
Minneapolis, MN 55407-3731
(612)863-4000

CHILDRENS HEALTH CARE - MINNEAPOLIS
2525 Chicago Avenue South
Minneapolis, MN 55404-4518
(612)813-6100

FAIRVIEW RIVERSIDE HOSPITAL
2312 South 6th St
Minneapolis, MN 55454-1395
(612)672-6000

FAIRVIEW UNIVERSITY MEDICAL CENTER
2450 Riverside Avenue
Minneapolis, MN 55454-1400
(612)672-6000

HENNEPIN COUNTY MEDICAL CENTER
701 Park Avenue
Minneapolis, MN 55415-1829
(612)347-2121

KINDRED HOSPITAL MINNEAPOLIS
1300 Hidden Lakes Pkwy
Minneapolis, MN 55422-4286
(763)588-2750

MERCY HOSPITAL
4050 Coon Rapids Boulevard Nw
Minneapolis, MN 55433-2522
(763)421-8888

PHILLIPS EYE INSTITUTE
2215 Park Avenue South
Minneapolis, MN 55404-3756
(612)336-6000

SAINT MARY'S HOSPITAL & REHABILITATION CENTER
2414 South 7th St
Minneapolis, MN 55454-1435
(612)338-2229

SHRINERS HOSPITAL
2025 E River Road
Minneapolis, MN 55414-3696
(612)596-6100

Hospital Telephone Directory   **MINNESOTA**

UNIVERSITY MEDICAL CENTER
420 Delaware St Se
Minneapolis, MN 55455-0341
(612)626-3000

VA MEDICAL CENTER - MINNEAPOLIS
1 Veterans Drive
Minneapolis, MN 55417-2309
(612)725-2000

MONTEVIDEO

CHIPPEWA COUNTY-MONTEVIDEO HOSPITAL
824 North 11th St
Montevideo, MN 56265-1629
(320)269-8877

MONTICELLO

MONTICELLO-BIG LAKE COMMUNITY HOSPITAL
1013 Hart Boulevard
Monticello, MN 55362-8230
(763)295-2945

MOOSE LAKE

MERCY HOSPITAL
710 South Kenwood Avenue, Box 469
Moose Lake, MN 55767-9405
(218)485-4481

MORA

KANABEC HOSPITAL
300 Clark Street
Mora, MN 55051-1590
(320)679-1212

MORRIS

STEVENS MEDICAL CENTER
PO Box 660
Morris, MN 56267-0660
(320)589-1313

NEW PRAGUE

QUEEN OF PEACE HOSPITAL
301 2nd St Ne
New Prague, MN 56071-1799
(952)758-4431

NEW ULM

NEW ULM MEDICAL CENTER
1324 5th Street North
New Ulm, MN 56073-1514
(507)354-2111

NORTHFIELD

NORTHFIELD CITY HOSPITAL
2000 North Ave
Northfield, MN 55057-1697
(507)645-6661

OLIVIA

RENVILLE COUNTY HOSPITAL
611 East Fairview
Olivia, MN 56277-4213
(320)523-1261

ONAMIA

MILLE LACS HEALTH SYSTEM
200 North Elm St
Onamia, MN 56359-7901
(320)532-3154

ORTONVILLE

ORTONVILLE MUNICIPAL HOSPITAL
750 Eastvold Avenue
Ortonville, MN 56278-1143
(320)839-2502

OWATONNA

OWATONNA HOSPITAL
903 South Oak Street
Owatonna, MN 55060-3200
(507)451-3850

PARK RAPIDS

SAINT JOSEPHS HOSPITAL
600 Pleasant Avenue
Park Rapids, MN 56470-1431
(218)732-3311

PAYNESVILLE

PAYNESVILLE HEALTHCARE HOSPITAL
200 First Street West
Paynesville, MN 56362-1496
(320)243-3767

PERHAM

PERHAM MEMORIAL HOSPITAL
665 3rd St Sw
Perham, MN 56573-1108
(218)346-4500

PINE CITY

LAKESIDE MEDICAL CENTER
129 E Sixth Avenue
Pine City, MN 55063-1999
(320)629-2542

PIPESTONE

PIPESTONE COUNTY MEDICAL CENTER
911 5th Avenue Sw
Pipestone, MN 56164-1054
(507)825-6125

PRINCETON

FAIRVIEW NORTHLAND REGIONAL HOSPITAL
911 Northland Drive
Princeton, MN 55371-2173
(763)389-6300

RED LAKE

PHS INDIAN HOSPITAL - RED LAKE
Red Lake, MN 56671
(218)679-3912

RED WING

FAIRVIEW REDWING HOSPITAL
PO Box 134
Red Wing, MN 55066-0134
(651)388-6721

REDWOOD FALLS

REDWOOD FALLS MUNICIPAL HOSPITAL
100 Fallwood Road
Redwood Falls, MN 56283-1828
(507)637-4500

ROBBINSDALE

NORTH MEMORIAL MEDICAL CENTER
3300 Oakdale North
Robbinsdale, MN 55422-2900
(763)520-5200

ROCHESTER

FEDERAL MEDICAL CENTER - ROCHESTER
PO Box 4600, 2110 East Center Street
Rochester, MN 55903-4600
(507)287-0674

MAYO CLINIC
200 1st Street Sw
Rochester, MN 55905-0002
(507)284-2511

OLMSTED HOSPITAL
1650 4th Street Se
Rochester, MN 55904-4700
(507)288-3443

ROCHESTER METHODIST HOSPITAL
201 W Center St
Rochester, MN 55902-3065
(507)266-7890

SAINT MARYS HOSPITAL
1216 2nd St Sw
Rochester, MN 55902-1970
(507)255-5123

ROSEAU

ROSEAU AREA HOSPITAL DISTRICT
715 Delmore Drive
Roseau, MN 56751-1599
(218)463-2500

SAINT CLOUD

SAINT CLOUD HOSPITAL
1406 6th Avenue North
Saint Cloud, MN 56303-1901
(320)251-2700

VA MEDICAL CENTER - SAINT CLOUD
4801 8th St N
Saint Cloud, MN 56303-2099
(320)252-1670

SAINT JAMES

SAINT JAMES HEALTH SERVICES
1207 6th Avenue South
Saint James, MN 56081-2415
(507)375-3261

SAINT LOUIS PARK

METHODIST HOSPITAL
6500 Excelsior Boulevard
Saint Louis Park, MN 55426-4700
(952)993-5000

SAINT PAUL

BETHESDA REHAB CENTER
559 Capitol Boulevard
Saint Paul, MN 55103-2101
(651)232-2000

CHILDRENS HEALTH CARE - SAINT PAUL
345 North Smith Avenue
Saint Paul, MN 55102-2346
(651)220-6000

GILLETTE CHILDRENS HOSPITAL
200 University Avenue East
Saint Paul, MN 55101-2598
(651)291-2848

REGIONS HOSPITAL
640 Jackson Street
Saint Paul, MN 55101-2595
(651)221-3456

SAINT JOSEPHS HOSPITAL
69 West Exchange Street
Saint Paul, MN 55102-1053
(651)232-3000

MISSISSIPPI — Hospital Telephone Directory

UNITED HOSPITALS
333 North Smith
Saint Paul, MN 55102-2389
(651)220-8000

SAINT PETER

MINNESOTA SECURITY HOSPITAL
Sheppard Drive
Saint Peter, MN 56082
(507)931-7100

SAINT PETER COMMUNITY HOSPITAL
618 West Broadway
Saint Peter, MN 56082-1327
(507)931-2200

SAINT PETER REGIONAL TREATMENT CENTER
2100 Freeman Drive
Saint Peter, MN 56082-1545
(507)931-7100

SANDSTONE

PINE MEDICAL CENTER
109 Court Avenue S
Sandstone, MN 55072-5120
(320)245-2212

SAUK CENTRE

SAINT MICHAELS HOSPITAL
425 North Elm Street
Sauk Centre, MN 56378-1010
(320)352-2221

SHAKOPEE

SAINT FRANCIS REGIONAL MEDICAL CENTER
1455 St Francis Avenue
Shakopee, MN 55379-3380
(952)403-3000

SLAYTON

MURRAY COUNTY HOSPITAL
2042 Juniper Avenue
Slayton, MN 56172-1008
(507)836-6111

SLEEPY EYE

SLEEPY EYE MUNICIPAL HOSPITAL
400 Fourth Avenue Northwest
Sleepy Eye, MN 56085-1109
(507)794-3571

SPRINGFIELD

SPRINGFIELD MEDICAL CENTER
625 N Jackson St
Springfield, MN 56087-1714
(507)723-6201

STAPLES

LAKEWOOD HEALTH SYSTEM
401 Prairie Avenue NE
Staples, MN 56479-3201
(218)894-0300

STARBUCK

MINNEWASKA DISTRICT HOSPITAL
610 West Sixth Street
Starbuck, MN 56381-9782
(320)239-2201

STILLWATER

LAKEVIEW MEMORIAL HOSPITAL
927 West Churchill Street
Stillwater, MN 55082-5999
(651)439-5330

THIEF RIVER FALLS

NORTHWEST MEDICAL CENTER
120 Labree Avenue S
Thief River Falls, MN 56701-2806
(218)681-4240

TRACY

TRACY MUNICIPAL HOSPITAL
5th St East
Tracy, MN 56175
(507)629-3200

TWO HARBORS

LAKEVIEW MEMORIAL HOSPITAL
325 - 11th Avenue
Two Harbors, MN 55616-1300
(218)834-7300

TYLER

TYLER HEALTH CARE CENTER
240 Willow Street
Tyler, MN 56178-1166
(507)247-5521

VIRGINIA

VIRGINIA REGIONAL MEDICAL CENTER
901 9th St N
Virginia, MN 55792-2398
(218)741-3340

WABASHA

SAINT ELIZABETH HOSPITAL
1200 5th Grant Boulevard West
Wabasha, MN 55981-1098
(651)565-4531

WACONIA

RIDGEVIEW MEDICAL CENTER
500 S Maple St
Waconia, MN 55387-1791
(952)442-2191

WADENA

TRI COUNTY HOSPITAL
415 Jefferson St N
Wadena, MN 56482-1297
(218)631-3510

WARREN

NORTH VALLEY HEALTH CENTER
109 South Minnesota Street
Warren, MN 56762-1461
(218)745-4211

WASECA

WASECA MEDICAL CENTER
100 5th Avenue Nw
Waseca, MN 56093-2422
(507)835-1210

WESTBROOK

WESTBROOK HEALTH CENTER
920 Bell Avenue
Westbrook, MN 56183-9669
(507)274-6121

WHEATON

WHEATON COMMUNITY HOSPITAL
401 12th Street North
Wheaton, MN 56296-1099
(320)563-8226

WILLMAR

RICE MEMORIAL HOSPITAL
301 Becker Avenue Sw
Willmar, MN 56201-3395
(320)235-4543

WILLMAR REGIONAL TREATMENT CENTER
1550 Highway 71 Ne
Willmar, MN 56201-9504
(320)231-5100

WINDOM

WINDOM AREA HOSPITAL
Highways 60 And 71 North, Box 339
Windom, MN 56101-0339
(507)831-2400

WINONA

WINONA HEALTH
855 Mankato Avenue, PO Box 5600
Winona, MN 55987-0600
(507)454-3650

WOODBURY

WOODWINDS HEALTH CAMPUS
1925 Woodwinds Drive
Woodbury, MN 55125-2504
(651)232-0110

WORTHINGTON

WORTHINGTON REGIONAL HOSPITAL
1018 6th Avenue
Worthington, MN 56187-2298
(507)372-2941

WYOMING

FAIRVIEW LAKES REGIONAL MEDICAL CENTER
5200 Fairview Boulevard
Wyoming, MN 55092-8013
(651)982-7000

ZUMBROTA

ZUMBROTA HOSPITAL
383 W 5th Street
Zumbrota, MN 55992-1699
(507)732-5131

MISSISSIPPI

ABERDEEN

PIONEER COMMUNITY HOSPITAL OF ABERDEEN
400 S Chestnut St
Aberdeen, MS 39730-3335
(662)369-2455

ACKERMAN

CHOCTAW COUNTY MEDICAL CENTER
148 Cherry St Box 417
Ackerman, MS 39735-0417
(662)285-3257

AMORY

GILMORE MEMORIAL HOSPITAL
S Boulevard Drive
Amory, MS 38821
(662)256-7111

BATESVILLE

TRI-LAKES MEDICAL CENTER
303 Medical Center Dr
Batesville, MS 38606-8608
(662)563-5611

Hospital Telephone Directory — **MISSISSIPPI**

BAY SAINT LOUIS
HANCOCK MEDICAL CENTER
PO Box 2790
Bay Saint Louis, MS 39521-2790
(228)467-8600

BAY SPRINGS
JASPER GENERAL HOSPITAL
PO Box 527
Bay Springs, MS 39422-0527
(601)764-2101

BELZONI
HUMPHREYS COUNTY MEMORIAL HOSPITAL
PO Box 510
Belzoni, MS 39038-0510
(662)247-3831

BILOXI
BILOXI REGIONAL MEDICAL CENTER
150 Reynoir Street
Biloxi, MS 39530-4199
(228)432-1571

GULF COAST MEDICAL CENTER
180 Debuys Road
Biloxi, MS 39531-4402
(228)388-6711

GULF OAKS HOSPITAL
180 Debuys Road Suite C
Biloxi, MS 39531-4402
(228)388-0600

SELECT SPECIALTY HOSPITAL - BILOXI
648 Beach Boulevard
Biloxi, MS 39530-4301
(228)374-7474

VA MEDICAL CENTER - BILOXI/GULFPORT
400 Veterans Avenue
Biloxi, MS 39531-2410
(228)523-5000

BOONEVILLE
BAPTIST MEMORIAL HOSPITAL BOONEVILLE
Washington And Second Streets
Booneville, MS 38829
(662)720-5000

BRANDON
RANKIN MEDICAL CENTER
350 Crossgates Boulevard
Brandon, MS 39042-2698
(601)825-2811

BROOKHAVEN
KINGS DAUGHTERS HOSPITAL
Highway 51 N Box 984
Brookhaven, MS 39602-0984
(601)833-6011

CALHOUN CITY
CALHOUN HEALTH SERVICES - HILLCREST HOSPITAL
140 Burke-Calhoon City Road
Calhoun City, MS 38916-9690
(662)628-6611

CANTON
MADISON COUNTY MEDICAL CENTER
Highway 16 E PO Box 1607
Canton, MS 39046-1607
(601)859-1331

CARTHAGE
LEAKE COUNTY MEMORIAL HOSPITAL
310 Ellis St PO Box 557
Carthage, MS 39051-0557
(601)267-1100

CENTREVILLE
FIELD MEMORIAL COMMUNITY HOSPITAL
PO Box 639
Centreville, MS 39631-0639
(601)645-5221

CHARLESTON
TALLAHATCHIE GENERAL HOSPITAL
4015 Market Street
Charleston, MS 38921
(662)647-5535

CLARKSDALE
NORTHWEST MISSISSIPPI REGIONAL MEDICAL CENTER
Hospital Drive PO Box 1218
Clarksdale, MS 38614-1218
(662)627-3211

CLEVELAND
BOLIVAR COUNTY MEDICAL-HOSPITAL
Highway 8 East
Cleveland, MS 38732
(662)846-0061

COLLINS
COVINGTON COUNTY HOSPITAL
PO Box 1149
Collins, MS 39428-1149
(601)765-6711

COLUMBIA
MARION GENERAL HOSPITAL
1560 Sumrall Road PO Box 630
Columbia, MS 39429-0630
(601)736-6303

COLUMBUS
BAPTIST MEMORIAL HOSPITAL/GOLDEN TRIANGLE
2520 5th St N
Columbus, MS 39701-5111
(662)244-1000

CORINTH
MAGNOLIA HOSPITAL
611 Alcorn Drive
Corinth, MS 38834-9368
(662)293-1000

EUPORA
WEBSTER GENERAL HOSPITAL
500 Highway 9 S
Eupora, MS 39744-2296
(662)258-6221

FAYETTE
JEFFERSON COUNTY HOSPITAL
809 S Main Box 577
Fayette, MS 39069-0577
(601)786-3401

FLOWOOD
WOMEN'S HOSPITAL AT RIVER OAKS
1026 North Flowood Drive
Flowood, MS 39232-9532
(601)932-1000

FOREST
LACKEY MEMORIAL HOSPITAL AND SWING BED
330 N Broad St Box 428
Forest, MS 39074-3508
(601)469-4151

GREENVILLE
DELTA REGIONAL MEDICAL CENTER
1400 E Union St
Greenville, MS 38703-3246
(662)378-3783

KINGS DAUGHTERS HOSPITAL
300 South Washington Avenue
Greenville, MS 38701-4723
(662)378-2020

GREENWOOD
GREENWOOD LEFLORE HOSPITAL
1401 River Road Drawer 1410
Greenwood, MS 38930-4030
(662)459-7000

GRENADA
GRENADA LAKE MEDICAL CENTER
960 Avent Drive
Grenada, MS 38901-5230
(662)227-7101

GULFPORT
GARDEN PARK MEDICAL CENTER
15200 Community Road
Gulfport, MS 39503-3085
(228)575-7000

MEMORIAL BEHAVIORAL HEALTH
11150 Highway 49 S
Gulfport, MS 39503-4110
(228)831-1700

MEMORIAL HOSPITAL AT GULFPORT
4500 13th St-PO Box 1810
Gulfport, MS 39502-1810
(228)867-4000

NAVAL BRANCH HOSPITAL
Naval Home
Gulfport, MS 39501
(228)871-2810

SELECT SPECIALTY HOSPITAL - GULFPORT
4500 13th Street
Gulfport, MS 39501-2515
(228)867-4820

HATTIESBURG
FORREST GENERAL HOSPITAL
400 S 28th Avenue
Hattiesburg, MS 39401-7234
(601)288-7000

WESLEY MEDICAL CENTER
5001 W Hardy St Box 16509
Hattiesburg, MS 39402-1308
(601)268-8000

HAZLEHURST
HARDY WILSON MEMORIAL HOSPITAL
233 Magnolia
Hazlehurst, MS 39083-2200
(601)894-4541

HOLLY SPRINGS
ALLIANCE HEALTHCARE SYSTEM
1430 Highway 4 E
Holly Springs, MS 38635-2140
(662)252-1212

MISSISSIPPI — Hospital Telephone Directory

HOUSTON
TRACE REGIONAL HOSPITAL AND SWING BED
Highway 8 E
Houston, MS 38851
(662)456-3700

INDIANOLA
SOUTH SUNFLOWER COUNTY HOSPITAL
121 E Baker St
Indianola, MS 38751-2498
(662)887-5235

IUKA
NORTH MISSISSIPPI MEDICAL CENTER - IUKA
1777 Curtis Drive
Iuka, MS 38852-1001
(662)423-6051

JACKSON
BAPTIST BEHAVIORAL HEALTH
1225 N State Street
Jackson, MS 39202-2064
(601)968-1102

BRENTWOOD BEHAVIORAL HEALTHCARE
3531 East Lakeland Drive
Jackson, MS 39232-8016
(601)936-2024

CENTRAL MISSISSIPPI MEDICAL CENTER
1850 Chadwick Drive
Jackson, MS 39204-3479
(601)376-1000

METHODIST REHAB CENTER
1350 E Woodrow Wilson Drive
Jackson, MS 39216-5198
(601)981-2611

MISSISSIPPI BAPTIST MEDICAL CENTER
1225 N State St
Jackson, MS 39202-2097
(601)968-1000

RESTORATIVE CARE HOSPITAL
1225 North State St
Jackson, MS 39202-2064
(601)968-100054

RIVER OAKS HOSPITAL
1030 River Oaks Drive Box 5100
Jackson, MS 39232-9729
(601)932-1030

SAINT DOMINIC JACKSON MEMORIAL HOSPITAL
969 Lakeland Drive
Jackson, MS 39216-4699
(601)982-0121

SELECT SPECIALTY HOSPITAL - JACKSON
1850 Chadwick Drive, Fifth Floor
Jackson, MS 39204-3404
(601)376-1005

UNIVERSITY OF MISSISSIPPI MEDICAL CENTER
2500 N State St
Jackson, MS 39216-4505
(601)984-1000

VA MEDICAL CENTER - G. V. MONTGOMERY
1500 E Woodrow Wilson Avenue
Jackson, MS 39216-5199
(601)362-1201

KEESLER AIR FORCE BASE
81ST MEDICAL GROUP, KEESLER MEDICAL CENTER
301 Fisher Street, Room 1a132
Keesler Air Force Base, MS 39534-2508
(228)377-6510

KILMICHAEL
KILMICHAEL HOSPITAL
Lamar St Box 188
Kilmichael, MS 39747-0188
(662)262-4311

KOSCIUSKO
MONTFORT JONES MEMORIAL HOSPITAL
Highway 12 W
Kosciusko, MS 39090
(662)289-4311

LAUREL
SOUTH CENTRAL REGIONAL MEDICAL CENTER
1220 Jefferson St Box 607
Laurel, MS 39440-4355
(601)426-4000

LEXINGTON
UNIVERSITY HOSPITAL
239 Bowling Green Road
Lexington, MS 39095-5167
(662)834-1321

LOUISVILLE
WINSTON MEDICAL CENTER
PO Box 967
Louisville, MS 39339-0967
(662)773-6211

LUCEDALE
GEORGE COUNTY HOSPITAL
859 Ratliss Street, PO Box 607
Lucedale, MS 39452-0607
(601)947-3161

MACON
NOXUBEE GENERAL HOSPITAL
606 N Jefferson St
Macon, MS 39341
(662)726-4231

MAGEE
MAGEE GENERAL HOSPITAL
300 Se 3rd Avenue
Magee, MS 39111-3698
(601)849-5070

MILLCREEK REHABILITATION CENTER
900 First Avenue Northeast
Magee, MS 39111-3255
(601)849-4221

MAGNOLIA
BEACHAM MEMORIAL HOSPITAL
203 N Cherry St
Magnolia, MS 39652-2819
(601)783-2351

MARKS
QUITMAN COUNTY HOSPITAL AND NH
340 Getwell Drive Box 330
Marks, MS 38646-9785
(662)326-8031

MCCOMB
SOUTHWEST MISSISSIPPI MEDICAL CENTER
215 Marion Avenue Box 1307
McComb, MS 39648-2705
(601)249-5500

MEADVILLE
FRANKLIN COUNTY MEMORIAL HOSPITAL
Highway 84 Box 636
Meadville, MS 39653-0636
(601)384-5801

MENDENHALL
SIMPSON GENERAL HOSPITAL
931 W Jackson Avenue
Mendenhall, MS 39114
(601)847-2221

MERIDIAN
ALLIANCE HEALTH CENTER
5000 Highway 39 N
Meridian, MS 39301-1021
(601)483-6211

EAST MISSISSIPPI STATE HOSPITAL
PO Box 4128
Meridian, MS 39304-4128
(601)482-6186

JEFF ANDERSON REGIONAL MEDICAL CENTER
2124 14 St
Meridian, MS 39301-4093
(601)553-6000

RILEY MEMORIAL HOSPITAL
1102 21st Avenue
Meridian, MS 39301-4096
(601)693-2511

RUSH FOUNDATION HOSPITAL
1314 19th Avenue
Meridian, MS 39301-4195
(601)483-0011

SPECIALITY HOSPITAL OF MERIDIAN
1314 19th Avenue
Meridian, MS 39301-4116
(601)486-4211

MONTICELLO
LAWRENCE COUNTY HOSPITAL
Highway 84 E
Monticello, MS 39654
(601)587-4051

MORTON
SCOTT REGIONAL HOSPITAL
Highway 13 South, PO Box 259
Morton, MS 39117-0259
(601)732-6301

NATCHEZ
NATCHEZ COMMUNITY HOSPITAL/SWING BED
129 Jeff Davis Boulevard Box 1203
Natchez, MS 39120-5100
(601)445-6200

NATCHEZ REGIONAL MEDICAL CENTER
PO Box 1488
Natchez, MS 39121-1488
(601)443-2100

NEW ALBANY
BAPTIST MEMORIAL HOSPITAL UNION COUNTY
Highway 30 W
New Albany, MS 38652
(662)538-7631

NEWTON
NEWTON REGIONAL HOSPITAL
PO Box 299
Newton, MS 39345-0299
(601)683-2031

Hospital Telephone Directory — MISSISSIPPI

OCEAN SPRINGS
OCEAN SPRINGS HOSPITAL
3109 Bienville Boulevard
Ocean Springs, MS 39564-4314
(228)818-1111

OKOLONA
OKOLONA COMMUNITY HOSPITAL
PO Box 419
Okolona, MS 38860-0419
(662)447-3311

OLIVE BRANCH
PARKWOOD HOSPITAL
8135 Goodman Road
Olive Branch, MS 38654-2199
(662)895-4900

OXFORD
BAPTIST MEMORIAL HOSPITAL NORTH MISSISSIPPI
Highway 7 S Box 946
Oxford, MS 38655-6002
(662)232-8100

PASCAGOULA
SINGING RIVER HOSPITAL
2809 Denny Avenue
Pascagoula, MS 39581-5300
(228)809-5000

PHILADELPHIA
CHOCTAW HEALTH CENTER
210 Hospital Cir
Philadelphia, MS 39350-6781
(601)656-2211

NESHOBA COUNTY GENERAL HOSPITAL
Highway 19 S/PO Box 648
Philadelphia, MS 39350-0648
(601)663-1200

PICAYUNE
CROSBY MEMORIAL HOSPITAL
801 Goodyear Boulevard
Picayune, MS 39466-3221
(601)798-4711

PONTOTOC
MILLCREEK OF PONTOTOC
1814 Highway 15 North
Pontotoc, MS 38863-6962
(662)488-8878

PONTOTOC HOSPITAL
PO Box 790/ 176 South Main Street
Pontotoc, MS 38863-0790
(662)489-5510

POPLARVILLE
PEARL RIVER COUNTY HOSPITAL
Moody St PO Box 392
Poplarville, MS 39470-0392
(601)795-4543

PORT GIBSON
CLAIBORNE COUNTY HOSPITAL
123 Mccomb Avenue
Port Gibson, MS 39150-2915
(601)437-5141

PRENTISS
PRENTISS COUNTY REGIONAL HOSPITAL
1102 Rose St
Prentiss, MS 39474
(601)792-4276

PURVIS
SOUTH MISSISSIPPI STATE HOSPITAL
823 Highway 589
Purvis, MS 39475-4194
(601)794-0100

QUITMAN
H C WATKINS MEMORIAL HOSPITAL
605 S Archusa Avenue
Quitman, MS 39355-2331
(601)776-6925

RICHTON
PERRY COUNTY GENERAL HOSPITAL
PO Drawer Y
Richton, MS 39476
(601)788-6316

RIPLEY
TIPPAH COUNTY HOSPITAL
1005 Highway 15 N
Ripley, MS 38663
(662)837-9221

ROLLING FORK
SHARKEY ISAQUENA COMMUNITY HOSPITAL
47 S Fourth St
Rolling Fork, MS 39159-5146
(662)873-4395

RULEVILLE
NORTH SUNFLOWER COUNTY HOSPITAL
840 N Oak Avenue
Ruleville, MS 38771-3227
(662)756-2711

SENATOBIA
NORTH OAK REGIONAL MEDICAL CENTER
401 Getwell Drive
Senatobia, MS 38668-2213
(662)562-3100

SOUTHAVEN
BAPTIST HOSPITAL DESOTO
7601 Southcrest Drive
Southaven, MS 38671-4739
(662)349-4000

STARKVILLE
OKTIBBEHA COUNTY HOSPITAL
PO Box 1506
Starkville, MS 39760-1506
(662)323-4320

TUPELO
NORTH MISSISSIPPI MEDICAL CENTER
830 S Gloster
Tupelo, MS 38801-4996
(662)377-3000

NORTH MISSISSIPPI STATE HOSPITAL
1937 Briar Ridge Road
Tupelo, MS 38804-5963
(662)690-4200

TYLERTOWN
WALTHALL COUNTY GENERAL HOSPITAL
100 Hospital Drive
Tylertown, MS 39667-2099
(601)876-2122

UNION
LAIRD HOSPITAL
108 Highway 15 Bypass N
Union, MS 39365
(601)774-8214

VICKSBURG
RIVER REGION MEDICAL CENTER
2100 Highway 61 North
Vicksburg, MS 39183-8211
(601)883-5000

RIVER REGION MEDICAL CENTER - WEST
1111 Frontage Road Box 1031
Vicksburg, MS 39180-5102
(601)636-2611

WATER VALLEY
YALOBUSHA GENERAL HOSPITAL
Highway 7 Box 728
Water Valley, MS 38965-0728
(662)473-1411

WAYNESBORO
WAYNE GENERAL HOSPITAL
950 Matthew Drive
Waynesboro, MS 39367-2590
(601)735-5151

WEST POINT
CLAY COUNTY MEDICAL CENTER
835 Medical Center Drive
West Point, MS 39773-9320
(662)495-2300

WHITFIELD
MISSISSIPPI STATE HOSPITAL
3550 Highway 468w
Whitfield, MS 39193
(601)351-8000

WHITFIELD MEDICAL SURGICAL HOSPITAL
PO Box 56
Whitfield, MS 39193-0056
(601)351-8023

WIGGINS
STONE COUNTY HOSPITAL
PO Box 97
Wiggins, MS 39577-0097
(601)928-6600

WINONA
TYLER HOLMES MEMORIAL HOSPITAL
Tyler Holmes Drive
Winona, MS 38967
(662)283-4114

YAZOO CITY
KINGS DAUGHTERS HOSPITAL SWING BED
823 Grand Avenue
Yazoo City, MS 39194-3233
(662)746-2261

MISSOURI   Hospital Telephone Directory

MISSOURI

ALBANY
GENTRY COUNTY MEMORIAL HOSPITAL
College And Clark Streets
Albany, MO 64402
(660)726-3941

APPLETON CITY
ELLETT MEMORIAL HOSPITAL
610 North Ohio Avenue
Appleton City, MO 64724-1609
(660)476-2111

AURORA
AURORA COMMUNITY HOSPITAL
500 Porter St
Aurora, MO 65605-2399
(417)678-2122

BELTON
RESEARCH BELTON HOSPITAL
17065 S Outer Road
Belton, MO 64012-2165
(816)348-1200

BETHANY
HARRISON COUNTY COMMUNITY HOSPITAL
2600 Miller St PO Box 428
Bethany, MO 64424-0428
(660)425-2211

BLUE SPRINGS
SAINT MARYS HOSPITAL OF BLUE SPRINGS
201 West R D Mize Road
Blue Springs, MO 64014-2533
(816)228-5900

BOLIVAR
CITIZENS MEMORIAL HOSPITAL
1500 N Oakland Box 67
Bolivar, MO 65613-3099
(417)326-6000

BONNE TERRE
PARKLAND HEALTH CENTER - BONNE TERRE
7245 Raider Road
Bonne Terre, MO 63628-3767
(573)358-1400

BOONVILLE
COOPER COUNTY MEMORIAL HOSPITAL
18668 Jackson Road
Boonville, MO 65233-2818
(660)882-7461

BRANSON
SKAGGS COMMUNITY HEALTH CENTER
Cahill Road Box 650
Branson, MO 65615-0600
(417)335-7000

BRIDGETON
ALL SAINTS SPECIAL CARE HOSPITAL
12303 Depaul Drive, 2nd Floor South
Bridgeton, MO 63044
(314)344-7830

DEPAUL HEALTH CENTER
12303 Depaul Drive
Bridgeton, MO 63044
(314)344-6000

BROOKFIELD
PERSHING MEMORIAL HOSPITAL
130 E Lockling
Brookfield, MO 64628-2337
(660)258-2222

BUTLER
BATES COUNTY MEMORIAL HOSPITAL
615 W Nursery St
Butler, MO 64730-1840
(660)679-4135

CAMERON
CAMERON COMMUNITY HOSPITAL
1015 W 4th St
Cameron, MO 64429-1498
(816)632-2101

CAPE GIRARDEAU
SAINT FRANCIS MEDICAL CENTER
211 St Francis Drive
Cape Girardeau, MO 63703-8399
(573)331-3000

SOUTHEAST MISSOURI HOSPITAL
1701 Lacey St
Cape Girardeau, MO 63701-5299
(573)334-4822

CARROLLTON
CARROLL COUNTY MEMORIAL HOSPITAL
1502 N Jefferson
Carrollton, MO 64633-1999
(660)542-1695

CARTHAGE
MCCUNE BROOKS HOSPITAL
627 W Centennial St
Carthage, MO 64836-2860
(417)358-8121

CASSVILLE
SOUTH BARRY COUNTY MEMORIAL
87 Gravel St
Cassville, MO 65625-1605
(417)847-6000

CHESTERFIELD
SAINT LUKES HOSPITAL
232 S Woods Mill Road
Chesterfield, MO 63017-3485
(314)434-1500

CHILLICOTHE
HEDRICK MEDICAL CENTER
100 Central St
Chillicothe, MO 64601-1599
(660)646-1480

CLINTON
GOLDEN VALLEY MEMORIAL HOSPITAL
1600 North Second
Clinton, MO 64735-1297
(660)885-5511

COLUMBIA
BOONE HOSPITAL CENTER
1600 E Broadway
Columbia, MO 65201-5897
(573)815-8000

COLUMBIA REGIONAL HOSPITAL
404 Keene St
Columbia, MO 65201-6698
(573)875-9000

ELLIS FISCHEL HEALTH CLINIC
115 Business Loop 70 W
Columbia, MO 65203-3299
(573)882-5460

MID MISSOURI MENTAL HEALTH
Three Hospital Drive
Columbia, MO 65201-5296
(573)884-1300

RUSK REHABILITATION CENTER
315 Business Loop 70 West
Columbia, MO 65203-3248
(573)817-2703

UNIVERSITY OF MISSOURI HOSPITAL AND CLINICS
One Hospital Drive
Columbia, MO 65212-0001
(573)882-4141

VA MEDICAL CENTER - HARRY S TRUMAN
800 Hospital Drive
Columbia, MO 65201-5275
(573)814-6000

CREVE COEUR
RANKEN JORDAN PEDIATRIC REHAB
10621 Ladue Road
Creve Coeur, MO 63141-8406
(314)993-1207

SAINT JOHNS MERCY MEDICAL CENTER
615 South New Ballas Road
Creve Coeur, MO 63141-8277
(314)569-6000

CRYSTAL CITY
JEFFERSON MEMORIAL HOSPITAL
Highway 61 South Box 350
Crystal City, MO 63019-0350
(636)933-1000

DEXTER
MISSOURI SOUTHERN HEALTHCARE
1200 One Mile Road Box 279
Dexter, MO 63841-1000
(573)624-5566

DONIPHAN
RIPLEY COUNTY MEMORIAL HOSPITAL
Grand And Plum Street
Doniphan, MO 63935
(573)996-2141

EL DORADO SPRINGS
CEDAR COUNTY MEMORIAL HOSPITAL
1401 S Park
El Dorado Springs, MO 64744-2037
(417)876-2511

ELLINGTON
REYNOLDS COUNTY GENERAL MEMORIAL HOSPITAL
Highway 21 S Box 250
Ellington, MO 63638-0250
(573)663-2511

EXCELSIOR SPRINGS
EXCELSIOR SPRINGS MEDICAL CENTER
1700 Rainbow Boulevard
Excelsior Springs, MO 64024-1190
(816)630-6081

FAIRFAX
COMMUNITY HOSPITAL ASSOCIATION
Highway 59
Fairfax, MO 64446
(660)686-2211

88

FARMINGTON

MINERAL AREA REGIONAL MEDICAL CENTER
1212 Weber Road
Farmington, MO 63640-3325
(573)701-7304 756-4581

PARKLAND HEALTH CENTER
1101 W Liberty
Farmington, MO 63640-1921
(573)756-6451

SOUTHEAST MISSOURI MENTAL HEALTH CENTER
1010 West Columbia Street
Farmington, MO 63640-2902
(573)218-6792

FLORISSANT

CHRISTIAN HOSPITAL NORTHWEST
1225 Graham Road
Florissant, MO 63031-8076
(314)953-6000

FORT LEONARD WOOD

GENERAL LEONARD WOOD ARMY COMMUNITY HOSPITAL
126 Missouri Avenue, Bldg 310
Fort Leonard Wood, MO 65473-8952
(573)596-0414

FREDERICKTOWN

MADISON MEDICAL CENTER
100 South Wood At West College
Fredericktown, MO 63645
(573)783-3341

FULTON

CALLAWAY MEMORIAL HOSPITAL
10 South Hospital Drive
Fulton, MO 65251-2513
(573)642-3376

FULTON STATE HOSPITAL
600 East 5th Street
Fulton, MO 65251-1798
(573)592-4100

HANNIBAL

HANNIBAL REGIONAL HOSPITAL
PO Box 551, Highway 36w
Hannibal, MO 63401-0551
(573)248-1300

HARRISONVILLE

CASS MEDICAL CENTER
1800 E Mechanic
Harrisonville, MO 64701-2017
(816)380-3474

HAYTI

PEMISCOT MEMORIAL HOSPITAL
Highway 61 And Reed, PO Box 489
Hayti, MO 63851-0489
(573)359-1372

HERMANN

HERMANN AREA DISTRICT HOSPITAL
521 W 18th St
Hermann, MO 65041-1547
(573)486-2191

HOUSTON

TEXAS COUNTY MEMORIAL HOSPITAL
1333 Sam Houston Boulevard
Houston, MO 65483-2046
(417)967-3311

INDEPENDENCE

INDEPENDENCE REGIONAL HEALTH CENTER
1509 W Truman Road
Independence, MO 64050-3498
(816)836-8100

MEDICAL CENTER OF INDEPENDENCE
17203 E 23rd St
Independence, MO 64057-1899
(816)478-5000

JEFFERSON CITY

CAPITAL REGION MEDICAL CENTER
PO Box 1128
Jefferson City, MO 65102-1128
(314)632-5000

SAINT MARYS HEALTH CENTER
100 St Mary's Medical Plaza
Jefferson City, MO 65101-1601
(573)761-7000

JOPLIN

FREEMAN HOSPITAL AND HEALTH SYSTEM-EAST
932 E 34th St
Joplin, MO 64804-3932
(417)347-2801

FREEMAN HOSPITAL AND HEALTH SYSTEM-WEST
1102 W 32nd St
Joplin, MO 64804-3594
(417)347-2801

SAINT JOHNS REGIONAL MEDICAL CENTER
2727 Mcclelland Boulevard
Joplin, MO 64804-1694
(417)781-2727

KANSAS CITY

BAPTIST MEDICAL CENTER
6601 Rockhill Road
Kansas City, MO 64131-1197
(816)276-7000

CANCER INSTITUTE, THE
2316 East Meyer Boulevard
Kansas City, MO 64132-1136
(816)932-2823

CHILDRENS MERCY HOSPITAL
2401 Gillham Road
Kansas City, MO 64108-4698
(816)234-3000

CRITTENTON CENTER
10918 Elm Avenue
Kansas City, MO 64134-4199
(816)765-6600

KINDRED HOSPITAL KANSAS CITY
8701 Troost Avenue
Kansas City, MO 64131-2767
(816)995-2000

REHAB INSTITUTE
3011 Baltimore Avenue
Kansas City, MO 64108-3465
(816)751-7700

RESEARCH MEDICAL CENTER
2316 E Meyer Boulevard
Kansas City, MO 64132-1199
(816)276-4000

RESEARCH PSYCHIATRIC CENTER
2323 E 63rd St
Kansas City, MO 64130-3495
(816)444-8161

SAINT JOSEPH HEALTH CENTER
1000 Carondelet Drive
Kansas City, MO 64114-4865
(816)942-4400

SAINT LUKE'S NORTHLAND HOSPITAL
5830 Nw Barry Road
Kansas City, MO 64154-2778
(816)891-6000

SAINT LUKES HOSPITAL OF KANSAS CITY
4400 Wornall Road Box 119000
Kansas City, MO 64111-3238
(816)932-2000

TRUMAN MEDICAL CENTER
2301 Holmes
Kansas City, MO 64108-2677
(816)556-3000

TRUMAN MEDICAL CENTER EAST
7900 Lee's Summit Road
Kansas City, MO 64139-1246
(816)373-4415

TWO RIVERS PSYCHIATRIC HOSPITAL
5121 Raytown Road
Kansas City, MO 64133-2141
(816)356-5688

VA MEDICAL CENTER - KANSAS CITY
4801 Linwood Boulevard
Kansas City, MO 64128-2226
(816)861-4700

WESTERN MISSOURI MHC
600 E 22nd St
Kansas City, MO 64108-2620
(816)512-4000

KENNETT

TWIN RIVERS REGIONAL MEDICAL CENTER
1301 First St
Kennett, MO 63857-2508
(573)888-4522

KIRKSVILLE

NORTHEAST REGIONAL MEDICAL CENTER
315 South Osteopathy
Kirksville, MO 63501-6401
(660)785-1000

KIRKWOOD

SAINT JOSEPH HOSPITAL
525 Couch Avenue
Kirkwood, MO 63122-5594
(314)966-1500

LAKE SAINT LOUIS

SAINT JOSEPH HOSPITAL WEST
100 Medical Plaza
Lake Saint Louis, MO 63367-1395
(636)625-5200

LAMAR

BARTON COUNTY MEMORIAL HOSPITAL
Second And Gulf St
Lamar, MO 64759
(417)682-6081

LEBANON

BREECH REGIONAL MEDICAL CENTER
100 Hospital Drive
Lebanon, MO 65536-9210
(417)533-6100

MISSOURI — Hospital Telephone Directory

LEES SUMMIT
LEES SUMMIT HOSPITAL
530 N Murray Road
Lees Summit, MO 64081-1497
(816)969-6000

LEXINGTON
LAFAYETTE REGIONAL HEALTH CENTER
15th And State St
Lexington, MO 64067
(660)259-2203

LIBERTY
LIBERTY HOSPITAL
2525 Glenn Hendren Drive
Liberty, MO 64068-9600
(816)781-7200

LOUISIANA
PIKE COUNTY MEMORIAL HOSPITAL
2305 W Georgia
Louisiana, MO 63353-2559
(573)754-5531

MACON
SAMARITAN MEMORIAL HOSPITAL
1205 N Missouri St
Macon, MO 63552-2099
(660)385-3151

MARSHALL
JOHN FITZGIBBON MEMORIAL HOSPITAL
2505 South 65 Highway
Marshall, MO 65340
(660)886-7431

MARYVILLE
SAINT FRANCIS HOSPITAL
2016 South Main St
Maryville, MO 64468-2693
(660)562-2600

MEMPHIS
SCOTLAND COUNTY MEMORIAL HOSPITAL
Sigler St Box 277
Memphis, MO 63555-0277
(660)465-8511

MEXICO
AUDRAIN MEDICAL CENTER
620 E Monroe
Mexico, MO 65265-2963
(573)582-5000

MILAN
SULLIVAN COUNTY MEMORIAL HOSPITAL
630 W 3rd St
Milan, MO 63556-1076
(660)265-4212

MOBERLY
MOBERLY REGIONAL MEDICAL CENTER
1515 Union Avenue
Moberly, MO 65270-9449
(660)263-8400

MONETT
COX-MONETT HOSPITAL
801 Lincoln Avenue
Monett, MO 65708-1698
(417)235-3144

MOUNT VERNON
MISSOURI REHABILITATION CENTER
600 N Main
Mount Vernon, MO 65712-1004
(417)466-3711

MOUNTAIN VIEW
SAINT FRANCIS HOSPITAL
PO Box 82
Mountain View, MO 65548-0082
(417)934-7000

NEOSHO
FREEMAN NEOSHO HOSPITAL
113 W Hickory
Neosho, MO 64850-1705
(417)451-1234

NEVADA
HEARTLAND BEHAVIORAL HEALTH SERVICES
1500 West Ashland
Nevada, MO 64772-1710
(417)667-2666

NEVADA REGIONAL MEDICAL CENTER
800 South Ash
Nevada, MO 64772-3223
(417)667-3355

NORTH KANSAS CITY
NORTH KANSAS CITY HOSPITAL
2800 Hospital Drive
North Kansas City, MO 64116-3280
(816)691-2000

OSAGE BEACH
LAKE REGIONAL HEALTH SYSTEM
54 Hospital Drive
Osage Beach, MO 65065-3051
(573)348-8000

OSCEOLA
SAC-OSAGE HOSPITAL
PO Box 426
Osceola, MO 64776-0426
(417)646-8181

PERRYVILLE
PERRY COUNTY MEMORIAL HOSPITAL
434 N West St
Perryville, MO 63775-1398
(573)547-2536

POPLAR BLUFF
THREE RIVERS HEALTHCARE - NORTH
2620 N Westwood Blvd
Poplar Bluff, MO 63901-3396
(573)785-7721

THREE RIVERS HEALTHCARE - SOUTH
621 Pine Boulevard
Poplar Bluff, MO 63901-5042
(573)686-4111

VA MEDICAL CENTER - JOHN J. PERSHING
1500 N Westwood Boulevard
Poplar Bluff, MO 63901-3318
(573)686-4151

POTOSI
WASHINGTON COUNTY MEMORIAL HOSPITAL
300 Health Way
Potosi, MO 63664-1499
(573)438-5451

RICHMOND
RAY COUNTY MEMORIAL HOSPITAL
Route 4 Box 45
Richmond, MO 64085-9804
(816)470-5432

RICHMOND HEIGHTS
SAINT MARYS HEALTH CENTER
6420 Clayton Road
Richmond Heights, MO 63117-1872
(314)768-8000

ROLLA
PHELPS COUNTY REGIONAL MEDICAL CENTER
1000 W 10th St
Rolla, MO 65401-2905
(573)364-3100

SAINT CHARLES
CENTER POINT HOSPITAL
5931 Highway 94 South
Saint Charles, MO 63304-5611
(636)441-7300

SAINT JOSEPH HEALTH CENTER
300 1st Capitol Drive
Saint Charles, MO 63301-2893
(636)947-5000

SAINT JOSEPH
HEARTLAND HEART CENTER-EAST CAMPUS
5325 Faraon St
Saint Joseph, MO 64506-3398
(816)271-6000

HEARTLAND REGIONAL MEDICAL CENTER WEST
801 Faraon Street
Saint Joseph, MO 64501-1868
(816)271-6000

NORTHWEST MISSOURI PSYCHIATRIC REHAB CENTER
3505 Frederick Avenue
Saint Joseph, MO 64506-2914
(785)387-2300

WOODSON CHILDREN'S PSYCHIATRIC UNIT
3510 Frederick
Saint Joseph, MO 64506-2987
(785)387-2320

SAINT LOUIS
BARNES JEWISH HOSPITAL
216 S Kings Highway
Saint Louis, MO 63110-1092
(314)747-3000

BARNES WEST COUNTY HOSPITAL
12634 Olive St Road
Saint Louis, MO 63141
(314)996-8000

CARDINAL GLENNON CHILDRENS HOSPITAL
1465 S Grand Boulevard
Saint Louis, MO 63104-1095
(314)577-5600

CHRISTIAN HOSPITAL NORTHEAST
11133 Dunn Road
Saint Louis, MO 63136-6119
(314)653-5000

DES PERES HOSPITAL
2345 Dougherty Ferry Road
Saint Louis, MO 63122-3313
(314)966-9100

HOMER G. PHILLIPS CLINIC
2425 Whittier #113
Saint Louis, MO 63113-2950
(314)371-3100

KINDRED HOSPITAL SAINT LOUIS
4930 Lindell Boulevard
Saint Louis, MO 63108-1510
(314)361-8700

METROPOLITAN SAINT LOUIS PSYCHIATRIC CENTER
5351 Delmar Boulevard
Saint Louis, MO 63112-3146
(314)877-0500

MISSOURI BAPTIST MEDICAL CENTER
3015 N Ballas Road
Saint Louis, MO 63131-2374
(314)996-5000

REHABILITATION INSTITUTE OF SAINT LOUIS
4455 Duncan Avenue
Saint Louis, MO 63110-1111
(314)658-3800

SAINT ALEXIUS HOSPITAL
3933 S Broadway
Saint Louis, MO 63118-4601
(314)865-3333

SAINT ALEXIUS HOSPITAL - JEFFERSON CAMPUS
2639 Miami Street
Saint Louis, MO 63118-3929
(314)772-1456

SAINT ANTHONYS MEDICAL CENTER
10010 Kennerly Road
Saint Louis, MO 63128-2185
(314)525-1000

SAINT LOUIS CHILDRENS HOSPITAL
1 Childrens Place
Saint Louis, MO 63110-1081
(314)454-6000

SAINT LOUIS CONNECT CARE MEDICAL CENTER
5535 Delmar Boulevard
Saint Louis, MO 63112-3005
(314)361-2273

SAINT LOUIS PSYCH REHAB HOSPITAL
5400 Arsenal St
Saint Louis, MO 63139-1403
(314)644-8000

SAINT LOUIS UNIVERSITY HOSPITAL
3635 Vista At Grand Boulevard Box 15250
Saint Louis, MO 63110-0250
(314)577-8000

SELECT SPECIALTY HOSPITAL - SAINT LOUIS
6150 Oakland Avenue, 5th Floor
Saint Louis, MO 63139-3215
(314)768-3400

SHRINERS HOSPITAL
2001 S Lindbergh Boulevard
Saint Louis, MO 63131-3597
(314)432-3600

SSM REHABILITATION INSTITUTE
6420 Clayton Road, Suite 600
Saint Louis, MO 63117-1811
(314)768-5300

VA MEDICAL CENTER - SAINT LOUIS
915 N Grand Boulevard
Saint Louis, MO 63106-1621
(314)652-4100

SAINT PETERS

BARNES-JEWISH SAINT PETERS HOSPITAL
10 Hospital Drive
Saint Peters, MO 63376-1691
(636)916-9000

SAINTE GENEVIEVE

STE GENEVIEVE COUNTY MEMORIAL HOSPITAL
Highway 61 And 32
Sainte Genevieve, MO 63670
(573)883-2751

SALEM

SALEM MEMORIAL HOSPITAL DISTRICT
Highway 72 North Box 774
Salem, MO 65560-0774
(573)729-6626

SEDALIA

BOTHWELL REGIONAL HEALTH CENTER
PO Box 1706
Sedalia, MO 65302-1706
(660)826-8833

SIKESTON

MISSOURI DELTA MEDICAL CENTER
1008 North Main St
Sikeston, MO 63801-5099
(573)471-1600

SMITHVILLE

SAINT LUKES NORTHLAND HOSPITAL
601 South 169 Hwy
Smithville, MO 64089-9317
(816)532-3700

SPRINGFIELD

DOCTORS HOSPITAL OF SPRINGFIELD
2828 North National St
Springfield, MO 65803-4306
(417)837-4000

LAKELAND REGIONAL HOSPITAL
440 S Market
Springfield, MO 65806-2090
(417)865-5581

LESTER E. COX MEDICAL CENTER - NORTH
1432 N Jefferson St
Springfield, MO 65802
(417)269-3000

LESTER E. COX MEDICAL CENTER SOUTH
3801 South National Avenue
Springfield, MO 65807-5297
(417)269-6000

SAINT JOHNS REGIONAL HEALTH CENTER
1235 E Cherokee
Springfield, MO 65804-2263
(417)885-2000

U.S. MEDICAL CENTER FOR FEDERAL PRISONERS
PO Box 4000
Springfield, MO 65801-4000
(417)862-7041

SULLIVAN

MISSOURI BAPTIST HOSPITAL SULLIVAN
751 Sappington Bridge Road
Sullivan, MO 63080-2354
(573)468-4186

TRENTON

WRIGHT MEMORIAL HOSPITAL
701 E First
Trenton, MO 64683-2402
(660)359-5621

TROY

LINCOLN COUNTY MEMORIAL HOSPITAL
1000 E Cherry
Troy, MO 63379-1599
(636)528-8551

UNIONVILLE

PUTNAM COUNTY MEMORIAL HOSPITAL
PO Box 389
Unionville, MO 63565-0389
(660)947-2411

WARRENSBURG

WESTERN MISSOURI MEDICAL CENTER
403 Burkarth Road
Warrensburg, MO 64093-3101
(660)747-2500

WASHINGTON

SAINT JOHNS MERCY HOSPITAL
901 E 5th St
Washington, MO 63090-3127
(636)239-8000

WENTZVILLE

CROSSROADS REGIONAL HOSPITAL
500 Medical Drive PO Box 711
Wentzville, MO 63385-3421
(636)327-1000

WEST PLAINS

OZARKS MEDICAL CENTER
1100 Kentucky Avenue, PO Box 1100
West Plains, MO 65775-1100
(417)256-9111

WHITEMAN AIR FORCE BASE

509TH MEDICAL GROUP
331 Sijan Avenue
Whiteman Air Force Base, MO 65305-1269
(660)687-4346

WINDSOR

ROYAL OAKS HOSPITAL
307 N Main
Windsor, MO 65360-1449
(660)647-2182

MONTANA

ANACONDA

COMMUNITY HOSPITAL OF ANACONDA
401 W Pennsylvania Avenue
Anaconda, MT 59711-1999
(406)563-8500

BAKER

FALLON COUNTY MEDICAL COMPLEX
PO Box 820
Baker, MT 59313-0820
(406)778-3331

BIG SANDY

BIG SANDY MEDICAL CENTER MAF
PO Box 530
Big Sandy, MT 59520-0530
(406)378-2188

BIG TIMBER

PIONEER MEDICAL CENTER MAF
PO Box 1228
Big Timber, MT 59011-1228
(406)932-4603

MONTANA — Hospital Telephone Directory

BILLINGS

DEACONESS HOSPITAL
2800 10th Avenue North
Billings, MT 59101-0799
(406)657-4000

SAINT VINCENT HOSPITAL AND HEALTH CENTER
1233 N 30th St PO Box 35200
Billings, MT 59107-5200
(406)237-7000

BOZEMAN

BOZEMAN DEACONESS HOSPITAL
915 Highland Boulevard
Bozeman, MT 59715-6999
(406)585-5000

BROWNING

PHS INDIAN HOSPITAL - BROWNING
Browning, MT 59417
(406)338-6200

BUTTE

SAINT JAMES COMMUNITY HOSPITAL
400 South Clark St Box 3300
Butte, MT 59701-9756
(406)723-2500

CHESTER

LIBERTY COUNTY HOSPITAL
Highway 223 And Monroe PO Box 705
Chester, MT 59522-0705
(406)759-5181

CHOTEAU

TETON MEDICAL CENTER MAF
915 4th St Nw
Choteau, MT 59422-9123
(406)466-5763

CIRCLE

MCCONE COUNTY MEDICAL ASSISTANCE FACILITY
205 Sullivan Avenue PO Box 48
Circle, MT 59215-0048
(406)485-3381

COLUMBUS

STILLWATER COMMUNITY HOSPITAL
44 W Fourth PO Box 959
Columbus, MT 59019-0959
(406)322-5316

CONRAD

PONDERA MEDICAL CENTER
805 Sunset Boulevard
Conrad, MT 59425-1721
(406)271-3211

CROW AGENCY

PHS INDIAN HOSPITAL - CROW AGENCY
PO Box 9
Crow Agency, MT 59022-0009
(406)638-2626

CULBERTSON

ROOSEVELT MEMORIAL MEDICAL CENTER
818 2nd Avenue E PO Box 419
Culbertson, MT 59218-0419
(406)787-6281

CUT BANK

NORTHERN ROCKIES MEDICAL CENTER
802 2nd St S E
Cut Bank, MT 59427-3329
(406)873-2251

DEER LODGE

POWELL COUNTY MEMORIAL HOSPITAL
1101 Texas Avenue
Deer Lodge, MT 59722-1899
(406)846-2212

DILLON

BARRETT MEMORIAL HOSPITAL
1260 S Atlantic
Dillon, MT 59725-3597
(406)683-3000

EKALAKA

DAHL MEMORIAL MAF
PO Box 46
Ekalaka, MT 59324-0046
(406)775-8738

ENNIS

MADISON VALLEY HOSPITAL
217 Us Highway 287 PO Box 397
Ennis, MT 59729-0397
(406)682-4222

FORSYTH

ROSEBUD HEALTH CARE CENTER
383 N 17th Avenue
Forsyth, MT 59327
(406)356-2161

FORT BENTON

MISSOURI RIVER MEDICAL CENTER MAF
PO Box 249
Fort Benton, MT 59442-0249
(406)622-3331

FORT HARRISON

VA HEALTHCARE SYSTEM - MONTANA
William St Off Highway 12 West
Fort Harrison, MT 59636
(406)442-6410

GLASGOW

FRANCES MAHON DEACONESS HOSPITAL
621 Third St South
Glasgow, MT 59230-2699
(406)228-3500

GLENDIVE

GLENDIVE MEDICAL CENTER
202 Prospect Drive
Glendive, MT 59330-1999
(406)345-3306

GREAT FALLS

BENEFIS HEALTHCARE
1101 26th Street South
Great Falls, MT 59405-5104
(406)455-5000

BENEFIS HEALTHCARE WEST CAMPUS
500 15th Avenue S
Great Falls, MT 59405-4324
(406)455-5000

HAMILTON

MARCUS DALY MEMORIAL HOSPITAL
1200 Westwood Drive
Hamilton, MT 59840-2395
(406)363-2211

HARDIN

BIG HORN COUNTY MEMORIAL HOSPITAL
17 N Miles
Hardin, MT 59034-2323
(406)665-2310

HARLEM

PHS INDIAN HOSPITAL - HARLEM
456 Gros Ventre Avenue, Rr 1 Box 67
Harlem, MT 59526-9705
(406)353-3100

HARLOWTON

WHEATLAND MEMORIAL HOSPITAL
530 Third St Nw
Harlowton, MT 59036
(406)632-4351

HAVRE

NORTHERN MONTANA HOSPITAL
PO Box 1231
Havre, MT 59501-1231
(406)265-2211

HELENA

SAINT PETERS COMMUNITY HOSPITAL
2475 Broadway
Helena, MT 59601-4999
(406)442-2480

SHODAIR CHILDRENS HOSPITAL
840 Helena Avenue PO Box 5539
Helena, MT 59604-5539
(406)444-7500

JORDAN

GARFIELD COUNTY CLINIC MAF
PO Box 389
Jordan, MT 59337-0389
(406)557-2500

KALISPELL

KALISPELL REGIONAL HOSPITAL
310 Sunnyview Lane
Kalispell, MT 59901-3199
(406)752-5111

PATHWAY TREATMENT CENTER
200 Heritage Way
Kalispell, MT 59901-3146
(406)756-3950

LEWISTOWN

CENTRAL MONTANA MEDICAL CENTER
408 Wendell Box 580
Lewistown, MT 59457-2261
(406)538-7711

LIBBY

SAINT JOHNS LUTHERAN HOSPITAL
350 Louisiana Avenue
Libby, MT 59923-2198
(406)293-0100

LIVINGSTON

LIVINGSTON MEMORIAL HOSPITAL
504 S 13th St
Livingston, MT 59047-3798
(406)222-3541

Hospital Telephone Directory — NEBRASKA

MALTA

PHILLIPS COUNTY MEDICAL CENTER-MAF
417 South Fourth East
Malta, MT 59538
(406)654-1100

MILES CITY

HOLY ROSARY HOSPITAL
2600 Wilson St
Miles City, MT 59301-5094
(406)233-2600

MISSOULA

COMMUNITY MEDICAL CENTER
2827 Fort Missoula Road
Missoula, MT 59804-7408
(406)728-4100

SAINT PATRICK HOSPITAL
500 W Broadway Box 4587
Missoula, MT 59802-4096
(406)543-7271

PHILIPSBURG

GRANITE COUNTY MEMORIAL MAF
310 Sansome PO Box 729
Philipsburg, MT 59858-0729
(406)859-3271

PLAINS

CLARK FORK VALLEY HOSPITAL
PO Box 768
Plains, MT 59859-0768
(406)826-3601

PLENTYWOOD

SHERIDAN MEMORIAL HOSPITAL
440 West Laurel Avenue
Plentywood, MT 59254-1596
(406)765-1420

POLSON

SAINT JOSEPH HOSPITAL
Box 1010 Skyline Drive
Polson, MT 59860-1010
(406)883-5377

POPLAR

POPLAR COMMUNITY HOSPITAL
PO Box 38
Poplar, MT 59255-0038
(406)768-3452

RED LODGE

BEAR TOOTH HOSPITAL AND HEALTH CENTER
600 W 20th St PO Box 590
Red Lodge, MT 59068-0590
(406)446-2345

RONAN

SAINT LUKE COMMUNITY HOSPITAL
107 6th Avenue Sw
Ronan, MT 59864-2634
(406)676-4441

ROUNDUP

ROUNDUP MEMORIAL HOSPITAL
1202 3rd St West, PO Box 40
Roundup, MT 59072-0040
(406)323-2302

SCOBEY

DANIELS MEMORIAL HOSPITAL
PO Box 400
Scobey, MT 59263-0400
(406)487-2296

SHELBY

MARIAS MEDICAL CENTER
640 Park Drive, PO Box 915
Shelby, MT 59474-0915
(406)434-3200

SHERIDAN

RUBY VALLEY HOSPITAL
220 E Crowfoot St Box 336
Sheridan, MT 59749-0336
(406)842-5453

SIDNEY

SIDNEY HEALTH CENTER
216 14th Ave Sw
Sidney, MT 59270-3586
(406)488-2100

SUPERIOR

MINERAL COMMUNITY HOSPITAL
Brooklyn And Roosevelt PO Box 66
Superior, MT 59872-0066
(406)822-4841

TERRY

PRAIRIE COMMUNITY HOSPITAL
312 S Adams, PO Box 156
Terry, MT 59349-0156
(406)635-5511

TOWNSEND

BROADWATER HEALTH CENTER
110 N Oak St
Townsend, MT 59644-2306
(406)266-3186

WARMSPRINGS

MONTANA STATE HOSPITAL
PO Box 300
Warmsprings, MT 59756-0300
(406)693-7000

WHITE SULPHUR SPRINGS

MOUNTAINVIEW MEDICAL CENTER MAF
16 W Main St PO Box Q
White Sulphur Springs, MT 59645-0817
(406)547-3321

WHITEFISH

NORTH VALLEY HOSPITAL
6575 Highway 93 South
Whitefish, MT 59937-2990
(406)863-3500

WOLF POINT

NORTHEAST MONTANA HEALTH SERVICES - TRINITY HOSPITAL
315 Knapp Street
Wolf Point, MT 59201-1826
(406)653-2100

NEBRASKA

AINSWORTH

BROWN COUNTY HOSPITAL
945 E Zero St
Ainsworth, NE 69210-1547
(402)387-2800

ALBION

BOONE COUNTY HEALTH CENTER
723 West Fairview St Box 151
Albion, NE 68620-1725
(402)395-2191

ALLIANCE

BOX BUTTE GENERAL HOSPITAL
2101 Box Butte Avenue
Alliance, NE 69301-4444
(308)762-6660

ALMA

HARLAN COUNTY HOSPITAL
717 North Brown, PO Box N
Alma, NE 68920-2132
(308)928-2151

ATKINSON

WEST HOLT MEDICAL CENTER
405 W Pearl St
Atkinson, NE 68713-4882
(402)925-2811

AUBURN

NEMAHA COUNTY HOSPITAL
2022 - 13th Street
Auburn, NE 68305-1799
(402)274-4366

AURORA

MEMORIAL HOSPITAL
1423 7th St
Aurora, NE 68818-1197
(402)694-3171

BASSETT

ROCK COUNTY HOSPITAL
Hc 75 Box 300
Bassett, NE 68714-9760
(402)684-3366

BEATRICE

BEATRICE COMMUNITY HOSPITAL AND HEALTH CENTER
1110 North 10th Street
Beatrice, NE 68310-2039
(402)228-3344

BEATRICE STATE DEVELOPMENTAL CENTER
3000 Lincoln Boulevard
Beatrice, NE 68310-3300
(402)223-6600

BENKELMAN

DUNDY COUNTY HOSPITAL
North Cheyenne Street PO Box 626
Benkelman, NE 69021-0626
(308)423-2204

BLAIR

MEMORIAL COMMUNITY HOSPITAL
810 N 22nd St
Blair, NE 68008-1199
(402)426-2182

NEBRASKA — Hospital Telephone Directory

BRIDGEPORT
MORRILL COUNTY COMMUNITY HOSPITAL
PO Box 579 1313 S Street
Bridgeport, NE 69336-0579
(308)262-1616

BROKEN BOW
JENNIE M MELHAM MEMORIAL MEDICAL CENTER
145 Memorial Drive
Broken Bow, NE 68822-1378
(308)872-6891

CALLAWAY
CALLAWAY DISTRICT HOSPITAL
211 Kimball PO Box 100
Callaway, NE 68825-0100
(308)836-2228

CAMBRIDGE
TRI VALLEY HEALTH SYSTEM
PO Box 488
Cambridge, NE 69022-0488
(308)697-3329

CENTRAL CITY
LITZENBERG MEMORIAL COUNTY HOSPITAL
1715 26th Street
Central City, NE 68826-9501
(308)946-3015

CHADRON
CHADRON COMMUNITY HOSPITAL
821 Morehead Street
Chadron, NE 69337-2599
(308)432-5586

COLUMBUS
COLUMBUS COMMUNITY HOSPITAL
PO Box 819
Columbus, NE 68602-0819
(402)564-7118

COZAD
COZAD COMMUNITY HOSPITAL
300 East 12th Street
Cozad, NE 69130-1532
(308)784-2261

CREIGHTON
CREIGHTON AREA HEALTH SERVICES
PO Box 186 1503 Main Street
Creighton, NE 68729-0186
(402)358-3322

CRETE
CRETE MUNICIPAL HOSPITAL
1540 Grove Street
Crete, NE 68333-1749
(402)826-6800

DAVID CITY
BUTLER COUNTY HOSPITAL
372 South 9th Street
David City, NE 68632-2199
(402)367-3115

FAIRBURY
JEFFERSON COMMUNITY HEALTH CENTER
2200 North H Street PO Box 277
Fairbury, NE 68352-0277
(402)729-3351

FALLS CITY
COMMUNITY MEDICAL CENTER
2307 Barada Street
Falls City, NE 68355-1599
(402)245-2428

FRANKLIN
FRANKLIN COUNTY MEMORIAL HOSPITAL
PO Box 315
Franklin, NE 68939-0315
(308)425-6221

FREMONT
FREMONT AREA MEDICAL CENTER
450 E 23rd St
Fremont, NE 68025-2387
(402)721-1610

FRIEND
WARREN MEMORIAL HOSPITAL
905 2nd St
Friend, NE 68359-1198
(402)947-2541

GENEVA
FILLMORE COUNTY HOSPITAL
1325 'h' St PO Box 193
Geneva, NE 68361-0193
(402)759-3167

GENOA
GENOA COMMUNITY HOSPITAL
706 Ewing Avenue
Genoa, NE 68640-3035
(402)993-2283

GORDON
GORDON MEMORIAL HOSPITAL
300 East 8th Street
Gordon, NE 69343-1199
(308)282-0401

GOTHENBURG
GOTHENBURG MEMORIAL HOSPITAL
910 20th Street PO Box 469
Gothenburg, NE 69138-0469
(308)537-3661

GRAND ISLAND
SAINT FRANCIS MEDICAL CENTER
2620 West Faidley
Grand Island, NE 68803-4297
(308)384-4600

VA MEDICAL CENTER - GRAND ISLAND
2201 N Broadwell
Grand Island, NE 68803-2196
(308)382-3660

GRANT
PERKINS COUNTY HOSPITAL
900 Lincoln Avenue
Grant, NE 69140-3095
(308)352-7200

HASTINGS
HASTINGS REGIONAL CENTER
PO Box 579
Hastings, NE 68902-0579
(308)462-1971

MARY LANNING MEMORIAL HOSPITAL
715 N St Joseph Avenue
Hastings, NE 68901-4497
(402)461-5110

HEBRON
THAYER COUNTY HEALTH SERVICES
121 Park Avenue PO Box 49
Hebron, NE 68370-0049
(402)768-6041

HENDERSON
HENDERSON HEALTH CARE SERVICES
1621 Front St PO Box 217
Henderson, NE 68371-0217
(402)723-4512

HOLDREGE
PHELPS MEMORIAL HEALTH CENTER
1215 Tibbals St
Holdrege, NE 68949-1255
(308)995-2211

HUMBOLDT
HUMBOLDT HOSPITAL
PO Box 578
Humboldt, NE 68376-0578
(402)862-2231

IMPERIAL
CHASE COUNTY COMMUNITY HOSPITAL
600 West 12th Street
Imperial, NE 69033-3131
(308)882-7111

KEARNEY
GOOD SAMARITAN HOSPITAL
10 E 31st Street
Kearney, NE 68847-2918
(308)865-7100

RICHARD H YOUNG HOSPITAL
PO Box 1750
Kearney, NE 68848-1750
(308)865-2000

KIMBALL
KIMBALL COUNTY HOSPITAL
505 South Burg Street
Kimball, NE 69145-1313
(308)235-1952

LEXINGTON
TRI COUNTY HOSPITAL
1201 North Erie Street PO Box 980
Lexington, NE 68850-0980
(308)324-5651

LINCOLN
BRYAN LGH EAST HOSPITAL
1600 South 48th Street
Lincoln, NE 68506-1299
(402)489-0200

BRYAN LGH WEST HOSPITAL
2300 S 16th St
Lincoln, NE 68502-3780
(402)475-1011

LINCOLN REGIONAL CENTER
PO Box 94949
Lincoln, NE 68509-4949
(402)471-4444

MADONNA REHABILITATION HOSPITAL
5401 South Street
Lincoln, NE 68506-2150
(402)489-7102

94

Hospital Telephone Directory — **NEBRASKA**

SAINT ELIZABETH COMMUNITY HEALTH CENTER
555 S 70th St
Lincoln, NE 68510-2494
(402)489-7181

LYNCH

NIOBRARA VALLEY HOSPITAL
PO Box 118
Lynch, NE 68746-0118
(402)569-2451

MC COOK

COMMUNITY HOSPITAL
PO Box 1328
Mc Cook, NE 69001-1328
(308)345-2650

MINDEN

KEARNEY COUNTY HEALTH SERVICES
727 East First Street
Minden, NE 68959-1700
(308)832-1440

NEBRASKA CITY

SAINT MARYS HOSPITAL
1314 Third Avenue
Nebraska City, NE 68410-1999
(402)873-3321

NELIGH

ANTELOPE MEMORIAL HOSPITAL
102 W 9th St PO Box 229
Neligh, NE 68756-0229
(402)887-4151

NORFOLK

FAITH REGIONAL HEALTH SERVICES - WEST CAMPUS
2700 Norfolk Avenue
Norfolk, NE 68701-4438
(402)644-7201

FAITH REGIONAL HOSPITAL
1500 Koenigstein Avenue
Norfolk, NE 68701-3664
(402)644-7201

NORFOLK REGIONAL CENTER
1700 N Victory Building 16
Norfolk, NE 68701-6859
(402)370-3400

NORTH PLATTE

GREAT PLAINS REGIONAL MEDICAL CENTER
601 W Leota St
North Platte, NE 69101-6598
(308)534-9310

O'NEILL

AVERA SAINT ANTHONYS HOSPITAL
2nd And Adams St
O'Neill, NE 68763
(402)336-2611

OAKLAND

OAKLAND MEMORIAL HOSPITAL
601 E 2nd St
Oakland, NE 68045-1499
(402)685-5601

OFFUTT AIR FORCE BASE

55TH MEDICAL GROUP, EHRLING BERGQUIST HOSPITAL
2501 Capehart Road
Offutt Air Force Base, NE 68113-2160
(402)294-7311

OGALLALA

OGALLALA COMMUNITY HOSPITAL
300 East 10th Street
Ogallala, NE 69153-1509
(308)284-4011

OMAHA

BERGAN MERCY MEDICAL CENTER
7500 Mercy Road
Omaha, NE 68124-2386
(402)343-4410

BOYS TOWN NATIONAL RESEARCH HOSPITAL
555 North 30th Street
Omaha, NE 68131-2136
(402)498-6511

CHILDRENS HOSPITAL
8301 Dodge St
Omaha, NE 68114-4114
(402)955-5400

CREIGHTON UNIVERSITY MEDICAL CENTER
601 N 30th St
Omaha, NE 68131-2137
(402)449-4000

DOUGLAS COUNTY HOSPITAL
4102 Woolworth Avenue
Omaha, NE 68105-1899
(402)444-7000

IMMANUEL MEDICAL CENTER
6901 N 72nd St
Omaha, NE 68122-1753
(402)572-2121

METHODIST RICHARD YOUNG
515 S 26th St
Omaha, NE 68105-4199
(402)354-6600

NEBRASKA MEDICAL CENTER
4350 Dewey Avenue
Omaha, NE 68105-1017
(402)552-2000

NEBRASKA METHODIST HOSPITAL
8303 Dodge Street
Omaha, NE 68114-4199
(402)354-4000

UNIVERSITY OF NEBRASKA MEDICAL CENTER
602 South 42nd Street
Omaha, NE 68198-1002
(402)559-4000

VA MEDICAL CENTER - OMAHA
4101 Woolworth Avenue
Omaha, NE 68105-1850
(402)449-0600

ORD

VALLEY COUNTY HOSPITAL
217 Westridge Drive
Ord, NE 68862-1665
(308)728-3211

OSCEOLA

ANNIE JEFFREY MEMORIAL COUNTY HEALTH CENTER
PO Box 428 531 Beebe Street
Osceola, NE 68651-0428
(402)747-2031

OSHKOSH

GARDEN COUNTY HEALTH SERVICES
North Highway 27 PO Box 320
Oshkosh, NE 69154-0320
(308)772-3283

OSMOND

OSMOND GENERAL HOSPITAL
5th And Maple Streets
Osmond, NE 68765
(402)748-3393

PAPILLION

MIDLANDS COMMUNITY HOSPITAL
11111 S 84th St
Papillion, NE 68046-4157
(402)593-3000

SELECT SPECIALTY HOSPITAL - OMAHA
11111 South 84th Street
Papillion, NE 68046-4122
(402)898-2700

PAWNEE CITY

PAWNEE COUNTY MEMORIAL HOSPITAL
600 I St PO Box 313
Pawnee City, NE 68420-0313
(402)852-2231

PENDER

PENDER COMMUNITY HOSPITAL
PO Box 100
Pender, NE 68047-0100
(402)385-3083

PLAINVIEW

PLAINVIEW AREA HEALTH SYSTEM
PO Box 489
Plainview, NE 68769-0489
(402)582-4245

RED CLOUD

WEBSTER COUNTY COMMUNITY HOSPITAL
6th And Franklin St
Red Cloud, NE 68970
(402)746-2291

SAINT PAUL

HOWARD COUNTY COMMUNITY HOSPITAL
PO Box 406
Saint Paul, NE 68873-0406
(308)754-4421

SCHUYLER

ALEGENT HEALTH - MEMORIAL HOSPITAL
104 W 17th St
Schuyler, NE 68661-1304
(402)352-2441

SCOTTSBLUFF

REGIONAL WEST MEDICAL CENTER
4021 Avenue B
Scottsbluff, NE 69361-4695
(308)635-3711

SEWARD

MEMORIAL HOSPITAL
300 N Columbia Avenue
Seward, NE 68434-2299
(402)643-2971

NEVADA

Hospital Telephone Directory

SIDNEY

MEMORIAL HEALTH CENTER
645 Osage Street
Sidney, NE 69162-1799
(308)254-5825

SUPERIOR

BRODSTONE MEMORIAL-NUCKOLLS CO
HOSPITAL
PO Box 187 520 East 10th Street
Superior, NE 68978-0187
(402)879-3281

SYRACUSE

COMMUNITY MEMORIAL HOSPITAL
1579 Midland St, PO Box N
Syracuse, NE 68446-0518
(402)269-2011

TECUMSEH

JOHNSON COUNTY HOSPITAL
202 High Street
Tecumseh, NE 68450-2443
(402)335-3361

TILDEN

TILDEN COMMUNITY HOSPITAL
2nd And Pine Street PO Box 340
Tilden, NE 68781-0340
(402)368-5343

VALENTINE

CHERRY COUNTY HOSPITAL
Green St And Highway 12
Valentine, NE 69201
(402)376-2525

WAHOO

SAUNDERS COUNTY COMMUNITY
HOSPITAL
805 West 10th Street
Wahoo, NE 68066-1102
(402)443-4191

WAYNE

PROVIDENCE MEDICAL CENTER
1200 Providence Road
Wayne, NE 68787-1299
(402)375-3800

WEST POINT

SAINT FRANCIS MEMORIAL HOSPITAL
430 North Monitor
West Point, NE 68788-1595
(402)372-2404

WINNEBAGO

PHS INDIAN HOSPITAL - WINNEBAGO
Winnebago, NE 68071
(402)878-2231

YORK

YORK GENERAL HOSPITAL
2222 Lincoln Avenue
York, NE 68467-1095
(402)362-0445

NEVADA

BATTLE MOUNTAIN

BATTLE MOUNTAIN GENERAL HOSPITAL
535 South Humboldt Street
Battle Mountain, NV 89820-1988
(775)635-2550

BOULDER CITY

BOULDER CITY HOSPITAL
901 Adams Boulevard
Boulder City, NV 89005-2299
(702)293-4111

CALIENTE

GROVER C DILS MEDICAL CENTER
Highway 93 North
Caliente, NV 89008
(775)726-3171

CARSON CITY

CARSON REHABILITATION CENTER
PO Box 2168
Carson City, NV 89702-2168
(775)881-7000

CARSON-TAHOE HOSPITAL
775 Fleischmann Way
Carson City, NV 89703-2995
(775)882-1361

EAST ELY

WILLIAM B. RIRIE HOSPITAL
PO Box 435
East Ely, NV 89315
(775)289-3001

ELKO

NORTHEASTERN NEVADA REGIONAL
HOSPITAL
1297 College Avenue
Elko, NV 89801-3425
(775)738-5151

FALLON

CHURCHILL COMMUNITY HOSPITAL
801 East Williams Avenue
Fallon, NV 89406-3052
(775)423-3151

HAWTHORNE

MOUNT GRANT GENERAL HOSPITAL
First And A Streets
Hawthorne, NV 89415
(775)945-2461

HENDERSON

HEALTHSOUTH REHABILITATION HOSPITAL
OF HENDERSON
10301 Jeffreys
Henderson, NV 89052-3922
(702)939-9400

SAINT ROSE DOMINICAN HOSPITAL - ROSE
DE LIMA CAMPUS
102 East Lake Mead Drive
Henderson, NV 89015-5524
(702)616-5000

SAINT ROSE DOMINICAN HOSPITAL - SIENA
CAMPUS
3001 Saint Rose Parkway
Henderson, NV 89052-3839
(702)616-5000

INCLINE VILLAGE

INCLINE VILLAGE HEALTH CENTER
880 Alder St
Incline Village, NV 89451-8215
(775)833-4100

LAS VEGAS

DESERT SPRINGS HOSPITAL
2075 East Flamingo Road
Las Vegas, NV 89119-5121
(702)733-8800

HARMON MEDICAL & REHABILATION
HOSPITAL
2170 East Harmon Avenue
Las Vegas, NV 89119-7840
(702)794-0100

HEALTHSOUTH HOSPITAL AT TENAYA
2500 Tenaya Way
Las Vegas, NV 89128-0482
(702)562-2021

HEALTHSOUTH REHABILITATION HOSPITAL
OF NEVADA
1250 South Valley View Boulevard
Las Vegas, NV 89102-1855
(702)877-8898

HORIZON SPECIALTY HOSPITAL
640 Desert Lane
Las Vegas, NV 89106-4200
(702)382-3155

KINDRED HOSPITAL LAS VEGAS
5110 W Sahara Avenue
Las Vegas, NV 89146-3406
(702)871-1418

KINDRED HOSPITAL LAS VEGAS -
FLAMINGO
2250 East Flamingo Road
Las Vegas, NV 89119-5117
(702)784-4300

MONTEVISTA HOSPITAL
5900 W Rochelle Avenue
Las Vegas, NV 89103-3327
(702)364-1111

MOUNTAINVIEW HOSPITAL
3100 N Tenaya Way
Las Vegas, NV 89128-0442
(702)255-5000

PROGRESSIVE HOSPITAL
4015 South McLeod
Las Vegas, NV 89121-4305
(702)433-2200

SOUTHERN NEVADA ADULT MENTAL
HEALTH
6161 West Charleston Boulevard
Las Vegas, NV 89146-1148
(702)486-6000

SPRING MOUNTAIN TREATMENT CENTER
7000 West Spring Mountain Road
Las Vegas, NV 89117-3816
(702)873-2400

SPRING VALLEY HOSPITAL MEDICAL
CENTER
5400 Rainbow Boulevard
Las Vegas, NV 89118-1859
(702)853-3000

SUMMERLIN HOSPITAL MEDICAL CENTER
657 Town Center Drive
Las Vegas, NV 89134
(702)233-7000

SUNRISE HOSPITAL AND MEDICAL CENTER
3186 S Maryland Parkway
Las Vegas, NV 89109-2306
(702)731-8000

Hospital Telephone Directory

NEW HAMPSHIRE

UNIVERSITY MEDICAL CENTER OF
SOUTHERN NEVADA
1800 West Charleston Boulevard
Las Vegas, NV 89102-2386
(702)383-2000

VA HEALTHCARE SYSTEM - SOUTHERN
NEVADA
1700 Vegas Drive
Las Vegas, NV 89106-2111
(702)636-3000

VALLEY HOSPITAL MEDICAL CENTER
620 Shadow Lane
Las Vegas, NV 89106-4194
(702)388-4000

LOVELOCK

PERSHING GENERAL HOSPITAL
855 6th St
Lovelock, NV 89419
(775)273-2621

NELLIS AIR FORCE BASE

99TH MEDICAL GROUP, MIKE
O'CALLAGHAN FEDERAL HOSPITAL
4700 Las Vegas Boulevard North, Suite 2419
Nellis Air Force Base, NV 89191-6601
(702)653-2000

NORTH LAS VEGAS

LAKE MEAD HOSPITAL MEDICAL CENTER
1409 East Lake Mead Boulevard
North Las Vegas, NV 89030-7197
(702)649-7711

OWYHEE

PHS/IHS OWYHEE COMMUNITY HOSPITAL
PO Box 130
Owyhee, NV 89832-0130
(775)757-2415

RENO

SAINT MARYS REGIONAL MEDICAL
CENTER
235 W 6th St
Reno, NV 89503-4548
(775)770-3000

TAHOE PACIFIC WEST
235 West 6th Street
Reno, NV 89503-4548
(775)770-7980

VA HEALTHCARE SYSTEM - RENO
1000 Locust St
Reno, NV 89502-2597
(775)786-7200

WAHOE REHABILITATION HOSPITAL
555 Gould St
Reno, NV 89502-1449
(775)348-5500

WASHOE MEDICAL CENTER
77 Pringle Way
Reno, NV 89502-1474
(775)982-4100

WASHOE VILLAGE ACUTE REHABILITATION
HOSPITAL
10101 Double R Blvd
Reno, NV 89521-5931
(775)982-7000

WEST HILLS HOSPITAL
1240 E Ninth St
Reno, NV 89512-2964
(775)323-0478

WILLOW SPRINGS CENTER
690 Edison Way
Reno, NV 89502-4135
(775)858-3303

SCHURZ

PHS/IHS INDIAN HEALTH CENTER - SCHURZ
Drawer A
Schurz, NV 89427-0500
(775)773-2345

SPARKS

NORTHERN NEVADA ADULT MENTAL
HEALTH SERVICE
480 Galleti Way
Sparks, NV 89431-5573
(775)688-2001

NORTHERN NEVADA MEDICAL CENTER
2375 Prater Way
Sparks, NV 89434-9665
(775)331-7000

TAHOE PACIFIC HOSPITAL
2385 Prater Way
Sparks, NV 89434-9629
(775)331-1044

TONOPAH

NYE REGIONAL MEDICAL CENTER
825 Erie Main St
Tonopah, NV 89049
(775)482-6233

WINNEMUCCA

HUMBOLDT GENERAL HOSPITAL
118 East Haskell Street
Winnemucca, NV 89445-3299
(775)623-5222

YERINGTON

SOUTH LYON MEDICAL CENTER
Surprise At Whitacre Avenue
Yerington, NV 89447
(775)463-2301

NEW HAMPSHIRE

BERLIN

ANDROSCOGGIN VALLEY HOSPITAL
59 Page Hill Road
Berlin, NH 03570-3542
(603)752-2200

CLAREMONT

VALLEY REGIONAL HOSPITAL
243 Elm St
Claremont, NH 03743-2099
(603)542-7771

COLEBROOK

UPPER CONNECTICUT VALLEY HOSPITAL
Corliss Lane
Colebrook, NH 03576
(603)237-4971

CONCORD

CONCORD HOSPITAL
250 Pleasant St
Concord, NH 03301-2598
(603)225-2711

HEALTHSOUTH REHABILITATION HOSPITAL
254 Pleasant St
Concord, NH 03301-2508
(603)226-9800

NEW HAMPSHIRE HOSPITAL
36 Clinton St
Concord, NH 03301-2359
(603)271-5200

STATE PSYCHIATRIC HOSPITAL
105 Pleasant St
Concord, NH 03301-3852
(603)271-5300

DERRY

PARKLAND MEDICAL CENTER
1 Parkland Drive
Derry, NH 03038-2750
(603)432-1500

DOVER

WENTWORTH-DOUGLASS HOSPITAL
789 Central Avenue
Dover, NH 03820-2589
(603)742-5252

EXETER

EXETER HOSPITAL
5 Alumni Dr
Exeter, NH 03833-2160
(603)778-7311

FRANKLIN

FRANKLIN REGIONAL HOSPITAL
15 Aiken Avenue
Franklin, NH 03235-1252
(603)934-2060

HAMPSTEAD

HAMPSTEAD HOSPITAL
East Road
Hampstead, NH 03841
(603)329-5311

KEENE

CHESHIRE MEDICAL CENTER
580 Court Street
Keene, NH 03431-1729
(603)354-5400

LACONIA

LAKES REGION GENERAL HOSPITAL
Highland St
Laconia, NH 03246
(603)524-3211

LANCASTER

WEEKS MEMORIAL HOSPITAL-SWING
173 Middle St
Lancaster, NH 03584
(603)788-4911

LEBANON

ALICE PECK DAY MEMORIAL HOSPITAL
125 Mascoma Street
Lebanon, NH 03766-2650
(603)448-3121

DARTMOUTH HITCHCOCK MEDICAL
CENTER
1 Medical Center Drive
Lebanon, NH 03756-0001
(603)650-5000

LITTLETON

LITTLETON REGIONAL HOSPITAL
600 Saint Johnsbury Rd
Littleton, NH 03561-3436
(603)444-7731

NEW JERSEY — Hospital Telephone Directory

MANCHESTER

CATHOLIC MEDICAL CENTER
100 Mcgregor Street
Manchester, NH 03102-3770
(603)668-3545

ELLIOT HOSPITAL
1 Elliot Way
Manchester, NH 03103-3599
(603)669-5300

VA MEDICAL CENTER - MANCHESTER
718 Smyth Road
Manchester, NH 03104-4098
(603)624-4366

NASHUA

SAINT JOSEPH HOSPITAL
172 Kinsley St
Nashua, NH 03060-3688
(603)882-3000

SOUTHERN NEW HAMPSHIRE MEDICAL CENTER
8 Prospect Street
Nashua, NH 03060-3925
(603)577-2000

NEW LONDON

NEW LONDON HOSPITAL ASSOCIATION
County Road
New London, NH 03257
(603)526-2911

NORTH CONWAY

MEMORIAL HOSPITAL
PO Box 5001 Intervale Road
North Conway, NH 03860-5001
(603)356-5461

PETERBOROUGH

MONADNOCK COMMUNITY HOSPITAL
452 Old Street Road
Peterborough, NH 03458-1295
(603)924-7191

PLYMOUTH

SPEARE MEMORIAL HOSPITAL
Hospital Road
Plymouth, NH 03264
(603)536-1120

PORTSMOUTH

PORTSMOUTH REGIONAL HOSPITAL
333-343 Borthwick Avenue, PO Box 7004
Portsmouth, NH 03802-7004
(603)436-5110

ROCHESTER

FRISBIE MEMORIAL HOSPITAL
Whitehall Road
Rochester, NH 03867
(603)332-5211

SALEM

NORTHEAST REHAB HEALTH NETWORK
70-78 Butler Street
Salem, NH 03079-3974
(603)893-2900

WOLFEBORO

HUGGINS HOSPITAL
South Main Street
Wolfeboro, NH 03894
(603)569-7500

WOODSVILLE

COTTAGE HOSPITAL
Swiftwater Road
Woodsville, NH 03785
(603)747-2761

NEW JERSEY

ATLANTIC CITY

ATLANTIC CITY MEDICAL CENTER
1925 Pacific Avenue
Atlantic City, NJ 08401-6784
(609)345-4000

BAYONNE

BAYONNE HOSPITAL
29 East 29th St
Bayonne, NJ 07002-4695
(201)858-5000

BELLE MEAD

CARRIER CLINIC FOUNDATION
PO Box 147
Belle Mead, NJ 08502-0147
(908)281-1000

BELLEVILLE

CLARA MAASS MEDICAL CENTER
One Franklin Avenue
Belleville, NJ 07109-3500
(973)450-2000

BERKELEY HEIGHTS

RUNNELLS SPECIALIZED HOSPITAL-UNION COUNTY
40 Watchung Way
Berkeley Heights, NJ 07922-2600
(908)771-5700

BERLIN

WEST JERSEY HOSPITAL-BERLIN
100 Townsend Avenue
Berlin, NJ 08009-9035
(856)322-3100

BLACKWOOD

CAMDEN COUNTY HEALTH SERVICES CENTER
20 N Woodbury Turnersville Rd
Blackwood, NJ 08012-2896
(856)374-6600

BOONTON TOWNSHIP

SAINT CLARE'S HOSPITAL - BOONTON TOWNSHIP
130 Powerville Road
Boonton Township, NJ 07005-8705
(973)316-1800

BRICK TOWNSHIP

MEDICAL CENTER OF OCEAN COUNTY
425 Jack Martin Blvd
Brick Township, NJ 08724-7732
(732)840-2200

BRIDGETON

SOUTH JERSEY HOSPITAL - BRIDGTON
333 Irving Avenue
Bridgeton, NJ 08302-2100
(856)575-4500

BROWNS MILLS

DEBORAH HEART AND LUNG CENTER
200 Trenton Road
Browns Mills, NJ 08015-1705
(609)893-6611

CAMDEN

COOPER HOSPITAL/UNIVERSITY MEDICAL CENTER
1 Cooper Plaza
Camden, NJ 08103-1489
(856)342-2000

OUR LADY OF LOURDES MEDICAL CENTER
1600 Haddon Avenue
Camden, NJ 08103-3117
(856)757-3500

WEST JERSEY HOSPITAL-CAMDEN
Mt Ephraim And Atlantic Aves
Camden, NJ 08104
(856)246-3000

CAPE MAY COURT HOUSE

BURDETE TOMLIN MEMORIAL HOSPITAL
Two Stone Harbor Boulevard
Cape May Court House, NJ 08210-2171
(609)463-2000

CEDAR GROVE

ESSEX COUNTY HOSPITAL CENTER
125 Fairview Avenue
Cedar Grove, NJ 07009-1345
(973)228-8000

CHERRY HILL

KENNEDY HEALTH SYSTEM
2201 Chapel Avenue W
Cherry Hill, NJ 08002-2048
(856)488-6500

DENVILLE

SAINT CLARES HOSPITAL-DENVILLE
Pocono Road
Denville, NJ 07834
(973)625-6000

DOVER

SAINT CLARES HOSPITAL
24 Jardine Street
Dover, NJ 07801
(973)989-3000

EAST ORANGE

EAST ORANGE GENERAL HOSPITAL
300 Central Avenue
East Orange, NJ 07018-2897
(973)672-8400

KESSLER INSTITUTE FOR REHABILITATION
Central Avenue At The Parkway
East Orange, NJ 07018
(973)414-4700

VA HEALTHCARE SYSTEM - EAST ORANGE
385 Tremont Avenue
East Orange, NJ 07018-1023
(973)676-1000

EDISON

JFK JOHNSON REHABILITATION INSTITUTE
65 James Street
Edison, NJ 08820-3947
(732)321-7050

Hospital Telephone Directory   **NEW JERSEY**

JOHN F KENNEDY MEDICAL CENTER
65 James Street
Edison, NJ 08820-3903
(732)321-7000

SOLARIS HEALTH SYSTEMS
80 James St
Edison, NJ 08820-3973
(732)632-1500

ELIZABETH

TRINITAS HOSPITAL
225 Williamson St
Elizabeth, NJ 07202-3600
(908)994-5000

TRINITAS HOSPITAL - JERSEY STREET
925 E Jersey St
Elizabeth, NJ 07201-2728
(908)289-8600

TRINITAS HOSPITAL - NEW POINT
655 East Jersey Street
Elizabeth, NJ 07206-1259
(908)351-9000

ELMER

SOUTH JERSEY HOSPITAL - ELMER
Front Street
Elmer, NJ 08318
(856)363-1000

ENGLEWOOD

ENGLEWOOD HOSPITAL AND MEDICAL CENTER
350 Engle St
Englewood, NJ 07631-1898
(201)894-3000

FLEMINGTON

HUNTERDON MEDICAL CENTER
Route 31
Flemington, NJ 08822
(908)788-6100

FLORHAM PARK

ATLANTIC HEALTH SYSTEMS
325 Columbia Turnpike
Florham Park, NJ 07932-1212
(973)660-3100

FORT DIX

305TH MEDICAL GROUP, WALSON AIRFORCE CLINIC
5250 New Jersey Avenue
Fort Dix, NJ 08640-5017
(609)562-9306

FREEHOLD

CENTRASTATE MEDICAL CENTER
Route 537 W Main St
Freehold, NJ 07728-2531
(732)431-2000

GLEN GARDNER

HAGEDORN PSYCHIATRIC HOSPITAL
Mt Kipp
Glen Gardner, NJ 08826
(908)537-2141

GREYSTONE PARK

GREYSTONE PARK PSYCH HOSPITAL
Central Avenue
Greystone Park, NJ 07950
(973)538-1800

HACKENSACK

HACKENSACK UNIVERSITY MEDICAL CENTER
30 Prospect Avenue
Hackensack, NJ 07601-1914
(201)996-2000

HACKETTSTOWN

HACKETTSTOWN COMMUNITY HOSPITAL
651 Willow Grove St
Hackettstown, NJ 07840-1798
(908)852-5100

HAMILTON

RWJ UNIVERSITY HOSPITAL AT HAMILTON
One Hamilton Health Plaza
Hamilton, NJ 08690-3542
(609)586-7900

HAMMONTON

ANCORA PSYCH HOSPITAL
Ancora Branch
Hammonton, NJ 08037
(609)561-1700

WILLIAM B KESSLER MEMORIAL HOSPITAL
600 South White Horse Pike
Hammonton, NJ 08037-2099
(609)561-6700

HOBOKEN

SAINT MARYS HOSPITAL
308 Willow Avenue
Hoboken, NJ 07030-3889
(201)418-1000

HOLMDEL

BAYSHORE COMMUNITY HOSPITAL
727 N Beers St
Holmdel, NJ 07733-1598
(732)739-5900

IRVINGTON

IRVINGTON GENERAL HOSPITAL
832 Chancellor Avenue
Irvington, NJ 07111-2299
(973)399-6000

JERSEY CITY

BON SECOURS HEALTH SYSTEMS
25 Mcwilliams Place
Jersey City, NJ 07302-1609
(201)418-1000

CHRIST HOSPITAL
176 Palisade Avenue
Jersey City, NJ 07306-1196
(201)795-8200

GREENVILLE HOSPITAL
1825 Kennedy Boulevard
Jersey City, NJ 07305-2198
(201)547-6100

JERSEY CITY MEDICAL CENTER
50 Baldwin Avenue
Jersey City, NJ 07304-3154
(201)915-2000

KEARNY

WEST HUDSON HOSPITAL
206 Bergen Avenue
Kearny, NJ 07032-3399
(201)955-7051

LAKELAND

CAMDEN COUNTY HEALTH SERVICES CENTER
PO Blackwood
Lakeland, NJ 08012
(856)227-3000

LAKEWOOD

KIMBALL MEDICAL CENTER
600 River Avenue
Lakewood, NJ 08701-5281
(732)363-1900

LAWRENCEVILLE

SAINT LAWRENCE REHABILITATION CENTER
2381 Lawrenceville Road
Lawrenceville, NJ 08648-2025
(609)896-9500

LIVINGSTON

SAINT BARNABAS MEDICAL CENTER
94 Old Short Hills Road
Livingston, NJ 07039-5672
(973)322-5000

LONG BRANCH

MONMOUTH MEDICAL CENTER
300 2nd Avenue
Long Branch, NJ 07740-6395
(732)222-5200

LYONS

VA HEALTHCARE SYSTEM - LYONS
151 Knollcroft Road
Lyons, NJ 07939-5001
(908)647-0180

MANAHAWKIN

SOUTHERN OCEAN COUNTY HOSPITAL
1140 W Bay Avenue
Manahawkin, NJ 08050
(609)978-8900

MARLTON

MEDIPLEX REHABILITATION HOSPITAL-MARLTON
300 Brick Road
Marlton, NJ 08053
(856)988-8778

VOORHEES PEDIATRIC REHABILITATION HOSPITAL
92 Brick Road, 3rd Floor
Marlton, NJ 08053-2177
(856)489-4520

WEST JERSEY HOSPITAL - MARLTON
90 Brick Road
Marlton, NJ 08053-2177
(856)355-6000

MONTCLAIR

ATLANTIC HEALTH SYSTEM/MOUNTAINSIDE HOSPITAL
Bay And Highland Avenue
Montclair, NJ 07042
(973)429-6000

MONTCLAIR COMMUNITY HOSPITAL
120 Harrison Avenue
Montclair, NJ 07042-2498
(973)744-7300

NEW JERSEY
Hospital Telephone Directory

MORRISTOWN

MORRISTOWN MEMORIAL HOSPITAL
100 Madison Avenue
Morristown, NJ 07960-6095
(973)971-5000

MOUNT HOLLY

BUTTONWOOD HOSPITAL OF BURLINGTON
COUNTY
PO Box 6000
Mount Holly, NJ 08060-6000
(609)726-7000

VIRTUA MEMORIAL HOSPITAL-BURLINGTON
COUNTY
175 Madison Avenue
Mount Holly, NJ 08060-2099
(609)267-0700

MOUNTAINSIDE

CHILDRENS SPECIALIZED HOSPITAL
150 New Providence Road
Mountainside, NJ 07092-2590
(908)233-3720

NEPTUNE

JERSEY SHORE MEDICAL CENTER
1945 Corlies Avenue
Neptune, NJ 07753-4889
(732)775-5500

NEW BRUNSWICK

ROBERT WOOD JOHNSON UNIVERSITY
HOSPITAL
One Robert Wood Johnson Pl
New Brunswick, NJ 08901-1966
(732)828-3000

SAINT PETERS UNIVERSITY HOSPITAL
254 Easton Avenue
New Brunswick, NJ 08901-1780
(732)745-8600

NEWARK

COLUMBUS HOSPITAL
495 North 13th St
Newark, NJ 07107-1397
(973)268-1400

MOUNT CARMEL GUILD
1160 Raymond Blvd
Newark, NJ 07102-4168
(973)596-4100

NEWARK BETH ISRAEL MEDICAL CENTER
201 Lyons Avenue
Newark, NJ 07112-2094
(973)926-7000

SAINT JAMES HOSPITAL
155 Jefferson St
Newark, NJ 07105-1791
(973)589-1300

SAINT MICHAELS MEDICAL CENTER
268 Doctor Martin Luther King Boulevard
Newark, NJ 07102
(973)877-5000

UNIVERSITY OF MEDICINE-DENTISTRY OF
NEW JERSEY HOSPITAL
150 Bergen St
Newark, NJ 07103-2496
(973)972-4300

NEWTON

NEWTON MEMORIAL HOSPITAL
175 High St
Newton, NJ 07860-1099
(973)383-2121

NORTH BERGEN

PALISADES MEDICAL CENTER
7600 River Road
North Bergen, NJ 07047-6217
(201)854-5000

OLD BRIDGE

RARITAN BAY MEDICAL CENTER
1 Hospital Plaza
Old Bridge, NJ 08857-3087
(732)360-1000

ORANGE

HOSPITAL CENTER AT ORANGE
188 S Essex Avenue
Orange, NJ 07050-3499
(973)266-2200

SAINT MARYS HOSPITAL
135 S Center St
Orange, NJ 07050-3599
(973)266-3000

PARAMUS

BERGEN REGIONAL MEDICAL CENTER
230 East Ridgewood Avenue
Paramus, NJ 07652-4131
(201)967-4000

PASSAIC

ATLANTIC HEALTH SYSTEM-GENERAL
HOSPITAL CENTER AT PASSAIC
350 Boulevard
Passaic, NJ 07055-2840
(973)365-4300

PASSAIC BETH ISRAEL HOSPITAL
70 Parker Avenue
Passaic, NJ 07055-7000
(973)365-5000

SAINT MARYS HOSPITAL
211 Pennington Avenue
Passaic, NJ 07055-4698
(973)470-3000

PATERSON

BARNERT HOSPITAL
680 Broadway
Paterson, NJ 07514-1472
(973)977-6600

SAINT JOSEPHS HOSPITAL
703 Main St
Paterson, NJ 07503-2691
(973)754-2000

PEAPACK

MATHENY SCHOOL AND HOSPITAL
Main St
Peapack, NJ 07977
(908)234-0011

PERTH AMBOY

RARITAN BAY MEDICAL CENTER
530 New Brunswick Avenue
Perth Amboy, NJ 08861-3685
(732)442-3700

PHILLIPSBURG

WARREN HOSPITAL
185 Roseberry St
Phillipsburg, NJ 08865-1684
(908)859-6700

PISCATAWAY

UNIVERSITY OF MEDICINE & DENTISTRY
OF NJ - UNIVERSITY BEHAVIORAL
HEALTHCARE
671 Hoes Lane
Piscataway, NJ 08854-5627
(732)235-5900

PLAINFIELD

MUHLENBERG REGIONAL MEDICAL
CENTER
Park Avenue Randolph Road
Plainfield, NJ 07061
(908)668-2000

POINT PLEASANT

SHORE REHABILITATION INSTITUTE
2121 Edgewater Place
Point Pleasant, NJ 08742-2212
(732)295-6500

POMONA

ATLANTIC CITY MEDICAL CENTER -
MAINLAND DIVISION
Jim Leeds Road
Pomona, NJ 08240
(609)652-1000

BETTY BACHARACH REHAB CENTER
61 W Jimmie Leeds Road
Pomona, NJ 08240
(609)652-7000

POMPTON PLAINS

CHILTON MEMORIAL HOSPITAL
97 W Parkway
Pompton Plains, NJ 07444-1696
(973)831-5000

PRINCETON

MEDICAL CENTER AT PRINCETON
253 Witherspoon St
Princeton, NJ 08540-3211
(609)497-4000

RAHWAY

RAHWAY MEMORIAL HOSPITAL
865 Stone St
Rahway, NJ 07065-2797
(732)381-4200

RED BANK

RIVERVIEW MEDICAL CENTER
One Riverview Plaza
Red Bank, NJ 07701-1872
(732)741-2700

RIDGEWOOD

VALLEY HOSPITAL
223 N Van Dien Avenue
Ridgewood, NJ 07450-2736
(201)447-8000

RIVERSIDE

RANCOCAS HOSPITAL
Hospital Plaza
Riverside, NJ 08075
(856)835-2900

SADDLE BROOK

KESSLER INSTITUTE FOR REHABILITATION
300 Market St
Saddle Brook, NJ 07663-5309
(201)857-8500

Hospital Telephone Directory

SALEM

MEMORIAL HOSPITAL OF SALEM COUNTY
310 Woodstown Road
Salem, NJ 08079-2080
(856)935-1000

SECAUCUS

HUDSON COUNTY MEADOWVIEW
PSYCHIATRIC HOSPITAL
595 County Avenue
Secaucus, NJ 07094-2605
(201)319-3660

MEADOWLANDS HOSPITAL MEDICAL
CENTER
Meadowland Parkway
Secaucus, NJ 07094
(201)392-3100

SOMERS POINT

SHORE MEMORIAL HOSPITAL
1 East New York Avenue
Somers Point, NJ 08244-2389
(609)653-3500

SOMERVILLE

SOMERSET MEDICAL CENTER
110 Rehill Avenue
Somerville, NJ 08876-2598
(908)685-2200

STRATFORD

KENNEDY MEMORIAL HOSPITAL-
UNIVERSITY MEDICAL CENTER
18 East Laurel Road
Stratford, NJ 08084-1339
(856)346-6000

SUMMIT

OVERLOOK HOSPITAL
99 Beauvior Avenue
Summit, NJ 07901-3595
(908)522-2000

SUMMIT HOSPITAL
19 Prospect St
Summit, NJ 07901-2531
(908)522-7000

SUSSEX

SAINT CLARES HOSPITAL-SUSSEX
20 Walnut St
Sussex, NJ 07461-2537
(973)702-2200

TEANECK

HOLY NAME HOSPITAL
718 Teaneck Road
Teaneck, NJ 07666-4281
(201)833-3000

TINTON FALLS

REHABILITATION HOSPITAL OF TINTON
FALLS
2 Centre Plaza
Tinton Falls, NJ 07724-9744
(732)460-5320

TOMS RIVER

CHILDREN'S SPECIALIZED HOSPITAL -
OCEAN
94 Stevens Road
Toms River, NJ 08755-1237
(732)914-1100

COMMUNITY MEDICAL CENTER
99 Route 37 West
Toms River, NJ 08755-6423
(732)557-8000

HEALTHSOUTH GARDEN STATE
REHABILITATION HOSPITAL
14 Hospital Drive
Toms River, NJ 08755-6402
(732)244-3100

SHORELINE BEHAVIORAL CENTER
1691 Highway 9
Toms River, NJ 08755-1245
(732)914-1688

TRENTON

CAPITAL HEALTH SYSTEM AT MERCER
446 Bellevue Avenue
Trenton, NJ 08618-4502
(609)394-4000

CAPITAL HEALTH SYSTEMS AT FULD
750 Brunswick Avenue
Trenton, NJ 08638-4143
(609)394-6000

NEW JERSEY STATE PRISON HOSPITAL
3rd & Federal Sts Cn-861
Trenton, NJ 08625
(609)292-9700

SAINT FRANCIS MEDICAL CENTER
601 Hamilton Avenue
Trenton, NJ 08629-1986
(609)599-5000

TRENTON PSYCHIATRIC HOSPITAL
Station A
Trenton, NJ 08625
(609)633-1500

TURNERSVILLE

KENNEDY HOSPITAL-WASHINGTON
435 Hurffville Cross Keys Road
Turnersville, NJ 08012-2499
(856)582-2500

UNION

UNION HOSPITAL
1000 Galloping Hill Road
Union, NJ 07083-7998
(908)687-1900

VINELAND

SOUTH JERSEY HOSPITAL - NEWCOMB
66 S State St
Vineland, NJ 08360-4851
(856)507-8500

VOORHEES

VIRTUA WEST JERSEY HOSPITAL-
VOORHEES
101 Carnie Boulevard
Voorhees, NJ 08043-1596
(856)325-3000

WAYNE

SAINT JOSEPH'S WAYNE HOSPITAL
224 Hamburg Turnpike
Wayne, NJ 07470-2111
(973)942-6900

WEST ORANGE

KESSLER INSTITUTE FOR REHABILITATION
1199 Pleasant Valley Way
West Orange, NJ 07052-1499
(973)731-3600

WEST TRENTON

ANNE KLEIN FORENSIC CENTER
Stuyvesant Avenue, PO Box 7717
West Trenton, NJ 08628-0717
(609)633-0900

WESTAMPTON

HAMPTON BEHAVIORAL HEALTH SYSTEM
650 Rancocas Road
Westampton, NJ 08060-5613
(609)267-7000

WESTWOOD

PASCACK VALLEY HOSPITAL
Old Hook Road
Westwood, NJ 07675
(201)358-3000

WILLINGBORO

LOURDES MEDICAL CENTER OF
BURLINGTON COUNTY
218A Sunset Road
Willingboro, NJ 08046-1110
(609)835-2900

WOODBRIDGE

WOODBRIDGE DEVELOPMENT CENTER
Rahway Avenue PO Box 189
Woodbridge, NJ 07095-0189
(732)499-5951

WOODBURY

UNDERWOOD MEMORIAL HOSPITAL
509 N Broad St
Woodbury, NJ 08096-1697
(856)845-0100

WYCKOFF

CHRISTIAN HEALTHCARE CENTER
301 Sycomac Avenue
Wyckoff, NJ 07481-2194
(201)848-5200

RAMAPO RIDGE PSYCHIATRIC HOSPITAL
301 Sycomac Avenue
Wyckoff, NJ 07481-2159
(201)848-5200

NEW MEXICO

ALAMOGORDO

GERALD CHAMPION MEMORIAL HOSPITAL
2669 Scenic Dr
Alamogordo, NM 88310-8799
(505)439-6100

ALBUQUERQUE

CARRIE TINGLEY HOSPITAL
1720 Louisiana Blvd Ne Ste 202
Albuquerque, NM 87110-7018
(505)272-5200

DESERT HILLS HOSPITAL
5310 Sequoia Road Nw
Albuquerque, NM 87120-1249
(505)836-7330

HEALTHSOUTH REHABILITATION HOSPITAL
7000 Jefferson Ne
Albuquerque, NM 87109-4357
(505)344-9478

HEART HOSPITAL OF NEW MEXICO
504 Elm Street
Albuquerque, NM 87102-2512
(505)242-5600

NEW MEXICO

Hospital Telephone Directory

INTEGRATED SPECIALTY HOSPITAL
235 Elm St Ne
Albuquerque, NM 87102-3672
(505)842-5550

KASEMAN PRESBYTERIAN HOSPITAL
8300 Constitution Ne
Albuquerque, NM 87110
(505)291-2000

KINDRED HOSPITAL ALBUQUERQUE
700 High St Nw
Albuquerque, NM 87102
(505)242-4444

LOVELACE HEALTH SYSTEMS
5400 Gibson Boulevard Se
Albuquerque, NM 87108-4763
(505)262-7000

MEMORIAL HOSPITAL
806 Central Avenue Se
Albuquerque, NM 87102-3671
(505)247-0220

PHS INDIAN HOSPITAL - ALBUQUERQUE
8807 Cottonwood Rd Ne
Albuquerque, NM 87111-4607
(505)248-4000

PRESBYTERIAN HOSPITAL
PO Box 26666
Albuquerque, NM 87125-6666
(505)841-1234

SAINT JOSEPH HEALTH CARE
601 Doctor Martin Luther King Jr Avenue Ne
Albuquerque, NM 87102
(505)727-8000

**SAINT JOSEPH HEALTH CARE -
NORTHWEST HEIGHTS**
4701 Montgomery Boulevard NE
Albuquerque, NM 87109-1219
(505)727-7800

SAINT JOSEPH REHAB THERAPY SERVICES
505 Elm Street Ne
Albuquerque, NM 87102-2500
(505)727-4700

SAINT JOSEPH WEST MESA HOSPITAL
10501 Golf Course Road Nw
Albuquerque, NM 87114-5000
(505)727-2000

**UNIVERSITY OF NEW MEXICO CHILDREN'S
PSYCHIATRIC HOSPITAL**
1001 Yale Blvd Ne
Albuquerque, NM 87131-0001
(505)272-2945

UNIVERSITY OF NEW MEXICO HOSPITAL
2211 Lomas Boulevard N E
Albuquerque, NM 87106-2745
(505)272-2111

**UNIVERSITY OF NEW MEXICO MENTAL
HEALTH**
2600 Marble Avenue Ne
Albuquerque, NM 87106-2058
(505)272-2263

VA HEALTHCARE SYSTEM - ALBUQUERQUE
1501 San Pedro Se
Albuquerque, NM 87108-5153
(505)265-1711

ARTESIA

ARTESIA GENERAL HOSPITAL
702 N 13th St
Artesia, NM 88210-1199
(505)748-3333

CANNON AIR FORCE BASE

27TH MEDICAL GROUP
208 West Casablanca Avenue
Cannon Air Force Base, NM 88103-5009
(505)784-6318

CARLSBAD

CARLSBAD MEDICAL CENTER
2430 W Pierce Street
Carlsbad, NM 88220-3597
(505)887-4100

CLAYTON

UNION COUNTY GENERAL HOSPITAL
PO Box 489
Clayton, NM 88415-0489
(505)374-2585

CLOVIS

**PLAINS REGIONAL MEDICAL CENTER
CLOVIS**
2100 North Thomas
Clovis, NM 88101-9412
(505)769-2141

CROWNPOINT

PHS/IHS INDIAN HOSPITAL - CROWNPOINT
PO Box 358
Crownpoint, NM 87313-0358
(505)786-5291

DEMING

MIMBRES MEMORIAL HOSPITAL
PO Box 710
Deming, NM 88031-0710
(505)546-2761

ESPANOLA

ESPANOLA MEDICAL CENTER
1010 Spruce Street
Espanola, NM 87532-3456
(505)753-7111

FARMINGTON

**LIFECOURSE CENTER FOR REHAB
SERVICES**
525 South Schwartz Avenue
Farmington, NM 87401-5955
(505)327-3422

SAN JUAN REGIONAL MEDICAL CENTER
801 W Maple
Farmington, NM 87401-5630
(505)325-5011

GALLUP

BEHAVIORAL HEALTH SERVICES
650 Vanden Bosch Parkway
Gallup, NM 87301-4538
(505)722-3804

**PHS/IHS INDIAN MEDICAL CENTER -
GALLUP**
PO Box 1337
Gallup, NM 87305-1337
(505)722-1000

**REHOBOTH MCKINLEY CHRISTIAN HEALTH
SERVICE**
1901 Red Rock Drive
Gallup, NM 87301-5683
(505)863-7000

GRANTS

CIBOLA GENERAL HOSPITAL
1212 Bonita Avenue Box 1057
Grants, NM 87020-2104
(505)287-4446

HOBBS

LEA REGIONAL HOSPITAL
5419 Lovington Highway PO Box 3000
Hobbs, NM 88241-9501
(505)392-6581

HOLLOMAN AIR FORCE BASE

49TH MEDICAL GROUP
280 First St
Holloman Air Force Base, NM 88330-8273
(505)572-5587

KIRTLAND AIR FORCE BASE

377TH MEDICAL GROUP
1951 Second St Se
Kirtland Air Force Base, NM 87117-5521
(505)846-3531

LAS CRUCES

MEMORIAL GENERAL MEDICAL CENTER
2450 South Telshor Boulevard
Las Cruces, NM 88011-5076
(505)522-8641

MESILLA VALLEY HOSPITAL
3751 Del Rey Boulevard
Las Cruces, NM 88012-8526
(505)382-3500

MOUNTAIN VIEW MEDICAL CENTER
4311 East Lohman Avenue
Las Cruces, NM 88011-8255
(505)556-7600

LAS VEGAS

LAS VEGAS MEDICAL CENTER
3695 Hot Springs Blvd
Las Vegas, NM 87701-9549
(505)454-2100

NORTHEASTERN REGIONAL HOSPITAL
1235 8th St
Las Vegas, NM 87701-4254
(505)425-6751

LOS ALAMOS

LOS ALAMOS MEDICAL CENTER
3917 West Road
Los Alamos, NM 87544-2275
(505)662-4201

LOVINGTON

NOR LEA GENERAL HOSPITAL
1600 North Main
Lovington, NM 88260-2871
(505)396-6611

MESCALERO

PHS INDIAN HOSPITAL - MESCALERO
PO Box 210
Mescalero, NM 88340-0210
(505)464-4441

PORTALES

ROOSEVELT GENERAL HOSPITAL
42121 US Highway 70
Portales, NM 88130
(505)359-1800

RATON

MINERS COLFAX MEDICAL CENTER
200 Hospital Drive
Raton, NM 87740-2099
(505)445-3661

Hospital Telephone Directory — NEW YORK

ROSWELL
EASTERN NEW MEXICO MEDICAL CENTER
405 W Country Club Road
Roswell, NM 88201-5265
(505)622-8170

NEW MEXICO REHABILITATION CENTER
31 Gail Harris Avenue
Roswell, NM 88203-8190
(505)347-3400

RUIDOSO
LINCOLN COUNTY MEDICAL CENTER
211 Sudderth
Ruidoso, NM 88345-6043
(505)257-7381

SAN FIDEL
PHS INDIAN HOSPITAL ACOMITA
CANONCITO LAQUNA
PO Box 130
San Fidel, NM 87049-0130
(505)552-5300

SANTA FE
PHS INDIAN HOSPITAL - SANTA FE
1700 Cerrillos Road
Santa Fe, NM 87505-3554
(505)988-9821

SAINT VINCENT HOSPITAL
455 St Michael's Drive
Santa Fe, NM 87505-7663
(505)983-3361

SANTA ROSA
GUADALUPE COUNTY HOSPITAL
535 Lake Drive
Santa Rosa, NM 88435-2542
(505)472-3417

SANTA TERESA
PEAK HOSPITAL
100 Laura Court Box 6
Santa Teresa, NM 88008-9439
(505)589-0033

POINTE RTC
100 Laura Court
Santa Teresa, NM 88008-9439
(505)589-0033

SHIPROCK
PHS/IHS NORTHERN NAVAJO MEDICAL CENTER
PO Box 160
Shiprock, NM 87420-0160
(505)368-6001

SILVER CITY
GILA REGIONAL MEDICAL CENTER
1313 E 32nd St
Silver City, NM 88061-7244
(505)538-4000

SOCORRO
SOCORRO GENERAL HOSPITAL
Highway 60 West
Socorro, NM 87801
(505)835-1140

TAOS
HOLY CROSS HOSPITAL
1397 Weimer Road
Taos, NM 87571-6284
(505)758-8883

TRUTH OR CONSEQUENCES
SIERRA VISTA HOSPITAL
800 East Ninth Avenue
Truth Or Consequences, NM 87901-1961
(505)894-2111

TUCUMCARI
TRIGG MEMORIAL HOSPITAL
301 E Miel De Luna
Tucumcari, NM 88401-3810
(505)461-0141

ZUNI
PHS INDIAN HOSPITAL - ZUNI
PO Box 467
Zuni, NM 87327-0467
(505)782-4431

NEW YORK

ALBANY
ALBANY MEDICAL CENTER
43 New Scotland Avenue
Albany, NY 12208-3478
(518)262-3125

ALBANY MEDICAL CENTER - SOUTH CLINICAL CAMPUS
25 Hackett Blvd
Albany, NY 12208-3420
(518)262-1200

ALBANY MEMORIAL HOSPITAL
600 Northern Boulevard
Albany, NY 12204-1083
(518)471-3221

CAPITAL DISTRICT PSYCH CENTER
75 New Scotland Avenue
Albany, NY 12208-3474
(518)447-9611

SAINT PETERS HOSPITAL
315 South Manning Boulevard
Albany, NY 12208-1789
(518)525-1550

VA MEDICAL CENTER - SAMUEL S. STRATTON
113 Holland Avenue
Albany, NY 12208-3410
(518)626-5000

ALEXANDRIA BAY
RIVER HOSPITAL
4 Fuller St
Alexandria Bay, NY 13607
(315)482-2511

AMITYVILLE
BRUNSWICK HALL
81 Loudan
Amityville, NY 11701
(631)789-7100

BRUNSWICK HOSPITAL
366 Broadway
Amityville, NY 11701-2778
(631)789-7000

SOUTH OAKS HOSPITAL
Sunrise Highway
Amityville, NY 11701
(631)264-4000

AMSTERDAM
AMSTERDAM MEMORIAL HOSPITAL
Upper Market St
Amsterdam, NY 12010
(518)842-3100

SAINT MARYS HOSPITAL
427 Guy Park Avenue
Amsterdam, NY 12010-1054
(518)842-1900

ASTORIA
MOUNT SINAI HOSPITAL - QUEENS
2510 30th Avenue
Astoria, NY 11102-2448
(718)932-1000

AUBURN
AUBURN MEMORIAL HOSPITAL
5-21 Lansing St
Auburn, NY 13021-1983
(315)255-7011

BATAVIA
UNITED MEMORIAL MEDICAL CENTER - BANK STREET
127 North St
Batavia, NY 14020-1697
(585)343-3131

UNITED MEMORIAL MEDICAL CENTER - NORTH STREET
16 Bank St
Batavia, NY 14020-2260
(585)343-3131

VA HEALTHCARE SYSTEM - BATAVIA
222 Richmond Avenue
Batavia, NY 14020-1227
(585)343-7500

BATH
DAVENPORT MEMORIAL HOSPITAL
Box 350 Route 54
Bath, NY 14810
(607)776-8500

VA MEDICAL CENTER - BATH
76 Veterans Avenue
Bath, NY 14810-0840
(607)664-4000

BAY SHORE
SOUTHSIDE HOSPITAL
301 East Main Street
Bay Shore, NY 11706-8458
(631)968-3000

BAYSIDE
SAINT MARYS HOSPITAL FOR CHILDREN
2901 216th St
Bayside, NY 11360-2899
(718)281-8800

BEACON
SAINT FRANCIS HOSPITAL - THE TURNING POINT
11 Hastings Drive
Beacon, NY 12508-2052
(845)838-4500

BELLEROSE
QUEENS CHILDRENS PSYCH CENTER
74-03 Commonwealth Boulevard
Bellerose, NY 11426-1890
(718)264-4500

BETHPAGE
NEW ISLAND HOSPITAL
4295 Hempstead Tpke
Bethpage, NY 11714-5769
(516)579-6000

NEW YORK — Hospital Telephone Directory

BINGHAMTON

BINGHAMTON GENERAL HOSPITAL
20-42 Mitchell Avenue
Binghamton, NY 13903-1678
(607)762-2200

BINGHAMTON PSYCH CENTER
425 Robinson St
Binghamton, NY 13901-4198
(607)724-1391

OUR LADY OF LOURDES MEMORIAL HOSPITAL
169 Riverside Drive
Binghamton, NY 13905-4198
(607)798-5111

BRENTWOOD

KINGS PARK PSYCHIATRIC CENTER
998 Crooked Hill Road
Brentwood, NY 11717-1043
(631)761-3500

PILGRIM PSYCHIATRIC CENTER
998 Crooked Hill Road
Brentwood, NY 11717-1043
(631)761-3500

BROCKPORT

LAKESIDE MEMORIAL HOSPITAL
156 West Avenue
Brockport, NY 14420-1229
(585)395-6095

BRONX

BRONX CHILDRENS PSYCH CENTER
1000 Waters Pl
Bronx, NY 10461-2799
(718)239-3600

BRONX PSYCHIATRIC CENTER
1500 Waters Place
Bronx, NY 10461-2796
(718)931-0600

BRONX-LEBANON HOSPITAL - CONCOURSE
1650 Grand Concourse
Bronx, NY 10457-7606
(718)590-1800

BRONX-LEBANON HOSPITAL CENTER
1276 Fulton Avenue
Bronx, NY 10456-3499
(718)590-1800

CALVARY HOSPITAL
1740-1770 Eastchester Road
Bronx, NY 10461-2392
(718)863-6900

JACK D. WEILER HOSPITAL OF ALBERT EINSTEIN COLLEGE
1825 Eastchester Road
Bronx, NY 10461-2301
(718)904-2000

JACOBI MEDICAL CENTER
Pelham Parkway And Eastchester Road
Bronx, NY 10461
(718)918-5000

LINCOLN MEDICAL AND MENTAL HEALTH CENTER
234 East 149th St
Bronx, NY 10451-5504
(718)579-5000

MONTEFIORE MEDICAL CENTER
3444 Kossuth Avenue
Bronx, NY 10467-2461
(718)920-4321A

NEW YORK WESTCHESTER SQUARE HOSPITAL
2475 St Raymond Avenue
Bronx, NY 10461-3198
(718)430-7300

NORTH CENTRAL BRONX HOSPITAL
3424 Kossuth Avenue
Bronx, NY 10467-2489
(718)519-5000

OUR LADY OF MERCY HOSPITAL - PELHAM BAY
1870 Pelham Parkway S
Bronx, NY 10461-3734
(718)430-6000

OUR LADY OF MERCY MEDICAL CENTER FLOR D'URSO
600 East 233rd Street
Bronx, NY 10466-2697
(718)920-9000

SAINT BARNABAS HOSPITAL
4422 Third Avenue
Bronx, NY 10457-2594
(718)960-9000

UNION COMMUNITY HEALTH CENTER
260 E 188th St
Bronx, NY 10458-5394
(718)220-2020

VA MEDICAL CENTER - BRONX
130 W Kingsbridge Road
Bronx, NY 10468-9938
(718)584-9000

BRONXVILLE

LAWRENCE HOSPITAL
55 Palmer Avenue
Bronxville, NY 10708-3491
(914)787-1000

BROOKLYN

BETH ISRAEL MEDICAL CENTER - KINGS HIGHWAY DIVISION
3201 Kings Highway
Brooklyn, NY 11234-2625
(718)252-3000

BROOKDALE UNIVERSITY HOSPITAL AND MEDICAL CENTER
1 Brookdale Plaza
Brooklyn, NY 11212-3198
(718)240-5000

BROOKLYN HOSPITAL CENTER
121 Dekalb Avenue
Brooklyn, NY 11201-5493
(718)250-8000

BROOKLYN HOSPITAL CENTER - CALEDONIAN CAMPUS
100 Parkside Avenue
Brooklyn, NY 11226-1192
(718)250-8000

CONEY ISLAND HOSPITAL
2601 Ocean Parkway
Brooklyn, NY 11235-7791
(718)616-3000

HOLY FAMILY HOME
1740 84th St
Brooklyn, NY 11214-2899
(718)232-3666

INTERFAITH MEDICAL CENTER
1545 Atlantic Avenue
Brooklyn, NY 11213-1122
(718)604-6000

KINGS COUNTY HOSPITAL CENTER
451 Clarkson Avenue
Brooklyn, NY 11203-2097
(718)245-3131

KINGSBORO PSYCHIATRIC CENTER
681 Clarkson Avenue
Brooklyn, NY 11203-2199
(718)221-7000

KINGSBROOK JEWISH MEDICAL CENTER
585 Schenectady Avenue
Brooklyn, NY 11203-1809
(718)604-5000

LONG ISLAND COLLEGE HOSPITAL
340 Henry St
Brooklyn, NY 11201-5591
(718)780-1000

LUTHERAN MEDICAL CENTER
150 55 St
Brooklyn, NY 11220-2559
(718)630-7000

MAIMONIDES MEDICAL CENTER
4802 Tenth Avenue
Brooklyn, NY 11219-2999
(718)283-6000

NEW YORK COMMUNITY HOSPITAL OF BROOKLYN
2525 Kings Highway
Brooklyn, NY 11229-1705
(718)692-5300

NEW YORK METHODIST HOSPITAL
506 Sixth St
Brooklyn, NY 11215-3645
(718)780-3000

SAINT MARYS HOSPITAL
170 Buffalo Avenue
Brooklyn, NY 11213-2421
(718)221-3000

UNIVERSITY HOSPITAL OF BROOKLYN
445 Lenox Road
Brooklyn, NY 11203-2017
(718)270-4762

VA HEALTHCARE SYSTEM - BROOKLYN
800 Poly Pl
Brooklyn, NY 11209-7104
(718)630-3500

VICTORY MEMORIAL HOSPITAL
9036 7th Avenue
Brooklyn, NY 11228-3699
(718)567-1234

WOODHULL MEDICAL/MENTAL HEALTH CENTER
760 Broadway
Brooklyn, NY 11206-5317
(718)963-8000

WYCKOFF HEIGHTS HOSPITAL
374 Stockholm St
Brooklyn, NY 11237-4006
(718)963-7272

BUFFALO

BRYLIN HOSPITAL
1263 Delaware Avenue
Buffalo, NY 14209-2497
(716)886-8200

BUFFALO GENERAL HOSPITAL
100 High St
Buffalo, NY 14203-1154
(716)859-5600

BUFFALO PSYCHIATRIC CENTER
400 Forest Avenue
Buffalo, NY 14213-1298
(716)885-2261

CHILDRENS HOSPITAL
219 Bryant St
Buffalo, NY 14222-2099
(716)878-7000

Hospital Telephone Directory — NEW YORK

ERIE COUNTY MEDICAL CENTER
462 Grider St
Buffalo, NY 14215-3098
(716)898-3000

MERCY HOSPITAL
565 Abbott Road
Buffalo, NY 14220-2095
(716)826-7000

MILLARD FILLMORE HOSPITAL
3 Gates Circle
Buffalo, NY 14209-1194
(716)887-4600

ROSWELL PARK CANCER INSTITUTE
Elm & Carlton Streets
Buffalo, NY 14263-0001
(716)845-2300

SHEEHAN MEMORIAL HOSPITAL
425 Michigan Avenue
Buffalo, NY 14203-2297
(716)848-2000

SISTERS OF CHARITY HOSPITAL
2157 Main St
Buffalo, NY 14214-2692
(716)862-1000

VA HEALTHCARE SYSTEM - BUFFALO
3495 Bailey Avenue
Buffalo, NY 14215-1129
(716)834-9200

WESTERN NEW YORK CHILDREN'S PSYCHIATRIC CENTER
1010 East & West Road
Buffalo, NY 14224-3602
(716)674-9730

CALLICOON

CATSKILL REGIONAL MEDICAL CENTER
Route 97
Callicoon, NY 12723
(845)887-5530

CANANDAIGUA

THOMPSON HEALTH
350 Parrish St
Canandaigua, NY 14424-1731
(585)396-6000

VA MEDICAL CENTER - CANANDAIGUA
400 Fort Hill Avenue
Canandaigua, NY 14424-1188
(585)394-2000

CARMEL

ARMS ACRES
75 Seminary Hill Road
Carmel, NY 10512-1921
(845)225-3400

PUTNAM HOSPITAL CENTER
Stoneleigh Avenue
Carmel, NY 10512
(845)279-5711

CARTHAGE

CARTHAGE AREA HOSPITAL
West St Road
Carthage, NY 13619
(315)493-1000

CASTLE POINT

VA HEALTHCARE SYSTEM - CASTLE POINT
Rte 9d
Castle Point, NY 12511
(845)831-2000

CHEEKTOWAGA

SAINT JOSEPH INTERCOMMUNITY HOSPITAL
2605 Harlem Road
Cheektowaga, NY 14225-4018
(716)891-2400

CLIFTON SPRINGS

CLIFTON SPRINGS HOSPITAL
2 Couler Road
Clifton Springs, NY 14432-1189
(315)462-9561

COBLESKILL

BASSETT HOSPITAL OF SCHOHARIE COUNTY
178 Grandview Dr
Cobleskill, NY 12043-5144
(518)234-2511

COHOES

EDDY COHOES REHABILITATION CENTER
421 Columbia St
Cohoes, NY 12047-2205
(518)237-5630

COOPERSTOWN

BASSETT HEALTH CARE
One Atwell Road
Cooperstown, NY 13326-1394
(607)547-3100

CORNING

CORNING HOSPITAL
176 Denison Parkway East
Corning, NY 14830-2899
(607)937-7200

CORNWALL

CORNWALL HOSPITAL
Laurel Avenue
Cornwall, NY 12518
(845)534-7711

CORTLAND

CORTLAND MEMORIAL HOSPITAL
134 Homer Avenue
Cortland, NY 13045-1254
(607)756-3500

CUBA

CUBA MEMORIAL HOSPITAL
140 W Main St
Cuba, NY 14727-1398
(585)968-2000

DANNEMORA

CLINTON CORRECTIONAL FACILITY
PO Box 2000
Dannemora, NY 12929-2000
(518)492-2511

DANSVILLE

NICHOLAS NOYES MEMORIAL HOSPITAL
111 Clara Barton St
Dansville, NY 14437-9527
(585)335-6001

DELHI

O'CONNOR HOSPITAL
Andes Road Box 205a
Delhi, NY 13753-0205
(607)746-0300

DOBBS FERRY

COMMUNITY HOSPITAL-DOBBS FERRY
128 Ashford Avenue
Dobbs Ferry, NY 10522-1896
(914)693-0700

DUNKIRK

BROOKS MEMORIAL HOSPITAL
529 Central Avenue
Dunkirk, NY 14048-2599
(716)366-1111

EAST MEADOW

NASSAU UNIVERSITY MEDICAL CENTER
2201 Hempstead Tnpk
East Meadow, NY 11554-5400
(516)572-0123

ELIZABETHTOWN

ELIZABETHTOWN COMMUNITY HOSPITAL
PO Box 277
Elizabethtown, NY 12932-0277
(518)873-6377

ELLENVILLE

ELLENVILLE REGIONAL HOSPITAL
Route 209
Ellenville, NY 12428
(845)647-6400

ELMHURST

CITY HOSPITAL CENTER AT ELMHURST
79-01 Broadway
Elmhurst, NY 11373-1329
(718)334-1141

ELMHURST HOSPITAL CENTER
7710 41st Ave
Elmhurst, NY 11373-1116
(718)334-4000

SAINT JOHN'S QUEENS HOSPITAL - DIV. OF CATHOLIC MEDICAL CENTER
90-02 Queens Blvd
Elmhurst, NY 11373-4998
(718)558-1000

ELMIRA

ARNOT OGDEN MEDICAL CENTER
600 Roe Avenue
Elmira, NY 14905-1676
(607)737-4100

ELMIRA PSYCH CENTER
Washington St
Elmira, NY 14901
(607)737-4739

SAINT JOSEPHS HOSPITAL
555 E Market St
Elmira, NY 14901-3256
(607)733-6541

FAR ROCKAWAY

PENINSULA HOSPITAL CENTER
51-15 Beach Channel Drive
Far Rockaway, NY 11691-1074
(718)734-2000

SAINT JOHN EPISCOPAL HOSPITAL
327 Beach 19th St
Far Rockaway, NY 11691-4423
(718)869-7000

NEW YORK — Hospital Telephone Directory

FLUSHING

FLUSHING HOSPITAL MEDICAL CENTER
45th Avenue And Parsons Boulevard
Flushing, NY 11355
(718)670-5000

NEW YORK HOSPITAL MEDICAL CENTER OF QUEENS
56-45 Main Street
Flushing, NY 11355-5060
(718)670-1231

SAINT JOSEPH'S HOSPITAL
158-40 79th Avenue
Flushing, NY 11366-1998
(718)558-6200

FOREST HILLS

NORTH SHORE UNIVERSITY HOSPITAL AT FOREST HILLS
102-01 66th Road
Forest Hills, NY 11375-2029
(718)830-4000

PARKWAY HOSPITAL
70-35 113th St
Forest Hills, NY 11375-4699
(718)990-4100

FULTON

ALBERT LINDLEY LEE MEMORIAL HOSPITAL
500 S Fourth St
Fulton, NY 13069-2904
(315)592-2224

GENEVA

GENEVA GENERAL HOSPITAL
196 198 North St
Geneva, NY 14456-1694
(315)787-4000

GLEN COVE

NORTH SHORE UNIVERSITY HOSPITAL AT GLEN COVE
St Andrews Lane
Glen Cove, NY 11542
(516)674-7300

GLEN OAKS

HILLSIDE HOSPITAL
75-59 263rd St
Glen Oaks, NY 11004-1150
(718)470-8000

GLENS FALLS

GLENS FALLS HOSPITAL
100 Park Street
Glens Falls, NY 12801-4447
(518)926-1000

GLENVILLE

CONIFER PARK
79 Glenridge Road
Glenville, NY 12302-4528
(518)399-6446

GLOVERSVILLE

NATHAN LITTAUER HOSPITAL
99 E State St
Gloversville, NY 12078-1293
(518)725-8621

GOSHEN

ORANGE REGIONAL MEDICAL CENTER-ARDEN HILL
Harriman Drive
Goshen, NY 10924
(845)294-5441

GOUVERNEUR

E J NOBLE-GOUVERNEUR
77 W Barney St
Gouverneur, NY 13642-1040
(315)287-1000

GOWANDA

TRI COUNTY MEMORIAL HOSPITAL
100 Memorial Drive
Gowanda, NY 14070-1194
(716)532-3377

GREENPORT

EASTERN LONG ISLAND HOSPITAL
201 Manor Place
Greenport, NY 11944-1298
(631)477-1000

HAMILTON

COMMUNITY MEMORIAL HOSPITAL
150 Broad St
Hamilton, NY 13346-9518
(315)824-1100

HARRIS

CATSKILL REGIONAL MEDICAL CENTER
Bushville Road PO Box 800
Harris, NY 12742-0800
(845)794-3300

HARRISON

SAINT VINCENT HOSPITAL
275 North St
Harrison, NY 10528-1524
(914)967-6500

HEMPSTEAD

ISLAND MEDICAL CENTER
800 Front St
Hempstead, NY 11550-4600
(516)560-1200

HORNELL

SAINT JAMES MERCY HOSPITAL
411 Canisted St
Hornell, NY 14843-2197
(607)324-8000

HUDSON

COLUMBIA MEMORIAL HOSPITAL
71 Prospect Avenue
Hudson, NY 12534-2907
(518)828-7601

HUNTINGTON

HUNTINGTON HOSPITAL
270 Park Avenue
Huntington, NY 11743-2799
(631)351-2200

HUNTINGTON STATION

SAGAMORE CHILDREN'S PSYCHIATRIC CENTERS
197 Half Hollow Road
Huntington Station, NY 11746-5861
(631)673-7700

IRVING

LAKE SHORE HEALTH CARE CENTER
Routes 5 And 20 At Seneca Road
Irving, NY 14081
(716)934-2654

ITHACA

CAYUGA MEDICAL CENTER AT ITHACA
101 Dates Drive
Ithaca, NY 14850-1383
(607)274-4011

JAMAICA

CREEDMOOR PSYCHIATRIC CENTER
80-45 Winchester Boulevard Building B
Jamaica, NY 11427-2193
(718)264-3300

HOLLISWOOD HOSPITAL
87-37 Palermo Street
Jamaica, NY 11423-1209
(718)776-8181

JAMAICA HOSPITAL
89th Avenue And Van Wyck Expressway
Jamaica, NY 11418
(718)206-6000

MARY IMMACULATE HOSPITAL
152-11 89th Avenue
Jamaica, NY 11432-3730
(718)558-2000

QUEENS HOSPITAL CENTER
82-68 164th St
Jamaica, NY 11432-1140
(718)883-3000

JAMESTOWN

WOMENS CHRISTIAN ASSOCIATION HOSPITAL
207 Foote Avenue
Jamestown, NY 14701-7077
(716)487-0141

JOHNSON CITY

UNITED HEALTH SERVICES-WILSON MEMORIAL HOSPITAL
33-57 Harrison St
Johnson City, NY 13790-2174
(607)763-6000

KATONAH

FOUR WINDS
Cross River Road
Katonah, NY 10536
(914)763-8151

KENMORE

KENMORE MERCY HOSPITAL
2950 Elmwood Avenue
Kenmore, NY 14217-1390
(716)447-6100

KINGSTON

BENEDICTINE HOSPITAL
105 St Mary Avenue
Kingston, NY 12401
(845)338-2500

KINGSTON HOSPITAL
396 Broadway
Kingston, NY 12401-4692
(845)331-3131

Hospital Telephone Directory **NEW YORK**

LACKAWANNA
OUR LADY OF VICTORY
55 Melroy At Ridge Road
Lackawanna, NY 14218
(716)828-9444

LEWISTON
MOUNT SAINT MARYS HOSPITAL OF NIAGARA FALLS
5300 Military Road
Lewiston, NY 14092-1997
(716)297-4800

LITTLE FALLS
LITTLE FALLS HOSPITAL
140 Burwell St
Little Falls, NY 13365-1794
(315)823-1000

LOCKPORT
LOCKPORT MEMORIAL HOSPITAL
521 East Avenue
Lockport, NY 14094-3299
(716)514-5700

LONG BEACH
LONG BEACH MEDICAL CENTER
455 E Bay Drive
Long Beach, NY 11561-2300
(516)897-1000

LONG ISLAND CITY
MOUNT SINAI HOSPITAL OF QUEENS
2510 30th Avenue
Long Island City, NY 11102-2418
(718)932-1000

LOWVILLE
LEWIS COUNTY GENERAL HOSPITAL
7785 North State St
Lowville, NY 13367-1297
(315)376-5200

MALONE
ALICE HYDE MEMORIAL HOSPITAL
115 Park St
Malone, NY 12953-1220
(518)483-3000

MANHASSET
MANHASSET AMBULATORY CARE PAVILION
1554 Northern Blvd
Manhasset, NY 11030-3006
(516)365-2070

NORTH SHORE UNIVERSITY HOSPITAL
300 Community Drive
Manhasset, NY 11030-3876
(516)562-0100

MARCY
CENTRAL NEW YORK PSYCHIATRIC CENTER
PO Box 300
Marcy, NY 13403-0300
(315)736-8271

MARGARETVILLE
MARGARETVILLE MEMORIAL HOSPITAL
Route 28
Margaretville, NY 12455
(845)586-2631

MASSENA
MASSENA MEMORIAL HOSPITAL
One Hospital Drive
Massena, NY 13662-1097
(315)764-1711

MEDINA
MEDINA MEMORIAL HOSPITAL
500 Ohio Street
Medina, NY 14103-1095
(585)798-2000

MIDDLETOWN
MIDDLETOWN PSYCH CENTER
PO Box 1453
Middletown, NY 10940
(845)342-5511

ORANGE REGIONAL MEDICAL CENTER-HORTON CAMPUS
60 Prospect Avenue
Middletown, NY 10940-4133
(845)343-2424

MINEOLA
WINTHROP UNIVERSITY HOSPITAL
259 1st St
Mineola, NY 11501-3987
(516)663-2244

MONTOUR FALLS
SCHUYLER HOSPITAL
220 Stuben Street
Montour Falls, NY 14865-9709
(607)535-7121

MOUNT KISCO
NORTHERN WESTCHESTER HOSPITAL
380 Main St
Mount Kisco, NY 10549-3016
(914)666-1200

MOUNT VERNON
MOUNT VERNON HOSPITAL
12 N 7th Avenue
Mount Vernon, NY 10550-2098
(914)664-8000

NEW HAMPTON
MID HUDSON PSYCHIATRIC CENTER
Box 158 Route 17M
New Hampton, NY 10958
(845)374-3171

NEW HYDE PARK
LONG ISLAND JEWISH MEDICAL CENTER
270-05 76th Avenue
New Hyde Park, NY 11040-1496
(718)470-7000

NEW ROCHELLE
SOUND SHORE MEDICAL CENTER
16 Guion Place
New Rochelle, NY 10801-5500
(914)632-5000

NEW YORK
BELLEVUE HOSPITAL CENTER
1st Avenue And 27th St
New York, NY 10016
(212)562-4141

BETH ISRAEL MEDICAL CENTER
First Avenue And 16th Street
New York, NY 10003
(212)420-2000

BETH ISRAEL SINGER DIVISION
170 E End Avenue
New York, NY 10128-7603
(212)870-9000

CABRINI MEDICAL CENTER
227 E 19th St
New York, NY 10003-2693
(212)995-6000

COLER MEMORIAL HOSPITAL
Roosevelt Island
New York, NY 10044
(212)848-6000

COLER-GOLDWATER SPECIALTY HOSPITAL
One Main Street
New York, NY 10044-0052
(212)318-8000

COLUMBIA PRESBYTERIAN MEDICAL CENTER - NEW YORK STATE PSYCHIATRIC INSTITUTE
722 W 168th St
New York, NY 10032-2603
(212)543-5000

CORNERSTONE OF MEDICAL ARTS CENTER HOSPITAL
57 West 57th St
New York, NY 10019-2802
(212)755-0200

GOLDWATER MEMORIAL HOSPITAL
Roosevelt Island
New York, NY 10044
(212)318-8000

GRACIE SQUARE HOSPITAL
420 East 76 St
New York, NY 10021-3104
(212)988-4400

HARLEM HOSPITAL CENTER
506 Lenox Avenue
New York, NY 10037-1889
(212)939-1000

HOSPITAL FOR JOINT DISEASES - ORTHOPAEDIC INSTITUTE
301 E 17th St
New York, NY 10003-3899
(212)598-6000

HOSPITAL FOR SPECIAL SURGERY
535 E 70th St
New York, NY 10021-4898
(212)606-1000

KIRBY FORENSIC PSYCHIATRIC CENTER
Ward Island
New York, NY 10035
(212)427-9003

LENOX HILL HOSPITAL
100 E 77th St
New York, NY 10021-1850
(212)434-2000

MANHATTAN EYE EAR THROAT HOSPITAL
210 E 64th St
New York, NY 10021-7498
(212)838-9200

MANHATTAN PSYCHIATRIC CENTER
Ward's Island
New York, NY 10035
(212)369-0500

MEMORIAL HOSPITAL FOR CANCER AND ALLIED DISEASES
1275 York Avenue
New York, NY 10021-6094
(212)639-2000

NEW YORK
Hospital Telephone Directory

METROPOLITAN HOSPITAL CENTER
1901 1st Avenue
New York, NY 10029-7491
(212)423-6262

MOUNT SINAI MEDICAL CENTER
One Gustave L Levy Place
New York, NY 10029-6500
(212)241-6500

NEW YORK EYE AND EAR INFIRMARY
310 E 14th St
New York, NY 10003-4297
(212)979-4000

NEW YORK PRESBYTERIAN HOSPITAL
525 E 68th St
New York, NY 10021-4885
(212)746-5454

NEW YORK PRESBYTERIAN HOSPITAL -
BABIES AND CHILDREN'S HOSPITAL
3959 Broadway
New York, NY 10032-1559
(212)305-2500

NEW YORK STATE PSYCHIATRIC INSTITUTE
722 West 168th St
New York, NY 10032-2695
(212)543-5000

NEW YORK UNIVERSITY - DOWNTOWN
HOSPITAL
170 William St
New York, NY 10038-2649
(212)312-5000

NEW YORK WEILL CORNELL MEDICAL
CENTER
525 East 68th Street
New York, NY 10021-4885
(212)746-5454

NORTH GENERAL HOSPITAL
1879 Madison Avenue
New York, NY 10035-2709
(212)423-4000

NYU MEDICAL CENTER-UNIVERSITY
HOSPITAL
550 First Avenue
New York, NY 10016-6402
(212)263-7300

PAYNE WHITNEY PSYCHIATRIC CLINIC
525 East 68th St Box 140
New York, NY 10021-4870
(212)932-5000

ROCKEFELLER UNIVERSITY HOSPITAL
1230 York Avenue
New York, NY 10021-6399
(212)327-8000

RUSK INSTITUTE OF REHABILITATION
MEDICINE
400 East 34th St
New York, NY 10016-4901
(212)263-7300

SAINT LUKES - ROOSEVELT HOSPITAL
1111 Amsterdam Avenue
New York, NY 10025-1716
(212)523-4000

SAINT LUKES ROOSEVELT HOSPITAL
CENTER
1000 10th Avenue
New York, NY 10019-1192
(212)523-4000

SAINT VINCENT MIDTOWN HOSPITAL
415 W 51st St
New York, NY 10019-6394
(212)459-8000

SAINT VINCENTS HOSPITAL MEDICAL
CENTER
153 W 11th Street
New York, NY 10011-8305
(212)604-7000

SCHNEIDER CHILDREN'S HOSPITAL
270-05 76th Avenue
New York, NY 11040-1433
(718)470-3000

SLOAN KETTERING CANCER CENTER
1275 York Avenue
New York, NY 10021-6094
(212)639-2000

TERRENCE CARDINAL COOKE HEALTH
CARE CENTER
1249 Fifth Avenue
New York, NY 10029-4413
(212)360-1000

VA HEALTHCARE SYSTEM - NEW YORK
423 E 23rd St
New York, NY 10010-5011
(212)686-7500

NEWARK

MYERS COMMUNITY HOSPITAL
PO Box 111
Newark, NY 14513-0111
(315)483-3000

NEWARK WAYNE COMMUNITY HOSPITAL
Driving Park Avenue
Newark, NY 14513
(315)332-2022

NEWBURGH

SAINT LUKES HOSPITAL OF NEWBURGH
70 Dubois St
Newburgh, NY 12550-4898
(845)561-4400

NEWFANE

NEWFANE INTER COMMUNITY MEMORIAL
HOSPITAL
2600 William St
Newfane, NY 14108-1026
(716)778-5111

NIAGARA FALLS

NIAGARA FALLS MEMORIAL MEDICAL
CENTER
621 10th St
Niagara Falls, NY 14301-1813
(716)278-4000

NISKAYUNA

BELLEVUE WOMENS HOSPITAL
2210 Troy Road
Niskayuna, NY 12309-4725
(518)346-9400

NORTH TARRYTOWN

PHELPS MEMORIAL HOSPITAL
701 North Broadway
North Tarrytown, NY 10591-1096
(914)366-3000

NORTH TONAWANDA

DEGRAFF MEMORIAL HOSPITAL
445 Tremont St
North Tonawanda, NY 14120-6196
(716)694-4500

NORTHPORT

VA MEDICAL CENTER - NORTHPORT
79 Middleville Road
Northport, NY 11768-2200
(631)261-4400

NORWICH

CHENANGO MEMORIAL HOSPITAL
179 N Broad St
Norwich, NY 13815-1097
(607)337-4111

NYACK

NYACK HOSPITAL
160 North Medland Avenue
Nyack, NY 10960
(845)348-2000

OCEANSIDE

SOUTH NASSAU COMMUNITY HOSPITAL
One Healthy Way
Oceanside, NY 11572-1500
(516)632-3000

OGDENSBURG

CLAXTON - HEPBURN MEDICAL CENTER
214 King St
Ogdensburg, NY 13669-1191
(315)393-3600

SAINT LAWRENCE PSYCH CENTER
Station A
Ogdensburg, NY 13669
(315)541-2001

OLEAN

OLEAN GENERAL HOSPITAL
515 Main St
Olean, NY 14760-1598
(716)373-2600

ONEIDA

ONEIDA CITY HOSPITAL
321 Genesse St
Oneida, NY 13421-2699
(315)363-6000

ONEONTA

FOX MEMORIAL HOSPITAL
One Norton Avenue
Oneonta, NY 13820-2697
(607)432-2000

ORANGEBURG

ROCKLAND CHILDREN'S PSYCHIATRIC
CENTER
599 Convent Road
Orangeburg, NY 10962
(845)359-7400

ROCKLAND PSYCH CENTER
140 Old Orangeburg Road
Orangeburg, NY 10962-1157
(845)359-1000

OSSINING

OSSINING CORRECTIONAL FACILITIES
HOSPITAL
354 Hunter St
Ossining, NY 10562-5498
(914)941-0108

STONY LODGE HOSPITAL
40 Croton Dam Road
Ossining, NY 10562-2644
(914)941-7400

OSWEGO

OSWEGO HOSPITAL
110 W 6th St
Oswego, NY 13126-2598
(315)349-5511

Hospital Telephone Directory   **NEW YORK**

PATCHOGUE

BROOKHAVEN MEMORIAL HOSPITAL
101 Hospital Road
Patchogue, NY 11772-4897
(631)654-7100

PEEKSKILL

HUDSON VALLEY HOSPITAL CENTER
1980 Crompond Road
Peekskill, NY 10567-4182
(914)737-9000

PENN YAN

SOLDIERS AND SAILORS MEMORIAL HOSPITAL
418 N Main St
Penn Yan, NY 14527-1070
(315)531-2000

PLAINVIEW

NORTH SHORE UNIVERSITY HOSPITAL AT PLAINVIEW
888 Old Country Road
Plainview, NY 11803-4914
(516)719-3000

PLATTSBURGH

CHAMPLAIN VALLEY PHYSICIANS HOSPITAL
100 Beekman St
Plattsburgh, NY 12901-1437
(518)561-2000

POMONA

SUMMIT PARK HOSPITAL
Sanatorium Road
Pomona, NY 10970-3518
(845)364-2700

PORT CHESTER

UNITED HOSPITAL MEDICAL CENTER
406 Boston Post Road
Port Chester, NY 10573-7300
(914)934-3000

PORT JEFFERSON

JOHN T MATHER MEMORIAL HOSPITAL
North Country Road
Port Jefferson, NY 11777
(631)473-1320

SAINT CHARLES HOSPITAL
200 Belle Terre Road
Port Jefferson, NY 11777-1968
(631)474-6000

PORT JERVIS

BON SECOURS COMMUNITY HOSPITAL
160 E Main St
Port Jervis, NY 12771-2253
(845)858-7000

POTSDAM

CANTON POTSDAM HOSPITAL
Potsdam Hospital Unit-50 Leroy St
Potsdam, NY 13676
(315)265-3300

POUGHKEEPSIE

HUDSON RIVER PSYCHIATRIC CENTER
Branch B
Poughkeepsie, NY 12601
(845)452-8000

SAINT FRANCIS HOSPITAL
North Road
Poughkeepsie, NY 12601
(845)483-5000

VASSAR BROTHERS HOSPITAL
Reade Place
Poughkeepsie, NY 12601
(845)454-8500

QUEENS VILLAGE

CREEDMOOR PSYCHIATRIC CENTER
8045 Winchester Boulevard
Queens Village, NY 11427-2193
(718)464-7500

RHINEBECK

NORTHERN DUTCHESS HOSPITAL
Springbrook Avenue
Rhinebeck, NY 12572-1179
(845)876-3001

RIVERDALE

HIGH RIDGE HOUSE
5959 Independence Avenue
Riverdale, NY 10471-1299
(718)796-4200

RIVERHEAD

CENTRAL SUFFOLK HOSPITAL
1300 Roanoke Avenue
Riverhead, NY 11901-2058
(631)548-6000

ROCHESTER

GENESEE HOSPITAL
244 Alexander St
Rochester, NY 14607-2502
(585)922-6568

HIGHLAND HOSPITAL
1000 South Avenue
Rochester, NY 14620-2782
(585)473-2200

MONROE COMMUNITY HOSPITAL
435 E Henrietta Road
Rochester, NY 14620-4684
(585)760-6500

PARK RIDGE HOSPITAL
1555 Long Pond Road
Rochester, NY 14626-4182
(585)723-7000

ROCHESTER GENERAL HOSPITAL
1425 Portland Avenue
Rochester, NY 14621-3095
(585)922-4000

ROCHESTER PSYCHIATRIC CENTER
1111 Elmwood Avenue
Rochester, NY 14620-3090
(585)241-1200

SAINT MARYS HOSPITAL
89 Genesee St
Rochester, NY 14611-3285
(585)723-7000

STRONG MEMORIAL HOSPITAL
601 Elmwood Avenue-Box 612
Rochester, NY 14642-0001
(585)275-2100

ROCKVILLE CENTRE

MERCY MEDICAL CENTER
1000 N Village Avenue
Rockville Centre, NY 11570-1000
(516)705-2525

ROME

ROME HOSPITAL AND MURPHY MEMORIAL HOSPITAL
1500 N James St
Rome, NY 13440-2899
(315)338-7000

ROSLYN

SAINT FRANCIS HOSPITAL
Port Washington Boulevard
Roslyn, NY 11576
(516)562-6000

RYE

RYE PSYCH HOSPITAL CENTER
754 Boston Post Road
Rye, NY 10580-2724
(914)967-4567

SARANAC LAKE

ADIRONDACK MEDICAL CENTER
Lake Colby Drive
Saranac Lake, NY 12983
(518)891-4141

SARATOGA SPRINGS

FOUR WINDS
30 Crescent Avenue
Saratoga Springs, NY 12866-5100
(518)584-3600

SARATOGA HOSPITAL
211 Church St
Saratoga Springs, NY 12866-1003
(518)587-3222

SCHENECTADY

BELLEVUE WOMENS HOSPITAL
2210 Troy Road
Schenectady, NY 12309-4725
(518)346-9400

ELLIS HOSPITAL
1101 Nott St
Schenectady, NY 12308-2489
(518)243-4000

SAINT CLARES HOSPITAL
600 Mcclellan St
Schenectady, NY 12304-1090
(518)382-2000

SUNNYVIEW HOSPITAL REHAB CENTER
1270 Belmont Avenue
Schenectady, NY 12308-2198
(518)382-4500

SIDNEY

HOSPITAL, THE
43 Pearl Street West
Sidney, NY 13838-1300
(607)561-2100

SMITHTOWN

SAINT CATHERINE OF SIENA MEDICAL CENTER
50 Route 25a
Smithtown, NY 11787-1398
(631)862-3000

SOUTHAMPTON

SOUTHAMPTON HOSPITAL
240 Meeting House Lane
Southampton, NY 11968-5090
(631)726-8200

NEW YORK — Hospital Telephone Directory

SPRINGVILLE

BERTRAND CHAFFEE HOSPITAL
224 E Main St
Springville, NY 14141-1497
(716)592-2871

STAR LAKE

CLIFTON FINE HOSPITAL
PO Box 10 Oswegatchie Trail
Star Lake, NY 13690-0010
(315)848-3351

STATEN ISLAND

SAINT VINCENT'S CATHOLIC MEDICAL CENTER - BAYLEY SETON CAMPUS
75 Vanderbilt Avenue
Staten Island, NY 10304-2604
(718)818-6000

SAINT VINCENTS CATHOLIC MEDICAL CENTER
355 Bard Avenue
Staten Island, NY 10310-1699
(718)818-1234

SOUTH BEACH PSYCHIATRIC CENTER
777 Seaview Avenue
Staten Island, NY 10305-3436
(718)667-2300

STATEN ISLAND UNIVERSITY HOSPITAL - CONCORD
1040 Targee
Staten Island, NY 10304
(718)390-1400

STATEN ISLAND UNIVERSITY HOSPITAL- NORTH
475 Seaview Avenue
Staten Island, NY 10305-3498
(718)226-9000

STATEN ISLAND UNIVERSITY HOSPITAL- SOUTH
375 Sequine Avenue
Staten Island, NY 10309-3998
(718)226-2000

STONY BROOK

UNIVERSITY HOSPITAL
SUNY At Stony Brook
Stony Brook, NY 11794-0001
(631)689-8333

SUFFERN

GOOD SAMARITAN HOSPITAL OF SUFFERN
255 Lafayette Avenue
Suffern, NY 10901-4869
(845)368-5000

SYOSSET

NORTH SHORE UNIVERSITY HOSPITAL SYOSSET
221 Jericho Turnpike
Syosset, NY 11791-4536
(516)496-6400

SYRACUSE

COMMUNITY GENERAL HOSPITAL
Broad Road
Syracuse, NY 13215-5100
(315)492-5011

CROUSE-IRVING MEMORIAL HOSPITAL
736 Irving Avenue
Syracuse, NY 13210-1687
(315)470-7111

FOUR WINDS HOSPITAL
650 S Salina St
Syracuse, NY 13202-3524
(315)476-2161

RICHARD H HUTCHINGS PSYCHIATRIC CENTER
620 Madison Street
Syracuse, NY 13210-2338
(315)473-4980

SAINT JOSEPHS HOSPITAL HEALTH CENTER
301 Prospect Avenue
Syracuse, NY 13203-1899
(315)448-5111

SUNY UPSTATE MEDICAL CENTER
750 E Adams St
Syracuse, NY 13210-1834
(315)464-5540

VA MEDICAL CENTER - SYRACUSE
800 Irving Avenue
Syracuse, NY 13210-2796
(315)425-4400

TICONDEROGA

MOSES LUDINGTON HOSPITAL
Montcalm Wicker Streets
Ticonderoga, NY 12883
(518)585-2831

TROY

SAMARITAN HOSPITAL
2215 Burdett Avenue
Troy, NY 12180-2475
(518)271-3300

SETON HEALTH - SAINT MARY'S HOSPITAL
1300 Massachusetts Avenue
Troy, NY 12180-1695
(518)268-5000

UTICA

FAXTON - SAINT LUKE'S HEALTHCARE
1676 Sunset Avenue
Utica, NY 13502-5416
(315)738-6200

MOHAWK VALLEY PSYCHIATRIC CENTER
1213 Court St
Utica, NY 13502-3803
(315)797-6800

SAINT ELIZABETHS HOSPITAL
2209 Genesee St
Utica, NY 13501-5999
(315)798-8100

SAINT LUKES MEMORIAL HOSPITAL CENTER
Box 479
Utica, NY 13503-0479
(315)798-6000

VALHALLA

BLYTHDALE CHILDRENS HOSPITAL
Bradhurst Avenue
Valhalla, NY 10595
(914)592-7555

WESTCHESTER MEDICAL CENTER
95 Grasslands Road
Valhalla, NY 10595-1646
(914)493-7000

VALLEY STREAM

FRANKLIN HOSPITAL MEDICAL CENTER
900 Franklin Avenue
Valley Stream, NY 11580-2190
(516)256-6000

WALTON

DELAWARE VALLEY HOSPITAL
1 Titus Place
Walton, NY 13856-1498
(607)865-2100

WARSAW

WYOMING COUNTY COMMUNITY HOSPITAL
400 N Main St
Warsaw, NY 14569-1097
(585)786-2233

WARWICK

SAINT ANTHONY COMMUNITY HOSPITAL
15-19 Maple Avenue
Warwick, NY 10990-1059
(845)986-2276

WATERTOWN

SAMARITAN MEDICAL CENTER
830 Washington St
Watertown, NY 13601-4099
(315)785-4121

WELLSVILLE

JONES MEMORIAL HOSPITAL
191 N Main St
Wellsville, NY 14895-1197
(585)596-4000

WEST HAVERSTRAW

HELEN HAYES HOSPITAL
Route 9 West
West Haverstraw, NY 10993
(845)786-4000

WEST ISLIP

GOOD SAMARITAN HOSPITAL
1000 Montauk Highway
West Islip, NY 11795-4958
(631)376-3000

WEST POINT

KELLER ARMY COMMUNITY HOSPITAL
Us Military Acad Building 900
West Point, NY 10996
(845)938-4837

WESTFIELD

WESTFIELD MEMORIAL HOSPITAL
189 E Main St
Westfield, NY 14787-1195
(716)326-4921

WHITE PLAINS

BURKE REHAB HOSPITAL
785 Mamaroneck Avenue
White Plains, NY 10605-2523
(914)597-2500

NEW YORK PRESBYTERIAN HOSPITAL - WESTCHESTER
21 Bloomingdale Road
White Plains, NY 10605-1504
(914)682-9100

WHITE PLAINS HOSPITAL MEDICAL CENTER
Davis Avenue At East Post Road
White Plains, NY 10601-4615
(914)681-0600

Hospital Telephone Directory — **NORTH CAROLINA**

WILLIAMSVILLE

MILLARD FILLMORE SUBURBAN HOSPITAL
1540 Maple Road
Williamsville, NY 14221-3698
(716)568-3600

YONKERS

SAINT JOHNS RIVERSIDE HOSPITAL
967 N Broadway
Yonkers, NY 10701-1302
(914)964-4444

SAINT JOSEPHS MEDICAL CENTER
127 S Broadway
Yonkers, NY 10701-4080
(914)378-7000

YONKERS GENERAL HOSPITAL
Two Park Avenue
Yonkers, NY 10703-3497
(914)964-7300

NORTH CAROLINA

AHOSKIE

ROANOKE CHOWAN HOSPITAL
500 S Academy St
Ahoskie, NC 27910-3261
(252)209-3000

ALBEMARLE

STANLY MEMORIAL HOSPITAL
301 Yadkin St Box 1489
Albemarle, NC 28001-3448
(704)984-4000

ASHEBORO

RANDOLPH HOSPITAL
PO Box 1048
Asheboro, NC 27204-1048
(336)625-5151

ASHEVILLE

MISSION SAINT JOSEPH'S HOSPITAL
509 Biltmore Avenue
Asheville, NC 28801-4690
(828)213-1111

SAINT JOSEPHS HOSPITAL
428 Biltmore Avenue
Asheville, NC 28801-4597
(828)213-1111

THOMS REHABILITATION HOSPITAL
68 Sweeten Creek Road
Asheville, NC 28803-2318
(828)274-2400

VA MEDICAL CENTER - ASHEVILLE
1100 Tunnel Road
Asheville, NC 28805-2043
(828)298-7911

BELHAVEN

PUNGO DISTRICT HOSPITAL
210 E Fromt St
Belhaven, NC 27810-1408
(252)943-2111

BLACK MOUNTAIN

JULIAN F. KEITH ALCOHOL AND DRUG
ABUSE TREATMENT CENTER
301 Tabernacle Road
Black Mountain, NC 28711-2537
(828)669-3402

BLOWING ROCK

BLOWING ROCK HOSPITAL
Chestnut Drive Box 148
Blowing Rock, NC 28605-0148
(828)295-3136

BOILING SPRINGS

CRAWLEY MEMORIAL HOSPITAL
315 W College Avenue Box 996
Boiling Springs, NC 28017-0996
(704)434-9466

BOONE

WATAUGA MEDICAL CENTER
PO Box 2600
Boone, NC 28607-2600
(828)262-4100

BREVARD

TRANSYLVANIA COMMUNITY HOSPITAL
Hospital Drive Box 1116
Brevard, NC 28712-1116
(828)884-9111

BRYSON CITY

SWAIN COUNTY HOSPITAL
45 Plateau St
Bryson City, NC 28713-6784
(828)488-2155

BURGAW

PENDER MEMORIAL HOSPITAL
507 Fremont Street
Burgaw, NC 28425
(910)259-5451

BURLINGTON

ALAMANCE REGIONAL MEDICAL CENTER
1240 Huffman Mill Road PO Box 202
Burlington, NC 27216-0202
(336)538-7000

BURNSVILLE

YANCEY COMMUNITY MEDICAL CENTER
320 Pensacola Road
Burnsville, NC 28714-3318
(828)682-6136

BUTNER

ALCOHOL & DRUG ABUSE TREATMENT
CENTER
205 West E St
Butner, NC 27509-1999
(919)575-7928

FEDERAL MEDICAL CENTER - BUTNER
PO Box 999, Old Oxford Hwy 75
Butner, NC 27509-0999
(919)575-3900

JOHN UMSTEAD HOSPITAL
1003 12th Street
Butner, NC 27509-1626
(919)575-7211

CAMP LEJEUNE

NAVAL HOSPITAL CAMP LEJEUNE
PO Box 10100
Camp Lejeune, NC 28547
(910)450-4300

CARY

WESTERN WAKE MEDICAL CENTER
1900 Kildare Farm Road
Cary, NC 27511-6616
(919)233-2300

CHAPEL HILL

UNIVERSITY OF NORTH CAROLINA
HOSPITAL
101 Manning Drive
Chapel Hill, NC 27514-4226
(919)966-4131

CHARLOTTE

BEHAVIORAL HEALTH CENTER - CMC-
RANDOLPH
501 Billingsley Road
Charlotte, NC 28211-1009
(704)358-2700

CAROLINAS MEDICAL CENTER
1000 Blythe Boulevard
Charlotte, NC 28203-5871
(704)355-2000

CAROLINAS MEDICAL CENTER - MERCY
2001 Vail Avenue
Charlotte, NC 28207-1219
(704)379-5100

CAROLINAS MEDICAL CENTER - PINEVILLE
10628 Park Road
Charlotte, NC 28210-8407
(704)543-2025

CAROLINAS MEDICAL CENTER -
UNIVERSITY
8800 North Tryon Street
Charlotte, NC 28262-8415
(704)548-6000

CCS/CHARLOTTE
1715 Sharon Road West
Charlotte, NC 28210-5663
(704)554-9874

CHARLOTTE INSTITUTE OF
REHABILITATION
1100 Blythe Boulevard
Charlotte, NC 28203-5864
(704)355-4300

PRESBYTERIAN HOSPITAL
200 Hawthorne Lane Box 33549
Charlotte, NC 28204-2528
(704)384-4000

PRESBYTERIAN-ORTHOPAEDIC HOSPITAL
200 Hawthorne Ln
Charlotte, NC 28204-2528
(704)316-2000

CHEROKEE

PHS INDIAN HOSPITAL - CHEROKEE
Cherokee, NC 28719
(828)497-9163

CHERRY POINT

NAVAL HOSPITAL CHERRY POINT
Psc Box 8023
Cherry Point, NC 28533
(252)466-0266

CLINTON

SAMPSON REGIONAL MEDICAL CENTER
607 Beaman St
Clinton, NC 28328-2603
(910)592-8511

NORTH CAROLINA — Hospital Telephone Directory

CLYDE

HAYWOOD REGIONAL MEDICAL CENTER
262 Leroy George Drive
Clyde, NC 28721-7430
(828)456-7311

COLUMBUS

SAINT LUKES HOSPITAL
220 Hospital Drive
Columbus, NC 28722-9473
(828)894-3311

CONCORD

NORTHEAST MEDICAL CENTER
920 Church St N
Concord, NC 28025-2983
(704)783-3000

DANBURY

STOKES-REYNOLDS MEMORIAL HOSPITAL
PO Box 10 Highway 8 And 89
Danbury, NC 27016-0010
(336)593-2831

DUNN

BETSY JOHNSON MEMORIAL HOSPITAL
800 Tilghman Drive
Dunn, NC 28334-5599
(910)892-7161

DURHAM

DUKE UNIVERSITY HOSPITAL
PO Box 3708 Dumc Erwin Road
Durham, NC 27710-0001
(919)684-8111

DURHAM REGIONAL HOSPITAL
3643 N Roxboro St
Durham, NC 27704-2763
(919)470-4000

NORTH CAROLINA EYE AND EAR HOSPITAL
1110 W Main St
Durham, NC 27701-2029
(919)682-9341

SELECT SPECIALTY HOSPITAL - DURHAM
3643 North Roxboro Road
Durham, NC 27704-2702
(919)470-9159

VA MEDICAL CENTER - DURHAM
508 Fulton St
Durham, NC 27705-3875
(919)286-0411

EDEN

MOREHEAD MEMORIAL HOSPITAL
117 E Kings Highway
Eden, NC 27288-5201
(336)623-9711

EDENTON

CHOWAN HOSPITAL
Virginia Road Box 629
Edenton, NC 27932-0629
(252)482-8451

ELIZABETH CITY

ALBEMARLE HOSPITAL
1144 N Road St
Elizabeth City, NC 27909-2622
(252)335-0531

ELIZABETHTOWN

BLADEN COUNTY HOSPITAL
Highway 701 N PO Box 398
Elizabethtown, NC 28337-0398
(910)862-5100

ELKIN

HUGH CHATHAM MEMORIAL HOSPITAL
180 Parkwood Drive
Elkin, NC 28621-2430
(336)527-7000

ERWIN

GOOD HOPE HOSPITAL
410 Denim Drive PO Box 668
Erwin, NC 28339-0668
(910)897-6151

FAYETTEVILLE

BEHAVIORAL HEALTH OF CAPE FEAR
VALLEY
3425 Melrose Road
Fayetteville, NC 28304-1608
(910)609-3000

CAPE FEAR VALLEY MEDICAL CENTER
1638 Owen Drive PO Box 2000
Fayetteville, NC 28302-2000
(910)609-4000

FAYETTEVILLE SPECIALTY HOSPITAL
150 Robeson Street, Fourth Floor
Fayetteville, NC 28301-5570
(910)609-1199

HIGHSMITH RAINEY MEMORIAL HOSPITAL
150 Robeson Street
Fayetteville, NC 28301-5519
(910)609-1000

VA MEDICAL CENTER - FAYETTEVILLE
2300 Ramsey St
Fayetteville, NC 28301-3856
(910)488-2120

FLETCHER

PARK RIDGE HOSPITAL
Naples Road Box 1569
Fletcher, NC 28732-1569
(828)684-8501

FORT BRAGG

WOMACK ARMY MEDICAL CENTER
2817 Reilly Road
Fort Bragg, NC 28310-0001
(910)907-6000

FRANKLIN

ANGEL MEDICAL CENTER
Riverview At White Oak St PO Box 1209
Franklin, NC 28744-1209
(828)524-8411

GASTONIA

GASTON MEMORIAL HOSPITAL
2525 Court Drive
Gastonia, NC 28054-2182
(704)834-2000

GOLDSBORO

CHERRY HOSPITAL
201 Stevens Mill Rd
Goldsboro, NC 27530-1057
(919)731-3200

WAYNE MEMORIAL HOSPITAL
2700 Wayne Memorial Drive
Goldsboro, NC 27534-9459
(919)736-1110

GREENSBORO

BEHAVIORAL HEALTH CENTER
700 Walter Reed Drive
Greensboro, NC 27403-1129
(336)852-4821

KINDRED HOSPITAL GREENSBORO
2401 Southside Boulevard
Greensboro, NC 27406-3311
(336)271-2800

MOSES H CONE MEMORIAL HOSPITAL
1200 N Elm St
Greensboro, NC 27401-1020
(336)832-7000

WESLEY LONG COMMUNITY HOSPITAL
501 N Elam Avenue
Greensboro, NC 27403-1199
(336)832-1000

WOMENS HOSPITAL OF GREENSBORO
801 Green Valley Road
Greensboro, NC 27408-7079
(336)832-6500

GREENVILLE

PITT COUNTY MEMORIAL HOSPITAL
2100 Stantonsburg Road PO Box 6028
Greenville, NC 27835-6028
(252)816-4100

WALTER B JONES ALCOHOL AND DRUG
ABUSE
2577 West Fifth Street
Greenville, NC 27834-7813
(252)830-3426

HAMLET

SANDHILLS REGIONAL MEDICAL CENTER
PO Box 1109
Hamlet, NC 28345-1109
(910)205-8000

HENDERSON

MARIA PARHAM HOSPITAL
PO Drawer 59 Ruin Creek Road
Henderson, NC 27536-0059
(252)438-4143

HENDERSONVLLE

MARGARET R PARDEE MEMORIAL
HOSPITAL
800 N Justice St
Hendersonvlle, NC 28791-3410
(828)696-1000

HICKORY

CATAWBA MEMORIAL HOSPITAL
810 Fairgrove Church Road
Hickory, NC 28602-9643
(828)326-3000

FRYE REGIONAL MEDICAL CENTER
420 N Center St
Hickory, NC 28601-5049
(828)322-6070

HIGH POINT

HIGH POINT REGIONAL HOSPITAL
601 N Elm St PO Box Hp-5
High Point, NC 27261-1899
(336)878-6000

Hospital Telephone Directory — NORTH CAROLINA

HIGHLANDS

HIGHLANDS-CASHIERS HOSPITAL
Highway 64 East PO Drawer 190
Highlands, NC 28741-0190
(828)526-1200

JACKSONVILLE

BRYNN MARR HOSPITAL
192 Village Drive
Jacksonville, NC 28546-7299
(910)577-1400

ONSLOW MEMORIAL HOSPITAL
317 Western Boulevard
Jacksonville, NC 28546-6379
(910)577-2345

JEFFERSON

ASHE MEMORIAL HOSPITAL
200 Hospital Avenue
Jefferson, NC 28640-9244
(336)246-7101

KENANSVILLE

DUPLIN GENERAL HOSPITAL
Duplin St Box 278
Kenansville, NC 28349-0278
(910)296-0941

KINGS MOUNTAIN

KINGS MOUNTAIN HOSPITAL
706 W King St
Kings Mountain, NC 28086-2708
(704)739-3601

KINSTON

CASWELL CENTER
2415 W Vernon Avenue
Kinston, NC 28504-3321
(252)208-4000

LENOIR MEMORIAL HOSPITAL
100 Airport Road
Kinston, NC 28501-1634
(252)522-7000

LAURINBURG

SCOTLAND MEMORIAL HOSPITAL
500 Lauchwood Drive
Laurinburg, NC 28352-5599
(910)291-7000

LENOIR

CALDWELL MEMORIAL HOSPITAL
321 Mulberry St Sw
Lenoir, NC 28645-5720
(828)757-5100

LEXINGTON

LEXINGTON MEMORIAL HOSPITAL
Old Salisbury Road Box 1817
Lexington, NC 27293-1817
(336)248-5161

LINCOLNTON

LINCOLN MEDICAL CENTER
Gamble Drive PO Box 677
Lincolnton, NC 28093-0677
(704)735-3071

LINVILLE

CHARLES A. CANNON JR. MEMORIAL HOSPITAL
434 Hospital Drive, PO Box 767
Linville, NC 28646-0767
(828)737-7000

LOUISBURG

FRANKLIN REGIONAL MEDICAL CENTER
100 Hospital Drive Box 609
Louisburg, NC 27549-2256
(919)496-5131

LUMBERTON

SOUTHEASTERN REGIONAL MEDICAL CENTER
300 W 27 St PO Box 1408
Lumberton, NC 28359-1408
(910)671-5000

MARION

MCDOWELL HOSPITAL
PO Box 730
Marion, NC 28752-0730
(828)659-5000

MATTHEWS

PRESBYTERIAN HOSPITAL MATTHEWS
1500 Matthews Township Parkway Box 3310
Matthews, NC 28105-4656
(704)384-6500

MCCAIN

MCCAIN CORRECTIONAL HOSPITAL
PO Box 5118
McCain, NC 28361-9798
(910)944-2351

MOCKSVILLE

DAVIE COUNTY HOSPITAL
223 Hospital St
Mocksville, NC 27028-2038
(336)751-8100

MONROE

UNION REGIONAL MEDICAL CENTER
600 Hospital Drive Box 5003
Monroe, NC 28112-6000
(704)283-3100

MOORESVILLE

LAKE NORMAN REGIONAL MEDICAL CENTER
630 East Center Avenue
Mooresville, NC 28115
(704)660-4000

MOREHEAD CITY

CARTERET GENERAL HOSPITAL
3500 Arendell St
Morehead City, NC 28557-2901
(252)808-6000

MORGANTON

BROUGHTON HOSPITAL
1000 S Sterling St
Morganton, NC 28655-3999
(828)433-2111

GRACE HOSPITAL
2201 S Sterling St
Morganton, NC 28655-4058
(828)580-5000

MOUNT AIRY

NORTHERN HOSPITAL OF SURRY COUNTY
830 Rockford St
Mount Airy, NC 27030-5365
(336)719-7000

MURPHY

DISTRICT MEMORIAL HOSPITAL OF SOUTHWEST NORTH CAROLINA
PO Box 770
Murphy, NC 28906-0770
(828)321-1200

MURPHY MEDICAL CENTER
4130 Us Highway 64 East
Murphy, NC 28906-6845
(828)837-8161

NAGS HEAD

OUTER BANKS HOSPITAL
4800 S Croatan Hwy
Nags Head, NC 27959-9704
(252)449-4500

NEW BERN

CRAVEN REGIONAL MEDICAL CENTER
2000 Neuse Boulevard
New Bern, NC 28560-3499
(252)633-8111

NORTH WILKESBORO

WILKES REGIONAL MEDICAL CENTER
1370 West D St
North Wilkesboro, NC 28659-3506
(336)651-8100

OXFORD

GRANVILLE MEDICAL CENTER
College St Box 947
Oxford, NC 27565-0947
(919)690-3000

PINEHURST

FIRSTHEALTH OF NORTH CAROLINA MOORE REGIONAL HOSPITAL
PO Box 3000
Pinehurst, NC 28374-3000
(910)215-1000

PLYMOUTH

WASHINGTON COUNTY HOSPITAL
PO Box 707
Plymouth, NC 27962-0707
(252)793-4135

RALEIGH

CENTRAL PRISON HOSPITAL
1300 Western Boulevard
Raleigh, NC 27606-2196
(919)733-0800

DOROTHEA DIX HOSPITAL
S Boylan Avenue
Raleigh, NC 27603
(919)733-5540

HOLLY HILL HOSPITAL
3019 Falstaff Road
Raleigh, NC 27610-1812
(919)250-7000

RALEIGH COMMUNITY HOSPITAL
3400 Wake Forest Road
Raleigh, NC 27609-7373
(919)954-3000

NORTH CAROLINA — Hospital Telephone Directory

REX HOSPITAL
4420 Lake Boone Trail
Raleigh, NC 27607-6599
(919)784-3100

WAKE COUNTY ALCOHOLISM TREATMENT CENTER
3000 Falstaff Road
Raleigh, NC 27610-1897
(919)250-1500

WAKE MEDICAL CENTER
3000 New Bern Avenue
Raleigh, NC 27610-1295
(919)350-8000

REIDSVILLE

ANNIE PENN MEMORIAL HOSPITAL
618 S Main St
Reidsville, NC 27320-5094
(336)634-1010

ROANOKE RAPIDS

HALIFAX REGIONAL MEDICAL CENTER
250 Smith Church Road
Roanoke Rapids, NC 27870-4928
(252)535-8011

ROCKINGHAM

RICHMOND MEMORIAL HOSPITAL
925 S Long Drive
Rockingham, NC 28379-4835
(910)417-3000

ROCKY MOUNT

LIFECARE HOSPITAL OF NORTH CAROLINA
1031 Noell Lane
Rocky Mount, NC 27804-1761
(252)451-2300

NASH GENERAL HOSPITAL
2460 Curtis Ellis Drive
Rocky Mount, NC 27804-2298
(252)443-8000

ROXBORO

PERSON COUNTY MEMORIAL HOSPITAL
615 Ridge Road
Roxboro, NC 27573-4629
(336)599-2121

RUTHERFORDTON

RUTHERFORD HOSPITAL
288 South Ridgecrest Avenue
Rutherfordton, NC 28139-2851
(828)286-5000

SALISBURY

ROWAN REGIONAL MEDICAL CENTER
612 Mocksville Avenue
Salisbury, NC 28144-2732
(704)210-5000

VA MEDICAL CENTER - BILL HEFNER
1601 Brenner Avenue
Salisbury, NC 28144-2515
(704)638-9000

SANFORD

CENTRAL CAROLINA HOSPITAL
1135 Carthage St
Sanford, NC 27330-4162
(919)774-2100

SCOTLAND NECK

OUR COMMUNITY HOSPITAL
921 Junior High School Road Box 405
Scotland Neck, NC 27874-0405
(252)826-4144

SEYMOUR JOHNSON AIR FORCE BASE

4TH MEDICAL GROUP, THOMAS KORITZ HOSPITAL
1050 Jabara Avenue
Seymour Johnson Air Force Base, NC 27531-2310
(919)722-1812

SHELBY

CLEVELAND REGIONAL MEDICAL CENTER
201 Grover St
Shelby, NC 28150-3940
(704)487-3000

SILER CITY

CHATHAM HOSPITAL
Third St And Ivey Avenue Box 649
Siler City, NC 27344-0649
(919)663-2113

SMITHFIELD

JOHNSTON MEMORIAL HOSPITAL
509 Brightleaf Blvd
Smithfield, NC 27577-4479
(919)934-8171

SOUTHPORT

J ARTHUR DOSHER MEMORIAL HOSPITAL
924 Howe St
Southport, NC 28461-3099
(910)457-3800

SPARTA

ALLEGHANY COUNTY MEMORIAL HOSPITAL
617 Doctors Street
Sparta, NC 28675
(336)372-5511

SPRUCE PINE

SPRUCE PINE COMMUNITY HOSPITAL
125 Hospital Drive
Spruce Pine, NC 28777-3035
(828)765-4201

STATESVILLE

DAVIS REGIONAL MEDICAL CENTER
218 Old Mocksbville Road PO Box 1823
Statesville, NC 28687-1823
(704)873-0281

IREDELL MEMORIAL HOSPITAL
557 Brookdale Drive PO Box 1828
Statesville, NC 28687-1828
(704)873-5661

SUPPLY

BRUNSWICK COMMUNITY HOSPITAL
1 Medical Center Drive PO Box 139
Supply, NC 28462-0139
(910)755-8121

SYLVA

HARRIS REGIONAL HOSPITAL
68 Hospital Road
Sylva, NC 28779-2722
(828)586-7000

TARBORO

HERITAGE HOSPITAL
111 Hospital Drive
Tarboro, NC 27886-2011
(252)641-7700

TAYLORSVILLE

ALEXANDER COUNTY HOSPITAL
326 Third St Sw
Taylorsville, NC 28681-3096
(828)632-4282

THOMASVILLE

THOMASVILLE MEDICAL CENTER
207 Old Lexington Rd
Thomasville, NC 27360-3419
(336)472-2000

TROY

FIRSTHEALTH MONTGOMERY MEMORIAL HOSPITAL
520 Allen St
Troy, NC 27371-2802
(910)572-1301

VALDESE

VALDESE GENERAL HOSPITAL
720 Malcolm Boulevard
Valdese, NC 28690
(828)874-2251

WADESBORO

ANSON COMMUNITY HOSPITAL
500 Morven Road
Wadesboro, NC 28170-2745
(704)694-5131

WASHINGTON

BEAUFORT COUNTY HOSPITAL
628 E 12th St
Washington, NC 27889-3409
(252)975-4100

WHITEVILLE

COLUMBUS COUNTY HOSPITAL
500 Jefferson St
Whiteville, NC 28472-3696
(910)642-8011

WILLIAMSTON

MARTIN GENERAL HOSPITAL
310 S Mccaskey Road PO Box 1128
Williamston, NC 27892-1128
(252)809-6179

WILMINGTON

CAPE FEAR MEMORIAL HOSPITAL
PO Box 9000
Wilmington, NC 28402-9000
(910)452-8100

NEW HANOVER REGIONAL MEDICAL CENTER
2131 S 17th St Box 9000
Wilmington, NC 28401-7483
(910)392-1498

WILMINGTON TREATMENT CENTER
2520 Troy Drive
Wilmington, NC 28401-7643
(910)762-2727

Hospital Telephone Directory — NORTH DAKOTA

WILSON

WILSON MEMORIAL HOSPITAL
1705 S Tarboro St
Wilson, NC 27893-3437
(252)399-8040

WINDSOR

BERTIE MEMORIAL HOSPITAL
401 Sterlingworth St
Windsor, NC 27983-1700
(252)794-6600

WINSTON-SALEM

AMOS COTTAGE REHABILITATION HOSPITAL
3325 Silas Creek Parkway
Winston-Salem, NC 27103-3013
(336)774-2400

FORSYTH MEDICAL CENTER
3333 Silas Creek Parkway
Winston-Salem, NC 27103-3013
(336)718-5000

MEDICAL PARK HOSPITAL
1950 S Hawthorne Road
Winston-Salem, NC 27103-3993
(336)718-0600

NORTH CAROLINA BAPTIST HOSPITAL
Medical Center Boulevard
Winston-Salem, NC 27157-0001
(336)716-2011

WAKE FOREST UNIVERSITY - BAPTIST BEHAVIORAL HEALTH CENTER
3637 Old Vineyard Road
Winston-Salem, NC 27104-4842
(336)794-3550

YADKINVILLE

HOOTS MEMORIAL HOSPITAL
625 W Main St Box 68
Yadkinville, NC 27055-7804
(336)679-2041

ZEBULON

WAKEMED ZEBULON/WENDELL
535 West Gannon Ave
Zebulon, NC 27597
(919)350-4700

NORTH DAKOTA

ASHLEY

ASHLEY MEDICAL CENTER
612 Center Avenue North
Ashley, ND 58413-7013
(701)288-3433

BELCOURT

PHS INDIAN HOSPITAL - BELCOURT
PO Box 160
Belcourt, ND 58316-0160
(701)477-6112

BISMARCK

MEDCENTER ONE
300 N 7th St
Bismarck, ND 58501-4400
(701)323-6000

SAINT ALEXIUS MEDICAL CENTER
900 E Broadway
Bismarck, ND 58501-4586
(701)530-7000

BOTTINEAU

SAINT ANDREWS HEALTH CENTER
316 Ohmer St
Bottineau, ND 58318-1097
(701)228-2255

BOWMAN

SOUTHWEST HEALTHCARE SERVICES
202 6th Avenue Sw
Bowman, ND 58623-4521
(701)523-5265

CANDO

TOWNER COUNTY MEDICAL CENTER
Highway 281 N Box 688
Cando, ND 58324-0688
(701)968-4411

CARRINGTON

CARRINGTON HEALTH CENTER
PO Box 461
Carrington, ND 58421-0461
(701)652-3141

CAVALIER

PEMBINA COUNTY MEMORIAL HOSPITAL
205 East 3rd Avenue Box M
Cavalier, ND 58220-4024
(701)265-8461

COOPERSTOWN

COOPERSTOWN MEDICAL CENTER
1200 Roberts Avenue Northeast
Cooperstown, ND 58425-7101
(701)797-2221

CROSBY

SAINT LUKES HOSPITAL
702 Sw 1st St Box 10
Crosby, ND 58730-0010
(701)965-6384

DEVILS LAKE

MERCY HOSPITAL
1031 7th St
Devils Lake, ND 58301-2719
(701)662-2131

DICKINSON

SAINT JOSEPHS HOSPITAL/HEALTH CENTER
30 West 7th St
Dickinson, ND 58601-4399
(701)264-4000

ELGIN

JACOBSON MEMORIAL HOSPITAL CARE CENTER
601 East St North
Elgin, ND 58533-7105
(701)584-2792

FARGO

CHILDRENS PSYCH/DBA PRAIRIE PSYCH CENTER
510 4th Street South
Fargo, ND 58103-1914
(701)232-3331

HEARTLAND HEALTH SYSTEM
1720 S University Drive
Fargo, ND 58103-4940
(701)280-4100

INNOVIS HOSPITAL
3000 32nd Avenue South
Fargo, ND 58103-6132
(701)364-8051

MERITCARE MEDICAL CENTER
720 4th St N
Fargo, ND 58122-4520
(701)234-6000

SCCI HOSPITAL
1720 University Drive South
Fargo, ND 58103-4940
(701)241-9099

VA MEDICAL CENTER - FARGO
2101 Elm St
Fargo, ND 58102-2417
(701)232-3241

FORT YATES

PHS INDIAN HOSPITAL - FORT YATES
Fort Yates
Fort Yates, ND 58538
(701)854-3831

GARRISON

GARRISON MEMORIAL HOSPITAL
407 3rd Avenue S E
Garrison, ND 58540-7235
(701)463-2275

GRAFTON

UNITY HOSPITAL
164 W 13th St
Grafton, ND 58237-1896
(701)352-1620

GRAND FORKS

ALTRU HEALTH INSTITUTE
1300 South Columbia Road
Grand Forks, ND 58201-4012
(701)780-2311

ALTRU HOSPITAL
1200 S Columbia Road
Grand Forks, ND 58201-4044
(701)780-5000

RICHARD P. STADTER PSYCHIATRIC CENTER
1451 44th Avenue South
Grand Forks, ND 58201-3407
(701)775-2500

GRAND FORKS AIR FORCE BAS

319TH MEDICAL GROUP
1599 J St
Grand Forks Air Force Bas, ND 58205-6306
(701)747-5325

HARVEY

SAINT ALOISIUS MEDICAL CENTER
325 East Brewster St
Harvey, ND 58341-1653
(701)324-4651

HAZEN

SAKAKAWEA MEDICAL CENTER
510 Eighth Avenue N E
Hazen, ND 58545-4600
(701)748-2225

HETTINGER

WEST RIVER REGIONAL MEDICAL CENTER
Route 2 Box 124 1000 Highway 12
Hettinger, ND 58639-7530
(701)567-4561

OHIO

Hospital Telephone Directory

HILLSBORO

HILLSBORO MEDICAL CENTER
12 3rd Street Southeast, PO Box 609
Hillsboro, ND 58045-0609
(701)436-4501

JAMESTOWN

JAMESTOWN HOSPITAL
419 5th Street N E
Jamestown, ND 58401-3360
(701)252-1050

NORTH DAKOTA STATE HOSPITAL
Box 476
Jamestown, ND 58402-0476
(701)253-3964

KENMARE

KENMARE COMMUNITY HOSPITAL
317 First Avenue N W
Kenmare, ND 58746-7104
(701)385-4296

LANGDON

CAVALIER COUNTY MEMORIAL HOSPITAL
909 Second St
Langdon, ND 58249-2407
(701)256-6100

LINTON

LINTON HOSPITAL
518 N Broadway
Linton, ND 58552-7308
(701)254-4511

LISBON

LISBON MEDICAL CENTER
905 Main St
Lisbon, ND 58054-4334
(701)683-5241

MANDAN

SCCI HOSPITAL - CENTRAL DAKOTAS
1000 18th Street Nw
Mandan, ND 58554-1612
(701)667-2000

MAYVILLE

UNION HOSPITAL
42 6th Avenue Sw
Mayville, ND 58257
(701)786-3800

MCVILLE

NELSON COUNTY HEALTH SYSTEM
Main St PO Box H
Mcville, ND 58254
(701)322-4328

MINOT

TRINITY HEALTH
Burdick Expressway At Main St
Minot, ND 58702
(701)857-5000

UNI-MED MEDICAL CENTER
Third St Se And Burdick Expy
Minot, ND 58701
(701)857-2000

MINOT AIR FORCE BASE

5TH MEDICAL GROUP
10 Missile Avenue
Minot Air Force Base, ND 58705-5024
(701)723-5103

NORTHWOOD

NORTHWOOD DEACONESS HEALTH
CENTER
4 N Park St
Northwood, ND 58267-4102
(701)587-6060

OAKES

OAKES COMMUNITY HOSPITAL
314 South 8th Street
Oakes, ND 58474-2099
(701)742-3291

PARK RIVER

FIRST CARE HEALTH CENTER
715 Vivian St
Park River, ND 58270
(701)284-7500

RICHARDTON

RICHARDTON HEALTH CENTER
212 Third Avenue W
Richardton, ND 58652-7103
(701)974-3304

ROLLA

PRESENTATION MEDICAL CENTER
213 Second Avenue Ne
Rolla, ND 58367-7153
(701)477-3161

RUGBY

HEART OF AMERICA MEDICAL CENTER
800 Main Street South
Rugby, ND 58368-2198
(701)776-5261

STANLEY

MOUNTRAIL COUNTY MEDICAL CENTER
502 Third St Se Box 399
Stanley, ND 58784-4023
(701)628-2424

TIOGA

TIOGA MEDICAL CENTER
810 N Welo St Box 159
Tioga, ND 58852-7157
(701)664-3305

TURTLE LAKE

COMMUNITY MEMORIAL HOSPITAL
220 5th Avenue
Turtle Lake, ND 58575-4005
(701)448-2331

VALLEY CITY

MERCY HOSPITAL
570 Chautauqua Boulevard
Valley City, ND 58072-3199
(701)845-6400

WATFORD CITY

MCKENZIE COUNTY MEMORIAL HOSPITAL
508 N Main PO Box 548
Watford City, ND 58854-0548
(701)842-3000

WILLISTON

MERCY MEDICAL CENTER
1301 15th Avenue W
Williston, ND 58801-3821
(701)774-7400

WISHEK

WISHEK COMMUNITY HOSPITAL
1007 4th Avenue S
Wishek, ND 58495-7527
(701)452-2326

OHIO

AKRON

AKRON GENERAL MEDICAL CENTER
400 Wabash Avenue
Akron, OH 44307-2463
(330)384-6000

CHILDRENS HOSPITAL MEDICAL CENTER
1 Perkins Square
Akron, OH 44308-1062
(330)543-1000

EDWIN SHAW HOSPITAL
1621 Flickinger Road
Akron, OH 44312-4495
(330)784-1271

SELECT SPECIALTY HOSPITAL - AKRON
400 Wabash Avenue
Akron, OH 44307-2433
(330)344-6910

SEMPERCARE HOSPITAL - AKRON
525 East Market Street
Akron, OH 44304-1619
(330)375-6500

SUMMA HEALTH - AKRON CITY HOSPITAL
525 East Market St
Akron, OH 44304-1698
(330)375-3000

SUMMA HEALTH - SAINT THOMAS
HOSPITAL
444 North Main Street
Akron, OH 44310-3110
(330)375-3000

ALLIANCE

ALLIANCE COMMUNITY HOSPITAL
264 East Rice Street
Alliance, OH 44601-4399
(330)829-4000

AMHERST

AMHERST HOSPITAL
254 Cleveland Avenue
Amherst, OH 44001-1699
(440)988-6000

ASHLAND

SAMARITAN REGIONAL HEALTH SYSTEM
1025 Center St
Ashland, OH 44805-4097
(419)289-0491

ASHTABULA

ASHTABULA COUNTY MEDICAL CENTER
PO Box 1400
Ashtabula, OH 44005-1400
(440)997-2262

ATHENS

APPALACHIAN BEHAVIORAL HEALTHCARE
100 Hospital Drive
Athens, OH 45701-2301
(740)594-5000

O BLENESS MEMORIAL HOSPITAL
Hospital Drive
Athens, OH 45701
(740)593-5551

Hospital Telephone Directory — OHIO

BARBERTON

BARBERTON CITIZENS HOSPITAL
155 5th Street Northeast
Barberton, OH 44203-3398
(330)745-1611

REGENCY HOSPITAL OF AKRON
155 Fifth St Ne
Barberton, OH 44203-3398
(330)861-2069

BARNESVILLE

BARNESVILLE HOSPITAL ASSOCIATION
639 West Main Street, PO Box 309
Barnesville, OH 43713-0309
(740)425-3941

BATAVIA

CLERMONT MERCY HOSPITAL
3000 Hospital Drive
Batavia, OH 45103-1998
(513)732-8200

BEDFORD

UNIVERSITY HOSPITAL-BEDFORD MEDICAL CENTER
44 Blaine St
Bedford, OH 44146-2709
(440)735-3900

BELLAIRE

BELMONT COMMUNITY HOSPITAL
4697 Harrison Street
Bellaire, OH 43906-1338
(740)671-1200

BELLEFONTAINE

MARY RUTAN HOSPITAL
205 Palmer Avenue
Bellefontaine, OH 43311-2298
(937)592-4015

BELLEVUE

BELLEVUE HOSPITAL
PO Box 297
Bellevue, OH 44811-0297
(419)483-4040

BLUFFTON

BLANCHARD VALLEY REGIONAL HEALTH CENTER - BLUFFTON
139 Garau St
Bluffton, OH 45817-1027
(419)358-9010

BOARDMAN

GREENBRIAR HOSPITAL FOR SPECIAL SERVICES
8064 South Avenue, Ste One
Boardman, OH 44512-6153
(330)965-6432

BOWLING GREEN

WOOD COUNTY HOSPITAL
950 W Wooster St
Bowling Green, OH 43402-2699
(419)354-8900

BRYAN

COMMUNITY HOSPITAL OF WILLIAMS COUNTY - BRYAN HOSPITAL
433 W High St
Bryan, OH 43506-1679
(419)636-1131

BUCYRUS

BUCYRUS COMMUNITY HOSPITAL
629 North Sandusky Avenue
Bucyrus, OH 44820-1821
(419)562-4677

CADIZ

HARRISON COMMUNITY HOSPITAL
951 East Market Street
Cadiz, OH 43907-9749
(740)942-4631

CAMBRIDGE

APPALACHIAN BEHAVIORAL HEALTHCARE
66737 Old Twenty-one Road
Cambridge, OH 43725-8987
(740)439-1371

SOUTHEASTERN OHIO REGIONAL MEDICAL CENTER
1341 North Clark Street
Cambridge, OH 43725-8911
(740)439-3561

CANTON

AULTMAN HOSPITAL
2600 Sixth Street Sw
Canton, OH 44710-1799
(330)452-9911

MERCY MEDICAL CENTER
1320 Mercy Drive Nw
Canton, OH 44708-2641
(330)489-1000

CHAGRIN FALLS

WINDSOR HOSPITAL
115 East Summit Avenue
Chagrin Falls, OH 44022-2750
(440)247-5300

CHARDON

HEATHER HILL HOSPITAL
12340 Bass Lake Road
Chardon, OH 44024-8327
(440)285-4040

UNIVERSITY HOSPITAL HEALTH SYSTEM GEAUGA REGIONAL HOSPITAL
13207 Ravenna Road
Chardon, OH 44024-7032
(440)269-6000

CHILLICOTHE

ADENA REGIONAL MEDICAL CENTER
272 Hospital Road
Chillicothe, OH 45601-9031
(740)779-7500

VA MEDICAL CENTER - CHILLICOTHE
17273 State Route 104
Chillicothe, OH 45601-8608
(740)773-1141

CINCINNATI

BETHESDA NORTH HOSPITALS
10500 Montgomery Road
Cincinnati, OH 45242-4415
(513)745-1111

CHILDRENS HOSPITAL MEDICAL CENTER
Elland And Bethesda Avenues
Cincinnati, OH 45229
(513)636-4200

CHRIST HOSPITAL
2139 Auburn Avenue
Cincinnati, OH 45219-2989
(513)585-2000

CONVALESCENT HOSPITAL FOR CHILDREN
3333 Burnet Avenue
Cincinnati, OH 45229-3026
(513)636-8778

DEACONESS HOSPITAL
311 Straight Street
Cincinnati, OH 45219-1099
(513)559-2100

DRAKE CENTER
151 Galbraith Road
Cincinnati, OH 45216
(513)948-2500

GOOD SAMARITAN HOSPITAL
375 Dixmth Avenue
Cincinnati, OH 45220-2489
(513)872-1400

JEWISH HOSPITAL KENWOOD
4777 E Galbraith Road
Cincinnati, OH 45236-2814
(513)686-3000

JEWISH HOSPITAL OF CINCINNATI
3200 Burnet Avenue
Cincinnati, OH 45229-3028
(513)686-3200

MERCY FRANCISCAN HOSPITAL-MOUNT AIRY
2446 Kipling Avenue
Cincinnati, OH 45239-6650
(513)853-5000

MERCY FRANCISCAN HOSPITAL-WESTERN HILLS CAMPUS
3131 Queen City Avenue
Cincinnati, OH 45238-2316
(513)389-5000

MERCY HOSPITAL ANDERSON
7500 State Road
Cincinnati, OH 45255-2492
(513)624-4500

SELECT SPECIALTY HOSPITAL - CINCINNATI
375 Dixmyth Avenue
Cincinnati, OH 45220-2475
(513)872-4444

SHRINERS HOSPITAL FOR CHILDREN
3229 Burnet Avenue
Cincinnati, OH 45229-3018
(513)872-6000

SUMMIT BEHAVIORAL HEALTHCARE
1101 Summit Road
Cincinnati, OH 45237-2621
(513)948-3600

UNIVERSITY HOSPITAL
234 Goodman Street
Cincinnati, OH 45267-1000
(513)584-1000

VA MEDICAL CENTER - CINCINNATI
3200 Vine St
Cincinnati, OH 45220-2213
(513)861-3100

CIRCLEVILLE

BERGER HOSPITAL
600 North Pickaway St
Circleville, OH 43113-2409
(740)474-2126

CLEVELAND

CLEVELAND CLINIC CHILDREN'S HOSPITAL FOR REHABILITATION
2801 Martin Luther King Jr Drive
Cleveland, OH 44104-3815
(216)721-5400

CLEVELAND CLINIC HOSPITAL
9500 Euclid Avenue
Cleveland, OH 44195-0002
(216)444-2200

OHIO
Hospital Telephone Directory

DEACONESS HOSPITAL
4229 Pearl Road
Cleveland, OH 44109-4272
(216)459-6300

FAIRVIEW GENERAL HOSPITAL
18101 Lorain Avenue
Cleveland, OH 44111-5656
(216)476-7000

GRACE HOSPITAL
2307 W 14th St
Cleveland, OH 44113-3698
(216)687-1500

HURON HOSPITAL
13951 Terrace Road
Cleveland, OH 44112-4399
(216)761-3300

KINDRED HOSPITAL CLEVELAND
2351 East 22nd Street, 7th Floor
Cleveland, OH 44115-3111
(216)363-2671

LAKEWOOD HOSPITAL
14519 Detroit Ave
Cleveland, OH 44107-4383
(216)521-4200

LUTHERAN HOSPITAL
1730 W 25th St
Cleveland, OH 44113-3170
(216)696-4300

METROHEALTH MEDICAL CENTER
2500 Metrohealth Drive
Cleveland, OH 44109-1998
(216)778-7800

NORTHCOAST BEHAVIORAL HEALTHCARE
1708 Southpoint Drive
Cleveland, OH 44109-1911
(216)787-0500

RAINBOW BABIES AND CHILDRENS
HOSPITAL
2101 Adelbert Road
Cleveland, OH 44106-2624
(216)844-1000

SAINT MICHAEL HOSPITAL
5163 Broadway
Cleveland, OH 44127-1532
(216)429-8000

SAINT VINCENT CHARITY HOSPITAL
2351 E 22nd St
Cleveland, OH 44115-3197
(216)861-6200

UNIVERSITY HOSPITALS-CLEVELAND
11100 Euclid Avenue
Cleveland, OH 44106-5000
(216)844-1000

VA MEDICAL CENTER - LOUIS STOKES
10701 East Boulevard
Cleveland, OH 44106-1782
(216)791-3800

COLDWATER

MERCER COUNTY COMMUNITY HOSPITAL
800 West Main Street
Coldwater, OH 45828-1613
(419)678-2341

COLUMBUS

ARTHUR G JAMES CANCER HOSPITAL AND
RESEARCH INSTITUTE
300 W Tenth Avenue
Columbus, OH 43210-1280
(614)293-5485

CHILDRENS HOSPITAL
700 Childrens Drive
Columbus, OH 43205-2696
(614)722-2000

DOCTORS HOSPITAL WEST/OHIO HEALTH
5100 West Broad St
Columbus, OH 43228-1672
(614)297-4000

DOCTORS HOSPITAL/OHIO HEALTH
1087 Dennison Avenue
Columbus, OH 43201-3496
(614)297-4000

GRANT MEDICAL CENTER
111 S Grant Avenue
Columbus, OH 43215-1898
(614)566-9000

MOUNT CARMEL EAST HOSPITAL
6001 E Broad St
Columbus, OH 43213-1570
(614)234-6000

MOUNT CARMEL MEDICAL CENTER
793 W State St
Columbus, OH 43222-1560
(614)234-5000

OHIO STATE UNIVERSITY MEDICAL CENTER
410 W 10th Avenue
Columbus, OH 43210-1228
(614)293-8000

OSU HOSPITAL - EAST
1492 East Broad Street
Columbus, OH 43205-1500
(614)257-3000

PARKSIDE BEHAVIORAL HEALTHCARE
349 Olde Ridenour Road
Columbus, OH 43230-2528
(614)471-2552

RIVERSIDE METHODIST HOSPITAL
3535 Olentangy River Road
Columbus, OH 43214-3998
(614)566-5000

SELECT SPECIALTY HOSPITAL - COLUMBUS
410 West 10th Avenue, 11th Floor, Doran Hall
Columbus, OH 43210-1240
(614)293-6931

SELECT SPECIALTY HOSPITAL - COLUMBUS
1492 E Broad St, 7th Floor Tower
Columbus, OH 43205-1546
(614)252-4440

SELECT SPECIALTY HOSPITAL -
COLUMBUS/GRANT
111 South Grant Avenue, Fifth Floor
Columbus, OH 43215-4701
(614)566-8211

SELECT SPECIALTY HOSPITAL -
COLUMBUS/RIVERSIDE
3535 Olentangy River Road, 5 South
Columbus, OH 43214-3908
(614)566-5017

TWIN VALLEY PSYCH SYSTEM-COLUMBUS
CAMPUS
1960 W Broad St
Columbus, OH 43223-1206
(614)752-0333

CONNEAUT

BROWN MEMORIAL HOSPITAL
158 W Main Road
Conneaut, OH 44030-2039
(440)593-1131

COSHOCTON

COSHOCTON COUNTY MEMORIAL
HOSPITAL
1460 Orange Street
Coshocton, OH 43812-2229
(740)622-6411

CRESTLINE

MEDICAL CENTRAL CRESTLINE HOSPITAL
700 Columbus St
Crestline, OH 44827
(419)683-1212

CUYAHOGA FALLS

CUYAHOGA FALLS GENERAL HOSPITAL
1900 23rd St
Cuyahoga Falls, OH 44223-1497
(330)971-7000

DAYTON

CHILDRENS MEDICAL CENTER
One Childrens Plaza
Dayton, OH 45404-1815
(937)641-3000

DAYTON HEART HOSPITAL
707 South Edwin C Moses Blvd
Dayton, OH 45408-1462
(937)221-8000

FRANCISCAN MEDICAL CENTER-DAYTON
CAMPUS
One Franciscan Way
Dayton, OH 45408-1470
(937)229-6035

GOOD SAMARITAN HOSPITAL AND HEALTH
CENTER
2222 Philadelphia Drive
Dayton, OH 45406-1891
(937)278-2612

GRANDVIEW HOSPITAL AND MEDICAL
CENTER
405 Grand Avenue
Dayton, OH 45405-4796
(937)226-3200

MIAMI VALLEY HOSPITAL
One Wyoming Street
Dayton, OH 45409-2711
(937)208-8000

SOUTHVIEW HOSPITAL
1997 Miamisburg Centerville Road
Dayton, OH 45459-3800
(937)439-6000

TWIN VALLEY PSYCH SYSTEM-DAYTON
CAMPUS
2611 Wayne Avenue
Dayton, OH 45420-1833
(937)258-0440

VA MEDICAL CENTER - DAYTON
4100 W 3rd St
Dayton, OH 45428-9000
(937)268-6511

DEFIANCE

DEFIANCE HOSPITAL
1200 Ralston Ave
Defiance, OH 43512-1396
(419)783-6955

DELAWARE

GRADY MEMORIAL HOSPITAL
561 W Central Avenue
Delaware, OH 43015-1489
(740)369-8711

DENNISON

TWIN CITY HOSPITAL
819 North First Street
Dennison, OH 44621-1098
(740)922-2800

Hospital Telephone Directory — OHIO

DOVER
UNION HOSPITAL
659 Boulevard
Dover, OH 44622-2077
(330)343-3311

EAST LIVERPOOL
EAST LIVERPOOL CITY HOSPITAL
425 W 5th Street
East Liverpool, OH 43920-2498
(330)385-7200

ELYRIA
EMH REGIONAL MEDICAL CENTER
630 East River Street
Elyria, OH 44035-5902
(440)329-7500

EUCLID
EUCLID HOSPITAL
18901 Lake Shore Boulevard
Euclid, OH 44119-1090
(216)531-9000

FAIRFIELD
MERCY HOSPITAL OF FAIRFIELD
3000 Mack Road
Fairfield, OH 45014-5399
(513)870-7000

FINDLAY
BLANCHARD VALLEY REGIONAL HEALTH CENTER - FINDLAY
145 W Wallace
Findlay, OH 45840-1299
(419)423-4500

FOSTORIA
FOSTORIA CITY HOSPITAL
PO Box 907
Fostoria, OH 44830-0907
(419)435-7734

FREMONT
MEMORIAL HOSPITAL
715 South Taft Avenue
Fremont, OH 43420-3296
(419)332-7321

GALION
GALION COMMUNITY HOSPITAL
Portland Way South
Galion, OH 44833-2399
(419)468-4841

GALLIPOLIS
HOLZER MEDICAL CENTER
100 Jackson Pike
Gallipolis, OH 45631-1563
(740)446-5000

VETERANS MEMORIAL HOSPITAL OF MEIGS CO
100 Jackson Pike
Gallipolis, OH 45631-1560
(740)992-2104

GARFIELD HEIGHTS
MARYMOUNT HOSPITAL
12300 Mccracken Road
Garfield Heights, OH 44125-2975
(216)581-0500

GENEVA
UHHS MEMORIAL HOSPITAL OF GENEVA
870 West Main Street
Geneva, OH 44041-1219
(440)466-1141

GEORGETOWN
BROWN COUNTY GENERAL HOSPITAL
Home Street
Georgetown, OH 45121-1449
(937)378-6121

GREEN SPRINGS
SAINT FRANCIS HEALTHCARE CENTER
401 N Broadway
Green Springs, OH 44836-9638
(419)639-2626

GREENFIELD
GREENFIELD AREA MEDICAL CENTER
550 Mirabeau St
Greenfield, OH 45123-1617
(937)981-9400

GREENVILLE
WAYNE HOSPITAL
835 Sweitzer St
Greenville, OH 45331-1077
(937)548-1141

GROVEPORT
BARIATIC CARE CENTER OF OHIO
3964 Hamilton Square Boulevard
Groveport, OH 43125-9119
(614)834-6800

HAMILTON
FORT HAMILTON HOSPITAL
630 Eaton Avenue
Hamilton, OH 45013-2767
(513)867-2000

HICKSVILLE
COMMUNITY MEMORIAL HOSPITAL
208 N Columbus St
Hicksville, OH 43526-1299
(419)542-6692

HILLIARD
GLENMONT
4599 Avery Road
Hilliard, OH 43026-9786
(614)876-0084

HILLSBORO
HIGHLAND DISTRICT HOSPITAL
1275 N High St
Hillsboro, OH 45133-5200
(937)393-6100

JACKSON
HOLZER MEDICAL CENTER - JACKSON
500 Burlington Road
Jackson, OH 45640-9360
(740)288-4625

KENTON
HARDIN MEMORIAL HOSPITAL
921 E Franklin Street
Kenton, OH 43326-2099
(419)673-0761

KETTERING
KETTERING HOSPITAL AND MEDICAL CENTER
3535 Southern Boulevard
Kettering, OH 45429-1298
(937)298-4331

LANCASTER
FAIRFIELD MEDICAL CENTER
401 N Ewing St
Lancaster, OH 43130-3371
(740)687-8000

LIMA
LIMA MEMORIAL HOSPITAL
1001 Bellefontaine Avenue
Lima, OH 45804-2899
(419)228-3335

OAKWOOD CORRECTIONAL FACILITY
3200 N West St
Lima, OH 45801-2048
(419)225-8052

SAINT RITAS MEDICAL CENTER
730 West Market Street
Lima, OH 45801-4667
(419)227-3361

SCCI HOSPITAL - LIMA
730 West Market Street, 6th Floor
Lima, OH 45801-4667
(419)224-1888

LODI
LODI COMMUNITY HOSPITAL
225 Elyria St
Lodi, OH 44254-1096
(330)948-1222

LOGAN
HOCKING VALLEY COMMUNITY HOSPITAL
State Route 664n Box966
Logan, OH 43138
(740)385-5631

LONDON
MADISON COUNTY HOSPITAL
210 North Main Street
London, OH 43140-2126
(740)852-1372

LORAIN
COMMUNITY HEALTH PARTNERS - EAST
205 West 20th St
Lorain, OH 44052-3779
(440)960-4000

COMMUNITY HEALTH PARTNERS OF OHIO
3700 Kolbe Road
Lorain, OH 44053-1611
(440)960-4000

SPECIALTY HOSPITAL OF LORAIN
205 West 20th Street, Ste 200
Lorain, OH 44052-3779
(440)204-3500

MANSFIELD
MEDCENTRAL MANSFIELD HOSPITAL
335 Glessner Avenue
Mansfield, OH 44903-2269
(419)526-8000

SCCI HOSPITAL - MANSFIELD
335 Glessner Avenue, 5th Floor
Mansfield, OH 44903-2269
(419)526-0777

OHIO — Hospital Telephone Directory

MARIETTA

MARIETTA MEMORIAL HOSPITAL
401 Matthew Street
Marietta, OH 45750-1699
(740)374-1400

SELBY GENERAL HOSPITAL
1106 Colegate Drive
Marietta, OH 45750-1399
(740)373-0582

MARION

MARION GENERAL HOSPITAL
Mckinley Park Drive
Marion, OH 43302
(740)383-8400

MEDICAL CENTER HOSPITAL
1050 Delaware Avenue
Marion, OH 43302-6482
(740)383-8000

MARTINS FERRY

EAST OHIO REGIONAL HOSPITAL
90 North 4th St
Martins Ferry, OH 43935-1669
(740)633-1100

MARYSVILLE

MEMORIAL HOSPITAL OF UNION COUNTY
500 London Avenue
Marysville, OH 43040-1594
(937)644-6115

MASSILLON

DOCTORS HOSPITAL OF STARK COUNTY
400 Austin Avenue Nw
Massillon, OH 44646-3598
(330)837-7200

HEARTLAND BEHAVIORAL HEALTHCARE
3000 Erie Sw, PO Box 540
Massillon, OH 44648-0540
(330)833-3135

MASSILLON COMMUNITY HOSPITAL
875 Eighth Street Ne
Massillon, OH 44646-8599
(330)832-8761

MAUMEE

FOCUS HEALTH CARE OF OHIO
1725 Timber Line Road
Maumee, OH 43537-4015
(419)891-9333

SAINT LUKES HOSPITAL
5901 Monclova Road
Maumee, OH 43537-1899
(419)893-5911

MAYFIELD HEIGHTS

HILLCREST HOSPITAL
6780 Mayfield Road
Mayfield Heights, OH 44124-2294
(440)449-4500

MEDINA

MEDINA GENERAL HOSPITAL
990 E Washington St
Medina, OH 44256-2167
(330)725-1000

MIAMISBURG

LIFECARE HOSPITAL - DAYTON
2150 Leiter Road
Miamisburg, OH 45342-3698
(937)384-8300

SYCAMORE HOSPITAL/MEDICAL CENTER
2150 Leiter Road
Miamisburg, OH 45342-3698
(937)866-0551

MIDDLEBURG HEIGHTS

SOUTHWEST GENERAL HEALTH CENTER
18697 Bagley Road
Middleburg Heights, OH 44130-3497
(440)816-8000

MIDDLETOWN

MIDDLETOWN REGIONAL HOSPITAL
105 Mcknight Drive
Middletown, OH 45044-4898
(513)424-2111

MILLERSBURG

POMERENE MEMORIAL HOSPITAL
981 Wooster Road
Millersburg, OH 44654-1536
(330)674-1015

MONTPELIER

COMMUNITY HOSPITAL-WILLIAMS COUNTY - MONTPELIER HOSPITAL
909 E Snyder Avenue
Montpelier, OH 43543-1251
(419)485-3154

MOUNT GILEAD

MORROW COUNTY HOSPITAL HOME HEALTH
651 W Marion Road
Mount Gilead, OH 43338-1096
(419)946-5015

MOUNT VERNON

KNOX COMMUNITY HOSPITAL
1330 Coshocton Road
Mount Vernon, OH 43050-1495
(740)393-9000

NAPOLEON

HENRY COUNTY HOSPITAL
11-600 State Road 424
Napoleon, OH 43545
(419)592-4015

NELSONVILLE

DOCTORS HOSPITAL OF NELSONVILLE
1950 Mount Saint Mary Drive
Nelsonville, OH 45764-1280
(740)753-1931

NEWARK

LICKING MEMORIAL HOSPITAL
1320 W Main St
Newark, OH 43055-3699
(740)348-4000

SHEPHERD HILL HOSPITAL
1320 W Main St
Newark, OH 43055-1822
(740)348-4870

NORTHFIELD

NORTHCOAST BEHAVIORAL HEALTHCARE - NORTHFIELD
1756 Sagamore Road, PO Box 305
Northfield, OH 44067-1086
(330)467-7131

NORWALK

FISHER TITUS MEMORIAL HOSPITAL
272 Benedict Avenue
Norwalk, OH 44857-2399
(419)668-8101

OBERLIN

ALLEN MEDICAL CENTER
200 W Lorain St
Oberlin, OH 44074-1026
(440)775-1211

OREGON

BAY PARK COMMUNITY HOSPITAL
2801 Bay Park Drive
Oregon, OH 43616-4925
(419)690-7900

SAINT CHARLES MERCY HOSPITAL
2600 Navarre Avenue
Oregon, OH 43616-3297
(419)696-7200

ORRVILLE

DUNLAP MEMORIAL HOSPITAL
832 South Main Street
Orrville, OH 44667-2208
(330)682-3010

OXFORD

MCCULLOUGH-HYDE MEMORIAL HOSPITAL
110 North Poplar Street
Oxford, OH 45056-1204
(513)523-2111

PAINESVILLE

LAKE HOSPITAL SYSTEM
10 East Washington St
Painesville, OH 44077-3472
(440)354-2400

PARMA

PARMA COMMUNITY GENERAL HOSPITAL
7007 Powers Boulevard
Parma, OH 44129-5495
(440)743-3000

PAULDING

PAULDING COUNTY HOSPITAL
11558 Sr 111
Paulding, OH 45879
(419)399-4080

PORT CLINTON

H B MAGRUDER MEMORIAL HOSPITAL
615 Fulton St
Port Clinton, OH 43452-2097
(419)734-3131

PORTSMOUTH

SOUTHERN OHIO MEDICAL CENTER
1805 27th Street
Portsmouth, OH 45662-2640
(740)354-5000

PROCTORVILLE

THREE GABLES SURGERY CENTER
5897 State Road 7
Proctorville, OH 45669
(740)886-9911

Hospital Telephone Directory — OHIO

RAVENNA
ROBINSON MEMORIAL HOSPITAL
6847 N Chestnut
Ravenna, OH 44266-3999
(330)297-0811

RICHMOND HEIGHTS
UNIVERSITY HOSPITAL - RICHMOND HEIGHTS
27100 Chardon Road
Richmond Heights, OH 44143-1192
(440)585-6500

ROCK CREEK
GLENBEIGH HOSPITAL OF ROCK CREEK
2863 State Route 45 PO Box 298
Rock Creek, OH 44084-0298
(440)563-3400

SAINT CLAIRSVILLE
FOX RUN HOSPITAL
67670 Traco Drive
Saint Clairsville, OH 43950-9375
(740)695-2131

SAINT MARYS
JOINT TOWNSHIP DISTRICT MEMORIAL HOSPITAL
200 Saint Clair Street
Saint Marys, OH 45885-2494
(419)394-3387

SALEM
SALEM COMMUNITY HOSPITAL
1995 East State Street
Salem, OH 44460-2400
(330)332-1551

SANDUSKY
FIRELANDS REGIONAL MEDICAL CENTER
1101 Decator St
Sandusky, OH 44870-3335
(419)626-7400

FIRELANDS REGIONAL MEDICAL CENTER - SOUTH
1912 South Hayes Avenue
Sandusky, OH 44870-4736
(419)621-7000

SHELBY
SHELBY HOSPITAL
20 Morris Road Box 608
Shelby, OH 44875-1163
(419)342-5015

SIDNEY
WILSON MEMORIAL HOSPITAL
915 W Michigan St
Sidney, OH 45365-2491
(937)498-2311

SPRINGFIELD
COMMUNITY HOSPITAL OF SPRINGFIELD
2615 East High Street
Springfield, OH 45505-1494
(937)325-0531

MENTAL HEALTH SERVICE - CLARK COUNTY
1345 Fountain Boulevard
Springfield, OH 45504-1422
(937)399-9500

MERCY MEDICAL CENTER OF SPRINGFIELD
1343 Fountain Boulevard
Springfield, OH 45504-1499
(937)390-5000

STEUBENVILLE
TRINITY MEDICAL CENTER EAST
380 Summit Avenue
Steubenville, OH 43952-2699
(740)283-7000

TRINITY MEDICAL CENTER WEST
4000 Johnson Road
Steubenville, OH 43952-2300
(740)264-8000

SYLVANIA
FLOWER HOSPITAL
5200 Harroun Road
Sylvania, OH 43560-2196
(419)824-1444

TIFFIN
MERCY HOSPITAL OF TIFFIN
485 W Market St
Tiffin, OH 44883-2673
(419)448-3133

TOLEDO
MEDICAL COLLEGE HOSPITAL OF OHIO-TOLEDO
3000 Arlington Avenue
Toledo, OH 43614-2598
(419)383-4000

MERCY CHILDREN'S HOSPITAL
2213 Cherry Street
Toledo, OH 43608-2603
(419)251-8000

NORTHCOAST BEHAVIORAL HEALTH CARE SYSTEM
930 S Detroit Avenue
Toledo, OH 43614-2701
(419)381-1881

RIVERSIDE MERCY HOSPITAL
3404 W Sylvania Ave
Toledo, OH 43623-4467
(419)729-6000

SAINT ANNE MERCY HOSPITAL
3404 Sylvania Avenue
Toledo, OH 43623-4480
(419)407-2663

SAINT VINCENTS MERCY MEDICAL CENTER
2213 Cherry St
Toledo, OH 43608-2691
(419)251-3232

TOLEDO CHILDREN'S HOSPITAL
2142 North Cove Boulevard
Toledo, OH 43606-3896
(419)291-4000

TOLEDO HOSPITAL
2142 North Cove Boulevard
Toledo, OH 43606-3896
(419)291-4000

TROY
DETTMER HOSPITAL
3130 N Dixie Highway
Troy, OH 45373-1337
(937)440-7500

UPPER VALLEY MEDICAL CENTER
3130 N Dixie Hwy
Troy, OH 45373-1300
(937)440-4000

UPPER SANDUSKY
WYANDOT MEMORIAL HOSPITAL
885 N Sandusky Avenue
Upper Sandusky, OH 43351-1098
(419)294-4991

URBANA
MERCY MEMORIAL HOSPITAL
904 Scioto Avenue
Urbana, OH 43078-2200
(937)653-5231

VAN WERT
VAN WERT COUNTY HOSPITAL
1250 S Washington Street
Van Wert, OH 45891-2599
(419)238-2390

WADSWORTH
WADSWORTH RITTMAN HOSPITAL
195 Wadsworth Road
Wadsworth, OH 44281-9505
(330)334-1504

WARREN
HILLSIDE REHAB HOSPITAL
8747 Squires Lane Ne
Warren, OH 44484-1697
(330)841-3700

SAINT JOSEPHS HEALTH CENTER
667 Eastland Avenue Se
Warren, OH 44484-4531
(330)841-4000

TRUMBULL MEMORIAL HOSPITAL
1350 East Market Street
Warren, OH 44483-6628
(330)841-9011

WARRENSVILLE HEIGHTS
SOUTH POINTE HOSPITAL
4110 Warrensville Center Road
Warrensville Heights, OH 44122-7099
(216)491-6000

WASHINGTON COURT HOUSE
FAYETTE COUNTY MEMORIAL HOSPITAL
1430 Columbus Road
Washington Court House, OH 43160-1791
(740)335-1210

WASHINGTON TOWNSHIP
KETTERING YOUTH SERVICES
3550 Lamme Road
Washington Township, OH 45439
(937)299-9511

WAUSEON
FULTON COUNTY HEALTH CENTER
725 S Shoop Avenue
Wauseon, OH 43567-1701
(419)335-2015

WAVERLY
PIKE COMMUNITY HOSPITAL
Dawn Lane
Waverly, OH 45690
(740)947-2186

WEST UNION
ADAMS COUNTY HOSPITAL
210 North Wilson Drive
West Union, OH 45693-1574
(937)544-5571

OKLAHOMA

Hospital Telephone Directory

WESTERVILLE

SAINT ANNS HOSPITAL OF COLUMBUS
500 South Cleveland Avenue
Westerville, OH 43081-8998
(614)898-4000

WESTLAKE

SAINT JOHN WEST SHORE HOSPITAL
29000 Center Ridge
Westlake, OH 44145-5293
(440)835-8000

WILLARD

MERCY HOSPITAL-WILLARD
110 E Howard St
Willard, OH 44890-1611
(419)964-5000

WILLOUGHBY

UNIVERSITY HOSPITAL - LAURELWOOD
35900 Euclid Avenue
Willoughby, OH 44094-4623
(440)953-3000

WILMINGTON

CLINTON MEMORIAL HOSPITAL
610 West Main Street
Wilmington, OH 45177-2194
(937)382-6611

WOOSTER

WOOSTER COMMUNITY HOSPITAL
1761 Beall Avenue
Wooster, OH 44691-2399
(330)263-8100

WORTHINGTON

OSU AND HARDING BEHAVIORAL
HEALTHCARE
445 East Granville Road
Worthington, OH 43085-3192
(614)293-9450

WRIGHT-PATTERSON AIR FORCE BASE

74TH MEDICAL GROUP
4881 Sugar Maple Drive
Wright-Patterson Air Force Base, OH 45433-5546
(937)257-9133

XENIA

GREENE MEMORIAL HOSPITAL
1141 N Monroe Drive
Xenia, OH 45385-1600
(937)372-8011

YOUNGSTOWN

BELMONT PINES HOSPITAL
615 Churchill - Hubbard Road
Youngstown, OH 44505-1332
(330)759-2700

SAINT ELIZABETH HEALTH CENTER
1044 Belmont Avenue
Youngstown, OH 44504-1096
(330)746-7211

SELECT SPECIALTY HOSPITAL -
YOUNGSTOWN
1044 Belmont Avenue
Youngstown, OH 44504-1006
(330)480-2349

SPECIALTY HOSPITAL OF MAHONING
VALLEY
345 Oak Hill Avenue, Suite 210
Youngstown, OH 44502-1454
(330)480-1200

TOD HOSPITAL FOR CHILDREN
500 Gypsy Lane
Youngstown, OH 44504-1315
(330)747-6700

WESTERN RESERVE CARE SYSTEM
500 Gypsy Lane
Youngstown, OH 44504-1315
(330)747-1444

ZANESVILLE

GENESIS HEALTHCARE SYSTEM -
BETHESDA HOSPITAL
2951 Maple Avenue
Zanesville, OH 43701-1465
(740)454-4000

GOOD SAMARITAN MEDICAL CENTER
800 Forest Avenue
Zanesville, OH 43701-2881
(740)454-5000

OKLAHOMA

ADA

PHS/IHS CARL ALBERT INDIAN HOSPITAL
1001 North Country Club Road
Ada, OK 74820-2599
(580)436-3980

ROLLING HILLS HOSPITAL
1000 Rolling Hills Lane
Ada, OK 74820-9415
(580)436-3600

VALLEY VIEW REGIONAL HOSPITAL
430 North Monta Vista
Ada, OK 74820-4657
(580)332-2323

ALTUS

JACKSON COUNTY MEMORIAL HOSPITAL
1200 East Pecan, PO Box
Altus, OK 73521-6141
(580)482-4781

ALTUS AIR FORCE BASE

97TH MEDICAL GROUP
301 North First St
Altus Air Force Base, OK 73523-5004
(580)481-5385

ALVA

SHARE MEDICAL CENTER
800 Share Drive
Alva, OK 73717-3699
(580)327-2800

ANADARKO

ANADARKO MUNICIPAL HOSPITAL
1002 East Central Boulevard
Anadarko, OK 73005-4496
(405)247-2551

ANTLERS

PUSHMATAHA COUNTY-TOWNN OF
ANTLERS HOSPITAL AUTHORITY
510 East Main Street, PO Box 518
Antlers, OK 74523-0518
(580)298-3342

ARDMORE

MERCY MEMORIAL HEALTH CENTER
1011 And 1012 14th Avenue, Northwest
Ardmore, OK 73401
(580)223-5400

ATOKA

ATOKA MEMORIAL HOSPITAL
1501 South Virginia Avenue
Atoka, OK 74525-3298
(580)889-3333

BARTLESVILLE

JANE PHILLIPS MEDICAL CENTER
3500 East Frank Phillips Boulevard
Bartlesville, OK 74006-2464
(918)333-7200

BEAVER

BEAVER COUNTY MEMORIAL HOSPITAL
212 East 8th Street, PO Box 640
Beaver, OK 73932-0640
(580)625-4551

BETHANY

CHILDREN'S CENTER
6800 Northwest 39th Expressway
Bethany, OK 73008-2513
(405)789-6711

BLACKWELL

INTEGRIS BLACKWELL REGIONAL
HOSPITAL
710 South 13th Street
Blackwell, OK 74631-3700
(580)363-2311

BOISE CITY

CIMARRON MEMORIAL HOSPITAL
100 South Ellis, PO Box 1059
Boise City, OK 73933-1059
(580)544-2501

BRISTOW

BRISTOW MEMORIAL HOSPITAL
Spruce And 7th Streets, PO Box 780
Bristow, OK 74010-0780
(918)367-2215

BROKEN ARROW

OKLAHOMA NEURORESTORATION CENTER
3000 South Elm Place
Broken Arrow, OK 74012-7917
(918)449-4090

SAINT FRANCIS HOSPITAL AT BROKEN
ARROW
3000 South Elm Place
Broken Arrow, OK 74012-7917
(918)455-3535

BUFFALO

HARPER COUNTY COMMUNITY HOSPITAL
U S Highway 64 North, PO Box 60
Buffalo, OK 73834-0060
(580)735-2555

CARNEGIE

CARNEGIE TRI COUNTY MUNICIPAL
HOSPITAL
102 North Broadway, PO Box 97
Carnegie, OK 73015-0097
(580)654-1050

Hospital Telephone Directory — OKLAHOMA

CHEYENNE
ROGER MILLS MEMORIAL HOSPITAL
501 South L L Males Avenue, PO Box 219
Cheyenne, OK 73628-0219
(580)497-3336

CHICKASHA
GRADY MEMORIAL HOSPITAL
2220 Iowa Street
Chickasha, OK 73018-2738
(405)224-2300

CLAREMORE
CLAREMORE REGIONAL HOSPITAL
1201 North Muskogee Street
Claremore, OK 74017
(918)341-2556

PHS/IHS INDIAN HOSPITAL - CLAREMORE
West Will Rogers and Moore
Claremore, OK 74017
(918)342-6200

CLEVELAND
CLEVELAND AREA HOSPITAL AUTHORITY
1401 West Pawnee
Cleveland, OK 74020-3019
(918)358-2501

CLINTON
INTEGRIS CLINTON REGIONAL HOSPITAL
100 North 30th Street, PO Box 1569
Clinton, OK 73601-1569
(580)323-2363

PHS INDIAN HOSPITAL - CLINTON
Route 1 Box 3060
Clinton, OK 73601-9303
(580)323-2884

COALGATE
MARY HURLEY HEALTH CENTER
PO Box 326
Coalgate, OK 74538-0326
(580)927-2327

CORDELL
CORDELL MEMORIAL HOSPITAL
1220 North Glenn English Street
Cordell, OK 73632-2099
(580)832-3339

CUSHING
CUSHING MUNICIPAL HOSPITAL
1027 East Cherry Street, PO Box 1409
Cushing, OK 74023-1409
(918)225-2915

DUNCAN
DUNCAN REGIONAL HOSPITAL
1407 Whisenant Drive, PO Box 2000
Duncan, OK 73534-2000
(580)252-5300

DURANT
MEDICAL CENTER OF SOUTHEASTERN
OKLAHOMA
1800 University Boulevard, PO Box 1207
Durant, OK 74702-1207
(580)924-3080

EDMOND
EDMOND HOSPITAL
1 South Bryant
Edmond, OK 73034-6309
(405)341-6100

INTEGRATED SPECIALTY HOSPITAL
1100 E 9th St
Edmond, OK 73034-5705
(405)341-8150

RENAISSANCE WOMENS HOSPITAL OF
EDMOND
1800 S Renaissance Boulevard
Edmond, OK 73013-3023
(405)359-9800

EL RENO
PARK VIEW HOSPITAL
2115 Park View Drive, PO Box 129
El Reno, OK 73036-0129
(405)262-2640

ELK CITY
GREAT PLAINS REGIONAL MEDICAL
CENTER
1705 West 2nd Street, PO Box 2339
Elk City, OK 73648-2339
(580)225-2511

ENID
INTEGRIS BASS BAPTIST HEALTH CENTER
600 South Monroe, 401 South 3rd Street
Enid, OK 73701
(580)233-2300

INTEGRIS BASS BEHAVIORAL HEALTH
SYSTEM
2216 S Van Buren St
Enid, OK 73703-8217
(580)234-2220

SAINT MARYS MERCY HOSPITAL
305 South 5th Street, PO Box 232
Enid, OK 73702-0232
(405)233-6100

EUFAULA
COMMUNITY HOSPITAL LAKEVIEW
1 Hospital Drive, Box 629
Eufaula, OK 74432-4010
(918)689-2535

FAIRFAX
FAIRFAX MEMORIAL HOSPITAL
State Highway 18 And Taft Avenue PO Box 219
Fairfax, OK 74637
(918)642-3291

FAIRVIEW
FAIRVIEW HOSPITAL
PO Box 548
Fairview, OK 73737-0548
(580)227-3721

FORT SILL
REYNOLDS ARMY COMMUNITY HOSPITAL
4301 Mow Way Road
Fort Sill, OK 73503
(580)458-3000

FORT SUPPLY
WESTERN STATE PSYCHIATRIC CENTER
1 Mile E Highway 270 PO Box 1
Fort Supply, OK 73841-0001
(580)766-2311

FREDERICK
MEMORIAL HOSPITAL AND PHYSICANS
GROUP
319 East Josephine
Frederick, OK 73542-2220
(580)335-7565

GROVE
INTEGRIS GROVE GENERAL HOSPITAL
1310 South Main Street
Grove, OK 74344-5324
(918)786-2243

GUTHRIE
LOGAN HOSPITAL AND MEDICAL CENTER
116 N Broad St
Guthrie, OK 73044-3363
(405)282-6700

GUYMON
MEMORIAL HOSPITAL OF TEXAS COUNTY
520 Medical Drive
Guymon, OK 73942-4499
(580)338-6515

HEALDTON
HEALDTON HOSPITAL
918 Sw 8th St
Healdton, OK 73438-2424
(580)229-0701

HENRYETTA
HENRYETTA MEDICAL CENTER
Dewey Bartlett And Main Streets, Box 1269
Henryetta, OK 74437-0126
(918)652-4463

HOBART
ELKVIEW GENERAL HOSPITAL
429 West Elm Street
Hobart, OK 73651-1699
(580)726-3324

HOLDENVILLE
HOLDENVILLE GENERAL HOSPITAL
100 Crestview Drive
Holdenville, OK 74848-2844
(405)379-6631

HOLLIS
HARMON MEMORIAL HOSPITAL
400 East Chestnut, PO Box 791
Hollis, OK 73550-0791
(580)688-3363

HUGO
CHOCTAW MEMORIAL HOSPITAL
1405 East Kirk Road
Hugo, OK 74743-3603
(580)326-6414

IDABEL
MCCURTAIN MEMORIAL HOSPITAL
1301 Memorial Road
Idabel, OK 74745
(580)286-7623

KINGFISHER
KINGFISHER REGIONAL HOSPITAL
500 South 9th Street, PO Box 59
Kingfisher, OK 73750-0059
(405)375-3141

123

OKLAHOMA — Hospital Telephone Directory

LAWTON

COMANCHE COUNTY MEMORIAL HOSPITAL
3401 West Gore Boulevard
Lawton, OK 73505-6300
(580)355-8620

JIM TALIAFERRO COMMUNITY MENTAL HEALTH CENTER
602 Southwest 38th Street
Lawton, OK 73505-6999
(580)248-5780

MEMORIAL PAVILION
1602 SW 82 Street
Lawton, OK 73505-9012
(580)357-7827

MILLER MANOR HALFWAY HOUSE
708 1/2 W Gore Blvd
Lawton, OK 73501-3717
(580)248-8526

PHS INDIAN HOSPITAL - LAWTON
1515 Lawrie Tatum Road
Lawton, OK 73507-3099
(580)353-0350

SOUTHWESTERN HOSPITAL
5602 Southwest Lee Boulevard, PO Box 7290
Lawton, OK 73502-0729
(580)531-4700

LINDSAY

LINDSAY MUNICIPAL HOSPITAL
State Highway 19 West, PO Box 888
Lindsay, OK 73052-0888
(405)756-1404

MADILL

INTEGRIS MARSHALL MEMORIAL HOSPITAL
1 Hospital Drive, PO Box 827
Madill, OK 73446-0827
(580)795-3384

MANGUM

MANGUM CITY HOSPITAL
One Wickersham Drive, PO Box 280
Mangum, OK 73554-0280
(580)782-3353

MARIETTA

MERCY HEALTH-LOVE COUNTY CENTER
300 Wanda Street
Marietta, OK 73448-1200
(580)276-3347

MC ALESTER

CARL ALBERT COMMUNITY MENTAL HEALTH CENTER
1100 East Monroe, PO Box 579
Mc Alester, OK 74502-0579
(918)426-1000

MC ALESTER REGIONAL HEALTH CENTER
1 Clark Bass Boulevard
Mc Alester, OK 74501-4255
(918)426-1800

MIAMI

INTEGRIS BAPTIST REGIONAL HEALTH CENTER
200 Second Avenue Southwest, Box 1207
Miami, OK 74354-6830
(918)542-6611

WILLOW CREST HOSPITAL
PO Box 1144
Miami, OK 74355-1144
(918)542-1836

MIDWEST CITY

INTERGRATED SPECIALTY HOSPITAL - MIDWEST CITY
8210 National Avenue
Midwest City, OK 73110-8518
(405)739-0800

MIDWEST CITY REGIONAL MEDICAL CENTER
2825 Parklawn Drive And 238 N Midwest Bv
Midwest City, OK 73110-4258
(405)610-4411

MUSKOGEE

MUSKOGEE REGIONAL MEDICAL CENTER
300 Edna M Rockefeller Drive
Muskogee, OK 74401
(918)682-5501

VA MEDICAL CENTER - MUSKOGEE
1011 Honor Heights Drive
Muskogee, OK 74401-1399
(918)683-3261

NORMAN

GRIFFIN MEMORIAL HOSPITAL
900 E Main St PO Box 151
Norman, OK 73070-0151
(405)321-4880

J D MCCARTY CENTER FOR CHILDREN
1125 East Alameda Street
Norman, OK 73071-5264
(405)321-4830

NORMAN REGIONAL HOSPITAL
901 North Porter, PO Box 1308
Norman, OK 73070-1308
(405)307-1000

NOWATA

JANE PHILLIPS NOWATA HEALTH CENTER
237 South Locust, PO Box 426
Nowata, OK 74048-0426
(918)273-3102

OKEENE

OKEENE MUNICIPAL HOSPITAL
207 East F Street, Box 489
Okeene, OK 73763-0489
(580)822-4417

OKEMAH

PHS/IHS CREEK NATION COMMUNITY HOSPITAL
309 North 14th Street
Okemah, OK 74859-2028
(918)623-1424

OKLAHOMA CITY

ADVANCE CARE HOSPITAL OF OKLAHOMA CITY
4300 West Memorial Road, Fifth Floor
Oklahoma City, OK 73120-8304
(405)486-8800

BONE AND JOINT HOSPITAL
1111 North Dewey Avenue
Oklahoma City, OK 73103-2652
(405)552-9100

CENTRIS
4401 South Western, 7th Floor
Oklahoma City, OK 73109-3413
(405)644-5007

CHILDREN'S HOSPITAL OF OKLAHOMA
940 NE 13th St
Oklahoma City, OK 73104-5099
(405)271-4700

DEACONESS HOSPITAL
5501 North Portland Avenue
Oklahoma City, OK 73112-2099
(405)604-6000

HEALTHSOUTH REHABILITATION HOSPITAL
700 NW 7th Street And 721 NW 6th Street
Oklahoma City, OK 73102-1212
(405)553-1195

HIGH POINTE HEALTHCARE
6501 Northeast 50th Street
Oklahoma City, OK 73141-9118
(405)424-3383

INTEGRIS BAPTIST MEDICAL CENTER
3300 Northwest Expressway
Oklahoma City, OK 73112-4999
(405)949-3011

INTEGRIS SOUTHWEST MEDICAL CENTER
4401 South Western Avenue
Oklahoma City, OK 73109-3413
(405)636-7000

KINDRED HOSPITAL OKLAHOMA CITY
1407 North Robinson Avenue
Oklahoma City, OK 73103-4899
(405)232-8000

LAKESIDE WOMEN'S HOSPITAL
11200 North Portland Avenue
Oklahoma City, OK 73120-5051
(405)936-1500

MERCY HEALTH CENTER
4300 West Memorial Road
Oklahoma City, OK 73120-8362
(405)755-1515

NORTHWEST SURGICAL HOSPITAL
9204 North May Avenue
Oklahoma City, OK 73120-4419
(405)848-1918

OKLAHOMA CENTER FOR ORTHOPAEDIC AND MULTI-SPECIALTY
8100 South Walker, Building C
Oklahoma City, OK 73139-9404
(405)602-6500

OKLAHOMA SPINE HOSPITAL
14101 Parkway Commons Drive
Oklahoma City, OK 73134-6012
(405)749-2700

OKLAHOMA UNIVERSITY MEDICAL CENTER - EVERETT TOWER
940 NE 13th St
Oklahoma City, OK 73104-5008
(405)271-4700

OKLAHOMA UNIVERSITY MEDICAL CENTER - PRESBYTERIAN TOWER
700 Northeast 13th Street
Oklahoma City, OK 73104-5004
(405)271-4700

PHYSICIANS HOSPITAL OF OKLAHOMA
3100 Sw 89th Street
Oklahoma City, OK 73159-7900
(405)602-8100

SAINT ANTHONY HOSPITAL
1000 North Lee Avenue, PO Box 205
Oklahoma City, OK 73101-0205
(405)272-7000

SAINT MICHAEL HOSPITAL
2129 Southwest 59th Street
Oklahoma City, OK 73119-7024
(405)685-6671

SELECT SPECIALTY HOSPITAL - OKLAHOMA CITY
5501 North Portland Avenue
Oklahoma City, OK 73112-2074
(405)951-4016

OKLAHOMA

SELECT SPECIALTY HOSPITAL - OKLAHOMA CITY EAST
3300 North West Expressway, 5 East, 601
Oklahoma City, OK 73112
(405)951-8100

SURGICAL HOSPITAL OF OKLAHOMA
100 Se 59th Street
Oklahoma City, OK 73129-3616
(405)634-9300

VA MEDICAL CENTER - OKLAHOMA CITY
921 Ne 13th St
Oklahoma City, OK 73104-5007
(405)270-0501

OKMULGEE

GEORGE NIGH REBAHILITATION INSTITUTE
900 East Airport Road, P O Box 1118
Okmulgee, OK 74447-1118
(918)756-9211

OKMULGEE HOSPITAL
1401 Morris Drive, PO Box 1038
Okmulgee, OK 74447-1038
(918)756-4233

PAULS VALLEY

PAULS VALLEY GENERAL HOSPITAL
100 Valley Drive, PO Box 368
Pauls Valley, OK 73075-0368
(405)238-5501

PAWHUSKA

PAWHUSKA HOSPITAL
1101 East 15th Street
Pawhuska, OK 74056-1920
(918)287-3232

PAWNEE

PAWNEE MUNICIPAL HOSPITAL AUTHORITY
1212 Fourth Street, PO Box 467
Pawnee, OK 74058-0467
(918)762-2577

PERRY

PERRY MEMORIAL HOSPITAL
501 14th Street
Perry, OK 73077-5099
(580)336-3541

PONCA CITY

VIA CHRISTI OKLAHOMA REGIONAL MEDICAL CENTER
1900 N 14th St P O Box 1270
Ponca City, OK 74602-1270
(580)765-3321

POTEAU

EASTERN OKLAHOMA MEDICAL CENTER
105 Wall Street, PO Box 1148
Poteau, OK 74953-1148
(918)647-8161

PRAGUE

PRAGUE MUNICIPAL HOSPITAL
1322 A Avenue, PO Drawer S
Prague, OK 74864-1090
(405)567-4922

PRYOR

INTEGRIS MAYES COUNTY MEDICAL CENTER
129 North Kentucky Avenue, PO Box 278
Pryor, OK 74362-0278
(918)825-1600

PURCELL

PURCELL MUNICIPAL HOSPITAL
1500 North Green Avenue, PO Box 511
Purcell, OK 73080-0511
(405)527-6524

SALLISAW

SEQUOYAH MEMORIAL HOSPITAL
213 East Redwood, PO Box 505
Sallisaw, OK 74955-0505
(918)774-1100

SAPULPA

SAINT JOHN SAPULPA
1004 East Bryan
Sapulpa, OK 74066-4513
(918)224-4280

SAYRE

SAYRE MEMORIAL HOSPITAL
501 E Washington Ave
Sayre, OK 73662-1337
(580)928-5541

SEILING

SEILING MUNICIPAL HOSPITAL AUTHORITY
Us Highway 60 Northeast, PO Box 720
Seiling, OK 73663-0720
(580)922-7361

SEMINOLE

SEMINOLE MEDICAL CENTER-HOSPITAL
2401 Wrangler Blvd
Seminole, OK 74868-1917
(405)303-4000

SHATTUCK

NEWMAN MEMORIAL HOSPITAL
905 South Main Street
Shattuck, OK 73858-9208
(580)938-2551

SHAWNEE

UNITY HEALTH CENTER - NORTH
1900 S Gordon Cooper Dr
Shawnee, OK 74801-8600
(405)273-2270

UNITY HEALTH CENTER - SOUTH
1900 Gordon Cooper Drive
Shawnee, OK 74801-8600
(405)273-2240

SPENCER

INTEGRIS MENTAL HEALTH SYSTEM - SPENCER
2601 North Spencer Road
Spencer, OK 73084-3649
(405)942-6100

STIGLER

HASKELL COUNTY HOSPITAL
PO Box 728
Stigler, OK 74462-0728
(918)967-4682

STILLWATER

STILLWATER MEDICAL CENTER
1323 West 6th Street, PO Box 2408
Stillwater, OK 74076-2408
(405)372-1480

STILWELL

MEMORIAL HOSPITAL
1401 West Locust, PO Box 272
Stilwell, OK 74960-0272
(918)696-3101

STROUD

STROUD MUNICIPAL HOSPITAL
U S Highway 66 West, PO Box 530
Stroud, OK 74079-0530
(918)968-3571

SULPHUR

ARBUCKLE MEMORIAL HOSPITAL
2011 West Broadway
Sulphur, OK 73086-4221
(580)622-2161

TAHLEQUAH

PHS/IHS W W HASTINGS INDIAN HOSPITAL
100 S Bliss
Tahlequah, OK 74464-2512
(918)458-3100

TAHLEQUAH CITY HOSPITAL
1400 East Downing Street, PO Box 1008
Tahlequah, OK 74465-1008
(918)456-0641

TALIHINA

PHS/IHS CHOCTAW NATION HEALTH CARE CENTER
Route 2 Box 1735
Talihina, OK 74571-9517
(918)567-7000

TINKER AIR FORCE BASE

72ND MEDICAL GROUP
5700 Arnold St, Blcg 5801
Tinker Air Force Base, OK 73145-8105
(405)736-2143

TISHOMINGO

JOHNSTON MEMORIAL HOSPITAL
1000 South Byrd
Tishomingo, OK 73460-3299
(580)371-2327

TULSA

BROOKHAVEN HOSPITAL
201 South Garnett Road
Tulsa, OK 74128-1800
(918)438-4257

BROWN SCHOOLS OF OKLAHOMA
6262 S Sheridan Road
Tulsa, OK 74133-4055
(918)492-8200

CANCER TREATMENT CENTER OF AMERICA
2408 East 81st Street
Tulsa, OK 74137-4208
(918)496-5000

CHILDRENS MEDICAL CENTER
1120 South Utica Avenue
Tulsa, OK 74104-4012
(918)579-3722

CONTINUOUS CARE CENTER OF TULSA
1923 S Utica Avenue
Tulsa, OK 74104-6520
(918)749-8930

HILLCREST MEDICAL CENTER
1120 South Utica Avenue
Tulsa, OK 74104-4090
(918)579-1000

OREGON
Hospital Telephone Directory

HILLCREST SPECIALTY HOSPITAL OF TULSA
2408 East 81st Street, Floors 24 And 25
Tulsa, OK 74137-4208
(918)491-2400

LAUREATE PSYCHIATRIC CLINIC AND HOSPITAL
6655 S Yale Avenue Box 470207
Tulsa, OK 74136-3329
(918)481-4000

MEADOWBROOK REHABILITATION HOSPITAL OF TULSA
3219 South 79th East Avenue
Tulsa, OK 74145-1343
(918)663-8183

ORTHOPEDIC HOSPITAL OF OKLAHOMA
2408 East 81st Street, Ste 900
Tulsa, OK 74137-4230
(918)477-5000

PARKSIDE HOSPITAL
1620 E 12th
Tulsa, OK 74120-5407
(918)582-2131

SAINT FRANCIS HOSPITAL
6161 South Yale And 4818 E 67th Street
Tulsa, OK 74136-1902
(918)494-2200

SAINT JOHN MEDICAL CENTER
1923 South Utica Avenue
Tulsa, OK 74104-6502
(918)744-2345

SELECT SPECIALTY HOSPITAL - TULSA
744 W 9th St 6th Floor West
Tulsa, OK 74127-9028
(918)699-2171

SOUTHCREST HOSPITAL
8801 South 101st Street, East Avenue
Tulsa, OK 74153
(405)294-4000

TULSA REGIONAL MEDICAL CENTER
744 West 9th Street
Tulsa, OK 74127-9028
(918)587-2561

VINITA

CRAIG GENERAL HOSPITAL
735 North Foreman, PO Box 326
Vinita, OK 74301-0326
(918)256-7551

EASTERN STATE HOSPITAL
2 Miles Northeast Of City, PO Box 69
Vinita, OK 74301-0069
(918)256-7841

WAGONER

WAGONER COMMUNITY HOSPITAL
1200 West Cherokee Street, PO Box 407
Wagoner, OK 74477-0407
(918)485-5514

WATONGA

OPPORTUNITIES INC - CHEMICAL DEPENDENCY TREATMENT CENTER
120 W First St PO Box 569
Watonga, OK 73772-0569
(580)623-2545

WATONGA MUNICIPAL HOSPITAL
500 N Clarence Nash Boulevard, Box 370
Watonga, OK 73772-2899
(580)623-7211

WAURIKA

JEFFERSON COUNTY HOSPITAL
U S Highways 81 And 70, PO Box 90
Waurika, OK 73573-0090
(580)228-2344

WEATHERFORD

SOUTHWESTERN MEMORIAL HOSPITAL
215 North Kansas
Weatherford, OK 73096-5499
(580)772-5551

WETUMKA

WETUMKA GENERAL HOSPITAL
325 South Washita Street
Wetumka, OK 74883-5500
(405)452-3276

WILBURTON

LATIMER COUNTY GENERAL HOSPITAL
806 State Highway 2 North
Wilburton, OK 74578
(918)465-2391

WOODARD

WESTERN STATE PSYCHIATRIC CENTER
1222 Tenth Street
Woodard, OK 73801-3156
(580)571-3233

WOODWARD

WOODWARD HOSPITAL AND HEALTH CENTER
900 17th Street
Woodward, OK 73801-2448
(580)256-5511

YUKON

INTERGRIS CANADIAN VALLEY REGIONAL HOSPITAL
1201 Health Center Parkway
Yukon, OK 73099-6392
(405)717-6800

OREGON

ALBANY

ALBANY GENERAL HOSPITAL
1046 6th Avenue Sw
Albany, OR 97321-1999
(541)812-4000

ASHLAND

ASHLAND COMMUNITY HOSPITAL
280 Maple Street, PO Box 98
Ashland, OR 97520-0069
(541)482-2441

ASTORIA

COLUMBIA MEMORIAL HOSPITAL
2111 Exchange Street
Astoria, OR 97103-3329
(503)325-4321

BAKER CITY

SAINT ELIZABETH HEALTH SERVICES
3325 Pocahontas Road
Baker City, OR 97814-1464
(541)523-6461

BANDON

SOUTHERN COOS HOSPITAL
900 11th Street SE
Bandon, OR 97411-9114
(541)347-2426

BEND

SAINT CHARLES MEDICAL CENTER
2500 Ne Neff Road
Bend, OR 97701-6015
(541)382-4321

BURNS

HARNEY DISTRICT HOSPITAL
557 W Washington St
Burns, OR 97720-1441
(541)573-7281

CLACKAMAS

KAISER SUNNYSIDE MEDICAL CENTER
10180 S E Sunnyside Road
Clackamas, OR 97015-9303
(503)652-2880

COOS BAY

BAY AREA HOSPITAL
1775 Thompson Road
Coos Bay, OR 97420-2125
(541)269-8111

COQUILLE

COQUILLE VALLEY HOSPITAL
940 East 5th Street
Coquille, OR 97423-1699
(541)396-3101

CORVALLIS

GOOD SAMARITAN HOSPITAL CORVALLIS
3600 Nw Samaritan Drive
Corvallis, OR 97330-3700
(541)768-5111

COTTAGE GROVE

COTTAGE GROVE COMMUNITY HOSPITAL
PO Box 128
Cottage Grove, OR 97424-0005
(541)942-0511

DALLAS

VALLEY COMMUNITY HOSPITAL
550 Se Clay Street, PO Box 378
Dallas, OR 97338-0378
(503)623-8301

ENTERPRISE

WALLOWA MEMORIAL HOSPITAL
401 Northeast First Street, PO Box 460
Enterprise, OR 97828-0460
(541)426-3111

EUGENE

LANE COUNTY PSYCHIATRIC HOSPITAL
151 W 5th Avenue (PO Box 10905)
Eugene, OR 97440-2905
(541)342-1697

SACRED HEART MEDICAL CENTER
1255 Hilyard Street
Eugene, OR 97401-3700
(541)686-7300

SERENITY LANE
616 East 16th St
Eugene, OR 97401-4357
(541)687-1110

Hospital Telephone Directory — **OREGON**

FLORENCE
PEACE HARBOR HOSPITAL
400 9th Street, PO Box 580
Florence, OR 97439-0020
(541)997-8412

FOREST GROVE
TUALITY FOREST GROVE HOSPITAL
1809 Maple St
Forest Grove, OR 97116-1995
(503)357-2173

GOLD BEACH
CURRY GENERAL HOSPITAL
94220 4th Street
Gold Beach, OR 97444-7772
(541)247-6621

GRANTS PASS
THREE RIVERS COMMUNITY HOSPITAL &
HEALTH CENTER - WASHINGTON
500 Ramsey Ave
Grants Pass, OR 97527-5554
(541)472-7000

GRESHAM
LEGACY MOUNT HOOD MEDICAL CENTER
24800 Se Stark Street
Gresham, OR 97030-3399
(503)667-1122

RECOVERY CENTER AT GRESHAM
4101 Northeast Division Street
Gresham, OR 97030-4617
(503)666-6575

HEPPNER
PIONEER MEMORIAL HOSPITAL
564 East Pioneer Drive, PO Box 9
Heppner, OR 97836-0009
(541)676-9133

HERMISTON
GOOD SHEPHERD COMMUNITY HOSPITAL
610 Nw 11th Avenue
Hermiston, OR 97838-6601
(541)667-3400

HILLSBORO
TUALITY COMMUNITY HOSPITAL
335 Se 8th Avenue
Hillsboro, OR 97123-4248
(503)681-1111

HOOD RIVER
PROVIDENCE HOOD RIVER MEMORIAL
HOSPITAL
13th And May Streets, PO Box 149
Hood River, OR 97031-0055
(541)386-3911

JOHN DAY
BLUE MOUNTAIN HOSPITAL
170 Ford Road
John Day, OR 97845-2009
(541)575-1311

KLAMATH FALLS
MERLE WEST MEDICAL CENTER
2865 Daggett Street
Klamath Falls, OR 97601-1106
(541)882-6311

LA GRANDE
GRANDE RONDE HOSPITAL
900 Sunset Drive, PO Box 3290
La Grande, OR 97850-7290
(541)963-8421

LAKEVIEW
LAKE DISTRICT HOSPITAL
700 South J Street
Lakeview, OR 97630-1623
(541)947-2114

LEBANON
LEBANON COMMUNITY HOSPITAL
525 N Santiam Highway, PO Box 739
Lebanon, OR 97355-0739
(541)258-2101

LINCOLN CITY
NORTH LINCOLN HOSPITAL
3043 Ne 28th Street, PO Box 767
Lincoln City, OR 97367-0767
(541)994-3661

MADRAS
MOUNTAIN VIEW HOSPITAL
470 Ne A Street
Madras, OR 97741-1899
(541)475-3882

MCMINNVILLE
WILLAMETTE VALLEY MEDICAL CENTER
2700 Three Mile Lane
McMinnville, OR 97128-6251
(503)472-6131

MEDFORD
PROVIDENCE MEDFORD MEDICAL CENTER
1111 Crater Lake Avenue
Medford, OR 97504-6241
(541)732-5000

ROGUE VALLEY MEDICAL CENTER
2825 Barnett Road
Medford, OR 97504-8389
(541)608-4900

MILWAUKIE
PROVIDENCE MILWAUKIE HOSPITAL
10150 Se 32nd Avenue
Milwaukie, OR 97222-6593
(503)513-8300

NEWBERG
PROVIDENCE NEWBERG HOSPITAL
501 Villa Road
Newberg, OR 97132-1832
(503)537-1555

NEWPORT
PACIFIC COMMUNITIES HOSPITAL
930 Sw Abbey Street
Newport, OR 97365-4820
(541)265-2244

ONTARIO
HOLY ROSARY MEDICAL CENTER
351 Sw 9th Street
Ontario, OR 97914-2639
(541)881-7000

OREGON CITY
WILLAMETTE FALLS HOSPITAL
1500 Division Street
Oregon City, OR 97045-1597
(503)656-1631

PENDLETON
EASTERN OREGON PSYCHIATRIC CENTER
2600 Westgate
Pendleton, OR 97801-9604
(541)276-4511

SAINT ANTHONY HOSPITAL
1601 Se Court Avenue
Pendleton, OR 97801-3217
(541)276-5121

PORTLAND
EASTMORELAND HOSPITAL
2900 S E Steele Street
Portland, OR 97202-4590
(503)234-0411

LEGACY EMANUEL HOSPITAL AND HEALTH
CENTER
2801 No Gantenbein Avenue
Portland, OR 97227-1623
(503)413-2200

LEGACY GOOD SAMARITAN HOSPITAL AND
MEDICAL CENTER
1015 Nw 22nd Avenue
Portland, OR 97210-3099
(503)413-7711

OHSU DOERNBECHER CHILDREN'S
HOSPITAL
3181 Southwest Sam Jackson Park Road
Portland, OR 97239-3011
(503)494-8311

OREGON HEALTH SERVICES UNIVERSITY
HOSPITAL AND CLINIC
3181 Sw Sam Jackson Park Road
Portland, OR 97239-3079
(503)494-8311

PORTLAND ADVENTIST MEDICAL CENTER
10123 Se Market
Portland, OR 97216-2599
(503)257-2500

PROVIDENCE PORTLAND MEDICAL
CENTER
4805 Ne Glisan
Portland, OR 97213-2933
(503)215-1111

PROVIDENCE SAINT VINCENT MEDICAL
CENTER
9205 Sw Barnes Road
Portland, OR 97225-6661
(503)216-1234

SHRINERS HOSPITAL FOR CHILDREN
3101 SW Sam Jackson Park Road
Portland, OR 97239-3009
(503)241-5090

VA MEDICAL CENTER - PORTLAND
3710 Sw Us Veterans Hospital Road, PO Box
1034
Portland, OR 97239-2964
(503)220-8262

WOODLAND PARK HOSPITAL
10300 Ne Hancock St
Portland, OR 97220-3899
(503)257-5500

PRINEVILLE
PIONEER MEMORIAL HOSPITAL
1201 North Elm Street
Prineville, OR 97754-1206
(541)447-6254

PENNSYLVANIA — Hospital Telephone Directory

REDMOND
CENTRAL OREGON DISTRICT HOSPITAL
1253 North Canal Boulevard
Redmond, OR 97756-1395
(541)548-8131

REEDSPORT
LOWER UMPQUA HOSPITAL
600 Ranch Road
Reedsport, OR 97467-1795
(541)271-2171

ROSEBURG
MERCY MEDICAL CENTER
2700 Stewart Parkway
Roseburg, OR 97470-1281
(541)673-0611

VA HEALTHCARE SYSTEM - ROSEBURG
913 N W Garden Valley Blvd
Roseburg, OR 97470-6523
(541)440-1000

SALEM
OREGON STATE HOSPITAL
2600 Center Street Ne
Salem, OR 97310-0001
(503)945-2870

SALEM HOSPITAL
665 Winter Street Southeast, PO Box 14001
Salem, OR 97301-3919
(503)561-5200

SALEM HOSPITAL - PSYCHIATRIC MEDICINE CENTER
1127 Oak St SE
Salem, OR 97301-4020
(503)370-5200

SALEM HOSPITAL REHAB CENTER
2561 Center St NE
Salem, OR 97301-4600
(503)370-5986

SEASIDE
PROVIDENCE SEASIDE HOSPITAL
725 S Wahanna Road
Seaside, OR 97138-7735
(503)717-7000

SILVERTON
SILVERTON HOSPITAL
342 Fairview Street
Silverton, OR 97381-1993
(503)873-1500

SPRINGFIELD
MCKENZIE-WILLAMETTE HOSPITAL
1460 G Street
Springfield, OR 97477-4197
(541)726-4400

STAYTON
SANTIAM MEMORIAL HOSPITAL
1401 North 10th Avenue
Stayton, OR 97383-1399
(503)769-2175

THE DALLES
MID COLUMBIA MEDICAL CENTER
1700 East 19th Street
The Dalles, OR 97058-3398
(541)296-1111

TILLAMOOK
TILLAMOOK COUNTY GENERAL HOSPITAL
1000 Third St
Tillamook, OR 97141-3498
(503)842-4444

TUALATIN
LEGACY MERIDIAN PARK HOSPITAL
19300 Sw 65th Avenue
Tualatin, OR 97062-9741
(503)692-1212

WHITE CITY
VA HEALTHCARE SYSTEM - SOUTHERN OREGON REHAB CENTER
8495 Crater Lake Highway
White City, OR 97503-3011
(541)826-2111

PENNSYLVANIA

ABINGTON
ABINGTON MEMORIAL HOSPITAL
1200 Old York Road
Abington, PA 19001-3788
(215)481-2000

ALIQUIPPA
ALIQUIPPA COMMUNITY HOSPITAL
2500 Hospital Drive
Aliquippa, PA 15001-2123
(724)857-1212

ALLENTOWN
ALLENTOWN STATE HOSPITAL
1600 Hanover Street
Allentown, PA 18109-2498
(610)740-3200

GOOD SHEPHERD REHABILITATION HOSPITAL
Fifth And St John Streets
Allentown, PA 18103
(610)776-3120

GOOD SHEPHERD SPECIALTY HOSPITAL
1200 Cedar Crest Blvd, 1st Floor, Anderson Wing
Allentown, PA 18105
(570)402-7670

LEHIGH VALLEY HOSPITAL
1200 S Cedar Crest Boulevard PO Box 689
Allentown, PA 18105-1556
(570)402-8000

SACRET HEART HOSPITAL
421 Chew St
Allentown, PA 18102-3490
(610)776-4500

SAINT LUKE'S HOSPITAL - ALLENTOWN CAMPUS
1736 Hamilton St
Allentown, PA 18104-5695
(610)770-8300

ALTOONA
ALTOONA CENTER
1515 4th St
Altoona, PA 16601-4595
(814)946-6900

ALTOONA HOSPITAL
620 Howard Avenue
Altoona, PA 16601-4899
(814)946-2011

BON SECOURS HOLY FAMILY HOSPITAL
2500 Seventh Avenue
Altoona, PA 16602-2099
(814)944-1681

HEALTHSOUTH REHABILITATION HOSPITAL ALTOONA
2005 Valley View Boulevard
Altoona, PA 16602-4548
(814)944-3535

VA MEDICAL CENTER - JAMES E. VAN ZANDT
2907 Pleasant Valley Road
Altoona, PA 16602-4305
(814)943-8164

AMBLER
HORSHAM CLINIC
Welsh Road And Butler Pike
Ambler, PA 19002
(215)643-7800

ASHLAND
ASHLAND REGIONAL MEDICAL CENTER
101 Broad Street
Ashland, PA 17921-2198
(570)875-2000

BEAVER
MEDICAL CENTER BEAVER
1000 Dutch Ridge Road
Beaver, PA 15009-9700
(724)728-7000

BENSALEM
LIVENGRIN FOUNDATION
4833 Hulmeville Road
Bensalem, PA 19020-3099
(215)638-5200

BERWICK
BERWICK HOSPITAL CENTER
701 East 16th St
Berwick, PA 18603-2397
(570)759-5000

BETHLEHEM
MUHLENBERG HOSPITAL CENTER
2545 Schoenersville Road
Bethlehem, PA 18017-7384
(610)884-2201

SAINT LUKES HOSPITAL OF BETHLEHEM
801 Ostrum St
Bethlehem, PA 18015-1000
(610)954-4000

BLOOMSBURG
BLOOMSBURG HOSPITAL
549 E Fair St
Bloomsburg, PA 17815-1498
(570)387-2100

BRADDOCK
UPMC - BRADDOCK HOSPITAL
400 Holland Avenue
Braddock, PA 15104-1598
(412)636-5000

BRADFORD
BRADFORD REGIONAL MEDICAL CENTER
116 Interstate Parkway Box 218
Bradford, PA 16701-1036
(814)368-4143

Hospital Telephone Directory — PENNSYLVANIA

BRIDGEVILLE
MAYVIEW STATE HOSPITAL
1601 Mayview Road
Bridgeville, PA 15017-1599
(412)257-6500

BRISTOL
TEMPLE LOWER BUCKS HOSPITAL
105 Bath Road
Bristol, PA 19007
(215)785-9200

BROOKVILLE
BROOKVILLE HOSPITAL
100 Hospital Road
Brookville, PA 15825-1363
(814)849-2312

BROWNSVILLE
BROWNSVILLE GENERAL HOSPITAL
125 Simpson Road
Brownsville, PA 15417-9699
(724)785-7200

BRYN MAWR
MAIN LINE HOSPITAL - BRYN MAWR
Bryn Mawr Avenue
Bryn Mawr, PA 19010
(610)526-3000

BUTLER
BUTLER MEMORIAL HOSPITAL
911 East Brady Street
Butler, PA 16001-4697
(724)283-6666

VA MEDICAL CENTER - BUTLER
325 New Castle Road
Butler, PA 16001-2464
(724)287-4781

CAMP HILL
HOLY SPIRIT HOSPITAL
N 21st St
Camp Hill, PA 17011
(717)763-2100

SELECT SPECIALTY HOSPITAL - CAMP HILL
503 North 21st Street, Fifth Floor
Camp Hill, PA 17011-2204
(717)972-4575

STATE CORRECTIONAL INSTITUTE AT CAMP HILL
Box 8834
Camp Hill, PA 17012-0001
(717)737-4531

CANONSBURG
CANONSBURG GENERAL HOSPITAL
100 Medical Boulevard
Canonsburg, PA 15317-9762
(724)745-6100

CARBONDALE
MARIAN COMMUNITY HOSPITAL
100 Lincoln Avenue
Carbondale, PA 18407-2198
(570)281-1000

CARLISLE
CARLISLE REGIONAL MEDICAL CENTER
246 Parker Street
Carlisle, PA 17013-3661
(717)249-1212

CENTRE HALL
MEADOWS PSYCHIATRIC CENTER
Earlystown Road Road 1 Box 259
Centre Hall, PA 16828-0259
(814)364-2161

CHAMBERSBURG
CHAMBERSBURG HOSPITAL
112 N 7 St PO Box 187
Chambersburg, PA 17201-0187
(717)267-3000

CHESTER
CROZER CHESTER MEDICAL CENTER
One Medical Center Boulevard
Chester, PA 19013-3995
(610)447-2000

KEYSTONE CENTER
2001 Providence Avenue
Chester, PA 19013-5504
(610)876-9000

CLARION
CLARION HOSPITAL
One Hospital Drive
Clarion, PA 16214-8599
(814)226-9500

CLARION PSYCH CENTER
Two Hospital Drive Road#3 Box 188
Clarion, PA 16214-0188
(814)226-9545

CLARKS SUMMIT
CLARKS SUMMIT STATE HOSPITAL
1451 Hillside Drive
Clarks Summit, PA 18411-9505
(570)586-2011

CLEARFIELD
CLEARFIELD HOSPITAL
809 Turnpike Avenue
Clearfield, PA 16830-1243
(814)765-5341

COAL TOWNSHIP
SHAMOKIN AREA COMMUNITY HOSPITAL
4200 Hospital Road
Coal Township, PA 17866-9697
(570)644-4200

COALDALE
SAINT LUKES MINERS MEMORIAL MEDICAL CENTER
360 West Ruddle Street
Coaldale, PA 18218-1027
(570)645-2131

COATESVILLE
BRANDYWINE HOSPITAL
201 Reeseville Road
Coatesville, PA 19320-1536
(610)383-8000

VA MEDICAL CENTER - COATESVILLE
1400 Blackhorse Hill Road
Coatesville, PA 19320-2040
(610)384-7711

COLUMBIA
LANCASTER GENERAL HOSPITAL - SUSQUEHANNA DIVISION
706 N 7th Street
Columbia, PA 17512
(717)684-2841

CONNELLSVILLE
HIGHLANDS HOSPITAL
401 East Murphy Avenue
Connellsville, PA 15425-2700
(724)628-1500

CONSHOHOCKEN
MERCY COMMUNITY HOSPITAL
1 W Elm St
Conshohocken, PA 19428-2007
(610)853-7000

MERCY HEALTH SYSTEM OF SOUTHWESTERN PENNSYLVANIA
1 W Elm St
Conshohocken, PA 19428-2007
(610)567-6000

CORRY
CORRY MEMORIAL HOSPITAL
612 W Smith St
Corry, PA 16407-1196
(814)664-4641

COUDERSPORT
CHARLES COLE MEMORIAL HOSPITAL
1001 East 2nd Street
Coudersport, PA 16915-8179
(814)274-9300

CRANBERRY TOWNSHIP
SAINT FRANCIS HOSPITAL - CRANBERRY
One Saint Francis Way
Cranberry Township, PA 16066-5119
(724)772-5300

DANVILLE
DANVILLE STATE HOSPITAL
200 State Hospital Dr
Danville, PA 17821-9198
(570)271-4500

GEISINGER HEALTHSOUTH REHAB HOSPITAL
2 Rehab Lane
Danville, PA 17821-8498
(570)271-6110

GEISINGER MEDICAL CENTER
100 N Academy Avenue
Danville, PA 17822-0001
(570)271-6211

DARBY
KINDRED HOSPITAL DELAWARE COUNTY
1500 Lansdowne Avenue, 6th Floor
Darby, PA 19023-1200
(610)237-4000

MERCY FITZGERALD HOSPITAL
Lansdowne And Baily Rds
Darby, PA 19023
(610)237-4000

DOWNINGTOWN
SAINT JOHN VIANNEY HOSPITAL
151 Woodbine Road
Downingtown, PA 19335-3057
(610)269-2600

DOYLESTOWN
DOYLESTOWN HOSPITAL
595 W State St
Doylestown, PA 18901-2597
(215)345-2200

PENNSYLVANIA   Hospital Telephone Directory

FOUNDATIONS BEHAVIORAL HEALTH
833 Butler Avenue
Doylestown, PA 18901-2280
(215)345-0444

DREXEL HILL

DELAWARE COUNTY MEMORIAL HOSPITAL
Lansdowne Keystone Aves
Drexel Hill, PA 19026
(610)284-8100

DUBOIS

DUBOIS REGIONAL MEDICAL CENTER
PO Box 447 Maple Avenue And 100 Hospital
Avenue
Dubois, PA 15801-0447
(814)371-2200

EAGLEVILLE

EAGLEVILLE HOSPITAL
100 Eagleville Road
Eagleville, PA 19403-1800
(610)539-6000

EAST STROUDSBURG

POCONO MEDICAL CENTER
206 E Brown St
East Stroudsburg, PA 18301-3094
(570)421-4000

EASTON

EASTON HOSPITAL
250 South 21st Street
Easton, PA 18042-3892
(610)250-4000

SCCI HOSPITAL - EASTON
250 South 21st Street
Easton, PA 18042-3851
(610)250-4708

ELKINS PARK

ELKINS PARK HOSPITAL
60 E Township Line
Elkins Park, PA 19027-2220
(215)663-6000

ELLWOOD CITY

ELLWOOD CITY HOSPITAL
724 Pershing St
Ellwood City, PA 16117-1499
(724)752-0081

EPHRATA

EPHRATA COMMUNITY HOSPITAL
169 Martin Avenue PO Box 1002
Ephrata, PA 17522-1002
(717)733-0311

ERIE

HAMOT MEDICAL CENTER
201 State St
Erie, PA 16550-0001
(814)877-6000

**HEALTHSOUTH REHABILITATION HOSPITAL
OF ERIE**
143 East Second Street
Erie, PA 16507-1501
(814)878-1200

METRO HEALTH CENTER
252 Eleventh St
Erie, PA 16501-1798
(814)870-3400

MILLCREEK COMMUNITY HOSPITAL
5515 Peach St
Erie, PA 16509-2695
(814)864-4031

SAINT VINCENT HEALTH CENTER
232 West 25th Street
Erie, PA 16544-0001
(814)452-5000

SELECT SPECIALTY HOSPITAL - ERIE
201 State Street
Erie, PA 16550-0002
(814)877-2774

SHRINERS HOSPITAL
1645 W 8th St
Erie, PA 16505-5097
(814)875-8700

VA MEDICAL CENTER - ERIE
135 E 38th St
Erie, PA 16504-1559
(814)860-2576

EVERETT

UPMC - BEDFORD MEMORIAL HOSPITAL
10455 Lincoln Highway
Everett, PA 15537-7046
(814)623-6161

FARRELL

**HORIZON HOSPITAL SYSTEM - SHENANGO
VALLEY**
2200 Memorial Drive
Farrell, PA 16121-1357
(724)981-3500

FORT WASHINGTON

**NORTHWESTERN INSTITUTE OF
PSYCHIATRY**
450 Bethlehem Pike
Fort Washington, PA 19034-2397
(215)641-5300

FRANKLIN

UPMC NORTHWEST
1 Spruce St
Franklin, PA 16323-2544
(814)437-7000

GETTYSBURG

GETTYSBURG HOSPITAL
147 Gettys St
Gettysburg, PA 17325-2534
(717)334-2121

GREENSBURG

**SELECT SPECIALTY HOSPITAL -
GREENSBURG**
532 West Pittsburgh Street
Greensburg, PA 15601-2239
(724)830-8649

WESTMORELAND REGIONAL HOSPITAL
532 W Pittsburgh St
Greensburg, PA 15601-2282
(724)832-4000

GREENVILLE

UPMC - HORIZON HOSPITAL
110 N Main St
Greenville, PA 16125-1726
(724)588-2100

GROVE CITY

UNITED COMMUNITY HOSPITAL
631 N Broad Street Ext
Grove City, PA 16127-4603
(724)458-5442

HANOVER

HANOVER GENERAL HOSPITAL
300 Highland Avenue
Hanover, PA 17331-2203
(717)637-3711

HARRISBURG

**COMMUNITY GENERAL OSTEOPATHIC
HOSPITAL**
4300 Londonderry Road
Harrisburg, PA 17109-5397
(717)652-3000

EDGEWATER PSYCHIATRIC CENTER
1829 N Front St
Harrisburg, PA 17102-2213
(717)238-8666

HARRISBURG STATE HOSPITAL
Cameron and Maclay Streets, PO Box 61260
Harrisburg, PA 17106-1260
(717)772-7455

PINNACLE HEALTH - POLYCLINIC HOSPITAL
2601 North Third Street
Harrisburg, PA 17110-2004
(717)782-4141

PINNACLE HEALTH HOSPITAL
111 S Front St
Harrisburg, PA 17101-2099
(717)782-3131

SCCI HOSPITAL - HARRISBURG
2601 North Third Street
Harrisburg, PA 17110-2004
(717)213-9944

HASTINGS

MINERS HOSPITAL
290 Haida Avenue, PO Box 689
Hastings, PA 16646-0689
(814)247-3100

HAZLETON

HAZLETON GENERAL HOSPITAL
700 E Broad St
Hazleton, PA 18201-6897
(570)501-4000

**HAZLETON-SAINT JOSEPH MEDICAL
CENTER**
687 N Church St
Hazleton, PA 18201-3187
(570)501-6000

HERSHEY

**PENNSYLVANIA STATE UNIVERSITY -
MILTON S HERSHEY MEDICAL CENTER**
500 University Drive
Hershey, PA 17033-2391
(717)531-8521

HONESDALE

WAYNE MEMORIAL HOSPITAL
601 Park Street
Honesdale, PA 18431-1498
(570)253-8100

HUNTINGDON

J C BLAIR MEMORIAL HOSPITAL
Warm Springs Avenue
Huntingdon, PA 16652
(814)643-2290

Hospital Telephone Directory — PENNSYLVANIA

INDIANA
INDIANA REGIONAL MEDICAL CENTER
Hospital Road, Box 788
Indiana, PA 15701-0788
(724)357-7000

JEANNETTE
JEANNETTE DISTRICT MEMORIAL HOSPITAL
600 Jefferson Avenue
Jeannette, PA 15644-2599
(724)527-3551

MONSOUR MEDICAL CENTER
70 Lincoln Way East
Jeannette, PA 15644-3185
(724)527-1511

JERSEY SHORE
JERSEY SHORE HOSPITAL
Thompson Street
Jersey Shore, PA 17740
(570)398-0100

JOHNSTOWN
CONEMAUGH VALLEY MEMORIAL HOSPITAL
1086 Franklin Street
Johnstown, PA 15905-4398
(814)534-9000

GOOD SAMARITAN MEDICAL CENTER
1020 Franklin St
Johnstown, PA 15905-4109
(814)533-1000

LEE HOSPITAL
320 Main St
Johnstown, PA 15901-1694
(814)533-0123

SELECT SPECIALTY HOSPITAL - JOHNSTOWN
1086 Franklin Street
Johnstown, PA 15905-4305
(814)534-5000

KANE
KANE COMMUNITY HOSPITAL
4372 Route 6
Kane, PA 16735-3099
(814)837-8585

KINGSTON
FIRST HOSPITAL WYOMING VALLEY
562 Wyoming Ave
Kingston, PA 18704-3721
(570)552-3900

NESBITT HOSPITAL-WYOMING VALLEY HEALTH CARE
562 Wyoming Avenue
Kingston, PA 18704-3779
(570)283-7000

KITTANNING
ARMSTRONG COUNTY MEMORIAL HOSPITAL
One Nolte Drive
Kittanning, PA 16201-7111
(724)543-8500

LAFAYETTE HILL
EUGENIA HOSPITAL
660 Thomas Road
Lafayette Hill, PA 19444-1199
(215)836-7700

LANCASTER
COMMUNITY HOSPITAL OF LANCASTER
1175 Clark St
Lancaster, PA 17602-3200
(717)397-3711

LANCASTER GENERAL HOSPITAL
555 N Duke St
Lancaster, PA 17602-2207
(717)290-5511

LANCASTER REGIONAL MEDICAL CENTER
250 College Avenue
Lancaster, PA 17603-3378
(717)291-8211

SEMPERCARE HOSPITAL OF LANCASTER
555 North Duke Street
Lancaster, PA 17602-2250
(717)290-5857

LANGHORNE
FRANKFORD HOSPITAL - BUCKS COUNTY
380 Oxford Valley Road
Langhorne, PA 19047-8399
(215)949-5000

SAINT MARY MEDICAL CENTER
Langhorne-newtown Road
Langhorne, PA 19047-1295
(215)750-2000

LANSDALE
CENTRAL MONTGOMERY MEDICAL CENTER
Medical Campus Drive
Lansdale, PA 19446
(215)368-2100

LATROBE
LATROBE AREA HOSPITAL
West Second Avenue
Latrobe, PA 15650
(724)537-1000

LEBANON
GOOD SAMARITAN HOSPITAL
Fourth Walnut Streets
Lebanon, PA 17042
(717)270-7500

PHILHAVEN HOSPITAL
Road 5 Box 345
Lebanon, PA 17042-0345
(717)273-8871

VA MEDICAL CENTER - LEBANON
1700 S Lincoln Avenue
Lebanon, PA 17042-7597
(717)272-6621

LEHIGHTON
GNADEN HUETTEN MEMORIAL HOSPITAL
11th And Hamilton Streets
Lehighton, PA 18235
(610)377-1300

LEWISBURG
EVANGELICAL COMMUNITY HOSPITAL
One Hospital Drive
Lewisburg, PA 17837-9318
(570)522-2000

LEWISTOWN
LEWISTOWN HOSPITAL
400 Highland Avenue
Lewistown, PA 17044-1198
(717)248-5411

LOCK HAVEN
LOCK HAVEN HOSPITAL
24 Cree Drive
Lock Haven, PA 17745-2699
(570)893-5000

MALVERN
BRYN MAWR HOSPITAL
Paoli Pike
Malvern, PA 19355
(610)251-5400

DEVEREUX CHILDREN'S BEHAVIORAL HEALTH CENTER
655 Sugartown Road
Malvern, PA 19355-3303
(484)595-6777

MALVERN INSTITUTE
940 W King Road
Malvern, PA 19355-3167
(610)647-0330

MC CONNELLSBURG
FULTON COUNTY MEDICAL CENTER
216 S 1st St
Mc Connellsburg, PA 17233-1399
(717)485-3155

MC KEES ROCKS
OHIO VALLEY GENERAL HOSPITAL
100 Heckel Road
Mc Kees Rocks, PA 15136
(412)777-6161

MC KEESPORT
UPMC MCKEESPORT HOSPITAL
1500 Fifth Avenue
Mc Keesport, PA 15132-2482
(412)664-2000

MEADOWBROOK
HOLY REDEEMER HOSPITAL & MEDICAL CENTER
1648 Huntingdon Pike
Meadowbrook, PA 19046-8099
(215)947-3000

MEADVILLE
MEADVILLE MEDICAL CENTER
751 Liberty St
Meadville, PA 16335-2591
(814)333-5000

MEADVILLE MEDICAL CENTER - GROVE STREET
1034 Grove St
Meadville, PA 16335-2945
(814)333-5000

MECHANICSBURG
HEALTHSOUTH REHAB HOSPITAL FOR SPECIAL SERVICES
4950 Wilson Lane
Mechanicsburg, PA 17055-4442
(717)697-7706

HEALTHSOUTH REHABILITATION HOSPITAL OF MECHANICSBURG
175 Lancaster Boulevard
Mechanicsburg, PA 17055-3562
(717)691-3700

SEIDLE MEMORIAL HOSPITAL
120 S Filbert St
Mechanicsburg, PA 17055-6591
(717)795-6760

PENNSYLVANIA — Hospital Telephone Directory

MEDIA

RIDDLE MEMORIAL HOSPITAL
Us Route 1
Media, PA 19063
(610)566-9400

MEYERSDALE

MEYERSDALE MEDICAL CENTER
200 Hospital Drive
Meyersdale, PA 15552-1247
(814)634-5911

MONONGAHELA

MONONGAHELA VALLEY HOSPITAL
Country Club Road Route 88
Monongahela, PA 15063
(724)258-1000

MONROEVILLE

FORBES REGIONAL HOSPITAL
2570 Haymaker Road
Monroeville, PA 15146-3513
(412)858-2000

HEALTHSOUTH REHAB OF GREATER PITTSBURGH
2380 McGinley Road
Monroeville, PA 15146-4400
(412)856-2400

MONTROSE

ENDLESS MOUNTAIN HEALTH SYSTEM
1-3 Grow Avenue
Montrose, PA 18801-1199
(570)278-3801

MOUNT GRETNA

PHILHAVEN HOSPITAL
283 South Butler Road
Mount Gretna, PA 17064
(717)273-8871

MOUNT PLEASANT

FRICK HOSPITAL
508 South Church St
Mount Pleasant, PA 15666-1790
(724)547-1500

MUNCY

MUNCY VALLEY HOSPITAL
PO Box 340
Muncy, PA 17756-0340
(570)546-8282

NANTICOKE

MERCY SPECIAL CARE
128 West Washington Street
Nanticoke, PA 18634-3113
(570)735-5000

NATRONA HEIGHTS

ALLE-KISKI MEDICAL CENTER
1301 Carlisle St
Natrona Heights, PA 15065-1152
(724)224-5100

NEW CASTLE

JAMESON MEMORIAL HOSPITAL
West Leisure Avenue
New Castle, PA 16101
(724)658-9001

SAINT FRANCIS HOSPITAL OF NEW CASTLE
1000 South Mercer Street
New Castle, PA 16101-4673
(724)658-3511

NORRISTOWN

MERCY SUBURBAN HOSPITAL
2701 Dekalb Pike
Norristown, PA 19401-1820
(610)278-2000

MONTGOMERY COUNTY EMERGENCY SERVICE
50 Beech Drive
Norristown, PA 19403-5421
(610)279-6100

MONTGOMERY HOSPITAL
Powell And Fornance Streets
Norristown, PA 19401-3377
(610)270-2000

NORRISTOWN STATE HOSPITAL
1001 Sterigere Street
Norristown, PA 19401-5397
(610)270-1000

VALLEY FORGE MEDICAL CENTER AND HOSPITAL
1033 W Germantown Pike
Norristown, PA 19403-3905
(610)539-8500

NORTH WARREN

WARREN STATE HOSPITAL
33 Main Drive
North Warren, PA 16365-5099
(814)723-5500

OAKDALE

KINDRED HOSPITAL PITTSBURGH
7777 Steubenville Pike
Oakdale, PA 15071-3409
(412)494-5500

OIL CITY

UPMC - OIL CITY
PO Box 1068
Oil City, PA 16301-0568
(814)677-1711

OREFIELD

NATIONAL HOSPITAL FOR KIDS IN CRISIS
5300 Kidspeace Drive
Orefield, PA 18069-2044
(610)799-8800

PALMERTON

PALMERTON HOSPITAL
135 Lafayette Avenue
Palmerton, PA 18071-1596
(610)826-3141

PAOLI

PAOLI MEMORIAL HOSPITAL
255 W Lancaster Avenue
Paoli, PA 19301-1793
(610)648-1000

PECKVILLE

MID VALLEY HOSPITAL ASSOCIATION
1400 Main St
Peckville, PA 18452-2098
(570)383-5500

PHILADELPHIA

ALBERT EINSTEIN MEDICAL CENTER
York And Tabor Rds
Philadelphia, PA 19141
(215)456-7890

BELMONT CENTER-COMPREHENSIVE TREATMENT
4200 Monument Avenue
Philadelphia, PA 19131-1625
(215)877-2000

CHILDRENS HOSPITAL OF PHILADELPHIA
34th And Civic Center Boulevard
Philadelphia, PA 19104
(215)590-1000

CHILDRENS SEASHORE HOUSE
3401 Civic Center Boulevard
Philadelphia, PA 19104-4302
(215)895-3600

CITY AVENUE HOSPITAL
4150 City Avenue
Philadelphia, PA 19131-1610
(215)871-1000

EASTERN PENNSYLVANIA PSYCH INSTITUTE
3200 Henry Avenue
Philadelphia, PA 19129-1137
(215)842-4000

FAIRMOUNT BEHAVIORAL HEALTH SYSTEM
561 Fairthorne Avenue
Philadelphia, PA 19128-2412
(215)487-4000

FOX CHASE CANCER CENTER
7701 Burholme Avenue
Philadelphia, PA 19111-2497
(215)728-6900

FRANKFORD HOSPITAL
Red Lion Knights Rds
Philadelphia, PA 19114
(215)612-4000

FRANKFORD HOSPITAL OF THE CITY OF PHILADELPHIA - FRANKFORD CAMPUS
Frankford Avenue & Wakeling St
Philadelphia, PA 19124
(215)831-2000

FRIEDMAN HOSPITAL OF THE HOME FOR JEWISH AGED
5301 Old York Road
Philadelphia, PA 19141-2912
(215)456-2900

FRIENDS HOSPITAL
4641 Roosevelt Boulevard
Philadelphia, PA 19124-2398
(215)831-4600

GERMANTOWN HOSPITAL
One Penn Center
Philadelphia, PA 19103-1834
(215)951-8000

GIRARD MEDICAL CENTER
8th Street And Girard Avenue
Philadelphia, PA 19122
(215)787-2000

GRADUATE HOSPITALS
One Graduate Plaza
Philadelphia, PA 19146-1497
(215)893-2000

HAHNEMANN UNIVERSITY HOSPITAL
230 N Broad St
Philadelphia, PA 19102-1178
(215)762-7000

JEANES HOSPITAL
7600 Central Avenue
Philadelphia, PA 19111-2499
(215)728-2000

Hospital Telephone Directory — PENNSYLVANIA

JOHN F KENNEDY MEMORIAL HOSPITAL
Langdon St And Cheltenham Avenue
Philadelphia, PA 19124
(215)831-7000

KENSINGTON HOSPITAL
136 W Diamond Street
Philadelphia, PA 19122-1797
(215)426-8100

KINDRED HOSPITAL PHILADELPHIA
6129 Palmetto Street
Philadelphia, PA 19111-5729
(215)722-8555

KIRKBRIDE CENTER
111 N 49th St
Philadelphia, PA 19139-2718
(215)471-2000

MAGEE REHABILITATION HOSPITAL
Six Franklin Plaza
Philadelphia, PA 19102-1177
(215)587-3000

MEDICAL COLLEGE OF PENN-MAIN CAMPUS
3300 Henry Avenue
Philadelphia, PA 19129-1191
(215)842-6000

MERCY HOSPITAL OF PHILADELPHIA
5301 Cedar Avenue
Philadelphia, PA 19143-1917
(215)748-9000

METHODIST HOSPITAL
2301 S Broad St
Philadelphia, PA 19148-3594
(215)952-9000

MOSS REHAB HOSPITAL
1200 W Tabor Road
Philadelphia, PA 19141-3099
(215)456-9070

NAZARETH HOSPITAL
2601 Holme Avenue
Philadelphia, PA 19152-2096
(215)335-6000

PARKVIEW HOSPITAL
1331 East Wyoming Avenue
Philadelphia, PA 19124-3895
(215)537-7400

PENNSYLVANIA HOSPITAL
800 Spruce Street
Philadelphia, PA 19107-6192
(215)829-3000

PRESBYTERIAN-UNIVERSITY OF PENNSYLVANIA MEDICAL CENTER
51 North 39th Street
Philadelphia, PA 19104-2640
(215)662-8000

RENFREW CENTER
475 Spring Lane
Philadelphia, PA 19128-3918
(215)482-5353

ROXBOROUGH MEMORIAL HOSPITAL
5800 Ridge Avenue
Philadelphia, PA 19128-1737
(215)483-9900

SAINT AGNES MEDICAL CENTER
1900 S Broad St
Philadelphia, PA 19145-3089
(215)339-4100

SAINT CHRISTOPHERS HOSPITAL FOR CHILDREN
3601 A Street
Philadelphia, PA 19134-1095
(215)427-5000

SAINT JOSEPH HOSPITAL
16th Street & Girard Avenue
Philadelphia, PA 19130
(215)787-9000

SELECT SPECIALTY HOSPITAL - PHILADELPHIA/AEMC
5501 Old York Road, 5 Levy Building
Philadelphia, PA 19141-3018
(215)456-6550

SHRINERS HOSPITAL
3551 N Broad St
Philadelphia, PA 19140-4131
(215)430-4000

TEMPLE EAST - NORTHEASTERN HOSPITAL
2301 E Allegheny Avenue
Philadelphia, PA 19134-4497
(215)291-3000

TEMPLE EAST NEUMANN MEDICAL CENTER
Frankford Avenue And Palmer Street
Philadelphia, PA 19125
(215)291-2000

TEMPLE UNIVERSITY CHILDREN'S MEDICAL CENTER
3509 North Broad Street
Philadelphia, PA 19140-4130
(215)707-6000

TEMPLE UNIVERSITY HOSPITAL
3401 N Broad St 400 Carnell Hall
Philadelphia, PA 19140-5103
(215)707-2000

TEMPLE UNIVERSITY HOSPITAL - EPISCOPAL
Front St, Lehigh Avenue
Philadelphia, PA 19125
(215)427-7000

THOMAS JEFFERSON UNIVERSITY HOSPITAL
3905 Ford Road
Philadelphia, PA 19131-2824
(215)578-3400

THOMAS JEFFERSON UNIVERSITY HOSPITAL
111 South 11th Street
Philadelphia, PA 19107-5084
(215)955-6000

UNIVERSITY OF PENNSYLVANIA HOSPITAL
34th And Spruce Streets
Philadelphia, PA 19104
(215)662-4000

VA MEDICAL CENTER - PHILADELPHIA
University And Woodland Avenue
Philadelphia, PA 19104
(215)823-5800

WILLS EYE HOSPITAL
9th Walnut St
Philadelphia, PA 19107
(215)928-3000

PHILIPSBURG

PHILIPSBURG AREA HOSPITAL
210 Loch Lomond Road
Philipsburg, PA 16866-1999
(814)342-7112

PHOENIXVILLE

PHOENIXVILLE HOSPITAL UNIVERSITY OF PA HEALTH SYSTEM
144 Nutt Road
Phoenixville, PA 19460-3906
(610)983-1000

PITTSBURGH

ALLEGHENY GENERAL HOSPITAL
320 East North Avenue
Pittsburgh, PA 15212-4772
(412)359-3131

CHILDREN'S INSTITUTE OF PITTSBURGH
6301 Northumberland St
Pittsburgh, PA 15217-1396
(412)420-2400

CHILDRENS HOME OF PITTSBURGH
5618 Kentucky Avenue
Pittsburgh, PA 15232-2696
(412)441-4884

CHILDRENS HOSPITAL OF PITTSBURGH
125 Desoto St
Pittsburgh, PA 15213-2583
(412)692-5325

HEALTHSOUTH HARMARVILLE REHAB HOSPITAL
Guys Run Road
Pittsburgh, PA 15238
(412)781-5700

JEFFERSON REGIONAL MEDICAL CENTER
Coal Valley Road
Pittsburgh, PA 15236
(412)469-5000

LIFECARE HOSPITAL OF PITTSBURGH
225 Penn Avenue
Pittsburgh, PA 15221-2148
(412)247-2424

MAGEE-WOMENS HOSPITAL
Forbes Avenue Halket St
Pittsburgh, PA 15213
(412)641-1000

MERCY HOSPITAL - PITTSBURGH
Pride And Locust Streets
Pittsburgh, PA 15219
(412)232-8111

MERCY PROVIDENCE HOSPITAL
1004 Arch St
Pittsburgh, PA 15212-5294
(412)323-5600

SAINT CLAIR MEMORIAL HOSPITAL
1000 Bower Hill Road
Pittsburgh, PA 15243-1899
(412)561-4900

SAINT FRANCIS MEDICAL CENTER
400 45th Street
Pittsburgh, PA 15201-1198
(412)622-4343

SELECT SPECIALTY HOSPITAL - PITTSBURGH
1400 Locust Street, Mpob Suite 104
Pittsburgh, PA 15219-5114
(412)485-4500

SOUTHWOOD PSYCHIATRIC HOSPITAL
2575 Boyce Plaza Road
Pittsburgh, PA 15241-3994
(412)257-2290

STATE CORRECTIONAL INSTITUTION HOSPITAL
Doerr St
Pittsburgh, PA 15233
(412)761-1955

SUBURBAN GENERAL HOSPITAL
100 S Jackson Avenue
Pittsburgh, PA 15202-3499
(412)734-6000

UPMC - PASSAVANT HOSPITAL
9100 Babcock Boulevard
Pittsburgh, PA 15237-5842
(412)367-6700

UPMC - PRESBYTERIAN
200 Lothrop Street
Pittsburgh, PA 15213-2582
(412)647-2345

UPMC - SAINT MARGARET
815 Freeport Road
Pittsburgh, PA 15215-3399
(412)784-4000

PENNSYLVANIA
Hospital Telephone Directory

UPMC - SOUTH SIDE
2000 Mary Street
Pittsburgh, PA 15203-2095
(412)488-5550

UPMC EYE AND EAR HOSPITAL OF
PITTSBURGH
200 Lothrop Street
Pittsburgh, PA 15213-2546
(412)647-2345

UPMC MONTEFIORE HOSPITAL
200 Lothrop Street
Pittsburgh, PA 15213-2582
(412)647-2345

UPMC REHABILITATION HOSPITAL
1405 Shady Avenue
Pittsburgh, PA 15217-1350
(412)521-9000

UPMC SHADYSIDE HOSPITAL
5230 Centre Avenue
Pittsburgh, PA 15232-1381
(412)623-2121

VA HEALTHCARE SYSTEM - PITTSBURGH
AT DELAFIELD
Delafield Road
Pittsburgh, PA 15240
(412)784-3900

VA HEALTHCARE SYSTEM - PITTSBURGH
AT HIGHLAND
7180 Highland Drive
Pittsburgh, PA 15206-1206
(412)365-4900

VA HEALTHCARE SYSTEM - PITTSBURGH
AT UNIVERSITY
University Drive
Pittsburgh, PA 15240
(412)688-6000

WESTERN PENNSYLVANIA HOSPITAL
4800 Friendship Avenue
Pittsburgh, PA 15224-1793
(412)578-5000

WESTERN PSYCHIATRIC INSTITUTE
3811 Ohara St
Pittsburgh, PA 15213-2593
(412)624-2100

PLEASANT GAP

HEALTHSOUTH NITTANY VALLEY
REHABILITATION HOSPITAL
550 West College Avenue
Pleasant Gap, PA 16823-7401
(814)359-3421

POTTSTOWN

POTTSTOWN MEMORIAL MEDICAL CENTER
High Street And Firestone Road
Pottstown, PA 19464
(610)327-7000

POTTSVILLE

GOOD SAMARITAN REGIONAL MEDICAL
CENTER
E Norwegian Tremont Streets
Pottsville, PA 17901
(570)621-4000

POTTSVILLE HOSPITAL-WARNE CLINIC
420 S Jackson St
Pottsville, PA 17901-3692
(570)621-5000

PUNXSUTAWNEY

PUNXSUTAWNEY AREA HOSPITAL
81 Hillcrest Drive
Punxsutawney, PA 15767-2616
(814)938-1881

QUAKERTOWN

SAINT LUKES QUAKERTOWN HOSPITAL
11th St And Park Avenue
Quakertown, PA 18951
(215)538-4510

READING

HEALTHSOUTH REHABILITATION HOSPITAL
OF READING
1623 Morgantown Road
Reading, PA 19607-9455
(610)796-6000

READING HOSPITAL AND MEDICAL CENTER
PO Box 16052
Reading, PA 19612-6052
(570)988-8000

SAINT JOSEPH MEDICAL CENTER
145 North 6th Street
Reading, PA 19601-3501
(610)378-2000

RENOVO

BUCKTAIL MEDICAL CENTER
1001 Pine St
Renovo, PA 17764-1620
(570)923-1000

RIDGWAY

ELK COUNTY REGIONAL MEDICAL CENTER
94 Hospital St
Ridgway, PA 15853-1931
(814)776-6111

RIDLEY PARK

TAYLOR HOSPITAL
175 E Chester Pike
Ridley Park, PA 19078-2284
(610)595-6000

ROARING SPRING

NASON HOSPITAL
Nason Drive
Roaring Spring, PA 16673
(814)224-2141

SAINT MARYS

ELK REGIONAL HEALTH CENTER
Johnsonburg Road
Saint Marys, PA 15857
(814)788-8000

SAYRE

ROBERT PACKER HOSPITAL
Guthrie Square
Sayre, PA 18840
(570)888-6666

SCRANTON

ALLIED REHAB MEDICINE
475 Morgan Highway PO Box 1103
Scranton, PA 18501-1103
(570)348-1300

COMMUNITY MEDICAL CENTER
1822 Mulberry St
Scranton, PA 18510-2375
(570)969-8000

MERCY HOSPITAL
746 Jefferson Avenue
Scranton, PA 18510-1697
(570)348-7100

MOSES TAYLOR HOSPITAL
700 Quincy Avenue
Scranton, PA 18510-1798
(570)340-2100

SELLERSVILLE

GRAND VIEW HOSPITAL
PO Box 902
Sellersville, PA 18960-0902
(215)453-4000

SEWICKLEY

HEALTHSOUTH REHAB HOSPITAL -
SEWICKLEY
303 Camp Meeting Road
Sewickley, PA 15143-8322
(412)741-9500

SEWICKLEY VALLEY HOSPITAL
720 Blackburn Road
Sewickley, PA 15143-1498
(412)741-6600

SHARON

SHARON REGIONAL HEALTH SYSTEM
740 East State Street
Sharon, PA 16146-3395
(724)983-3911

SHICKSHINNY

CLEAR BROOK LODGE
890 Bethel Hill Rd
Shickshinny, PA 18655-3706
(570)864-3116

SOMERSET

SCI LAUREL HIGHLANDS PRISON
Road 5 PO Box 631
Somerset, PA 15501-0631
(814)443-0231

SOMERSET COMMUNITY HOSPITAL
225 S Center Avenue
Somerset, PA 15501-2088
(814)443-5000

SPRINGFIELD

SPRINGFIELD HOSPITAL
190 W Sproul Road
Springfield, PA 19064-2097
(610)328-8700

STATE COLLEGE

CENTRE COMMUNITY HOSPITAL
1800 E Park Avenue
State College, PA 16803-6797
(814)231-7000

SUNBURY

SUNBURY COMMUNITY HOSPITAL
350 North 11th Street
Sunbury, PA 17801-1600
(570)286-3333

SUSQUEHANNA

BARNES KASSON COUNTY HOSPITAL
400 Turnpike St
Susquehanna, PA 18847-1699
(570)853-3135

TITUSVILLE

TITUSVILLE HOSPITAL
406 W Oak St
Titusville, PA 16354-1499
(814)827-1851

Hospital Telephone Directory — PUERTO RICO

TORRANCE

TORRANCE STATE HOSPITAL
PO Box 105
Torrance, PA 15779-0105
(724)459-8000

TOWANDA

MEMORIAL HOSPITAL
One Hospital Drive
Towanda, PA 18848-9703
(570)265-2191

TROY

TROY COMMUNITY HOSPITAL
100 John St
Troy, PA 16947-1134
(570)297-2121

TUNKHANNOCK

TYLER MEMORIAL HOSPITAL
Route 6 Road 1
Tunkhannock, PA 18657
(570)836-2161

TYRONE

TYRONE HOSPITAL
Clay Avenue Extension
Tyrone, PA 16686
(814)684-1255

UNION CITY

UNION CITY MEMORIAL HOSPITAL
130 N Main St
Union City, PA 16438-1094
(814)438-1000

UNIONTOWN

UNIONTOWN HOSPITAL
500 W Berkley St
Uniontown, PA 15401-5596
(724)430-5000

WARMINSTER

WARMINSTER HOSPITAL
225 Newtown Road
Warminster, PA 18974-5221
(215)441-6600

WARREN

WARREN GENERAL HOSPITAL
Crescent Park West
Warren, PA 16365
(814)723-4973

WARREN STATE HOSPITAL
PO Box 249
Warren, PA 16365-0249
(814)723-5500

WASHINGTON

WASHINGTON HOSPITAL
155 Wilson Avenue
Washington, PA 15301-3398
(724)225-7000

WAYMART

STATE CORRECTIONAL INSTITUTE-WAYMART
PO Box 256
Waymart, PA 18472-0256
(570)488-5811

WAYNESBORO

WAYNESBORO HOSPITAL
E Main St
Waynesboro, PA 17268
(717)765-4000

WAYNESBURG

GREENE COUNTY MEMORIAL HOSPITAL
Seventh Bonar Streets
Waynesburg, PA 15370
(724)627-3101

WELLSBORO

SOLDIERS AND SAILORS MEMORIAL HOSPITAL
32-36 Central Avenue
Wellsboro, PA 16901-1840
(570)724-1631

WERNERSVILLE

CARON FOUNDATION
Box 277 Galen Hall Road
Wernersville, PA 19565-9331
(610)678-2332

WERNERSVILLE STATE HOSPITAL
PO Box 300
Wernersville, PA 19565-0300
(610)670-4111

WEST CHESTER

CHESTER COUNTY HOSPITAL
701 East Marshall St
West Chester, PA 19380-4421
(610)431-5000

WEST GROVE

SOUTHERN CHESTER COUNTY MEDICAL CENTER
1015 W Baltimore Pk
West Grove, PA 19390-9459
(610)869-1000

WILKES-BARRE

CLEAR BROOK MANOR
1100 E Northampton St
Wilkes-Barre, PA 18706-9511
(570)823-1171

GEISINGER WYOMING VALLEY MEDICAL CENTER
1000 East Mountain Drive
Wilkes-Barre, PA 18711-0002
(570)826-7300

JOHN HEINZ INSTITUTE OF REHAB MEDICINE
150 Mundy St
Wilkes-Barre, PA 18702-6830
(570)826-3800

KINDRED HOSPITAL WYOMING VALLEY
575 North River Street
Wilkes-Barre, PA 18764-0999
(570)552-7620

MERCY HOSPITAL
25 Church St PO Bx 658
Wilkes-Barre, PA 18703-0658
(570)826-3100

VA MEDICAL CENTER - WILKES BARRE
1111 East End Boulevard
Wilkes-Barre, PA 18711-0026
(570)824-3521

WILKES BARRE GENERAL HOSPITAL
575 N River St
Wilkes-Barre, PA 18764-0999
(570)829-8111

WILLIAMSBURG

COVE FORGE BEHAVIORAL HELATH SYSTEM
Route 1 Box 79
Williamsburg, PA 16693-9673
(814)832-2121

WILLIAMSPORT

DIVINE PROVIDENCE HOSPITAL
1100 Grampian Boulevard
Williamsport, PA 17701-1995
(570)326-8000

WILLIAMSPORT HOSPITAL
777 Rural Avenue
Williamsport, PA 17701-3198
(570)321-1000

WINDBER

WINDBER MEDICAL CENTER
600 Somerset Avenue
Windber, PA 15963-1331
(814)467-6611

WYNDMOOR

CHESTNUT HILL HOSPITAL
8601 Stenton Avenue
Wyndmoor, PA 1903808395
(215)248-8200

CHESTNUT HILL REHAB HOSPITAL
8601 Stenton Avenue
Wyndmoor, PA 19038-8395
(215)233-6200

WYNNEWOOD

LANKENAU HOSPITAL
Lancaster And City Line Avenue
Wynnewood, PA 19096
(610)645-2000

YORK

HEALTHSOUTH REHABILITATION HOSPITAL YORK
1850 Normandie Drive
York, PA 17404-1534
(717)767-6941

MEMORIAL HOSPITAL
325 Belmont St
York, PA 17403-2609
(717)843-8623

SELECT SPECIALTY HOSPITAL - YORK
1001 South George Street
York, PA 17403-3676
(717)812-2421

YORK HOSPITAL
1001 South George St
York, PA 17403-3645
(717)851-2345

PUERTO RICO

AGUADILLA

AGUADILLA REGIONAL HOSPITAL
Bo Camaseyes PO Box 3968
Aguadilla, PR 00605-3968
(787)891-0972

AIBONITO

MENNONITE GENERAL HOSPITAL INC
PO Box 1379
Aibonito, PR 00705-1379
(787)735-8001

PENNSYLVANIA
Hospital Telephone Directory

ARECIBO

HOSPITAL DR SUSONI INC
55 Palm St PO Box 1298
Arecibo, PR 00613-1298
(787)878-1010

HOSPITAL REGIONAL DR CAYETANO COLL
Y TOSTE
Box 9976 Cotto Station
Arecibo, PR 00613-9976
(787)878-7272

ARROYO

LAFAYETTE HOSPITAL
Box 207
Arroyo, PR 00714-0207
(787)839-3232

BAYAMON

HOSPITAL HERMANOS MELENDEZ
PO Box 306
Bayamon, PR 00960-6006
(787)785-6715

HOSPITAL MATILDE BRENES
9 J Street Ext Hermanas Davila
Bayamon, PR 00960
(787)786-6315

HOSPITAL UNIVERSITARIO DR RUIZ ARNAU
Laurel Ave Santa Juanita
Bayamon, PR 00956-3273
(787)787-0179

MEPSI CENTER
Rd Num 2 KM 8 2
Bayamon, PR 00956
(787)793-3030

SAN PABLO HOSPITAL
70 Santa Cruz St, Box 236
Bayamon, PR 00960-6036
(787)786-7474

CAGUAS

HOSPITAL INTERAMERICANO DE MEDICINA
PO Box 1744
Caguas, PR 00726-1744
(787)743-3434

SAN JUAN BAUTISTA MEDICAL CENTER
Carr 172 Urb Turabo Gardens
Caguas, PR 00725
(787)744-2500

CAPARRA

HOSPITAL PSIQUIATRIA DR RAMON
FERNANDEZ
Bo Monacillos
Caparra, PR 00922
(787)759-8132

CAROLINA

CAROLINA AREA HOSPITAL
Ave 65th Infanteria Box 3747
Carolina, PR 00984-3747
(787)757-1800

CASTANER

CASTANER GENERAL HOSPITAL
PO Box 1003
Castaner, PR 00631-1003
(787)829-5010

CAYEY

HOSPITAL MENONITA DE CAYEY
PO Box 967
Cayey, PR 00737-0967
(787)738-2181

CIDRA

FIRST HOSPITAL PANAMERICANO
Box 6425
Cidra, PR 00739
(787)739-5555

COTO LAUREL

HOSPITAL SAN CRISTOBAL
Carr 506 Bo
Coto Laurel, PR 00780
(787)848-2100

FAJARDO

HOSPITAL SAN PABLO DEL ESTE
PO Box 1028
Fajardo, PR 00738-1028
(787)863-0505

GUAYAMA

GUAYAMA AREA HOSPITAL
PO Box 910
Guayama, PR 00785-0910
(787)864-4300

SANTA ROSA CLINIC
PO Box 988
Guayama, PR 00785-0988
(787)864-0101

HATO REY

AUXILIO MUTUO HOSPITAL
Ponce De Leon Avenue Stop 36 1/2
Hato Rey, PR 00919
(787)758-2000

HUMACAO

FONT MARTELLO HOSPITAL
Box 639
Humacao, PR 00792-0639
(787)852-2424

HOSPITAL DR DOMINGUEZ
300 Font Martello Street
Humacao, PR 00792
(787)852-0505

HUMACAO AREA HOSPITAL
Box 115
Humacao, PR 00792-0115
(787)852-2727

RYDER MEMORIAL HOSPITAL
Call Box 489
Humacao, PR 00792-0489
(787)852-0768

MANATI

DOCTORS CENTER HOSPITAL
PO Box 532
Manati, PR 00674-0532
(787)854-3372

DR ALEJANDRO OTERO LOPEZ HOSPITAL
Calle Hernandez Carrion 668
Manati, PR 00674
(787)854-3700

HOSPITAL SAN AGUSTIN INC
Box 991
Manati, PR 00674-0991
(787)854-2091

MAYAGUEZ

BELLA VISTA HOSPITAL
Box 1750
Mayaguez, PR 00681-1750
(787)834-2350

CLINICA DR PEREA, INC
Box 170
Mayaguez, PR 00681-0170
(787)834-0101

CLINICA ESPANOLA INC
Box 490 La Quinta
Mayaguez, PR 00681-0490
(787)832-2094

DR RAMON EMETERIO BETANCES
Road Two KM 157
Mayaguez, PR 00680
(787)832-8686

MOCA

HOSPITAL SAN CARLOS BORROMEO
Rd 110 KM 12 2
Moca, PR 00676
(787)877-8000

PONCE

CLINICA DR PILA
PO Box 1910 Las Americas Ave
Ponce, PR 00731
(787)848-5600

CLINICA ONCOLOGICA
Terrenos Centro Medico Barrio Machuelo
Ponce, PR 00731
(787)843-0800

SANTO ASILO DE DAMAS HOSPITAL
Ponce By Pass
Ponce, PR 00731
(787)840-8686

ST LUKE'S EPISCOPAL HOSPITAL
Bo Machuelo
Ponce, PR 00731
(787)844-2080

ST LUKES EPISCOPAL HOSPITAL
PO Box 2027 Ponce
Ponce, PR 00733-2027
(787)840-4545

RIO PIEDRAS

CENTRO CARDIOVASCULAR
Centro Medico Box 366528
Rio Piedras, PR 00936-6528
(787)754-8500

HEALTHSOUTH REHABILITATION HOSPITAL
University District Hospital — 3rd Floor
Rio Piedras, PR 00935
(787)274-5100

HOSPITAL SAN FRANCISCO
371 De Diego Ave
Rio Piedras, PR 00923-3002
(787)767-5100

HOSPITAL SAN GERARDO
Road No 844 KM 0 5 PO Cupey Bajo
Rio Piedras, PR 00928
(787)761-8383

SAN JUAN CAPESTRANO PSYCHIATRIC
HOSPITAL
Carr 877 Km 1 6 Camino Las Lomas RR2
Rio Piedras, PR 00926-9803
(787)760-0222

SAN JUAN MUNICIPAL HOSPITAL
Centro Medico, Box 21405
Rio Piedras, PR 00928-1405
(787)765-9995

UNIVERSITY DISTRICT HOSPITAL
Barrio Monacillos
Rio Piedras, PR 00935
(787)754-0101

Hospital Telephone Directory — RHODE ISLAND

SAN GERMAN

HOSPITAL DE LA CONCEPCION
41 Luna St, Box 285
San German, PR 00683-0285
(787)892-1860

HOSPITAL METROPOLITANO SAN GERMAN
Calle Javilla Al Costado Parque De Bombas
San German, PR 00683
(787)892-5300

SAN JUAN

ADMIN DE SERVICIOS MEDICOS PUERTO RIC
Monacillo Ward Building # 1
San Juan, PR 00922
(787)777-3400

ASHFORD PRESBYTERIAN COMMUNITY HOSPITAL
PO Box 32
San Juan, PR 00902
(787)721-2160

DEL MAESTRO HOSPITAL
PO Box 4708
San Juan, PR 00936
(787)758-8383

DR I GONZALEZ MARTINEZ ONCOLOGY HOSPITAL
Box 1811 Centro Medico
San Juan, PR 00919
(787)863-4149

METROPOLITAN HOSPITAL
Box 11981
San Juan, PR 00922-1981
(787)783-6200

UNIVERSITY PEDIATRIC HOSPITAL
PO Box 191079
San Juan, PR 00919-1079
(787)754-3700

SANTURCE

DOCTORS HOSPITAL
PO Box 11338
Santurce, PR 00907
(787)724-2950

PAVIA HOSPITAL
PO Box 11137
Santurce, PR 00909
(787)727-6060

SAN CARLOS GENERAL HOSPITAL
1822 Ponce De Leon Ave
Santurce, PR 00909-1906
(787)727-5858

VEGA BAJA

HOSPITAL WILMA N VAZQUEZ
Calle Bx 7001
Vega Baja, PR 00694-7001
(787)858-1580

YAUCO

HOSPITAL DR TITO MATTEI
Road 128 PO Box 68
Yauco, PR 00698-0068
(787)856-2050

RHODE ISLAND

CRANSTON

ELEANOR SLATER HOSPITAL
Box 8269
Cranston, RI 02920-0269
(401)462-3085

INSTITUTE OF MENTAL HEALTH
PO Box 8281
Cranston, RI 02920-0281
(401)464-2495

NEWPORT

NAVAL HOSPITAL NEWPORT
Newport, RI 02841
(401)841-3771

NEWPORT HOSPITAL
11 Freindship Street
Newport, RI 02840-2299
(401)846-6400

NORTH PROVIDENCE

SAINT JOSEPH HEALTH SERVICES OF RHODE ISLAND - OUR LADY OF FATIMA HOSPITAL
200 High Service Avenue
North Providence, RI 02904-5113
(401)456-3000

NORTH SMITHFIELD

LANDMARK MEDICAL CENTER - FOGARTY
Eddie Dowling Highway
North Smithfield, RI 02896
(401)766-0800

REHABILITATION HOSPITAL OF RHODE ISLAND
Eddie Dowling Highway
North Smithfield, RI 02896
(401)766-0800

PAWTUCKET

MEMORIAL HOSPITAL OF RHODE ISLAND
111 Brewster Street
Pawtucket, RI 02860-4499
(401)729-2000

PROVIDENCE

BUTLER HOSPITAL
345 Blackstone Boulevard
Providence, RI 02906-4861
(401)455-6200

MIRIAM HOSPITAL
164 Summit Avenue
Providence, RI 02906-2894
(401)793-2500

RHODE ISLAND HOSPITAL
593 Eddy St
Providence, RI 02903-4970
(401)444-4000

ROGER WILLIAMS HOSPITAL
825 Chalkstone Avenue
Providence, RI 02908-4735
(401)456-2000

SAINT JOSEPH HOSPITAL FOR SPECIALTY CARE
21 Peace St
Providence, RI 02907-1510
(401)456-3000

VA MEDICAL CENTER - PROVIDENCE
830 Chalkstone Avenue
Providence, RI 02908-4799
(401)457-3042

WOMEN AND INFANTS HOSPITAL OF RHODE ISLAND
101 Dudley Street
Providence, RI 02905-2401
(401)274-1100

RIVERSIDE

EMMA PENDLETON BRADLEY HOSPITAL
1011 Veterans Memorial Parkway
Riverside, RI 02915-5061
(401)432-1000

WAKEFIELD

SOUTH COUNTY HOSPITAL
95 Kenyon Avenue
Wakefield, RI 02879-4213
(401)782-8000

WARWICK

KENT COUNTY MEMORIAL HOSPITAL
455 Toll Gate Road
Warwick, RI 02886-2770
(401)737-7000

WESTERLY

WESTERLY HOSPITAL
Wells St
Westerly, RI 02891
(401)596-6000

WOONSOCKET

LANDMARK MEDICAL CENTER
115 Cass Avenue
Woonsocket, RI 02895-4731
(401)769-4100

SOUTH CAROLINA

ABBEVILLE

ABBEVILLE COUNTY MEMORIAL HOSPITAL
Highway 72 West Box 887
Abbeville, SC 29620-0887
(864)459-5011

AIKEN

AIKEN REGIONAL MEDICAL CENTER
202 University Parkway
Aiken, SC 29801
(803)641-5000

AURORA PAVILION
PO Box 1117
Aiken, SC 29802-1117
(803)641-5900

ANDERSON

ANDERSON AREA MEDICAL CENTER
800 N Fant St
Anderson, SC 29621-5793
(864)261-1000

PATRICK B HARRIS PSYCHIATRIC HOSPITAL
PO Box 2907
Anderson, SC 29622-2907
(864)231-2600

BAMBERG

BAMBERG COUNTY MEMORIAL HOSPITAL
600 North St Box 507
Bamberg, SC 29003-1374
(803)245-4321

BARNWELL

BARNWELL COUNTY HOSPITAL
811 Reynolds Rd
Barnwell, SC 29812-1555
(803)259-1000

SOUTH CAROLINA
Hospital Telephone Directory

BEAUFORT

BEAUFORT MEMORIAL HOSPITAL
955 Ribaut Road
Beaufort, SC 29902-5454
(843)522-5200

LOW COUNTRY GENERAL HOSPITAL
PO Box 1068
Beaufort, SC 29901-1068
(843)717-3300

NAVAL HOSPITAL BEAUFORT
1 Pinckney Boulevard
Beaufort, SC 29902-6122
(843)228-5301

BENNETTSVILLE

MARLBORO PARK HOSPITAL
PO Box 738
Bennettsville, SC 29512-0738
(843)479-2881

CAMDEN

KERSHAW COUNTY MEDICAL CENTER
Haile And Roberts Streets, Box 7003
Camden, SC 29020-7003
(803)432-4311

CHARLESTON

BON SECOURS-SAINT FRANCIS XAVIER HOSPITAL
2095 Henry Tecklenburg Drive
Charleston, SC 29414-5734
(843)402-1000

CHARLESTON MEMORIAL HOSPITAL
326 Calhoun St
Charleston, SC 29401-1189
(843)953-8300

KINDRED HOSPITAL - CHARLESTON
326 Calhoun Street, 3rd Floor
Charleston, SC 29401-1124
(843)953-8340

MEDICAL UNIVERSITY HOSPITAL
171 Ashley Avenue
Charleston, SC 29425-0100
(843)792-2300

PALMETTO LOWCOUNTRY BEHAVIORAL HEALTH SYSTEM
2777 Speissegger Drive
Charleston, SC 29405-8229
(843)747-5830

ROPER HOSPITAL NORTH
325 Calhoun St
Charleston, SC 29401-1114
(843)744-2110

TRIDENT MEDICAL CENTER
9330 Medical Plaza Drive
Charleston, SC 29406-9195
(843)797-7000

VA MEDICAL CENTER - RALPH H JOHNSON
109 Bee St
Charleston, SC 29401-5703
(843)577-5011

CHERAW

CHESTERFIELD GENERAL HOSPITAL
Highway 9 Box 151
Cheraw, SC 29520-0151
(843)537-7881

CHESTER

CHESTER COUNTY HOSPITAL
1 Medical Park Drive
Chester, SC 29706-9776
(803)581-9400

CLINTON

LAURENS COUNTY HOSPITAL
Us Highway 76 PO Drawer 976
Clinton, SC 29325-0976
(864)833-9100

WHITTEN CENTER HOSPITAL
PO Box 239
Clinton, SC 29325-0239
(864)833-2733

COLUMBIA

CHILDREN'S HOSPITAL
5 Richland Medical Park
Columbia, SC 29203-8000
(803)434-7000

G WERBER BRYAN PSYCH HOSPITAL
220 Faison Drive
Columbia, SC 29203-3210
(803)935-7140

HEALTHSOUTH REHABILITATION HOSPITAL/COLUMBIA
2935 Colonial Drive
Columbia, SC 29203-6811
(803)254-7777

INTERMEDICAL HOSPITAL OF SOUTH CAROLINA
Taylor At Marion Street
Columbia, SC 29220-0001
(803)296-3701

MIDLANDS CENTER
8301 Farrow Road
Columbia, SC 29203-3294
(803)935-7508

PALMETTO BAPTIST MEDICAL CENTER AT COLUMBIA
Taylor At Marion Street
Columbia, SC 29220-0001
(803)296-5010

PALMETTO RICHLAND HOSPITAL
5 Richland Medical Park
Columbia, SC 29203-6897
(803)434-7000

PROVIDENCE HOSPITAL
2435 Forest Drive
Columbia, SC 29204-2098
(803)865-4500

PROVIDENCE HOSPITAL NORTHEAST
120 Gateway Corporate Boulevard
Columbia, SC 29203-9802
(803)865-4500

SOUTH CAROLINA STATE HOSPITAL
PO Box 119
Columbia, SC 29202-0119
(803)898-2261

VA MEDICAL CENTER - WM JENNINGS BRYAN DORN
6439 Garner's Ferry Road
Columbia, SC 29209-1638
(803)776-4000

WILLIAM S HALL PSYCHIATRIC INSTITUTE
1800 Colonial Drive
Columbia, SC 29203-6827
(803)898-1725

CONWAY

CONWAY HOSPITAL
300 Singleton Ridge Road
Conway, SC 29526-9142
(843)347-7111

DARLINGTON

WILSON MEDICAL CENTER
PO Box 1859
Darlington, SC 29540-1859
(843)395-1100

DILLON

SAINT EUGENE MEDICAL CENTER
301 E Jackson St
Dillon, SC 29536-2509
(843)774-4111

EASLEY

PALMETTO BAPTIST MEDICAL CENTER-EASLEY
200 Fleetwood Drive
Easley, SC 29640-2076
(864)442-7200

EDGEFIELD

EDGEFIELD COUNTY HOSPITAL
PO Box 590 Bauskett St
Edgefield, SC 29824-0590
(803)637-3174

FAIRFAX

ALLENDALE COUNTY HOSPITAL
Highway 278 W Box 218
Fairfax, SC 29827-0218
(803)632-3311

FLORENCE

CAROLINAS HOSPITAL SYSTEM
805 Pamplico Hwy, PO Box 100550
Florence, SC 29501-0550
(843)674-5000

HEALTHSOUTH REHAB HOSPITAL/FLORENCE
900 East Cheves Street
Florence, SC 29506-2704
(843)679-9000

MCLEOD REGIONAL MEDICAL CENTER
555 E Cheves St Box 8700
Florence, SC 29506-2606
(843)667-2000

REGENCY HOSPITAL OF FLORENCE
121 East Cedar Street
Florence, SC 29506-2576
(843)661-3480

FORT JACKSON

MONCRIEF ARMY COMMUNITY HOSPITAL - U.S.A. MEDDAC
4500 Stuart Street
Fort Jackson, SC 29207-5700
(803)751-2284

GAFFNEY

UPSTATE CAROLINA MEDICAL CENTER
1530 N Limestone St
Gaffney, SC 29340-4738
(864)487-4271

GEORGETOWN

GEORGETOWN MEMORIAL HOSPITAL
606 Black River Road Drawer 1718
Georgetown, SC 29440-3368
(843)527-7000

Hospital Telephone Directory — SOUTH CAROLINA

GREENVILLE

BON SECOURS SAINT FRANCIS HEALTH CARE
1 St Francis Drive
Greenville, SC 29601-3955
(864)255-1000

GREENVILLE HOSPITAL SYSTEM
701 Grove Road
Greenville, SC 29605-5611
(864)455-7000

MARSHALL I. PICKENS HOSPITAL
701 Grove Road
Greenville, SC 29605-5611
(864)455-7000

ROGER C. PEACE REHAB HOSPITAL
701 Grove Road
Greenville, SC 29605-5611
(864)455-7000

SAINT FRANCIS WOMEN'S & FAMILY HOSPITAL
125 Commonwealth Drive
Greenville, SC 29615-4880
(864)675-4000

SHRINERS HOSPITAL FOR CHILDREN
950 W Faris Road
Greenville, SC 29605-4277
(864)271-3444

W. J. BARGE MEMORIAL HOSPITAL
Wade Hampton Blvd
Greenville, SC 29614-0001
(864)242-5100

GREENWOOD

SELF MEMORIAL HOSPITAL
1325 Spring Street
Greenwood, SC 29646-3860
(864)227-4111

GREER

ALLEN BENNETT MEMORIAL HOSPITAL
313 Memorial Drive Box 1149
Greer, SC 29650-1599
(864)968-6300

CAROLINA CENTER FOR BEHAVORIAL HEALTH
2700 E Phillips Road
Greer, SC 29650-4815
(864)235-2335

HARTSVILLE

CAROLINA PINES REGIONAL HOSPITAL
1304 W Bobo Newsom Hwy
Hartsville, SC 29550-4399
(843)339-2100

HILTON HEAD ISLAND

HILTON HEAD MEDICAL CENTER AND CLINICS
25 Hospital Center Boulevard
Hilton Head Island, SC 29926-2738
(843)681-6122

KINGSTREE

WILLIAMSBURG REGIONAL HOSPITAL
500 Nelson Boulevard
Kingstree, SC 29556-4027
(843)355-8888

LAKE CITY

CAROLINAS HOSPITAL SYSTEM-LAKE CITY
258 N Ron Mcnair Boulevard
Lake City, SC 29560-2462
(843)394-2036

LANCASTER

SPRINGS MEMORIAL HOSPITAL
800 W Meeting St
Lancaster, SC 29720-2298
(803)286-1214

LITTLE RIVER

SEACOAST MEDICAL CENTER
4000 Highway 9-East
Little River, SC 29566-7833
(843)390-8100

LOCKHART

HOPE HOSPITAL
PO Box 280
Lockhart, SC 29364-0280
(864)545-6500

LORIS

LORIS COMMUNITY HOSPITAL
3655 Mitchell St
Loris, SC 29569-2844
(843)716-7000

MANNING

CLARENDON MEMORIAL HOSPITAL
10 Hospital Street PO Box 550
Manning, SC 29102-0550
(803)435-8463

MARION

MARION COUNTY MEDICAL CENTER
2829 E Highway 76 PO Box 1150
Marion, SC 29571-1150
(843)431-2000

MOUNT PLEASANT

EAST COOPER REGIONAL MEDICAL CENTER
1200 Johnnie Dodds Boulevard
Mount Pleasant, SC 29464-3294
(843)881-0100

MURRELLS INLET

WACCAMAW COMMUNITY HOSPITAL
4070 Highway 17-South Bypass
Murrells Inlet, SC 29576-5033
(843)652-1000

MYRTLE BEACH

GRAND STRAND REGIONAL MEDICAL CENTER
809 82nd Parkway Box 7500
Myrtle Beach, SC 29572-4607
(843)692-1000

NEWBERRY

NEWBERRY COUNTY MEMORIAL HOSPITAL
2669 Kinard St PO Box 497
Newberry, SC 29108-0497
(803)276-7570

NORTH CHARLESTON

HEALTHSOUTH REHAB HOSPITAL OF CHARLESTON
9181 Medcom Drive
North Charleston, SC 29406-9168
(843)820-7777

NAVAL HOSPITAL CHARLESTON
3600 Rivers Avenue
North Charleston, SC 29405-7769
(843)743-7000

ORANGEBURG

REGIONAL MEDICAL CENTER OF ORANGEBURG AND CALHOUN
3000 St Matthews Road Box 1806
Orangeburg, SC 29118-1442
(803)533-2200

PICKENS

CANNON MEMORIAL HOSPITAL
123 Medical Park Drive Box 188
Pickens, SC 29671-2739
(864)878-4791

ROCK HILL

HEALTHSOUTH REHABILITATION HOSPITAL
PO Box 36488
Rock Hill, SC 29732-0508
(803)326-3500

PIEDMONT HEALTH CARE SYSTEM
222 S Herlong Avenue
Rock Hill, SC 29732-1158
(803)329-1234

SENECA

OCONEE MEMORIAL HOSPITAL
298 Memorial Drive
Seneca, SC 29672-9499
(864)882-3351

SHAW AIR FORCE BASE

20TH MEDICAL GROUP
431 Meadowlark St
Shaw Air Force Base, SC 29152-5019
(803)895-6324

SIMPSONVILLE

HILLCREST HOSPITAL
729 South East Main Street
Simpsonville, SC 29681-3280
(864)967-6100

SPARTANBURG

MARY BLACK MEMORIAL HOSPITAL
1700 Skylyn Drive Box 3217
Spartanburg, SC 29307-1061
(864)573-3000

SPARTANBURG HOSPITAL FOR RESTORATIVE CARE
389 Serpentine Drive
Spartanburg, SC 29303-3074
(864)560-3280

SPARTANBURG REGIONAL MEDICAL CENTER
101 E Wood St
Spartanburg, SC 29303-3072
(864)560-6000

SUMMERVILLE

SUMMERVILLE MEDICAL CENTER
295 Midland Parkway
Summerville, SC 29485-8104
(843)832-5000

SUMTER

TUOMEY HEALTH CARE SYSTEM
129 N Washington St
Sumter, SC 29150-4949
(803)778-9000

SOUTH DAKOTA — Hospital Telephone Directory

TRAVELERS REST

NORTH GREENVILLE HOSPITAL
807 N Main St
Travelers Rest, SC 29690-1598
(864)834-5132

SPRINGBROOK BEHAVIORAL HEALTHCARE
PO Box 1005
Travelers Rest, SC 29690-1005
(864)834-8013

UNION

WALLACE THOMSON HOSPITAL
322 W South St PO Drawer 789
Union, SC 29379-2857
(864)429-2600

VARNVILLE

HAMPTON REGIONAL MEDICAL CENTER
503 Carolina Avenue West
Varnville, SC 29944
(803)943-2771

WALTERBORO

COLLETON MEDICAL CENTER
501 Robertson Boulevard
Walterboro, SC 29488-2787
(843)549-2000

WEST COLUMBIA

LEXINGTON MEDICAL CENTER
2720 Sunset Boulevard
West Columbia, SC 29169-4810
(803)791-2000

THREE RIVERS BEHAVIORAL HEALTH
SYSTEM
2900 Sunset Boulevard
West Columbia, SC 29169-3422
(803)796-9911

WINNSBORO

FAIRFIELD MEMORIAL HOSPITAL
Highway 321 By-pass Box 620
Winnsboro, SC 29180-0620
(803)635-5548

WOODRUFF

B J WORKMAN MEMORIAL HOSPITAL
751 E Georgia Street
Woodruff, SC 29388-1991
(864)560-9100

SOUTH DAKOTA

ABERDEEN

AVERA SAINT LUKES HOSPITAL
305 S State St
Aberdeen, SD 57401-4590
(605)622-5000

DAKOTA PLAINS SURGICAL CENTER
701 8th Avenue Nw, Suite C
Aberdeen, SD 57401-1803
(605)225-3300

ARMOUR

DOUGLAS COUNTY MEMORIAL HOSPITAL-
RPCH
Box 26
Armour, SD 57313-0026
(605)724-2159

BOWDLE

BOWDLE HOSPITAL
PO Box 556
Bowdle, SD 57428-0556
(605)285-6146

BRITTON

MARSHALL COUNTY
HEALTHCARE/HOSPITAL
413 9th Street
Britton, SD 57430-2274
(605)448-2253

BROOKINGS

BROOKINGS HOSPITAL
300 22nd Avenue
Brookings, SD 57006-2474
(605)696-9000

BURKE

COMMUNITY MEMORIAL HOSPITAL - RPCH
8th And Jackson, PO Box 319
Burke, SD 57523-0319
(605)775-2621

CANTON

CANTON-INWOOD MEMORIAL HOSPITAL
Highway 18 East PO Box 9
Canton, SD 57013-0009
(605)987-2621

CHAMBERLAIN

MID DAKOTA HOSPITAL
PO Box 307
Chamberlain, SD 57325-0307
(605)734-5511

CLEAR LAKE

DEUEL COUNTY MEMORIAL HOSPITAL -
RPCH
701 3rd Ave S
Clear Lake, SD 57226-2016
(605)874-2141

CUSTER

CUSTER COMMUNITY HOSPITAL
1039 Montgomery St
Custer, SD 57730-1304
(605)673-2229

DAKOTA DUNES

SIOUXLAND SURGERY CENTER LTD
PARTNERSHIP
600 Sioux Point Road
Dakota Dunes, SD 57049-5000
(605)232-3332

DE SMET

DESMET MEMORIAL HOSPITAL
306 Prairie Avenue Sw
De Smet, SD 57231-2285
(605)854-3329

DEADWOOD

NORTHERN HILLS GENERAL HOSPITAL
61 Charles St
Deadwood, SD 57732-1303
(605)722-6101

DELL RAPIDS

DELLS AREA HEALTH CENTER
909 N Iowa
Dell Rapids, SD 57022-1231
(605)428-5431

EAGLE BUTTE

PHS INDIAN HOSPITAL - EAGLE BUTTE
PO Box 1012
Eagle Butte, SD 57625-1012
(605)964-7724

ELLSWORTH AIR FORCE BASE

28TH MEDICAL GROUP
2900 Doolittle Drive
Ellsworth Air Force Base, SD 57706-4821
(605)385-3328

EUREKA

EUREKA COMMUNITY HOSPITAL - RPCH
E Avenue And 9th Street
Eureka, SD 57437
(605)284-2661

FAULKTON

FAULK COUNTY MEMORIAL HOSPITAL
Box 100
Faulkton, SD 57438-0100
(605)598-6263

FLANDREAU

FLANDREAU MUNICIPAL HOSPITAL
214 N Prairie
Flandreau, SD 57028-1243
(605)997-2433

FORT MEADE

VA MEDICAL CENTER - FORT MEADE
113 Comanche Road
Fort Meade, SD 57741-1002
(605)347-2511

FREEMAN

FREEMAN COMMUNITY HOSPITAL
PO Box 370
Freeman, SD 57029-0370
(605)925-4000

GETTYSBURG

GETTYSBURG MEDICAL CENTER
700 East Garfield Avenue
Gettysburg, SD 57442-1327
(605)765-2480

GREGORY

GREGORY COMMUNITY HOSPITAL
400 Park Avenue PO Box 408
Gregory, SD 57533-0408
(605)835-839402

HOT SPRINGS

FALL RIVER HOSPITAL
209 North 16th Street PO Box 940
Hot Springs, SD 57747-0940
(605)745-3159

VA HEALTHCARE SYSTEM - BLACK HILLS
AT HOT SPRINGS
500 North 5th Street
Hot Springs, SD 57747-1480
(605)745-2052

Hospital Telephone Directory — SOUTH DAKOTA

HOVEN
HOLY INFANT HOSPITAL
158 Main Street PO Box 158
Hoven, SD 57450-0158
(605)948-2262

HURON
HURON REGIONAL MEDICAL CENTER
4th And Iowa Se
Huron, SD 57350
(605)353-6200

LEMMON
FIVE COUNTIES HOSPITAL - RPCH
405 Sixth Avenue W PO Box 479
Lemmon, SD 57638-0479
(605)374-3871

MADISON
MADISON COMMUNITY HOSPITAL
917 N Washington
Madison, SD 57042-1696
(605)256-6551

MARTIN
BENNETT COUNTY HEALTHCARE CENTER
102 Major Allen, PO Box 70-d
Martin, SD 57551-0070
(605)685-6622

MILBANK
SAINT BERNARDS PROVIDENCE HOSPITAL
901 E Virgil Avenue
Milbank, SD 57252-2124
(605)432-4538

MILLER
HAND COUNTY MEMORIAL HOSPITAL
300 W Fifth Street
Miller, SD 57362-1299
(605)853-2421

MITCHELL
AVERA QUEEN OF PEACE HOSPITAL - EACH
525 N Foster
Mitchell, SD 57301-2966
(605)995-2000

MOBRIDGE
MOBRIDGE REGIONAL HOSPITAL
PO Box 580
Mobridge, SD 57601-0580
(605)845-3693

PARKSTON
AVERA SAINT BENEDICT HOSPITAL
401 W Glynn Drive, PO Box B
Parkston, SD 57366-1202
(605)928-3311

PHILIP
HANS P PETERSON MEMORIAL HOSPITAL
503 West Pine PO Box 790
Philip, SD 57567-0790
(605)859-2511

PIERRE
SAINT MARYS HOSPITAL
803 E Dakota
Pierre, SD 57501-3312
(605)224-3100

PINE RIDGE
PHS INDIAN HOSPITAL - PINE RIDGE
Pine Ridge - Shannon
Pine Ridge, SD 57770
(605)867-5131

PLATTE
PLATTE COMMUNITY MEMORIAL HOSPITAL
601 E 7th, PO Box 818
Platte, SD 57369-0818
(605)337-3364

RAPID CITY
BLACK HILLS SURGERY CENTER LLP
1868 Lombardy Dr
Rapid City, SD 57703-4130
(605)721-4900

PHS INDIAN HOSPITAL - RAPID CITY
3200 Canyon Lake Drive
Rapid City, SD 57702-8114
(605)355-2500

RAPID CITY REGIONAL HOSPITAL
353 Fairmont Boulevard PO Box 6000
Rapid City, SD 57709-6000
(605)719-1000

SAME DAY SURGERY CENTER
651 Cathedral Drive
Rapid City, SD 57701-7368
(605)719-5000

REDFIELD
COMMUNITY MEMORIAL HOSPITAL
111 W 10th Avenue PO Box 420
Redfield, SD 57469-0420
(605)472-1111

ROSEBUD
PHS INDIAN HOSPITAL - ROSEBUD
PO Box 400
Rosebud, SD 57570-0400
(605)747-2231

SCOTLAND
SCOTLAND LANDMANN-JUNGMAN MEMORIAL HOSPITAL
600 Billars Street
Scotland, SD 57059-2026
(605)583-2226

SIOUX FALLS
AVERA MCKENNAN HOSPITAL
800 E 21st St
Sioux Falls, SD 57105-1096
(605)322-8000

CHILDRENS CARE HOSPITAL/SCHOOL
2501 W 26th St
Sioux Falls, SD 57105-2498
(605)782-2300

HEART HOSPITAL OF SOUTH DAKOTA
4500 West 69th Street
Sioux Falls, SD 57108-8148
(605)977-7000

SELECT SPECIALTY HOSPITAL - SIOUX FALLS
800 E 21st St Suite 300
Sioux Falls, SD 57105-1016
(605)322-3500

SIOUX FALLS SURGICAL CENTER LLP
910 East 20th Street
Sioux Falls, SD 57105-1079
(605)334-6730

SIOUX VALLEY BEHAVIORAL HEALTH SYSTEM
2812 S Louise Avenue
Sioux Falls, SD 57106-4300
(605)361-8111

SIOUX VALLEY HOSPITAL
1305 W 18th St
Sioux Falls, SD 57105-0496
(605)333-1000

VA MEDICAL CENTER - SIOUX FALLS
2501 W 22nd St
Sioux Falls, SD 57105-1305
(605)336-3230

SISSETON
COTEAU DES PRAIRIES HOSPITAL
205 Orchard Drive
Sisseton, SD 57262-2398
(605)698-7647

PHS INDIAN HOSPITAL - SISSETON
PO Box 189
Sisseton, SD 57262-0189
(605)698-7606

SPEARFISH
LOOKOUT MEMORIAL HOSPITAL
1440 N Main
Spearfish, SD 57783-1504
(605)644-4000

SPEARFISH SURGERY CENTER
1316 10th Street
Spearfish, SD 57783-1530
(605)642-3113

STURGIS
STURGIS COMMUNITY HEALTH CARE CENTER
949 Harmon Box 279
Sturgis, SD 57785-2452
(605)347-2536

TYNDALL
SAINT MICHAELS HOSPITAL
PO Box 27
Tyndall, SD 57066-0027
(605)589-3341

VERMILLION
SIOUX VALLEY MEDICAL CENTER
20 South Plum
Vermillion, SD 57069-3346
(605)624-2611

VIBORG
PIONEER MEMORIAL HOSPITAL
Washington St Box 368
Viborg, SD 57070-0368
(605)326-5161

WAGNER
PHS INDIAN HOSPITAL - WAGNER
110 Washington St
Wagner, SD 57380
(605)384-3621

WAGNER COMMUNITY MEMORIAL HOSPITAL
3rd St And Wagner Heights
Wagner, SD 57380
(605)384-3611

TENNESSEE

Hospital Telephone Directory

WATERTOWN

MEMORIAL CARE UNIT
400 10th Avenue Nw
Watertown, SD 57201-1561
(605)882-7701

PRAIRIE LAKES HOSPITAL AND CARE
CENTER - EACH
400 10th Avenue Nw
Watertown, SD 57201-1599
(605)882-7000

WEBSTER

LAKE AREA HOSPITAL
North First St PO Box 489
Webster, SD 57274-0489
(605)345-3336

WESSINGTON SPRINGS

AVERA WESKOTA MEMORIAL MEDICAL
CENTER
604 1st St Ne
Wessington Springs, SD 57382-2134
(605)539-1201

WINNER

WINNER REGIONAL HEALTHCARE CENTER
745 East 8th St
Winner, SD 57580-2677
(605)842-7100

YANKTON

AVERA SACRED HEART HOSPITAL
501 Summit
Yankton, SD 57078-3855
(605)668-8000

LEWIS AND CLARK SPECIALTY HOSPITAL
2605 Fox Run Pkwy
Yankton, SD 57078-5341
(605)665-5100

SOUTH DAKOTA HUMAN SERVICES
CENTER
PO Box 76 3515 Broadway Avenue
Yankton, SD 57078-0076
(605)668-3102

TENNESSEE

ASHLAND CITY

CENTENNIAL MEDICAL CENTER
313 N Main St
Ashland City, TN 37015-1319
(615)792-3030

ATHENS

ATHENS REGIONAL MEDICAL CENTER
1114 West Madison Avenue
Athens, TN 37303-4150
(423)745-1411

BOLIVAR

BOLIVAR GENERAL HOSPITAL
650 Nuckolls Road
Bolivar, TN 38008-1532
(731)658-3100

WESTERN MENTAL HEALTH INSTITUTE
Highway 64
Bolivar, TN 38074
(901)228-2000

BRISTOL

BRISTOL REGIONAL MEDICAL CENTER
1 Medical Park Boulevard
Bristol, TN 37620-7430
(423)844-1121

SELECT SPECIALTY HOSPITAL - TRI-CITY
One Medical Park Boulevard
Bristol, TN 37620-7430
(423)844-5900

BROWNSVILLE

METHODIST HAYWOOD PARK HOSPITAL
2545 N Washington Avenue
Brownsville, TN 38012-1697
(731)772-4110

CAMDEN

CAMDEN GENERAL HOSPITAL
175 Hospital Drive
Camden, TN 38320-1617
(731)584-6135

CARTHAGE

CARTHAGE GENERAL HOSPITAL
PO Box 319, 130 Lebanon Highway
Carthage, TN 37030-0319
(615)735-9815

SMITH COUNTY MEMORIAL HOSPITAL
158 Hospital Drive
Carthage, TN 37030-1096
(615)735-1560

CELINA

CUMBERLAND RIVER HOSPITAL
100 Old Jefferson St
Celina, TN 38551-4040
(931)243-3581

CENTERVILLE

BAPTIST HICKMAN COMMUNITY HOSPITAL
135 E Swan St
Centerville, TN 37033-1417
(931)729-4271

CHATTANOOGA

EAST RIDGE HOSPITAL
941 Spring Creek Road
Chattanooga, TN 37412-3997
(423)855-3500

ERLANGER MEDICAL CENTER
975 East Third St
Chattanooga, TN 37403-2163
(423)778-7000

ERLANGER NORTH HEALTH
SYSTEM/HOSPITAL
632 Morrison Springs Road
Chattanooga, TN 37415-3498
(423)778-3300

FHC CUMBERLAND HALL PSYCHIATRIC
HOSPITAL
7351 Standifer Gap Road
Chattanooga, TN 37421-8404
(423)499-9007

HEALTHSOUTH CHATTANOOGA REHAB
HOSPITAL
2412 McCallie Avenue
Chattanooga, TN 37404-3398
(423)698-0221

KINDRED HOSPITAL CHATTANOOGA
709 Walnut Street
Chattanooga, TN 37402-1916
(423)266-7721

MEMORIAL HOSPITAL
2525 Desales Avenue
Chattanooga, TN 37404-1102
(423)495-8656

MOCASSIN BEND MENTAL HEALTH
INSTITUTE
Moccasin Bend Road
Chattanooga, TN 37405
(423)785-3400

PARKRIDGE MEDICAL CENTER
2333 McCallie Avenue
Chattanooga, TN 37404-3285
(423)698-6061

SISKIN HOSPITAL FOR PHYSICAL REHAB
1 Siskin Plaza
Chattanooga, TN 37403-1306
(423)634-1200

T. C. THOMPSON CHILDREN'S HOSPITAL
910 Blackford St
Chattanooga, TN 37403-1499
(423)778-6011

VALLEY BEHAVIORAL HEALTH SYSTEM
2200 Morris Hill Road
Chattanooga, TN 37421-2818
(423)499-1204

WOMENS EAST PAVILION
1751 Gunbarrel Road
Chattanooga, TN 37421-7177
(423)954-8700

CLARKSVILLE

GATEWAY HEALTH SYSTEMS
1771 Madison St
Clarksville, TN 37043-4990
(931)552-6622

CLEVELAND

BRADLEY MEMORIAL HOSPITAL
2305 N Chambliss Avenue, Box 3060
Cleveland, TN 37311-3847
(423)559-6000

CLEVELAND COMMUNITY HOSPITAL
2800 West Side Drive Nw
Cleveland, TN 37312-3599
(423)339-4100

COLLIERVILLE

BAPTIST MEMORIAL HOSPITAL -
COLLIERVILLE
1500 West Poplar Avenue
Collierville, TN 38017-0601
(901)227-8140

COLUMBIA

MAURY REGIONAL HOSPITAL
1224 Trotwood Avenue
Columbia, TN 38401-4802
(931)381-1111

COOKEVILLE

COOKEVILLE REGIONAL HOSPITAL
142 W 5th St
Cookeville, TN 38501-1760
(931)528-2541

COPPERHILL

COPPER BASIN MEDICAL CENTER
Highway 68 Box X
Copperhill, TN 37317
(423)496-5511

Hospital Telephone Directory — TENNESSEE

COVINGTON

BAPTIST MEMORIAL HOSPITAL TIPTON
1995 Highway 51 S Box 737
Covington, TN 38019-3635
(901)476-2621

CROSSVILLE

CUMBERLAND MEDICAL CENTER
811 S Main St
Crossville, TN 38555-5011
(931)484-9511

DAYTON

RHEA MEDICAL CENTER
7900 Rhea County Highway Box 609
Dayton, TN 37321-5912
(423)775-1121

DICKSON

HORIZON MEDICAL CENTER
111 Highway 70 E
Dickson, TN 37055-2080
(615)446-0446

DYERSBURG

METHODIST HEALTHCARE/HOSPITAL OF DYERSBURG
400 Tickle St
Dyersburg, TN 38024-3120
(731)285-2410

ELIZABETHTON

SYCAMORE SHOALS HOSPITAL
1501 West Elk Avenue
Elizabethton, TN 37643-2854
(423)542-1300

ERIN

TRINITY HOSPITAL
353 Main St Box 489
Erin, TN 37061-0489
(931)289-4211

ERWIN

UNICOI COUNTY MEMORIAL HOSPITAL
Greenway Circle
Erwin, TN 37650
(423)743-3141

ETOWAH

WOODS MEMORIAL HOSPITAL
PO Box 410
Etowah, TN 37331-0410
(423)263-3600

FAYETTEVILLE

LINCOLN REGIONAL HOSPITAL
106 Medical Center Blvd
Fayetteville, TN 37334-2684
(931)438-1100

FRANKLIN

WILLIAMSON MEDICAL CENTER
2021 Carothers Road Box 681600
Franklin, TN 37067-8542
(615)791-0500

GALLATIN

SUMNER REGIONAL MEDICAL CENTER
555 Hartsville Pike
Gallatin, TN 37066-2400
(615)452-4210

TENNESSEE NEURORESTORATION CENTER
300 Stream Plant Road, Ste 410
Gallatin, TN 37066-3065
(615)451-6670

GERMANTOWN

BAPTIST REHABILITATION GERMANTOWN
2100 Exeter Road
Germantown, TN 38138-3922
(901)757-1350

METHODIST HOSPITAL - GERMANTOWN
7691 Poplar Avenue
Germantown, TN 38138-3983
(901)754-6418

GREENEVILLE

LAUGHLIN MEMORIAL HOSPITAL
1420 Tusculum Boulevard
Greeneville, TN 37745-5825
(423)787-5000

TAKOMA ADVENTIST HOSPITAL
401 Takoma Avenue
Greeneville, TN 37743-4668
(423)639-3151

HARRIMAN

ROANE MEDICAL CENTER
412 Devonia St
Harriman, TN 37748-2009
(865)882-1323

HARTSVILLE

TROUSDALE MEDICAL CENTER
500 Church St
Hartsville, TN 37074-1744
(615)374-2221

HENDERSONVILLE

HENDERSONVILLE MEDICAL CENTER
355 New Shackle Island Road
Hendersonville, TN 37075-2300
(615)264-4000

HERMITAGE

SUMMIT MEDICAL CENTER
5655 Frist Boulevard
Hermitage, TN 37076-2053
(615)316-3000

HIXSON

MEMORIAL NORTH PARK HOSPITAL
2051 Hamill Road
Hixson, TN 37343-6606
(423)870-6100

HUMBOLDT

HUMBOLDT GENERAL HOSPITAL
3525 Chere Carol Road
Humboldt, TN 38343-3638
(731)784-0301

HUNTINGDON

BAPTIST MEMORIAL HOSPITAL HUNTINGDON
631 R B Wilson Drive
Huntingdon, TN 38344-1727
(731)986-4461

JACKSON

JACKSON-MADISON COUNTY GENERAL HOSPITAL
708 W Forest
Jackson, TN 38301-3901
(731)425-5000

METHODIST HEALTHCARE - JACKSON HOSPITAL
367 Hospital Boulevard Box 3310
Jackson, TN 38305-2080
(731)661-2000

PATHWAYS OF TENNESSEE
238 Summar Drive
Jackson, TN 38301-3906
(731)935-8200

JAMESTOWN

JAMESTOWN REGIONAL MEDICAL CENTER
436 Central Avenue West
Jamestown, TN 38556-3031
(931)879-8171

JASPER

GRANDVIEW MEDICAL CENTER
1000 Highway 28
Jasper, TN 37347-3638
(423)837-9500

JEFFERSON CITY

JEFFERSON MEMORIAL HOSPITAL
110 Hospital Drive
Jefferson City, TN 37760-5282
(865)471-2400

JELLICO

JELLICO COMMUNITY HOSPITAL
188 Hospital Lane
Jellico, TN 37762-4432
(423)784-7252

JOHNSON CITY

JOHNSON CITY MEDICAL CENTER HOSPITAL
400 State Of Franklin Road
Johnson City, TN 37601
(423)431-6111

JOHNSON CITY SPECIALTY HOSPITAL
203 E Watauga Avenue
Johnson City, TN 37601-4677
(423)434-1400

NORTHSIDE HOSPITAL
401 Princeton Road
Johnson City, TN 37601-2097
(423)854-5600

QUILLEN REHAB HOSPITAL
2511 Wesley St Box 5340
Johnson City, TN 37601-1763
(423)283-0700

WOODRIDGE HOSPITAL
403 State Of Franklin Road
Johnson City, TN 37601
(423)928-7111

KINGSPORT

HEALTHSOUTH REHABILITATION HOSPITAL
113 Cassel Drive
Kingsport, TN 37660-3766
(423)246-7240

INDIAN PATH MEDICAL CENTER
2000 Brookside Road
Kingsport, TN 37660-4682
(423)392-7000

TENNESSEE — Hospital Telephone Directory

INDIAN PATH PAVILION
2300 Pavilion Drive
Kingsport, TN 37660-4622
(423)378-7500

WELLMONT HOLSTON VALLEY MEDICAL CENTER
W Ravine St
Kingsport, TN 37660-3831
(423)224-4000

KNOXVILLE

BAPTIST HOSPITAL OF EAST TENNESSEE
137 Blount Avenue Box 1788
Knoxville, TN 37920-1643
(865)632-5011

EAST TENNESSEE CHILDRENS HOSPITAL
2018 Clinch Avenue Sw
Knoxville, TN 37916-2393
(865)541-8000

FORT SANDERS PARK WEST MEDICAL CENTER
9352 Park West Boulevard
Knoxville, TN 37923-4325
(865)693-5151

FORT SANDERS REGIONAL MEDICAL CENTER
1901 Clinch Avenue
Knoxville, TN 37916-2398
(865)541-1111

LAKESHORE MENTAL HEALTH INSTITUTE
5908 Lyons View Pike
Knoxville, TN 37919-7598
(865)450-5200

SAINT MARYS MEDICAL CENTER
900 E Oak Hill Avenue
Knoxville, TN 37917-4556
(865)545-8000

SELECT SPECIALTY HOSPITAL - KNOXVILLE
1901 Clinch Avenue, 4th Floor North
Knoxville, TN 37916-2307
(865)541-2600

SELECT SPECIALTY HOSPITAL - NORTH KNOXVILLE
900 East Oak Hill Avenue
Knoxville, TN 37917-4505
(865)545-8527

UNIVERSITY OF TENNESSEE MEDICAL CENTER/HOSPITAL
1924 Alcoa Highway
Knoxville, TN 37920-6900
(865)544-9000

LA FOLLETTE

SAINT MARY'S MEDICAL CENTER
Box 1301 East Central Avenue
La Follette, TN 37766-2880
(423)907-1200

LAFAYETTE

MACON COUNTY GENERAL HOSPITAL
PO Box 378
Lafayette, TN 37083-0378
(615)666-2147

LAWRENCEBURG

CROCKETT HOSPTIAL
Highway 43 S Box 847
Lawrenceburg, TN 38464-0847
(931)762-6571

LEBANON

MCFARLAND SPECIALTY HOSPITAL
500 Park Avenue
Lebanon, TN 37087-3721
(615)449-0500

UNIVERSITY MEDICAL CENTER
1411 Baddour Parkway
Lebanon, TN 37087-2573
(615)444-8262

LEWISBURG

MARSHALL MEDICAL CENTER
1080 N Ellington Parkway
Lewisburg, TN 37091-2227
(931)359-6241

LEXINGTON

METHODIST HEALTHCARE/LEXINGTON HOSPITAL
200 W Church St
Lexington, TN 38351-2014
(731)968-3646

LINDEN

PERRY COMMUNITY HOSPITAL
805 Squirrel Drive
Linden, TN 37096
(931)589-2121

LIVINGSTON

LIVINGSTON REGIONAL HOSPITAL
315 Oak St Box 550
Livingston, TN 38570-1734
(931)823-5611

LOUDON

FORT SANDERS LOUDON MEDICAL CENTER
Vonore Road Box 217
Loudon, TN 37774-0217
(865)458-8222

LOUISVILLE

PENINSULA HEALTH CARE
Jones Bend Road Box 2000
Louisville, TN 37777-2000
(865)970-9800

MADISON

TENNESSEE CHRISTIAN MEDICAL CENTER
500 Hospital Drive
Madison, TN 37115-5032
(615)865-2373

MANCHESTER

COFFEE MEDICAL CENTER
1001 Mcarthur Drive Box 1079
Manchester, TN 37355-2455
(931)728-3586

MEDICAL CENTER OF MANCHESTER
481 Interstate Drive Box 1409
Manchester, TN 37355-3108
(931)728-6354

MARTIN

HEALTHSOUTH CANE CREEK REHAB HOSPITAL
180 Pelia Road
Martin, TN 38237
(731)587-4231

METHODIST VOLUNTEER GENERAL HOSPITAL
161 Mount Pelia Road
Martin, TN 38237-3811
(731)587-4261

MARYVILLE

BLOUNT MEMORIAL HOSPITAL
907 E Lamar Alexander Parkway
Maryville, TN 37804-5016
(865)983-7211

MC KENZIE

METHODIST HEALTHCARE HOSPITAL - MC KENZIE
945 N Highland
Mc Kenzie, TN 38201
(731)352-5344

MC MINNVILLE

RIVER PARK HOSPITAL
1510 Sparta Road
Mc Minnville, TN 37110-1317
(931)815-4000

MEMPHIS

BAPTIST MEMORIAL HOSPITAL FOR WOMEN
6225 Humphreys Boulevard
Memphis, TN 38120-2373
(901)227-9000

BAPTIST MEMORIAL HOSPITAL MEMPHIS
6019 Walnut Grove Road
Memphis, TN 38120-2173
(901)226-5000

BAPTIST MEMORIAL RESTORATIVE CARE HOSPITAL
6019 Walnut Grove Road, One-West
Memphis, TN 38120-2113
(901)226-1400

DELTA MEDICAL CENTER
3000 Getwell Road
Memphis, TN 38118-2299
(901)369-8500

HEALTHSOUTH REHABILITATION HOSPITAL - MEMPHIS
1282 Union Avenue
Memphis, TN 38104-3414
(901)722-2000

HEALTHSOUTH REHABILITATION HOSPITAL - MEMPHIS NORTH
4100 Austin Peay Highway
Memphis, TN 38128-2502
(901)213-5400

LAKESIDE BEHAVIORAL HEALTH SYSTEM
2911 Brunswick Road
Memphis, TN 38133-4105
(901)377-4700

LE BONHEUR CHILDREN'S MEDICAL CENTER
One Children's Plaza
Memphis, TN 38103
(901)572-3000

MEMPHIS MENTAL HEALTH INSTITUTE
865 Poplar Avenue
Memphis, TN 38105-4626
(901)524-1200

METHODIST ALLIANCE EXTENDED CARE HOSPITAL
225 South Claybrook
Memphis, TN 38104-3537
(901)726-7000

METHODIST CENTRAL HOSPITALS OF MEMPHIS
1265 Union Avenue
Memphis, TN 38104-3499
(901)726-7000

Hospital Telephone Directory — TENNESSEE

METHODIST HEALTHCARE SOUTH
1300 Wesley Drive
Memphis, TN 38116-6499
(901)346-3700

METHODIST HOSPITAL NORTH - J. HARRIS HOSPITAL
3960 New Covington Pike
Memphis, TN 38128-2589
(901)372-5200

REGIONAL MEDICAL CENTER AT MEMPHIS
877 Jefferson Avenue
Memphis, TN 38103-2897
(901)545-7100

SAINT FRANCIS HOSPITAL
5959 Park Avenue
Memphis, TN 38119-5198
(901)765-1000

SAINT JUDE CHILDRENS RESEARCH HOSPITAL
332 North Lauderdale St
Memphis, TN 38105-2729
(901)495-3300

SELECT SPECIALTY HOSPITAL - MEMPHIS
5959 Park Avenue, 12th Floor
Memphis, TN 38119-5200
(901)765-1245

UNIVERSITY OF TENNESSEE - BOWLD HOSPITAL
951 Court Avenue
Memphis, TN 38103-2813
(901)448-4000

VA MEDICAL CENTER - MEMPHIS
1030 Jefferson Avenue
Memphis, TN 38104-2127
(901)523-8990

MILAN

MILAN GENERAL HOSPITAL
4039 South Highland
Milan, TN 38358-3485
(731)686-1591

MORRISTOWN

LAKEWAY REGIONAL HOSPITAL
726 McFarland St
Morristown, TN 37814-3990
(423)586-2302

MORRISTOWN HAMBLEN HOSPITAL ASSOCIATION
908 W 4th North St
Morristown, TN 37814-3890
(423)586-4231

MOUNTAIN CITY

JOHNSON COUNTY HEALTH CENTER
Hospital Drive
Mountain City, TN 37683
(423)727-7731

MOUNTAIN HOME

VA MEDICAL CENTER - MOUNTAIN HOME
Sidney And Lamont St
Mountain Home, TN 37684
(423)926-1171

MURFREESBORO

MIDDLE TENNESSEE MEDICAL CENTER
400 N Highland Avenue
Murfreesboro, TN 37130-3837
(615)849-4100

VA MEDICAL CENTER - ALVIN C YORK
3400 Lebanon Road
Murfreesboro, TN 37129-1236
(615)867-6100

NASHVILLE

BAPTIST HOSPITAL
2000 Church St
Nashville, TN 37236-0002
(615)284-5555

BAPTIST WOMEN'S PAVILION
2011 Murphy Avenue
Nashville, TN 37203-2023
(615)284-2970

CENTENNIAL MEDICAL CENTER AND PARTHENON PAVILION
2300 Patterson Street
Nashville, TN 37203-1528
(615)342-1000

METRO NASHVILLE GENERAL HOSPITAL
1818 Albion St
Nashville, TN 37208-2918
(615)341-4000

MIDDLE TENNESSEE MENTAL HEALTH INSTITUTE
221 Stewarts Ferry Pike
Nashville, TN 37214-3325
(615)902-7535

NASHVILLE METROPOLITAN BORDEAUX NURSING HOME/HOSPITAL
1414 County Hospital Road
Nashville, TN 37218-3023
(615)862-7000

NASHVILLE REHAB HOSPITAL
610 Gallatin Road
Nashville, TN 37206-3225
(615)226-4330

PSYCHIATRIC HOSPITAL AT VANDERBILT
1601 23rd Avenue South
Nashville, TN 37212-3180
(615)320-7770

RALEIGH COMMUNITY HOSPITAL
1114 17th Ave S
Nashville, TN 37212-2215
(615)782-4203

SAINT THOMAS HOSPITAL
4220 Harding Road, PO Box 380
Nashville, TN 37202-0380
(423)222-2111

SELECT SPECIALTY HOSPITAL - NASHVILLE
2000 Church Street, 4th Floor
Nashville, TN 37236-0002
(615)284-4599

SKYLINE MEDICAL CENTER
3441 Dickerson Pike
Nashville, TN 37207-2539
(615)769-2000

SOUTHERN HILLS MEDICAL CENTER
391 Wallace Road
Nashville, TN 37211-4859
(615)781-4000

VA MEDICAL CENTER - NASHVILLE
1310 24th Avenue S
Nashville, TN 37212-2637
(615)327-4751

VANDERBILT STALLWORTH REHAB HOSPITAL LP
2201 Capers Avenue
Nashville, TN 37212-3165
(615)320-7600

VANDERBILT UNIVERSITY MEDICAL CENTER
1211 22nd Avenue South
Nashville, TN 37232-0002
(615)322-5000

NEWPORT

BAPTIST HOSPITAL OF COCKE COUNTY
702-710 2nd St
Newport, TN 37821-3703
(423)625-2200

OAK RIDGE

METHODIST MEDICAL CENTER OF OAK RIDGE
990 Oak Ridge Turnpike Box 529
Oak Ridge, TN 37830-6942
(865)481-1000

RIDGEVIEW PSYCHIATRIC HOSPITAL AND CENTER
240 W Tyrone Road
Oak Ridge, TN 37830-6571
(865)482-1076

ONEIDA

SCOTT COUNTY HOSPITAL
Highway 27 Box 308
Oneida, TN 37841
(423)569-8521

PARIS

HENRY COUNTY MEDICAL CENTER
301 Tyson Avenue
Paris, TN 38242-4544
(731)642-1220

PARSONS

DECATUR COUNTY GENERAL HOSPITAL
1200 Tennessee St S Box 250
Parsons, TN 38363-0250
(731)847-3031

PIKEVILLE

BLEDSOE COUNTY HOSPITAL
Highway 30 Box 428
Pikeville, TN 37367-0428
(423)447-2112

PORTLAND

TENNESSEE CHRISTIAN MEDICAL CENTER
105 Redbud Drive
Portland, TN 37148-1673
(615)325-7301

PULASKI

HILLSIDE HOSPITAL
1265 E College St
Pulaski, TN 38478-4548
(931)363-7531

RIPLEY

BAPTIST MEMORIAL HOSPITAL LAUDERDALE
326 Asbury Road
Ripley, TN 38063-5544
(731)221-2200

ROGERSVILLE

WELLMONT HAWKINS COUNTY MEMORIAL HOSPITAL
851 Locust St
Rogersville, TN 37857-2498
(423)272-2671

SAVANNAH

HARDIN COUNTY GENERAL HOSPITAL
2006 Wayne Road
Savannah, TN 38372-2294
(731)925-4954

TEXAS — Hospital Telephone Directory

SELMER
MCNAIRY METHODIST HEALTHCARE HOSPITAL
705 E Poplar Avenue
Selmer, TN 38375-1828
(731)645-3221

SEVIERVILLE
FORT SANDERS SEVIER MEDICAL CENTER
709 Middle Creek Road
Sevierville, TN 37862-5038
(865)429-6100

SEWANEE
EMERALD - HODGSON HOSPITAL
University Avenue
Sewanee, TN 37375
(931)598-5691

SHELBYVILLE
BEDFORD COUNTY MEDICAL CENTER
845 Union St
Shelbyville, TN 37160-2609
(931)685-5433

SMITHVILLE
BAPTIST DEKALB GENERAL HOSPITAL
520 W Main St
Smithville, TN 37166-1138
(615)597-7171

SMYRNA
STONECREST MEDICAL CENTER
542 Chaney Road
Smyrna, TN 37167-6136
(615)220-3992

SOMERVILLE
METHODIST HEALTHCARE HOSPITAL OF FAYETTE
214 Lakeview Rd
Somerville, TN 38068-9737
(901)465-3594

SPARTA
WHITE COUNTY COMMUNITY HOSPITAL
401 Sewell Road
Sparta, TN 38583-1299
(931)738-9211

SPRINGFIELD
NORTHCREST MEDICAL CENTER-HOSPITAL
100 Northcrest Drive
Springfield, TN 37172-3961
(615)384-2411

SWEETWATER
SWEETWATER HOSPITAL
304 Church St
Sweetwater, TN 37874-1181
(423)337-6171

TAZEWELL
CLAIBORNE COUNTY HOSPITAL
1000 Old Knoxville Road
Tazewell, TN 37879-3625
(423)626-4211

TRENTON
GIBSON GENERAL HOSPITAL
200 Hospital Drive
Trenton, TN 38382-3322
(731)855-7900

TULLAHOMA
HARTON REGIONAL MEDICAL CENTER
1801 N Jackson St Box 460
Tullahoma, TN 37388-2201
(931)393-3000

UNION CITY
BAPTIST MEMORIAL HOSPITAL UNION CITY
1201 Bishop St, PO Box 310
Union City, TN 38281-0310
(731)884-8601

WAVERLY
THREE RIVERS HOSPITAL
451 Highway 13 South
Waverly, TN 37185-2109
(931)296-4203

WAYNESBORO
WAYNE MEDICAL CENTER
103 J V Mangubat Drive
Waynesboro, TN 38485
(931)722-5411

WINCHESTER
SOUTHERN TENNESSEE MEDICAL CENTER
609 Hospital Road
Winchester, TN 37398-2407
(931)967-8200

WOODBURY
STONES RIVER HOSPITAL
324 Doolittle Road
Woodbury, TN 37190-1139
(615)563-4001

TEXAS

ABILENE
ABILENE PSYCHIATRIC HOSPITAL
4225 Woods Place
Abilene, TX 79602-7991
(915)698-6600

ABILENE REGIONAL MEDICAL CENTER
6250 Highway 83-84 At Antilley Road
Abilene, TX 79606
(325)695-9900

HENDRICK HEALTH SYSTEM
1242 N 19th St
Abilene, TX 79601-2316
(325)670-2000

ALICE
ALICE REGIONAL HOSPITAL
2500 E Main St
Alice, TX 78332-4169
(361)664-4376

CHRISTUS SPOHN HOSPITAL - ALICE
700 North Flourndy Road
Alice, TX 78332-4087
(361)661-8000

ALLEN
PRESBYTERIAN HOSPITAL OF ALLEN
1105 Central Expressway North
Allen, TX 75013-6103
(972)747-1000

ALPINE
BIG BEND REGIONAL MEDICAL CENTER
2600 N Highway 118
Alpine, TX 79830-2002
(423)837-3447

AMARILLO
BAPTIST SAINT ANTHONYS HOSPITAL
200 N W 7th St
Amarillo, TX 79107-5290
(806)356-2000

BAPTIST/SAINT ANTHONYS HEALTH SYSTEM
1600 Wallace Boulevard
Amarillo, TX 79106-1789
(806)212-2000

BSA PANHANDLE SURGICAL HOSPITAL
7100 West 9th Avenue
Amarillo, TX 79106-1704
(806)212-0247

NORTHWEST TEXAS HEALTHCARE SYSTEM - PSYCHIATRIC PAVILION
7201 Evan
Amarillo, TX 79106-1707
(806)354-1000

NORTHWEST TEXAS HEART HOSPITAL
1501 Coulter Road
Amarillo, TX 79106-1770
(806)354-1000

NORTHWEST TEXAS HOSPITAL
1501 Coulter Road PO Box 1110
Amarillo, TX 79106-1770
(806)354-1000

NORTHWEST TEXAS SURGICAL CENTER
3501 Soncy Road, Suite 118
Amarillo, TX 79119-6405
(806)359-7999

PLUM CREEK SPECIALTY HOSPITAL
5601 Plum Creek Drive
Amarillo, TX 79124-1801
(806)351-1000

SCCI HOSPITAL OF AMARILLO
2828 Sw 27th St
Amarillo, TX 79109-1782
(806)351-1600

VA HEALTHCARE SYSTEM - AMARILLO
6010 W Amarillo Boulevard
Amarillo, TX 79106-1992
(806)355-9703

ANAHUAC
BAYSIDE COMMUNITY HOSPITAL
200 Hospital Drive Box 398
Anahuac, TX 77514-0398
(409)267-3143

ANDREWS
PERMIAN GENERAL HOSPITAL
720 Hospital Drive Box 2108
Andrews, TX 79714-3617
(432)523-2200

ANGLETON
ANGLETON-DANBURY GENERAL HOSPITAL
132 Hospital Drive
Angleton, TX 77515-4197
(979)849-7721

ANSON
ANSON GENERAL HOSPITAL
101 Avenue J
Anson, TX 79501-2198
(325)823-3231

ARANSAS PASS
NORTH BAY HOSPITAL
1711 W Wheeler Avenue
Aransas Pass, TX 78336-4536
(361)758-8585

Hospital Telephone Directory — TEXAS

ARLINGTON

ARLINGTON MEMORIAL HOSPITAL
800 W Randol Mill Road
Arlington, TX 76012-2503
(817)548-6100

HEALTHSOUTH REHAB HOSPITAL OF ARLINGTON
3200 Matlock Road
Arlington, TX 76015-2911
(817)468-4000

KINDRED HOSPITAL ARLINGTON
1000 N Cooper St
Arlington, TX 76011-5540
(817)548-3400

MEDICAL CENTER OF ARLINGTON
3301 Matlock Road
Arlington, TX 76015-2998
(817)465-3241

MILLWOOD HOSPITAL
1011 North Cooper Street
Arlington, TX 76011-5517
(817)261-3121

ASPERMONT

STONEWALL MEMORIAL HOSPITAL
Washington Avenue Highway 83 No Drawer C
Aspermont, TX 79502-0902
(940)989-3551

ATHENS

EAST TEXAS MEDICAL CENTER ATHENS
2000 South Palestine
Athens, TX 75751-5610
(903)676-1000

ATLANTA

ATLANTA MEMORIAL HOSPITAL
PO Box 1049
Atlanta, TX 75551-1049
(903)799-3000

AUSTIN

AUSTIN STATE HOSPITAL
4110 Guadalupe
Austin, TX 78751-4223
(512)452-0381

BRACKENRIDGE HOSPITAL
601 E 15th St
Austin, TX 78701-1996
(512)324-7000

CHILDREN'S HOSPITAL OF AUSTIN
One Children's Place
Austin, TX 78701
(512)324-8000

CHRISTOPHER HOUSE
2820 East Martin Luther King
Austin, TX 78702-1544
(512)322-0747

CORNERSTONE HOSPITAL OF AUSTIN
4207 Burnet Road
Austin, TX 78756-3396
(512)706-1900

CORNERSTONE HOSPITAL OF AUSTIN
8402 Cross Park Drive
Austin, TX 78754-4595
(512)837-6233

HEALTHSOUTH REHAB HOSPITAL OF AUSTIN
1215 Red River
Austin, TX 78701-1921
(512)474-5700

HEALTHSOUTH SURGERY HOSPITAL OF AUSTIN
6818 Austin Center Boulevard Suite 100
Austin, TX 78731-3199
(512)346-1994

HEART HOSPITAL OF AUSTIN
3801 North Lamar Boulevard
Austin, TX 78756-4080
(512)407-7000

NORTH AUSTIN MEDICAL CENTER
12221 Mopac Expressway North
Austin, TX 78758
(512)901-1000

OAKS TREATMENT CENTER
1407 West Stassney Lane
Austin, TX 78745-2947
(512)464-0400

SAINT DAVIDS MEDICAL CENTER
919 E 32nd St
Austin, TX 78705-2703
(512)476-7111

SAINT DAVIDS PAVILION
1025 East 32nd Street
Austin, TX 78705-2705
(512)867-5800

SAINT DAVIDS REHABILITATION CENTER
1005 E 32nd St
Austin, TX 78705-2705
(512)867-5100

SETON MEDICAL CENTER
1201 W 38th St
Austin, TX 78705-1056
(512)324-1000

SETON NORTHWEST HOSPITAL
11113 Research Boulevards
Austin, TX 78759-5297
(512)324-6000

SETON SHOAL CREEK HOSPITAL
3501 Mills Avenue
Austin, TX 78731-6391
(512)324-2000

SOUTH AUSTIN HOSPITAL
901 West Ben White Boulevard
Austin, TX 78704-6999
(512)447-2211

TEXAS NEURO REHAB CENTER
1106 W Dittmar Road
Austin, TX 78745-6328
(512)444-4835

AZLE

HARRIS METHODIST NORTHWEST
108 Denver Trail
Azle, TX 76020-3697
(817)444-8600

BALLINGER

BALLINGER MEMORIAL HOSPITAL
608 Avenue B
Ballinger, TX 76821-2406
(325)365-2531

BAY CITY

MATAGORDA GENERAL HOSPITAL
1115 Avenue G
Bay City, TX 77414-3544
(979)245-6383

BAYTOWN

SAN JACINTO METHODIST HOSPITAL
4401 Garth Road
Baytown, TX 77521-2179
(281)420-8600

SAN JACINTO METHODIST HOSPITAL - ALEXANDER
1700 James Bowie Drive Box 1451
Baytown, TX 77520-3302
(281)420-6100

BEAUMONT

CHRISTUS SAINT ELIZABETH HOSPITAL
2830 Calder Avenue
Beaumont, TX 77702-1892
(409)892-7171

DUBUIS HOSPITAL - BEAUMONT
2830 Calder Avenue 4th Floor
Beaumont, TX 77702-1809
(409)899-8154

HEALTHSOUTH REHAB HOSPITAL
3340 Plaza 10 Boulevard
Beaumont, TX 77707-2551
(409)835-0835

MEMORIAL HERMANN BAPTIST HOSPITAL - BEAUMONT
3576 College Street
Beaumont, TX 77701-4614
(409)835-3781

MEMORIAL HERMANN BAPTIST HOSPITAL - EAST
PO Box 1591
Beaumont, TX 77704-1591
(409)833-1411

MEMORIAL HERMANN BEHAVIORAL HEALTH
3250 Fannin St
Beaumont, TX 77701-3903
(409)833-1411

BEDFORD

HARRIS METHODIST - SPRINGWOOD
1608 Hospital Parkway
Bedford, TX 76022-6913
(817)355-7700

HARRIS METHODIST H E B
1600 Hospital Parkway
Bedford, TX 76022-6913
(817)685-4000

BEEVILLE

CHRISTUS SPOHN HOSPITAL
1500 E Houston Highway
Beeville, TX 78102-5312
(361)354-2000

BELLVILLE

BELLVILLE GENERAL HOSPITAL
44 N Cummings PO Box 977
Bellville, TX 77418-0977
(979)865-3141

BIG LAKE

REAGAN MEMORIAL HOSPITAL
805 N Main
Big Lake, TX 76932-3938
(325)884-2561

BIG SPRING

BIG SPRING STATE HOSPITAL
1901 North Highway 87
Big Spring, TX 79720-0283
(432)267-8216

SCENIC MOUNTAIN MEDICAL CENTER
1601 W 11th Place
Big Spring, TX 79720-4198
(432)263-1211

147

TEXAS — Hospital Telephone Directory

VA MEDICAL CENTER - WEST TEXAS
300 W Veterans Boulevard
Big Spring, TX 79720-5566
(432)263-7361

BONHAM

NORTHEAST MEDICAL CENTER
504 Lipscomb
Bonham, TX 75418-4096
(903)583-8585

VA HEALTHCARE SYSTEM - SAM RAYBURN
1201 East Ninth Street
Bonham, TX 75418-4059
(903)583-2111

BORGER

GOLDEN PLAINS HEALTH CENTER/HOSPITAL
200 S Mc Gee
Borger, TX 79007-4095
(806)273-1100

BOWIE

BOWIE MEMORIAL HOSPITAL
705 East Greenwood Avenue
Bowie, TX 76230-3199
(940)872-1126

BRADY

HEART OF TEXAS MEMORIAL HOSPITAL
Nine Road PO Box 1150
Brady, TX 76825-1150
(325)597-2901

BRECKENRIDGE

STEPHENS MEMORIAL HOSPITAL
200 South Geneva
Breckenridge, TX 76424-4702
(254)559-2241

BRENHAM

TRINITY COMMUNITY MEDICAL CENTER OF BRENHAM
700 Medical Parkway
Brenham, TX 77833-5498
(979)836-6173

BROWNFIELD

BROWNFIELD REGIONAL MEDICAL CENTER
705 E Felt St
Brownfield, TX 79316-3439
(806)637-3551

BROWNSVILLE

BROWNSVILLE MEDICAL CENTER
1040 W Jefferson St
Brownsville, TX 78520-6399
(956)544-1400

BROWNSVILLE SURGICAL HOSPITAL
4750 North Expressway
Brownsville, TX 78526-4120
(956)554-2000

VALLEY REGIONAL MEDICAL CENTER
100A Alton Gloor Blvd
Brownsville, TX 78526
(956)350-7000

BROWNWOOD

BROWNWOOD REGIONAL MEDICAL CENTER
1501 Burnet Drive
Brownwood, TX 76801-6424
(325)646-8541

BRYAN

PHYSICIANS CENTER
3131 University Drive East
Bryan, TX 77802-3473
(979)731-3100

SAINT JOSEPH REGIONAL HEALTH CENTER
2801 Franciscan Drive
Bryan, TX 77802-2544
(979)776-3777

BURNET

SETON HIGHLAND LAKES MEDICAL CENTER
3201 South Water St PO Box 840
Burnet, TX 78611-0840
(512)756-6000

CALDWELL

BURLESON SAINT JOSEPH HEALTH CENTER
1101 Woodson Drive
Caldwell, TX 77836
(979)567-3245

CAMERON

CENTRAL TEXAS HOSPITAL
806 N Crockett Box 947
Cameron, TX 76520-2599
(254)697-6591

CANADIAN

HEMPHILL COUNTY HOSPITAL
1020 S 4th St
Canadian, TX 79014-3315
(806)323-6422

CARRIZO SPRINGS

DIMMIT COUNTY MEMORIAL HOSPITAL
704 Hospital Drive
Carrizo Springs, TX 78834-3836
(830)876-2424

CARROLLTON

SELECT SPECIALTY HOSPITAL - NORTH DALLAS
4343 Josey Lane, Fourth Floor
Carrollton, TX 75010-4603
(972)395-7350

TRINITY MEDICAL CENTER
4343 North Josey Lane
Carrollton, TX 75010-4691
(972)492-1010

CARTHAGE

EAST TEXAS MEDICAL CENTER-CARTHAGE
409 Cottage Road At Daniel PO Box 549
Carthage, TX 75633-0549
(903)693-3841

CENTER

SHELBY REGIONAL MEDICAL CENTER
602 Hurst Street
Center, TX 75935-3414
(936)598-2781

CENTER POINT

STARLITE VILLAGE HOSPITAL
Elm Pass Road Box 317
Center Point, TX 78010-0317
(830)634-2212

CHANNELVIEW

TRIUMPH HOSPITAL - EAST HOUSTON
15101 East Freeway
Channelview, TX 77530-4104
(832)200-5000

CHILDRESS

CHILDRESS REGIONAL MEDICAL CENTER
Highway 83 North Box 1030
Childress, TX 79201-1030
(940)937-6371

CHILLICOTHE

CHILLICOTHE HOSPITAL
303 Avenue I Box 370
Chillicothe, TX 79225-0370
(940)852-5131

CLARKSVILLE

EAST TEXAS MEDICAL CENTER - CLARKSVILLE
PO Drawer 1270 Highway 82 West
Clarksville, TX 75426-1270
(903)427-3851

CLEBURNE

WALLS REGIONAL HOSPITAL
201 Walls Drive
Cleburne, TX 76033-4008
(817)641-2551

CLEVELAND

CLEVELAND REGIONAL MEDICAL CENTER
300 E Crockett
Cleveland, TX 77327-4062
(281)593-1811

CLIFTON

GOODALL WITCHER HEALTHCARE FOUNDATION
101 S Avenue T
Clifton, TX 76634-1832
(254)675-8322

COLEMAN

COLEMAN COUNTY MEDICAL CENTER
310 S Pecos St
Coleman, TX 76834-4159
(325)625-2135

COLLEGE STATION

COLLEGE STATION MEDICAL CENTER
PO Box 10000
College Station, TX 77842-3500
(979)764-5100

COLORADO CITY

MITCHELL COUNTY HOSPITAL
1543 Chestnut Street
Colorado City, TX 79512-3998
(325)728-3431

COLUMBUS

COLUMBUS COMMUNITY HOSPITAL
110 Shult Drive PO Box 865
Columbus, TX 78934-0865
(979)732-2371

COMANCHE

COMANCHE COMMUNITY HOSPITAL
211 South Austin PO Box 443
Comanche, TX 76442-0443
(325)356-5241

COMMERCE

PRESBYTERIAN HOSPITAL OF COMMERCE
2900 Sterling Hart Drive
Commerce, TX 75428-3912
(903)886-3161

CONROE

CONROE REGIONAL MEDICAL CENTER
504 Medical Center Boulevard
Conroe, TX 77304-2808
(936)539-1111

HEALTHSOUTH REHAB HOSPITAL NORTH HOUSTON
18550 Interstate 45 S
Conroe, TX 77384-4108
(281)364-2000

SELECT SPECIALTY HOSPITAL
504 Medical Center Boulevard
Conroe, TX 77304-2808
(936)538-3195

CORPUS CHRISTI

CHRISTUS SPOHN HOSPITAL - SHORELINE
600 Elizabeth St
Corpus Christi, TX 78404-2235
(361)881-3000

CHRISTUS SPOHN HOSPITAL - SOUTH
5950 Saratoga Blvd
Corpus Christi, TX 78414-4199
(361)985-5000

CHRISTUS SPOHN MEMORIAL HOSPITAL
2606 Hospital Boulevard
Corpus Christi, TX 78405-1818
(361)902-4000

CORPUS CHRISTI MEDICAL CENTER
3315 South Alameda
Corpus Christi, TX 78411-1820
(361)857-1400

CORPUS CHRISTI MEDICAL CENTER - BAY AREA
7101 S Padre Island Drive
Corpus Christi, TX 78412-4913
(361)985-1200

CORPUS CHRISTI MEDICAL CENTER - HEART HOSPITAL
7002 Williams Drive
Corpus Christi, TX 78412-4911
(361)761-6800

CORPUS CHRISTI WARM SPRINGS REHAB HOSPITAL
2606 Hospital Boulevard 8th Floor
Corpus Christi, TX 78405-1818
(361)888-4458

DRISCOLL CHILDRENS HOSPITAL
3533 S Alameda Box 6530
Corpus Christi, TX 78411-1785
(361)694-5000

IHS - CORPUS CHRISTI
1310 3rd St
Corpus Christi, TX 78404-2208
(361)888-4323

NAVAL HOSPITAL CORPUS CHRISTI
10651 East Street
Corpus Christi, TX 78419-5130
(361)961-2688

NORTHWEST REGIONAL HOSPITAL
13725 Northwest Boulevard
Corpus Christi, TX 78410-5127
(361)241-4243

PADRE BEHAVIORAL HEALTH SYSTEM
6629 Woolridge Road
Corpus Christi, TX 78414-2909
(361)986-9444

CORSICANA

NAVARRO REGIONAL HOSPITAL
3201 West Highway 22
Corsicana, TX 75110-2469
(903)654-6800

CRANE

CRANE MEMORIAL HOSPITAL
1310 S Alford St
Crane, TX 79731-3800
(432)558-3555

CROCKETT

EAST TEXAS MEDICAL CENTER CROCKETT
1100 Loop 304 East Box 1129
Crockett, TX 75835-1810
(936)546-3862

CROSBYTON

CROSBYTON CLINIC HOSPITAL
710 West Main Street
Crosbyton, TX 79322-2143
(806)675-2382

CUERO

CUERO COMMUNITY HOSPITAL
2550 N Esplanade
Cuero, TX 77954-4716
(361)275-6191

DALHART

COON MEMORIAL HOSPITAL AND HOME
PO Box 2014
Dalhart, TX 79022-6014
(806)244-4571

DALLAS

BAYLOR HEART AND VASCULAR CENTER
621 North Hall Street
Dallas, TX 75226-1339
(214)820-0600

BAYLOR INSTITUTE FOR REHAB AT GASTON
3505 Gaston Avenue
Dallas, TX 75246-2094
(214)820-9300

BAYLOR SPECIALTY HOSPITAL
3504 Swiss Avenue
Dallas, TX 75204-6224
(214)820-9700

BAYLOR UNIVERSITY MEDICAL CENTER
3500 Gaston Avenue
Dallas, TX 75246-2088
(214)820-0111

CHARLTON METHODIST HOSPITAL
3500 W Wheatland Road Box 225357
Dallas, TX 75237-3499
(214)947-7777

CHILDRENS MEDICAL CENTER OF DALLAS
1935 Motor Street
Dallas, TX 75235-7794
(214)456-7000

DALLAS SOUTHWEST MEDICAL CENTER
2929 S Hampton Road
Dallas, TX 75224-3026
(214)330-4611

DOCTORS HOSPITAL
9440 Poppy Drive
Dallas, TX 75218-3694
(214)324-6562

GREEN OAKS HOSPITAL
7808 Clodus Fields Drive
Dallas, TX 75251-2206
(972)991-9504

HEALTHSOUTH MEDICAL CENTER
2124 Research Row
Dallas, TX 75235-2524
(214)904-6100

IHS HOSPITAL-DALLAS
7955 Harry Hines Blvd
Dallas, TX 75235-3305
(214)637-0000

KINDRED HOSPITAL DALLAS
9525 Greenville Ave
Dallas, TX 75243-4116
(214)355-2600

KINDRED HOSPITAL WHITE ROCK
9440 Poppy Drive, 5th Floor
Dallas, TX 75218-3652
(214)324-6730

LIFECARE HOSPITAL OF DALLAS
6161 Harry Hines Boulevard Suite 110
Dallas, TX 75235-5306
(214)525-6300

MARY SHIELS HOSPITAL
3515 Howell Street
Dallas, TX 75204-2895
(214)443-3000

MEDICAL CITY HOSPITAL - DALLAS
7777 Forest Lane
Dallas, TX 75230-2505
(972)566-7000

METHODIST MEDICAL CENTER
1441 N Beckley Avenue
Dallas, TX 75203-1201
(214)947-8181

NORTH DALLAS REHABILITATION HOSPITAL
8383 Meadow Road
Dallas, TX 75231-3701
(214)891-0880

OUR CHILDREN'S HOUSE AT BAYLOR
3301 Swiss Avenue
Dallas, TX 75204
(214)820-9838

PARKLAND HEALTH AND HOSPITAL SYSTEM
5201 Harry Hines Boulevard
Dallas, TX 75235-7793
(214)590-8000

PRESBYTERIAN HEALTH CARE SYSTEM
8200 Walnut Hill Lane
Dallas, TX 75231-4426
(214)345-6789

RHD MEMORIAL MEDICAL CENTER
7 Medical Parkway
Dallas, TX 75234-7829
(972)247-1000

SAINT PAUL MEDICAL CENTER
5909 Harry Hines Boulevard
Dallas, TX 75235-6209
(214)879-1000

SCCI HOSPITAL OF KOKOMO
12300 Ford Rd
Dallas, TX 75234-7248
(972)452-6730

SELECT SPECIALTY HOSPITAL - DALLAS
10 Medical Parkway, Suite 205
Dallas, TX 75234-7845
(972)488-9167

TEXAS SCOTTISH RITE HOSPITAL
2222 Welborn St
Dallas, TX 75219-3993
(214)559-5000

TEXAS — Hospital Telephone Directory

TIMBERLAWN MENTAL HEALTH SYSTEM
4600 Samuell Boulevard PO Box 151489
Dallas, TX 75315-1489
(214)381-7181

VA MEDICAL CENTER - DALLAS
4500 S Lancaster Road
Dallas, TX 75216-7167
(214)742-8387

ZALE LIPSHY UNIVERSITY HOSPITAL
5151 Harry Hines Boulevard
Dallas, TX 75235-7786
(214)590-3000

DE LEON

DELEON HOSPITAL
407 S Texas St
De Leon, TX 76444-1947
(254)893-2011

DE SOTO

CEDARS HOSPITAL
2000 N Old Hickory Trail
De Soto, TX 75115-2242
(972)298-7323

SELECT SPECIALTY HOSPITAL - SOUTH DALLAS
800 Kirnwood Drive
De Soto, TX 75115-2000
(972)780-6500

DECATUR

WISE REGIONAL HEALTH SYSTEM
2000 S Fm 51
Decatur, TX 76234-3702
(940)627-5921

DEL RIO

VAL VERDE REGIONAL MEDICAL CENTER
801 Bedell Avenue
Del Rio, TX 78840-4112
(830)775-8566

DENISON

TEXOMA MEDICAL CENTER
1000 Memorial Drive PO Box 890
Denison, TX 75021-0890
(903)416-4000

TEXOMA MEDICAL CENTER RESTORATIVE CARE
1000 Memorial Drive, 4th Floor, PO Box 890
Denison, TX 75021-0008
(903)416-4441

DENTON

DENTON COMMUNITY HOSPITAL
207 N Bonnie Brae
Denton, TX 76201-3798
(940)898-7000

DENTON REGIONAL MEDICAL CENTER
3535 South I-35 East
Denton, TX 76207
(940)384-3535

DENVER CITY

YOAKUM COUNTY HOSPITAL
412 Mustang Avenue Drawer 1130
Denver City, TX 79323-2750
(806)592-5484

DILLEY

COMMUNITY GENERAL HOSPITAL
230 West Miller
Dilley, TX 78017-3818
(830)965-2003

DIMMITT

PLAINS MEMORIAL HOSPITAL
310 W Halsell St Box 278
Dimmitt, TX 79027-1846
(806)647-2191

DUMAS

MOORE COUNTY HOSPITAL DISTRICT
224 E Second Street
Dumas, TX 79029-3808
(806)935-7171

DYESS AIR FORCE BASE

7TH MEDICAL GROUP
697 Hospital Road
Dyess Air Force Base, TX 79607-1367
(915)696-2346

EAGLE LAKE

RICE MEDICAL CENTER
600 South Austin Road
Eagle Lake, TX 77434-3202
(979)234-5571

EAGLE PASS

EAGLE PASS HEALTH CENTER
HC 1, Box 9700
Eagle Pass, TX 78852-9752
(830)757-6793

FORT DUNCAN MEDICAL CENTER
350 S Adams St
Eagle Pass, TX 78852-5110
(830)773-5321

EASTLAND

EASTLAND MEMORIAL HOSPITAL
304 S Daugherty Box 897
Eastland, TX 76448-2609
(254)629-2601

EDEN

CONCHO COUNTY HOSPITAL
Eaker And Burleson Streets Drawer L
Eden, TX 76837
(325)869-5911

EDINBURG

CORNERSTONE REGIONAL HOSPITAL
2302 Cornerstone Blvd
Edinburg, TX 78539-8471
(956)618-4444

CORNERSTONE REHABILITATION
2655 Cornerstone Blvd
Edinburg, TX 78539-8479
(956)686-0411

EDINBURG REGIONAL MEDICAL CENTER
1102 W Trenton Road
Edinburg, TX 78539
(956)388-6000

LIFECARE HOSPITAL OF SOUTH TEXAS
333 West Freddy Gonzales Drive
Edinburg, TX 78539-6132
(956)388-1800

EDNA

JACKSON COUNTY HOSPITAL
1013 S Wells
Edna, TX 77957-4098
(361)782-5241

EL CAMPO

EL CAMPO MEMORIAL HOSPITAL
303 Sandy Corner Road
El Campo, TX 77437-9535
(979)543-6251

EL PASO

DEL SOL MEDICAL CENTER
10301 Gateway West
El Paso, TX 79925-7798
(915)595-9000

DEL SOL REHABILITATION HOSPITAL
300 Waymore Drive
El Paso, TX 79902-1604
(915)577-2600

EL PASO PSYCHIATRIC CENTER
4615 Alameda Avenue
El Paso, TX 79905-2702
(915)532-2202

EL PASO SPECIALTY HOSPITAL
1755 Curie, Ste A
El Paso, TX 79902-2920
(915)544-3636

HIGHLANDS REGIONAL REHABILITATION HOSPITAL
1395 George Dieter
El Paso, TX 79936-7410
(915)298-7222

MESA HILLS SPECIALITY HOSPITAL
2311 N Oregon
El Paso, TX 79902-3216
(915)545-1823

NCED MENTAL HEALTH CENTER
1801 North Oregon
El Paso, TX 79902-3524
(915)521-1200

NCED MENTAL HEALTH CENTER
1900 Denver Street
El Paso, TX 79902-3008
(915)544-4000

PAN AMERICAN COMMUNITY HOSPITAL
1221 N Cotton
El Paso, TX 79902-3096
(915)496-9600

PROVIDENCE MEMORIAL HOSPITAL
2001 N Oregon St
El Paso, TX 79902-3320
(915)577-6011

R E THOMASON GENERAL HOSPITAL
4815 Alameda Avenue
El Paso, TX 79905-2794
(915)544-1200

RIO VISTA REHAB HOSPITAL
1740 Curie Drive
El Paso, TX 79902-2900
(915)544-3399

SCCI HOSPITAL - EL PASO
1740 Curie Drive
El Paso, TX 79902-2901
(915)351-9044

SIERRA MEDICAL CENTER
1625 Medical Center Drive
El Paso, TX 79902-5044
(915)747-4000

VA HEALTHCARE SYSTEM - EL PASO
5001 North Piedras Street
El Paso, TX 79930-4210
(915)564-6100

WILLIAM BEAUMONT ARMY MEDICAL CENTER
5005 N Piedras St
El Paso, TX 79920-5000
(915)569-2121

Hospital Telephone Directory — TEXAS

ELDORADO
SCHLEICHER COUNTY MEDICAL CENTER
PO Box V
Eldorado, TX 76936-1246
(325)853-2507

ELECTRA
ELECTRA MEMORIAL HOSPITAL
1207 S Bailey St Box 1112
Electra, TX 76360-3221
(940)495-3981

ENNIS
ENNIS REGIONAL MEDICAL CENTER
803 West Lampasas
Ennis, TX 75119-4535
(972)875-0900

FAIRFIELD
EAST TEXAS MEDICAL CENTER
125 Newman St
Fairfield, TX 75840-1419
(903)389-2121

FLORESVILLE
WILSON MEMORIAL HOSPITAL
1301 Hospital Boulevard
Floresville, TX 78114-2798
(830)393-3122

FORT HOOD
DARNALL ARMY COMMUNITY HOSPITAL
36000 Darnall Loop
Fort Hood, TX 76544-5095
(254)288-8000

FORT SAM HOUSTON
BROOKE ARMY MEDICAL CENTER
3851 Roger Brooke Drive, Bldg 3600
Fort Sam Houston, TX 78234-4501
(210)916-2225

FORT STOCKTON
PECOS COUNTY MEMORIAL HOSPITAL
1648 Sanderson Highway
Fort Stockton, TX 79735
(432)336-2241

FORT WORTH
BAYLOR ALL SAINTS HOSPITAL-CITYVIEW
7100 Oakmont Boulevard
Fort Worth, TX 76132-3999
(817)346-5700

BAYLOR ALL SAINTS MEDICAL CENTER
1400 Eighth Avenue
Fort Worth, TX 76104-4110
(817)926-2544

COOK CHILDRENS MEDICAL CENTER
801 Seventh Avenue
Fort Worth, TX 76104-2796
(682)885-4000

FEDERAL MEDICAL CENTER - CARSWELL
PO Box 27066, J Street, Bld 3000
Fort Worth, TX 76127-0066
(817)782-4002

FEDERAL MEDICAL CENTER - FORT WORTH
3150 Horton Road
Fort Worth, TX 76119-5905
(817)534-8400

HARRIS CONTINUED CARE HOSPITAL
1300 Pennsylvania 4th Floor Main Building
Fort Worth, TX 76104-2111
(817)878-5500

HARRIS METHODIST FORT WORTH
1301 Pennsylvania
Fort Worth, TX 76104-2122
(817)882-2000

HARRIS METHODIST SOUTHWEST
6100 Harris Parkway
Fort Worth, TX 76132-4199
(817)3433-5000

HEALTHSOUTH REHAB CENTER
1212 W Lancaster Avenue
Fort Worth, TX 76102-4510
(817)870-2336

HEALTHSOUTH REHAB HOSPITAL - CITY VIEW
6701 Oakmont Boulevard
Fort Worth, TX 76132-2957
(817)370-4700

HUGULEY HEALTH SYSTEM
11801 S Freeway PO Box 6337
Fort Worth, TX 76115-0337
(817)293-9110

JPS HEALTH NETWORK
1500 S Main St
Fort Worth, TX 76104-4917
(817)921-3431

KINDRED HOSPITAL FORT WORTH
815 Eighth Avenue
Fort Worth, TX 76104-2609
(817)332-4812

KINDRED HOSPITAL FORT WORTH SOUTHWEST
7800 Oakmont Blvd
Fort Worth, TX 76132-4203
(817)346-0094

KINDRED HOSPITAL MANSFIELD
815 8th Ave
Fort Worth, TX 76104-2609
(817)473-6101

LIFECARE HOSPITAL OF NORTH TEXAS - FORT WORTH
6201 Overton Ridge Boulevard
Fort Worth, TX 76132-3613
(817)370-6078

OSTEOPATHIC MEDICAL CENTER OF TEXAS
1000 Montgomery St
Fort Worth, TX 76107-2691
(817)731-4311

PLAZA MEDICAL CENTER HOSPITAL FORT WORTH
900 Eighth Avenue
Fort Worth, TX 76104-3902
(817)336-2100

TRINITY SPRINGS EAST PAVILION
1500 S Main St
Fort Worth, TX 76104-4917
(817)927-3636

FREDERICKSBURG
HILL COUNTRY MEMORIAL HOSPITAL
1020 Kerrville Highway PO Box 835
Fredericksburg, TX 78624-0835
(830)997-4353

FRIONA
PARMER COUNTY COMMUNITY HOSPITAL
1307 Cleveland
Friona, TX 79035-1121
(806)250-2754

GAINESVILLE
GAINESVILLE MEMORIAL HOSPITAL
1016 Ritchey St
Gainesville, TX 76240-3599
(940)665-1751

GALVESTON
SHRINERS BURN INSTITUTE
815 Market St
Galveston, TX 77550-2720
(409)770-6600

UNIVERSITY OF TEXAS MEDICAL BRANCH GALVESTON
301 University Boulevard
Galveston, TX 77555-5302
(409)772-1011

GARLAND
BAYLOR MEDICAL CENTER AT GARLAND
PO Box 469009
Garland, TX 75046-9009
(214)487-5000

GATESVILLE
CORYELL MEMORIAL HOSPITAL
1507 W Main St
Gatesville, TX 76528-1098
(254)865-8251

GEORGETOWN
GEORGETOWN HOSPITAL
2000 Scenic Drive
Georgetown, TX 78626-7793
(512)943-3000

GLEN ROSE
GLEN ROSE MEDICAL CENTER
1021 Holden Street Box 2159
Glen Rose, TX 76043-4937
(254)897-2215

GONZALES
MEMORIAL HOSPITAL
Highway 90A Bypass Box 587
Gonzales, TX 78629-0587
(830)672-7581

WARM SPRINGS SPECIALTY HOSPITAL
200 Memorial Dr
Gonzales, TX 78648
(830)875-8400

GRAHAM
GRAHAM GENERAL HOSPITAL
1301 Montgomery Road, PO Box 1390
Graham, TX 76450-1390
(940)549-3400

GRANBURY
LAKE GRANBURY MEDICAL CENTER
1310 Paluxy Road
Granbury, TX 76048-5655
(817)573-2683

GRAND SALINE
COZBY GERMANY HOSPITAL
707 N Waldrip
Grand Saline, TX 75140-1555
(903)962-4242

TEXAS — Hospital Telephone Directory

GRAPEVINE

BAYLOR MEDICAL CENTER AT GRAPEVINE
1650 W College St
Grapevine, TX 76051-3596
(817)481-1588

GREENVILLE

GLEN OAKS HOSPITAL
301 E Division Box 1885
Greenville, TX 75402-4199
(903)454-6000

HUNT MEMORIAL HOSPITAL DISTRICT
4215 Joe Ramsey Boulevard
Greenville, TX 75401-7852
(903)408-5000

PRESBYTERIAN HOSPITAL OF GREENVILLE
4215 Joe Ramsey Boulevard
Greenville, TX 75401-7852
(903)408-5000

GROESBECK

LIMESTONE MEDICAL CENTER
701 Mcclintic Dr
Groesbeck, TX 76642-2128
(254)729-3281

GROVES

DOCTORS HOSPITAL
5500 39th St
Groves, TX 77619-2999
(409)962-5733

HALLETTSVILLE

LAVACA MEDICAL CENTER
1400 North Texana Street
Hallettsville, TX 77964-2099
(361)798-3671

HAMILTON

HAMILTON GENERAL HOSPITAL
400 N Brown
Hamilton, TX 76531-1598
(254)386-3151

HAMLIN

HAMLIN MEMORIAL HOSPITAL
632 N W Second St Box 387
Hamlin, TX 79520-3831
(325)576-3646

HARLINGEN

HARLINGEN MEDICAL CENTER
5501 South Expressway 77
Harlingen, TX 78550-3213
(956)365-1000

RIO GRANDE STATE MENTAL HEALTH CENTER
1401 S Rangerville Road
Harlingen, TX 78552-7638
(956)425-8900

SOUTH TEXAS HOSPITAL
1301 Rangerville Road
Harlingen, TX 78552-7610
(956)423-3420

VALLEY BAPTIST MEDICAL CENTER
2101 Pease St Box 2588
Harlingen, TX 78550-8307
(956)389-1100

HASKELL

HASKELL MEMORIAL HOSPITAL
1 North Avenue N
Haskell, TX 79521-5499
(940)864-2621

HEMPHILL

SABINE COUNTY HOSPITAL
PO Drawer W Highway 83 West
Hemphill, TX 75948
(409)787-3300

HENDERSON

HENDERSON MEMORIAL HOSPITAL
300 Wilson Street
Henderson, TX 75652-5956
(903)657-7541

HENRIETTA

CLAY COUNTY MEMORIAL HOSPITAL
310 W South Street
Henrietta, TX 76365-3346
(940)538-5621

HEREFORD

HEREFORD REGIONAL MEDICAL CENTER
801 East Third
Hereford, TX 79045-5727
(806)364-2141

HILLSBORO

HILL REGIONAL HOSPITAL
101 Circle Drive
Hillsboro, TX 76645-2670
(254)580-8500

HONDO

MEDINA COMMUNITY HOSPITAL
3100 Avenue E
Hondo, TX 78861-3599
(830)741-4677

HOUSTON

BELLAIRE MEDICAL CENTER
5314 Dashwood
Houston, TX 77081-4603
(713)512-1200

BEN TAUB GENERAL HOSPITAL
1504 Taub Loop
Houston, TX 77030-1608
(713)873-2000

CHARLES R DREW MEDICAL CENTER
4514 Lyons Avenue
Houston, TX 77020-2649
(713)675-1711

CHRISTUS SAINT JOHN HOSPITAL
2050 Space Park Drive
Houston, TX 77058-3605
(281)333-5503

CHRISTUS SAINT JOSEPH HOSPITAL
1919 Labranch
Houston, TX 77002-8393
(713)757-1000

CORNERSTONE HOSPITAL OF HOUSTON
5556 Gasmer
Houston, TX 77035-4598
(713)551-5300

CYPRESS CREEK HOSPITAL
17750 Cali Dr
Houston, TX 77090-2705
(281)586-7600

CYPRESS FAIRBANKS MEDICAL CENTER HOSPITAL
10655 Steepletop Drive
Houston, TX 77065-4297
(281)890-4285

DOCTORS HOSPITAL - PARKWAY
510 W Tidwell Rd
Houston, TX 77091-4339
(713)765-2600

DOCTORS HOSPITAL - TIDWELL
510 W Tidwell
Houston, TX 77091-4399
(713)691-1111

DUBUIS HOSPITAL AT HOUSTON
1919 Labranch
Houston, TX 77002-8321
(713)756-8660

EAST HOUSTON MEDICAL CENTER
13111 East Freeway
Houston, TX 77015-5820
(713)393-2000

HARRIS COUNTY PSYCHIATRIC CENTER
2800 MacGregor Way
Houston, TX 77021-1000
(713)741-5000

HEALTH BRIDGE CHILDRENS HOSPITAL
2929 Woodland Park Drive
Houston, TX 77082-2687
(281)293-7774

HEALTHSOUTH HOSPITAL FOR SPECIALIZED SURGERY
5445 Labranch Street
Houston, TX 77004-6835
(713)528-6800

HEALTHSOUTH REHAB INSTITUTE
17506 Red Oak Drive
Houston, TX 77090-7721
(281)580-1212

HOUSTON COMMUNITY HOSPITAL
PO Box 11527
Houston, TX 77293-1527
(281)697-7777

HOUSTON COMMUNITY HOSPITAL
2807 Little York Road
Houston, TX 77093-3405
(713)697-2961

HOUSTON NORTHWEST MEDICAL CENTER
710 Fm 1960 West
Houston, TX 77090-3420
(281)440-1000

IHS HOSPITAL AT HOUSTON
6160 S Loop East
Houston, TX 77087-1010
(713)640-2400

INSTITUTE FOR REHAB AND RESEARCH
1333 Moursund Avenue
Houston, TX 77030-3405
(713)799-5000

INTRACARE HOSPITAL
7601 Fannin
Houston, TX 77054-1905
(713)790-0949

INTRACARE NORTH HOSPITAL
1120 Cypress Station Drive
Houston, TX 77090-3002
(281)893-7200

KINDRED HOSPITAL HOUSTON
6441 Main St
Houston, TX 77030-1502
(713)790-0500

KINDRED HOSPITAL HOUSTON NORTHWEST
11297 Fallbrook
Houston, TX 77065-4230
(281)897-8114

Hospital Telephone Directory — TEXAS

LYNDON B. JOHNSON GENERAL HOSPITAL
5656 Kelly St
Houston, TX 77026-1967
(713)566-5000

MEMORIAL HERMANN CHILDRENS HOSPITAL
6411 Fannin
Houston, TX 77030-1501
(713)704-5437

MEMORIAL HERMANN CONTINUING CARE HOSPITAL
3043 North Gessner Drive
Houston, TX 77080-1000
(713)744-3004

MEMORIAL HERMANN HOSPITAL
6411 Fannin
Houston, TX 77030-1599
(713)704-4000

MEMORIAL HERMANN MEMORIAL CITY HOSPITAL
920 Frostwood Drive
Houston, TX 77024-2314
(713)932-3000

MEMORIAL HERMANN SOUTHWEST HOSPITAL
7600 Beechnut St
Houston, TX 77074-4302
(713)776-5000

MEMORIAL HOSPITAL NORTHWEST
1635 North Loop West
Houston, TX 77008-1532
(713)867-2000

MEMORIAL HOSPITAL SOUTHEAST
11800 Astoria Boulevard
Houston, TX 77089-6041
(281)929-6100

METHODIST DIAGNOSTIC HOSPITAL
6565 Fannin
Houston, TX 77030-2707
(713)790-3311

METHODIST HOSPITAL
6565 Fannin
Houston, TX 77030-2707
(713)790-3311

METHODIST WILLOWBROOK HOSPITAL
18220 Tomcall Parkway
Houston, TX 77070-4347
(281)477-1000

PARK PLAZA HOSPITAL
1313 Hermann Drive
Houston, TX 77004-7092
(713)527-5000

PLAZA SPECIALTY HOSPITAL
1300 Binz St
Houston, TX 77004
(713)285-1000

QUENTIN MEASE HOSPITAL
3601 N Macgregor
Houston, TX 77004-8004
(713)873-3700

RIVERSIDE GENERAL HOSPITAL
3204 Ennis St
Houston, TX 77004-3299
(713)526-2441

SAINT LUKES EPISCOPAL HOSPITAL
6720 Bertner Avenue
Houston, TX 77030-2697
(713)785-8537

SCCI HOSPITAL HOUSTON CENTRAL
105 Drew
Houston, TX 77006-1527
(713)529-8922

SELECT SPECIALTY HOSPITAL - HOUSTON HEIGHTS
1917 Ashland Street
Houston, TX 77008-3907
(713)861-6161

SELECT SPECIALTY HOSPITAL - HOUSTON MEDICAL CENTER
6447 Main Street
Houston, TX 77030-1502
(713)363-9393

SELECT SPECIALTY HOSPITAL - HOUSTON WEST
8850 Long Point Road, 6th Floor Tower
Houston, TX 77055-3006
(713)984-2273

SHRINERS HOSPITAL FOR CHILDREN
6977 Main St
Houston, TX 77030-3701
(713)797-1616

SPRING BRANCH MEDICAL CENTER
8850 Long Point Road PO Box 55227
Houston, TX 77255-5227
(713)467-6555

TEXAS CHILDRENS HOSPITAL
6621 Fannin Street
Houston, TX 77030-2399
(823)824-1000

TEXAS ORTHOPEDIC HOSPITAL
7401 S Main
Houston, TX 77030-4509
(713)799-8600

TOPS SURGICAL SPECIALTY HOSPITAL
17080 Red Oak Drive Box 73409
Houston, TX 77090-2602
(281)539-2900

TRIUMPH HOSPITAL OF NORTH HOUSTON
7407 I-45 North
Houston, TX 77076-1314
(832)200-6000

TWELVE OAKS
6700 Bellaire
Houston, TX 77074-4906
(713)774-7611

TWELVE OAKS MEDICAL CENTER
4200 Twelve Oaks Drive
Houston, TX 77027
(713)623-2500

UNIVERSITY OF TX M D ANDERSON CANCER CENTER
1515 Holcombe Boulevard
Houston, TX 77030-4009
(713)792-2121

VA MEDICAL CENTER - HOUSTON
2002 Holcombe Boulevard
Houston, TX 77030-4211
(713)791-1414

WEST HOUSTON MEDICAL CENTER
12141 Richmond Avenue
Houston, TX 77082-2499
(281)558-3444

WEST OAKS HOSPITAL
6500 Hornwood
Houston, TX 77074-5095
(713)995-0909

WOMANS HOSPITAL OF TEXAS
7600 Fannin
Houston, TX 77054-1987
(713)790-1234

HUMBLE

HEALTHSOUTH REHABILITATION HOSPITAL
19002 McKay Drive
Humble, TX 77338-5701
(281)446-6148

NORTHEAST MEDICAL CENTER HOSPITAL
18951 Memorial North
Humble, TX 77338-4297
(281)540-7700

HUNT

LA HACIENDA TREATMENT CENTER
PO Box 1
Hunt, TX 78024-0001
(830)238-4222

HUNTSVILLE

HUNTSVILLE MEMORIAL HOSPITAL
3000 Interstate 45 PO Box 4001
Huntsville, TX 77342-4001
(936)291-3411

IRAAN

PECOS COUNTY GENERAL HOSPITAL
305 West 5th Street
Iraan, TX 79744
(432)639-2575

IRVING

BAYLOR MEDICAL CENTER - IRVING
1901 N Macarthur Boulevard
Irving, TX 75061-2220
(972)579-8100

LAS COLINAS MEDICAL CENTER
6800 N Macarthur Blvd
Irving, TX 75039-2422
(972)969-2000

JACKSBORO

FAITH COMMUNITY HOSPITAL
717 Magnolia St
Jacksboro, TX 76458-1111
(940)567-6633

JACKSONVILLE

MOTHER FRANCES HOSPITAL - JACKSONVILLE
2026 South Jackson Street
Jacksonville, TX 75766-5822
(903)541-4500

JASPER

CHRISTUS JASPER MEMORIAL HOSPITAL
1275 Marvin Hancock Drive
Jasper, TX 75951-4995
(409)384-5461

DICKERSON MEMORIAL HOSPITAL
1001 Dickerson Drive
Jasper, TX 75951-5110
(409)489-0600

JOURDANTON

SOUTH TEXAS REGIONAL MEDICAL CENTER
1905 Highway 97 East, Box 189
Jourdanton, TX 78026-1504
(830)769-3515

JUNCTION

KIMBLE HOSPITAL
2101 Main St
Junction, TX 76849-3097
(325)446-3321

KATY

MEMORIAL HERMANN KATY HOSPITAL
5602 Medical Center Drive
Katy, TX 77494-6325
(281)392-1111

TEXAS — Hospital Telephone Directory

SAINT CATHERINE HEALTH CENTER
701 South Fry Road
Katy, TX 77450-2237
(281)599-5700

KAUFMAN

PRESBYTERIAN HOSPITAL OF KAUFMAN
Highway 243 W At Highway 175 PO Box 310
Kaufman, TX 75142-0310
(972)932-7200

KENEDY

OTTO KAISER MEMORIAL HOSPITAL
3349 S Highway 181
Kenedy, TX 78119-5241
(830)583-3401

KERMIT

WINKLER COUNTY MEMORIAL HOSPITAL
821 Jeffee Drive
Kermit, TX 79745-4696
(432)586-5864

KERRVILLE

KERRVILLE STATE HOSPITAL
721 Thompson Drive Box 1465
Kerrville, TX 78028-5199
(830)896-2211

SID PETERSON MEMORIAL HOSPITAL
710 Water St
Kerrville, TX 78028-5329
(830)896-4200

KILGORE

LAIRD MEMORIAL HOSPITAL
1612 South Henderson Boulevard
Kilgore, TX 75662-3518
(903)984-3505

KILLEEN

METROPLEX ADVENTIST HOSPITAL
2201 S Clear Creek Road
Killeen, TX 76549-4110
(254)526-7523

KINGSVILLE

CHRISTUS SPOHN HOSPITAL - KLEBERG
1300 General Cavazos Boulevard
Kingsville, TX 78363-7116
(361)595-1661

KINGWOOD

KINGWOOD HEALTH CENTER
2001 Ladbrook
Kingwood, TX 77339-3004
(281)358-1495

KINGWOOD MEDICAL CENTER
22999 Us Highway 59
Kingwood, TX 77339-4438
(281)348-8000

KNOX CITY

KNOX COUNTY HOSPITAL
701 South 5th Street Box 608
Knox City, TX 79529-2107
(940)657-3535

LA GRANGE

FAYETTE MEMORIAL HOSPITAL
543 N Jackson
La Grange, TX 78945-2040
(979)968-3166

LACKLAND AIR FORCE BASE

59TH MEDICAL WING, WILFORD HALL MEDICAL CENTER
2200 Bergquist Drive
Lackland Air Force Base, TX 78236-9907
(210)292-7412

LAKE JACKSON

BRAZOSPORT MEMORIAL HOSPITAL
100 Medical Drive
Lake Jackson, TX 77566-5690
(979)297-4411

LAMESA

MEDICAL ARTS HOSPITAL
1600 N Bryan Avenue
Lamesa, TX 79331-3145
(806)872-2183

LAMPASAS

ROLLINS-BROOK COMMUNITY HOSPITAL
PO Box 589
Lampasas, TX 76550-0032
(512)556-3682

LANCASTER

MEDICAL CENTER AT LANCASTER
2600 W Pleasant Run Road
Lancaster, TX 75146-1199
(972)223-9600

LAREDO

DOCTORS HOSPITAL OF LAREDO
500 E Mann Road
Laredo, TX 78041-2630
(956)523-2000

MERCY HEALTH CENTER
1700 East Saunders
Laredo, TX 78041-5401
(956)796-5000

LAUGHLIN AIR FORCE BASE

47TH MEDICAL GROUP
590 Mitchell Boulevard Building 375
Laughlin Air Force Base, TX 78843-5242
(830)298-6311

LEAGUE CITY

DEVEREUX TEXAS TREATMENT NETWORK
1150 Devereux Drive
League City, TX 77573-2043
(281)335-1000

LEVELLAND

COVENANT HOSPITAL LEVELLAND
1900 College Avenue
Levelland, TX 79336-6508
(806)894-4963

LEWISVILLE

MEDICAL CENTER OF LEWISVILLE
500 West Main Street
Lewisville, TX 75057-3629
(972)420-1000

LIBERTY

LIBERTY DAYTON HOSPITAL
1353 North Travis Street
Liberty, TX 77575-3549
(936)336-7316

LINDEN

LINDEN MUNICIPAL HOSPITAL
404 N Kaufman St
Linden, TX 75563-5234
(903)756-5561

LITTLEFIELD

LAMB HEALTHCARE CENTER
1500 S Sunset
Littlefield, TX 79339-4899
(806)385-6411

LIVINGSTON

MEMORIAL MEDICAL CENTER LIVINGSTON
PO Box 1257
Livingston, TX 77351-0022
(936)327-4381

LLANO

LLANO MEMORIAL HOSPITAL
200 W Ollie
Llano, TX 78643-2628
(325)247-5040

LOCKNEY

W J MANGOLD MEMORIAL HOSPITAL
320 N Main St Box 37
Lockney, TX 79241-0037
(806)652-3373

LONGVIEW

GOOD SHEPHERD MEDICAL CENTER
700 East Marshall Avenue
Longview, TX 75601-5572
(903)315-2000

LONGVIEW REGIONAL MEDICAL CENTER
2901 N Fourth St
Longview, TX 75605-5191
(903)758-1818

MEADOW PINES HOSPITAL
22 Bermuda Lane
Longview, TX 75605-2900
(903)663-4411

LUBBOCK

COVENANT CHILDRENS HOSPITAL
3610 21st St
Lubbock, TX 79410-1218
(806)725-1011

COVENANT LAKESIDE MEDICAL CENTER
4000 24th Street
Lubbock, TX 79410-1894
(806)725-6000

COVENANT MEDICAL CENTER
3615 19th St
Lubbock, TX 79410-1209
(806)725-1011

HIGHLAND MEDICAL CENTER
2412 50th St
Lubbock, TX 79412-2504
(806)788-4100

SOUTHWEST REGIONAL MEDICAL COMPLEX
1409 9th St
Lubbock, TX 79401-2601
(806)767-9133

SUNRISE CANYON HOSPITAL
PO Box 2828
Lubbock, TX 79408-2828
(806)740-1400

Hospital Telephone Directory — TEXAS

UNIVERSITY MEDICAL CENTER
602 Indiana Avenue PO Box 5980
Lubbock, TX 79408-5980
(806)775-8200

LUFKIN

MEMORIAL HEALTH SYSTEMS OF EAST TEXAS
1201 W Frank Street
Lufkin, TX 75904-3357
(936)634-8111

MEMORIAL SPECIALTY HOSPITAL
1201 West Frank Street Ste D5
Lufkin, TX 75904-3357
(936)639-7975

WOODLAND HEIGHTS MEDICAL CENTER
505 S John Redditt Dr
Lufkin, TX 75904-3157
(936)634-8311

LULING

SETON EDGAR B DAVIS MEMORIAL HOSPITAL
130 Hays St
Luling, TX 78648-3207
(830)875-7000

MADISONVILLE

MADISON SAINT JOSEPH HEALTH CENTER
100 W Cross St Box 698
Madisonville, TX 77864-2432
(936)348-2631

MARLIN

FALLS COMMUNITY HOSPITAL AND CLINIC
322 Coleman St Box 60
Marlin, TX 76661-2358
(254)803-3561

MARSHALL

MARSHALL REGIONAL MEDICAL CENTER
811 S Washington Box 1599
Marshall, TX 75670-5336
(903)927-6000

MC ALLEN

MC ALLEN HEART HOSPITAL
301 W Expressway 83
Mc Allen, TX 78503-3045
(956)994-2000

MC ALLEN MEDICAL CENTER
301 W Expressway 83
Mc Allen, TX 78503-3098
(956)632-4000

RIO GRANDE REGIONAL HOSPITAL
101 E Ridge Road
Mc Allen, TX 78503-1299
(956)632-6000

MC CAMEY

MCCAMEY HOSPITAL AND CONVALESCENT CENTER
2500 South Highway 305 PO Box 1200
Mc Camey, TX 79752-1200
(432)652-8626

MC KINNEY

NORTH CENTRAL MEDICAL CENTER OF MC KINNEY
4500 Medical Center Drive
Mc Kinney, TX 75069-1650
(972)547-8000

WESTPARK SURGERY CENTER
130 South Central Expressway
Mc Kinney, TX 75070-3797
(972)548-5300

MESQUITE

MEDICAL CENTER OF MESQUITE
1011 N Galloway Box 1008
Mesquite, TX 75149-2760
(214)320-7000

MESQUITE COMMUNITY HOSPITAL
3500 Interstate 30 At Motley Drive
Mesquite, TX 75150
(972)698-3300

MEXIA

PARKVIEW REGIONAL HOSPITAL
312 East Glendale St
Mexia, TX 76667-3699
(254)562-0408

MIDLAND

DESERT SPRINGS MEDICAL CENTER
3300 S FM 1788
Midland, TX 79706-2608
(432)563-1200

HEALTHSOUTH REHAB HOSPITAL OF MIDLAND/ODESSA
1800 Heritage Boulevard
Midland, TX 79707-9750
(432)520-1600

HEART PLACE HOSPITAL
Wall and Andrews Highway
Midland, TX 79703
(432)683-2255

MEMORIAL REHABILITATION HOSPITAL
1010 South County Road
Midland, TX 79704
(432)520-2333

MIDLAND MEMORIAL HOSPITAL
2200 West Illinois Avenue
Midland, TX 79701-6499
(432)685-1111

MIDLAND MEMORIAL HOSPITAL - WEST
4214 Andrews Highway
Midland, TX 79703-4861
(432)522-2273

MINEOLA

EAST TEXAS MEDICAL CENTER
5875 South State Highway 37
Mineola, TX 75773-7910
(903)569-6124

MINERAL WELLS

PALO PINTO GENERAL HOSPITAL
400 Southwest 25 Avenue
Mineral Wells, TX 76067-8285
(940)325-7891

MISSION

MISSION HOSPITAL
900 South Bryan Road
Mission, TX 78572-6613
(956)580-9000

MISSOURI CITY

MEMORIAL HERMANN FORT BEND MEDICAL CENTER
3803 Fm 1092 At Highway 6
Missouri City, TX 77459
(281)499-4800

MONAHANS

WARD MEMORIAL HOSPITAL
406 S Gary St
Monahans, TX 79756-4798
(432)943-2511

MORTON

COCHRAN MEMORIAL HOSPITAL
201 East Grant
Morton, TX 79346-3444
(806)266-5565

MOUNT PLEASANT

TITUS COUNTY MEMORIAL HOSPITAL
2001 N Jefferson
Mount Pleasant, TX 75455-2371
(903)577-6000

MOUNT VERNON

EAST TEXAS MEDICAL CENTER MOUNT VERNON
Highway 37 South Box 477
Mount Vernon, TX 75457-0477
(903)537-8000

MUENSTER

MUENSTER MEMORIAL HOSPITAL
605 N Maple Avenue Box 370
Muenster, TX 76252-2424
(940)759-2271

MULESHOE

MULESHOE AREA MEDICAL CENTER
708 S 1st St
Muleshoe, TX 79347-3627
(806)272-4524

NACOGDOCHES

NACOGDOCHES MEDICAL CENTER HOSPITAL
4920 Ne Stallings Drive
Nacogdoches, TX 75965-1254
(936)569-9481

NACOGDOCHES MEMORIAL HOSPITAL
1204 Mound St
Nacogdoches, TX 75961-4061
(936)564-4611

NASSAU BAY

CHRISTUS SAINT JOHN HOSPITAL
18300 Saint John Drive
Nassau Bay, TX 77058-6302
(281)333-5503

NAVASOTA

GRIMES SAINT JOSEPH HEALTH CENTER
210 South Judson St
Navasota, TX 77868-3704
(936)825-6585

NEDERLAND

MID JEFFERSON HOSPITAL
Highway 365 And 27th St
Nederland, TX 77627
(409)727-2321

NEW BOSTON

DOCTORS HOSPITAL
520 Hospital Drive Box 7
New Boston, TX 75570-2301
(903)628-5531

155

TEXAS — Hospital Telephone Directory

NEW BRAUNFELS
MCKENNA MEMORIAL HOSPITAL
600 N Union Avenue
New Braunfels, TX 78130-4191
(830)606-9111

NOCONA
NOCONA GENERAL HOSPITAL
100 Park Road
Nocona, TX 76255-3616
(940)825-3235

NORTH RICHLAND HILLS
NORTH HILLS HOSPITAL
4401 Booth Calloway Road
North Richland Hills, TX 76180-7399
(817)255-1000

ODESSA
MEDICAL CENTER HOSPITAL
500 W 4th St Drawer 7239
Odessa, TX 79761-5059
(432)640-4000

ODESSA REGIONAL HOSPITAL
520 E 6th St Box 4859 79760
Odessa, TX 79761-4527
(432)334-8200

OLNEY
HAMILTON HOSPITAL
901 W Hamilton St Box 158
Olney, TX 76374-1799
(940)564-5521

ORANGE
MEMORIAL HERMANN BAPTIST - ORANGE
608 Strickland Drive
Orange, TX 77630-4717
(409)883-9361

PALACIOS
PALACIOS COMMUNITY MEDICAL CENTER
310 Green Avenue Box 859
Palacios, TX 77465-3214
(361)972-2511

PALESTINE
PALESTINE REGIONAL MEDICAL CENTER - EAST
2900 S Loop 256
Palestine, TX 75801-6958
(903)731-1000

PALESTINE REGIONAL REHAB HOSPITAL
4000 South Loop 256
Palestine, TX 75801-8467
(903)731-1000

PAMPA
PAMPA REGIONAL MEDICAL CENTER
1 Medical Plaza
Pampa, TX 79066
(806)665-3721

PARIS
CHRISTUS SAINT JOSEPH HOSPITAL - NORTH
PO Box 9070
Paris, TX 75461-9070
(903)737-1111

CHRISTUS SAINT JOSEPHS HOSPITAL AND HEALTH CENTER
820 Clarksville St PO Box 9070 75461
Paris, TX 75461-9070
(903)785-4521

PASADENA
BAYSHORE MEDICAL CENTER
4000 Spencer Highway
Pasadena, TX 77504-1202
(713)359-2000

KINDRED HOSPITAL BAY AREA
1004 Seymour Street
Pasadena, TX 77506-2637
(713)473-9700

VISTA MEDICAL CENTER
4301 Vista
Pasadena, TX 77504-2117
(713)378-3000

PEARSALL
FRIO HOSPITAL
200 S Interstate 35
Pearsall, TX 78061-6601
(830)334-3617

PECOS
REEVES COUNTY HOSPITAL
2323 Texas St Box 2058
Pecos, TX 79772-7338
(432)447-3551

PERRYTON
OCHILTREE GENERAL HOSPITAL
3101 Garrett Drive
Perryton, TX 79070-5323
(806)435-3606

PITTSBURG
EAST TEXAS MEDICAL CENTER PITTSBURG
414 Quitman Street
Pittsburg, TX 75686-1032
(903)856-6663

PLAINVIEW
COVENANT HOSPITAL PLAINVIEW
2601 Dimmitt Road
Plainview, TX 79072-1833
(806)296-5531

PLANO
HEALTHSOUTH PLANO REHAB HOSPITAL
2800 W 15th St
Plano, TX 75075-7526
(972)612-9000

IHS HOSPITAL AT PLANO
1621 Coit Road
Plano, TX 75075-6141
(972)758-5200

LELAND MEDICAL PLAZA
5800 Granite Pkwy Ste 850
Plano, TX 75024-6612
(972)276-7116

MEDICAL CENTER OF PLANO
3901 W 15th St
Plano, TX 75075-7738
(972)596-6800

PRESBYTERIAN HOSPITAL OF PLANO
6200 W Parker Boulevard
Plano, TX 75093-7939
(972)981-8000

PORT ARTHUR
CHRISTUS SAINT MARY HOSPITAL
3600 Gates Boulevard
Port Arthur, TX 77642-3858
(409)985-7431

DUBUIS HOSPITAL - PORT ARTHUR
3600 Gates Boulevard
Port Arthur, TX 77642-3858
(409)989-5300

PARK PLACE MEDICAL CENTER
3050 39th Street
Port Arthur, TX 77642-5535
(409)983-4951

PORT LAVACA
MEMORIAL MEDICAL CENTER
815 N Virginia Street
Port Lavaca, TX 77979-3025
(361)552-6713

QUANAH
HARDEMAN COUNTY MEMORIAL HOSPITAL
402 Mercer St
Quanah, TX 79252-4026
(940)663-2795

QUITMAN
EAST TEXAS MEDICAL CENTER QUITMAN
117 Winnsboro Box 1000
Quitman, TX 75783-2144
(903)763-4505

RANKIN
RANKIN COUNTY HOSPITAL DISTRICT
1105 Elizabeth St Box 327
Rankin, TX 79778-0327
(432)693-2443

REFUGIO
REFUGIO MEMORIAL HOSPITAL
107 Swift St
Refugio, TX 78377-2425
(361)526-2321

RICHARDSON
LEAVES
1230 West Spring Valley Road
Richardson, TX 75080-7709
(972)231-4864

RICHARDSON REGIONAL MEDICAL CENTER
401 W Campbell Road
Richardson, TX 75080-3499
(972)498-4000

RICHMOND
POLLY RYON MEMORIAL HOSPITAL
1705 Jackson St
Richmond, TX 77469-3289
(281)341-3000

RIO GRANDE CITY
STARR COUNTY MEMORIAL HOSPITAL
Fm Road 3167 Box 78
Rio Grande City, TX 78582-0078
(956)487-5561

ROCKDALE
RICHARDS MEMORIAL HOSPITAL
1700 Brazos St
Rockdale, TX 76567-2517
(512)446-2513

ROTAN

FISHER COUNTY HOSPITAL DISTRICT
Drawer F Roby Highway 70
Rotan, TX 79546-0485
(432)735-2256

ROUND ROCK

ROUND ROCK MEDICAL CENTER
2400 Round Rock Avenue
Round Rock, TX 78681-4097
(512)341-1000

ROWLETT

LAKE POINTE MEDICAL CENTER
6800 Scenic Drive
Rowlett, TX 75088-4552
(972)412-2273

RUSK

EAST TEXAS MEDICAL CENTER
JACKSONVILLE
PO Box 226
Rusk, TX 75785-0226
(903)541-5000

RUSK STATE HOSPITAL
Highway 69 North PO Box 318
Rusk, TX 75785-0318
(903)683-3421

SAN ANGELO

RIVER CREST HOSPITAL
1636 Hunters Glen Road
San Angelo, TX 76901-5016
(432)949-5722

SAN ANGELO COMMUNITY MEDICAL
CENTER
3501 Knickerbocker Road
San Angelo, TX 76904-7697
(432)949-9511

SCCI HOSPITAL - SAN ANGELO
2018 Pulliam Street
San Angelo, TX 76905-5148
(432)659-3906

SHANNON MEDICAL CENTER-SAINT JOHN
CAMPUS
2018 Pulliam St
San Angelo, TX 76905-5148
(432)659-7100

SHANNON WEST TEXAS MEMORIAL
HOSPITAL
120 East Harris Street
San Angelo, TX 76903-5904
(432)653-6741

SAN ANTONIO

BAPTIST MEDICAL CENTER
111 Dallas St
San Antonio, TX 78205-1230
(210)297-7000

CHRISTUS SANTA ROSA CHILDRENS
HOSPITAL
519 W Houston Street, PO Box 839942
San Antonio, TX 78283-3942
(210)704-2011

CHRISTUS SANTA ROSA HEALTH CARE-
DOWNTOWN DIVISION
519 W Houston St
San Antonio, TX 78207-3106
(210)704-2011

CHRISTUS SANTA ROSA NORTHWEST
HOSPITAL
2827 Babcock Road
San Antonio, TX 78229-6098
(210)705-6300

COMPASS HOSPITAL OF SAN ANTONIO
14743 Jones Maltsberger
San Antonio, TX 78247-3713
(210)402-0029

HEALTHSOUTH REHAB INSTITUTE OF SAN
ANTONIO
9119 Cinnamon Hill
San Antonio, TX 78240-5401
(210)691-0737

IHS HOSPITAL AT SAN ANTONIO
7310 Oak Manor
San Antonio, TX 78229-4509
(210)308-0261

KINDRED HOSPITAL SAN ANTONIO
3636 Medical Drive
San Antonio, TX 78229-2183
(210)616-0616

LAUREL RIDGE HOSPITAL-BROWN
SCHOOLS
17720 Corporate Woods Drive
San Antonio, TX 78259-3509
(210)491-9400

LIFECARE HOSPITAL OF SAN ANTONIO
8026 Floyd Curl Drive, 2-west
San Antonio, TX 78229-3915
(210)692-8080

METHODIST AMBULATORY SURGERY
HOSPITAL NW
9150 Huebner Road Suite 900
San Antonio, TX 78240-1558
(210)691-8000

METHODIST CHILDRENS HOSPITAL OF
SOUTH TEXAS
7700 Floyd Curl Dr
San Antonio, TX 78229-3979
(210)575-7138

METHODIST SPECIALTY AND TRANSPLANT
HOSPITAL
8026 Floyd Curl Drive
San Antonio, TX 78229-3915
(210)575-8110

METROPOLITAN METHODIST HOSPITAL
1310 McCullough Avenue
San Antonio, TX 78212-5699
(210)208-2200

MISSION VISTA HOSPITAL
14747 Jones Maltsberger
San Antonio, TX 78247-3713
(210)490-0000

NIX MEDICAL CENTER
414 Navarro
San Antonio, TX 78205-2516
(210)271-1800

NORTH CENTRAL BAPTIST HOSPITAL
520 Madison Oak Drive
San Antonio, TX 78258-3912
(210)297-4000

NORTHEAST BAPTIST HOSPITAL
8811 Village Drive
San Antonio, TX 78217-5415
(210)297-2000

NORTHEAST METHODIST HOSPITAL
12412 Judson Road
San Antonio, TX 78233-3272
(210)650-4949

SAINT LUKES BAPTIST HOSPITAL
7930 Floyd Curl Drive
San Antonio, TX 78229-3950
(210)297-5000

SAN ANTONIO STATE HOSPITAL
6711 S New Braunfels Ave Ste 500
San Antonio, TX 78223-3009
(210)532-8811

SELECT SPECIALTY HOSPITAL - SAN
ANTONIO
111 Dallas Street
San Antonio, TX 78205-1201
(210)297-7195

SOUTHEAST BAPTIST HOSPITAL
4214 E Southcross Boulevard
San Antonio, TX 78222-3740
(210)297-3000

SOUTHWEST GENERAL HOSPITAL
7400 Barlite Boulevard
San Antonio, TX 78224-1399
(210)921-2000

SOUTHWEST MENTAL HEALTH CENTER
8535 Tom Slick
San Antonio, TX 78229-3367
(210)616-0300

SOUTHWEST TEXAS METHODIST HOSPITAL
7700 Floyd Curl Drive
San Antonio, TX 78229-3993
(210)575-4000

SPINE HOSPITAL OF SOUTH TEXAS
18600 Hardy Oak Boulevard
San Antonio, TX 78258-4206
(210)404-0800

TEXAS CENTER FOR INFECTIOUS DISEASE
2303 Se Military Dr
San Antonio, TX 78223-3542
(210)534-8857

TEXSAN HEART HOSPITAL
6700 IH 10 West
San Antonio, TX 78201-2009
(210)736-6700

UNIVERSITY HEALTH SYSTEM
4502 Medical Drive
San Antonio, TX 78229-4492
(210)358-4000

VA HEALTHCARE SYSTEM - SAN ANTONIO
7400 Merton Minter Blvd
San Antonio, TX 78284-5700
(210)617-5300

WARM SPRINGS AND BAPTIST REHAB
NETWORK
5101 Medical Drive
San Antonio, TX 78229-4801
(210)616-0100

SAN AUGUSTINE

SAN AUGUSTINE MEMORIAL HOSPITAL
511 Hospital St Box 658
San Augustine, TX 75972-2121
(936)275-3446

SAN BENITO

DOLLY VINSANT MEMORIAL HOSPITAL
400 E Highway 77 PO Box 42
San Benito, TX 78586-0001
(956)399-1313

SAN MARCOS

CENTRAL TEXAS MEDICAL CENTER
1301 Wonder World Drive
San Marcos, TX 78666-7544
(512)353-8979

SAN MARCOS TREATMENT CENTER
120 Bert Brown Road
San Marcos, TX 78666-5803
(512)396-8500

SEGUIN

GUADALUPE VALLEY HOSPITAL
1215 E Court St
Seguin, TX 78155-5189
(830)379-2411

TEXAS — Hospital Telephone Directory

SEMINOLE
MEMORIAL HOSPITAL
209 N W 8th St
Seminole, TX 79360-3447
(432)758-5811

SEYMOUR
SEYMOUR HOSPITAL
200 Stadium Dr
Seymour, TX 76380-2344
(940)889-5572

SHAMROCK
SHAMROCK GENERAL HOSPITAL
PO Box 511
Shamrock, TX 79079-0511
(806)256-2114

SHEPPARD AIR FORCE BASE
82ND MEDICAL GROUP
149 Hart St, Suite 1
Sheppard Air Force Base, TX 76311-3479
(940)676-5874

SHERMAN
TEXOMA MEDICAL CENTER
2601 Cornerstone
Sherman, TX 75092-2551
(903)416-4000

WILSON N JONES MEDICAL CENTER - NORTH
1111 Gallagher Road
Sherman, TX 75090-1713
(903)870-7000

WILSON N JONES MEMORIAL HOSPITAL
500 N Highland
Sherman, TX 75092-7354
(903)870-4611

SMITHVILLE
SMITHVILLE REGIONAL HOSPITAL
800 Highway 71 E
Smithville, TX 78957-1730
(512)237-3214

SNYDER
D M COGDELL MEMORIAL HOSPITAL
1700 Cogdell Boulevard
Snyder, TX 79549-6198
(432)573-6374

SONORA
LILLIAN M HUDSPETH MEMORIAL HOSPITAL
308 Hudspeth Avenue
Sonora, TX 76950-8003
(432)387-2521

SPEARMAN
HANSFORD HOSPITAL
707 S Roland
Spearman, TX 79081-3441
(806)659-2535

STAMFORD
STAMFORD MEMORIAL HOSPITAL
Highway 6 East Box 911
Stamford, TX 79553-0911
(325)773-2725

STANTON
MARTIN COUNTY HOSPITAL DISTRICT
610 N St Peter St Box 640
Stanton, TX 79782-0640
(432)756-3345

STEPHENVILLE
HARRIS METHODIST ERATH COUNTY
411 N Belknap St
Stephenville, TX 76401-3415
(254)965-1500

SUGAR LAND
METHODIST HEALTH CENTER - SUGAR LAND
16655 Southwest Freeway
Sugar Land, TX 77479-2343
(281)274-8000

SULPHUR SPRINGS
HOPKINS COUNTY MEMORIAL HOSPITAL
115 Airport Road
Sulphur Springs, TX 75482-2105
(903)885-7671

SWEENY
SWEENY COMMUNITY HOSPITAL
305 N Mckinney St
Sweeny, TX 77480-2801
(979)548-3311

SWEETWATER
ROLLING PLAINS MEMORIAL HOSPITAL
PO Box 690
Sweetwater, TX 79556-0690
(325)235-1701

TAHOKA
LYNN COUNTY HOSPITAL DISTRICT
2600 Lockwood Box 1310
Tahoka, TX 79373-1310
(806)998-4533

TAYLOR
JOHNS COMMUNITY HOSPITAL
305 Mallard Lane
Taylor, TX 76574-1296
(512)352-7611

TEMPLE
KINGS DAUGHTERS HOSPITAL
1901 Sw H K Dodgen Loop
Temple, TX 76502-1896
(254)771-8600

SCOTT AND WHITE HOSPITAL
2401 S 31st St
Temple, TX 76508
(254)724-2558

VA MEDICAL CENTER - OLIN E. TEAGUE
1901 Veterans Memorial Drive
Temple, TX 76504-7451
(254)778-4811

TERRELL
MEDICAL CENTER AT TERRELL
1551 Highway 34 S
Terrell, TX 75160-4833
(972)563-7611

TERRELL STATE HOSPITAL
1200 E Brin St Box 70
Terrell, TX 75160-2938
(972)524-6452

TEXARKANA
CHRISTUS SAINT MICHAEL HEALTH CARE CENTER
2600 St Michael Drive
Texarkana, TX 75503-2372
(903)614-1000

CHRISTUS SAINT MICHAEL REHAB HOSPITAL
2400 St Michael Drive
Texarkana, TX 75503-2374
(903)614-4000

DUBUIS HOSPITAL - TEXARKANA
2600 Saint Michael Drive
Texarkana, TX 75503-2372
(903)614-7600

HEALTHSOUTH REHAB HOSPITAL OF TEXARKANA
515 W 12th St
Texarkana, TX 75501-4416
(903)793-0088

WADLEY REGIONAL MEDICAL CENTER
1000 Pine Street
Texarkana, TX 75501-5170
(903)798-8000

TEXAS CITY
MAINLAND MEDICAL CENTER
6801 Emmett Lowry Expressway
Texas City, TX 77591
(409)938-5000

THE WOODLANDS
MEMORIAL HERMANN HOSPITAL - WOODLANDS
9250 Pinecroft Drive
The Woodlands, TX 77380-3218
(281)364-2300

THROCKMORTON
THROCKMORTON COUNTY MEMORIAL HOSPITAL
1100 N Minter Avenue Box 729
Throckmorton, TX 76483-4400
(940)849-2151

TOMBALL
TOMBALL REGIONAL HOSPITAL
605 Holderrieth
Tomball, TX 77375-6490
(281)351-1623

TRINITY
EAST TEXAS MEDICAL CENTER TRINITY
317 Prospect Drive, PO Box 3169
Trinity, TX 75862-3169
(936)594-3541

TULIA
SWISHER MEMORIAL HOSPITAL
539 Southeast Second Street
Tulia, TX 79088-2400
(806)995-8200

TYLER
EAST TEXAS MEDICAL CENTER
1000 S Beckham Box 6400
Tyler, TX 75701-1908
(903)597-0351

EAST TEXAS MEDICAL CENTER REHABILITATION CENTER
701 Olympic Plaza Circle
Tyler, TX 75701-1950
(903)596-3000

EAST TEXAS MEDICAL CENTER SPECIALTY HOSPITAL
1000 S Beckham 5th Floor
Tyler, TX 75701-1908
(903)597-0351

EAST TEXAS MEDICAL CENTER-BEHAVIORAL HEALTH CENTER
4101 University Boulevard
Tyler, TX 75701-6623
(903)566-8668

HEALTHSOUTH REHAB HOSPITAL OF TYLER
3131 Troup Highway
Tyler, TX 75701-8350
(903)510-7000

MOTHER FRANCES HOSPITAL
800 East Dawson
Tyler, TX 75701-2093
(903)593-8441

UNIVERSITY OF TEXAS HEALTH CENTER
11937 US Highway 271
Tyler, TX 75708-3154
(903)877-3451

UVALDE

UVALDE MEMORIAL HOSPITAL
1025 Garner Field Road
Uvalde, TX 78801-4895
(830)278-6251

VAN HORN

CULBERSON COUNTY HOSPITAL DISTRICT
Eisenhower Road And Fm 2185 Box 609
Van Horn, TX 79855-0609
(432)283-2760

VERNON

VERNON STATE HOSPITAL
PO Box 2231
Vernon, TX 76385-2231
(940)552-9901

WILBARGER GENERAL HOSPITAL
920 Hillcrest Drive
Vernon, TX 76384-3196
(940)552-9351

VICTORIA

CITIZENS MEDICAL CENTER
2701 Hospital Drive
Victoria, TX 77901-5748
(361)573-9181

DETAR HOSPITAL
506 E San Antonio St
Victoria, TX 77901-6060
(361)575-7441

DETAR HOSPITAL - NORTH
PO Box 2575
Victoria, TX 77902-2575
(361)573-6100

SCCI HOSPITAL OF VICTORIA
506 East San Antonio Street, 3-East
Victoria, TX 77901-6060
(361)575-1445

VICTORIA WARM SPRINGS REHAB HOSPITAL
102 Medical Drive
Victoria, TX 77904-3101
(361)576-6200

WACO

DE PAUL CENTER
301 Londonberry Drive
Waco, TX 76712-8097
(254)776-5970

HILLCREST BAPTIST MEDICAL CENTER
3000 Herring
Waco, TX 76708-3239
(254)202-2000

PROVIDENCE HEALTH CENTER
6901 Medical Parkway PO Box 2589 78702
Waco, TX 76702-2589
(254)751-4000

VA MEDICAL CENTER - WACO
4800 Memorial Drive
Waco, TX 76711-1397
(254)752-6581

WAXAHACHIE

BAYLOR MEDICAL CENTER-ELLIS COUNTY
1405 W Jefferson St
Waxahachie, TX 75165-2275
(972)923-7000

WEATHERFORD

CAMPBELL HEALTH SYSTEM
713 E Anderson St
Weatherford, TX 76086-5705
(817)596-8751

WEBSTER

CLEAR LAKE REGIONAL MEDICAL CENTER
500 Medical Center Boulevard
Webster, TX 77598-4220
(281)332-2511

CORNERSTONE HOSPITAL OF HOUSTON
709 Medical Center Boulevard
Webster, TX 77598-4005
(281)332-3322

HEALTHSOUTH CLEAR LAKE REHAB HOSPITAL
655 E Medical Center Boulevard
Webster, TX 77598-4328
(281)286-1500

WEIMAR

COLORADO FAYETTE MEDICAL CENTER
400 Youens Drive
Weimar, TX 78962-9563
(979)725-9531

WELLINGTON

COLLINGSWORTH GENERAL HOSPITAL
PO Box 1112
Wellington, TX 79095-1112
(806)447-2521

WESLACO

KNAPP MEDICAL CENTER
1401 East Eight Street PO Box 1110
Weslaco, TX 78599-1110
(956)968-8567

WHARTON

GULF COAST MEDICAL CENTER
1400 U S 59 N Bypass PO Box 3004
Wharton, TX 77488-0079
(979)532-2500

WHEELER

PARKVIEW HOSPITAL
901 Sweetwater PO Box 1030
Wheeler, TX 79096-1030
(806)826-5581

WHITNEY

LAKE WHITNEY MEDICAL CENTER
200 N San Jacinto St Box 458
Whitney, TX 76692-2388
(254)694-3165

WICHITA FALLS

HEALTHSOUTH REHAB HOSPITAL - WICHITA
3901 Armory Road, PO Box 3449
Wichita Falls, TX 76301-0449
(940)720-5700

IHS HOSPITAL AT WICHITA FALLS
1103 Grace St
Wichita Falls, TX 76301-4414
(940)720-6633

KELL WEST REGIONAL HOSPITAL
5420 Kell West Blvd
Wichita Falls, TX 76310-1610
(940)692-5888

NORTH TEXAS STATE HOSPITAL
PO Box 300, 6515 Lake Road
Wichita Falls, TX 76307-0300
(940)692-1220

RED RIVER BEHAVIORAL HEALTH SERVICES
1505 8th St
Wichita Falls, TX 76301-3106
(940)322-3171

UNITED REGIONAL HEALTH CARE SYSTEM
1600 11th Street
Wichita Falls, TX 76301-4388
(940)764-0055

UNITED REGIONAL HEALTH CARE SYSTEM
1600 8th Street
Wichita Falls, TX 76301-3164
(940)764-0055

WICHITA VALLEY REHAB HOSPITAL
300 Loop 11
Wichita Falls, TX 76306-3705
(940)397-8200

WINNIE

WINNIE COMMUNITY HOSPITAL
538 Broadway
Winnie, TX 77665-7600
(409)296-6000

WINNSBORO

PRESBYTERIAN HOSPITAL OF WINNSBORO
719 West Coke Road Box 106
Winnsboro, TX 75494-3098
(903)342-5227

WINTERS

NORTH RUNNELS HOSPITAL
Highway 153 East Box 185
Winters, TX 79567-0185
(325)754-5551

WOODVILLE

TYLER COUNTY HOSPITAL
1100 West Bluff
Woodville, TX 75979-4799
(409)283-8141

WYLIE

BARIATRIC CARE CENTER OF TEXAS
801 South Highway 78
Wylie, TX 75098-5502
(972)429-8000

UTAH

Hospital Telephone Directory

YOAKUM

YOAKUM COMMUNITY HOSPITAL
1200 Fm 3475
Yoakum, TX 77995
(361)293-2321

UTAH

AMERICAN FORK

AMERICAN FORK HOSPITAL
170 North 1100 East
American Fork, UT 84003-2961
(801)763-3300

BEAVER

BEAVER VALLEY HOSPITAL
PO Box 1670
Beaver, UT 84713-1670
(435)438-2531

BOUNTIFUL

LAKEVIEW HOSPITAL
630 East Medical Drive
Bountiful, UT 84010-4908
(801)292-6231

SOUTH DAVIS COMMUNITY HOSPITAL
401 South 400 East
Bountiful, UT 84010-4933
(801)295-2361

BRIGHAM CITY

BRIGHAM CITY COMMUNITY HOSPITAL
950 S 500 West
Brigham City, UT 84302-4724
(435)734-9471

CEDAR CITY

VALLEY VIEW MEDICAL CENTER
1303 N Main St
Cedar City, UT 84720-9746
(435)586-6587

DELTA

DELTA COMMUNITY MEDICAL CENTER
126 South White Sage Avenue
Delta, UT 84624-8937
(435)864-5591

FILLMORE

FILLMORE COMMUNITY MEDICAL CENTER
674 South Highway 99
Fillmore, UT 84631-5013
(435)743-5591

GUNNISON

GUNNISON VALLEY HOSPITAL
60 East 100 North
Gunnison, UT 84634
(435)528-7246

HEBER CITY

HEBER VALLEY MEDICAL CENTER
1485 S Highway 40
Heber City, UT 84032-3522
(435)654-2500

HILL AIR FORCE BASE

75TH MEDICAL GROUP
7321 11th St Building 570
Hill Air Force Base, UT 84056-5012
(801)777-6205

KANAB

KANE COUNTY HOSPITAL
355 N Main St
Kanab, UT 84741-3260
(435)644-5811

LAYTON

DAVIS HOSPITAL AND MEDICAL CENTER
1600 West Antelope Drive
Layton, UT 84041-1120
(801)825-9561

LOGAN

LOGAN HOSPITAL
500 East 1400 North
Logan, UT 84341-2465
(435)716-1000

MIDVALE

HIGHLAND RIDGE HOSPITAL
7309 S 180 W
Midvale, UT 84047-1020
(801)569-2153

MILFORD

MILFORD VALLEY MEMORIAL HOSPITAL
451 Main St
Milford, UT 84751
(435)387-2411

MOAB

ALLEN MEMORIAL HOSPITAL
719 West 4th North
Moab, UT 84532-2239
(435)259-7191

MONTICELLO

SAN JUAN HOSPITAL
364 West 100 North
Monticello, UT 84535
(435)587-2116

MOUNT PLEASANT

SANPETE HOSPITAL
1100 S Medical Drive
Mount Pleasant, UT 84647-2222
(435)462-2441

NEPHI

CENTRAL VALLEY MEDICAL CENTER
PO Box 412
Nephi, UT 84648-0412
(435)623-1242

NORTH LOGAN

CACHE VALLEY SPECIALTY HOSPITAL
2380 North 400 East
North Logan, UT 84341-1749
(435)713-9700

OGDEN

MCKAY-DEE HOSPITAL CENTER
PO Box 9370
Ogden, UT 84409-0370
(801)387-2800

OGDEN REGIONAL MEDICAL CENTER
5475 South 500 East
Ogden, UT 84405-6905
(801)479-2111

OREM

OREM COMMUNITY HOSPITAL
331 North 400 West
Orem, UT 84057-1999
(801)224-4080

PROVO CANYON SCHOOL
1350 East 750 North
Orem, UT 84097-4345
(801)227-2000

TIMPANOGOS REGIONAL HOSPITAL
750 West 800 North
Orem, UT 84057-3660
(801)714-6000

PANGUITCH

GARFIELD MEMORIAL HOSPITAL
200 N 400 E
Panguitch, UT 84759
(435)676-8811

PAYSON

MOUNTAIN VIEW HOSPITAL
1000 East 100 North
Payson, UT 84651-1600
(801)465-7000

PRICE

CASTLEVIEW HOSPITAL
300 North Hospital Drive
Price, UT 84501-4200
(435)637-4800

PROVO

UTAH STATE HOSPITAL-PSYCHIATRIC
1300 East Center Street PO Box 270
Provo, UT 84603-0270
(801)344-4400

UTAH VALLEY REGIONAL MEDICAL CENTER
1034 North 500 West
Provo, UT 84604-3380
(801)373-7850

RICHFIELD

SEVIER VALLEY HOSPITAL
70 E 1000 N Ste B
Richfield, UT 84701-1850
(435)896-8271

ROOSEVELT

UINTAH BASIN MEDICAL CENTER
250 West 300 North
Roosevelt, UT 84066-2336
(435)722-6163

SAINT GEORGE

DIXIE REGIONAL MEDICAL CENTER
544 South 400 East
Saint George, UT 84770-3799
(435)634-4000

SALT LAKE CITY

COTTONWOOD HOSPITAL
PO Box 57800
Salt Lake City, UT 84157-0800
(801)314-6300

LATTER-DAY SAINTS HOSPITAL
325 Eighth Avenue
Salt Lake City, UT 84143-0001
(801)408-1100

ORTHOPEDIC SPECIALTY HOSPITAL
5848 South 300 East
Salt Lake City, UT 84107-6121
(801)269-4100

PRIMARY CHILDRENS MEDICAL CENTER
100 North Medical Drive
Salt Lake City, UT 84113-1100
(801)588-2000

SAINT MARKS HOSPITAL
1200 East 3900 South
Salt Lake City, UT 84124-1390
(801)268-7111

SALT LAKE REGIONAL MEDICAL CENTER
1050 East South Temple
Salt Lake City, UT 84102-1507
(801)350-4111

SHRINERS HOSPITAL FOR CHILDREN
1275 Fairfax Road
Salt Lake City, UT 84103-4399
(801)536-3500

UNIVERSITY OF UTAH HOSPITAL
50 N Medical Drive
Salt Lake City, UT 84132-0001
(801)581-2380

UNIVERSITY OF UTAH NEUROPSYCHIATRIC INSTITUTE
501 Chipeta Way
Salt Lake City, UT 84108-1222
(801)583-2500

VA HEALTHCARE SYSTEM - SALT LAKE CITY
500 Foothill Drive
Salt Lake City, UT 84148-0001
(801)582-1565

SANDY

ALTA VIEW HOSPITAL
9660 South 1300 East
Sandy, UT 84094-3793
(801)501-2600

HEALTHSOUTH REHAB INSTITUTE
8074 South 1300 East
Sandy, UT 84094-0743
(801)561-3400

TOOELE

MOUNTAIN WEST MEDICAL CENTER
211 South 100 East
Tooele, UT 84074-2736
(435)843-3600

TREMONTON

BEAR RIVER VALLEY HOSPITAL
440 W 600 N
Tremonton, UT 84337-2497
(435)257-7441

VERNAL

ASHLEY VALLEY MEDICAL CENTER
151 West 200 North
Vernal, UT 84078-1907
(435)789-3342

WEST JORDAN

COPPER HILLS YOUTH CENTER
5899 West Rivendell Drive
West Jordan, UT 84088-5700
(801)561-3377

JORDAN VALLEY HOSPITAL
3580 West 9000 South
West Jordan, UT 84088-8899
(801)561-8888

WEST VALLEY CITY

PIONEER VALLEY HOSPITAL
3460 South Pioneer Parkway
West Valley City, UT 84120-2098
(801)964-3100

SALT LAKE SPECIALTY MEDICAL CENTER
3460 South Pioneer Parkway
West Valley City, UT 84120-2049
(801)964-3551

WOODS CROSS

BENCHMARK REGIONAL HOSPITAL
592 West 1350 South
Woods Cross, UT 84010-8111
(801)299-5300

VERMONT

BARRE

CENTRAL VERMONT HOSPITAL
Box 547
Barre, VT 05641-0547
(802)371-4100

BENNINGTON

SOUTHWESTERN VERMONT MEDICAL CENTER
100 Hospital Drive East
Bennington, VT 05201-5013
(802)442-6361

BRATTLEBORO

BRATTLEBORO MEMORIAL HOSPITAL
9 Belmont Avenue
Brattleboro, VT 05301-3460
(802)257-0341

BRATTLEBORO RETREAT
Anna Marsh Lane
Brattleboro, VT 05301
(802)257-7785

BURLINGTON

FLETCHER ALLEN HEALTH CARE
111 Colchester Avenue
Burlington, VT 05401-1416
(802)847-2345

COLCHESTER

FLETCHER ALLEN HOSPITAL-FANNY ALLEN CAMPUS
790 College Pkwy
Colchester, VT 05446-3035
(802)655-1234

MIDDLEBURY

PORTER MEDICAL CENTER
South St
Middlebury, VT 05753
(802)388-4701

MORRISVILLE

COPLEY HOSPITAL
Washington Highway
Morrisville, VT 05661
(802)888-4231

NEWPORT

NORTH COUNTRY HOSPITAL AND HEALTH CENTER
189 Prouty Drive
Newport, VT 05855-9820
(802)334-7331

RANDOLPH

GIFFORD MEDICAL CENTER
44 S Main St
Randolph, VT 05060-1381
(802)728-4441

RUTLAND

RUTLAND REGIONAL MEDICAL CENTER
160 Allen St
Rutland, VT 05701-4595
(802)775-7111

SAINT ALBANS

NORTHWESTERN MEDICAL CENTER
PO Box 1370
Saint Albans, VT 05478-1370
(802)524-5911

SAINT JOHNSBURY

NORTHEASTERN VERMONT REGIONAL HOSPITAL
Hospital Drive
Saint Johnsbury, VT 05819
(802)748-8141

SPRINGFIELD

SPRINGFIELD HOSPITAL
25 Ridgewood Road
Springfield, VT 05156-3057
(802)885-2151

TOWNSHEND

GRACE COTTAGE HOSPITAL
Route 35
Townshend, VT 05353
(802)365-7357

WATERBURY

VERMONT STATE HOSPITAL
103 South Main St
Waterbury, VT 05676-1531
(802)241-1000

WHITE RIVER JUNCTION

VA MEDICAL CENTER - WHITE RIVER JUNCTION
N Hartland Road
White River Junction, VT 05009-0001
(802)295-9363

WINDSOR

MOUNT ASCUTNEY HOSPITAL HEALTH CENTER
Box 375
Windsor, VT 05089-0375
(802)674-6711

VIRGINIA

ABINGDON

JOHNSTON MEMORIAL HOSPITAL
351 N Court St
Abingdon, VA 24210-2955
(276)676-7000

ALEXANDRIA

INOVA ALEXANDRIA HOSPITAL
4320 Seminary Road
Alexandria, VA 22304-1592
(703)504-3000

LYNN HOUSE OF POTOMAC VALLEY
4400 W Braddock Road
Alexandria, VA 22304-1099
(703)379-6001

MOUNT VERNON HOSPITAL
2501 Parkers Lane
Alexandria, VA 22306-3281
(703)664-7000

VIRGINIA — Hospital Telephone Directory

ARLINGTON

HOSPICE OF NORTHERN VIRGINIA
4715 North 15th Street
Arlington, VA 22205-2699
(703)525-7070

NORTHERN VIRGINIA COMMUNITY
HOSPITAL
601 Carlin Springs Road
Arlington, VA 22204-1023
(703)671-1200

VIRGINIA HOSPITAL CENTER - ARLINGTON
1701 N George Mason Drive
Arlington, VA 22205-3610
(703)558-5000

BEDFORD

BEDFORD MEMORIAL HOSPITAL
1613 Oakwood Street Box 688
Bedford, VA 24523-1213
(540)586-2441

BIG STONE GAP

WELMONT LONESOME PINE HOSPITAL
1990 Holton Avenue East PO Drawer 1
Big Stone Gap, VA 24219-3350
(276)523-3111

BLACKSBURG

MONTGOMERY REGIONAL HOSPITAL
Route 460 South
Blacksburg, VA 24060
(540)951-1111

BURKEVILLE

PIEDMONT GERIATRIC HOSPITAL
Highway 360 And 460
Burkeville, VA 23922
(434)767-4401

CATAWBA

CATAWBA HOSPITAL
PO Box 200
Catawba, VA 24070-0200
(540)375-4200

CHARLOTTESVILLE

BROWN SCHOOLS OF VIRGINIA
2101 Arlington Boulevard
Charlottesville, VA 22903-1521
(434)977-1523

MARTHA JEFFERSON HOSPITAL
459 Locust Avenue
Charlottesville, VA 22902-4808
(434)982-7000

UNIVERSITY OF VIRGINIA HOSPITAL
1215 Lee Street
Charlottesville, VA 22908-0001
(434)924-0211

UVA/HEALTHSOUTH REHABILITATION
HOSPITAL
515 Ray C Hunt Drive
Charlottesville, VA 22903-2981
(434)244-2000

CHESAPEAKE

CHESAPEAKE GENERAL HOSPITAL
736 Battlefield Boulevard N
Chesapeake, VA 23320-4906
(757)312-8121

CHRISTIANSBURG

CARILION NEW RIVER VALLEY MEDICAL
CENTER
2900 Lamb Circle
Christiansburg, VA 24073-6344
(540)731-2000

CULPEPER

CULPEPER MEMORIAL HOSPITAL
501 Sunset Lane
Culpeper, VA 22701-3917
(540)829-4100

DANVILLE

DANVILLE REGIONAL MEDICAL CENTER
142 S Main St
Danville, VA 24541-2987
(434)799-2100

SOUTHERN VIRGINIA MENTAL HEALTH
INSTITUTE
382 Taylor Drive
Danville, VA 24541-4023
(434)799-6220

EMPORIA

GREENSVILLE MEMORIAL HOSPITAL
214 Weaver Avenue
Emporia, VA 23847-1224
(434)348-2000

FAIRFAX

INOVA FAIR OAKS HOSPITAL
3600 Joseph Diewick Drive
Fairfax, VA 22033-1798
(703)391-3600

FALLS CHURCH

DOMINION HOSPITAL
2960 Sleepy Hollow Road
Falls Church, VA 22044-2030
(703)536-2000

HOSPICE OF NORTHERN VIRGINIA
6565 Arlington Boulevard
Falls Church, VA 22042-3013
(703)534-7070

INOVA FAIRFAX HOSPITAL
3300 Gallows Road
Falls Church, VA 22042-3300
(703)698-1110

NORTHERN VIRGINIA MENTAL HEALTH
INSTITUTE
3302 Gallows Road
Falls Church, VA 22042-3353
(703)207-7110

FARMVILLE

SOUTHSIDE COMMUNITY HOSPITAL
800 Oak St
Farmville, VA 23901-1199
(434)392-8811

FISHERSVILLE

AUGUSTA MEDICAL CENTER
96 Medical Center Drive
Fishersville, VA 22939-2332
(540)932-4000

WOODROW WILSON REHABILITATION
CENTER
PO Box 1500
Fishersville, VA 22939-1500
(540)332-7000

FORT BELVOIR

DEWITT ARMY COMMUNITY HOSPITAL
9501 Farrell Road Suite Gc11
Fort Belvoir, VA 22060-5901
(703)805-0510

FORT EUSTIS

MCDONALD ARMY COMMUNITY HOSPITAL
Jefferson Avenue, Building 576
Fort Eustis, VA 23604
(757)314-7500

FRANKLIN

SOUTHAMPTON MEMORIAL HOSPITAL
100 Fairview Drive
Franklin, VA 23851-1238
(757)569-6100

FREDERICKSBURG

MARY WASHINGTON HOSPITAL
1001 Sam Perry Boulevard
Fredericksburg, VA 22401-3354
(540)741-1100

SNOWDEN AT FREDERICKSBURG
1900 Sam Perry Boulevard
Fredericksburg, VA 22401
(540)372-3900

FRONT ROYAL

WARREN MEMORIAL HOSPITAL
1000 Shenandoah Avenue
Front Royal, VA 22630-3598
(540)636-0300

GALAX

TWIN COUNTY REGIONAL HOSPITAL
200 Hospital Drive
Galax, VA 24333-2227
(276)236-8181

GLOUCESTER

RIVERSIDE WALTER REED HOSPITAL
Route 17 Box 1130
Gloucester, VA 23061
(804)693-8800

GRUNDY

BUCHANAN GENERAL HOSPITAL
Route 5 Box 20
Grundy, VA 24614-9611
(276)935-1000

HAMPTON

PENINSULA BEHAVIORAL CENTER
2244 Executive Drive
Hampton, VA 23666-2430
(757)827-1001

SENTARA CAREPLEX HOSPITAL
3000 Coliseum Drive
Hampton, VA 23666-5963
(757)727-7000

VA MEDICAL CENTER - HAMPTON
100 Emancipation Drive
Hampton, VA 23667-0001
(757)722-9961

HARRISONBURG

ROCKINGHAM MEMORIAL HOSPITAL
235 Cantrell Avenue
Harrisonburg, VA 22801-3293
(540)433-4100

Hospital Telephone Directory — **VIRGINIA**

HOPEWELL

JOHN RANDOLPH MEDICAL CENTER
411 W Randolph Road
Hopewell, VA 23860-2938
(804)541-1600

HOT SPRINGS

BATH COUNTY COMMUNITY HOSPITAL
Route 220 Drawer Z
Hot Springs, VA 24445
(540)839-7000

KILMARNOCK

RAPPAHANNOCK GENERAL HOSPITAL
Harris Drive PO Box 1449
Kilmarnock, VA 22482-1449
(804)435-8000

LANGLEY AIR FORCE BASE

1ST MEDICAL GROUP
45 Pine Road
Langley Air Force Base, VA 23665-2025
(757)764-6969

LEBANON

RUSSELL COUNTY MEDICAL CENTER
Carrol Tate Streets
Lebanon, VA 24266
(276)889-1224

LEESBURG

GRAYDON MANOR
801 Childrens Center Road Sw
Leesburg, VA 20175-2545
(703)777-3485

LOUDOUN HOSPITAL CENTER
44045 Riverside Parkway
Leesburg, VA 20176-5101
(703)858-6000

PIEDMONT BEHAVIORAL HEALTH CENTER
42009 Charter Springwood Lane
Leesburg, VA 20176
(703)777-0800

WOODSIDE HOSPITAL
PO Box 2577
Leesburg, VA 20177-7771
(703)888-0400

LEXINGTON

STONEWALL JACKSON HOSPITAL
102 Spotswood Road
Lexington, VA 24450-2430
(540)462-1200

LOWMOOR

ALLEGHENY REGIONAL HOSPITAL
1 Arh Lane PO Box 7
Lowmoor, VA 24457-0007
(540)862-6011

LURAY

PAGE MEMORIAL HOSPITAL
200 Memorial Drive
Luray, VA 22835-1000
(540)743-4561

LYNCHBURG

CENTRAL VIRGINIA TRAINING CENTER
PO Box 1098
Lynchburg, VA 24505-1098
(434)947-6326

LYNCHBURG GENERAL HOSPITAL
1901 Tate Springs Road
Lynchburg, VA 24501-1167
(434)947-3000

VIRGINIA BAPTIST HOSPITAL
3300 Rivermont Avenue
Lynchburg, VA 24503-2053
(434)947-4000

MANASSAS

PRINCE WILLIAM HOSPITAL
8700 Sudley Road
Manassas, VA 20110-4415
(703)369-8000

MARION

SMYTH COUNTY COMMUNITY HOSPITAL
700 Park Boulevard
Marion, VA 24354-3526
(276)782-1234

SOUTHWESTERN VIRGINIA MENTAL HEALTH INSTITUTE
502 East Main Street
Marion, VA 24354
(276)783-1200

MARTINSVILLE

MEMORIAL HOSPITAL MARTINSVILLE
PO Box 4788
Martinsville, VA 24115-4788
(276)666-7200

MECHANICSVILLE

MEMORIAL REGIONAL HOSPITAL
8260 Atlee Road
Mechanicsville, VA 23116-1844
(804)764-6102

SHELTERING ARMS HOSPITAL
8254 Atlee Rd
Mechanicsville, VA 23116-1844
(804)764-6000

NASSAWADOX

SHORE MEMORIAL HOSPITAL
9507 Hospital Avenue PO Box 17
Nassawadox, VA 23413-0017
(757)414-8000

NEW KENT

CUMBERLAND HOSPITAL FOR CHILDREN/ADOLESCENTS
PO Box 150 Route 637
New Kent, VA 23124-0150
(804)966-2242

NEWPORT NEWS

MARY IMMACULATE HOSPITAL
2 Bernadine Drive
Newport News, VA 23602-4499
(757)886-6000

NEWPORT NEWS GENERAL HOSPITAL
5100 Marshall Avenue
Newport News, VA 23605-2600
(757)247-7200

RIVERSIDE PSYCHIATRIC INSTITUTE
420 J Clyde Morris Blvd
Newport News, VA 23601-1927
(757)594-3100

RIVERSIDE REGIONAL MEDICAL CENTER
500 J Clyde Morris Boulevard
Newport News, VA 23601-1975
(757)594-2000

RIVERSIDE REHAB INSTITUTE
245 Chesapeake Avenue
Newport News, VA 23607-6038
(757)928-8000

NORFOLK

BON SECOURS - DEPAUL MEDICAL CENTER
150 Kingsley Lane
Norfolk, VA 23505-4602
(757)889-5000

CHILDRENS HOSPITAL OF KINGS DAUGHTERS
601 Children's Lane
Norfolk, VA 23507-1971
(757)668-7700

HOSPITAL FOR EXTENDED RECOVERY
600 Gresham Drive Ste 700
Norfolk, VA 23507-1904
(757)668-1700

LAKE TAYLOR HOSPITAL
1309 Kempsville Road
Norfolk, VA 23502-2286
(757)461-5001

SENTARA LEIGH HOSPITAL
830 Kempsville Road
Norfolk, VA 23502-3981
(757)466-6000

SENTARA NORFOLK GENERAL HOSPITAL
600 Gresham Drive
Norfolk, VA 23507-1999
(757)668-3000

NORTON

NORTON COMMUNITY HOSPITAL
100 15th St Nw
Norton, VA 24273-1699
(276)679-9600

SAINT MARYS HOSPITAL
Third Street Ne
Norton, VA 24273
(276)679-9100

PEARISBURG

CARILION GILES MEMORIAL HOSPITAL
One Taylor Avenue
Pearisburg, VA 24134-1932
(540)921-6000

PENNINGTON GAP

LEE COUNTY COMMUNITY HOSPITAL
PO Box 70
Pennington Gap, VA 24277-0070
(276)546-1440

PETERSBURG

CENTRAL STATE HOSPITAL
PO Box 4030
Petersburg, VA 23803-0030
(804)524-7000

HIRAM W DAVIS MEDICAL CENTER
PO Box 4030
Petersburg, VA 23803-0030
(804)524-7420

POPLAR SPRINGS HOSPITAL
350 Poplar Drive PO Box 3060
Petersburg, VA 23805-3060
(804)733-6874

SOUTHSIDE REGIONAL MEDICAL CENTER
801 S Adams Street
Petersburg, VA 23803-5133
(804)862-5000

VIRGINIA
Hospital Telephone Directory

PORTSMOUTH

MARYVIEW MEDICAL
CENTER/PORTSMOUTH GENERAL
Portsmouth, VA 23707
(757)398-2200

NAVAL MEDICAL CENTER PORTSMOUTH
620 John Paul Jones Circle
Portsmouth, VA 23708-2111
(757)953-7424

PULASKI

PULASKI COMMUNITY HOSPITAL
2400 Lee Highway
Pulaski, VA 24301-2332
(540)994-8100

RADFORD

CARILION SAINT ALBANS HOSPITAL
PO Box 3608
Radford, VA 24143-3608
(276)639-2481

RESTON

RESTON HOSPITAL CENTER
1850 Town Center Parkway
Reston, VA 20190-3298
(703)689-9000

RICHLANDS

CLINCH VALLEY MEDICAL CENTER
2949 W Front St
Richlands, VA 24641-2099
(276)596-6000

RICHMOND

CAPITOL MEDICAL CENTER
700 West Grace St
Richmond, VA 23220-4120
(804)775-4100

CHILDRENS HOSPITAL
2924 Brook Road
Richmond, VA 23220-1298
(804)321-7474

CJW MEDICAL CENTER - CHIPPENHAM
7101 Jahnke Road
Richmond, VA 23225-4044
(804)320-3911

CJW MEDICAL CENTER - JOHNSTON WILLIS
1401 Johnson-Willis Drive
Richmond, VA 23235-4730
(804)330-2000

HALLMARK YOUTH CARE
12800 West Creek Parkway
Richmond, VA 23238-1116
(804)784-2200

HEALTHSOUTH REHAB HOSPITAL OF
VIRGINIA
5700 Fitzhugh Avenue
Richmond, VA 23226-1800
(804)288-5700

HENRICO DOCTORS HOSPITAL - FOREST
1602 Skipwith Road
Richmond, VA 23229-5298
(804)289-4500

HENRICO DOCTORS HOSPITAL - PARHAM
7700 Parham Road
Richmond, VA 23294-4301
(804)747-5600

RETREAT HOSPITAL
2621 Grove Avenue
Richmond, VA 23220-4300
(804)254-5100

RICHMOND COMMUNITY HOSPITAL
1500 N 28th St
Richmond, VA 23223-5396
(804)225-1700

RICHMOND EYE AND EAR HOSPITAL
8700 Stony Point Pkwy Ste 100
Richmond, VA 23235-1968
(804)775-4500

SAINT MARYS HOSPITAL OF RICHMOND
5801 Bremo Road
Richmond, VA 23226-1900
(804)285-2011

VA MEDICAL CENTER - HUNTER HOLMES
MCGUIRE
1201 Broad Rock Road
Richmond, VA 23249-0002
(804)675-5000

VCU HEALTH SYSTEMS
1250 East Marshall, Mcv Station Box 510
Richmond, VA 23298-5051
(804)828-9000

ROANOKE

CARILION ROANOKE COMMUNITY
HOSPITAL
101 Elm Avenue SE
Roanoke, VA 24013-2222
(540)985-8000

ROANOKE MEMORIAL REHAB CENTER
Belleview And Jefferson Streets PO Box 13367
Roanoke, VA 24002-0001
(540)981-7000

ROCKY MOUNT

CARILION FRANKLIN MEMORIAL HOSPITAL
124 Floyd Avenue
Rocky Mount, VA 24151-1318
(540)483-5277

SALEM

LEWIS-GALE MEDICAL CENTER
1900 Electric Road
Salem, VA 24153-7494
(540)776-4000

MOUNT REGIS CENTER
405 Kimball Avenue
Salem, VA 24153-6251
(540)389-4761

VA MEDICAL CENTER - SALEM
1970 Roanoke Boulevard
Salem, VA 24153-6478
(540)982-2463

SOUTH BOSTON

HALIFAX REGIONAL HOSPITAL
2204 Wilborn Avenue
South Boston, VA 24592-1638
(434)517-3100

SOUTH HILL

COMMUNITY MEMORIAL HEALTH CENTER
125 Buena Vista Circle
South Hill, VA 23970-1499
(434)447-3151

STAUNTON

DE JARNETTE CENTER
1355 Richmond Road
Staunton, VA 24401-9146
(540)332-2100

WESTERN STATE HOSPITAL
PO Box 2500
Staunton, VA 24402-2500
(540)332-8000

STUART

R J REYNOLDS-PATRICK COMMUNITY
HOSPITAL
18688 Jeb Stuart Highway
Stuart, VA 24171-1559
(276)694-3151

SUFFOLK

LOUISE OBICI MEMORIAL HOSPITAL
PO Box 1100
Suffolk, VA 23439-1100
(757)934-4000

TAPPAHANNOCK

RIVERSIDE TAPPAHANNOCK HOSPITAL
Route 2 Box 612
Tappahannock, VA 22560
(804)443-3311

TAZEWELL

TAZEWELL COMMUNITY HOSPITAL
PO Box 60 141 Ben Bolt Avenue
Tazewell, VA 24651-0060
(276)988-2506

VIRGINIA BEACH

SENTARA BAYSIDE HOSPITAL
800 Independence Boulevard
Virginia Beach, VA 23455-6076
(757)363-6100

VIRGINIA BEACH GENERAL HOSPITAL
1060 First Colonial Road
Virginia Beach, VA 23454-0685
(757)395-8000

VIRGINIA BEACH PSYCHIATRIC CENTER
1100 First Colonial Road
Virginia Beach, VA 23454-2403
(757)496-6000

WARRENTON

FAUQUIER HOSPITAL
500 Hospital Drive
Warrenton, VA 20186-3099
(540)349-0531

WILLIAMSBURG

EASTERN STATE HOSPITAL
4601 Ironbound Road, PO Box 8791
Williamsburg, VA 23187-8791
(757)253-5161

WILLIAMSBURG COMMUNITY HOSPITAL
1238 Mount Vernon Avenue
Williamsburg, VA 23185-2836
(757)259-6000

WINCHESTER

WINCHESTER MEDICAL CENTER
1840 Amherst St
Winchester, VA 22601-2808
(540)536-8000

WOODBRIDGE

POTOMAC HOSPITAL
2300 Opitz Boulevard
Woodbridge, VA 22191-3398
(703)670-1313

WOODSTOCK

SHENANDOAH COUNTY MEMORIAL
HOSPITAL
PO Box 508 Route 11
Woodstock, VA 22664-0508
(540)459-4021

Hospital Telephone Directory — WASHINGTON

WYTHEVILLE

WYTHE COUNTY COMMUNITY HOSPITAL
600 W Ridge Road
Wytheville, VA 24382-1099
(276)228-0200

WASHINGTON

ABERDEEN

GRAYS HARBOR COMMUNITY HOSPITAL
915 Anderson Drive
Aberdeen, WA 98520-1097
(360)532-8330

ANACORTES

ISLAND HOSPITAL
11211-24th Street
Anacortes, WA 98221
(360)299-1300

ARLINGTON

CASCADE VALLEY HOSPITAL
330 S Stillaguamish Avenue
Arlington, WA 98223-1603
(360)435-2133

AUBURN

AUBURN REGIONAL MEDICAL CENTER
202 North Division, Plaza One
Auburn, WA 98001-4939
(253)833-7711

BELLEVUE

OVERLAKE HOSPITAL MEDICAL CENTER
1035-116th Avenue Ne
Bellevue, WA 98004-4604
(425)688-5000

BELLINGHAM

SAINT JOSEPHS HOSPITAL
3201 Ellis St
Bellingham, WA 98225-1905
(360)734-5400

BREMERTON

HARRISON MEMORIAL HOSPITAL
2520 Cherry Avenue
Bremerton, WA 98310-4270
(360)377-3911

NAVAL HOSPITAL BREMERTON
Hp01 Boone Road
Bremerton, WA 98312
(360)475-4000

BREWSTER

OKANOGAN-DOUGLAS DISTRICT HOSPITAL
507 Hospital Way, PO Box 577
Brewster, WA 98812-0577
(509)689-2517

BURIEN

HIGHLINE COMMUNITY HOSPITAL
16251 Sylvester Road Sw
Burien, WA 98166-3052
(206)244-9970

CENTRALIA

PROVIDENCE HOSPITAL
914 South Scheuber Road
Centralia, WA 98531-9027
(360)736-2803

CHELAN

LAKE CHELAN COMMUNITY HOSPITAL
503 E Highland
Chelan, WA 98816-8631
(509)682-2531

CHEWELAH

SAINT JOSEPHS HOSPITAL
PO Box 197
Chewelah, WA 99109-0197
(509)935-8211

CLARKSTON

TRI STATE MEMORIAL HOSPITAL
1221 Highland Avenue (PO Box 189)
Clarkston, WA 99403-0189
(509)758-5511

COLFAX

WHITMAN HOSPITAL AND MEDICAL CENTER
1200 Almota Road
Colfax, WA 99111-9509
(509)397-3435

COLVILLE

MOUNT CARMEL HOSPITAL
982 E Columbia Ave
Colville, WA 99114-3352
(509)684-2561

COUPEVILLE

WHIDBEY GENERAL HOSPITAL
101 N Main St
Coupeville, WA 98239-3413
(360)678-5151

DAVENPORT

LINCOLN HOSPITAL
10 Nichols Street
Davenport, WA 99122-9729
(509)725-7101

DAYTON

DAYTON GENERAL HOSPITAL
1012 S Third St
Dayton, WA 99328-1696
(509)382-2531

DEER PARK

DEER PARK HEALTH CENTER AND HOSPITAL
East 1015 D Street (PO Box 742)
Deer Park, WA 99006-0742
(509)276-5061

EDMONDS

STEVENS MEMORIAL HOSPITAL
21601 76th Avenue West
Edmonds, WA 98026-7506
(425)640-4000

ELLENSBURG

KITTITAS VALLEY COMMUNITY HOSPITAL
603 S Chestnut
Ellensburg, WA 98926-3897
(509)962-7302

ENUMCLAW

ENUMCLAW COMMUNITY HOSPITAL
1450 Battersby Avenue/PO Box 218
Enumclaw, WA 98022-0218
(360)825-2505

EPHRATA

COLUMBIA BASIN HOSPITAL
200 Southeast Boulevard
Ephrata, WA 98823-1997
(509)754-4631

EVERETT

PROVIDENCE EVERETT MEDICAL CENTER
916 Pacific Avenue
Everett, WA 98201-4147
(425)258-7123

PROVIDENCE EVERETT MEDICAL CENTER-COLBY
1321 Colby Avenue PO Box 1147
Everett, WA 98206-1147
(206)261-2000

FEDERAL WAY

SAINT FRANCIS COMMUNITY HOSPITAL
34515 - 9th Avenue South
Federal Way, WA 98003-6761
(253)927-9700

FORKS

FORKS COMMUNITY HOSPITAL
530 Bogachiel Way
Forks, WA 98331-9120
(360)374-6271

GOLDENDALE

KLICKITAT VALLEY HOSPITAL
310 S Roosevelt Street
Goldendale, WA 98620-9201
(509)773-4022

GRAND COULEE

COULEE COMMUNITY HOSPITAL
411 Fortuyn Rd
Grand Coulee, WA 99133-8718
(509)633-1753

ILWACO

OCEAN BEACH HOSPITAL
First And Fir, Drawer H
Ilwaco, WA 98624-0258
(360)642-3181

KENNEWICK

KENNEWICK GENERAL HOSPITAL
900 South Auburn St
Kennewick, WA 99336-5652
(509)586-6111

KIRKLAND

EVERGREEN HOSPITAL MEDICAL CENTER
12040 Ne 128th Street
Kirkland, WA 98034-3098
(425)899-1000

FAIRFAX HOSPITAL
10200 Ne 132nd Street
Kirkland, WA 98034-2899
(425)821-2000

LACEY

SAINT PETER CHEMICAL DEPENDENCY CENTER
4800 College St Se
Lacey, WA 98503-4389
(360)456-7575

165

WASHINGTON
Hospital Telephone Directory

LAKEWOOD

SAINT CLARE HOSPITAL
11315 Bridgeport Way Sw
Lakewood, WA 98499-3070
(253)588-1711

LEAVENWORTH

CASCADE MEDICAL CENTER
817 Commercial St (PO Box 330)
Leavenworth, WA 98826-0330
(509)548-5815

LONGVIEW

HOSPICE CARE CENTER HOSPITAL
1035 - 11th Avenue
Longview, WA 98632-2505
(360)425-8510

PEACEHEALTH SAINT JOHN MEDICAL
CENTER
1615 Delaware Street, (PO Box 3002)
Longview, WA 98632-0302
(360)414-2000

MCCLEARY

MARK REED HOSPITAL
322 South Birch Street
McCleary, WA 98557-9522
(360)495-3244

MEDICAL LAKE

EASTERN STATE HOSPITAL
Maple Street Box A
Medical Lake, WA 99022-0045
(509)299-3121

MONROE

VALLEY GENERAL HOSPITAL
14701 179th Se
Monroe, WA 98272-1152
(360)794-7497

MORTON

MORTON GENERAL HOSPITAL
521 Adams
Morton, WA 98356
(360)496-5112

MOSES LAKE

SAMARITAN HOSPITAL
801 East Wheeler Road
Moses Lake, WA 98837-1899
(509)765-5606

MOUNT VERNON

AFFILIATED HEALTH SERVICES - SKAGIT
VALLEY HOSPITAL
1415 E Kincaid Street
Mount Vernon, WA 98274-4126
(360)424-4111

NEWPORT

NEWPORT COMMUNITY HOSPITAL
714 W Pine PO Box 667
Newport, WA 99156-0667
(509)447-2441

OAK HARBOR

NAVAL HOSPITAL OAK HARBOR
3475 North Saratoga St
Oak Harbor, WA 98278-8800
(360)257-9500

ODESSA

ODESSA MEMORIAL HOSPITAL
502 E Amende
Odessa, WA 99159
(509)982-2611

OLYMPIA

CAPITAL MEDICAL CENTER
3900 Capital Mall Drive Sw
Olympia, WA 98502-5026
(360)754-5858

PROVIDENCE SAINT PETER HOSPITAL
413 N Lilly Road
Olympia, WA 98501-2108
(360)491-9480

OMAK

MID VALLEY HOSPITAL
810 Jasmine Street
Omak, WA 98841-9578
(509)826-1760

OTHELLO

OTHELLO COMMUNITY HOSPITAL
315 North 14th Street
Othello, WA 99344-1297
(509)488-2636

PASCO

LOURDES MEDICAL CENTER
520 North Fourth Avenue
Pasco, WA 99301-5257
(509)547-7704

POMEROY

GARFIELD COUNTY HOSPITAL
North 66 Sixth St
Pomeroy, WA 99347
(509)843-1591

PORT ANGELES

OLYMPIC MEMORIAL HOSPITAL
939 Caroline St
Port Angeles, WA 98362-3997
(360)417-7000

PORT TOWNSEND

JEFFERSON GENERAL HOSPITAL
834 Sheridan
Port Townsend, WA 98368-2499
(360)385-2200

PROSSER

PROSSER MEMORIAL HOSPITAL
723 Memorial Street
Prosser, WA 99350-1593
(509)786-2222

PULLMAN

PULLMAN MEMORIAL HOSPITAL
NE 1125 Washington Avenue
Pullman, WA 99163-4237
(509)332-2541

PUYALLUP

GOOD SAMARITAN HOSPITAL
407 14th Avenue Se
Puyallup, WA 98372-3795
(253)848-6661

QUINCY

QUINCY VALLEY MEDICAL CENTER
908 Tenth Avenue Sw
Quincy, WA 98848-1376
(509)787-3531

REDMOND

GROUP HEALTH COOPERATIVE
2700 152nd Avenue NE
Redmond, WA 98052-5560
(425)883-5151

RENTON

VALLEY MEDICAL CENTER
PO Box 50010
Renton, WA 98058-5010
(425)228-3450

REPUBLIC

FERRY COUNTY MEMORIAL HOSPITAL
470 N Klondike Road PO Box 365
Republic, WA 99166-0365
(509)775-3333

RICHLAND

KADLEC MEDICAL CENTER
888 Swift Boulevard
Richland, WA 99352-3583
(509)946-4611

LOURDES COUNSELING CENTER
1175 Carondelet Drive
Richland, WA 99352-3300
(509)943-9104

RITZVILLE

EAST ADAMS RURAL HOSPITAL
903 South Adams
Ritzville, WA 99169-2227
(509)659-1200

SEATTLE

CHILDRENS HOSPITAL AND REGIONAL
MEDICAL CENTER
4800 Sand Point Way Ne
Seattle, WA 98105-3916
(206)526-2000

FRED HUTCHINSON CANCER RESEARCH
CENTER
PO Box 19024
Seattle, WA 98109-1024
(206)667-5000

GROUP HEALTH - METROPOLITAN PARK
EAST
1730 Minor Avenue
Seattle, WA 98101-1498
(206)287-2500

GROUP HEALTH CENTRAL HOSPITAL
201 16th Avenue E
Seattle, WA 98112-5226
(206)326-3000

HARBORVIEW MEDICAL CENTER
325 9th Avenue
Seattle, WA 98104-2499
(206)731-3000

HIGHLINE SPECIALITY CENTER
12844 Military Road South
Seattle, WA 98168-3045
(206)244-0180

KINDRED HOSPITAL SEATTLE
10560 5th Avenue Ne
Seattle, WA 98125-7202
(206)364-2050

Hospital Telephone Directory — WASHINGTON

NORTHWEST HOSPITAL
1550 North 115th Street
Seattle, WA 98133-8498
(206)364-0500

PACIFIC MEDICAL CENTER & CLINICS
1200 12th Avenue South
Seattle, WA 98144-2712
(206)621-4000

REGIONAL HOSPITAL FOR RESP AND COMPLEX CARE
12844 Military Road South
Seattle, WA 98168-3045
(206)248-4548

SCHICK-SHADEL HOSPITAL
12101 Ambaum Boulevard S W
Seattle, WA 98146-2651
(206)244-8100

SEATTLE CANCER CARE ALLIANCE
825 Eastlake Avenue East, PO Box 19023
Seattle, WA 98109-1023
(206)288-1400

SWEDISH AND PROVIDENCE MEDICAL CENTER
500 17th Avenue/PO Box 34008
Seattle, WA 98124-1008
(206)320-2000

SWEDISH MEDICAL CENTER
747 Broadway
Seattle, WA 98122-4307
(206)386-6000

SWEDISH MEDICAL CENTER-BALLARD
PO Box 70707, 5300 Tallman Avenue Nw
Seattle, WA 98127-1507
(206)782-2700

UNIVERSITY OF WASHINGTON MEDICAL CENTER
1959 Ne Pacific St
Seattle, WA 98195-0001
(206)598-3300

VA HEALTHCARE SYSTEM - PUGET SOUND
1660 S Columbian Way
Seattle, WA 98108-1532
(206)762-1010

VIRGINIA MASON MEDICAL CENTER
925 Seneca Street
Seattle, WA 98101-2798
(206)223-6600

WEST SEATTLE PSYCHIATRIC HOSPITAL
2600 Southwest Holden
Seattle, WA 98126-3505
(206)933-7199

SEDRO WOOLLEY

UNITED GENERAL HOSPITAL
1971 State Route 20
Sedro Woolley, WA 98284-9381
(360)856-6021

SHELTON

MASON GENERAL HOSPITAL
2100 Sherwood Lane/PO Box 1668
Shelton, WA 98584-5001
(360)426-1611

SNOQUALMIE

SNOQUALMIE VALLEY HOSPITAL
9575 Ethan Wade Way SE, PO Box 2021
Snoqualmie, WA 98065-2021
(425)831-2300

SOUTH BEND

WILLAPA HARBOR HOSPITAL
PO Box 187
South Bend, WA 98586-0187
(360)875-4502

SPOKANE

DEACONESS MEDICAL CENTER
W 800 Fifth Avenue/PO Box 248
Spokane, WA 99210-0248
(509)458-5800

HOLY FAMILY HOSPITAL
N 5633 Lidgerwood
Spokane, WA 99208-1295
(509)482-0111

SACRED HEART MEDICAL CENTER
101 West 8th Avenue/PO Box 2555
Spokane, WA 99220-2555
(509)474-3040

SAINT LUKES REHABILITATION INSTITUTE
711 South Cowley
Spokane, WA 99202-1388
(509)838-4771

SHRINERS HOSPITALS FOR CHILDREN - SPOKANE
911 West Fifth Avenue
Spokane, WA 99204-2910
(509)455-7844

SOUTH HILL MEDICAL CENTER
South 2830 Grand Blvd
Spokane, WA 99203-2528
(509)747-0770

VA MEDICAL CENTER - SPOKANE
4815 N Assembly St
Spokane, WA 99205-6197
(509)434-7200

VALLEY HOSPITAL AND MEDICAL CENTER
12606 East Mission Avenue
Spokane, WA 99216-1090
(509)924-6650

STEILACOOM

MC NEIL ISLAND CORRECTION CENTER - HEALTH SERVICES
Box 88900
Steilacoom, WA 98388-0499
(253)512-6640

SUNNYSIDE

SUNNYSIDE COMMUNITY HOSPITAL
10th And Tacoma
Sunnyside, WA 98944
(509)837-1650

TACOMA

ALLENMORE HOSPITAL
1901 South Union
Tacoma, WA 98405-1702
(253)403-2323

MADIGAN ARMY MEDICAL CENTER
9040 Reid St Fort Lewis
Tacoma, WA 98431-1100
(253)968-1110

MARY BRIDGE CHILDRENS HEALTH CENTER
311 South L St
Tacoma, WA 98405-4289
(253)403-1400

PUGET SOUND HOSPITAL
3580 Pacific Ave
Tacoma, WA 98418-7915
(253)474-0561

SAINT JOSEPH HOSPITAL AND MEDICAL CENTER
1718 South I Street
Tacoma, WA 98405
(253)627-4101

TACOMA GENERAL HOSPITAL
315 S Martin Luther King Jr Way
Tacoma, WA 98405-4291
(253)403-1000

WESTERN STATE HOSPITAL
9601 Steilacoom Boulevard SW
Tacoma, WA 98498-7213
(253)582-8900

TONASKET

NORTH VALLEY HOSPITAL
203 S Western Ave
Tonasket, WA 98855-8803
(509)486-2151

TOPPENISH

PROVIDENCE TOPPENISH HOSPITAL
502 W Fourth Avenue/PO Box 672
Toppenish, WA 98948-0672
(509)865-3105

VANCOUVER

SOUTHWEST WASHINGTON MEDICAL CENTER
400 NE Mother Joseph Place
Vancouver, WA 98664-3200
(360)256-2000

WALLA WALLA

SAINT MARY MEDICAL CENTER
401 W Poplar St
Walla Walla, WA 99362-2862
(509)525-3320

VA MEDICAL CENTER - J.M. WAINWRIGHT
77 Wainwright Drive
Walla Walla, WA 99362-3994
(509)525-5200

WALLA WALLA GENERAL HOSPITAL
1025 S Second Avenue
Walla Walla, WA 99362-4164
(509)525-0480

WASHINGTON STATE PENITENTIARY HOSPITAL
1313 N 13th Avenue
Walla Walla, WA 99362-8817
(509)525-3610

WENATCHEE

CENTRAL WASHINGTON HOSPITAL
1300 Fuller Street
Wenatchee, WA 98801-3329
(509)662-1511

WENATCHEE VALLEY HOSPITAL
820 North Chelan Street
Wenatchee, WA 98801-2028
(509)663-8711

WHITE SALMON

SKYLINE HOSPITAL
211 Skyline Drive
White Salmon, WA 98672
(509)493-1101

YAKIMA

PROVIDENCE YAKIMA MEDICAL CENTER
110 South Ninth Avenue
Yakima, WA 98902-3397
(509)575-5000

WEST VIRGINIA — Hospital Telephone Directory

YAKIMA VALLEY MEMORIAL HOSPITAL
2811 Tieton Drive
Yakima, WA 98902-3799
(509)575-8000

WEST VIRGINIA

BECKLEY

BECKLEY APPALACHIAN REGIONAL HOSPITAL
306 Stanaford Road
Beckley, WV 25801-3186
(304)255-3000

RALEIGH GENERAL HOSPITAL-BECKLEY CAMPUS
1710 Harper Road
Beckley, WV 25801-3397
(304)256-4100

VA MEDICAL CENTER - BECKLEY
200 Veterans Avenue
Beckley, WV 25801-6444
(304)255-2121

BERKELEY SPRINGS

MORGAN COUNTY WAR MEMORIAL HOSPITAL
109 War Memorial Dr
Berkeley Springs, WV 25411-1743
(304)258-1234

BLUEFIELD

BLUEFIELD REGIONAL MEDICAL CENTER
500 Cherry St
Bluefield, WV 24701-3390
(304)327-1100

SAINT LUKES HOSPITAL
1333 Southview Drive
Bluefield, WV 24701-4399
(304)327-2900

BUCKEYE

POCAHONTAS MEMORIAL HOSPITAL
Route 2, Box 52 West
Buckeye, WV 24924-9639
(304)799-7400

BUCKHANNON

SAINT JOSEPH HOSPITAL
Amalia Drive
Buckhannon, WV 26201
(304)473-2000

CHARLESTON

CHARLESTON AREA MEDICAL CENTER - GENERAL DIVISION
501 Morris St
Charleston, WV 25301-1326
(304)388-5432

CHARLESTON AREA MEDICAL CENTER - MEMORIAL DIVISION
3200 Maccorkle Avenue SE
Charleston, WV 25304-1227
(304)388-5432

CHARLESTON AREA MEDICAL CENTER - WOMEN AND CHILDRENS HOSPITAL
800 Pennsylvania Avenue
Charleston, WV 25302-3351
(304)388-5432

EYE AND EAR CLINIC OF CHARLESTON
1306 Kanawha Bl E
Charleston, WV 25301-3001
(304)343-4371

HIGHLAND HOSPITAL
300 56th Street Se, PO Box 4107
Charleston, WV 25364-4107
(304)926-1600

SAINT FRANCIS HOSPITAL
333 Laidley St
Charleston, WV 25301-1628
(304)347-6500

SELECT SPECIALTY HOSPITAL - CHARLESTON
501 Morris Street, 3-East
Charleston, WV 25301-1326
(304)388-6600

CLARKSBURG

UNITED HOSPITAL CENTER
PO Box 1605
Clarksburg, WV 26302-1605
(304)624-2121

VA MEDICAL CENTER - LOUIS A JOHNSON
1 Medical Center Drive
Clarksburg, WV 26301
(304)623-3461

ELKINS

DAVIS MEMORIAL HOSPITAL
PO Box 1484
Elkins, WV 26241-1484
(304)636-3300

FAIRMONT

FAIRMONT GENERAL HOSPITAL
1325 Locust Avenue
Fairmont, WV 26554-1482
(304)367-7100

GASSAWAY

BRAXTON COUNTY MEMORIAL HOSPITAL
100 Hoylman Drive
Gassaway, WV 26624-9320
(304)364-5156

GLEN DALE

REYNOLDS MEMORIAL HOSPITAL
800 Wheeling Avenue
Glen Dale, WV 26038-1697
(304)845-3211

GRAFTON

GRAFTON CITY HOSPITAL
Route 50 And Market St
Grafton, WV 26354
(304)265-0400

GRANTSVILLE

MINNIE HAMILTON HEALTHCARE CENTER
High St
Grantsville, WV 26147
(304)354-9244

HINTON

SUMMERS COUNTY APPALACHIAN REGIONAL HOSPITAL
PO Box 940 Terrace St
Hinton, WV 25951-0940
(304)466-1000

HUNTINGTON

CABELL-HUNTINGTON HOSPITAL
1340 Hal Greer Boulevard
Huntington, WV 25701-0195
(304)526-2000

HEALTHSOUTH HUNTINGTON REHAB HOSPITAL
6900 West Country Club Drive
Huntington, WV 25705-2000
(304)733-1060

MILDRED MITCHELL-BATEMAN HOSPITAL
1530 Norway Avenue
Huntington, WV 25705-1336
(304)525-7801

RIVER PARK HOSPITAL
1230 Sixth Avenue
Huntington, WV 25701-2312
(304)526-9111

SAINT MARYS HOSPITAL
2900 1st Avenue
Huntington, WV 25702-1271
(304)526-1234

VA MEDICAL CENTER - HUNTINGTON
1540 Spring Valley Drive
Huntington, WV 25704-9399
(304)429-6741

HURRICANE

PUTNAM GENERAL HOSPITAL
1400 Hospital Drive
Hurricane, WV 25526-9205
(304)757-1700

INSTITUTE

WEST VIRGINIA REHAB HOSPITAL
Barron Drive
Institute, WV 25112
(304)766-4600

KEYSER

POTOMAC VALLEY HOSPITAL
South Mineral Street
Keyser, WV 26726
(304)788-3141

KINGWOOD

PRESTON MEMORIAL HOSPITAL
300 South Price St
Kingwood, WV 26537-1495
(304)329-1400

LOGAN

GUYAN VALLEY HOSPITAL
396 Dingess St
Logan, WV 25601-3624
(304)792-1700

LOGAN GENERAL HOSPITAL
20 Hospital Drive
Logan, WV 25601-3497
(304)792-1101

MADISON

BOONE MEMORIAL HOSPITAL
701 Madison Avenue
Madison, WV 25130-1699
(304)369-1230

MARTINSBURG

CITY HOSPITAL
Tavern And Dry Run Road
Martinsburg, WV 25401
(304)264-1000

VA MEDICAL CENTER - MARTINSBURG
Route 9
Martinsburg, WV 25401-9809
(304)263-0811

Hospital Telephone Directory — WISCONSIN

MONTGOMERY
MONTGOMERY GENERAL HOSPITAL
Washington St And Sixth Avenue
Montgomery, WV 25136
(304)442-5151

MORGANTOWN
CHESTNUT RIDGE BEHAVIORAL HEALTH SYSTEM
930 Chestnut Ridge Road
Morgantown, WV 26505-2854
(304)293-4000

HEALTHSOUTH MOUNTAINVIEW REHAB HOSPITAL
1160 Van Voorhis Road
Morgantown, WV 26505-3437
(304)598-1100

MONONGALIA COUNTY GENERAL HOSPITAL
1200 JD Anderson Drive
Morgantown, WV 26505-3494
(304)598-1200

WEST VIRGINIA UNIVERSITY HOSPITAL
Medical Center Drive
Morgantown, WV 26506
(304)598-4000

NEW MARTINSVILLE
WETZEL COUNTY HOSPITAL
3 East Benjamin Drive, PO Box 237
New Martinsville, WV 26155-0237
(304)455-8000

OAK HILL
PLATEAU MEDICAL CENTERS
430 Main St W
Oak Hill, WV 25901-3455
(304)469-8600

PARKERSBURG
CAMDEN CLARK MEMORIAL HOSPITAL
800 Garfield Avenue
Parkersburg, WV 26101-5378
(304)424-2111

HEALTHSOUTH WESTERN HILLS REGIONAL REHAB HOSPITAL
3 Western Hills Drive
Parkersburg, WV 26105-8122
(304)420-1300

SAINT JOSEPHS HOSPITAL
1824 Murdock Avenue
Parkersburg, WV 26101-3246
(304)424-4111

PETERSBURG
GRANT MEMORIAL HOSPITAL
Route 55 PO Box 1019
Petersburg, WV 26847-1019
(304)257-1026

PHILIPPI
BROADDUS HOSPITAL
PO Box 930
Philippi, WV 26416-0930
(304)457-1760

POINT PLEASANT
PLEASANT VALLEY HOSPITAL
Valley Drive
Point Pleasant, WV 25550
(304)675-4340

PRINCETON
HEALTHSOUTH SOUTHERN HILLS REGIONAL REHAB HOSPITAL
120 12th Street
Princeton, WV 24740-2352
(304)487-8000

PRINCETON COMMUNITY HOSPITAL
12th St Extension
Princeton, WV 24740
(304)487-7000

RANSON
JEFFERSON MEMORIAL HOSPITAL
300 S Preston St
Ranson, WV 25438-1631
(304)728-1600

RICHMOND
RICHWOOD AREA COMMUNITY HOSPITAL
Riverside Addition
Richmond, WV 26261
(304)846-2573

RIPLEY
JACKSON GENERAL HOSPITAL
Pinnell St
Ripley, WV 25271
(304)372-2731

ROMNEY
HAMPSHIRE MEMORIAL HOSPITAL
PO Box 555 549 Center Avenue
Romney, WV 26757-0555
(304)822-4561

RONCEVERTE
GREENBRIER VALLEY MEDICAL CENTER
202 Maplewood Avenue PO Box 497
Ronceverte, WV 24970-0497
(304)647-4411

SISTERSVILLE
SISTERSVILLE GENERAL HOSPITAL
314 S Wells St
Sistersville, WV 26175-1098
(304)652-2611

SOUTH CHARLESTON
THOMAS MEMORIAL HOSPITAL
4605 Maccorkle Avenue Sw
South Charleston, WV 25309-1398
(304)766-3600

SPENCER
ROANE GENERAL HOSPITAL
200 Hospital Drive
Spencer, WV 25276-1060
(304)927-4444

SUMMERSVILLE
SUMMERSVILLE MEMORIAL HOSPITAL
400 Fairview Heights Road
Summersville, WV 26651-9300
(304)872-2891

TERRA ALTA
HOPEMONT STATE HOSPITAL
Route 1 Box 330
Terra Alta, WV 26764-9801
(304)789-2411

WEBSTER SPRINGS
WEBSTER COUNTY MEMORIAL HOSPITAL
PO Box 312
Webster Springs, WV 26288-0312
(304)847-5682

WEIRTON
WEIRTON MEDICAL CENTER
601 Colliers Way
Weirton, WV 26062-5091
(304)797-6000

WELCH
WELCH EMERGENCY HOSPITAL
454 McDowell Street
Welch, WV 24801-2097
(304)436-8461

WESTON
STONEWALL JACKSON MEMORIAL HOSPITAL
230 Hospital Plz
Weston, WV 26452-8558
(304)269-8000

WILLIAM R SHARPE HOSPITAL AT WESTON
936 Sharpe Hospital Rd
Weston, WV 26452-8550
(304)269-1210

WHEELING
OHIO VALLEY GENERAL MEDICAL CENTER
2000 Eoff Street
Wheeling, WV 26003-3870
(304)234-0123

PETERSON HOSPITAL
Homestead Avenue
Wheeling, WV 26003
(304)234-0500

WHEELING HOSPITAL
Medical Park
Wheeling, WV 26003
(304)243-3000

WILLIAMSON
WILLIAMSON MEMORIAL HOSPITAL
859 Alderson Street
Williamson, WV 25661-3215
(304)235-2500

WISCONSIN

AMERY
AMERY REGIONAL MEDICAL CENTER
230 Deronda Street
Amery, WI 54001-1412
(715)268-8000

ANTIGO
LANGLADE MEMORIAL HOSPITAL
112 East Fifth Avenue
Antigo, WI 54409-2710
(715)623-2331

APPLETON
APPLETON MEDICAL CENTER
1818 North Meade Street
Appleton, WI 54911-3496
(920)731-4101

SAINT ELIZABETH HOSPITAL
1506 S Oneida St
Appleton, WI 54915-1396
(920)738-2000

WISCONSIN
Hospital Telephone Directory

ARCADIA

FRANCISCAN SKEMP MEDICAL CENTER
ARCADIA
464 S St Joseph Avenue
Arcadia, WI 54612-1401
(608)323-3341

ASHLAND

MEMORIAL MEDICAL CENTER
1615 Maple Lane
Ashland, WI 54806-3689
(715)682-4563

BALDWIN

BALDWIN HOSPITAL
730 10th Avenue
Baldwin, WI 54002-9214
(715)684-3311

BARABOO

SAINT CLARE HOSPITAL AND HEALTH
SERVICES
707 14th Street
Baraboo, WI 53913-1597
(608)356-1400

BARRON

BARRON MEMORIAL MEDICAL CENTER
1222 Woodland Avenue
Barron, WI 54812-1798
(715)537-3186

BEAVER DAM

BEAVER DAM COMMUNITY HOSPITALS
707 S University Avenue
Beaver Dam, WI 53916-3089
(920)887-7181

BELOIT

BELOIT MEMORIAL HOSPITAL
1969 West Hart Road
Beloit, WI 53511-2298
(608)364-5011

BERLIN

BERLIN MEMORIAL HOSPITAL
225 Memorial Drive
Berlin, WI 54923-1295
(920)361-1313

BLACK RIVER FALLS

BLACK RIVER FALLS MEMORIAL HOSPITAL
711 W Adams St
Black River Falls, WI 54615-9108
(715)284-5361

BLOOMER

BLOOMER COMMUNITY MEDICAL
CENTER/HOSPITAL
1501 Thompson Street
Bloomer, WI 54724-1257
(715)568-2000

BOSCOBEL

BOSCOBEL AREA HEALTH CARE
205 Parker Street
Boscobel, WI 53805-1642
(608)375-4112

BROOKFIELD

ELMBROOK MEMORIAL HOSPITAL
19333 West North Avenue
Brookfield, WI 53045-4198
(262)785-2000

BURLINGTON

MEMORIAL HOSPITAL BURLINGTON
252 McHenry Street
Burlington, WI 53105-1828
(262)767-6000

CHILTON

CALUMET MEDICAL CENTER
614 Memorial Drive
Chilton, WI 53014-1597
(920)849-2386

CHIPPEWA FALLS

SAINT JOSEPHS HOSPITAL
2661 County Trunk I
Chippewa Falls, WI 54729
(715)723-1811

COLUMBUS

COLUMBUS COMMUNITY HOSPITAL
1515 Park Avenue
Columbus, WI 53925-1618
(920)623-2200

CUBA CITY

EVERGREEN ADULT CENTER
808 S Washington St
Cuba City, WI 53807-1439
(608)854-2231

SOUTHWEST HEALTH CENTER
808 South Washington St
Cuba City, WI 53807-1494
(608)744-2161

CUDAHY

SAINT LUKES SOUTHSHORE
5900 S Lake Drive
Cudahy, WI 53110-3171
(414)769-9000

CUMBERLAND

CUMBERLAND MEMORIAL HOSPITAL
1110 7th Avenue
Cumberland, WI 54829-9133
(715)822-2741

DARLINGTON

MEMORIAL HOSPITAL OF LAFAYETTE
COUNTY
800 Clay St
Darlington, WI 53530-1228
(608)776-4466

DELAFIELD

CLEARVIEW HOME
935 Main Street
Delafield, WI 53018-1613
(262)646-3361

DODGEVILLE

UPLAND HILLS HEALTH
800 Compassion Way
Dodgeville, WI 53533-1956
(608)930-8000

DURAND

CHIPPEWA VALLEY HOSPITAL
1220 Third Avenue West
Durand, WI 54736-1600
(715)672-4211

EAGLE RIVER

EAGLE RIVER MEMORIAL HOSPITAL
201 Hospital Road PO Box 129
Eagle River, WI 54521-0129
(715)479-7411

EAU CLAIRE

LUTHER HOSPITAL
1221 Whipple St
Eau Claire, WI 54703-5200
(715)838-3311

OAK LEAF SURGICAL HOSPITAL
3802 West Oakwood Mall Drive
Eau Claire, WI 54701-3016
(715)831-8130

SACRED HEART HOSPITAL
900 W Clairemont Avenue
Eau Claire, WI 54701-5105
(715)839-4121

EDGERTON

MEMORIAL COMMUNITY HOSPITAL
PO Box 334
Edgerton, WI 53534-0334
(608)884-3441

ELKHORN

LAKELAND MEDICAL CENTER
County Trunk Nn PO Box 1002
Elkhorn, WI 53121-1002
(262)741-2000

FOND DU LAC

FOND DU LAC HEALTH CARE CENTER
459 E First Street
Fond Du Lac, WI 54935-4505
(920)929-3000

SAINT AGNES HOSPITAL
430 East Divison Street
Fond Du Lac, WI 54935-4597
(920)929-2300

FORT ATKINSON

FORT ATKINSON MEMORIAL HEALTH
SERVICES
PO Box 249
Fort Atkinson, WI 53538-0249
(920)568-5000

FRIENDSHIP

ADAMS COUNTY MEMORIAL HOSPITAL
402 W Lake St
Friendship, WI 53934-9699
(608)339-3331

GLENDALE

HEART HOSPITAL OF MILWAUKEE
375 West River Woods Parkway
Glendale, WI 53212-1080
(414)963-7000

ORTHOPAEDIC HOSPITAL OF WISCONSIN
575 West River Woods Parkway
Glendale, WI 53212-1003
(414)961-6800

Hospital Telephone Directory — WISCONSIN

GRANTSBURG
BURNETT MEDICAL CENTER
257 W St George Avenue
Grantsburg, WI 54840-7827
(715)463-5353

GREEN BAY
AURORA BAYCARE MEDICAL CENTER
2845 Greenbrier Road, PO Box 8900
Green Bay, WI 54308-8900
(608)288-8000

BELLIN MEMORIAL HOSPITAL
744 S Webster Avenue PO Box 23400
Green Bay, WI 54305-3400
(920)433-3500

BELLIN PSYCHIATRIC CENTER
301 E St Joseph Street
Green Bay, WI 54301-2241
(920)433-3630

BROWN COUNTY MENTAL HEALTH CENTER
2900 St Anthony Drive
Green Bay, WI 54311-5899
(920)468-1136

SAINT MARYS HOSPITAL MEDICAL CENTER
1726 Shawano Avenue
Green Bay, WI 54303-3282
(920)498-4200

SAINT VINCENT HOSPITAL
835 S Van Buren PO Box 13508
Green Bay, WI 54307-3508
(608)433-0111

GREENFIELD
KINDRED HOSPITAL MILWAUKEE
5017 S 110th St
Greenfield, WI 53228-3131
(414)427-8282

HARTFORD
AURORA MEDICAL CENTER OF WASHINGTON COUNTY
1032 E Sumner Street
Hartford, WI 53027-1608
(262)673-2300

HAYWARD
HAYWARD AREA MEMORIAL HOSPITAL
11040 N State Road 77
Hayward, WI 54843-6391
(715)634-8911

HILLSBORO
SAINT JOSEPHS MEMORIAL HOSPITAL
400 Water Avenue
Hillsboro, WI 54634-9051
(608)489-2211

HUDSON
HUDSON MEDICAL CENTER
405 Stageline Road
Hudson, WI 54016-7757
(715)531-6000

JANESVILLE
MERCY HOSPITAL OF JANESVILLE
1000 Mineral Point Avenue
Janesville, WI 53548-2982
(608)756-6000

ROCK COUNTY MENTAL HEALTH SERV
3512 N Parker Drive PO Box 351
Janesville, WI 53547-0351
(262)757-5225

KENOSHA
AURORA MEDICAL CENTER - KENOSHA
10400 75th Street
Kenosha, WI 53142-8323
(262)697-7000

CHILDREN'S HOSPITAL OF WISCONSIN - KENOSHA
6308 8th Avenue, 6th Floor
Kenosha, WI 53143-5031
(262)656-2261

KENOSHA HOSPITAL AND MEDICAL CENTER
6308 Eighth Avenue
Kenosha, WI 53143-5082
(262)656-2011

SAINT CATHERINES HOSPITAL
3556 7th Avenue
Kenosha, WI 53140-2595
(262)656-3011

LA CROSSE
FRANCISCAN SKEMP FOUNDATION LACROSSE
700 West Avenue South
La Crosse, WI 54601-4783
(608)785-0940

GUNDERSEN LUTHERAN MEDICAL CENTER
1910 South Avenue
La Crosse, WI 54601-5467
(608)785-0530

LADYSMITH
RUSK COUNTY MEMORIAL HOSPITAL
900 College Avenue West
Ladysmith, WI 54848-2116
(715)532-5561

LANCASTER
GRANT REGIONAL HEALTH CENTER
507 S Monroe St
Lancaster, WI 53813-2054
(608)723-2143

MADISON
MENDOTA MENTAL HEALTH INSTITUTE
301 Troy Drive
Madison, WI 53704-1599
(608)301-1000

MERITER HOSPITAL
202 S Park St
Madison, WI 53715-1596
(608)267-6000

SAINT MARYS HOSPITAL MEDICAL CENTER
707 South Mills Street
Madison, WI 53715-1893
(608)251-6100

UNIVERSITY OF WISCONSIN HOSPITALS/CLINICS AUTHORITY
600 Highland Avenue
Madison, WI 53792-3284
(608)263-8000

VA MEDICAL CENTER - WILLIAM S MIDDLETON MEMORIAL
2500 Overlook Terrace
Madison, WI 53705-2254
(608)256-1901

MANITOWOC
HOLY FAMILY MEMORIAL MEDICAL CENTER
2300 Western Avenue
Manitowoc, WI 54220-3712
(920)684-2011

MARINETTE
BAY AREA MEDICAL CENTER MARINETTE
3100 Shore Drive
Marinette, WI 54143-4297
(715)735-6621

MARSHFIELD
NORWOOD HEALTH CENTER
1600 North Chestnut Avenue
Marshfield, WI 54449-1499
(715)384-2188

SAINT JOSEPHS HOSPITAL
611 St Joseph Avenue
Marshfield, WI 54449-1898
(715)387-1713

MAUSTON
MILE BLUFF MEDICAL CENTER - HESS MEMORIAL
1050 Division St
Mauston, WI 53948-1931
(608)847-6161

MEDFORD
MEMORIAL HOSPITAL OF TAYLOR COUNTY
135 South Gibson Street
Medford, WI 54451-1696
(715)748-8100

MENOMONEE FALLS
COMMUNITY MEMORIAL HOSPITAL
W180 N8085 Town Hall Road
Menomonee Falls, WI 53051-3558
(262)251-1000

MENOMONIE
MYRTLE WERTH HOSPITAL MAYO HEALTH SYSTEM
2321 Stout Road
Menomonie, WI 54751-7003
(715)235-5531

MEQUON
SAINT MARYS HOSPITAL OZAUKEE
13111 North Port Washington
Mequon, WI 53097-2417
(262)243-7300

MERRILL
GOOD SAMARITAN HEALTH CENTER OF MERRILL
601 S Center Street
Merrill, WI 54452-3404
(715)536-5511

MILWAUKEE
AURORA SINAI MEDICAL CENTER
945 N 12th Street, Box 342
Milwaukee, WI 53233-1337
(414)219-2000

CHILDRENS HOSPITAL OF WISCONSIN
9000 W Wisconsin Avenue
Milwaukee, WI 53226-4810
(414)266-2000

COLUMBIA HOSPITAL
2025 East Newport Avenue
Milwaukee, WI 53211-2990
(414)961-3300

FROEDTERT MEMORIAL LUTHERAN HOSPITAL
9200 W Wisconsin Avenue
Milwaukee, WI 53226-3596
(414)259-3000

WISCONSIN — Hospital Telephone Directory

KINDRED HOSPITAL MILWAUKEE
5700 West Layton Avenue
Milwaukee, WI 53220-4016
(414)427-8282

LIFECARE HOSPITAL OF MILWAUKEE AT
SAINT JOSEPH
5000 West Chambers Street, 8th Floor
Milwaukee, WI 53210-1650
(414)447-3600

LIFECARE HOSPITAL OF MILWAUKEE AT
SAINT MICHAEL
2400 West Villard Avenue, 3rd Floor South
Milwaukee, WI 53209-4901
(414)527-5825

MILWAUKEE COUNTY MENTAL HEALTH
COMPLEX
9455 W Watertown Plank Road
Milwaukee, WI 53226-4805
(414)257-6995

ROGERS MEMORIAL HOSPITAL
11101 W Lincoln Avenue
Milwaukee, WI 53227-1166
(414)327-3000

SACRED HEART REHAB INSTITUTE
PO Box 392
Milwaukee, WI 53201-0392
(262)298-6700

SAINT FRANCIS HOSPITAL
3237 South 16th Street
Milwaukee, WI 53215-4592
(414)647-5000

SAINT JOSEPHS HOSPITAL
5000 West Chambers Street
Milwaukee, WI 53210-1688
(414)447-2000

SAINT LUKES MEDICAL CENTER
2900 W Oklahoma Avenue
Milwaukee, WI 53215-4330
(414)649-6000

SAINT MARY'S HOSPITAL - BEHAVIORAL
MEDICINE
2350 N Lake Drive
Milwaukee, WI 53211-4507
(414)291-1661

SAINT MARYS HOSPITAL OF MILWAUKEE
2323 N Lake Drive
Milwaukee, WI 53211-4562
(414)291-1000

SAINT MICHAEL HOSPITAL
2400 West Villard Avenue
Milwaukee, WI 53209-4999
(414)527-8000

SELECT SPECIALTY HOSPITAL -
MILWAUKEE/SAINT LUKES
2900 West Oklahoma Avenue
Milwaukee, WI 53215-4330
(414)649-6991

VA MEDICAL CENTER - CLEMENT ZABLOCKI
5000 W National Avenue
Milwaukee, WI 53295-0002
(414)384-2000

MONROE

MONROE CLINIC HOSPITAL
515 22nd Avenue
Monroe, WI 53566-1598
(608)324-1000

NEENAH

CHILDREN'S HOSPITAL OF WISCONSIN -
FOX VALLEY
130 Second Street
Neenah, WI 54956-2883
(920)969-7900

THEDA CLARK MEMORIAL HOSPITAL
130 2nd St
Neenah, WI 54956-2883
(920)729-3100

NEILLSVILLE

MEMORIAL MEDICAL CENTER
216 Sunset Place
Neillsville, WI 54456-1706
(715)743-3101

NEW LONDON

NEW LONDON FAMILY MEDICAL CENTER
1405 Mill St
New London, WI 54961-2155
(920)982-5330

NEW RICHMOND

HOLY FAMILY HOSPITAL
535 Hospital Road
New Richmond, WI 54017-1495
(715)246-2101

OCONOMOWOC

MEMORIAL HOSPITAL - OCONOMOWOC
791 East Summit Auenue
Oconomowoc, WI 53066-3844
(262)569-9400

ROGERS MEMORIAL HOSPITAL
34700 Valley Road
Oconomowoc, WI 53066-4599
(262)646-4411

OCONTO

OCONTO MEMORIAL HOSPITAL
405 First Street
Oconto, WI 54153-1264
(920)834-8806

OCONTO FALLS

COMMUNITY MEMORIAL HOSPITAL
855 S Main Street
Oconto Falls, WI 54154-1296
(920)846-3444

OSCEOLA

OSCEOLA MEDICAL CENTER
301 River Street PO Box 218
Osceola, WI 54020-0218
(715)294-2111

OSHKOSH

MERCY MEDICAL CENTER OF OSHKOSH
500 South Oakwood Road
Oshkosh, WI 54904-7944
(920)236-2000

OSSEO

OSSEO MEDICAL CENTER/NURSING HOME
674 E Eighth Street
Osseo, WI 54758
(715)597-3121

PARK FALLS

FLAMBEAU HOSPITAL
98 Sherry Avenue
Park Falls, WI 54552-1467
(715)762-2484

PLATTEVILLE

SOUTHWEST HEALTH CENTER
250 Camp St
Platteville, WI 53818-1299
(608)348-2331

PLYMOUTH

VALLEY VIEW/AURORA MEDICAL CENTERS
OF SHEBOYGAN COUNTY
901 Reed Street
Plymouth, WI 53073-2409
(920)893-1771

PORTAGE

DIVINE SAVIOR HOSPITAL
PO Box 387
Portage, WI 53901-0387
(608)742-4131

PRAIRIE DU CHIEN

PRAIRIE DU CHIEN MEMORIAL HOSPITAL
705 East Taylor Street
Prairie Du Chien, WI 53821-2110
(608)357-2000

PRAIRIE DU SAC

SAUK PRAIRIE MEMORIAL HOSPITAL
80 1st St
Prairie Du Sac, WI 53578-1599
(608)643-7166

RACINE

ALL SAINTS - SAINT LUKES HOSPITAL
1320 Wisconsin Avenue
Racine, WI 53403-1978
(262)687-2011

ALL SAINTS - SAINT MARYS MEDICAL
CENTER
3801 Spring St
Racine, WI 53405-1688
(262)687-4011

REEDSBURG

REEDSBURG AREA MEDICAL CENTER
2000 North Dewey Avenue
Reedsburg, WI 53959-1097
(608)524-6487

RHINELANDER

SACRED HEART SAINT MARYS HOSPITAL
1044 Kabel Avenue
Rhinelander, WI 54501-3998
(715)369-6600

RICE LAKE

LAKEVIEW MEDICAL CENTER
1100 N Main St
Rice Lake, WI 54868-1203
(715)234-1515

RICHLAND CTR

RICHLAND HOSPITAL
300 E 2nd St
Richland Ctr, WI 53581-1913
(608)647-6321

RIPON

RIPON MEDICAL CENTER
933 Newbury St PO Box 390
Ripon, WI 54971-0390
(920)748-3101

RIVER FALLS

RIVER FALLS AREA HOSPITAL
1629 E Division Street
River Falls, WI 54022-1571
(715)425-6155

Hospital Telephone Directory — WYOMING

SAINT CROIX FALLS
SAINT CROIX VALLEY MEMORIAL HOSPITAL
204 S Adams
Saint Croix Falls, WI 54024-9449
(715)483-3261

SHAWANO
SHAWANO MEDICAL CENTER
2629 North 7th Street
Shawano, WI 54166
(715)526-2111

SHEBOYGAN
SAINT NICHOLAS HOSPITAL
1601 N Taylor Drive
Sheboygan, WI 53081-1999
(920)459-8300

SHEBOYGAN MEMORIAL MEDICAL CENTER
2629 N 7th St
Sheboygan, WI 53083-4998
(920)451-5000

SHELL LAKE
INDIANHEAD MEDICAL CENTER
113 4th Avenue, PO Box 300
Shell Lake, WI 54871-0300
(715)468-7833

SPARTA
FRANCISCAN SKEMP MEDICAL CENTER SPARTA
310 West Main Street
Sparta, WI 54656-2170
(608)269-2132

SPOONER
SPOONER HEALTH SYSTEM AND NURSING HOME
819 Ash Street
Spooner, WI 54801-1201
(715)635-2111

STANLEY
VICTORY MEDICAL CENTER
230 E Fourth Avenue
Stanley, WI 54768-1298
(715)644-5571

STEVENS POINT
SAINT MICHAELS HOSPITAL
900 Illinois Avenue
Stevens Point, WI 54481-3196
(715)346-5000

STOUGHTON
STOUGHTON HOSPITAL
900 Ridge Street
Stoughton, WI 53589-1897
(608)873-6611

STURGEON BAY
DOOR COUNTY MEMORIAL HOSPITAL
330 South 16th Place
Sturgeon Bay, WI 54235-1457
(920)743-5566

SUPERIOR
SAINT MARYS HOSPITAL OF SUPERIOR
3500 Tower Avenue
Superior, WI 54880-5395
(715)392-8281

TOMAH
TOMAH MEMORIAL HOSPITAL
321 Butts Avenue
Tomah, WI 54660-1412
(608)372-2181

VA MEDICAL CENTER - TOMAH
500 E Veterans St
Tomah, WI 54660-3105
(608)372-3971

TOMAHAWK
SACRED HEART HOSPITAL
401 W Mohawk Dr Ste 100
Tomahawk, WI 54487-2273
(715)453-7700

TWO RIVERS
AURORA MEDICAL CENTER - MANITOWOC
5000 Memorial Dr
Two Rivers, WI 54241-3900
(920)794-5000

VIROQUA
VERNON MEMORIAL HOSPITAL
507 South Main Street
Viroqua, WI 54665-2096
(608)637-2101

WATERFORD
LAKEVIEW NEUROREHAB CENTER MIDWEST
1701 Sharp Road
Waterford, WI 53185-5214
(262)534-7297

WATERTOWN
WATERTOWN MEMORIAL HOSPITAL
125 Hospital Drive
Watertown, WI 53098-3384
(920)261-4210

WAUKESHA
WAUKESHA COUNTY MENTAL HEALTH CENTER
1501 Airport Road
Waukesha, WI 53188-2461
(262)548-7950

WAUKESHA MEMORIAL HOSPITAL
725 American Avenue
Waukesha, WI 53188-5099
(262)928-1000

WAUPACA
RIVERSIDE MEDICAL CENTER
800 Riverside Drive
Waupaca, WI 54981-1999
(715)258-1000

WAUPUN
WAUPUN MEMORIAL HOSPITAL
620 W Brown St
Waupun, WI 53963-1799
(920)324-5581

WAUSAU
NORTH CENTRAL HEALTH CARE FACILITIES
1100 Lakeview Drive
Wausau, WI 54403-6799
(715)848-4600

WAUSAU HOSPITAL
333 Pine Ridge Boulevard
Wausau, WI 54401-4187
(715)847-2121

WAUWATOSA
AURORA PSYCHIATRIC HOSPITAL
1220 Dewey Avenue, PO Box 13199
Wauwatosa, WI 53213-0199
(414)454-6600

WEST ALLIS
SELECT SPECIALTY HOSPITAL - MILWAUKEE
8901 West Lincoln Avenue
West Allis, WI 53227-2409
(414)328-7700

WEST ALLIS MEMORIAL HOSPITAL
8901 West Lincoln Avenue
West Allis, WI 53227-2477
(414)328-6000

WEST BEND
SAINT JOSEPHS COMMUNITY HOSPITAL OF WEST BEND
551 South Silverbrook Drive
West Bend, WI 53095-3898
(262)334-5533

WHITEHALL
TRI COUNTY MEMORIAL HOSPITAL
1801 Lincoln Street
Whitehall, WI 54773-9508
(715)538-4361

WILD ROSE
WILD ROSE COMMUNITY MEMORIAL HOSPITAL
601 Grove Avenue PO Box 243
Wild Rose, WI 54984-0243
(920)622-3257

WINNEBAGO
WINNEBAGO MENTAL HEALTH INSTITUTE
Mains St, Box 9
Winnebago, WI 54985-0009
(920)235-4910

WISCONSIN RAPIDS
RIVERVIEW HOSPITAL ASSOCIATION
410 Dewey Street-PO Box 8080
Wisconsin Rapids, WI 54494-4715
(715)423-6060

WOODRUFF
HOWARD YOUNG MEDICAL CENTER
240 Maple St - PO Box 470
Woodruff, WI 54568-0470
(715)356-8000

WYOMING

AFTON
STAR VALLEY HOSPITAL
110 Hospital Lane
Afton, WY 83110
(307)885-5800

BUFFALO
JOHNSON COUNTY HEALTH CARE
497 W Lott St
Buffalo, WY 82834-1609
(307)684-5521

US POSSESSIONS — Hospital Telephone Directory

CASPER

WYOMING BEHAVIORAL INSTITUTE
2521 East 15th Street
Casper, WY 82609-4126
(307)237-7444

WYOMING MEDICAL CENTER
1233 East 2nd St
Casper, WY 82601-2988
(307)577-7201

CHEYENNE

DE PAUL HOSPITAL
2600 East 18th Street
Cheyenne, WY 82001-5597
(307)634-2273

UNITED MEDICAL CENTER
214 East 23rd St
Cheyenne, WY 82001-3748
(307)634-2273

VA MEDICAL CENTER - CHEYENNE
2360 E Pershing Boulevard
Cheyenne, WY 82001-5356
(307)778-7550

CODY

WEST PARK HOSPITAL DISTRICT
707 Sheridan Avenue
Cody, WY 82414-3409
(307)527-7501

DOUGLAS

MEMORIAL HOSPITAL OF CONVERSE
COUNTY
111 S 5th St
Douglas, WY 82633-2434
(307)358-2122

EVANSTON

EVANSTON REGIONAL HOSPITAL
190 Arrowhead Drive
Evanston, WY 82930-9266
(307)789-3636

WYOMING STATE HOSPITAL
831 S Highway 150 PO Box 177
Evanston, WY 82931-0177
(307)789-3464

F.E. WARREN AIR FORCE BASE

90TH MEDICAL GROUP
6900 Alden Drive
F.E. Warren Air Force Base, WY 82005-3906
(307)773-3788

GILLETTE

CAMPBELL COUNTY MEMORIAL HOSPITAL
501 S Burma Avenue
Gillette, WY 82716-3426
(307)682-8811

GREYBULL

SOUTH BIG HORN COUNTY HOSPITAL
388 South US Highway 20
Greybull, WY 82426
(307)568-3311

JACKSON

SAINT JOHNS HOSPITAL
625 E Broadway, PO Box 428
Jackson, WY 83001-0428
(307)733-3636

KEMMERER

SOUTH LINCOLN MEDICAL CENTER
PO Box 390 (Moose and Onyx Streets)
Kemmerer, WY 83101-0390
(307)877-4401

LANDER

LANDER VALLEY MEDICAL CENTER
1320 Bishop Randall Drive
Lander, WY 82520-3996
(307)335-6330

LARAMIE

IVINSON MEMORIAL HOSPITAL
255 N 30th
Laramie, WY 82072-5195
(307)742-2141

LOVELL

NORTH BIG HORN HOSPITAL
1115 Lane 12
Lovell, WY 82431-9537
(307)548-2771

NEWCASTLE

WESTON COUNTY HEALTH SERVICES
1124 Washington Boulevard
Newcastle, WY 82701-2972
(307)746-4491

POWELL

POWELL HOSPITAL
777 Avenue H
Powell, WY 82435-2296
(307)754-2267

RAWLINS

MEMORIAL HOSPITAL OF CARBON COUNTY
2221 Elm St PO Box 460
Rawlins, WY 82301-0460
(307)324-8213

RIVERTON

RIVERTON MEMORIAL HOSPITAL
2100 W Sunset Drive
Riverton, WY 82501-2274
(307)856-4161

ROCK SPRINGS

MEMORIAL HOSPITAL SWEETWATER
COUNTY
1200 College Drive
Rock Springs, WY 82901-5868
(307)362-3711

SHERIDAN

MEMORIAL HOSPITAL OF SHERIDAN
COUNTY
1401 W 5th St
Sheridan, WY 82801-2799
(307)672-1000

VA MEDICAL CENTER - SHERIDAN
1898 Fort Road
Sheridan, WY 82801-8320
(307)672-3473

SUNDANCE

CROOK COUNTY MEMORIAL HOSPITAL
PO Box 517
Sundance, WY 82729-0517
(307)283-3501

THERMOPOLIS

HOT SPRINGS COUNTY MEMORIAL
HOSPITAL
150 E Arapahoe
Thermopolis, WY 82443-2498
(307)864-3121

TORRINGTON

TORRINGTON COMMUNITY HOSPITAL
2000 Campbell Drive
Torrington, WY 82240-1597
(307)532-4181

WHEATLAND

PLATTE COUNTY MEMORIAL HOSPITAL
201 14th St, PO Drawer 848
Wheatland, WY 82201-3201
(307)322-3636

WORLAND

WASHAKIE COUNTY MEMORIAL HOSPITAL
400 South 15th St, PO Box 700
Worland, WY 82401-0700
(307)347-3221

US POSSESSIONS

PAGO PAGO

LBJ TROPICAL MEDICAL CENTER
Pago Pago, AS 96799
(808)633-1222

SAINT CROIX

GOV JUAN F LUIS HOSPITAL AND MEDICAL
CENTER
#4007 Est Diamond Ruby, Christiansted
Saint Croix, U 00820
(809)778-6311

SAINT THOMAS

ROY LESTER SCHNEIDER HOSPITAL
9048 Sugar Estate
Saint Thomas, U 00801
(809)776-8311

SAIPAN MARIANA ISLANDS

COMMONWEALTH HEALTH CENTER
PO Box 409 Ck (Navy Hill Road)
Saipan Mariana Islands, MA 96950
(670)234-8950

TAMUNING

GUAM MEMORIAL AUTHORITY HOSPITAL
850 Gov Carlos G Camacho Road
Tamuning, GU 96913-3128
(671)647-2108

Alphabetical Index

A G Holley State Hospital ....Lantana FL
Abbeville County Memorial Hospital ....Abbeville SC
Abbeville General Hospital ....Abbeville LA
Abbott - Northwestern Hospital ....Minneapolis MN
Abilene Psychiatric Hospital ....Abilene TX
Abilene Regional Medical Center ....Abilene TX
Abington Memorial Hospital ....Abington PA
Abraham Lincoln Memorial Hospital ....Lincoln IL
Abram Kaplan Memorial Hospital ....Kaplan LA
Acadia Hospital ....Bangor ME
Acadia Rehabilitation Hospital ....Crowley LA
Acadia Saint Landry Parish Hospital ....Church Point LA
Adair County Memorial Hospital ....Greenfield IA
Adams County Hospital ....West Union OH
Adams County Memorial Hospital ....Decatur IN
Adams County Memorial Hospital ....Friendship WI
Adcare Hospital of Worcester ....Worcester MA
Addison Gilbert Hospital ....Gloucester MA
Adena Regional Medical Center ....Chillicothe OH
Adirondack Medical Center ....Saranac Lake NY
Admin De Servicios Medicos Puerto Rico ....San Juan PR
Advance Care Hospital ....Hot Springs AR
Advance Care Hospital ..Marrero LA
Advance Care Hospital of Oklahoma City ....Oklahoma City OK
Adventist Health - Redbud Community Hospital ...Clearlake CA
Advocate Christ Medical Center and Hope Children's Hospital ....Oak Lawn IL
Affiliated Health Services - Skagit Valley Hospital ...Mount Vernon WA
Agnews State Hospital .San Jose CA
Aguadilla Regional Hospital ....Aguadilla PR
Aiken Regional Medical Center ....Aiken SC
Akron General Medical Center ....Akron OH
Alabama Clinical Schools ....Birmingham AL

Alamance Regional Medical Center ....Burlington NC
Alameda County Medical Center ....Oakland CA
Alameda County Medical Center ....San Leandro CA
Alameda Hospital ......Alameda CA
Alaska Psychiatric Institute ....Anchorage AK
Alaska Regional Hospital ....Anchorage AK
Albany Area Hospital ....Albany MN
Albany General Hospital ..Albany OR
Albany Medical Center ...Albany NY
Albany Medical Center - South Clinical Campus ....Albany NY
Albany Memorial Hospital ....Albany NY
Albemarle Hospital ....Elizabeth City NC
Albert Einstein Medical Center ....Philadelphia PA
Albert Lea Medical Center ....Albert Lea MN
Albert Lindley Lee Memorial Hospital ....Fulton NY
Alcohol & Drug Abuse Treatment Center ....Butner NC
Alegent Health - Memorial Hospital ....Schuyler NE
Alexander County Hospital ....Taylorsville NC
Alexian Brothers Behavioral Health Hospital ....Hoffman Estates IL
Alexian Brothers Medical Center ....Elk Grove Village IL
Alfred I Dupont Institute For Children ....Wilmington DE
Alhambra Hospital ....Alhambra CA
Alhambra Hospital ...Rosemead CA
Alice Hyde Memorial Hospital ....Malone NY
Alice Peck Day Memorial Hospital ....Lebanon NH
Alice Regional Hospital .....Alice TX
Aliquippa Community Hospital ....Aliquippa PA
All Childrens Hospital ....Saint Petersburg FL
All Saints - Saint Lukes Hospital ....Racine WI
All Saints - Saint Marys Medical Center ....Racine WI
All Saints Special Care Hospital ....Bridgeton MO
Alle-Kiski Medical Center ....Natrona Heights PA
Allegan General Hospital ....Allegan MI
Alleghany County Memorial Hospital ....Sparta NC
Allegheny General Hospital ....Pittsburgh PA

Allegheny Regional Hospital ....Lowmoor VA
Allen Bennett Memorial Hospital ....Greer SC
Allen County Hospital ....Iola KS
Allen Medical Center ....Oberlin OH
Allen Memorial Hospital ..Waterloo IA
Allen Memorial Hospital ...Moab UT
Allen Parish Hospital .....Kinder LA
Allendale County Hospital ....Fairfax SC
Allenmore Hospital .....Tacoma WA
Allentown State Hospital ....Allentown PA
Alliance Community Hospital ....Alliance OH
Alliance Health Center ..Meridian MS
Alliance Healthcare System ....Holly Springs MS
Allied Rehab Medicine ..Scranton PA
Alpena General Hospital ..Alpena MI
Alta Bates Medical Center-Ashby Campus ....Berkeley CA
Alta Bellwood General Hospital Inc ....Bellflower CA
Alta View Hospital ....Sandy UT
Alton Memorial Hospital .....Alton IL
Alton Mental Health Center ..Alton IL
Altoona Center ....Altoona PA
Altoona Hospital ....Altoona PA
Altru Health Institute ....Grand Forks ND
Altru Hospital ......Grand Forks ND
Alvarado Hospital Medical Center ....San Diego CA
Alvarado Parkway Institute - San Diego ....La Mesa CA
American Fork Hospital ....American Fork UT
American Legion Hospital ....Crowley LA
Amery Regional Medical Center ....Amery WI
Amherst Hospital .....Amherst OH
Amos Cottage Rehabilitation Hospital ....Winston-Salem NC
Amsterdam Memorial Hospital ....Amsterdam NY
Anadarko Municipal Hospital ....Anadarko OK
Anaheim General Hospital ....Anaheim CA
Anaheim General Hospital-Buena Park Campus ......Buena Park CA
Anaheim Memorial Hospital ....Anaheim CA
Anchor Hospital ....Atlanta GA
Ancora Psych Hospital ....Hammonton NJ
Andalusia Regional Hospital ....Andalusia AL
Anderson Area Medical Center ....Anderson SC

Alphabetical Index

Anderson County Hospital
...................Garnett KS
Anderson Hospital ......Maryville IL
Andrew Mcfarland Mental Health
Center ....Springfield IL
Androscoggin Valley Hospital
....................Berlin NH
Angel Medical Center ...Franklin NC
Angleton-Danbury General
Hospital ....Angleton TX
Anna Jaques Hospital
.................Newburyport MA
Anne Arundel Medical Center
.................Annapolis MD
Anne Klein Forensic Center
.................West Trenton NJ
Annie Jeffrey Memorial County
Health Center ....Osceola NE
Annie Penn Memorial Hospital
.................Reidsville NC
Anoka-Metro Regional Treatment
Center ....Anoka MN
Anson Community Hospital
.................Wadesboro NC
Anson General Hospital ...Anson TX
Antelope Memorial Hospital
.....................Neligh NE
Antelope Valley Hospital Medical
Center ....Lancaster CA
Antioch Convalescent Hospital
...................Antioch CA
Appalachian Behavioral Healthcare
...................Athens OH
Appalachian Behavioral Healthcare
.................Cambridge OH
Appleton Medical Center
...................Appleton WI
Appleton Municipal Hospital
...................Appleton MN
Appling Health Care Systems
....................Baxley GA
Arbour Hospital ...Jamaica Plain MA
Arbour Human Resource Institute
of Boston ....Brookline MA
Arbour-Fuller Hospital
.............South Attleboro MA
Arbuckle Memorial Hospital
...................Sulphur OK
Arizona Heart Hospital ...Phoenix AZ
Arizona Spine and Joint
Hospital ....Mesa AZ
Arizona State Hospital ...Phoenix AZ
Arizona Surgical Hospital
...................Phoenix AZ
Arkansas Childrens Hospital
.................Little Rock AR
Arkansas Heart Hospital
.................Little Rock AR
Arkansas Methodist Hospital
.................Paragould AR
Arkansas State Hospital Psychiatric
Division ....Little Rock AR

Arkansas Valley Regional Medical
Center ....La Junta CO
Arlington Memorial Hospital
...................Arlington TX
Arms Acres ....Carmel NY
Armstrong County Memorial
Hospital ....Kittanning PA
Arnold Memorial Hospital
...................Adrian MN
Arnold Palmer Hospital For Children
& Women ....Orlando FL
Arnot Ogden Medical Center
...................Elmira NY
Aroostook Health Center
.................Mars Hill ME
Aroostook Medical Center
.................Presque Isle ME
Arrowhead Community Hospital
...................Glendale AZ
Arrowhead Regional Medical
Center ....Colton CA
Arroyo Grande Community
Hospital ....Arroyo Grande CA
Artesia General Hospital
...................Artesia NM
Arthur G James Cancer Hospital and
Research Institute ....Columbus OH
Arthur R. Gould Memorial
Hospital ....Presque Isle ME
Ascension Hospital ....Gonzales LA
Ashe Memorial Hospital
...................Jefferson NC
Ashford Presbyterian Community
Hospital ....San Juan PR
Ashland Community Hospital
...................Ashland OR
Ashland District Hospital
...................Ashland KS
Ashland Regional Medical
Center ....Ashland PA
Ashley County Medical Center
...................Crossett AR
Ashley Medical Center ...Ashley ND
Ashley Valley Medical Center
...................Vernal UT
Ashtabula County Medical
Center ....Ashtabula OH
Ashton Woods Rehab ...Atlanta GA
Aspen Valley Hospital ....Aspen CO
Assumption Community Hospital
.................Napoleonville LA
Atascadero State Hospital
.................Atascadero CA
Atchison Hospital ......Atchison KS
Athens Regional Medical Center
...................Athens GA
Athens Regional Medical Center
...................Athens TN
Athens-Limestone Hospital
...................Athens AL
Athol Memorial Hospital ...Athol MA
Atlanta Medical Center ..Atlanta GA

Atlanta Memorial Hospital
...................Atlanta TX
Atlantic City Medical Center
.................Atlantic City NJ
Atlantic City Medical Center -
Mainland Division ......Pomona NJ
Atlantic General Hospital ..Berlin MD
Atlantic Health System-General
Hospital Center at Passaic
...................Passaic NJ
Atlantic Health System/mountainside
Hospital ....Montclair NJ
Atlantic Health Systems
.................Florham Park NJ
Atlantic Shores Hospital
.................Fort Lauderdale FL
Atmore Community Hospital
...................Atmore AL
Atoka Memorial Hospital ...Atoka OK
Attica District Hospital .....Attica KS
Auburn Memorial Hospital
...................Auburn NY
Auburn Regional Medical
Center ....Auburn WA
Audrain Medical Center ..Mexico MO
Audubon County Memorial
Hospital ....Audubon IA
Augusta Medical Center
.................Fishersville VA
Augusta Medical Complex
...................Augusta KS
Augusta Mental Health Institute
...................Augusta ME
Aultman Hospital ......Canton OH
Aurora Baycare Medical
Center ....Green Bay WI
Aurora Behavioral Health Care -
Charter Oak ....Covina CA
Aurora Community Hospital
...................Aurora MO
Aurora Medical Center -
Kenosha ....Kenosha WI
Aurora Medical Center -
Manitowoc ....Two Rivers WI
Aurora Medical Center of
Washington County ....Hartford WI
Aurora Pavilion ....Aiken SC
Aurora Psychiatric Hospital
...................Wauwatosa WI
Aurora San Diego ....San Diego CA
Aurora Sinai Medical Center
...................Milwaukee WI
Austen Riggs Center
...................Stockbridge MA
Austin Medical Center ....Austin MN
Austin State Hospital .....Austin TX
Auxilio Mutuo Hospital ..Hato Rey PR
Avalon Municipal Hospital
...................Avalon CA
Aventura Hospital and Medical
Center ....Aventura FL
Avera Mckennan Hospital
.................Sioux Falls SD

Alphabetical Index

Avera Queen of Peace Hospital - Each . . . . .Mitchell SD
Avera Sacred Heart Hospital . . . . .Yankton SD
Avera Saint Anthonys Hospital . . . . .O'Neill NE
Avera Saint Benedict Hospital . . . . .Parkston SD
Avera Saint Lukes Hospital . . . . .Aberdeen SD
Avera Weskota Memorial Medical Center . . . . .Wessington Springs SD
Avista Adventist Hospital . . . . .Louisville CO
Avoyelles Hospital . . . .Marksville LA
B J Workman Memorial Hospital . . . . .Woodruff SC
Bacon County Hospital . . . .Alma GA
Bakersfield Heart Hospital . . . . .Bakersfield CA
Bakersfield Memorial Hospital . . . . .Bakersfield CA
Baldpate Hospital . . .Georgetown MA
Baldwin Hospital . . . . . . .Baldwin WI
Ball Memorial Hospital . . . .Muncie IN
Ballinger Memorial Hospital . . . . .Ballinger TX
Bamberg County Memorial Hospital . . . . .Bamberg SC
Bangor Mental Health Institute . . . . .Bangor ME
Banks-Jackson-Commerce Hospital . . . . .Commerce GA
Banner Lassen Medical Center . . . . .Susanville CA
Baptisi Montclair Medical Center . . . . .Birmingham AL
Baptist Behavioral Health . . . . .Jackson MS
Baptist Dekalb General Hospital . . . . .Smithville TN
Baptist Hickman Community Hospital . . . . .Centerville TN
Baptist Hospital . . . . . .Pensacola FL
Baptist Hospital . . . . . .Nashville TN
Baptist Hospital Desoto . . . . .Southaven MS
Baptist Hospital East . . .Louisville KY
Baptist Hospital of Cocke County . . . . .Newport TN
Baptist Hospital of East Tennessee . . . . .Knoxville TN
Baptist Hospital of Miami . . .Miami FL
Baptist Medical Cente . . . . .Little Rock AR
Baptist Medical Center . . . . .Jacksonville FL
Baptist Medical Center . . . . .Kansas City MO
Baptist Medical Center . . . . .San Antonio TX
Baptist Medical Center Arkadelphia . . . . . .Arkadelphia AR

Baptist Medical Center Beaches . . . . .Jacksonville Beach FL
Baptist Medical Center Cherokee . . . . .Centre AL
Baptist Medical Center Dekalb . . . . .Fort Payne AL
Baptist Medical Center Heber Springs . . .Heber Springs AR
Baptist Medical Center Nassau . . . . .Fernandina Beach FL
Baptist Medical Center Princeton . . . . .Birmingham AL
Baptist Medical Center-East . . . . .Montgomery AL
Baptist Medical Center-South . . . . .Montgomery AL
Baptist Memorial Hospital - Collierville . . . . .Collierville TN
Baptist Memorial Hospital Blytheville . . . . .Blytheville AR
Baptist Memorial Hospital Booneville . . . . .Booneville MS
Baptist Memorial Hospital For Women . . . . .Memphis TN
Baptist Memorial Hospital Forrest City . . . . . .Forrest City AR
Baptist Memorial Hospital Huntingdon . . . . .Huntingdon TN
Baptist Memorial Hospital Lauderdale . . . . .Ripley TN
Baptist Memorial Hospital Memphis . . . . .Memphis TN
Baptist Memorial Hospital North Mississippi . . . . .Oxford MS
Baptist Memorial Hospital Osceola . . . . .Osceola AR
Baptist Memorial Hospital Tipton . . . . .Covington TN
Baptist Memorial Hospital Union City . . . . .Union City TN
Baptist Memorial Hospital Union County . . . . .New Albany MS
Baptist Memorial Hospital/Golden Triangle . . . . .Columbus MS
Baptist Memorial Medical Center . . . . . .North Little Rock AR
Baptist Memorial Restorative Care Hospital . . . . .Memphis TN
Baptist Regional Medical Center . . . . .Corbin KY
Baptist Rehab Institute of Arkansas . . . . .Little Rock AR
Baptist Rehabilitation Germantown . . . . . .Germantown TN
Baptist Saint Anthonys Hospital . . . . .Amarillo TX
Baptist Women's Pavilion . . . . .Nashville TN
Baptist/Saint Anthonys Health System . . . . .Amarillo TX
Baraga County Memorial Hospital . . . . .L'anse MI

Barberton Citizens Hospital . . . . .Barberton OH
Bariatic Care Center of Ohio . . . . .Groveport OH
Bariatric Care Center of Texas .Wylie TX
Barlow Respiratory Hospital . . . . .Los Angeles CA
Barnert Hospital . . . . . . .Paterson NJ
Barnes Jewish Hospital . . . . .Saint Louis MO
Barnes Kasson County Hospital . . . . .Susquehanna PA
Barnes West County Hospital . . . . .Saint Louis MO
Barnes-Jewish Saint Peters Hospital . . . . .Saint Peters MO
Barnesville Hospital Association . . . . .Barnesville OH
Barnstable County Hospital . . . . .Barnstable MA
Barnwell County Hospital . . . . .Barnwell SC
Barrett Memorial Hospital . .Dillon MT
Barron Memorial Medical Center . . . . .Barron WI
Barrow Medical Center . . .Winder GA
Barstow Community Hospital . . . . .Barstow CA
Bartlett Regional Hospital . . . . .Juneau AK
Barton County Memorial Hospital . . . . .Lamar MO
Barton Memorial Hospital . . . . .South Lake Tahoe CA
Bartow Memorial Hospital . . . . .Bartow FL
Bascom Palmer Eye Institute - Anne Bates Leach Eye Hospital . .Miami FL
Bassett Army Community Hospital . . . . . .Fort Wainwright AK
Bassett Health Care . . . . .Cooperstown NY
Bassett Hospital of Schoharie County . . . . .Cobleskill NY
Bastrop Rehab Hospital . .Bastrop LA
Bates County Memorial Hospital . . . . .Butler MO
Bates Medical Center . . . . .Bentonville AR
Bath County Community Hospital . . . . .Hot Springs VA
Baton Rouge General Medical Center - Bluebonnet . . . . . .Baton Rouge LA
Baton Rouge General Medical Center - Mid-City . . . . .Baton Rouge LA
Battle Creek Health System . . . . .Battle Creek MI
Battle Mountain General Hospital . . . . . .Battle Mountain NV
Baum Harmon Memorial Hospital . . . . .Primghar IA

177

Alphabetical Index

Baxter County Regional Hospital
.............Mountain Home AR
Bay Area Hospital ....Coos Bay OR
Bay Area Medical Center Marinette
..................Marinette WI
Bay Health Medical Center at Kent
General Hospital ....Dover DE
Bay Health Medical Center at Milford
Memorial Hospital ....Milford DE
Bay Medical Center
................Panama City FL
Bay Medical Center ....Bay City MI
Bay Medical Center - Samaritan
..................Bay City MI
Bay Park Community Hospital
.....................Oregon OH
Bay Ridge Hospital ......Lynn MA
Bay Special Care Center
......................Bay City MI
Bayfront Medical Center
............Saint Petersburg FL
Baylor All Saints Hospital-Cityview
................Fort Worth TX
Baylor All Saints Medical Center
................Fort Worth TX
Baylor Heart and Vascular Center
..................Dallas TX
Baylor Institute For Rehab
at Gaston ....Dallas TX
Baylor Medical Center - Irving
......................Irving TX
Baylor Medical Center at Garland
....................Garland TX
Baylor Medical Center at
Grapevine ....Grapevine TX
Baylor Medical Center-Ellis
County ....Waxahachie TX
Baylor Specialty Hospital ..Dallas TX
Baylor University Medical Center
.......................Dallas TX
Bayne Jones Army Community
Hospital ....Fort Polk LA
Bayonne Hospital .....Bayonne NJ
Bayshore Community Hospital
....................Holmdel NJ
Bayshore Medical Center
....................Pasadena TX
Bayside Community Hospital
....................Anahuac TX
Baystate Medical Center
..................Springfield MA
Bayview Hospital and Mental Health
System ....Chula Vista CA
Beacham Memorial Hospital
....................Magnolia MS
Bear Lake Memorial Hospital
..................Montpelier ID
Bear River Valley Hospital
.....................Tremonton UT
Bear Tooth Hospital and Health
Center ....Red Lodge MT
Bear Valley Community Hospital
..............Big Bear Lake CA

Beatrice Community Hospital and
Health Center ....Beatrice NE
Beatrice State Developmental
Center ....Beatrice NE
Beaufort County Hospital
..................Washington NC
Beaufort Memorial Hospital
....................Beaufort SC
Beauregard Memorial Hospital
....................Deridder LA
Beaver County Memorial
Hospital ....Beaver OK
Beaver Dam Community
Hospitals ....Beaver Dam WI
Beaver Valley Hospital ...Beaver UT
Beckley Appalachian Regional
Hospital ....Beckley WV
Bedford County Medical Center
................Shelbyville TN
Bedford Memorial Hospital
....................Bedford VA
Bedford Regional Medical
Center ....Bedford IN
Beebe Medical Center ....Lewes DE
Behavioral Health Center
..................Greensboro NC
Behavioral Health Center - Cmc-
Randolph ....Charlotte NC
Behavioral Health of Cape Fear
Valley ....Fayetteville NC
Behavioral Health Services
..................Winfield IL
Behavioral Health Services
....................Gallup NM
Behavioral Healthcare - Columbus
....................Columbus IN
Behavioral Healthcare of Northern
Indiana ....Plymouth IN
Bell Memorial Hospital
....................Ishpeming MI
Bella Vista Hospital ...Mayaguez PR
Bellaire Medical Center ..Houston TX
Bellevue Hospital .....Bellevue OH
Bellevue Hospital Center
....................New York NY
Bellevue Womens Hospital
....................Niskayuna NY
Bellevue Womens Hospital
..................Schenectady NY
Bellflower Medical Center
....................Bellflower CA
Bellin Memorial Hospital
....................Green Bay WI
Bellin Psychiatric Center
....................Green Bay WI
Bellville General Hospital
....................Bellville TX
Belmond Community Hospital
....................Belmond IA
Belmont Center-comprehensive
Treatment ....Philadelphia PA
Belmont Community Hospital
....................Bellaire OH

Belmont Pines Hospital
................Youngstown OH
Beloit Memorial Hospital ...Beloit WI
Ben Taub General Hospital
....................Houston TX
Benchmark Regional Hospital
................Woods Cross UT
Benedictine Hospital ...Kingston NY
Benefis Healthcare ...Great Falls MT
Benefis Healthcare West
Campus ....Great Falls MT
Benewah Community Hospital
................Saint Maries ID
Bennett County Healthcare
Center ....Martin SD
Benson Hospital ....Benson AZ
Benton Rehabilitation Hospital
................Baton Rouge LA
Berea Hospital ....Berea KY
Bergan Mercy Medical Center
....................Omaha NE
Bergen Regional Medical
Center ....Paramus NJ
Berger Hospital ......Circleville OH
Berkshire Medical Center
....................Pittsfield MA
Berlin Memorial Hospital ...Berlin WI
Bernice Community Rehab
Hospital ....Minden LA
Berrien County Hospital
....................Nashville GA
Bert Fish Medical Center
..........New Smyrna Beach FL
Bertie Memorial Hospital
....................Windsor NC
Bertrand Chaffee Hospital
...................Springville NY
Berwick Hospital Center ..Berwick PA
Beth Israel Deaconess Medical
Center ....Boston MA
Beth Israel Deaconess Medical
Center - West Campus ..Boston MA
Beth Israel Medical Center
....................New York NY
Beth Israel Medical Center - Kings
Highway Division ......Brooklyn NY
Beth Israel Singer Division
....................New York NY
Bethany Healthcare Center
..................Framingham MA
Bethany Hospital ......Chicago IL
Bethesda Memorial Hospital
................Boynton Beach FL
Bethesda North Hospitals
....................Cincinnati OH
Bethesda Rehab Center
....................Saint Paul MN
Betsy Johnson Memorial
Hospital ....Dunn NC
Betty Bacharach Rehab
Center ....Pomona NJ
Betty Ford Center
.............Rancho Mirage CA

Alphabetical Index

Beverly Hospital . . . . .Montebello CA
Beverly Hospital . . . . . . .Beverly MA
Bi-County Community
Hospital . . . . .Warren MI
Bibb Medical Center Hospital
. . . . .Centreville AL
Big Bend Regional Medical
Center . . . . .Alpine TX
Big Horn County Memorial
Hospital . . . . .Hardin MT
Big Sandy Medical Center Maf
. . . . .Big Sandy MT
Big Spring State Hospital
. . . . .Big Spring TX
Biggs-Gridley Memorial Hospital
. . . . .Gridley CA
Biloxi Regional Medical Center
. . . . .Biloxi MS
Bingham Memorial Hospital
. . . . .Blackfoot ID
Binghamton General Hospital
. . . . .Binghamton NY
Binghamton Psych Center
. . . . .Binghamton NY
Bixby Medical Center . . . . .Adrian MI
Black Hills Surgery Center Llp
. . . . .Rapid City SD
Black River Falls Memorial
Hospital . . . . . .Black River Falls WI
Blackford County Hospital
. . . . .Hartford City IN
Bladen County Hospital
. . . . .Elizabethtown NC
Blake Medical Center . .Bradenton FL
Blanchard Valley Regional Health
Center - Bluffton . . . . . . .Bluffton OH
Blanchard Valley Regional Health
Center - Findlay . . . . .Findlay OH
Bleckley Memorial Hospital
. . . . .Cochran GA
Bledsoe County Hospital
. . . . .Pikeville TN
Blessing Hospital . . . . . . .Quincy IL
Bloomer Community Medical
Center/hospital . . . . . . .Bloomer WI
Bloomington Hospital
. . . . .Bloomington IN
Bloomington Hospital . . . . .Paoli IN
Bloomsburg Hospital
. . . . .Bloomsburg PA
Blount Memorial Hospital
. . . . .Maryville TN
Blowing Rock Hospital
. . . . .Blowing Rock NC
Blue Grass Community
Hospital . . . . .Versailles KY
Blue Hill Memorial Hospital
. . . . .Blue Hill ME
Blue Mountain Hospital
. . . . .John Day OR
Bluefield Regional Medical
Center . . . . .Bluefield WV

Bluffton Regional Medical
Center . . . . .Bluffton IN
Blythdale Childrens Hospital
. . . . .Valhalla NY
Bob Wilson Memorial Grant County
Hospital . . . . .Ulysses KS
Boca Raton Community
Hospital . . . . .Boca Raton FL
Bogalusa Community Medical
Center . . . . .Bogalusa LA
Bogalusa Community Rehab
Hospital . . . . .Bogalusa LA
Bolivar County Medical-Hospital
. . . . .Cleveland MS
Bolivar General Hospital . .Bolivar TN
Bon Secours - Depaul Medical
Center . . . . .Norfolk VA
Bon Secours - Saint Joseph Hospital
Port Charlotte . . . . .Port Charlotte FL
Bon Secours Community
Hospital . . . . .Port Jervis NY
Bon Secours Cottage
Hospital . . .Grosse Pointe Farms MI
Bon Secours Health Systems
. . . . .Jersey City NJ
Bon Secours Holy Family
Hospital . . . . .Altoona PA
Bon Secours Hospital . .Baltimore MD
Bon Secours Hospital
. . . . .Grosse Pointe MI
Bon Secours Saint Francis
Health Care . . . . . . .Greenville SC
Bon Secours Venice Hospital
. . . . .Venice FL
Bon Secours-Saint Francis Xavier
Hospital . . . . .Charleston SC
Bone and Joint Hospital
. . . . .Oklahoma City OK
Bonner General Hospital
. . . . .Sandpoint ID
Boone County Health Center
. . . . .Albion NE
Boone County Hospital . . . .Boone IA
Boone Hospital Center
. . . . .Columbia MO
Boone Memorial Hospital
. . . . .Madison WV
Booneville Community Hospital
. . . . .Booneville AR
Borgess Medical Center
. . . . .Kalamazoo MI
Borgess Pipp Health Center
. . . . .Plainwell MI
Borgess-Lee Memorial Hospital
. . . . .Dowagiac MI
Boscobel Area Health Care
. . . . .Boscobel WI
Bossier Medical Center
. . . . .Bossier City LA
Boston Medical Center - Hac
. . . . .Boston MA
Boston University Medical Center
. . . . .Boston MA

Bothwell Regional Health Center
. . . . .Sedalia MO
Botsford General Hospital
. . . . .Farmington MI
Boulder City Hospital
. . . . .Boulder City NV
Boulder Community Hospital
. . . . .Boulder CO
Boundary County Community
Hospital . . . . .Bonners Ferry ID
Bourbon Community
Hospital . . . . .Paris KY
Bournewood Hospital . .Brookline MA
Bournewood Hospital
. . . . .Chestnut Hill MA
Bowdle Hospital . . . . . . .Bowdle SD
Bowie Memorial Hospital . .Bowie TX
Box Butte General Hospital
. . . . .Alliance NE
Boys Town National Research
Hospital . . . . .Omaha NE
Bozeman Deaconess Hospital
. . . . .Bozeman MT
Brackenridge Hospital . . . .Austin TX
Bradford Health Services
. . . . .Madison AL
Bradford Health Services at Oak
Mountain . . . . .Pelham AL
Bradford Health Services,
Birmingham Lodge . . . . . .Warrior AL
Bradford Regional Medical
Center . . . . .Bradford PA
Bradley Center of Saint Francis
. . . . .Columbus GA
Bradley County Medical Center
. . . . .Warren AR
Bradley Memorial Hospital
. . . . .Cleveland TN
Bradley Memorial Hospital and Health
Center . . . . .Southington CT
Brainerd Regional Human Services
Center . . . . .Brainerd MN
Brandon Regional Hospital
. . . . .Brandon FL
Brandywine Hospital . .Coatesville PA
Brattleboro Memorial Hospital
. . . . .Brattleboro VT
Brattleboro Retreat . . .Brattleboro VT
Braxton County Memorial
Hospital . . . . .Gassaway WV
Brazosport Memorial Hospital
. . . . .Lake Jackson TX
Brea Community Hospital . . .Brea CA
Breckinridge Memorial Hospital
. . . . .Hardinsburg KY
Breech Regional Medical
Center . . . . .Lebanon MO
Brentwood Behavioral Healthcare
. . . . .Shreveport LA
Brentwood Behavioral Healthcare
. . . . .Jackson MS
Bridgeport Hospital . . .Bridgeport CT
Bridges Medical Services . . .Ada MN

179

Alphabetical Index

Bridgewater State Hospital . . . . .Bridgewater MA
Bridgeway . . . . .North Little Rock AR
Bridgton Hospital . . . . . .Bridgton ME
Brigham and Womens Hospital . . . . .Boston MA
Brigham City Community Hospital . . . . .Brigham City UT
Brighton Hospital . . . . . . .Brighton MI
Bristol Hospital . . . . .Bristol CT
Bristol Regional Medical Center . . . . .Bristol TN
Bristow Memorial Hospital . . . . .Bristow OK
Broad Horizons of Ramona . . . . .Ramona CA
Broaddus Hospital . . . . . .Philippi WV
Broadlawns Medical Center . . . . .Des Moines IA
Broadwater Health Center . . . . .Townsend MT
Brockton Hospital . . . . .Brockton MA
Brodstone Memorial-Nuckolls Co Hospital . . . . .Superior NE
Bromenn Healthcare . . . . .Normal IL
Bronson Methodist Hospital . . . . .Kalamazoo MI
Bronson Vicksburg Hospital . . . . .Vicksburg MI
Bronx Childrens Psych Center . . . . .Bronx NY
Bronx Psychiatric Center . .Bronx NY
Bronx-Lebanon Hospital - Concourse . . . . .Bronx NY
Bronx-Lebanon Hospital Center . . . . .Bronx NY
Brook Lane Psychiatric Center . . . . .Hagerstown MD
Brookdale University Hospital and Medical Center . . . . .Brooklyn NY
Brooke Army Medical Center . . . . .Fort Sam Houston TX
Brookhaven Hospital . . . . . .Tulsa OK
Brookhaven Memorial Hospital . . . . .Patchogue NY
Brookings Hospital . . . .Brookings SD
Brooklyn Hospital Center . . . . .Brooklyn NY
Brooklyn Hospital Center - Caledonian Campus . . .Brooklyn NY
Brooks County Hospital . . . . .Quitman GA
Brooks Memorial Hospital . . . . .Dunkirk NY
Brooks Rehabilitation Hospital . . . . .Jacksonville FL
Brooksville Regional Hospital . . . . .Brooksville FL
Brookville Hospital . . . .Brookville PA
Brookwood Medical Center . . . . .Birmingham AL
Brotman Medical Center . . . . .Culver City CA

Broughton Hospital . . .Morganton NC
Broward General Medical Center . . . . .Fort Lauderdale FL
Brown County General Hospital . . . . .Georgetown OH
Brown County Hospital . . . . .Ainsworth NE
Brown County Mental Health Center . . . . .Green Bay WI
Brown Memorial Hospital . . . . .Conneaut OH
Brown Schools of Oklahoma . . . . .Tulsa OK
Brown Schools of Virginia . . . . .Charlottesville VA
Brownfield Regional Medical Center . . . . .Brownfield TX
Brownsville General Hospital . . . . .Brownsville PA
Brownsville Medical Center . . . . .Brownsville TX
Brownsville Surgical Hospital . . . . .Brownsville TX
Brownwood Regional Medical Center . . . . .Brownwood TX
Brunswick Community Hospital . . . . .Supply NC
Brunswick Hall . . . . . .Amityville NY
Brunswick Hospital . . . .Amityville NY
Bryan Lgh East Hospital .Lincoln NE
Bryan Lgh West Hospital .Lincoln NE
Bryan W Whitfield Memorial Hospital . . . . .Demopolis AL
Bryce Hospital . . . . .Tuscaloosa AL
Brylin Hospital . . . . .Buffalo NY
Bryn Mawr Hospital . . . . .Malvern PA
Brynn Marr Hospital . . . . .Jacksonville NC
Bsa Panhandle Surgical Hospital . . . . .Amarillo TX
Buchanan General Hospital . . . . .Grundy VA
Bucktail Medical Center . .Renovo PA
Bucyrus Community Hospital . . . . .Bucyrus OH
Buena Vista County Hospital . . . . .Storm Lake IA
Buffalo General Hospital . .Buffalo NY
Buffalo Hospital . . . . . . .Buffalo MN
Buffalo Psychiatric Center . . . . .Buffalo NY
Bullock County Hospital . . . . .Union Springs AL
Bunkie General Hospital . .Bunkie LA
Burdete Tomlin Memorial Hospital . . . . .Cape May Court House NJ
Burgess Memorial Hospital . . . . .Onawa IA
Burke County Hospital . . . . .Waynesboro GA
Burke Rehab Hospital . . . . .White Plains NY

Burleson Saint Joseph Health Center . . . . . . .Caldwell TX
Burnett Medical Center . . . . .Grantsburg WI
Butler County Hospital . . . . .David City NE
Butler Hospital . . . . . .Providence RI
Butler Memorial Hospital . . .Butler PA
Buttonwood Hospital of Burlington County . . . . .Mount Holly NJ
Byrd Regional Hospital . .Leesville LA
C S Mott Children's Hospital . . . . .Ann Arbor MI
Cabell-Huntington Hospital . . . . .Huntington WV
Cabrini Medical Center . . . . .New York NY
Cache Valley Specialty Hospital . . . . .North Logan UT
Calais Regional Hospital . .Calais ME
Calcasieu Oaks . . . .Lake Charles LA
Caldwell County Hospital . . . . .Princeton KY
Caldwell Memorial Hospital . . . . .Columbia LA
Caldwell Memorial Hospital . . . . .Lenoir NC
Calhoun Health Services - Hillcrest Hospital . . . . .Calhoun City MS
Calhoun Liberty Hospital . . . . .Blountstown FL
Calhoun Memorial Hospital . . . . .Arlington GA
California Hospital Medical Center La . . . . .Los Angeles CA
California Medical Facility . . . . .Vacaville CA
California Mens Colony . . . . .San Luis Obispo CA
California Pacific Medical Center . . . . .San Francisco CA
California Pacific Medical Center - East . . . . .San Francisco CA
California Pacific Medical Center Davies Campus . . .San Francisco CA
California Pacific Medical Center Pacific Campus . . .San Francisco CA
California Speciality Hospital . . . . .Vallejo CA
Callahan Eye Foundation Hospital . . . . .Birmingham AL
Callaway District Hospital . . . . .Callaway NE
Callaway Memorial Hospital . . . . .Fulton MO
Calumet Medical Center . .Chilton WI
Calvary Hospital . . . . .Bronx NY
Calvert Memorial Hospital . . . . .Prince Frederick MD
Cambridge Hospital . .Cambridge MA
Cambridge Medical Center . . . . .Cambridge MN

Alphabetical Index

Camden Clark Memorial Hospital . . . . .Parkersburg WV
Camden County Health Services Center . . . . .Blackwood NJ
Camden County Health Services Center . . . . .Lakeland NJ
Camden General Hospital . . . . .Camden TN
Camden Medical Center . . . . .Saint Marys GA
Cameron Community Hospital . . . . .Cameron MO
Cameron Hospital and Home Health Care . . . . .Angola IN
Campbell County Memorial Hospital . . . . .Gillette WY
Campbell Health System . . . . .Weatherford TX
Campbellton Graceville Hospital . . . . .Graceville FL
Cancer Institute, The . . . . .Kansas City MO
Cancer Treatment Center of America . . . . .Tulsa OK
Candler County Hospital . .Metter GA
Candler Hospital . . . . .Savannah GA
Cannon Falls Community Hospital . . . . .Cannon Falls MN
Cannon Memorial Hospital . . . . .Pickens SC
Canonsburg General Hospital . . . . .Canonsburg PA
Canton Potsdam Hospital . . . . .Potsdam NY
Canton-Inwood Memorial Hospital . . . . .Canton SD
Canyon Ridge Hospital . . . .Chino CA
Canyon View Hospital . .Twin Falls ID
Cape Canaveral Hospital . . . . .Cocoa Beach FL
Cape Cod and Islands Community Mental Health Center . .Pocasset MA
Cape Cod Hospital . . . . .Hyannis MA
Cape Coral Hospital . .Cape Coral FL
Cape Fear Memorial Hospital . . . . .Wilmington NC
Cape Fear Valley Medical Center . . . . .Fayetteville NC
Capital District Psych Center . . . . .Albany NY
Capital Health System at Mercer . . . . .Trenton NJ
Capital Health Systems at Fuld . . . . .Trenton NJ
Capital Medical Center . .Olympia WA
Capital Region Medical Center . . . . .Jefferson City MO
Capitol Medical Center . . . . .Richmond VA
Capitol Regional Medical Center . . . . .Tallahassee FL
Cardinal Glennon Childrens Hospital . . . . .Saint Louis MO

Cardinal Hill Rehabilitation Hospital . . . . .Lexington KY
Caribou Memorial Hospital . . . . .Soda Springs ID
Carilion Franklin Memorial Hospital . . . . .Rocky Mount VA
Carilion Giles Memorial Hospital . . . . .Pearisburg VA
Carilion New River Valley Medical Center . . . . .Christiansburg VA
Carilion Roanoke Community Hospital . . . . .Roanoke VA
Carilion Saint Albans Hospital . . . . .Radford VA
Caritas Medical Center . . . . .Louisville KY
Caritas Norwood Hospital . . . . .Norwood MA
Caritas Saint Elizabeths Medical Center . . . . .Boston MA
Carl Albert Community Mental Health Center . . . . .Mc Alester OK
Carle Foundation Hospital . . . . .Urbana IL
Carlinville Area Hospital . . . . .Carlinville IL
Carlisle Regional Medical Center . . . . .Carlisle PA
Carlsbad Medical Center . . . . .Carlsbad NM
Carnegie Tri County Municipal Hospital . . . . .Carnegie OK
Carney Hospital . . . . . . .Boston MA
Caro Community Hospital . . .Caro MI
Caro Regional Mental Health Center . . . . .Caro MI
Carolina Area Hospital . .Carolina PR
Carolina Center For Behavorial Health . . . . .Greer SC
Carolina Pines Regional Hospital . . . . .Hartsville SC
Carolinas Hospital System . . . . .Florence SC
Carolinas Hospital System-Lake City . . . . .Lake City SC
Carolinas Medical Center . . . . .Charlotte NC
Carolinas Medical Center - Mercy . . . . .Charlotte NC
Carolinas Medical Center - Pineville . . . . .Charlotte NC
Carolinas Medical Center - University . . . . .Charlotte NC
Caron Foundation . . .Wernersville PA
Carondelet Holy Cross Hospital . . . . .Nogales AZ
Carondelet Saint Josephs Hospital . . . . .Tucson AZ
Carondelet Saint Marys Hospital . . . . .Tucson AZ
Carraway Methodist Medical Center . . . . .Birmingham AL

Carraway Northwest Medical Center . . . . .Winfield AL
Carrie Tingley Hospital . . . . .Albuquerque NM
Carrier Clinic Foundation . . . . .Belle Mead NJ
Carrington Health Center . . . . .Carrington ND
Carroll County General Hospital . . . . .Westminster MD
Carroll County Memorial Hospital . . . . .Carrollton KY
Carroll County Memorial Hospital . . . . .Carrollton MO
Carroll Regional Medical Center . . . . .Berryville AR
Carson City Hospital . .Carson City MI
Carson Rehabilitation Center . . . . .Carson City NV
Carson-Tahoe Hospital . . . . .Carson City NV
Carteret General Hospital . . . . .Morehead City NC
Carthage Area Hospital . . . . .Carthage NY
Carthage General Hospital . . . . .Carthage TN
Cary Medical Center . . . .Caribou ME
Casa Colina Hospital For Rehab Medicine . . . . .Pomona CA
Casa Grande Regional Medical Center . . . . .Casa Grande AZ
Cascade Medical Center . . . . .Cascade ID
Cascade Medical Center . . . . .Leavenworth WA
Cascade Valley Hospital . . . . .Arlington WA
Casey County Hospital . . .Liberty KY
Cass County Memorial Hospital . . . . .Atlantic IA
Cass Medical Center . . . . .Harrisonville MO
Cassia Regional Medical Center . . . . .Burley ID
Castaner General Hospital . . . . .Castaner PR
Castle Medical Center . . . . .Kailua HI
Castleview Hospital . . . . . .Price UT
Caswell Center . . . . . . .Kinston NC
Catawba Hospital . . . . . .Catawba VA
Catawba Memorial Hospital . . . . .Hickory NC
Catholic Medical Center . . . . .Manchester NH
Catskill Regional Medical Center . . . . .Callicoon NY
Catskill Regional Medical Center . . . . .Harris NY
Cavalier County Memorial Hospital . . . . .Langdon ND
Caverna Memorial Hospital . . . . .Horse Cave KY

Alphabetical Index

Caylor-Nickel Medical Center
..................Bluffton IN
Cayuga Medical Center at Ithaca
..................Ithaca NY
Ccs/Charlotte ....Charlotte NC
Cedar County Memorial Hospital
..........El Dorado Springs MO
Cedar Springs Hospital
..........Colorado Springs CO
Cedar Vale Community Hospital
..................Cedar Vale KS
Cedar Vista Hospital .....Fresno CA
Cedarcrest Regional Hospital
..................Newington CT
Cedars Hospital ....De Soto TX
Cedars Medical Center ....Miami FL
Cedars-Sinai Medical Center
..................Los Angeles CA
Centennial Medical Center
..................Ashland City TN
Centennial Medical Center and
Parthenon Pavilion ....Nashville TN
Centennial Peaks Hospital
..................Louisville CO
Center Point Hospital
..................Saint Charles MO
Centinela Hospital Medical Center
..................Inglewood CA
Central Arkansas Hospital
..................Searcy AR
Central Baptist Hospital
..................Lexington KY
Central Carolina Hospital
..................Sanford NC
Central Community Hospital
..................Elkader IA
Central Dupage Hospital ..Winfield IL
Central Florida Regional Hospital
..................Sanford FL
Central Kansas Medical Center
..................Great Bend KS
Central Kansas Medical Center -
Saint Joseph Campus ....Larned KS
Central Louisiana State Hospital
..................Pineville LA
Central Maine Medical Center
..................Lewiston ME
Central Michigan Community
Hospital ....Mount Pleasant MI
Central Mississippi Medical
Center ....Jackson MS
Central Montana Medical
Center ....Lewistown MT
Central Montgomery Medical
Center ....Lansdale PA
Central New York Psychiatric
Center ....Marcy NY
Central Oregon District Hospital
..................Redmond OR
Central Peninsula General
Hospital ....Soldotna AK
Central Prison Hospital ..Raleigh NC

Central State Hospital
..................Milledgeville GA
Central State Hospital ..Louisville KY
Central State Hospital
..................Petersburg VA
Central Suffolk Hospital
..................Riverhead NY
Central Texas Hospital ..Cameron TX
Central Texas Medical Center
..................San Marcos TX
Central Valley General Hospital
..................Hanford CA
Central Valley Medical Center
..................Nephi UT
Central Vermont Hospital ...Barre VT
Central Virginia Training Center
..................Lynchburg VA
Central Washington Hospital
..................Wenatchee WA
Centrastate Medical Center
..................Freehold NJ
Centre Community Hospital
..................State College PA
Centris ....Oklahoma City OK
Centro Cardiovascular
..................Rio Piedras PR
Century City Hospital
..................Los Angeles CA
Cgh Medical Center ......Sterling IL
Chadron Community
Hospital ....Chadron NE
Chalmette Medical Center
..................Chalmette LA
Chambersburg Hospital
..................Chambersburg PA
Champlain Valley Physicians
Hospital ....Plattsburgh NY
Chandler Regional Hospital
..................Chandler AZ
Chapman Medical Center
..................Orange CA
Charles A Dean Memorial
Hospital ....Greenville ME
Charles A. Cannon Jr. Memorial
Hospital ....Linville NC
Charles Cole Memorial Hospital
..................Coudersport PA
Charles R Drew Medical Center
..................Houston TX
Charles River Hospital ...Nahant MA
Charleston Area Medical Center -
General Division ....Charleston WV
Charleston Area Medical Center -
Memorial Division ....Charleston WV
Charleston Area Medical Center -
Women and Childrens Hospital
..................Charleston WV
Charleston Memorial Hospital
..................Charleston SC
Charlevoix Area Hospital
..................Charlevoix MI
Charlotte Hungerford Hospital
..................Torrington CT

Charlotte Institute of Rehabilitation
..................Charlotte NC
Charlotte Regional Medical
Center ....Punta Gorda FL
Charlton Memorial Hospital
..................Folkston GA
Charlton Memorial Hospital
..................Fall River MA
Charlton Methodist Hospital
..................Dallas TX
Chase County Community
Hospital ....Imperial NE
Chatham Hospital .....Siler City NC
Chatuge Regional Hospital
..................Hiawassee GA
Cheboygan Memorial Hospital
..................Cheboygan MI
Chelsea Community Hospital
..................Chelsea MI
Chenango Memorial Hospital
..................Norwich NY
Cherry County Hospital
..................Valentine NE
Cherry Hospital ......Goldsboro NC
Chesapeake General Hospital
..................Chesapeake VA
Cheshire Medical Center ..Keene NH
Chestatee Regional Hospital
..................Dahlonega GA
Chester County Hospital
..................West Chester PA
Chester County Hospital .Chester SC
Chester Mental Health
Center ....Chester IL
Chesterfield General Hospital
..................Cheraw SC
Chestnut Hill Hospital
..................Wyndmoor PA
Chestnut Hill Rehab Hospital
..................Wyndmoor PA
Chestnut Ridge Behavioral Health
System ....Morgantown WV
Cheyenne County Hospital
..................Saint Francis KS
Chicago Lakeshore Hospital
..................Chicago IL
Chicago-Read Mental Health
Center ....Chicago IL
Chicot Memorial Hospital
..................Lake Village AR
Children's Center ......Bethany OK
Children's Healthcare of Atlanta at
Egleston ....Atlanta GA
Children's Hospital ....Columbia SC
Children's Hospital Central
California ....Madera CA
Children's Hospital of Austin
..................Austin TX
Children's Hospital of Oklahoma
..................Oklahoma City OK
Children's Hospital of Wisconsin -
Fox Valley ....Neenah WI

Alphabetical Index

Children's Hospital of Wisconsin - Kenosha . . . . .Kenosha WI
Children's Institute of Pittsburgh . . . . .Pittsburgh PA
Children's National Medical Center . . . . .Washington DC
Children's Recovery Center of North California . . . . .Campbell CA
Children's Specialized Hospital - Ocean . . . . .Toms River NJ
Childrens Care Hospital/School . . . . .Sioux Falls SD
Childrens Health Care - Minneapolis . . . . . . .Minneapolis MN
Childrens Health Care - Saint Paul . . . . .Saint Paul MN
Childrens Healthcare Atlanta . . . . .Atlanta GA
Childrens Home of Pittsburgh . . . . .Pittsburgh PA
Childrens Hospital . . . . . .Denver CO
Childrens Hospital . .New Orleans LA
Childrens Hospital . . . . .Boston MA
Childrens Hospital . . . . .Omaha NE
Childrens Hospital . . . . .Buffalo NY
Childrens Hospital . . . .Columbus OH
Childrens Hospital . . . .Richmond VA
Childrens Hospital and Health Center . . . . .San Diego CA
Childrens Hospital and Regional Medical Center . . . . .Seattle WA
Childrens Hospital at Mission . . . . .Mission Viejo CA
Childrens Hospital Medical Center . . . . .Oakland CA
Childrens Hospital Medical Center . . . . .Akron OH
Childrens Hospital Medical Center . . . . .Cincinnati OH
Childrens Hospital of Alabama . . . . .Birmingham AL
Childrens Hospital of Kings Daughters . . . . .Norfolk VA
Childrens Hospital of Los Angeles . . . . .Los Angeles CA
Childrens Hospital of Michigan . . . . .Detroit MI
Childrens Hospital of Orange County . . . . .Orange CA
Childrens Hospital of Philadelphia . . . . .Philadelphia PA
Childrens Hospital of Pittsburgh . . . . .Pittsburgh PA
Childrens Hospital of Wisconsin . . . . .Milwaukee WI
Childrens Medical Center . . . . .Dayton OH
Childrens Medical Center . .Tulsa OK
Childrens Medical Center of Dallas . . . . .Dallas TX
Childrens Memorial Hospital . . . . .Chicago IL

Childrens Mercy Hospital . . . . .Kansas City MO
Childrens Mercy Hospital South . . . . .Overland Park KS
Childrens Psych/dba Prairie Psych Center . . . . .Fargo ND
Childrens Seashore House . . . . .Philadelphia PA
Childrens Specialized Hospital . . . . .Mountainside NJ
Childress Regional Medical Center . . . . .Childress TX
Chillicothe Hospital . . .Chillicothe TX
Chilton Medical Center . . .Clanton AL
Chilton Memorial Hospital . . . . .Pompton Plains NJ
Chinese Hospital . .San Francisco CA
Chino Valley Medical Center . . . . .Chino CA
Chippewa County War Memorial Hospital . . . . .Sault Sainte Marie MI
Chippewa County-Montevideo Hospital . . . . .Montevideo MN
Chippewa Valley Hospital . . . . .Durand WI
Choate Mental Health & Development Center . . . . . .Anna IL
Choctaw County Medical Center . . . . .Ackerman MS
Choctaw Health Center . . . . .Philadelphia MS
Choctaw Memorial Hospital . . . . .Hugo OK
Chowan Hospital . . . . .Edenton NC
Chowchilla District Memorial Hospital . . . . .Chowchilla CA
Christ Hospital . . . . .Jersey City NJ
Christ Hospital . . . . . .Cincinnati OH
Christian Healthcare Center . . . . .Wyckoff NJ
Christian Hospital Northeast . . . . .Saint Louis MO
Christian Hospital Northwest . . . . .Florissant MO
Christiana Hospital . . . . . .Newark DE
Christopher House . . . . . . .Austin TX
Christus Coushatta Health Care . . . . .Coushatta LA
Christus Jasper Memorial Hospital . . . . .Jasper TX
Christus Saint Elizabeth Hospital . . . . .Beaumont TX
Christus Saint Frances Cabrini Hospital . . . . .Alexandria LA
Christus Saint John Hospital . . . . .Houston TX
Christus Saint John Hospital . . . . .Nassau Bay TX
Christus Saint Joseph Hospital . . . . .Houston TX
Christus Saint Joseph Hospital - North . . . . .Paris TX

Christus Saint Josephs Hospital and Health Center . . . . .Paris TX
Christus Saint Mary Hospital . . . . .Port Arthur TX
Christus Saint Michael Health Care Center . . . . . . .Texarkana TX
Christus Saint Michael Rehab Hospital . . . . .Texarkana TX
Christus Santa Rosa Childrens Hospital . . . . .San Antonio TX
Christus Santa Rosa Health Care-Downtown Division . .San Antonio TX
Christus Santa Rosa Northwest Hospital . . . . .San Antonio TX
Christus Spohn Hospital . . . . .Beeville TX
Christus Spohn Hospital - Alice . . . . .Alice TX
Christus Spohn Hospital - Kleberg . . . . .Kingsville TX
Christus Spohn Hospital - Shoreline . . . . . . .Corpus Christi TX
Christus Spohn Hospital - South . . . . .Corpus Christi TX
Christus Spohn Memorial Hospital . . . . . . .Corpus Christi TX
Churchill Community Hospital . . . . .Fallon NV
Cibola General Hospital . .Grants NM
Cimarron Memorial Hospital . . . . .Boise City OK
Circles of Care . . . . . .Melbourne FL
Citizens Baptist Medical Center . . . . .Talladega AL
Citizens Medical Center . . .Colby KS
Citizens Medical Center . . . . .Columbia LA
Citizens Medical Center . .Victoria TX
Citizens Memorial Hospital . . . . .Bolivar MO
Citrus Memorial Hospital . . . . .Inverness FL
Citrus Valley Medical Center . . . . .West Covina CA
Citrus Valley Medical Center-IC Campus . . . . .Covina CA
City Avenue Hospital . . . . .Philadelphia PA
City Hospital . . . . . .Martinsburg WV
City Hospital Center at Elmhurst . . . . .Elmhurst NY
City of Angels Medical Center . . . . .Los Angeles CA
City of Hope National Medical Center . . . . .Duarte CA
Civista Medical Center . .La Plata MD
Cjw Medical Center - Chippenham . . . . .Richmond VA
Cjw Medical Center - Johnston Willis . . . . .Richmond VA
Claiborne County Hospital . . . . .Port Gibson MS

Alphabetical Index

Claiborne County Hospital . . . . .Tazewell TN
Clara Barton Hospital . . . . .Hoisington KS
Clara Maass Medical Center . . . . .Belleville NJ
Claremore Regional Hospital . . . . .Claremore OK
Clarendon Memorial Hospital . . . . .Manning SC
Clarian Health Partners . . . . .Indianapolis IN
Clarinda Mental Health Institute . . . . .Clarinda IA
Clarinda Regional Health Center . . . . .Clarinda IA
Clarion Hospital . . . . . . .Clarion PA
Clarion Psych Center . . . .Clarion PA
Clark County Memorial Hospital . . . . .Jeffersonville IN
Clark Fork Valley Hospital . . . . .Plains MT
Clark Regional Medical Center . . . . .Winchester KY
Clarke County Public Hospital . . . . .Osceola IA
Clarks Summit State Hospital . . . . .Clarks Summit PA
Claxton - Hepburn Medical Center . . . . .Ogdensburg NY
Clay County Hospital . . . .Ashland AL
Clay County Hospital . . . . . . .Flora IL
Clay County Hospital and Medical Center . . . . .Clay Center KS
Clay County Medical Center . . . . .West Point MS
Clay County Memorial Hospital . . . . .Henrietta TX
Clear Brook Lodge . .Shickshinny PA
Clear Brook Manor . .Wilkes-Barre PA
Clear Lake Regional Medical Center . . . . .Webster TX
Clearfield Hospital . . . . .Clearfield PA
Clearview Home . . . . . . .Delafield WI
Clearwater County Memorial Hospital . . . . .Bagley MN
Clearwater Valley Hospital . . . . .Orofino ID
Cleo Wallace Center Hospital . . . . .Westminster CO
Cleo Wallace Centers . . . . .Broomfield CO
Clermont Mercy Hospital . . . . .Batavia OH
Cleveland Area Hospital Authority . . . . .Cleveland OK
Cleveland Clinic Children's Hospital For Rehabilitation . . . .Cleveland OH
Cleveland Clinic Florida Hospital . . . . .Naples FL
Cleveland Clinic Hospital . . . . .Weston FL

Cleveland Clinic Hospital . . . . .Cleveland OH
Cleveland Community Hospital . . . . .Cleveland TN
Cleveland Regional Medical Center . . . . .Shelby NC
Cleveland Regional Medical Center . . . . .Cleveland TX
Clifton Fine Hospital . . .Star Lake NY
Clifton Springs Hospital . . . . .Clifton Springs NY
Clifton T Perkins Center . .Jessup MD
Clinch Memorial Hospital . . . . .Homerville GA
Clinch Valley Medical Center . . . . .Richlands VA
Clinica Dr Perea, Inc . .Mayaguez PR
Clinica Dr Pila . . . . .Ponce PR
Clinica Espanola Inc . .Mayaguez PR
Clinica Oncologica . . . . . .Ponce PR
Clinton Correctional Facility . . . . .Dannemora NY
Clinton County Hospital . . .Albany KY
Clinton Hospital Association . . . . .Clinton MA
Clinton Memorial Hospital . . . . .Saint Johns MI
Clinton Memorial Hospital . . . . .Wilmington OH
Clinton Rehabilitation Hospital . . . . .Clinton LA
Cloud County Health Center . . . . .Concordia KS
Clovis Community Medical Center . . . . .Clovis CA
Coalinga Regional Medical Center . . . . .Coalinga CA
Coast Plaza Doctors Hospital . . . . .Norwalk CA
Coastal Communities Hospital . . . . .Santa Ana CA
Coastal Harbor Treatment Center . . . . .Savannah GA
Cobb Memorial Hospital . . . . .Royston GA
Cobre Valley Community Hospital . . . . .Globe AZ
Cochran Memorial Hospital . . . . .Morton TX
Coffee Medical Center . . . . .Manchester TN
Coffee Regional Medical Center . . . . .Douglas GA
Coffey County Hospital . . . . .Burlington KS
Coffeyville Regional Medical Center . . . . .Coffeyville KS
Coleman County Medical Center . . . . .Coleman TX
Coler Memorial Hospital . . . . .New York NY
Coler-Goldwater Specialty Hospital . . . . . . .New York NY

Coliseum Medical Centers . . . . .Macon GA
Coliseum Psychiatric Hospital . . . . .Macon GA
College Hospital . . . . . .Cerritos CA
College Hospital Costa Mesa . . . . .Costa Mesa CA
College Station Medical Center . . . . .College Station TX
Colleton Medical Center . . . . .Walterboro SC
Collingsworth General Hospital . . . . .Wellington TX
Colonel Florence A Blanchfield Army Community Hospital . . . . .Fort Campbell KY
Colorado Fayette Medical Center . . . . .Weimar TX
Colorado Mental Health Center at Fort Logan . . . . . .Denver CO
Colorado Mental Health Institute at Pueblo . . . . .Pueblo CO
Colorado Plains Medical Center . . . . .Fort Morgan CO
Colorado River Medical Center . . . . .Needles CA
Colquitt Regional Medical Center . . . . .Moultrie GA
Columbia Basin Hospital . . . . .Ephrata WA
Columbia Hospital . . . . .West Palm Beach FL
Columbia Hospital . . . .Milwaukee WI
Columbia Hospital For Women . . . . .Gaithersburg MD
Columbia Memorial Hospital . . . . .Hudson NY
Columbia Memorial Hospital . . . . .Astoria OR
Columbia Presbyterian Medical Center - New York State Psychiatric Institute . . . . .New York NY
Columbia Regional Hospital . . . . .Columbia MO
Columbus Community Hospital . . . . .Columbus NE
Columbus Community Hospital . . . . .Columbus TX
Columbus Community Hospital . . . . .Columbus WI
Columbus County Hospital . . . . .Whiteville NC
Columbus Hospital . . . . . .Chicago IL
Columbus Hospital . . . . . .Newark NJ
Columbus Regional Hospital . . . . .Columbus IN
Columbus Specialty Hospital . . . . .Columbus GA
Colusa Regional Medical Center . . . . .Colusa CA
Comanche Community Hospital . . . . .Comanche TX

Alphabetical Index

Comanche County Hospital . . . . .Coldwater KS
Comanche County Memorial Hospital . . . . .Lawton OK
Commonwealth Health Center . . . . .Saipan Mariana Islands MA
Community Care Hospital . . . . .New Orleans LA
Community General Hospital . . . . .Fort Fairfield ME
Community General Hospital . . . . .Syracuse NY
Community General Hospital . . . . .Dilley TX
Community General Osteopathic Hospital . . . . .Harrisburg PA
Community Health Center of Branch County . . . . .Coldwater MI
Community Health Partners - East . . . . .Lorain OH
Community Health Partners of Ohio . . . . .Lorain OH
Community Hospital . . . .Tallassee AL
Community Hospital . . . . .Grand Junction CO
Community Hospital . . .Watervliet MI
Community Hospital . . . .Mc Cook NE
Community Hospital and Health Center . . . . .Sioux Center IA
Community Hospital Association . . . . .Fairfax MO
Community Hospital Indianapolis . . . . .Indianapolis IN
Community Hospital Lakeview . . . . .Eufaula OK
Community Hospital Los Gatos . . . . .Los Gatos CA
Community Hospital North . . . . .Indianapolis IN
Community Hospital of Anaconda . . . . .Anaconda MT
Community Hospital of Anderson . . . . .Anderson IN
Community Hospital of Bremen . . . . .Bremen IN
Community Hospital of Gardena . . . . .Gardena CA
Community Hospital of Huntington Park . . . . .Huntington Park CA
Community Hospital of Lancaster . . . . .Lancaster PA
Community Hospital of Long Beach . . . . .Long Beach CA
Community Hospital of Monterey Peninsula . . . . .Monterey CA
Community Hospital of Munster . . . . .Munster IN
Community Hospital of New Port Richey . . . . .New Port Richey FL
Community Hospital of Ottawa . . . . .Ottawa IL
Community Hospital of San Bernardino . . . . .San Bernardino CA

Community Hospital of Springfield . . . . .Springfield OH
Community Hospital of Williams County - Bryan Hospital . . .Bryan OH
Community Hospital Onaga . . . . .Onaga KS
Community Hospital South . . . . .Indianapolis IN
Community Hospital-Dobbs Ferry . . . . .Dobbs Ferry NY
Community Hospital-Williams County - Montpelier Hospital . .Montpelier OH
Community Medical Center . . . . .Monmouth IL
Community Medical Center . . . . .Missoula MT
Community Medical Center . . . . .Falls City NE
Community Medical Center . . . . .Toms River NJ
Community Medical Center . . . . .Scranton PA
Community Medical Center - Fresno . . . . .Fresno CA
Community Medical Center of Izard County . . . . .Calico Rock AR
Community Memorial Health Care . . . . .Marysville KS
Community Memorial Health Center . . . . .South Hill VA
Community Memorial Hospital . . . . .Staunton IL
Community Memorial Hospital . . . . .Missouri Valley IA
Community Memorial Hospital . . . . .Sumner IA
Community Memorial Hospital . . . . .Cloquet MN
Community Memorial Hospital . . . . .Syracuse NE
Community Memorial Hospital . . . . .Hamilton NY
Community Memorial Hospital . . . . .Turtle Lake ND
Community Memorial Hospital . . . . .Hicksville OH
Community Memorial Hospital . . . . .Redfield SD
Community Memorial Hospital . . . . .Menomonee Falls WI
Community Memorial Hospital . . . . .Oconto Falls WI
Community Memorial Hospital - Rpch . . . . .Burke SD
Community Memorial Hospital of San Buenaventura . . . . .Ventura CA
Community Mental Health Center . . . . .Lawrenceburg IN
Community Rehabilitation Hospital of Coushatta . . . . .Coushatta LA
Community Rehabilitation of Lafayette . . . . .Lafayette LA

Compass Hospital of San Antonio . . . . .San Antonio TX
Concho County Hospital . . .Eden TX
Concord Hospital . . . . .Concord NH
Condell Medical Center . . . . .Libertyville IL
Conejos County Hospital . . . . .La Jara CO
Conemaugh Valley Memorial Hospital . . . . .Johnstown PA
Coney Island Hospital . .Brooklyn NY
Conifer Park . . . . .Glenville NY
Connecticut Childrens Medical Center . . . . .Hartford CT
Connecticut Department of Corrections Hospital . . . .Somers CT
Connecticut Hospice . . . .Branford CT
Connecticut Mental Health Center . . . . .New Haven CT
Connecticut Valley Hospital . . . . .Middletown CT
Conroe Regional Medical Center . . . . .Conroe TX
Continental Rehab Hospital of San Diego . . . . .San Diego CA
Continuing Care Hospital at Saint Joseph East . . . . .Lexington KY
Continuous Care Center of Tulsa . . . . .Tulsa OK
Contra Costa Regional Medical Center . . . . .Martinez CA
Convalescent Hospital For Children . . . . .Cincinnati OH
Conway Hospital . . . . . . .Conway SC
Conway Regional Medical Center . . . . .Conway AR
Cook Childrens Medical Center . . . . .Fort Worth TX
Cook Community Hospital . .Cook MN
Cook County Hospital . . . .Chicago IL
Cook County North Shore Hospital . . . . .Grand Marais MN
Cookeville Regional Hospital . . . . .Cookeville TN
Cooley Dickinson Hospital . . . . .Northampton MA
Coon Memorial Hospital and Home . . . . .Dalhart TX
Cooper County Memorial Hospital . . . . .Boonville MO
Cooper Green Hospital . . . . .Birmingham AL
Cooper Hospital/university Medical Center . . . . .Camden NJ
Cooperstown Medical Center . . . . .Cooperstown ND
Coosa Valley Baptist Medical Center . . . . .Sylacauga AL
Copley Hospital . . . . . .Morrisville VT
Copper Basin Medical Center . . . . .Copperhill TN
Copper Hills Youth Center . . . . .West Jordan UT

Alphabetical Index

Copper Queen Community Hospital . . . . .Bisbee AZ
Coquille Valley Hospital . . . . .Coquille OR
Coral Gables Hospital . . . . .Coral Gables FL
Coral Springs Medical Center . . . . .Coral Springs FL
Corcoran District Hospital . . . . .Corcoran CA
Cordell Memorial Hospital . . . . .Cordell OK
Cordilleras Mental Health Rehabilitation Center . . . . .Redwood City CA
Cordova Community Medical Center . . . . .Cordova AK
Cornerstone Hospital of Austin . . . . .Austin TX
Cornerstone Hospital of Austin . . . . .Austin TX
Cornerstone Hospital of Houston . . . . .Houston TX
Cornerstone Hospital of Houston . . . . .Webster TX
Cornerstone Hospital of North Louisiana . . . . . . .West Monroe LA
Cornerstone of Medical Arts Center Hospital . . . . .New York NY
Cornerstone Regional Hospital . . . . .Edinburg TX
Cornerstone Rehabilitation . . . . .Edinburg TX
Cornerstone-Grant-Blackford Mental Health . . . . .Marion IN
Corning Hospital . . . . . . .Corning NY
Cornwall Hospital . . . . . .Cornwall NY
Corona Regional Medical Center . . . . .Corona CA
Corona Regional Medical Center-Rehab . . . . .Corona CA
Corpus Christi Medical Center . . . . .Corpus Christi TX
Corpus Christi Medical Center - Bay Area . . . . .Corpus Christi TX
Corpus Christi Medical Center - Heart Hospital . . . . .Corpus Christi TX
Corpus Christi Warm Springs Rehab Hospital . . . . .Corpus Christi TX
Corry Memorial Hospital . . .Corry PA
Cortland Memorial Hospital . . . . .Cortland NY
Coryell Memorial Hospital . . . . .Gatesville TX
Coshocton County Memorial Hospital . . . . .Coshocton OH
Coteau Des Prairies Hospital . . . . .Sisseton SD
Cottage Grove Community Hospital . . . . . . .Cottage Grove OR
Cottage Hospital . . . . .Woodsville NH
Cottonwood Hospital . . . . .Salt Lake City UT

Coulee Community Hospital . . . . .Grand Coulee WA
Council Community Hospital . . . . .Council ID
Cove Forge Behavioral Helath System . . . . .Williamsburg PA
Covenant Childrens Hospital . . . . .Lubbock TX
Covenant Health Care System . . . . .Saginaw MI
Covenant Hospital Levelland . . . . .Levelland TX
Covenant Hospital Plainview . . . . .Plainview TX
Covenant Lakeside Medical Center . . . . .Lubbock TX
Covenant Medical Center . . . . .Waterloo IA
Covenant Medical Center . . . . .Lubbock TX
Covenant Medical Center - Michigan . . . . .Saginaw MI
Covington County Hospital . . . . .Collins MS
Cox-Monett Hospital . . . . .Monett MO
Cozad Community Hospital Cozad NE
Cozby Germany Hospital . . . . .Grand Saline TX
Craig General Hospital . . . .Vinita OK
Craig Hospital . . . . . .Englewood CO
Crane Memorial Hospital . .Crane TX
Craven Regional Medical Center . . . . .New Bern NC
Crawford County Memorial Hospital . . . . .Van Buren AR
Crawford County Memorial Hospital . . . . .Denison IA
Crawford Long Hospital . .Atlanta GA
Crawford Memorial Hospital . . . . .Robinson IL
Crawley Memorial Hospital . . . . .Boiling Springs NC
Creedmoor Psychiatric Center . . . . .Jamaica NY
Creedmoor Psychiatric Center . . . . . . .Queens Village NY
Creighton Area Health Services . . . . .Creighton NE
Creighton University Medical Center . . . . .Omaha NE
Crenshaw Baptist Hospital . . . . .Luverne AL
Cresta Loma Mental Health Center . . . . .Lemon Grove CA
Crestwood Medical Center . . . . .Huntsville AL
Crete Municipal Hospital . . .Crete NE
Crisp Regional Hospital . .Cordele GA
Crittenden County Hospital . . . . .Marion KY
Crittenden Memorial Hospital . . . . .West Memphis AR
Crittenton Center . . .Kansas City MO

Crittenton Hospital . . . .Rochester MI
Crockett Hosptial . .Lawrenceburg TN
Crook County Memorial Hospital . . . . .Sundance WY
Crosby Memorial Hospital . . . . .Picayune MS
Crosbyton Clinic Hospital . . . . .Crosbyton TX
Crossridge Community Hospital . . . . .Wynne AR
Crossroad Regional Hospital . . . . .Alexandria LA
Crossroads Community Hospital . . . . .Mount Vernon IL
Crossroads Regional Hospital . . . . .Wentzville MO
Crouse-Irving Memorial Hospital . . . . .Syracuse NY
Crownsville Hospital Center . . . . .Crownsville MD
Crozer Chester Medical Center . . . . .Chester PA
Cuba Memorial Hospital . . .Cuba NY
Cuero Community Hospital . . . . .Cuero TX
Culberson County Hospital District . . . . .Van Horn TX
Cullman Regional Medical Center . . . . .Cullman AL
Culpeper Memorial Hospital . . . . .Culpeper VA
Cumberland County Hospital . . . . .Burkesville KY
Cumberland Hospital For Children/adolescents . .New Kent VA
Cumberland Medical Center . . . . .Crossville TN
Cumberland Memorial Hospital . . . . .Cumberland WI
Cumberland River Hospital . . . . .Celina TN
Curry General Hospital . . . . .Gold Beach OR
Cushing Memorial Hospital . . . . .Leavenworth KS
Cushing Municipal Hospital . . . . .Cushing OK
Custer Community Hospital . . . . .Custer SD
Cuyahoga Falls General Hospital . . . . . .Cuyahoga Falls OH
Cuyuna Regional Medical Center . . . . .Crosby MN
Cypress Creek Hospital . .Houston TX
Cypress Fairbanks Medical Center Hospital . . . . .Houston TX
D M Cogdell Memorial Hospital . . . . .Snyder TX
D W Mcmillan Memorial Hospital . . . . .Brewton AL
Dahl Memorial Maf . . . . .Ekalaka MT
Dakota Plains Surgical Center . . . . .Aberdeen SD

186

Alphabetical Index

Dale Medical Center . . . . . .Ozark AL
Dallas County Hospital . .Fordyce AR
Dallas County Hospital . . . . .Perry IA
Dallas Southwest Medical Center
. . . . .Dallas TX
Dameron Hospital Association
. . . . .Stockton CA
Dana-Farber Cancer Institute
. . . . .Boston MA
Danbury Hospital . . . . . .Danbury CT
Daniel Freeman Marina Hospital
. . . . .Marina Del Rey CA
Daniel Freeman Memorial Hospital
. . . . .Inglewood CA
Daniels Memorial Hospital
. . . . .Scobey MT
Danville Regional Medica
Center . . . . .Danville VA
Danville State Hospital . . .Danville PA
Dardanelle Hospital . .Dardanelle AR
Darnall Army Community
Hospital . . . . .Fort Hood TX
Dartmouth Hitchcock Medical
Center . . . . .Lebanon NH
Dauterive Hospital . . . .New Iberia LA
Davenport Memorial Hospital
. . . . .Bath NY
Davie County Hospital
. . . . .Mocksville NC
Daviess County Hospital
. . . . .Washington IN
Davis County Hospital . .Bloomfield IA
Davis Hospital and Medical
Center . . . . .Layton UT
Davis Memorial Hospital . .Elkins WV
Davis Regional Medical Center
. . . . .Statesville NC
Day Kimball Hospital . . . .Putnam CT
Daystar . . . . . . .Fort Lauderdale FL
Dayton General Hospital
. . . . .Dayton WA
Dayton Heart Hospital . . .Dayton OH
Dch Regional Medical Center
. . . . .Tuscaloosa AL
De Jarnette Center . . . . .Staunton VA
De Paul Center . . . . .Waco TX
De Paul Hospital . . . . .Cheyenne WY
De Paul Tulane Behavioral Health
Center . . . . .New Orleans LA
De Poo Hospital . . . . . .Key West FL
De Queen Regional Medical
Center . . . . .De Queen AR
Deaconess - Nashoba Hospital
. . . . .Ayer MA
Deaconess Cross Pointe Center
. . . . .Evansville IN
Deaconess Hospital . . .Evansville IN
Deaconess Hospital . . . . .Billings MT
Deaconess Hospital . . .Cincinnati OH
Deaconess Hospital . . .Cleveland OH
Deaconess Hospital
. . . . .Oklahoma City OK

Deaconess Medical Center
. . . . .Spokane WA
Deaconess-Glover Hospital
. . . . .Needham MA
Dearborn County Hospital
. . . . .Lawrenceburg IN
Deborah Heart and Lung
Center . . . . .Browns Mills NJ
Decatur County General
Hospital . . . . .Parsons TN
Decatur County Hospital . . . .Leon IA
Decatur County Hospital . .Oberlin KS
Decatur County Memorial Hospital
. . . . .Greensburg IN
Decatur General Hospital
. . . . .Decatur AL
Decatur General Hospital -
West . . . . .Decatur AL
Decatur Hospital . . . . . . .Decatur GA
Decatur Memorial Hospital
. . . . .Decatur IL
Deckerville Community Hospital
. . . . .Deckerville MI
Deer Park Health Center and
Hospital . . . . .Deer Park WA
Deer River Healthcare Center
. . . . .Deer River MN
Deers Head Center . . . .Salisbury MD
Defiance Hospital . . . . .Defiance OH
Degraff Memorial Hospital
. . . . .North Tonawanda NY
Dekalb Medical Center . .Decatur GA
Dekalb Memorial Hospital
. . . . .Auburn IN
Del Amo Hospital . . . . . .Torrance CA
Del E Webb Memorial Hospital
. . . . .Sun City West AZ
Del Maestro Hospital . .San Juan PR
Del Sol Medical Center . .El Paso TX
Del Sol Rehabilitation Hospital
. . . . .El Paso TX
Delano Regional Medical
Center . . . . .Delano CA
Delaware County Memorial
Hospital . . . . .Drexel Hill PA
Delaware Hospital-Chronically Ill
. . . . .Smyrna DE
Delaware Psychiatric Center
. . . . .New Castle DE
Delaware Valley Hospital
. . . . .Walton NY
Deleon Hospital . . . . . . .De Leon TX
Dells Area Health Center
. . . . .Dell Rapids SD
Delnor Community Hospital
. . . . .Geneva IL
Delray Medical Hospital
. . . . .Delray Beach FL
Delta Community Medical Center
. . . . .Delta UT
Delta County Memorial Hospital
. . . . .Delta CO
Delta Medical Center . . .Memphis TN

Delta Memorial Hospital . .Dumas AR
Delta Memorial Hospital . .Antioch CA
Delta Regional Medical Center
. . . . .Greenville MS
Denton Community Hospital
. . . . .Denton TX
Denton Regional Medical Center
. . . . .Denton TX
Denver Health Medical Center
. . . . .Denver CO
Depaul Health Center
. . . . .Bridgeton MO
Dequincy Memorial Hospital
. . . . .Dequincy LA
Des Peres Hospital . .Saint Louis MO
Desert Hills Hospital
. . . . .Albuquerque NM
Desert Regional Medica
Center . . . . .Palm Springs CA
Desert Samaritan Medical
Center . . . . .Mesa AZ
Desert Springs Hospital
. . . . .Las Vegas NV
Desert Springs Medical Center
. . . . .Midland TX
Desert Valley Hospital . .Victorville CA
Desmet Memorial Hospital
. . . . .De Smet SD
Desoto Memorial Hospital
. . . . .Arcadia FL
Desoto Regional Health System
. . . . .Mansfield LA
Detar Hospital . . . . .Victoria TX
Detar Hospital - North . . . .Victoria TX
Detroit Receiving Hospital and
University Health Center . . .Detroit MI
Dettmer Hospital . . . . .Troy OH
Deuel County Memorial Hospital -
Rpch . . . . .Clear Lake SD
Devereux Children's Behavioral
Health Center . . . . .Malvern PA
Devereux Georgia Treatment
Network . . . . .Kennesaw GA
Devereux Hospital and Children
Center . . . . .Viera FL
Devereux Texas Treatment
Network . . . . .League City TX
Devonshire Care Center . .Hemet CA
Dewitt Army Community
Hospital . . . . .Fort Belvoir VA
Dewitt Community Hospital
. . . . .De Witt IA
Dewitt Hospital and Nursing
Home . . . . .De Witt AR
Dickenson County Medical
Center . . . . .Fort Lauderdale FL
Dickerson Memorial Hospital
. . . . .Jasper TX
Dickinson County Memorial
Hospital . . . . .Iron Mountain MI
Dimmit County Memorial Hospital
. . . . .Carrizo Springs TX

Alphabetical Index

District Memorial Hospital of Southwest North Carolina . . . . Murphy NC

District of Columbia General Hospital . . . . Washington DC

Divine Providence Health Center . . . . Ivanhoe MN

Divine Providence Hospital . . . . Williamsport PA

Divine Savior Hospital . . . Portage WI

Dixie Regional Medical Center . . . . Saint George UT

Dixon Medical Center . . Covington LA

Dixon Medical Center . . . . Denham Springs LA

Doctors Center Hospital . . Manati PR

Doctors Community Hospital . . . . Lanham MD

Doctors Hospital . . . . . Montclair CA

Doctors Hospital . . . . . . Augusta GA

Doctors Hospital . . . . Columbus GA

Doctors Hospital . . . . . Springfield IL

Doctors Hospital . . . . . Santurce PR

Doctors Hospital . . . . Dallas TX

Doctors Hospital . . . . Groves TX

Doctors Hospital . . . New Boston TX

Doctors Hospital - Parkway . . . . Houston TX

Doctors Hospital - Tidwell . . . . Houston TX

Doctors Hospital of Jackson . . . . Jackson MI

Doctors Hospital of Jefferson . . . . Metairie LA

Doctors Hospital of Laredo . . . . Laredo TX

Doctors Hospital of Manteca . . . . Manteca CA

Doctors Hospital of Nelsonville . . . . Nelsonville OH

Doctors Hospital of Opelousas . . . . Opelousas LA

Doctors Hospital of Sarasota . . . . Sarasota FL

Doctors Hospital of Shreveport . . . . Shreveport LA

Doctors Hospital of Springfield . . . . Springfield MO

Doctors Hospital of Stark County . . . . Massillon OH

Doctors Hospital of West Covina . . . . West Covina CA

Doctors Hospital West/ohio Health . . . . Columbus OH

Doctors Hospital/ohio Health . . . . Columbus OH

Doctors Medical Center . . . . Modesto CA

Doctors Medical Center Pinole Campus . . . . Pinole CA

Doctors Medical Center San Pablo Campus . . . . San Pablo CA

Doctors Memorial Hospital . . . . Bonifay FL

Doctors Memorial Hospital . . Perry FL

Doctors Specialty Hospital . . . . Leawood KS

Dodge County Hospital . . . . Eastman GA

Dolly Vinsant Memorial Hospital . . . . San Benito TX

Dominican Hospital . . Santa Cruz CA

Dominion Hospital . . Falls Church VA

Donalsonville Hospital . . . . Donalsonville GA

Door County Memorial Hospital . . . . Sturgeon Bay WI

Dorchester General Hospital . . . . Cambridge MD

Dorminy Medical Center . . . . Fitzgerald GA

Dorothea Dix Hospital . . . Raleigh NC

Dos Palos Memorial Hospital . . . . Dos Palos CA

Douglas County Hospital . . . . Alexandria MN

Douglas County Hospital . . . . Omaha NE

Douglas County Memorial Hospital-Rpch . . . . Armour SD

Down East Community Hospital . . . . Machias ME

Downey Regional Medical Center . . . . Downey CA

Doylestown Hospital . . Doylestown PA

Dr Ramon Emeterio Betances . . . . Mayaguez PR

Dr Alejandro Otero Lopez Hospital . . . . Manati PR

Dr Harry Solomon Mhc . . . Lowell MA

Dr I Gonzalez Martinez Oncology Hospital . . . . San Juan PR

Dr John C Corrigan Mental Health Center . . . . Fall River MA

Dr John Warner Hospital . . . Clinton IL

Dr Solomon Carter Fuller M H Center . . . . Boston MA

Drake Center . . . . Cincinnati OH

Drew Memorial Hospital . . . . Monticello AR

Driscoll Childrens Hospital . . . . Corpus Christi TX

Duane L Waters Hospital . . . . Jackson MI

Dubois Regional Medical Center . . . . Dubois PA

Dubuis Continuing Care - Lake Charles . . . . Lake Charles LA

Dubuis Hospital - Beaumont . . . . Beaumont TX

Dubuis Hospital - Continuing Care . . . . Shreveport LA

Dubuis Hospital - Port Arthur . . . . Port Arthur TX

Dubuis Hospital - Texarkana . . . . Texarkana TX

Dubuis Hospital at Houston . . . . Houston TX

Dubuis Hospital For Continuing Care . . . . Alexandria LA

Duke University Hospital . . . . Durham NC

Dukes Memorial Hospital . . . . Peru IN

Duncan Regional Hospital . . . . Duncan OK

Dundy County Hospital . . . . Benkelman NE

Dunlap Memorial Hospital . . . . Orrville OH

Dunn Memorial Hospital . . Bedford IN

Duplin General Hospital . . . . Kenansville NC

Dupont Hospital . . . . . Fort Wayne IN

Durham Regional Hospital . . . . Durham NC

Dwight David Eisenhower Army Medical Center . . . . . Fort Gordon GA

E J Noble-Gouverneur . . . . Gouverneur NY

Eagle Pass Health Center . . . . Eagle Pass TX

Eagle River Memorial Hospital . . . . Eagle River WI

Eagleville Hospital . . . . . Eagleville PA

Earl K Long Medical Center . . . . Baton Rouge LA

Early Memorial Hospital . . Blakely GA

East Adams Rural Hospital . . . . Ritzville WA

East Alabama Medical Center . . . . Opelika AL

East Carroll Parish Hospital . . . . Lake Providence LA

East Central Regional Hospital . . . . Augusta GA

East Cooper Regional Medical Center . . Mount Pleasant SC

East Georgia Regional Hospital . . . . Statesboro GA

East Houston Medical Center . . . . Houston TX

East Jefferson General Hospital . . . . Metairie LA

East Liverpool City Hospital . . . . East Liverpool OH

East Los Angeles Doctors Hospital . . . . Los Angeles CA

East Louisiana Mental Health System . . . . Jackson LA

East Mississippi State Hospital . . . . Meridian MS

East Morgan County Hospital . . . . Brush CO

East Ohio Regional Hospital . . . . Martins Ferry OH

East Orange General Hospital . . . . East Orange NJ

Alphabetical Index

East Pasco Medical Center
.................Zephyrhills FL
East Ridge Hospital
.............Chattanooga TN
East Tennessee Childrens
Hospital ....Knoxville TN
East Texas Medical Center
...................Fairfield TX
East Texas Medical Center
...................Mineola TX
East Texas Medical Center ..Tyler TX
East Texas Medical Center -
Clarksville ....Clarksville TX
East Texas Medical Center
Athens ....Athens TX
East Texas Medical Center
Crockett ....Crockett TX
East Texas Medical Center
Jacksonville ....Rusk TX
East Texas Medical Center Mount
Vernon ....Mount Vernon TX
East Texas Medical Center
Pittsburg ....Pittsburg TX
East Texas Medical Center
Quitman ....Quitman TX
East Texas Medical Center
Rehabilitation Center ......Tyler TX
East Texas Medical Center Specialty
Hospital ....Tyler TX
East Texas Medical Center
Trinity ....Trinity TX
East Texas Medical Center-
Behavioral Health Center ...Tyler TX
East Texas Medical Center-
Carthage ....Carthage TX
East Valley Hospital Medical
Center ....Glendora CA
Eastern Idaho Regional Medical
Center ....Idaho Falls ID
Eastern Long Island Hospital
..................Greenport NY
Eastern Maine Medical Cente
..................Bangor ME
Eastern Neuro Rehabilitation
Hospital ....Rockville MD
Eastern New Mexico Medical
Center ....Roswell NM
Eastern Oklahoma Medical
Center ....Poteau OK
Eastern Oregon Psychiatric
Center ....Pendleton OR
Eastern Ozarks Regional Health
System ......Cherokee Village AR
Eastern Pennsylvania Psych
Institute ....Philadelphia PA
Eastern Plumas Health Care
....................Portola CA
Eastern Shore Hospital Center
.................Cambridge MD
Eastern State Hospital
................Lexington KY
Eastern State Hospital ....Vinita OK

Eastern State Hospital
...............Williamsburg VA
Eastern State Hospital
.............Medical Lake WA
Eastland Memorial Hospital
...................Eastland TX
Eastmoreland Hospital ..Portland OR
Easton Hospital ....Easton PA
Eastside Psychiatric Hospital
.................Tallahassee FL
Eaton Rapids Community
Hospital ....Eaton Rapids MI
Ed Fraser Memorial Hospital and
Baker Community Health Center
.................MacClenny FL
Eddy Cohoes Rehabilitation
Center ....Cohoes NY
Eden Medical Center
.................Castro Valley CA
Edgefield County Hospital
...................Edgefield SC
Edgewater Psychiatric
Center ....Harrisburg PA
Edinburg Regional Medical
Center ....Edinburg TX
Edmond Hospital ......Edmond OK
Edward A Utlaut Memorial
Hospital ....Greenville IL
Edward Hospital ......Naperville IL
Edward Mccready Memorial
Hospital ....Crisfield MD
Edward W Sparrow Hospital
..................Lansing MI
Edward White Hospital
.............Saint Petersburg FL
Edwards County Hospital
...................Kinsley KS
Edwin Shaw Hospital .....Akron OH
Effingham County Hospital
.................Springfield GA
81st Medical Group, Keesler Medical
Center ...Keesler Air Force Base MS
89th Medical Group, Malcolm Grow
U.S. Air Force Medical Center
......Andrews Air Force Base MD
82nd Medical Group
......Sheppard Air Force Base TX
Eisenhower Medical Center
.............Rancho Mirage CA
El Camino Hospital
.............Mountain View CA
El Campo Memorial Hospital
...................El Campo TX
El Centro Regional Medical
Center ....El Centro CA
El Dorado Hospital .....Tucson AZ
El Paso Psychiatric Center
...................El Paso TX
El Paso Specialty Hospital
...................El Paso TX
Elastar Community Hospital
.................Los Angeles CA
Elba General Hospital .....Elba AL

Elbert Memorial Hospital
...................Elberton GA
Eleah Medical Center
.................Elbow Lake MN
Eleanor Slater Hospital ..Cranston RI
Electra Memorial Hospital
...................Electra TX
Elgin Mental Health Center ..Elgin IL
Eliza Coffee Memorial Hospital
...................Florence AL
Eliza Coffee Memorial Hospital -
East ....Florence AL
Elizabethtown Community
Hospital ....Elizabethtown NY
Elk County Regional Medical
Center ....Ridgway PA
Elk Regional Health Center
.................Saint Marys PA
Elkhart General Hospital ..Elkhart IN
Elkins Park Hospital ..Elkins Park PA
Elkview General Hospital
...................Hobart OK
Ellenville Regional Hospital
.................Ellenville NY
Ellett Memorial Hospital
.............Appleton City MO
Ellinwood District Hospital
...................Ellinwood KS
Elliot Hospital .....Manchester NH
Ellis Fischel Health Clinic
...................Columbia MO
Ellis Hospital ......Schenectady NY
Ellsworth County Hospital
...................Ellsworth KS
Ellsworth Municipal Hospital
...................Iowa Falls IA
Ellwood City Hospital
.................Ellwood City PA
Elmbrook Memorial Hospital
...................Brookfield WI
Elmhurst Hospital Center
...................Elmhurst NY
Elmhurst Memorial Hospital
...................Elmhurst IL
Elmira Psych Center .....Elmira NY
Elmore Community Hospital
...................Wetumpka AL
Elmore Memorial Hospital
.................Mountain Home ID
Ely Bloomenson Community
Hospital ....Ely MN
Emanuel County Hospital
...................Swainsboro GA
Emanuel Medical Center
...................Turlock CA
Emerald - Hodgson Hospital
...................Sewanee TN
Emerson Hospital .....Concord MA
Emh Regional Medical Center
...................Elyria OH
Emma Pendleton Bradley
Hospital ....Riverside RI

Alphabetical Index

Emory Cartersville Medical
Center . . . . .Cartersville GA
Emory Dunwoody Medical
Center . . . . .Atlanta GA
Emory Eastside Medical Center
. . . . .Snellville GA
Emory Northlake Regional Medical
Center . . . . .Tucker GA
Emory University Hospital
. . . . .Atlanta GA
Emory-adventist Hospital
. . . . .Smyrna GA
Emporia Surgical Hospital
. . . . .Emporia KS
Encino-Tarzana Regional Medical
Center . . . . .Encino CA
Encino-Tarzana Regional Medical
Center . . . . Tarzana CA
Endless Mountain Health System
. . . . .Montrose PA
Englewood Community Hospital
. . . . .Englewood FL
Englewood Hospital and Medical
Center . . . . .Englewood NJ
Enloe Medical Center-Cohasset
. . . . .Chico CA
Enloe Medical Center-Esplanade
. . . . .Chico CA
Enloe Rehabilitation Center
. . . . .Chico CA
Ennis Regional Medical Center
. . . . .Ennis TX
Enumclaw Community Hospital
. . . . .Enumclaw WA
Ephraim Mcdowell Regional Medical
Center . . . . .Danville KY
Ephrata Community Hospital
. . . . .Ephrata PA
Erich Lindemann Mental Health
Center . . . . .Boston MA
Erie County Medical Center
. . . . .Buffalo NY
Erlanger Medical Center
. . . . .Chattanooga TN
Erlanger North Health
System/hospital . . . .Chattanooga TN
Espanola Medical Center
. . . . .Espanola NM
Essex County Hospital Center
. . . . .Cedar Grove NJ
Estes Park Medical Center
. . . . .Estes Park CO
Euclid Hospital . . . . .Euclid OH
Eugene Dupont Memorial Division
Hospital . . . . .Wilmington DE
Eugenia Hospital . . .Lafayette Hill PA
Eunice Community Medical
Center . . . . .Eunice LA
Eureka Community Hospital
. . . . .Eureka IL
Eureka Community Hospital -
Rpch . . . . .Eureka SD

Eureka Springs Hospital
. . . . .Eureka Springs AR
Evangelical Community Hospital
. . . . .Lewisburg PA
Evans Army Community
Hospital . . . . .Fort Carson CO
Evans Memorial Hospital
. . . . .Claxton GA
Evanston Hospital . . . . . .Evanston IL
Evanston Northwestern Health Care
and Glenbrook Hospital . .Glenview IL
Evanston Regional Hospital
. . . . .Evanston WY
Evansville State Hospital
. . . . .Evansville IN
Eveleth Health Services
. . . . .Eveleth MN
Evergreen Adult Center
. . . . .Cuba City WI
Evergreen Hospital Medical
Center . . . . .Kirkland WA
Evergreen Medical Center
. . . . .Evergreen AL
Excelsior Springs Medical
Center . . . . . .Excelsior Springs MO
Exempla Healthcare Saint Joseph
Hospital . . . . .Denver CO
Exempla Lutheran Medical
Center . . . . .Wheat Ridge CO
Exempla West Pines at Lutheran
Medical Center . . . .Wheat Ridge CO
Exeter Hospital . . . . .Exeter NH
Extended Care of Southwest
Louisiana . . . . .Lake Charles LA
Eye and Ear Clinic of Charleston
. . . . .Charleston WV
Fair Oaks Hospital . .Delray Beach FL
Fairbanks Hospital . . .Indianapolis IN
Fairbanks Memorial Hospital
. . . . .Fairbanks AK
Fairchild Medical Center . . .Yreka CA
Fairfax Hospital . . . . . .Kirkland WA
Fairfax Memorial Hospital
. . . . .Fairfax OK
Fairfield Medical Center
. . . . .Lancaster OH
Fairfield Memorial Hospital
. . . . .Fairfield IL
Fairfield Memorial Hospital
. . . . .Winnsboro SC
Fairlawn Rehabilitation Hospital
. . . . .Worcester MA
Fairmont Community Hospital
. . . . .Fairmont MN
Fairmont General Hospital
. . . . .Fairmont WV
Fairmount Behavioral Health
System . . . . .Philadelphia PA
Fairview Developmental Center
. . . . .Costa Mesa CA
Fairview General Hospital
. . . . .Cleveland OH

Fairview Hospital
. . . . .Great Barrington MA
Fairview Hospital . . . . .Fairview OK
Fairview Lake Regional Medical
Center . . . . .Chisago City MN
Fairview Lakes Regional Medical
Center . . . . .Wyoming MN
Fairview Northland Regional
Hospital . . . . .Princeton MN
Fairview Park Hospital . . . .Dublin GA
Fairview Redwing Hospital
. . . . .Red Wing MN
Fairview Ridges Hospital
. . . . .Burnsville MN
Fairview Riverside Hospital
. . . . .Minneapolis MN
Fairview Southdale Hospital
. . . . .Edina MN
Fairview University Medical
Center . . . . .Minneapolis MN
Fairview University Medical Center-
Mesabi . . . . .Hibbing MN
Faith Community Hospital
. . . . .Jacksboro TX
Faith Regional Health Services -
West Campus . . . . .Norfolk NE
Faith Regional Hospital . . .Norfolk NE
Fall River Hospital . . .Hot Springs SD
Fallbrook Hospital . . . . .Fallbrook CA
Fallon County Medical
Complex . . . . .Baker MT
Falls Community Hospital
and Clinic . . . . .Marlin TX
Falls Memorial Hospital
. . . . .International Falls MN
Falmouth Hospital . . . . .Falmouth MA
Family Health West - Rpch
. . . . .Fruita CO
Fannin Regional Hospital
. . . . .Blue Ridge GA
Faulk County Memorial Hospital
. . . . .Faulkton SD
Faulkner Hospital . . . . . .Boston MA
Fauquier Hospital . . . . .Warrenton VA
Fawcett Memorial Hospital
. . . . .Port Charlotte FL
Faxton - Saint Luke's
Healthcare . . . . .Utica NY
Fayette Community Hospital
. . . . .Fayetteville GA
Fayette County Hospital . .Vandalia IL
Fayette County Memorial Hospital
. . . . . .Washington Court House OH
Fayette Medical Center and Long
Term Care Unit . . . . .Fayette AL
Fayette Memorial Hospital
. . . . .La Grange TX
Fayette Memorial Hospital
Association . . . . .Connersville IN
Fayetteville City Hospital and
Geriatric Center . . . . .Fayetteville AR
Fayetteville Specialty Hospital
. . . . .Fayetteville NC

Alphabetical Index

Feather River Hospital . .Paradise CA
Federal Medical Center -
Butner . . . . .Butner NC
Federal Medical Center -
Carswell . . . . .Fort Worth TX
Federal Medical Center - Devens
. . . . .Devens MA
Federal Medical Center - Fort
Worth . . . . .Fort Worth TX
Federal Medical Center -
Lexington . . . . .Lexington KY
Federal Medical Center -
Rochester . . . . .Rochester MN
Fergus Falls Regional Treatment
Center . . . . .Fergus Falls MN
Ferrell Hospital . . . . . . .Eldorado IL
Ferry County Memorial Hospital
. . . . .Republic WA
Fhc Cumberland Hall
. . . . .Hopkinsville KY
Fhc Cumberland Hall Psychiatric
Hospital . . . . .Chattanooga TN
Field Memorial Community
Hospital . . . . .Centreville MS
Fieldstone Center . . .Battle Creek MI
5th Medical Group
. . . . .Minot Air Force Base ND
55th Medical Group, Ehrling Bergquist
Hospital . . .Offutt Air Force Base NE
59th Medical Wing, Wilford Hall
Medical Center
. . . . . . .Lackland Air Force Base TX
56th Medical Grou
. . . . .Luke Air Force Base AZ
Fillmore Community Medica
Center . . . . .Fillmore UT
Fillmore County Hospital
. . . . .Geneva NE
Finley Hospital . . . . . . .Dubuque IA
Firelands Regional Medical
Center . . . . .Sandusky OH
Firelands Regional Medical Center -
South . . . . .Sandusky OH
First Care Health Center
. . . . .Park River ND
First Care Medical Services
. . . . .Fosston MN
First Hospital Panamericano
. . . . .Cidra PR
First Hospital Wyoming Valley
. . . . .Kingston PA
1st Medical Group
. . . . . . .Langley Air Force Base VA
Firsthealth Montgomery Memorial
Hospital . . . . .Troy NC
Firsthealth of North Carolina Moore
Regional Hospital . . . . .Pinehurst NC
Fisher County Hospital District
. . . . .Rotan TX
Fisher Titus Memorial Hospital
. . . . .Norwalk OH
Fishermens Hospital . . .Marathon FL

Five Counties Hospital - Rpch
. . . . .Lemmon SD
509th Medical Group
. . . . . .Whiteman Air Force Base MO
Flaget Memorial Hospital
. . . . .Bardstown KY
Flagler Hospital West
. . . . .Saint Augustine FL
Flagler Psychiatric Center
. . . . .Saint Augustine FL
Flagstaff Medical Center
. . . . .Flagstaff AZ
Flambeau Hospital . . . .Park Falls WI
Flandreau Municipal Hospital
. . . . .Flandreau SD
Fleming County Hospital
. . . . .Flemingsburg KY
Fletcher Allen Health Care
. . . . .Burlington VT
Fletcher Allen Hospital-Fanny Allen
Campus . . . . .Colchester VT
Flint River Community Hospital
. . . . .Montezuma GA
Florala Memorial Hospital .Florala AL
Florida Hospital Altamonte
. . . . .Altamonte Springs FL
Florida Hospital Apopka . .Apopka FL
Florida Hospital Celebration
Health . . . . .Celebration FL
Florida Hospital Deland . . .Deland FL
Florida Hospital East Orlando
. . . . .Orlando FL
Florida Hospital Fish Memorial Orange
City FL
Florida Hospital Heartland Medical
Center . . . . .Sebring FL
Florida Hospital Kissimee
. . . . .Kissimmee FL
Florida Hospital Lake Placid
. . . . .Lake Placid FL
Florida Hospital Oceanside
. . . . .Ormond Beach FL
Florida Hospital Orlando .Orlando FL
Florida Hospital Ormond
Beach . . . . .Ormond Beach FL
Florida Hospital Waterman
. . . . .Eustis FL
Florida Hospital Wauchula
. . . . .Wauchula FL
Florida Hosptial Flagler
. . . . .Palm Coast FL
Florida Medical Center
. . . . .Fort Lauderdale FL
Florida State Hospital
. . . . .Chattahoochee FL
Flower Hospital . . . . . .Sylvania OH
Flowers Hospital . . . . . . .Dothan AL
Floyd County Memorial
Hospital . . . . .Charles City IA
Floyd Medical Center . . . . .Rome GA
Floyd Memorial Hospital and Health
Services . . . . .New Albany IN
Floyd Valley Hospital . . . .Le Mars IA

Flushing Hospital Medical
Center . . . . .Flushing NY
Focus By-the-Sea
. . . . .Saint Simons Island GA
Focus Health Care of Ohio
. . . . .Maumee OH
Fond Du Lac Health Care Center
. . . . .Fond Du Lac WI
Font Martello Hospital . .Humacao PR
Foote Health System . . . .Jackson MI
Foothill Presbyterian Hospital
. . . . .Glendora CA
Forbes Regional Hospital
. . . . .Monroeville PA
Forest Health Medical Center
. . . . .Ypsilanti MI
Forest View Hospital
. . . . .Grand Rapids MI
Forks Community Hospital
. . . . .Forks WA
Forrest General Hospital
. . . . .Hattiesburg MS
Forsyth Medical Center
. . . . .Winston-Salem NC
Fort Atkinson Memorial Health
Services . . . . .Fort Atkinson WI
Fort Duncan Medical Center
. . . . .Eagle Pass TX
Fort Hamilton Hospital . .Hamilton OH
Fort Lauderdale Hospital
. . . . .Fort Lauderdale FL
Fort Logan Hospital . . . .Stanford KY
Fort Madison Community
Hospital . . . . .Fort Madison IA
Fort Sanders Loudon Medical
Center . . . . .Loudon TN
Fort Sanders Park West Medical
Center . . . . .Knoxville TN
Fort Sanders Regional Medical
Center . . . . .Knoxville TN
Fort Sanders Sevier Medical
Center . . . . .Sevierville TN
Fort Walton Beach Medical
Center . . . . . .Fort Walton Beach FL
Fort Washington Medical Center
. . . . .Fort Washington MD
49th Medical Group
. . . . . .Holloman Air Force Base NM
47th Medical Group
. . . . .Laughlin Air Force Base TX
Fostoria City Hospital . . .Fostoria OH
Foundations Behavioral Health
. . . . .Doylestown PA
Fountain Valley Regional
Hospital . . . . . . .Fountain Valley CA
Four County Counseling
Center . . . . .Logansport IN
Four Winds . . . . .Katonah NY
Four Winds . . . .Saratoga Springs NY
Four Winds Hospital . . .Syracuse NY
4th Medical Group, Thomas Koritz
Hospital
Seymour Johnson Air Force Base NC

Alphabetical Index

Fox Chase Cancer Center . . . . .Philadelphia PA
Fox Memorial Hospital . .Oneonta NY
Fox Run Hospital . . . . .Saint Clairsville OH
Frances Mahon Deaconess Hospital . . . . .Glasgow MT
Franciscan Childrens Hospital . . . . .Boston MA
Franciscan Medical Center-Dayton Campus . . . . .Dayton OH
Franciscan Skemp Foundation Lacrosse . . . . .La Crosse WI
Franciscan Skemp Medical Center Arcadia . . . . .Arcadia WI
Franciscan Skemp Medical Center Sparta . . . . .Sparta WI
Frank R Howard Memorial Hospital . . . . .Willits CA
Frankford Hospital . . .Philadelphia PA
Frankford Hospital - Bucks County . . . . .Langhorne PA
Frankford Hospital of The City of Philadelphia - Frankford Campus . . . . .Philadelphia PA
Frankfort Regional Medical Center . . . . .Frankfort KY
Franklin County Medical Center . . . . .Preston ID
Franklin County Memorial Hospital . . . . .Meadville MS
Franklin County Memorial Hospital . . . . .Franklin NE
Franklin Foundation Hospital . . . . .Franklin LA
Franklin General Hospital . . . . .Hampton IA
Franklin Hospital . . . . . . .Benton IL
Franklin Hospital Medical Center . . . . .Valley Stream NY
Franklin Medical Center . . . . .Greenfield MA
Franklin Memorial Hospital . . . . .Farmington ME
Franklin Parish Medical Center . . . . .Winnsboro LA
Franklin Regional Hospital . . . . .Franklin NH
Franklin Regional Medical Center . . . . .Louisburg NC
Franklin Square Hospital . . . . .Baltimore MD
Frazier Rehab Center . .Louisville KY
Fred Hutchinson Cancer Research Center . . . . .Seattle WA
Frederick Memorial Hospital . . . . .Frederick MD
Fredonia Regional Hospital . . . . .Fredonia KS
Freeman Community Hospital . . . . .Freeman SD
Freeman Hospital and Health System-East . . . . .Joplin MO

Freeman Hospital and Health System-West . . . . .Joplin MO
Freeman Neosho Hospital . . . . .Neosho MO
Freeport Memorial Hospital . . . . .Freeport IL
Fremont Area Medical Center . . . . .Fremont NE
Fremont Hospital . . . . . .Fremont CA
Fremont Medical Center . . . . .Yuba City CA
French Hospital . . . . .San Luis Obispo CA
Fresno Surgery Center . . .Fresno CA
Friary of Baptist Health Center . . . . .Gulf Breeze FL
Frick Hospital . . . .Mount Pleasant PA
Friedman Hospital of The Home For Jewish Aged . . . . . .Philadelphia PA
Friends Hospital . . . .Philadelphia PA
Frio Hospital . . . . .Pearsall TX
Frisbie Memorial Hospital . . . . .Rochester NH
Froedtert Memorial Lutheran Hospital . . . . .Milwaukee WI
Frye Regional Medical Center . . . . .Hickory NC
Fulton County Health Center . . . . .Wauseon OH
Fulton County Hospital . . .Salem AR
Fulton County Medical Center . . . . .Mc Connellsburg PA
Fulton State Hospital . . . . .Fulton MO
G Werber Bryan Psych Hospital . . . . .Columbia SC
Gadsden Community Hospital . . . . .Quincy FL
Gadsden Regional Medical Center . . . . .Gadsden AL
Gainesville Memorial Hospital . . . . .Gainesville TX
Galena-Stauss Hospital . . .Galena IL
Galesburg Cottage Hospital . . . . .Galesburg IL
Galichia Heart Hospital . . .Wichita KS
Galion Community Hospital . . . . .Galion OH
Garden City Osteopathic Hospital . . . . .Garden City MI
Garden County Health Services . . . . .Oshkosh NE
Garden Grove Hospital . . . . .Garden Grove CA
Garden Park Medical Center . . . . .Gulfport MS
Garfield County Clinic Maf . . . . .Jordan MT
Garfield County Hospital . . . . .Pomeroy WA
Garfield Medical Center . . . . .Monterey Park CA
Garfield Memorial Hospital . . . . .Panguitch UT

Garfield Neurobehavioral Center . . . . .Oakland CA
Garrard County Memorial Hospital . . . . .Lancaster KY
Garrett County Memorial Hospital . . . . .Oakland MD
Garrison Memorial Hospital . . . . .Garrison ND
Gaston Memorial Hospital . . . . .Gastonia NC
Gateway Health Systems . . . . .Clarksville TN
Gateway Regional Medical Center . . . . .Granite City IL
Gateway Rehabilitation Hospital . . . . .Florence KY
Gateway Rehabilitation Hospital . . . . .Louisville KY
Gateways Hospital and Mental Health Center . . . . . . .Los Angeles CA
Gaylord Hospital . . . . .Wallingford CT
Geary Community Hospital . . . . .Junction City KS
Geisinger Healthsouth Rehab Hospital . . . . .Danville PA
Geisinger Medical Center . . . . .Danville PA
Geisinger Wyoming Valley Medical Center . . . . . . .Wilkes-Barre PA
General Hospital . . . . . . .Eureka CA
General Leonard Wood Army Community Hospital . . . . .Fort Leonard Wood MO
Genesee Hospital . . . .Rochester NY
Genesis Healthcare System - Bethesda Hospital . . . .Zanesville OH
Genesis Medical Center . . . . .Davenport IA
Genesis Medical Center-West . . . . .Davenport IA
Genesis Specialty Hospital . . . . .New Orleans LA
Genesys Regional Medical Center . . . . .Grand Blanc MI
Geneva General Hospital . . . . .Geneva NY
Genoa Community Hospital . . . . .Genoa NE
Gentry County Memorial Hospital . . . . .Albany MO
George A Zeller Mental Health Center . . . . .Peoria IL
George County Hospital . . . . .Lucedale MS
George E Weems Memorial Hospital . . . . .Apalachicola FL
George H Lanier Memorial Hospital . . . . .Valley AL
George L Mee Memorial Hospital . . . . .King City CA
George Nigh Rebabilitation Institute . . . . .Okmulgee OK

Alphabetical Index

George Washington University Hospital ....Washington DC
Georgetown Communit Hospital ....Georgetown KY
Georgetown Hospital ....Georgetown TX
Georgetown Memorial Hospital ....Georgetown SC
Georgetown University Hospital ....Washington DC
Georgia Baptist Meriwether Hospital ....Warm Springs GA
Georgia Regional Hospital Atlanta ....Decatur GA
Georgia Regional Hospital Savannah ....Savannah GA
Georgiana Doctors Hospital ....Georgiana AL
Gerald Champion Memorial Hospital ....Alamogordo NM
Gerber Memorial Hospital ....Fremont MI
Germantown Hospital ....Philadelphia PA
Gettysburg Hospital ..Gettysburg PA
Gettysburg Medical Center ....Gettysburg SD
Gibson Community Hospital ....Gibson City IL
Gibson General Hospital ....Princeton IN
Gibson General Hospital ....Trenton TN
Gifford Medical Center ....Randolph VT
Gila Regional Medical Center ....Silver City NM
Gillette Childrens Hospital ....Saint Paul MN
Gilmore Memorial Hospital ....Amory MS
Girard Medical Center ....Philadelphia PA
Glacial Ridge Hospital ....Glenwood MN
Glades General Hospital ....Belle Glade FL
Gladman Psych Health Facility ....Oakland CA
Gladys Spellman Specialty Hospital & Nursing Center ......Hyattsville MD
Glen Oaks Hospital ...Greenville TX
Glen Rose Medical Center ....Glen Rose TX
Glenbeigh Hospital of Rock Creek ....Rock Creek OH
Glencoe Area Health Center ....Glencoe MN
Glendale Adventist Medical Center ....Glendale CA
Glendale Memorial Hospital and Health Center ....Glendale CA
Glendive Medical Center Glendive MT

Glenmont ....Hilliard OH
Glenn General Hospital and Medical Center ....Willows CA
Glenoaks Hospital and Medical Center ....Glendale Heights IL
Glens Falls Hospital ..Glens Falls NY
Glenwood Regional Medical Center ....West Monroe LA
Glenwood Resource Center ....Glenwood IA
Gnaden Huetten Memorial Hospital ....Lehighton PA
Golden Plains Health Center/Hospital ....Borger TX
Golden Valley Memorial Hospital ....Clinton MO
Goldwater Memorial Hospital ....New York NY
Goleta Valley Cottage Hospital ....Santa Barbara CA
Good Hope Hospital ......Erwin NC
Good Samaritan and Mission Oaks Hospital ....San Jose CA
Good Samaritan Health Center of Merrill ....Merrill WI
Good Samaritan Hospital ....Bakersfield CA
Good Samaritan Hospital ....Los Angeles CA
Good Samaritan Hospital ....San Jose CA
Good Samaritan Hospital ....Vincennes IN
Good Samaritan Hospital ....Baltimore MD
Good Samaritan Hospital ....Kearney NE
Good Samaritan Hospital ....West Islip NY
Good Samaritan Hospital ....Cincinnati OH
Good Samaritan Hospital ....Lebanon PA
Good Samaritan Hospital ....Puyallup WA
Good Samaritan Hospital and Health Center ....Dayton OH
Good Samaritan Hospital Corvallis ....Corvallis OR
Good Samaritan Hospital of Suffern ....Suffern NY
Good Samaritan Hospital-Advocate ....Downers Grove IL
Good Samaritan Medical Center ....West Palm Beach FL
Good Samaritan Medical Center ....Brockton MA
Good Samaritan Medical Center ....Zanesville OH
Good Samaritan Medical Center ....Johnstown PA
Good Samaritan Regional Health Center ....Mount Vernon IL

Good Samaritan Regional Medical Center ....Phoenix AZ
Good Samaritan Regional Medical Center ....Pottsville PA
Good Shepherd Communit Hospital ....Hermiston OR
Good Shepherd Hospital ....Barrington IL
Good Shepherd Medical Center ....Longview TX
Good Shepherd Rehabilitation Hospital ....Allentown PA
Good Shepherd Specialty Hospital ....Allentown PA
Goodall Witcher Healthcare Foundation ....Clifton TX
Gooding County Memorial Hospital ....Gooding ID
Goodland Regional Medical Center ....Goodland KS
Gordon Hospital ....Calhoun GA
Gordon Memorial Hospital ....Gordon NE
Goshen General Hospital ....Goshen IN
Gothenburg Memorial Hospital ....Gothenburg NE
Gottlieb Memorial Hospital ....Melrose Park IL
Gov Juan F Luis Hospital and Medical Center ....Saint Croix
Gove County Medical Center ....Quinter KS
Grace Cottage Hospital ....Townshend VT
Grace Hospital ......Morganton NC
Grace Hospital ....Cleveland OH
Graceville Health Center ....Graceville MN
Gracewood State School and Hospital ....Gracewood GA
Gracie Square Hospital ....New York NY
Graduate Hospitals ..Philadelphia PA
Grady General Hospital ....Cairo GA
Grady Memorial Hospital ....Atlanta GA
Grady Memorial Hospital ....Delaware OH
Grady Memorial Hospital ....Chickasha OK
Grafton City Hospital ....Grafton WV
Graham County Hospital ....Hill City KS
Graham General Hospital ....Graham TX
Graham Hospital Association ....Canton IL
Granada Hills Communit Hospital ....Granada Hills CA
Grand River Hospital ......Rifle CO
Grand Strand Regional Medical Center ....Myrtle Beach SC

Alphabetical Index

Grand View Hospital . . .Ironwood MI
Grand View Hospital . .Sellersville PA
Grande Ronde Hospital
. . . . .La Grande OR
Grandview Hospital and Medical
Center . . . . .Dayton OH
Grandview Medical Center
. . . . .Jasper TN
Granite County Memorial Maf
. . . . .Philipsburg MT
Granite Falls Municipal Hospital
. . . . .Granite Falls MN
Grant Hospital of Chicago
. . . . .Chicago IL
Grant Medical Center
. . . . .Columbus OH
Grant Memorial Hospital
. . . . .Petersburg WV
Grant Regional Health Center
. . . . .Lancaster WI
Granville Medical Center . .Oxford NC
Grape Community Hospital
. . . . .Hamburg IA
Gratiot Community Hospital
. . . . .Alma MI
Gravette Medical Center Hospital . . .
Gravette AR
Graydon Manor . . . . . . .Leesburg VA
Grays Harbor Community Hospital
. . . . .Aberdeen WA
Great Lakes Regional Rehab
Hospital . . . . .Southfield MI
Great Plains of Greeley County
. . . . .Tribune KS
Great Plains of Kiowa County
. . . . .Greensburg KS
Great Plains Regional Medical
Center . . . . .North Platte NE
Great Plains Regional Medical
Center . . . . .Elk City OK
Great River Medical Center
. . . . .West Burlington IA
Greater Baltimore Medical Center
. . . . .Baltimore MD
Greater Community Hospital
. . . . .Creston IA
Greater El Monte Community
Hospital . . . . . . .South El Monte CA
Greater Southeast Hospital
. . . . .Washington DC
Green Hill Hospital . . . .Stonewall LA
Green Oaks Hospital . . . . .Dallas TX
Greenbriar Hospital For Special
Services . . . . .Boardman OH
Greenbrier Hospital . . .Covington LA
Greenbrier Valley Medical
Center . . . . .Ronceverte WV
Greene County General Hospital
. . . . .Linton IN
Greene County Hospital and Nursing
Home . . . . .Eutaw AL
Greene County Medical Center
. . . . .Jefferson IA

Greene County Memorial
Hospital . . . . .Waynesburg PA
Greene Memorial Hospital
. . . . .Xenia OH
Greenfield Area Medical Center
. . . . .Greenfield OH
Greenleaf Center . . . . . .Valdosta GA
Greensville Memorial Hospital
. . . . .Emporia VA
Greenview Regional Hospital
. . . . .Bowling Green KY
Greenville Hospital . . .Jersey City NJ
Greenville Hospital System
. . . . .Greenville SC
Greenwell Springs Hospital
. . . . .Greenwell Springs LA
Greenwich Hospital . . .Greenwich CT
Greenwood County Hospital
. . . . .Eureka KS
Greenwood Leflore Hospital
. . . . .Greenwood MS
Gregory Community Hospital
. . . . .Gregory SD
Greil Memorial Psychiatric
Hospital . . . . .Montgomery AL
Grenada Lake Medical Center
. . . . .Grenada MS
Greystone Park Psych Hospital
. . . . .Greystone Park NJ
Griffin Hospital . . . . .Derby CT
Griffin Memorial Hospital
. . . . .Norman OK
Grimes Saint Joseph Health
Center . . . . .Navasota TX
Grinnell Regional Medical
Center . . . . .Grinnell IA
Grisell Memorial Hospital
District #1 . . . . .Ransom KS
Gritman Memorial Hospital
. . . . .Moscow ID
Grossmont Hospital . . . .La Mesa CA
Group Health - Metropolitan Park
East . . . . .Seattle WA
Group Health Central Hospital
. . . . .Seattle WA
Group Health Cooperative
. . . . .Redmond WA
Grove Hill Memorial Hospital
. . . . .Grove Hill AL
Grover C Dils Medical Center
. . . . .Caliente NV
Grundy County Memorial
Hospital . . . . .Grundy Center IA
Guadalupe County Hospital
. . . . .Santa Rosa NM
Guadalupe Valley Hospital
. . . . .Seguin TX
Guam Memorial Authority
Hospital . . . . .Tamuning GU
Guayama Area Hospital
. . . . .Guayama PR
Guidance Center, The . . .Flagstaff AZ

Gulf Breeze Hospital
. . . . .Gulf Breeze FL
Gulf Coast Hospital . . .Fort Myers FL
Gulf Coast Medical Center
. . . . .Panama City FL
Gulf Coast Medical Center
. . . . .Biloxi MS
Gulf Coast Medical Center
. . . . .Wharton TX
Gulf Coast Treatment Center
. . . . .Fort Walton Beach FL
Gulf Oaks Hospital . . . . . .Biloxi MS
Gulf Pines Hospital
. . . . .Port Saint Joe FL
Gundersen Lutheran Medical
Center . . . . .La Crosse WI
Gunnison Valley Hospital
. . . . .Gunnison CO
Gunnison Valley Hospital
. . . . .Gunnison UT
Guthrie County Hospital
. . . . .Guthrie Center IA
Guttenberg Municipal Hospital
. . . . .Guttenberg IA
Guyan Valley Hospital . . . .Logan WV
Gwinnett Medical Center
. . . . .Lawrenceville GA
H B Magruder Memorial
Hospital . . . . .Port Clinton OH
H C Watkins Memorial Hospital
. . . . .Quitman MS
H Douglas Singer Mental Health
Center . . . . .Rockford IL
Habersham County Medica
Center . . . . .Demorest GA
Hacienda De Los Ninos . .Phoenix AZ
Hackensack University Medical
Center . . . . .Hackensack NJ
Hackettstown Community
Hospital . . . . .Hackettstown NJ
Hackley Hospital . . . . . .Muskegon MI
Hadley Memorial Hospital
. . . . .Washington DC
Hagedorn Psychiatric Hospital
. . . . .Glen Gardner NJ
Hahnemann University Hospital
. . . . .Philadelphia PA
Hale County Hospital
. . . . .Greensboro AL
Hale Hoola Hamakua . . .Honokaa HI
Hale Mohalu Hospital . . .Honolulu HI
Halifax Behavioral Services
. . . . .Daytona Beach FL
Halifax Medical Center
. . . . .Daytona Beach FL
Halifax Regional Hospital
. . . . .South Boston VA
Halifax Regional Medical
Center . . . . . . .Roanoke Rapids NC
Hall-Brooke Hospital . . .Westport CT
Hallmark Health - Malden Medical
Center . . . . .Malden MA
Hallmark Youth Care . .Richmond VA

Alphabetical Index

Hallmark Youth Care of Atlanta ....Atlanta GA
Hamilton Center .....Terre Haute IN
Hamilton County Hospital ....Syracuse KS
Hamilton County Public Hospital ....Webster City IA
Hamilton General Hospital ....Hamilton TX
Hamilton Hospital ....Olney TX
Hamilton Medical Center ..Dalton GA
Hamilton Memorial Hospital ....Mcleansboro IL
Hamlin Memorial Hospital ....Hamlin TX
Hammond Rehabilitation Hospital ....Hammond LA
Hammond-Henry Hospital ....Geneseo IL
Hamot Medical Center ......Erie PA
Hampshire Memorial Hospital ....Romney WV
Hampstead Hospital ....Hampstead NH
Hampton Behavioral Health System ....Westampton NJ
Hampton Regional Medical Center ....Varnville SC
Hana Medical Center .....Hana HI
Hancock County Memorial Hospital ....Britt IA
Hancock Medical Center ....Bay Saint Louis MS
Hancock Memorial Hospital and Health Services .....Greenfield IN
Hand County Memorial Hospital ....Miller SD
Hanford Community Medical Center ....Hanford CA
Hannibal Regional Hospital ....Hannibal MO
Hanover General Hospital ....Hanover PA
Hanover Hospital ......Hanover KS
Hans P Peterson Memorial Hospital ....Philip SD
Hansford Hospital ....Spearman TX
Harbor Beach Community Hospital ....Harbor Beach MI
Harbor Hospital Center ....Baltimore MD
Harbor Oaks Hospital ....New Baltimore MI
Harbor View Mercy Hospital ....Fort Smith AR
Harborview Medical Center ....Seattle WA
Hardeman County Memorial Hospital ....Quanah TX
Hardin County General Hospital ....Rosiclare IL
Hardin County General Hospital ....Savannah TN

Hardin Memorial Hospital ....Elizabethtown KY
Hardin Memorial Hospital ....Kenton OH
Hardtner Medical Center ....Olla LA
Hardy Wilson Memorial Hospital ....Hazlehurst MS
Harford Memorial Hospital ....Havre De Grace MD
Harlan Arh Hospital ......Harlan KY
Harlan County Hospital ....Alma NE
Harlem Hospital Center ....New York NY
Harlingen Medical Center ....Harlingen TX
Harmon Medical & Rehabilation Hospital ....Las Vegas NV
Harmon Memorial Hospital ....Hollis OK
Harms Memorial Hospital ....American Falls ID
Harney District Hospital ...Burns OR
Harper County Community Hospital ....Buffalo OK
Harper Hospital ....Harper KS
Harper Hospital ....Detroit MI
Harrington Memorial Hospital ....Southbridge MA
Harris Continued Care Hospital ....Fort Worth TX
Harris County Psychiatric Center ....Houston TX
Harris Hospital ....Newport AR
Harris Methodist - Springwood ....Bedford TX
Harris Methodist Erath County ....Stephenville TX
Harris Methodist Fort Worth ....Fort Worth TX
Harris Methodist H E B ..Bedford TX
Harris Methodist Northwest ..Azle TX
Harris Methodist Southwest ....Fort Worth TX
Harris Regional Hospital ...Sylva NC
Harrisburg Medical Center ....Harrisburg IL
Harrisburg State Hospital ....Harrisburg PA
Harrison Community Hospital ....Cadiz OH
Harrison County Community Hospital ....Bethany MO
Harrison County Hospital ....Corydon IN
Harrison Memorial Hospital ....Cynthiana KY
Harrison Memorial Hospital ....Bremerton WA
Hart County Hospital ....Hartwell GA
Hartford Hospital ......Hartford CT
Hartgrove Hospital .....Chicago IL
Harton Regional Medical Center ....Tullahoma TN

Hartselle Medical Center ....Hartselle AL
Harvard Community Memorial Hospital ....Harvard IL
Haskell County Hospital ..Stigler OK
Haskell Memorial Hospital ....Haskell TX
Hastings Regional Center ....Hastings NE
Havasu Regional Medical Center ....Lake Havasu City AZ
Havenwyck Hospital ....Auburn Hills MI
Hawaii State Hospital ...Kaneohe HI
Hawarden Community Hospital ....Hawarden IA
Hawthorn Center ......Northville MI
Haxtun Hospital/Heritage Liv Center ....Haxtun CO
Hayes Green Beach Memorial Hospital ....Charlotte MI
Hays Medical Center ......Hays KS
Hayward Area Memorial Hospital ....Hayward WI
Haywood Regional Medical Center ....Clyde NC
Hazard Arh Regional Medical Center ....Hazard KY
Hazel Hawkins Memorial Hospital ....Hollister CA
Hazleton General Hospital ....Hazleton PA
Hazleton-Saint Joseph Medical Center ....Hazleton PA
Healdsburg District Hospital ....Healdsburg CA
Healdton Hospital .....Healdton OK
Health Alliance Burbank Hospital ....Fitchburg MA
Health Alliance Leominster Hospital ....Leominster MA
Health Bridge Childrens Hospital ....Houston TX
Health Central ....Ocoee FL
Health Paradigm Medical Center ....Ruston LA
Healthbridge Children's Rehab Hospital ....Orange CA
Healthmark Regional Medical Center ....Defuniak Springs FL
Healthpark ....Owensboro KY
Healthsource Saginaw ..Saginaw MI
Healthsouth Bakersfield Rehab Hospital ....Bakersfield CA
Healthsouth Braintree Rehab Hospital ....Braintree MA
Healthsouth Cane Creek Rehab Hospital ....Martin TN
Healthsouth Central Georgia Rehabilitation Hospital ...Macon GA
Healthsouth Chattanooga Rehab Hospital ....Chattanooga TN

195

Alphabetical Index

Healthsouth Chesapeake Rehab Hospital . . . . Salisbury MD

Healthsouth Clear Lake Rehab Hospital . . . . Webster TX

Healthsouth Doctors Hospital . . . . Coral Gables FL

Healthsouth Emerald Coast Rehab Hospital . . . . Panama City FL

Healthsouth Garden State Rehabilitation Hospital . . . . Toms River NJ

Healthsouth Harmarville Rehab Hospital . . . . Pittsburgh PA

Healthsouth Hospital at Tenaya . . . . Las Vegas NV

Healthsouth Hospital For Specialized Surgery . . . . Houston TX

Healthsouth Hospital of Western Massachusetts . . . . Ludlow MA

Healthsouth Huntington Rehab Hospital . . . . Huntington WV

Healthsouth Lakeshore Rehab Hospital . . . . Birmingham AL

Healthsouth Medical Center . . . . Birmingham AL

Healthsouth Medical Center . . . . Dallas TX

Healthsouth Metro West Hospital . . . . Fairfield AL

Healthsouth Mountainview Rehab Hospital . . . . Morgantown WV

Healthsouth New England Rehab Hospital . . . . Woburn MA

Healthsouth Nittany Valley Rehabilitation Hospital . . . . Pleasant Gap PA

Healthsouth North Louisiana Rehab Hospital . . . . Ruston LA

Healthsouth Northern Kentucky Rehabilitation Hospital . . . . Edgewood KY

Healthsouth Plano Rehab Hospital . . . . Plano TX

Healthsouth Rehab Center . . . . Fort Worth TX

Healthsouth Rehab Hospital . . . . Kokomo IN

Healthsouth Rehab Hospital . . . . Beaumont TX

Healthsouth Rehab Hospital - City View . . . . Fort Worth TX

Healthsouth Rehab Hospital - Sewickley . . . . Sewickley PA

Healthsouth Rehab Hospital - Wichita . . . . Wichita Falls TX

Healthsouth Rehab Hospital For Special Services . . Mechanicsburg PA

Healthsouth Rehab Hospital North Houston . . . . Conroe TX

Healthsouth Rehab Hospital of Alexandria . . . . Alexandria LA

Healthsouth Rehab Hospital of Arlington . . . . Arlington TX

Healthsouth Rehab Hospital of Austin . . . . Austin TX

Healthsouth Rehab Hospital of Baton Rouge . . . . . Baton Rouge LA

Healthsouth Rehab Hospital of Charleston . . . . North Charleston SC

Healthsouth Rehab Hospital of Fort Smith . . . . Fort Smith AR

Healthsouth Rehab Hospital of Midland/odessa . . . . Midland TX

Healthsouth Rehab Hospital of Montgomery . . . . . . Montgomery AL

Healthsouth Rehab Hospital of North Alabama . . . . Huntsville AL

Healthsouth Rehab Hospital of Sarasota . . . . Sarasota FL

Healthsouth Rehab Hospital of Tallahassee . . . . Tallahassee FL

Healthsouth Rehab Hospital of Texarkana . . . . Texarkana TX

Healthsouth Rehab Hospital of Tyler . . . . Tyler TX

Healthsouth Rehab Hospital of Virginia . . . . Richmond VA

Healthsouth Rehab Hospital/Florence . . . . . Florence SC

Healthsouth Rehab Institute . . . . Houston TX

Healthsouth Rehab Institute . . . . Sandy UT

Healthsouth Rehab Institute of San Antonio . . . . San Antonio TX

Healthsouth Rehab Institute of Tucson . . . . Tucson AZ

Healthsouth Rehab of Greater Pittsburgh . . . . Monroeville PA

Healthsouth Rehabilitation Center . . . . Largo FL

Healthsouth Rehabilitation Hospital . . . . Dothan AL

Healthsouth Rehabilitation Hospital . . . . Gadsden AL

Healthsouth Rehabilitation Hospital . . . . Fayetteville AR

Healthsouth Rehabilitation Hospital . . . . Jonesboro AR

Healthsouth Rehabilitation Hospital . . . . Miami FL

Healthsouth Rehabilitation Hospital . . . . Terre Haute IN

Healthsouth Rehabilitation Hospital . . . . Concord NH

Healthsouth Rehabilitation Hospital . . . . Albuquerque NM

Healthsouth Rehabilitation Hospital . . . . Oklahoma City OK

Healthsouth Rehabilitation Hospital . . . . Rio Piedras PR

Healthsouth Rehabilitation Hospital . . . . Rock Hill SC

Healthsouth Rehabilitation Hospital . . . . Kingsport TN

Healthsouth Rehabilitation Hospital . . . . Humble TX

Healthsouth Rehabilitation Hospital - Memphis . . . . Memphis TN

Healthsouth Rehabilitation Hospital - Memphis North . . . . . . Memphis TN

Healthsouth Rehabilitation Hospital Altoona . . . . Altoona PA

Healthsouth Rehabilitation Hospital of Central Kentucky . . Elizabethtown KY

Healthsouth Rehabilitation Hospital of Colorado Springs . . . . Colorado Springs CO

Healthsouth Rehabilitation Hospital of Erie . . . . Erie PA

Healthsouth Rehabilitation Hospital of Henderson . . . . Henderson NV

Healthsouth Rehabilitation Hospital of Mechanicsburg . . . Mechanicsburg PA

Healthsouth Rehabilitation Hospital of Nevada . . . . Las Vegas NV

Healthsouth Rehabilitation Hospital of Reading . . . . Reading PA

Healthsouth Rehabilitation Hospital of Southern Arizona . . . . Tucson AZ

Healthsouth Rehabilitation Hospital York . . . . York PA

Healthsouth Rehabilitation Hospital/Columbia . . . . . Columbia SC

Healthsouth Saint Joseph Healthcare Center . . . . . . Lowell MA

Healthsouth Scottsdale Rehab Hospital . . . . Scottsdale AZ

Healthsouth Sea Pines Hospital . . . . Melbourne FL

Healthsouth Southern Hills Regional Rehab Hospital . . . . . . Princeton WV

Healthsouth Sunrise Rehab Hospital . . . . Sunrise FL

Healthsouth Surgery Hospital of Austin . . . . Austin TX

Healthsouth Treasure Coast Rehab Hospital . . . . . . Vero Beach FL

Healthsouth Treasure Valley Hospital . . . . Boise ID

Healthsouth Tri State Rehab Hospital . . . . Evansville IN

Healthsouth Tustin Rehabilitation Hospital . . . . Tustin CA

Healthsouth Valley of Sun Rehab . . . . Glendale AZ

Healthsouth Western Hills Regional Rehab Hospital . . . . Parkersburg WV

Healthwest Rehabilitation Hospital . . . . Gretna LA

Heart Hospital of Austin . . . Austin TX

Heart Hospital of Milwaukee . . . . Glendale WI

Heart Hospital of New Mexico . . . . Albuquerque NM

Heart Hospital of South Dakota . . . . Sioux Falls SD

Alphabetical Index

Heart of America Medical Center . . . . .Rugby ND
Heart of Florida Regional Medical Center . . . . .Davenport FL
Heart of Texas Memorial Hospital . . . . .Brady TX
Heart of The Rockies Regional Medical Center . . . . .Salida CO
Heart Place Hospital . . . .Midland TX
Heartland Behavioral Health Services . . . . .Nevada MO
Heartland Behavioral Healthcare . . . . .Massillon OH
Heartland Health System . .Fargo ND
Heartland Heart Center-East Campus . . . . .Saint Joseph MO
Heartland Regional Medical Center West . . . . .Saint Joseph MO
Heather Hill Hospital . . .Chardon OH
Heber Valley Medical Center . . . . .Heber City UT
Hebrew Home and Hospital . . . . .West Hartford CT
Hebrew Home For The Aged Disabled . . . . .San Francisco CA
Hebrew Rehabilitation Center For The Aged . . . . .Boston MA
Hedrick Medical Center . . . . .Chillicothe MO
Hegg Memorial Health Center . . . . .Rock Valley IA
Helen Ellis Memorial Hospital . . . . .Tarpon Springs FL
Helen Hayes Hospital . . . . .West Haverstraw NY
Helen Keller Memorial Hospital . . . . .Sheffield AL
Helen Newberry Joy Hospital . . . . .Newberry MI
Helena Regional Medical Center . . . . .Helena AR
Hemet Valley Medical Center . . . . .Hemet CA
Hemphill County Hospital . . . . .Canadian TX
Henderson Health Care Services . . . . .Henderson NE
Henderson Memorial Hospital . . . . .Henderson TX
Hendersonville Medical Center . . . . .Hendersonville TN
Hendrick Health System . .Abilene TX
Hendricks Community Hospital . . . . .Danville IN
Hendricks Community Hospital . . . . .Hendricks MN
Hendry Regional Medical Center . . . . .Clewiston FL
Hennepin County Medical Center . . . . .Minneapolis MN
Henrico Doctors Hospital - Forest . . . . .Richmond VA

Henrico Doctors Hospital - Parham . . . . .Richmond VA
Henrietta D Goodall Hospital . . . . .Sanford ME
Henry County Health Center . . . . .Mount Pleasant IA
Henry County Hospital . . . . .Napoleon OH
Henry County Medical Center . . . . .Paris TN
Henry County Memorial Hospital . . . . .New Castle IN
Henry Ford Hospital . . . . .Detroit MI
Henry Ford Medical Center . . . . .Detroit MI
Henry Ford Wyandotte Hospital . . . . .Wyandotte MI
Henry Ford-Kingswood Hospital . . . . .Ferndale MI
Henry General Hospital . . . . .Stockbridge GA
Henry Mayo Newhall Memorial Hospital . . . . .Valencia CA
Henryetta Medical Center . . . . .Henryetta OK
Hereford Regional Medical Center . . . . .Hereford TX
Herington Municipal Hospital . . . . .Herington KS
Heritage Behavioral Health Center . . . . .Decatur IL
Heritage Hospital . . . . . . .Tarboro NC
Heritage Oaks Hospital . . . . .Sacramento CA
Hermann Area District Hospital . . . . .Hermann MO
Herrick Memorial Hospital . . . . .Tecumseh MI
Herrin Hospital . . . . .Herrin IL
Heywood Hospital . . . . .Gardner MA
Hi-Desert Medical Center . . . . .Joshua Tree CA
Hialeah Hospital . . . . . . .Hialeah FL
Hiawatha Community Hospital . . . . .Hiawatha KS
Higgins General Hospital . . . . .Bremen GA
High Point Regional Hospital . . . . .High Point NC
High Pointe Healthcare . . . . .Oklahoma City OK
High Ridge House . . . . .Riverdale NY
Highland District Hospital . . . . .Hillsboro OH
Highland Hills Hospital . . . . .Shreveport LA
Highland Hospital . . . .Shreveport LA
Highland Hospital . . . .Rochester NY
Highland Hospital . . . .Charleston WV
Highland Medical Center . . . . .Lubbock TX
Highland Park Hospital . . . . .Highland Park IL

Highland Park Pavilion . . . .Miami FL
Highland Ridge Hospital . . . . .Midvale UT
Highlands Hospital . .Connellsville PA
Highlands Regional Medical Center . . . . .Sebring FL
Highlands Regional Medical Center . . . . .Prestonsburg KY
Highlands Regional Rehabilitation Hospital . . . . .El Paso TX
Highlands-Cashiers Hospital . . . . .Highlands NC
Highline Community Hospital . . . . .Burien WA
Highline Speciality Center . . . . .Seattle WA
Highsmith Rainey Memorial Hospital . . . . .Fayetteville NC
Hill Country Memorial Hospital . . . . .Fredericksburg TX
Hill Crest Behavioral Health Services . . . . .Birmingham AL
Hill Hospital of Sumter County . . . . .York AL
Hill Regional Hospital . . .Hillsboro TX
Hillcrest Baptist Medical Center . . . . .Waco TX
Hillcrest Hospital . . . . . .Pittsfield MA
Hillcrest Hospital . . . . .Mayfield Heights OH
Hillcrest Hospital . . .Simpsonville SC
Hillcrest Medical Center . . .Tulsa OK
Hillcrest Specialty Hospital of Tulsa . . . . .Tulsa OK
Hills and Dales General Hospital . . . . .Cass City MI
Hillsboro Area Hospital . . .Hillsboro IL
Hillsboro Community Medical Center . . . . .Hillsboro KS
Hillsboro Medical Center . . . . .Hillsboro ND
Hillsdale Community Health Center . . . . .Hillsdale MI
Hillside Hospital . . . . . . .Atlanta GA
Hillside Hospital . . . .Glen Oaks NY
Hillside Hospital . . . . . . .Pulaski TN
Hillside Rehab Hospital . .Warren OH
Hilo Medical Center . . . . . . .Hilo HI
Hilton Head Medical Center and Clinics . . . . . . .Hilton Head Island SC
Hinsdale Hospital . . . . . . .Hinsdale IL
Hiram W Davis Medical Center . . . . .Petersburg VA
Hoag Memorial Hospital Presbyterian . . . .Newport Beach CA
Hocking Valley Community Hospital . . . . .Logan OH
Hodgeman County Health Center . . . . .Jetmore KS
Holdenville General Hospital . . . . .Holdenville OK
Holland Community Hospital . . . . .Holland MI

Alphabetical Index

Holliswood Hospital . . . .Jamaica NY
Holly Hill Hospital . . . . .Raleigh NC
Hollywood Community Hospital
. . . . .Hollywood CA
Hollywood Community Hospital-Van
Nuys . . . . .Van Nuys CA
Hollywood Medical Center
. . . . .Hollywood FL
Hollywood Pavilion Hospital
. . . . .Hollywood FL
Holmes Regional Medical Center
. . . . .Melbourne FL
Holton City Hospital . . . . .Holton KS
Holy Cross Hospital
. . . . .Fort Lauderdale FL
Holy Cross Hospital . . . .Chicago IL
Holy Cross Hospital
. . . . .Silver Spring MD
Holy Cross Hospital . . . . .Taos NM
Holy Family Home . . . .Brooklyn NY
Holy Family Hospital . . .Estherville IA
Holy Family Hospital . . .Spokane WA
Holy Family Hospital
. . . . .New Richmond WI
Holy Family Hospital and Medical
Center . . . . .Methuen MA
Holy Family Medical Center
. . . . .Des Plaines IL
Holy Family Memorial Medical
Center . . . . .Manitowoc WI
Holy Infant Hospital . . . . .Hoven SD
Holy Name Hospital . . . .Teaneck NJ
Holy Redeemer Hospital & Medical
Center . . . . .Meadowbrook PA
Holy Rosary Hospital . .Miles City MT
Holy Rosary Medical Center
. . . . .Ontario OR
Holy Spirit Hospital . . . .Camp Hill PA
Holyoke Hospital Inc . . . .Holyoke MA
Holzer Medical Center . .Gallipolis OH
Holzer Medical Center -
Jackson . . . . .Jackson OH
Homer G. Phillips Clinic
. . . . .Saint Louis MO
Homer Memorial Hospital
. . . . .Homer LA
Homestead Hospital . .Homestead FL
Hood Memorial Hospital . . .Amite LA
Hoopeston Community Memorial
Hospital . . . . .Hoopeston IL
Hoots Memorial Hospital
. . . . .Yadkinville NC
Hope Hospital . . . . .Lockhart SC
Hopedale Hospital . . . . .Hopedale IL
Hopemont State Hospital
. . . . .Terra Alta WV
Hopkins County Memorial
Hospital . . . . . . .Sulphur Springs TX
Horizon Hospital System - Shenango
Valley . . . . .Farrell PA
Horizon Medical Center . .Dickson TN
Horizon Specialty Hospital
. . . . .Las Vegas NV

Horn Memorial Hospital
. . . . .Ida Grove IA
Horsham Clinic . . . . .Ambler PA
Hospice Care Center Hospital
. . . . .Longview WA
Hospice of Northern Virginia
. . . . .Arlington VA
Hospice of Northern Virginia
. . . . .Falls Church VA
Hospice of Palm Beach County
. . . . .West Palm Beach FL
Hospital Center at Orange
. . . . .Orange NJ
Hospital De La Concepcion
. . . . .San German PR
Hospital District #1 of Rice
County . . . . .Lyons KS
Hospital District #6 of Harper
County . . . . .Anthony KS
Hospital District 1 Crawford
County . . . . .Girard KS
Hospital Dr Dominguez
. . . . .Humacao PR
Hospital Dr Susoni Inc . . .Arecibo PR
Hospital Dr Tito Mattei . . . .Yauco PR
Hospital For Extended Recovery
. . . . .Norfolk VA
Hospital For Joint Diseases -
Orthopaedic Institute . . .New York NY
Hospital For Sick Children
. . . . .Washington DC
Hospital For Special Care
. . . . .New Britain CT
Hospital For Special Surgery
. . . . .New York NY
Hospital Hermanos Melendez
. . . . .Bayamon PR
Hospital Interamericano De
Medicina . . . . .Caguas PR
Hospital Matilde Brenes
. . . . .Bayamon PR
Hospital Menonita De Cayey
. . . . .Cayey PR
Hospital Metropolitano San
German . . . . .San German PR
Hospital of Saint Raphael
. . . . .New Haven CT
Hospital of The California Institute
For Men . . . . .Chino CA
Hospital Psiquiatria Dr Ramon
Fernandez . . . . .Caparra PR
Hospital Regional Dr Cayetano
Coll Y Toste . . . . .Arecibo PR
Hospital San Agustin Inc . .Manati PR
Hospital San Carlos Borromeo
. . . . .Moca PR
Hospital San Cristobal
. . . . .Coto Laurel PR
Hospital San Francisco
. . . . .Rio Piedras PR
Hospital San Gerardo
. . . . .Rio Piedras PR

Hospital San Pablo Del Este
. . . . .Fajardo PR
Hospital Universitario Dr Ruiz
Arnau . . . . .Bayamon PR
Hospital Wilma N Vazquez
. . . . .Vega Baja PR
Hospital, The . . . . .Sidney NY
Hot Spring County Medical
Center . . . . .Malvern AR
Hot Springs County Memorial
Hospital . . . . .Thermopolis WY
Hot Springs Rehabilitation
Center . . . . .Hot Springs AR
Hot Springs Surgical Hospital
. . . . .Hot Springs AR
Houlton Regional Hospital
. . . . .Houlton ME
Houston Community Hospital
. . . . .Houston TX
Houston Community Hospital
. . . . .Houston TX
Houston Medical Center
. . . . .Warner Robins GA
Houston Northwest Medical
Center . . . . .Houston TX
Howard Community Hospital
. . . . .Kokomo IN
Howard County Community
Hospital . . . . .Saint Paul NE
Howard County General
Hospital . . . . .Columbia MD
Howard Memorial Hospital
. . . . .Nashville AR
Howard University Hospital
. . . . .Washington DC
Howard Young Medical Center
. . . . .Woodruff WI
Hubbard Regional Hospital
. . . . .Webster MA
Hudson County Meadowview
Psychiatric Hospital . . . .Secaucus NJ
Hudson Medical Center . .Hudson WI
Hudson River Psychiatric Center
. . . . .Poughkeepsie NY
Hudson Valley Hospital Center
. . . . .Peekskill NY
Huey P Long Memorial Center
. . . . .Pineville LA
Huggins Hospital . . . . .Wolfeboro NH
Hugh Chatham Memorial
Hospital . . . . .Elkin NC
Hughes Spalding Children's
Hospital . . . . .Atlanta GA
Hughston Sports Medicine
Hospital . . . . .Columbus GA
Huguley Health System
. . . . .Fort Worth TX
Humacao Area Hospital
. . . . .Humacao PR
Humboldt County Memorial
Hospital . . . . .Humboldt IA
Humboldt General Hospital
. . . . .Winnemucca NV

Alphabetical Index

Humboldt General Hospital . . . . Humboldt TN
Humboldt Hospital . . . .Humboldt NE
Humphreys County Memorial Hospital . . . . .Belzoni MS
Hunt Memorial Hospital District . . . . .Greenville TX
Hunterdon Medical Center . . . . .Flemington NJ
Huntington Beach Hospital . . . . .Huntington Beach CA
Huntington Hospital . .Huntington NY
Huntington Memorial Hospital .Pasadena CA
Huntsville Hospital . . . .Huntsville AL
Huntsville Hospital East . . . . .Huntsville AL
Huntsville Memorial Hospital .Huntsville TX
Hurley Medical Center . . . . .Flint MI
Huron Hospital . . . . . .Cleveland OH
Huron Memorial Hospital . . . . .Bad Axe MI
Huron Regional Medical Center . . . . .Huron SD
Huron Valley-sinai Hospital .Commerce MI
Hutcheson Medical Center . . . . .Fort Oglethorpe GA
Hutchinson Community Hospital . . . . .Hutchinson MN
Hutchinson Hospital . .Hutchinson KS
Hutzel Hospital . . . . .Detroit MI
Iberia Medical Center .New Iberia LA
Idaho Elks Rehabilitation Hospital . . . . .Boise ID
Idaho Falls Recovery Center . . . . .Idaho Falls ID
Idaho State Hospital South . . . . .Blackfoot ID
Ihs - Corpus Christi . . . . .Corpus Christi TX
Ihs Hospital at Houston . .Houston TX
Ihs Hospital at Plano . . . . .Plano TX
Ihs Hospital at San Antonio . . . . .San Antonio TX
Ihs Hospital at Wichita Falls . . . . .Wichita Falls TX
Ihs Hospital-Dallas . . . . . .Dallas TX
Illiana Surgery and Medical Center . . . . .Munster IN
Illini Community Hospital . . . . .Pittsfield IL
Illini Hospital . . . . .Silvis IL
Illinois Masonic Medical Center . . . . .Chicago IL
Illinois Valley Community Hospital . . . . .Peru IL
Immanuel Medical Center . . . . .Omaha NE
Immanuel-saint Josephs-Mayo Health Systems . . . . . .Mankato MN

Impact Drug & Alcohol Treatment Center . . . . .Pasadena CA
Imperial Point Medical Center . . . . .Fort Lauderdale FL
Incline Village Health Center . . . . .Incline Village NV
Independence Regional Health Center . . . . .Independence MO
Indian Path Medical Center .Kingsport TN
Indian Path Pavilion . . .Kingsport TN
Indian River Memorial Hospital . . . . .Vero Beach FL
Indian Valley District Hospital . . . . .Greenville CA
Indiana Regional Medical Center . . . . .Indiana PA
Indiana University Medical Center . . . . .Indianapolis IN
Indianhead Medical Center . . . . .Shell Lake WI
Ingalls Memorial Hospital . .Harvey IL
Ingham Regional Medical Center . . . . .Lansing MI
Ingham Regional Medical Center - Greenlawn Campus . . . . .Lansing MI
Ingleside Hospital . . . .Rosemead CA
Inland Hospital . . . . . .Waterville ME
Inland Valley Regional Medical Center . . . . .Wildomar CA
Inner Harbour Hospitals . . . . .Douglasville GA
Innovis Hospital . . . . .Fargo ND
Inova Alexandria Hospital . . . . .Alexandria VA
Inova Fair Oaks Hospital . .Fairfax VA
Inova Fairfax Hospital . . . . .Falls Church VA
Institute For Rehab and Research . . . . .Houston TX
Institute of Living . . . . . .Hartford CT
Institute of Mental Health . . . . .Cranston RI
Integrated Specialty Hospital . . . . .Albuquerque NM
Integrated Specialty Hospital . . . . .Edmond OK
Integris Baptist Medical Center . . . . .Oklahoma City OK
Integris Baptist Regional Health Center . . . . .Miami OK
Integris Bass Baptist Health Center . . . . .Enid OK
Integris Bass Behavioral Health System . . . . .Enid OK
Integris Blackwell Regional Hospital . . . . .Blackwell OK
Integris Clinton Regional Hospital . . . . .Clinton OK
Integris Grove General Hospital . . . . .Grove OK
Integris Marshall Memorial Hospital . . . . .Madill OK

Integris Mayes County Medical Center . . . . .Pryor OK
Integris Mental Health System - Spencer . . . . .Spencer OK
Integris Southwest Medical Center . . . . .Oklahoma City OK
Interfaith Medical Center .Brooklyn NY
Intergrated Specialty Hospital - Midwest City . . . . .Midwest City OK
Intergris Canadian Valley Regional Hospital . . . . . . .Yukon OK
Intermedical Hospital of South Carolina . . . . .Columbia SC
Intermountain Hospital . . . .Boise ID
Intracare Hospital . . . . . .Houston TX
Intracare North Hospital .Houston TX
Ionia County Memorial Hospital . . . . .Ionia MI
Iowa Lutheran Hospital . . . . .Des Moines IA
Iowa Medical & Classification Center . . . . .Oakdale IA
Iowa Methodist Medical Center . . . . .Des Moines IA
Iredell Memorial Hospital . . . . .Statesville NC
Ireland Army Community Hospital . . . . .Fort Knox KY
Iron County General Hospital .Iron River MI
Iroquois Memorial Hospital . . . . .Watseka IL
Irvine Regional Hospital . . .Irvine CA
Irvington General Hospital .Irvington NJ
Irwin Army Community Hospital . . . . .Fort Riley KS
Irwin County Hospital . . . .Ocilla GA
Isham Health Center . . .Andover MA
Island Hospital . . . . . .Anacortes WA
Island Medical Center . . . . .Hempstead NY
Itasca Medical Center . . . . .Grand Rapids MN
Ivinson Memorial Hospital . . . . .Laramie WY
J Arthur Dosher Memorial Hospital . . . . .Southport NC
J C Blair Memorial Hospital . . . . .Huntingdon PA
J D Mccarty Center For Children . . . . .Norman OK
J Paul Jones Hospital . . .Camden AL
Jack D. Weiler Hospital of Albert Einstein College . . . . .Bronx NY
Jackson County Hospital . . . . .Marianna FL
Jackson County Hospital . . .Edna TX
Jackson County Hospital and Nursing Home . . . . .Scottsboro AL

Alphabetical Index

Jackson County Memorial Hospital ....Altus OK

Jackson County Public Hospital ....Maquoketa IA

Jackson General Hospital ....Ripley WV

Jackson Hospital and Clinic ....Montgomery AL

Jackson Medical Center ....Jackson AL

Jackson Memorial Hospital ....Miami FL

Jackson Municipal Hospital ....Jackson MN

Jackson Parish Hospital ....Jonesboro LA

Jackson Park Hospital Foundation ....Chicago IL

Jackson Purchase Medical Center ....Mayfield KY

Jackson South Community Hospital ....Miami FL

Jackson-Madison County General Hospital ....Jackson TN

Jacksonville Hospital ....Jacksonville AL

Jacobi Medical Center .... Bronx NY

Jacobson Memorial Hospital Care Center ....Elgin ND

Jamaica Hospital .....Jamaica NY

James B Haggin Memorial Hospital ....Harrodsburg KY

James Lawrence Kernan Hospital ....Baltimore MD

Jameson Memorial Hospital ....New Castle PA

Jamestown Hospital ..Jamestown ND

Jamestown Regional Medical Center ....Jamestown TN

Jane Phillips Medical Center ....Bartlesville OK

Jane Phillips Nowata Health Center ....Nowata OK

Jane Todd Crawford Memorial Hospital ....Greensburg KY

Jasper County Hospital ....Rensselaer IN

Jasper General Hospital ....Bay Springs MS

Jasper Memorial Hospital ....Monticello GA

Jay County Hospital .....Portland IN

Jay Hospital ....Jay FL

Jeanes Hospital ....Philadelphia PA

Jeannette District Memorial Hospital ....Jeannette PA

Jeff Anderson Regional Medical Center ....Meridian MS

Jeff Davis Hospital ..Hazlehurst GA

Jefferson Community Health Center ....Fairbury NE

Jefferson County Hospital ....Fairfield IA

Jefferson County Hospital ....Fayette MS

Jefferson County Hospital ....Waurika OK

Jefferson County Memorial Hospital ....Winchester KS

Jefferson General Hospital ....Port Townsend WA

Jefferson Hospital .....Louisville GA

Jefferson Memorial Hospital ....Crystal City MO

Jefferson Memorial Hospital ....Jefferson City TN

Jefferson Memorial Hospital ....Ranson WV

Jefferson Regional Medical Center ....Pine Bluff AR

Jefferson Regional Medical Center ....Pittsburgh PA

Jellico Community Hospital ....Jellico TN

Jenkins Community Hospital ....Jenkins KY

Jenkins County Hospital ...Millen GA

Jennie Edmundson Hospital ....Council Bluffs IA

Jennie M Melham Memorial Medical Center ....Broken Bow NE

Jennie Stuart Medical Center ....Hopkinsville KY

Jennings American Legion Hospital ....Jennings LA

Jerold Phelps Community Hospital ....Garberville CA

Jersey City Medical Center ....Jersey City NJ

Jersey Community Hospital ....Jerseyville IL

Jersey Shore Hospital ....Jersey Shore PA

Jersey Shore Medical Center ....Neptune NJ

Jewell County Hospital ..Mankato KS

Jewish Hospital ....Louisville KY

Jewish Hospital Kenwood ....Cincinnati OH

Jewish Hospital of Cincinnati ....Cincinnati OH

Jewish Hospital Shelbyville ....Shelbyville KY

Jewish Memorial Hospital ....Boston MA

JFK Johnson Rehabilitation Institute ....Edison NJ

JFK Medical Center .....Atlantis FL

Jim Taliaferro Community Mental Health Center ....Lawton OK

Joan Glancy Memorial Hospital ....Duluth GA

Joe Dimaggio Children's Hospital ....Hollywood FL

John and Mary Kirby Hospital ....Monticello IL

John C Fremont Medical Clinic ....Mariposa CA

John C Lincoln Hospital and Health Center ....Phoenix AZ

John C Lincoln Hospital-Deer Valley ....Phoenix AZ

John D Archbold Memorial Hospital ....Thomasville GA

John Ed Chambers Memorial Hospital ....Danville AR

John F Kennedy Medical Center ....Edison NJ

John F Kennedy Memorial Hospital ....Indio CA

John F Kennedy Memoria Hospital ....Philadelphia PA

John Fitzgibbon Memorial Hospital ....Marshall MO

John Heinz Institute of Rehab Medicine ....Wilkes-Barre PA

John J Madden Mental Health Center ....Hines IL

John Muir Medical Center ....Walnut Creek CA

John Randolph Medical Center ....Hopewell VA

John T Mather Memorial Hospital ....Port Jefferson NY

John Umstead Hospital ...Butner NC

Johns Community Hospital ....Taylor TX

Johns Hopkins Bayview Medical Center ....Baltimore MD

Johns Hopkins Hospital ....Baltimore MD

Johnson City Medical Center Hospital ....Johnson City TN

Johnson City Specialty Hospital ....Johnson City TN

Johnson County Health Care ....Buffalo WY

Johnson County Health Center ....Mountain City TN

Johnson County Hospital ....Tecumseh NE

Johnson Memorial Hospital ....Stafford Springs CT

Johnson Memorial Hospital ....Franklin IN

Johnson Memorial Hospital ....Dawson MN

Johnson Regional Medical Center ....Clarksville AR

Johnston Memorial Hospital ....Smithfield NC

Johnston Memorial Hospital ....Tishomingo OK

Johnston Memorial Hospital ....Abingdon VA

Johnston R. Bowman Health Center ....Chicago IL

Joint Township District Memorial Hospital ....Saint Marys OH

Alphabetical Index

Jones Memorial Hospital
. . . . .Wellsville NY
Jones Regional Medical Center
. . . . .Anamosa IA
Jordan Hospital . . . . . .Plymouth MA
Jordan Valley Hospital
. . . . .West Jordan UT
Jps Health Network . . .Fort Worth TX
Julian F. Keith Alcohol and Drug
Abuse Treatment Center
. . . . .Black Mountain NC
Juneau Recovery Hospital
. . . . .Juneau AK
Jupiter Medical Center . . . .Jupiter FL
Kadlec Medical Center
. . . . .Richland WA
Kahi Mohala . . . . . . .Ewa Beach HI
Kahuku Hospital . . . . . . .Kahuku HI
Kaiser Foundation Hospital
. . . . .Panorama City CA
Kaiser Foundation Hospital
. . . . .Redwood City CA
Kaiser Foundation Hospital
. . . . .San Rafael CA
Kaiser Foundation Hospital
. . . . .Santa Clara CA
Kaiser Foundation Hospital
. . . . .South San Francisco CA
Kaiser Foundation Hospital
. . . . .Walnut Creek CA
Kaiser Foundation Hospital -
Carson . . . . .Carson CA
Kaiser Foundation Hospital -
Fresno . . . . .Fresno CA
Kaiser Foundation Hospital -
Riverside . . . . .Riverside CA
Kaiser Foundation Hospital -
Sacramento . . . . . . .Sacramento CA
Kaiser Foundation Hospital
Fontana . . . . .Fontana CA
Kaiser Foundation Hospital Mental
Health Center . . . . .Los Angeles CA
Kaiser Foundation Hospital
Vallejo . . . . .Vallejo CA
Kaiser Foundation Hospital-Santa
Rosa . . . . .Santa Rosa CA
Kaiser Medical Center . .Hayward CA
Kaiser Medical Center . .Martinez CA
Kaiser Permanente
. . . . .Baldwin Park CA
Kaiser Permanente Foundation
Hospital . . . . .Honolulu HI
Kaiser Permanente Hospital
. . . . .San Diego CA
Kaiser Permanente Hospital
. . . . .San Francisco CA
Kaiser Permanente Hospital
. . . . .Woodland Hills CA
Kaiser Permanente Los Angeles
Medical Center . . . . .Los Angeles CA
Kaiser Permanente Medical
Center . . . . .Harbor City CA

Kaiser Permanente Medical Center
Bellflower . . . . .Bellflower CA
Kaiser Permanente Medical Center
Oakland Campus . . . . .Oakland CA
Kaiser Permanente Orange County
Medical Center . . . . . .Anaheim CA
Kaiser Permanente Sacramento
. . . . .Sacramento CA
Kaiser Permanente West Los Angeles
Medical Center . . . . .Los Angeles CA
Kaiser Sunnyside Medical
Center . . . . .Clackamas OR
Kalamazoo Psychiatric Hospital
. . . . .Kalamazoo MI
Kalispell Regional Hospital
. . . . .Kalispell MT
Kalkaska Memorial Health
Center . . . . .Kalkaska MI
Kanabec Hospital . . . . . . .Mora MN
Kane Community Hospital . .Kane PA
Kane County Hospital . . . .Kanab UT
Kansas City Orthopedic Institute
. . . . .Leawood KS
Kansas Heart Hospital . . .Wichita KS
Kansas Neurological Institute
. . . . .Topeka KS
Kansas Rehabilitation Hospital
. . . . .Topeka KS
Kansas Surgery and Recovery
Center Lp . . . . .Wichita KS
Kapiolani Medical Center at Pali
Momi . . . . .Aiea HI
Kapiolani Womens and Childrens
Medical Center . . . . . . .Honolulu HI
Kaplan Rehab Hospital . . .Kaplan LA
Kaseman Presbyterian Hospital
. . . . .Albuquerque NM
Katherine Shaw Bethea Hospital
. . . . .Dixon IL
Kau Hospital . . . . .Pahala HI
Kauai Veterans Memorial Hospital
. . . . .Waimea HI
Kaweah Delta and Visalia Hospital
. . . . .Visalia CA
Kearney County Health Services
. . . . .Minden NE
Kearny County Hospital . . . .Lakin KS
Kedren Community Health
Center . . . . .Los Angeles CA
Keefe Memorial Hospital
. . . . .Cheyenne Wells CO
Kell West Regional Hospital
. . . . .Wichita Falls TX
Keller Army Community Hospital
. . . . .West Point NY
Kelsey Memorial Hospital
. . . . .Lakeview MI
Kendall Medical Center . . .Miami FL
Kenmare Community Hospital
. . . . .Kenmare ND
Kenmore Mercy Hospital
. . . . .Kenmore NY

Kennedy Health System
. . . . .Cherry Hill NJ
Kennedy Hospital-Washington
. . . . .Turnersville NJ
Kennedy Krieger Children's
Hospital . . . . .Baltimore MD
Kennedy Memorial Hospital-University
Medical Center . . . . .Stratford NJ
Kenner Regional Medical Center
. . . . .Kenner LA
Kennewick General Hospital
. . . . .Kennewick WA
Kenosha Hospital and Medica
Center . . . . .Kenosha WI
Kensington Hospita
. . . . .Philadelphia PA
Kent and Queen Annes Hospital
. . . . .Chestertown MD
Kent County Memorial Hospital
. . . . .Warwick RI
Kentfield Medical Hospital
. . . . .Kentfield CA
Kentucky Correctional Psych
Center . . . . .La Grange KY
Kentucky River Medical Center
. . . . .Jackson KY
Kentucky State Penitentiary Medical
Clinic . . . . .Eddyville KY
Keokuk Area Hospital . . . .Keokuk IA
Keokuk County Health Center
. . . . .Sigourney IA
Kern Hospital and Medical
Center . . . . .Warren MI
Kern Medical Center . .Bakersfield CA
Kern Valley Hospital
. . . . .Lake Isabella CA
Kerrville State Hospital . .Kerrville TX
Kershaw County Medical
Center . . . . .Camden SC
Kessler Adventist Rehab
Hospital . . . . .Rockville MD
Kessler Institute For Rehabilitation
. . . . .East Orange NJ
Kessler Institute For Rehabilitation
. . . . .Saddle Brook NJ
Kessler Institute For Rehabilitation
. . . . .West Orange NJ
Ketchikan General Hospital
. . . . .Ketchikan AK
Kettering Hospital and Medical
Center . . . . .Kettering OH
Kettering Youth Services
. . . . .Washington Township OH
Kewanee Hospital . . . . . .Kewanee IL
Keweenaw Memorial Medical
Center . . . . .Laurium MI
Keystone Center . . . . . . .Chester PA
Kilmichael Hospital . .Kilmichael MS
Kimball - Ridge Center . .Waterloo IA
Kimball County Hospital . .Kimball NE
Kimball Medical Center
. . . . .Lakewood NJ
Kimble Hospital . . . . . . .Junction TX

Alphabetical Index

Kindred Hospital ....Atlanta GA
Kindred Hospital Los Angeles ....Los Angeles CA
Kindred Hospital Ontario ....Ontario CA
Kindred Hospital Sacramento ....Folsom CA
Kindred Hospital San Diego ....San Diego CA
Kindred Hospital San Francisco Bay Area ....San Leandro CA
Kindred Hospital - Charleston ....Charleston SC
Kindred Hospital Albuquerque ....Albuquerque NM
Kindred Hospital Arizona - Scottsdale ....Scottsdale AZ
Kindred Hospital Arlington ....Arlington TX
Kindred Hospital at Santa Ana ....Santa Ana CA
Kindred Hospital Bay Area ....Pasadena TX
Kindred Hospital Boston ..Boston MA
Kindred Hospital Boston North Shore Hospital ....Peabody MA
Kindred Hospital Brea .....Brea CA
Kindred Hospital Central Tampa ....Tampa FL
Kindred Hospital Chattanooga ....Chattanooga TN
Kindred Hospital Chicago - Lake Shore ....Chicago IL
Kindred Hospital Chicago Central ....Chicago IL
Kindred Hospital Chicago North ....Chicago IL
Kindred Hospital Cleveland ....Cleveland OH
Kindred Hospital Coral Gables ....Coral Gables FL
Kindred Hospital Dallas ...Dallas TX
Kindred Hospital Delaware County ....Darby PA
Kindred Hospital Denver ....Denver CO
Kindred Hospital Detroit ....Lincoln Park MI
Kindred Hospital Fort Lauderdale ....Fort Lauderdale FL
Kindred Hospital Fort Worth ....Fort Worth TX
Kindred Hospital Fort Worth Southwest ....Fort Worth TX
Kindred Hospital Greensboro ....Greensboro NC
Kindred Hospital Hollywood ....Hollywood FL
Kindred Hospital Houston ....Houston TX
Kindred Hospital Houston Northwest ....Houston TX

Kindred Hospital Indianapolis ....Indianapolis IN
Kindred Hospital Indianapolis South ....Greenwood IN
Kindred Hospital Kansas City ....Kansas City MO
Kindred Hospital Las Vegas ....Las Vegas NV
Kindred Hospital Las Vegas - Flamingo ....Las Vegas NV
Kindred Hospital Louisville ....Louisville KY
Kindred Hospital Mansfield ....Fort Worth TX
Kindred Hospital Metro Detroit ....Detroit MI
Kindred Hospital Milwaukee ....Greenfield WI
Kindred Hospital Milwaukee ....Milwaukee WI
Kindred Hospital Minneapolis ....Minneapolis MN
Kindred Hospital New Orleans ....New Orleans LA
Kindred Hospital North Florida ....Green Cove Springs FL
Kindred Hospital Northlake ....Northlake IL
Kindred Hospital of La Mirada ....La Mirada CA
Kindred Hospital of Southern California ....West Covina CA
Kindred Hospital Oklahoma City ....Oklahoma City OK
Kindred Hospital Philadelphia ....Philadelphia PA
Kindred Hospital Phoenix ....Phoenix AZ
Kindred Hospital Pittsburgh ....Oakdale PA
Kindred Hospital Saint Louis ....Saint Louis MO
Kindred Hospital Saint Petersburg ....Saint Petersburg FL
Kindred Hospital San Antonio ....San Antonio TX
Kindred Hospital Seattle ..Seattle WA
Kindred Hospital Sycamore ....Sycamore IL
Kindred Hospital Tampa ...Tampa FL
Kindred Hospital Tucson ..Tucson AZ
Kindred Hospital Westminster ....Westminster CA
Kindred Hospital White Rock ....Dallas TX
Kindred Hospital Wyoming Valley ....Wilkes-Barre PA
Kingfisher Regional Hospital ....Kingfisher OK
Kingman Community Hospital ....Kingman KS
Kingman Regional Medical Center ....Kingman AZ

Kings County Hospital Center ....Brooklyn NY
Kings Daughters Hospital ....Madison IN
Kings Daughters Hospital ....Brookhaven MS
Kings Daughters Hospital ....Greenville MS
Kings Daughters Hospital ....Temple TX
Kings Daughters Hospital Swing Bed ....Yazoo City MS
Kings Daughters Medical Center ....Ashland KY
Kings Mountain Hospital ....Kings Mountain NC
Kings Park Psychiatric Center ....Brentwood NY
Kingsboro Psychiatric Center ....Brooklyn NY
Kingsbrook Jewish Medical Center ....Brooklyn NY
Kingsburg Medical Center ....Kingsburg CA
Kingston Hospital .....Kingston NY
Kingwood Health Center ....Kingwood TX
Kingwood Medical Center ....Kingwood TX
Kino Community Hospital ....Tucson AZ
Kiowa District Hospital ....Kiowa KS
Kirby Forensic Psychiatric Center ....New York NY
Kirkbride Center ....Philadelphia PA
Kishwaukee Community Hospital ....De Kalb IL
Kit Carson County Memorial Hospital ....Burlington CO
Kittitas Valley Community Hospital ....Ellensburg WA
Kittson Memorial Health Care Center ....Hallock MN
Klickitat Valley Hospital ....Goldendale WA
Knapp Medical Center ..Weslaco TX
Knollwood Psych and Chemical Dependency Center ...Riverside CA
Knox Community Hospital ....Mount Vernon OH
Knox County Hospital ....Barbourville KY
Knox County Hospital ..Knox City TX
Knoxville Area Community Hospital ....Knoxville IA
Kohala Hospital ....Kapaau HI
Kona Community Hospital ....Kealakekua HI
Kootenai Medical Center ....Coeur D'alene ID
Kosciusko Community Hospital ....Warsaw IN
Kossuth County Hospital ..Algona IA

Alphabetical Index

Kremmling Memorial Hospital . . . . Kremmling CO
Kuakini Medical Center . . Honolulu HI
Kula Hospital . . . . Kula HI
L V Stabler Memorial Hospital . . . . Greenville AL
La Amistad Behavioral Health Services . . . . Maitland FL
La Casa Mental Health Rehabilitation Center . . . . Long Beach CA
La Casa Psychiatric Healthcare Facility . . . . Long Beach CA
La Grange Memorial Hospital . . . . La Grange IL
La Hacienda Treatment Center . . . . Hunt TX
La Palma Intercommunity Hospital . . . . La Palma CA
La Paz Regional Hospital . . . . Parker AZ
La Place Rehabilitation Hospital . . . . La Place LA
La Porte Hospital . . . . . . La Porte IN
Labette County Medical Center . . . . Parsons KS
Lac High Desert Hospital . . . . Lancaster CA
Lac/ Harbor-ucla Medical Center . . . . Torrance CA
Lac/King - Drew Medical Center . . . . Los Angeles CA
Lac/Olive View - UCLA . . . Sylmar CA
Lackey Memorial Hospital and Swing Bed . . . . Forest MS
Lady of The Sea General Hospital . . . . Cut Off LA
Lafayette General Medical Center . . . . Lafayette LA
Lafayette Home Hospital . . . . Lafayette IN
Lafayette Hospital . . . . . . Arroyo PR
Lafayette Regional Health Center . . . . Lexington MO
Lagniappe Hospital . . . Shreveport LA
Lagrange Community Hospital . . . . Lagrange IN
Laguna Honda Hospital . . . . San Francisco CA
Lahey Clinic . . . . Burlington MA
Laird Hospital . . . . Union MS
Laird Memorial Hospital . . Kilgore TX
Lake Area Hospital . . . . . Webster SD
Lake Butler Hospital - Hand Surgery Center . . . . Lake Butler FL
Lake Charles Memorial Hospital . . . . Lake Charles LA
Lake Chelan Community Hospital . . . . Chelan WA
Lake City Medical Center . . . . Lake City FL
Lake City Medical Center . . . . Lake City MN

Lake Cumberland Regional Hospital . . . . Somerset KY
Lake District Hospital . . Lakeview OR
Lake Forest Hospital . . Lake Forest IL
Lake Granbury Medical Center . . . . Granbury TX
Lake Hospital System . . . . Painesville OH
Lake Martin Community Hospital . . . . Dadeville AL
Lake Mead Hospital Medica Center . . . . . . North Las Vegas NV
Lake Norman Regional Medical Center . . . . Mooresville NC
Lake Pointe Medical Center . . . . Rowlett TX
Lake Region Hospital . . . . Fergus Falls MN
Lake Regional Health System . . . . Osage Beach MO
Lake Shore Health Care Center . . . . Irving NY
Lake Taylor Hospital . . . . Norfolk VA
Lake Wales Medical Center . . . . Lake Wales FL
Lake Whitney Medical Center . . . . Whitney TX
Lakeland Community Hospital . . . . Haleyville AL
Lakeland Hospital - Niles . . . Niles MI
Lakeland Hospital - Saint Joseph . . . . Saint Joseph MI
Lakeland Medical Center . . . . New Orleans LA
Lakeland Medical Center . . . . Elkhorn WI
Lakeland Regional Hospital . . . . Springfield MO
Lakeland Regional Medical Center . . . . Lakeland FL
Lakeland Specialty Hospital - Berrien . . . . Berrien Center MI
Lakes Region General Hospital . . . . Laconia NH
Lakes Regional Healthcare . . . . Spirit Lake IA
Lakeshore Community Hospital . . . . Shelby MI
Lakeshore Mental Health Institute . . . . Knoxville TN
Lakeside Alternatives Hospital . . . . Orlando FL
Lakeside Behavioral Health System . . . . Memphis TN
Lakeside Hospital . . . . . Metairie LA
Lakeside Medical Center . . . . Pine City MN
Lakeside Memorial Hospital . . . . Brockport NY
Lakeside Women's Hospital . . . . Oklahoma City OK
Lakeview Community Hospital . . . . Eufaula AL

Lakeview Community Hospital . . . . Paw Paw MI
Lakeview Hospital . . . . Bountiful UT
Lakeview Medical Center . . . . Rice Lake WI
Lakeview Memorial Hospital . . . . Stillwater MN
Lakeview Memorial Hospital . . . . Two Harbors MN
Lakeview Neurorehab Center Midwest . . . . Waterford WI
Lakeview Regional Medical Center . . . . Covington LA
Lakeway Regional Hospital . . . . Morristown TN
Lakewood Health Center . . . . Baudette MN
Lakewood Health System . . . . Staples MN
Lakewood Hospital . . . Cleveland OH
Lakewood Regional Medical Center . . . . Lakewood CA
Lallie Kemp Regional Medical Center . . . . Independence LA
Lamb Healthcare Center . . . . Littlefield TX
Lanai Community Hospital . . . . Lanai City HI
Lancaster Community Hospital . . . . Lancaster CA
Lancaster General Hospital . . . . Lancaster PA
Lancaster General Hospital - Susquehanna Division . . Columbia PA
Lancaster Regional Medical Center . . . . Lancaster PA
Lander Valley Medical Center . . . . Lander WY
Landmark Medical Center . . . . Pomona CA
Landmark Medical Center . . . . Woonsocket RI
Landmark Medical Center - Fogarty . . . . . North Smithfield RI
Lane County Hospital . . . Dighton KS
Lane County Psychiatric Hospital . . . . Eugene OR
Lane Memorial Hospital . . Zachary LA
Langlade Memorial Hospital . . . . Antigo WI
Langley Porter Psych Institute . . . . San Francisco CA
Lanier Park Hospital . . Gainesville GA
Lankenau Hospital . . Wynnewood PA
Lanterman Developmental Center . . . . Pomona CA
Lapeer Regional Hospital . . Lapeer MI
Larabida Childrens Hospital . . . . Chicago IL
Largo Medical Center . . . . Largo FL
Larkin Community Hospital . . . . South Miami FL
Larned State Hospital . . . Larned KS

Alphabetical Index

Larue D Carter Memorial Hospital ....Indianapolis IN
Las Colinas Medical Center ....Irving TX
Las Encinas Hospital ..Pasadena CA
Las Vegas Medical Center ....Las Vegas NM
Lasalle General Hospital ....Jena LA
Latimer County General Hospital ....Wilburton OK
Latrobe Area Hospital ...Latrobe PA
Latter-day Saints Hospital ....Salt Lake City UT
Laughlin Memorial Hospital ....Greeneville TN
Laureate Psychiatric Clinic and Hospital ....Tulsa OK
Laurel Heights Hospital ..Atlanta GA
Laurel Regional Hospital ..Laurel MD
Laurel Ridge Hospital-Brown Schools ....San Antonio TX
Laurens County Hospital ..Clinton SC
Lavaca Medical Center ....Hallettsville TX
Lawnwood Pavilion ...Fort Pierce FL
Lawnwood Regional Medical Center ....Fort Pierce FL
Lawrence and Memorial Hospital ....New London CT
Lawrence Baptist Medical Center ....Moulton AL
Lawrence County Hospital ....Monticello MS
Lawrence County Memorial Hospital ....Lawrenceville IL
Lawrence F. Quigley Memorial Hospital ....Chelsea MA
Lawrence General Hospital ....Lawrence MA
Lawrence Hospital ....Bronxville NY
Lawrence Memorial Hospital ....Walnut Ridge AR
Lawrence Memorial Hospital ....Lawrence KS
Lawrence Memorial Hospital of Medford ....Medford MA
LBJ Tropical Medical Center ....Pago Pago AS
Le Bonheur Children's Medical Center ....Memphis TN
Lea Regional Hospital ....Hobbs NM
Leahi Hospital ....Honolulu HI
Leake County Memorial Hospital ....Carthage MS
Leaves ....Richardson TX
Lebanon Community Hospital ....Lebanon OR
Lee County Community Hospital ....Pennington Gap VA
Lee Hospital ....Johnstown PA
Lee Memorial Health System ....Fort Myers FL

Lee Moffitt Cancer Center and Research Institute ......Tampa FL
Leelanau Memorial Health Center ....Northport MI
Lees Summit Hospital ....Lees Summit MO
Leesburg Regional Medical Center ....Leesburg FL
Legacy Emanuel Hospital and Health Center ....Portland OR
Legacy Good Samaritan Hospital and Medical Center ....Portland OR
Legacy Meridian Park Hospital ....Tualatin OR
Legacy Mount Hood Medical Center ....Gresham OR
Lehigh Regional Medical Center ....Lehigh Acres FL
Lehigh Valley Hospital ..Allentown PA
Leland Medical Plaza .....Plano TX
Lemuel Shattuck Hospital ....Boston MA
Lenoir Memorial Hospital ....Kinston NC
Lenox Hill Hospital ....New York NY
Leo N Levi National Arthritis Hospital ....Hot Springs AR
Leonard J Chaubert Medical Center ....Houma LA
Lester E. Cox Medical Center - North ....Springfield MO
Lester E. Cox Medical Center South ....Springfield MO
Levindale Hebrew Geriatric Center ....Baltimore MD
Lewis and Clark Specialty Hospital ....Yankton SD
Lewis County General Hospital ....Lowville NY
Lewis-Gale Medical Center ....Salem VA
Lewistown Hospital ...Lewistown PA
Lexington Medical Center ....West Columbia SC
Lexington Memorial Hospital ....Lexington NC
Liberty County Hospital ..Chester MT
Liberty Dayton Hospital ...Liberty TX
Liberty Hospital ....Liberty MO
Liberty Regional Medical Center ....Hinesville GA
Licking Memorial Hospital ....Newark OH
Lifecare Hospital .....Muskegon MI
Lifecare Hospital - Dayton ....Miamisburg OH
Lifecare Hospital - Doctors ....Shreveport LA
Lifecare Hospital - Main ....Shreveport LA
Lifecare Hospital - Pierremont ....Shreveport LA

Lifecare Hospital of Dallas ....Dallas TX
Lifecare Hospital of Denver ....Denver CO
Lifecare Hospital of Milwaukee at Saint Joseph ....Milwaukee WI
Lifecare Hospital of Milwaukee at Saint Michael ....Milwaukee WI
Lifecare Hospital of New Orleans ....New Orleans LA
Lifecare Hospital of New Orleans - Chalmette ....Chalmette LA
Lifecare Hospital of New Orleans - Kenner ....Kenner LA
Lifecare Hospital of North Carolina ....Rocky Mount NC
Lifecare Hospital of North Texas - Fort Worth ....Fort Worth TX
Lifecare Hospital of Pittsburgh ....Pittsburgh PA
Lifecare Hospital of San Antonio ....San Antonio TX
Lifecare Hospital of South Texas ....Edinburg TX
Lifecourse Center For Rehab Services ....Farmington NM
Lifestream Behavioral Center ....Leesburg FL
Lillian M Hudspeth Memorial Hospital ....Sonora TX
Lima Memorial Hospital ....Lima OH
Limestone Medical Center ....Groesbeck TX
Lincoln Community Hospital ....Hugo CO
Lincoln County Hospital ..Lincoln KS
Lincoln County Medical Center ....Ruidoso NM
Lincoln County Memorial Hospital ....Troy MO
Lincoln Developmental Center ....Springfield IL
Lincoln General Hospital ..Ruston LA
Lincoln Hospital .....Davenport WA
Lincoln Hospital Medical Center ....Los Angeles CA
Lincoln Medical and Mental Health Center ....Bronx NY
Lincoln Medical Center ....Lincolnton NC
Lincoln Regional Center ..Lincoln NE
Lincoln Regional Hospital ....Fayetteville TN
Lincoln Trail Behavioral Health System ....Radcliff KY
Linden Municipal Hospital ....Linden TX
Linden Oaks Hospital ...Naperville IL
Lindsay Municipal Hospital ....Lindsay OK
Lindsborg Community Hospital ....Lindsborg KS
Linton Hospital ....Linton ND

Alphabetical Index

Lisbon Medical Center . . .Lisbon ND
Little Company of Mary Hospital
. . . . .Torrance CA
Little Company of Mary Hospital
. . . . .Evergreen Park IL
Little Falls Hospital . . . .Little Falls NY
Little River Memorial Hospital
. . . . .Ashdown AR
Littleton Adventist Hospital
. . . . .Littleton CO
Littleton Regional Hospital
. . . . .Littleton NH
Litzenberg Memorial County
Hospital . . . . .Central City NE
Livengrin Foundation . .Bensalem PA
Living Hope Texarkana
. . . . .Texarkana AR
Livingston Hospital and Healthcare
Service . . . . .Salem KY
Livingston Memorial Hospital
. . . . .Livingston MT
Livingston Regional Hospital
. . . . .Livingston TN
Llano Memorial Hospital . . .Llano TX
Lock Haven Hospital
. . . . .Lock Haven PA
Lockport Memorial Hospital
. . . . .Lockport NY
Lodi Community Hospital . . .Lodi OH
Lodi Memorial Hospital . . . .Lodi CA
Lodi Memorial Hospital West
. . . . .Lodi CA
Logan County Hospital . . .Oakley KS
Logan General Hospital . .Logan WV
Logan Hospital . . . . .Logan UT
Logan Hospital and Medical Center
. . . . .Guthrie OK
Logan Memorial Hospital
. . . . .Russellville KY
Logansport State Hospital
. . . . .Logansport IN
Loma Linda University Behavioral
Medicine Center . . . . . .Redlands CA
Loma Linda University Community
Medical Center . . . . .Loma Linda CA
Loma Linda University Medical
Center . . . . .Loma Linda CA
Lompoc Hospital District
. . . . .Lompoc CA
Long Beach Medical Center
. . . . .Long Beach NY
Long Beach Memorial Hospital
. . . . .Long Beach CA
Long Island College Hospital
. . . . .Brooklyn NY
Long Island Jewish Medical
Center . . . . .New Hyde Park NY
Long Prairie Memorial Hospital
. . . . .Long Prairie MN
Long Term Care Hospital of
Jackson . . . . .Montgomery AL
Longmont United Hospital
. . . . .Longmont CO

Longview Regional Medical
Center . . . . .Longview TX
Lookout Memorial Hospital
. . . . .Spearfish SD
Loretto Hospital . . . . . . .Chicago IL
Loring Hospital . . . . .Sac City IA
Loris Community Hospital
. . . . .Loris SC
Los Alamitos Medical Center
. . . . .Los Alamitos CA
Los Alamos Medical Center
. . . . .Los Alamos NM
Los Angeles Community
Hospital . . . . .Los Angeles CA
Los Angeles Community Hospital of
Norwalk . . . . .Los Angeles CA
Los Angeles County - University of
Southern California . .Los Angeles CA
Los Angeles Metropolitan Medical
Center - Hawthorn . . .Hawthorne CA
Los Angeles Metropolitan Medical
Center - La Campus
. . . . .Los Angeles CA
Los Angeles Sheriffs Department
Medical . . . . .Los Angeles CA
Los Robles Regional Medical
Center . . . . .Thousand Oaks CA
Lost Rivers District Hospital . .Arco ID
Loudoun Hospital Center
. . . . .Leesburg VA
Louis A Weiss Memorial Hospital
. . . . .Chicago IL
Louis Smith Memorial Hospital
. . . . .Lakeland GA
Louise Obici Memorial Hospital
. . . . .Suffolk VA
Louisiana Extended Care Hospital
. . . . .Arcadia LA
Louisiana Health Care Specialty
Hospital . . . . .Natchitoches LA
Louisiana Heart Hospital
. . . . .Lacomb LA
Louisiana State University Medical
Center . . . . .Shreveport LA
Lourdes Counseling Center
. . . . .Richland WA
Lourdes Hospital . . . . .Paducah KY
Lourdes Medical Center . .Pasco WA
Lourdes Medical Center of Burlington
County . . . . .Willingboro NJ
Lovelace Health Systems
. . . . .Albuquerque NM
Low Country General Hospital
. . . . .Beaufort SC
Lowell General Hospital . . .Lowell MA
Lower Florida Keys Health
Systems . . . . .Key West FL
Lower Umpqua Hospital
. . . . .Reedsport OR
Loyola University Center and Ronald
McDonald Childrens Hospital
. . . . .Maywood IL

LSU - E.A. Conway Medical
Center . . . . .Monroe LA
Lucas County Health Center
. . . . .Chariton IA
Lucerne Medical Center . .Orlando FL
Lucille Salter Packard Childrens
Hospital . . . . .Palo Alto CA
Luling Rehab Hospital . . . . .Luling LA
Luther Hospital . . . . . .Eau Claire WI
Lutheran General Hospital
. . . . .Park Ridge IL
Lutheran Heart Hospital . . . .Mesa AZ
Lutheran Hospital . . . .Fort Wayne IN
Lutheran Hospital . . . .Cleveland OH
Lutheran Medical Center
. . . . .Brooklyn NY
Luverne Community Hospital
. . . . .Luverne MN
Lynchburg General Hospital
. . . . .Lynchburg VA
Lyndon B. Johnson General
Hospital . . . . .Houston TX
Lynn County Hospital District
. . . . .Tahoka TX
Lynn House of Potomac Valley
. . . . .Alexandria VA
Lyster Army Community
Hospital . . . . .Fort Rucker AL
Mac Neal Memorial Hospital
. . . . .Berwyn IL
Mackinac Straits Hospital and Health
Center . . . . .Saint Ignace MI
Macon County General Hospital
. . . . .Lafayette TN
Macon Northside Hospital
. . . . .Macon GA
Mad River Community
Hospital . . . . .Arcata CA
Madelia Community Hospital
. . . . .Madelia MN
Madera Community Hospital
. . . . .Madera CA
Madigan Army Medical Center
. . . . .Tacoma WA
Madison Community Hospital
. . . . .Madison Hts MI
Madison Community Hospital
. . . . .Madison SD
Madison County Hospital
. . . . .London OH
Madison County Medical Center
. . . . .Canton MS
Madison County Memorial
Hospital . . . . .Madison FL
Madison County Memorial
Hospital . . . . .Winterset IA
Madison Hospital . . . .South Bend IN
Madison Hospital . . . . .Madison MN
Madison Medical Center
. . . . .Fredericktown MO
Madison Memorial Hospital
. . . . .Rexburg ID
Madison Parish Hospital . .Tallulah LA

Alphabetical Index

Madison Saint Joseph Health Center . . . . .Madisonville TX
Madison State Hospital . .Madison IN
Madison Valley Hospital . . .Ennis MT
Madonna Rehabilitation Hospital . . . . .Lincoln NE
Magee General Hospital . .Magee MS
Magee Rehabilitation Hospital . . . . .Philadelphia PA
Magee-Womens Hospital . . . . .Pittsburgh PA
Magic Valley Regional Medical Center . . . . .Twin Falls ID
Magnolia Hospital . . . . .Magnolia AR
Magnolia Hospital . . . . . .Corinth MS
Mahaska County Hospital . . . . .Oskaloosa IA
Mahnomen Health Center . . . . .Mahnomen MN
Maimonides Medical Center . . . . .Brooklyn NY
Main Line Hospital - Bryn Mawr . . . . .Bryn Mawr PA
Maine Coast Memorial Hospital . . . . .Ellsworth ME
Maine General Medical Center . . . . .Waterville ME
Maine General Medical Center - Augusta Campus . . . . . .Augusta ME
Maine Medical Center . .Portland ME
Mainland Medical Center . . . . .Texas City TX
Major Hospital . . . . . . .Shelbyville IN
Malvern Institute . . . . . . .Malvern PA
Mammoth Hospital . . . . .Mammoth Lakes CA
Manatee Glen Hospital . . . . .Bradenton FL
Manatee Memorial Hospital . . . . .Bradenton FL
Manatee Palms Youth Services . . . . .Bradenton FL
Manchester Memorial Hospital . . . . .Manchester CT
Mangum City Hospital . .Mangum OK
Manhasset Ambulatory Care Pavilion . . . . .Manhasset NY
Manhattan Eye Ear Throat Hospital . . . . .New York NY
Manhattan Psychiatric Center . . . . .New York NY
Manhattan Surgical Hospital . . . . .Manhattan KS
Maniilaq Association and Health Center . . . . .Kotzebue AK
Manning Regional Healthcare Center . . . . .Manning IA
Marcum and Wallace Memorial Hospital . . . . .Irvine KY
Marcus Daly Memorial Hospital . . . . .Hamilton MT
Marengo Memorial Hospital . . . . .Marengo IA

Margaret Mary Community Hospital . . . . .Batesville IN
Margaret R Pardee Memorial Hospital . . . . . . .Hendersonvlle NC
Margaretville Memorial Hospital . . . . .Margaretville NY
Maria Parham Hospital . . . . .Henderson NC
Marian Community Hospital . . . . .Carbondale PA
Marian Medical Center . . . . .Santa Maria CA
Marianjoy Rehabilitation Center . . . . .Wheaton IL
Marias Medical Center . . .Shelby MT
Maricopa Medical Center . . . . .Phoenix AZ
Marietta Memorial Hospital . . . . .Marietta OH
Marin General Hospital . . . . .San Rafael CA
Mariners Hospital . . . . . .Tavernier FL
Marion County Medical Center . . . . .Marion SC
Marion General Hospital . . .Marion IN
Marion General Hospital . . . . .Columbia MS
Marion General Hospital . .Marion OH
Marion Memorial Hospital . .Marion IL
Mark Reed Hospital . . .McCleary WA
Mark Twain Saint Josephs Hospital . . . . .San Andreas CA
Marlboro Park Hospital . . . . .Bennettsville SC
Marlborough Hospital . . . . .Marlborough MA
Marlette Community Hospital . . . . .Marlette MI
Marquette General Hospital . . . . .Marquette MI
Marshall Browning Hospital . . . . .Du Quoin IL
Marshall County Healthcare/Hospital . . . . .Britton SD
Marshall County Hospital . . . . .Benton KY
Marshall Hospital . . . . .Placerville CA
Marshall I. Pickens Hospital . . . . .Greenville SC
Marshall Medical Center . . . . .Lewisburg TN
Marshall Medical Center North . . . . .Guntersville AL
Marshall Medical Center South . . . . .Boaz AL
Marshall Regional Medical Center . . . . .Marshall TX
Marshalltown Medical and Surgical Center . . . . .Marshalltown IA
Martha Jefferson Hospital . . . . .Charlottesville VA
Marthas Vineyard Hospital . . . . .Oak Bluffs MA

Martin Army Community Hospital . . . . .Fort Benning GA
Martin County Hospital District . . . . .Stanton TX
Martin General Hospital . . . . .Williamston NC
Martin Memorial Hospital - South . . . . .Stuart FL
Martin Memorial Medical Center . . . . .Stuart FL
Mary Black Memorial Hospital . . . . .Spartanburg SC
Mary Breckinridge Hospital . . . . .Hyden KY
Mary Bridge Childrens Health Center . . . . .Tacoma WA
Mary Chiles Hospital . . . . .Mount Sterling KY
Mary Free Bed Hospital and Rehab . . . . .Grand Rapids MI
Mary Greeley Medical Center . . . . .Ames IA
Mary Hurley Health Center . . . . .Coalgate OK
Mary Immaculate Hospital . . . . .Jamaica NY
Mary Immaculate Hospital . . . . .Newport News VA
Mary Lane Hospital . . . . . . .Ware MA
Mary Lanning Memorial Hospital . . . . .Hastings NE
Mary Rutan Hospital . . . . .Bellefontaine OH
Mary S Harper Geriatric Psychiatry Center . . . . .Tuscaloosa AL
Mary Shiels Hospital . . . .Dallas TX
Mary Washington Hospital . . . . .Fredericksburg VA
Maryland General Hospital . . . . .Baltimore MD
Maryland Penitentiary Hospital . . . . .Baltimore MD
Marymount Hospital . . . . .Garfield Heights OH
Marymount Medical Center . . . . .London KY
Maryvale Hospital Medical Center . . . . .Phoenix AZ
Maryview Medical Center/Portsmouth General . . . . .Portsmouth VA
Mason District Hospital . . .Havana IL
Mason General Hospital . . . . .Shelton WA
Masonic Geriatric Health Care Center . . . . . . .Wallingford CT
Massac Memorial Hospital . . . . .Metropolis IL
Massachusetts Correctional Institution . . . . .Norfolk MA
Massachusetts Eye and Ear Infirmary . . . . . . .Boston MA
Massachusetts General Hospital . . . . .Boston MA

Alphabetical Index

Massachusetts Hospital School .Canton MA
Massena Memorial Hospital . . . . .Massena NY
Massillon Community Hospital . . . . .Massillon OH
Matagorda General Hospital . . . . .Bay City TX
Matheny School and Hospital . . . . .Peapack NJ
Maude Norton Memorial City Hospital . . . . .Columbus KS
Maui Memorial Hospital . .Wailuku HI
Maury Regional Hospital . . . . .Columbia TN
Mayers Memorial Hospital . . . . .Fall River Mills CA
Mayo Clinic . . . . .Rochester MN
Mayo Clinic Hospital . . . .Phoenix AZ
Mayo Regional Hospital . . . . .Dover Foxcroft ME
Mayview State Hospital . . . . .Bridgeville PA
Mc Alester Regional Health Center . . . . .Mc Alester OK
Mc Allen Heart Hospital . . . . .Mc Allen TX
Mc Allen Medical Center . . . . .Mc Allen TX
Mc Donough District Hospital .Macomb IL
Mc Neil Island Correction Center - Health Services . . . . .Steilacoom WA
McCain Correctional Hospital . . . . .McCain NC
McCall Memorial Hospital . . . . .Mc Call ID
McCamey Hospital and Convalescent Center . . . . .Mc Camey TX
McCone County Medical Assistance Facility . . . . .Circle MT
McCullough-Hyde Memorial Hospital . . . . .Oxford OH
McCune Brooks Hospital . . . . .Carthage MO
McCurtain Memorial Hospital .Idabel OK
McDonald Army Community Hospital . . . . .Fort Eustis VA
McDowell Appalachian Regional Hospital . . . . .Mc Dowell KY
McDowell Hospital . . . . .Marion NC
McDuffie Regional Medical Center . . . . .Thomson GA
McFarland Specialty Hospital . . . . .Lebanon TN
McGehee Desha County Hospital . . . . .McGehee AR
McKay-Dee Hospital Center . . . . .Ogden UT
McKee Medical Center . . . . .Loveland CO

McKenna Memorial Hospital . . . . .New Braunfels TX
McKenzie County Memorial Hospital . . . . .Watford City ND
McKenzie Memorial Hospital . . . . .Sandusky MI
McKenzie-Willamette Hospital . . . . .Springfield OR
McLaren Regional Medical Center . . . . .Flint MI
McLean Hospital . . . . . .Belmont MA
McLeod Regional Medical Center . . . . .Florence SC
McNairy Methodist Healthcare Hospital . . . . .Selmer TN
Meade District Hospital . . .Meade KS
Meadow Pines Hospital . . . . .Longview TX
Meadow Wood Hospital . . . . .New Castle DE
Meadowbrook Hospital . .Gardner KS
Meadowbrook Rehab Hospital . . . . .Lafayette LA
Meadowbrook Rehab Hospital of West Gables . . . . .Miami FL
Meadowbrook Rehabilitation Hospital of Tulsa . . . . .Tulsa OK
Meadowcrest Hospital . . . .Gretna LA
Meadowlands Hospital Medical Center . . . . .Secaucus NJ
Meadows Hospital . . .Bloomington IN
Meadows Psychiatric Center . . . . .Centre Hall PA
Meadows Regional Medical Center . . . . .Vidalia GA
Meadowview Regional Medical Center . . . . .Maysville KY
Meadville Medical Center . . . . .Meadville PA
Meadville Medical Center - Grove Street . . . . .Meadville PA
Mease Countryside Hospital . . . . .Safety Harbor FL
Mease Hospital Dunedin .Dunedin FL
Mecosta County General Hospital . . . . .Big Rapids MI
Medcenter One . . . . . . .Bismarck ND
Medcentral Mansfield Hospital . . . . .Mansfield OH
Medfield State Hospital . . . . .Westborough MA
Medical Arts Hospital . . . .Lamesa TX
Medical Behavioral Center . . . . .Panama City FL
Medical Center . . . . .Columbus GA
Medical Center . . .Bowling Green KY
Medical Center at Franklin . . . . .Franklin KY
Medical Center at Lancaster . . . . .Lancaster TX
Medical Center at Princeton . . . . .Princeton NJ

Medical Center at Scottsville . . . . .Scottsville KY
Medical Center at Terrell . . .Terrell TX
Medical Center Beaver . .Beaver PA
Medical Center Blount . .Oneonta AL
Medical Center East . . . . .Birmingham AL
Medical Center Enterprise . . . . .Enterprise AL
Medical Center Hospital . .Marion OH
Medical Center Hospital . .Odessa TX
Medical Center of Arlington . . . . .Arlington TX
Medical Center of Aurora - North Campus . . . . .Aurora CO
Medical Center of Aurora - South Campus . . . . .Aurora CO
Medical Center of Central Georgia . . . . .Macon GA
Medical Center of Independence . . . . .Independence MO
Medical Center of Lewisville . . . . .Lewisville TX
Medical Center of Louisiana - Charity Hospital . . . . .New Orleans LA
Medical Center of Louisiana at New Orleans . . . . .New Orleans LA
Medical Center of Manchester . . . . .Manchester TN
Medical Center of Mesquite . . . . .Mesquite TX
Medical Center of Ocean County . . . . .Brick Township NJ
Medical Center of Plano . . .Plano TX
Medical Center of South Arkansas . . . . .El Dorado AR
Medical Center of Southeastern Oklahoma . . . . .Durant OK
Medical Center of Southern Indiana . . . . .Charlestown IN
Medical Center of Southwest Louisiana . . . . .Lafayette LA
Medical Central Crestline Hospital . . . . .Crestline OH
Medical City Hospital - Dallas .Dallas TX
Medical College Hospital of Ohio-toledo . . . . .Toledo OH
Medical College of Georgia . . . . .Augusta GA
Medical College of Penn-Main Campus . . . . .Philadelphia PA
Medical Park Hospital . . . . . .Hope AR
Medical Park Hospital . . . . .Winston-Salem NC
Medical Surgical Hospital . . . . .Milledgeville GA
Medical University Hospital . . . . .Charleston SC
Medicine Lodge Memorial Hospital . . . . . . .Medicine Lodge KS
Medina Community Hospital .Hondo TX

Alphabetical Index

Medina General Hospital ....Medina OH
Medina Memorial Hospital ....Medina NY
Mediplex Rehab Bowling Green ....Bowling Green KY
Mediplex Rehabilitation Hospital-Marlton ....Marlton NJ
Medlink Hospital of Capitol Hill ....Washington DC
Meeker County Memorial Hospital ....Litchfield MN
Melissa Memorial Hospital ....Holyoke CO
Melrose Area Hospital - Centracare ....Melrose MN
Melrose-Wakefield Hospital ....Melrose MA
Memorial Behavioral Health ....Gulfport MS
Memorial Care Unit ...Watertown SD
Memorial Center .....Bakersfield CA
Memorial Community Hospital ....Blair NE
Memorial Community Hospital ....Edgerton WI
Memorial General Medical Center ....Las Cruces NM
Memorial Health Center ..Sidney NE
Memorial Health Systems of East Texas ....Lufkin TX
Memorial Healthcare Center ....Owosso MI
Memorial Hermann Baptist - Orange ....Orange TX
Memorial Hermann Baptist Hospital - Beaumont ....Beaumont TX
Memorial Hermann Baptist Hospital - East ....Beaumont TX
Memorial Hermann Behavioral Health ....Beaumont TX
Memorial Hermann Childrens Hospital ....Houston TX
Memorial Hermann Continuing Care Hospital ....Houston TX
Memorial Hermann Fort Bend Medical Center ....Missouri City TX
Memorial Hermann Hospital ....Houston TX
Memorial Hermann Hospital - Woodlands .....The Woodlands TX
Memorial Hermann Katy Hospital ....Katy TX
Memorial Hermann Memorial City Hospital ....Houston TX
Memorial Hermann Southwest Hospital ....Houston TX
Memorial Hospital ....Colorado Springs CO
Memorial Hospital ....Craig CO
Memorial Hospital ....Bainbridge GA
Memorial Hospital .....Belleville IL
Memorial Hospital ....Carbondale IL

Memorial Hospital ......Carthage IL
Memorial Hospital ....Chester IL
Memorial Hospital ...Logansport IN
Memorial Hospital .....Seymour IN
Memorial Hospital .....Abilene KS
Memorial Hospital ..McPherson KS
Memorial Hospital ..Manchester KY
Memorial Hospital ..Aurora NE
Memorial Hospital ......Seward NE
Memorial Hospital .North Conway NH
Memorial Hospital .Albuquerque NM
Memorial Hospital ....Fremont OH
Memorial Hospital ......Stilwell OK
Memorial Hospital ....Towanda PA
Memorial Hospital ....York PA
Memorial Hospital ..Chattanooga TN
Memorial Hospital ....Gonzales TX
Memorial Hospital ....Seminole TX
Memorial Hospital - Oconomowoc ....Oconomowoc WI
Memorial Hospital and Health Care Center ....Jasper IN
Memorial Hospital and Medical Center Cumberland ....Cumberland MD
Memorial Hospital and Physicans Group ....Frederick OK
Memorial Hospital at Easton ....Easton MD
Memorial Hospital at Gulfport ....Gulfport MS
Memorial Hospital Burlington ....Burlington WI
Memorial Hospital For Cancer and Allied Diseases ......New York NY
Memorial Hospital Jacksonville ....Jacksonville FL
Memorial Hospital Los Banos ....Los Banos CA
Memorial Hospital Martinsville ....Martinsville VA
Memorial Hospital Northwest ....Houston TX
Memorial Hospital of Adel ...Adel GA
Memorial Hospital of Carbon County ....Rawlins WY
Memorial Hospital of Converse County ....Douglas WY
Memorial Hospital of Gardena ....Gardena CA
Memorial Hospital of Lafayette County ....Darlington WI
Memorial Hospital of Rhode Island ....Pawtucket RI
Memorial Hospital of Salem County ....Salem NJ
Memorial Hospital of Sheridan County ....Sheridan WY
Memorial Hospital of South Bend ....South Bend IN
Memorial Hospital of Tampa ....Tampa FL

Memorial Hospital of Taylor County ....Medford WI
Memorial Hospital of Texas County ....Guymon OK
Memorial Hospital of Union County ....Marysville OH
Memorial Hospital Pembroke ....Pembroke Pines FL
Memorial Hospital Southeast ....Houston TX
Memorial Hospital Sweetwater County ....Rock Springs WY
Memorial Hospital West ....Pembroke Pines FL
Memorial Medical Center ....Modesto CA
Memorial Medical Center ....Savannah GA
Memorial Medical Center ....Springfield IL
Memorial Medical Center ....Woodstock IL
Memorial Medical Center ....Port Lavaca TX
Memorial Medical Center ....Ashland WI
Memorial Medical Center ....Neillsville WI
Memorial Medical Center - Baptist ....New Orleans LA
Memorial Medical Center - Mercy ....New Orleans LA
Memorial Medical Center Livingston ....Livingston TX
Memorial Medical Center of West Michigan ....Ludington MI
Memorial North Park Hospital ....Hixson TN
Memorial Pavilion ......Lawton OK
Memorial Regional Hospital ....Hollywood FL
Memorial Regional Hospital ....Mechanicsville VA
Memorial Rehabilitation Hospital ....Midland TX
Memorial Specialty Hospital ....Lufkin TX
Memphis Mental Health Institute ....Memphis TN
Mena Medical Center .....Mena AR
Mendocino Coast District Hospital ....Fort Bragg CA
Mendota Community Hospital ....Mendota IL
Mendota Mental Health Institute ....Madison WI
Menifee Valley Medical Center ....Sun City CA
Menlo Park Surgical Hospital ....Menlo Park CA
Menninger Cf Memorial Hospital ....Topeka KS

Alphabetical Index

Mennonite General Hospital Inc . . . . .Aibonito PR
Menorah Medical Center . . . . .Overland Park KS
Mental Health Institute . .Cherokee IA
Mental Health Institute . . . . .Independence IA
Mental Health Service - Clark County . . . . .Springfield OH
Mepsi Center . . . . .Bayamon PR
Mercer County Community Hospital . . . . .Coldwater OH
Mercer County Hospital . . . .Aledo IL
Mercy Behavioral Health Center . . . . .Sioux City IA
Mercy Capital . . . . . . .Des Moines IA
Mercy Children's Hospital . . . . .Toledo OH
Mercy Community Hospital . . . . .Conshohocken PA
Mercy Fitzgerald Hospital . .Darby PA
Mercy Franciscan Hospital-Mount Airy . . . . .Cincinnati OH
Mercy Franciscan Hospital-Western Hills Campus . . . . .Cincinnati OH
Mercy Franklin Center . . . . .Des Moines IA
Mercy General Health Partners . . . . .Muskegon MI
Mercy General Hospital . . . . .Sacramento CA
Mercy General Hospital . . . . .Muskegon MI
Mercy Health Center . . . .Dubuque IA
Mercy Health Center . . .Sioux City IA
Mercy Health Center . .Manhattan KS
Mercy Health Center . . . . .Oklahoma City OK
Mercy Health Center . . . . .Laredo TX
Mercy Health Center - North Iowa . . . . .Mason City IA
Mercy Health Center-Saint Marys . . . . .Dyersville IA
Mercy Health System of Southwestern Pennsylvania . . . . .Conshohocken PA
Mercy Health-love County Center . . . . .Marietta OK
Mercy Hospital . . . . . .Bakersfield CA
Mercy Hospital . . . . .Miami FL
Mercy Hospital . . . . .Corning IA
Mercy Hospital . . . . .Council Bluffs IA
Mercy Hospital . . . . .Iowa City IA
Mercy Hospital . . . . . . .Fort Scott KS
Mercy Hospital . . . . . .Moundridge KS
Mercy Hospital . . . . . . .Portland ME
Mercy Hospital . . . . . .Springfield MA
Mercy Hospital . . . . .Grayling MI
Mercy Hospital . . . . . .Port Huron MI
Mercy Hospital . . . .Coon Rapids MN
Mercy Hospital . . . . .Minneapolis MN
Mercy Hospital . . . .Moose Lake MN
Mercy Hospital . . . . .Buffalo NY

Mercy Hospital . . . . .Devils Lake ND
Mercy Hospital . . . . . .Valley City ND
Mercy Hospital . . . . .Scranton PA
Mercy Hospital . . . . .Wilkes-Barre PA
Mercy Hospital - Pittsburgh . . . . .Pittsburgh PA
Mercy Hospital and Medical Center . . . . .Chicago IL
Mercy Hospital Anderson . . . . .Cincinnati OH
Mercy Hospital Independence . . . . .Independence KS
Mercy Hospital Medical Center . . . . .Des Moines IA
Mercy Hospital of Fairfield . . . . .Fairfield OH
Mercy Hospital of Folsom . . . . .Folsom CA
Mercy Hospital of Franciscan Sisters . . . . .Oelwein IA
Mercy Hospital of Janesville . . . . .Janesville WI
Mercy Hospital of Philadelphia . . . . .Philadelphia PA
Mercy Hospital of Scott County . . . . .Waldron AR
Mercy Hospital of Tiffin . . . .Tiffin OH
Mercy Hospital Turner Memorial . . . . .Ozark AR
Mercy Hospital-Cadillac . .Cadillac MI
Mercy Hospital-Willard . . .Willard OH
Mercy Medical . . . . .Daphne AL
Mercy Medical Center . . . .Nampa ID
Mercy Medical Center . . . . .Cedar Rapids IA
Mercy Medical Center . . . .Clinton IA
Mercy Medical Center . . . . .Baltimore MD
Mercy Medical Center . . . . .Rockville Centre NY
Mercy Medical Center . . .Williston ND
Mercy Medical Center . . .Canton OH
Mercy Medical Center .Roseburg OR
Mercy Medical Center - Dominican Campus . . . . .Merced CA
Mercy Medical Center - Merced . . . . .Merced CA
Mercy Medical Center - New Hampton . . . . .New Hampton IA
Mercy Medical Center - South . . . . .Clinton IA
Mercy Medical Center Mount Shasta . . . . .Mount Shasta CA
Mercy Medical Center of Durango . . . . .Durango CO
Mercy Medical Center of Oshkosh . . . . .Oshkosh WI
Mercy Medical Center of Springfield . . . . .Springfield OH
Mercy Medical Center Redding . . . . .Redding CA
Mercy Memorial Health Center . . . . .Ardmore OK

Mercy Memorial Hospital . . . . .Manhattan KS
Mercy Memorial Hospital . . . . .Urbana OH
Mercy Providence Hospital . . . . .Pittsburgh PA
Mercy San Juan Hospital . . . . .Carmichael CA
Mercy Southwest Hospital . . . . .Bakersfield CA
Mercy Special Care . . .Nanticoke PA
Mercy Suburban Hospital . . . . .Norristown PA
Mercy West Side District Hospital . . . . .Taft CA
Mercy-Memorial Hospital . . . . .Monroe MI
Meritcare Medical Center . .Fargo ND
Meriter Hospital . . . . .Madison WI
Merle West Medical Center . . . . .Klamath Falls OR
Merrill Pioneer Community Hospital . . . . .Rock Rapids IA
Merrimack Valley Hospital . . . . .Haverhill MA
Mesa General Hospital . . . .Mesa AZ
Mesa Hills Speciality Hospital . . . . .El Paso TX
Mesa Lutheran Hospital . . . .Mesa AZ
Mesilla Valley Hospital . . . . .Las Cruces NM
Mesquite Community Hospital . . . . .Mesquite TX
Methodist Alliance Extended Care Hospital . . . . .Memphis TN
Methodist Ambulatory Surgery Hospital Nw . . . . .San Antonio TX
Methodist Behavioral Hospital . . . . .Maumelle AR
Methodist Behavioral Resources . . . . .New Orleans LA
Methodist Central Hospitals of Memphis . . . . .Memphis TN
Methodist Childrens Hospital of South Texas . . . . .San Antonio TX
Methodist Diagnostic Hospital . . . . .Houston TX
Methodist Haywood Park Hospital . . . . .Brownsville TN
Methodist Health Center - Sugar Land . . . . .Sugar Land TX
Methodist Healthcare - Jackson Hospital . . . . .Jackson TN
Methodist Healthcare Hospital - Mc Kenzie . . . . .Mc Kenzie TN
Methodist Healthcare Hospital of Fayette . . . . .Somerville TN
Methodist Healthcare South . . . . .Memphis TN
Methodist Healthcare/hospital of Dyersburg . . . . .Dyersburg TN
Methodist Healthcare/lexington Hospital . . . . .Lexington TN

Alphabetical Index

Methodist Hospital . .Sacramento CA
Methodist Hospital . . .Henderson KY
Methodist Hospital . . .Morganfield KY
Methodist Hospital
. . . . .Saint Louis Park MN
Methodist Hospital . .Philadelphia PA
Methodist Hospital . . . . .Houston TX
Methodist Hospital - Germantown
. . . . .Germantown TN
Methodist Hospital North - J. Harris
Hospital . . . . .Memphis TN
Methodist Hospital of Chicago
. . . . .Chicago IL
Methodist Hospital of Indiana
. . . . .Indianapolis IN
Methodist Hospital of Southern
California . . . . .Arcadia CA
Methodist Hospitals North Lake
. . . . .Gary IN
Methodist Hospitals Southlake
. . . . .Merrillville IN
Methodist Medical Center . .Dallas TX
Methodist Medical Center of Illinois
. . . . .Peoria IL
Methodist Medical Center of Oak
Ridge . . . . .Oak Ridge TN
Methodist Rehab Center
. . . . .Jackson MS
Methodist Richard Young
. . . . .Omaha NE
Methodist Specialty and Transplant
Hospital . . . . .San Antonio TX
Methodist Volunteer General
Hospital . . . . .Martin TN
Methodist Willowbrook Hospital
. . . . .Houston TX
Metro Health Center . . . . . .Erie PA
Metro Nashville General Hospital
. . . . .Nashville TN
Metrohealth Medical Center
. . . . .Cleveland OH
Metroplex Adventist Hospital
. . . . .Killeen TX
Metropolitan Hospital   . .San Juan PR
Metropolitan Hospital Center
. . . . .New York NY
Metropolitan Methodist Hospital
. . . . .San Antonio TX
Metropolitan Saint Louis Psychiatric
Center . . . . .Saint Louis MO
Metropolitan State Hospital
. . . . .Norwalk CA
Metropolitian Hospital
. . . . .Grand Rapids MI
Metrowest Medical Center -
Framingham Union Hospital
. . . . .Framingham MA
Metrowest Medical Center - Leonard
Morse Hospital . . . . .Natick MA
Meyersdale Medical Center
. . . . .Meyersdale PA
Miami Childrens Hospital . . .Miami FL

Miami County Medical Center
. . . . .Paola KS
Miami Heart Institute & Medical
Center - South Campus   . . .Miami FL
Miami Heart Institute and Medical
Center South . . . . . .Miami Beach FL
Miami Jewish Home and Hospital -
Douglas Gardens . . . . . . .Miami FL
Miami Valley Hospital . . . .Dayton OH
Michael Reese Hospital and Medical
Center . . . . .Chicago IL
Mid America Rehabilitation
Hospital . . . . .Overland Park KS
Mid Coast Hospital   . . .Brunswick ME
Mid Columbia Medical Center
. . . . .The Dalles OR
Mid Dakota Hospital
. . . . .Chamberlain SD
Mid Hudson Psychiatric Center
. . . . .New Hampton NY
Mid Jefferson Hospital
. . . . .Nederland TX
Mid Missouri Mental Health
. . . . .Columbia MO
Mid Valley Hospital . . . . .Omak WA
Mid Valley Hospital Association
. . . . .Peckville PA
Middle Tennessee Medical
Center . . . . .Murfreesboro TN
Middle Tennessee Mental Health
Institute . . . . .Nashville TN
Middlesboro Appalachian Regional
Hospital . . . . .Middlesboro KY
Middlesex Hospital . . .Middletown CT
Middletown Psych Center
. . . . .Middletown NY
Middletown Regional Hospital
. . . . .Middletown OH
Midland Memorial Hospital
. . . . .Midland TX
Midland Memorial Hospital - West
. . . . .Midland TX
Midlands Center . . . . . .Columbia SC
Midlands Community Hospital
. . . . .Papillion NE
Midmichigan Regional Medical
Center . . . . .Midland MI
Midmichigan Regional Medical
Center-clare . . . . .Clare MI
Midmichigan Regional Medical
Center-gladwin . . . . .Gladwin MI
Midstate Medical Center
. . . . .Meriden CT
Midstate Medical Center - East
. . . . .Meriden CT
Midway Hospital Medical Center
. . . . .Los Angeles CA
Midwest City Regional Medical
Center . . . . .Midwest City OK
Midwestern Region Medical Center
. . . . .Zion IL
Milan General Hospital . . . .Milan TN

Mildred Mitchell-bateman Hospital
. . . . .Huntington WV
Mile Bluff Medical Center - Hess
Memorial . . . . .Mauston WI
Miles Memorial Hospital
. . . . .Damariscotta ME
Milford Hospital . . . . .Milford CT
Milford Valley Memorial Hospital
. . . . .Milford UT
Milford Whitinsville Regional
Hospital . . . . .Milford MA
Millard Fillmore Hospital . .Buffalo NY
Millard Fillmore Suburban
Hospital . . . . .Williamsville NY
Millcreek Community Hospital
. . . . .Erie PA
Millcreek Habilitation Center
. . . . .Fordyce AR
Millcreek of Pontotoc . . .Pontotoc MS
Millcreek Rehabilitation
Center . . . . .Magee MS
Mille Lacs Health System
. . . . .Onamia MN
Miller Children's Hospital
. . . . .Long Beach CA
Miller County Hospital . . .Colquitt GA
Miller Dwan Medical Center
. . . . .Duluth MN
Miller Manor Halfway House
. . . . .Lawton OK
Millinocket Regional Hospital
. . . . .Millinocket ME
Mills Hospital . . . . . . .San Mateo CA
Millwood Hospital . . . . .Arlington TX
Milton Medical Center . . . .Milton MA
Milwaukee County Mental Health
Complex . . . . .Milwaukee WI
Mimbres Memorial Hospital
. . . . .Deming NM
Minden Medical Center . . .Minden LA
Mineral Area Regional Medical
Center . . . . .Farmington MO
Mineral Community Hospital
. . . . .Superior MT
Miners Colfax Medical Center
. . . . .Raton NM
Miners Hospital . . . . . . .Hastings PA
Minidoka Memorial Hospital
. . . . .Rupert ID
Minneola District Hospital
. . . . .Minneola KS
Minnesota Neuro Rehabilitation
Hospital . . . . .Brainerd MN
Minnesota Security Hospital
. . . . .Saint Peter MN
Minnesota Valley Memorial
Hospital . . . . .Le Sueur MN
Minnewaska District Hospital
. . . . .Starbuck MN
Minnie G Boswell Memorial
Hospital . . . . .Greensboro GA
Minnie Hamilton Healthcare
Center . . . . .Grantsville WV

Alphabetical Index

Miriam Hospital . . . . . .Providence RI
Mission Community Hospital
. . . . .Panorama City CA
Mission Hospital . . . . . . .Mission TX
Mission Hospital of Huntington
Park . . . . .Huntington Park CA
Mission Hospital Regional Medical
Center . . . . .Mission Viejo CA
Mission Saint Joseph's Hospital
. . . . .Asheville NC
Mission Vista Hospital
. . . . .San Antonio TX
Mississippi Baptist Medical
Center . . . . .Jackson MS
Mississippi State Hospital
. . . . .Whitfield MS
Missouri Baptist Hospital
Sullivan . . . . .Sullivan MO
Missouri Baptist Medica
Center . . . . .Saint Louis MO
Missouri Delta Medical Center
. . . . .Sikeston MO
Missouri Rehabilitation Center
. . . . .Mount Vernon MO
Missouri River Medical Center
Maf . . . . .Fort Benton MT
Missouri Southern Healthcare
. . . . .Dexter MO
Mit Medical Department
. . . . .Cambridge MA
Mitchell County Hospital .Camilla GA
Mitchell County Hospital . . .Beloit KS
Mitchell County Hospital
. . . . .Colorado City TX
Mitchell County Memorial
Hospital . . . . .Osage IA
Mizell Memorial Hospital . . . .Opp AL
Moberly Regional Medical
Center . . . . .Moberly MO
Mobile Infirmary Medical
Center . . . . .Mobile AL
Mobridge Regional Hospital
. . . . .Mobridge SD
Mocassin Bend Mental Health
Institute . . . . .Chattanooga TN
Modesto Rehab Hospital
. . . . .Modesto CA
Modoc Medical Center . . .Alturas CA
Mohawk Valley Psychiatric
Center . . . . .Utica NY
Molokai General Hospita
. . . . .Kaunakakai HI
Monadnock Community
Hospital . . . . .Peterborough NH
Moncrief Army Community Hospital -
U.S.A. Meddac . . . .Fort Jackson SC
Monmouth Medical Cente
. . . . .Long Branch NJ
Monongahela Valley Hospital
. . . . .Monongahela PA
Monongalia County General
Hospital . . . . . . .Morgantown WV
Monroe Clinic Hospital . . .Monroe WI

Monroe Community Hospital
. . . . .Rochester NY
Monroe County Hospital
. . . . .Monroeville AL
Monroe County Hospital
. . . . .Forsyth GA
Monroe County Hospital . . . .Albia IA
Monroe County Medical Center
. . . . .Tompkinsville KY
Monroe Surgical Hospital
. . . . .Monroe LA
Monrovia Community Hospital
. . . . .Monrovia CA
Monsour Medical Center
. . . . .Jeannette PA
Montana State Hospital
. . . . .Warmsprings MT
Montclair Community Hospital
. . . . .Montclair NJ
Montefiore Medical Center
. . . . .Bronx NY
Monterey Park Hospital
. . . . .Monterey Park CA
Montevista Hospital . . .Las Vegas NV
Montfort Jones Memorial
Hospital . . . . .Kosciusko MS
Montgomery County Emergency
Service . . . . .Norristown PA
Montgomery County Memorial
Hospital . . . . .Red Oak IA
Montgomery General Hospital
. . . . .Olney MD
Montgomery General Hospital
. . . . .Montgomery WV
Montgomery Hospital . .Norristown PA
Montgomery Regional Hospital
. . . . .Blacksburg VA
Monticello-Big Lake Community
Hospital . . . . .Monticello MN
Montrose Memorial Hospital
. . . . .Montrose CO
Moore County Hospital
District . . . . .Dumas TX
Morehead Memorial Hospital
. . . . .Eden NC
Morehouse General Hospital
. . . . .Bastrop LA
Morenci Health Care Center
. . . . .Morenci AZ
Moreno Valley Medical Center
. . . . .Moreno Valley CA
Morgan County Appalachian Regional
Hospital . . . . .West Liberty KY
Morgan County Memorial
Hospital . . . . .Martinsville IN
Morgan County War Memorial
Hospital . . . . . .Berkeley Springs WV
Morgan Memorial Hospital
. . . . .Madison GA
Morrill County Community
Hospital . . . . .Bridgeport NE
Morris County Hospital
. . . . .Council Grove KS

Morris Hospital . . . . .Morris IL
Morrison Community Hospital
. . . . .Morrison IL
Morristown Hamblen Hospital
Association . . . . . . .Morristown TN
Morristown Memorial Hospital
. . . . .Morristown NJ
Morrow County Hospital Home
Health . . . . .Mount Gilead OH
Morton Bakar Center . . .Hayward CA
Morton County Hospital . . .Elkhart KS
Morton General Hospital .Morton WA
Morton Hospital and Medical
Center . . . . .Taunton MA
Morton Plant Hospital
. . . . .Clearwater FL
Moses H Cone Memorial
Hospital . . . . .Greensboro NC
Moses Ludington Hospital
. . . . .Ticonderoga NY
Moses Taylor Hospital . .Scranton PA
Moss Regional Medical Center
. . . . .Lake Charles LA
Moss Rehab Hospital
. . . . .Philadelphia PA
Mother Frances Hospital . . .Tyler TX
Mother Frances Hospital -
Jacksonville . . . . . .Jacksonville TX
Motion Picture and Television
Hospital . . . . .Woodland Hills CA
Mount Ascutney Hospital Health
Center . . . . .Windsor VT
Mount Auburn Hospital
. . . . .Cambridge MA
Mount Carmel East Hospital
. . . . .Columbus OH
Mount Carmel Guild . . . .Newark NJ
Mount Carmel Hospital . .Colville WA
Mount Carmel Medical Center
. . . . .Pittsburg KS
Mount Carmel Medical Center
. . . . .Columbus OH
Mount Clemens General
Hospital . . . . . . .Mount Clemens MI
Mount Desert Island Hospital
. . . . .Bar Harbor ME
Mount Diablo Hospital Medical
Center . . . . .Concord CA
Mount Diablo Medical Pavilion
. . . . .Concord CA
Mount Graham Community
Hospital . . . . .Safford AZ
Mount Grant General Hospital
. . . . .Hawthorne NV
Mount Pleasant Mental Health
Institute . . . . .Mount Pleasant IA
Mount Regis Center . . . . . .Salem VA
Mount Saint Marys Hospital of
Niagara Falls . . . . .Lewiston NY
Mount San Rafael Hospital
. . . . .Trinidad CO
Mount Sinai Hospital
. . . . .Miami Beach FL

Alphabetical Index

Mount Sinai Hospital - Queens .Astoria NY
Mount Sinai Hospital Medical Center . . . . .Chicago IL
Mount Sinai Hospital of Queens . . . . .Long Island City NY
Mount Sinai Medical Center . . . . .New York NY
Mount Vernon Hospital . . . . .Mount Vernon NY
Mount Vernon Hospital . . . . .Alexandria VA
Mount Washington Pediatric Hospital . . . . .Baltimore MD
Mountain Crest Hospital . . . . .Fort Collins CO
Mountain Manor Treatment Center . . . . .Emmitsburg MD
Mountain View Hospital .Gadsden AL
Mountain View Hospital . .Madras OR
Mountain View Hospital . .Payson UT
Mountain View Medical Center . . . . .Las Cruces NM
Mountain West Medical Center . . . . .Tooele UT
Mountains Community Hospital . . . . .Lake Arrowhead CA
Mountainside Medical Center Hospital . . . . .Jasper GA
Mountainview Hospital . . . . .Las Vegas NV
Mountainview Medical Center Maf . . . . .White Sulphur Springs MT
Mountrail County Medical Center . . . . .Stanley ND
Mpi Treatment Services - Chemical Dependency Recovery Hospital . . . . .Oakland CA
Muenster Memorial Hospital . . . . .Muenster TX
Muhlenberg Community Hospital . . . . .Greenville KY
Muhlenberg Hospital Center . . . . .Bethlehem PA
Muhlenberg Regional Medical Center . . . . .Plainfield NJ
Muleshoe Area Medical Center . . . . .Muleshoe TX
Muncy Valley Hospital . . . .Muncy PA
Munising Memorial Hospital . . . . .Munising MI
Munroe Regional Medical Center . . . . .Ocala FL
Munson Health Care . . . . .Traverse City MI
Murphy Medical Center . .Murphy NC
Murray County Hospital . .Slayton MN
Murray Medical Center . . . . .Chatsworth GA
Murray-Calloway County Hospital . . . . .Murray KY
Muskogee Regional Medical Center . . . . .Muskogee OK

Myers Community Hospital . . . . .Newark NY
Myrtle Werth Hospital Mayo Health System . . . . .Menomonie WI
Nacogdoches Medical Center Hospital . . . . .Nacogdoches TX
Nacogdoches Memorial Hospital . . . . .Nacogdoches TX
Nanticoke Memorial Hospital . . . . .Seaford DE
Nantucket Cottage Hospital . . . . .Nantucket MA
Napa State Hospital . . . . .Napa CA
Naples Community Hospital . . . . .Naples FL
Nash General Hospital . . . . .Rocky Mount NC
Nashville Metropolitan Bordeaux Nursing Home/hospital . .Nashville TN
Nashville Rehab Hospital . . . . .Nashville TN
Nason Hospital . . .Roaring Spring PA
Nassau University Medical Center . . . . .East Meadow NY
Natchaug Hospital . . . . .Mansfield Center CT
Natchez Community Hospital/Swing Bed . . . . .Natchez MS
Natchez Regional Medical Center . . . . .Natchez MS
Natchitoches Parish Hospital . . . . .Natchitoches LA
Nathan Littauer Hospital . . . . .Gloversville NY
National Hospital For Kids In Crisis . . . . .Orefield PA
National Jewish Medical Center . . . . .Denver CO
National Naval Medical Center . . . . .Bethesda MD
National Park Medical Center . . . . .Hot Springs AR
National Rehab Hospital . . . . .Washington DC
Natividad Medical Center . . . . .Salinas CA
Nature Coast Regional Hospital . . . . .Williston FL
Naval Branch Hospital . .Gulfport MS
Naval Hospital . . . . .Groton CT
Naval Hospital Beaufort . . . . .Beaufort SC
Naval Hospital Bremerton . . . . .Bremerton WA
Naval Hospital Camp Lejeune . . . . .Camp Lejeune NC
Naval Hospital Camp Pendleton . . . . .Camp Pendleton CA
Naval Hospital Charleston . . . . .North Charleston SC
Naval Hospital Cherry Point . . . . .Cherry Point NC

Naval Hospital Corpus Christi . . . . .Corpus Christi TX
Naval Hospital Great Lakes . . . . .Great Lakes IL
Naval Hospital Jacksonville . . . . .Jacksonville FL
Naval Hospital Lemoore . . . . .Lemoore CA
Naval Hospital Newport . .Newport RI
Naval Hospital Oak Harbor . . . . .Oak Harbor WA
Naval Hospital Pensacola . . . . .Pensacola FL
Naval Medical Center Patuxent River . . . . .Patuxent River MD
Naval Medical Center Portsmouth . . . . .Portsmouth VA
Naval Medical Center San Diego . . . . .San Diego CA
Navapache Hospital . . .Show Low AZ
Navarro Regional Hospital . . . . .Corsicana TX
Nazareth Hospital . . .Philadelphia PA
Nced Mental Health Center . . . . .El Paso TX
Nced Mental Health Center . . . . .El Paso TX
Nebraska Medical Center . . . . .Omaha NE
Nebraska Methodist Hospital . . . . .Omaha NE
Nelson County Health System . . . . .Mcville ND
Nelson Holderman Hospital . . . . .Yountville CA
Nemaha County Hospital . . . . .Auburn NE
Nemaha Valley Community Hospital . . . . .Seneca KS
Neosho Memorial Hospital . . . . .Chanute KS
Nesbitt Hospital-Wyoming Valley Health Care . . . . .Kingston PA
Neshoba County General Hospital . . . . .Philadelphia MS
Ness County Hospital . .Ness City KS
Nevada Regional Medical Center . . . . .Nevada MO
New Bedford Rehab Hospital . . . . .New Bedford MA
New Britain General Hospital . . . . .New Britain CT
New England Baptist Hospital . . . . .Boston MA
New England Rehab Hospital of Portland . . . . .Portland ME
New England Sinai Hospital and Rehab Center . . . . . .Stoughton MA
New Hampshire Hospital . . . . .Concord NH
New Hanover Regional Medical Center . . . . .Wilmington NC

Alphabetical Index

New Horizons Health Systems ....Owenton KY
New Island Hospital ...Bethpage NY
New Jersey State Prison Hospital ....Trenton NJ
New London Family Medical Center ....New London WI
New London Hospital Association ....New London NH
New Mexico Rehabilitation Center ....Roswell NM
New Milford Hospital ....New Milford CT
New Orleans Adolescent Hospital ....New Orleans LA
New Ulm Medical Center ....New Ulm MN
New York Community Hospital of Brooklyn ....Brooklyn NY
New York Eye and Ear Infirmary ....New York NY
New York Hospital Medical Center of Queens ....Flushing NY
New York Methodist Hospital ....Brooklyn NY
New York Presbyterian Hospital ....New York NY
New York Presbyterian Hospital - Babies and Children's Hospital ....New York NY
New York Presbyterian Hospital - Westchester ......White Plains NY
New York State Psychiatric Institute ....New York NY
New York University - Downtown Hospital ....New York NY
New York Weill Cornell Medical Center ....New York NY
New York Westchester Square Hospital ....Bronx NY
Newark Beth Israel Medical Center ....Newark NJ
Newark Wayne Community Hospital ....Newark NY
Newberry County Memorial Hospital ....Newberry SC
Newfane Inter Community Memorial Hospital ....Newfane NY
Newman Memorial County Hospital ....Emporia KS
Newman Memorial Hospital ....Shattuck OK
Newnan Hospital .....Newnan GA
Newport Bay Hospital ....Newport Beach CA
Newport Community Hospital ....Newport WA
Newport Hospital ......Newport RI
Newport Hospital and Clinic ....Newport AR
Newport News General Hospital ....Newport News VA

Newton General Hospital ....Covington GA
Newton Medical Center ..Newton KS
Newton Memorial Hospital ....Newton NJ
Newton Regional Hospital ....Newton MS
Newton-Wellesley Hospital ....Newton Lower Falls MA
Niagara Falls Memorial Medical Center ....Niagara Falls NY
Nicholas County Hospital ....Carlisle KY
Nicholas Noyes Memorial Hospital ....Dansville NY
90th Medical Group ....F.E. Warren Air Force Base WY
9th Medical Group ....Beale Air Force Base CA
95th Medical Group ....Edwards Air Force Base CA
99th Medical Group, Mike O'Callaghan Federal Hospital ....Nellis Air Force Base NV
97th Medical Group ....Altus Air Force Base OK
96th Medical Group ....Eglin Air Force Base FL
Niobrara Valley Hospital ...Lynch NE
Nix Medical Center ..San Antonio TX
Noble Hospital ......Westfield MA
Nocona General Hospital ....Nocona TX
Nor Lea General Hospital ....Lovington NM
Norfolk Regional Center ..Norfolk NE
Norman Regional Hospital ....Norman OK
Norristown State Hospital ....Norristown PA
North Adams Regional Hospital ....North Adams MA
North Alabama Regional Hospital ....Decatur AL
North Arkansas Regional Medical Center ....Harrison AR
North Arundel Hospital ....Glen Burnie MD
North Austin Medical Center ....Austin TX
North Baldwin Hospital ....Bay Minette AL
North Bay Hospital ....Aransas Pass TX
North Bay Medical Center ....New Port Richey FL
North Big Horn Hospital ...Lovell WY
North Broward Medical Center ....Pompano Beach FL
North Caddo Medical Center ....Vivian LA
North Carolina Baptist Hospital ....Winston-Salem NC

North Carolina Eye and Ear Hospital ....Durham NC
North Central Baptist Hospital ....San Antonio TX
North Central Bronx Hospital ....Bronx NY
North Central Health Care Facilities ....Wausau WI
North Central Medical Center of Mc Kinney ....Mc Kinney TX
North Coast Health Care Centers ....Santa Rosa CA
North Colorado Medical Center ....Greeley CO
North Country Hospital and Health Center ....Newport VT
North Country Regional Hospital ....Bemidji MN
North Dakota State Hospital ....Jamestown ND
North Dallas Rehabilitation Hospital ....Dallas TX
North Florida Reception Center Hospital ....Lake Butler FL
North Florida Regional Medical Center ....Gainesville FL
North Fulton Regional Hospital ....Roswell GA
North General Hospital ....New York NY
North Georgia Medical Center ....Ellijay GA
North Greenville Hospital ....Travelers Rest SC
North Hawaii Community Hospital ....Kamuela HI
North Hills Hospital ....North Richland Hills TX
North Idaho Behavioral Health Institute ....Coeur D'alene ID
North Kansas City Hospital ....North Kansas City MO
North Lincoln Hospital ....Lincoln City OR
North Logan Mercy Hospital ....Paris AR
North Memorial Medical Center ....Robbinsdale MN
North Mississippi Medical Center ....Tupelo MS
North Mississippi Medical Center - Iuka ....Iuka MS
North Mississippi Medical Center- Hamilton ....Hamilton AL
North Mississippi State Hospital ....Tupelo MS
North Monroe Hospital ...Monroe LA
North Oak Regional Medical Center ....Senatobia MS
North Oakland Medical Centers ....Pontiac MI
North Oaks Medical Center ....Hammond LA

Alphabetical Index

North Oaks Rehab Hospital ....Hammond LA
North Okaloosa Medical Center ....Crestview FL
North Ottawa Community Hospital ....Grand Haven MI
North Ridge Medical Center ....Fort Lauderdale FL
North Runnels Hospital ..Winters TX
North Shore Children's Hospital ....Salem MA
North Shore Medical Center ....Miami FL
North Shore University Hospital ....Manhasset NY
North Shore University Hospital at Forest Hills ....Forest Hills NY
North Shore University Hospital at Glen Cove ....Glen Cove NY
North Shore University Hospital at Plainview ....Plainview NY
North Shore University Hospital Syosset ....Syosset NY
North Star Behavioral Health System ....Anchorage AK
North Star Hospital ..Anchorage AK
North Suburban Medical Center ....Thornton CO
North Sunflower County Hospital ....Ruleville MS
North Texas State Hospital ....Wichita Falls TX
North Valley Health Center ....Warren MN
North Valley Hospital ..Whitefish MT
North Valley Hospital ..Tonasket WA
North Valley Rehab Center ....Thornton CO
Northbay Medical Center ....Fairfield CA
Northcoast Behavioral Health Care System ....Toledo OH
Northcoast Behavioral Healthcare ....Cleveland OH
Northcoast Behavioral Healthcare - Northfield ....Northfield OH
Northcrest Medical Center-Hospital ....Springfield TN
Northeast Alabama Regional Medical Center ....Anniston AL
Northeast Baptist Hospital ....San Antonio TX
Northeast Florida State Hospital ....MacClenny FL
Northeast Georgia Medical Center ....Gainesville GA
Northeast Kansas Center For Health ....Horton KS
Northeast Medical Center ....Concord NC
Northeast Medical Center ....Bonham TX

Northeast Medical Center Hospital ....Humble TX
Northeast Methodist Hospital ....San Antonio TX
Northeast Montana Health Services - Trinity Hospital ......Wolf Point MT
Northeast Regional Medical Center ....Kirksville MO
Northeast Rehab Health Network ....Salem NH
Northeast Specialty Hospital ....Braintree MA
Northeastern Nevada Regional Hospital ....Elko NV
Northeastern Regional Hospital ....Las Vegas NM
Northeastern Vermont Regional Hospital ....Saint Johnsbury VT
Northern California Rehab Hospital ....Redding CA
Northern Cochise Community Hospital ....Willcox AZ
Northern Dutchess Hospital ....Rhinebeck NY
Northern Hills General Hospital ....Deadwood SD
Northern Hospital of Surry County ....Mount Airy NC
Northern Illinois Medical Center ....Mc Henry IL
Northern Inyo Hospital ...Bishop CA
Northern Itasca Hospital ..Bigfork MN
Northern Maine Medical Center ....Fort Kent ME
Northern Michigan Hospital ....Petoskey MI
Northern Montana Hospital ....Havre MT
Northern Nevada Adult Mental Health Service ....Sparks NV
Northern Nevada Medical Center ....Sparks NV
Northern Rockies Medical Center ....Cut Bank MT
Northern Virginia Community Hospital ....Arlington VA
Northern Virginia Mental Health Institute ....Falls Church VA
Northern Westchester Hospital ....Mount Kisco NY
Northfield City Hospital ....Northfield MN
Northkey Community Care - Children's Intensive Services ....Covington KY
Northport Medical Center ....Northport AL
Northridge Hospital Medical Center ....Northridge CA
Northridge Hospital Medical Center, Sherman ....Van Nuys CA
Northshore Psychiatric Hospital ....Slidell LA

Northshore Regional Medical Center ....Slidell LA
Northside Hospital ....Saint Petersburg FL
Northside Hospital ......Atlanta GA
Northside Hospital ..Johnson City TN
Northside Hospital Cherokee ....Canton GA
Northside Hospital Forsythe ....Cumming GA
Northville Psychiatric Hospital ....Northville MI
Northwest Community Hospital ....Arlington Heights IL
Northwest Florida Community Hospital ....Chipley FL
Northwest Georgia Regional Hospital ....Rome GA
Northwest Hospital ......Seattle WA
Northwest Hospital Center ....Randallstown MD
Northwest Iowa Health Center ....Sheldon IA
Northwest Medical Center ....Tucson AZ
Northwest Medical Center ....Springdale AR
Northwest Medical Center ....Margate FL
Northwest Medical Center ....Thief River Falls MN
Northwest Mississippi Regional Medical Center ......Clarksdale MS
Northwest Missouri Psychiatric Rehab Center ....Saint Joseph MO
Northwest Regional Hospital ....Corpus Christi TX
Northwest Specialty Hospital ....Post Falls ID
Northwest Suburban Community Hospital ....Belvidere IL
Northwest Surgical Hospital ....Oklahoma City OK
Northwest Texas Healthcare System - Psychiatric Pavilion .....Amarillo TX
Northwest Texas Heart Hospital ....Amarillo TX
Northwest Texas Hospital ....Amarillo TX
Northwest Texas Surgical Center ....Amarillo TX
Northwestern Institute of Psychiatry .....Fort Washington PA
Northwestern Medical Center ....Saint Albans VT
Northwestern Memorial Hospital ....Chicago IL
Northwood Deaconess Health Center ...Northwood ND
Norton Audubon Hospital ....Louisville KY
Norton Community Hospital ....Norton VA

Alphabetical Index

Norton County Hospital . . .Norton KS
Norton Health Care Pavilion
. . . . .Louisville KY
Norton Hospital . . . . . .Louisville KY
Norton Southwest Hospital
. . . . .Louisville KY
Norton Spring View Hospital
. . . . .Lebanon KY
Norton Suburban Hospital
. . . . .Louisville KY
Norton-Kosair Childrens
 Hospital . . . . .Louisville KY
Norwalk Hospital . . . . . .Norwalk CT
Norwegian-American Hospital
. . . . .Chicago IL
Norwood Health Center
. . . . .Marshfield WI
Novato Community Hospital
. . . . .Novato CA
Noxubee General Hospital
. . . . .Macon MS
Nyack Hospital . . . . .Nyack NY
Nye Regional Medical Center
. . . . .Tonopah NV
NYU Medical Center-University
Hospital . . . . .New York NY
O Bleness Memorial Hospital
. . . . .Athens OH
O'Connor Hospital . . . . .San Jose CA
O'Connor Hospital . . . . . . .Delhi NY
Oak Forest Hospital . . .Oak Forest IL
Oak Hill Hospital . . . . . .Spring Hill FL
Oak Leaf Surgical Hospital
. . . . .Eau Claire WI
Oak Park Hospital . . . . . .Oak Park IL
Oak Valley District Hospital
. . . . .Oakdale CA
Oakdale Community Hospital
. . . . .Oakdale LA
Oakes Community Hospital
. . . . .Oakes ND
Oakland Memorial Hospital
. . . . .Oakland NE
Oaklawn Hospital . . . . .Marshall MI
Oaklawn Psychiatric Center
. . . . .Goshen IN
Oaks Treatment Center . . .Austin TX
Oakwood Center of Palm Beach
. . . . .West Palm Beach FL
Oakwood Correctional Facility
. . . . .Lima OH
Oakwood Health Care Systems
Heritage . . . . .Taylor MI
Oakwood Healthcare Center-Allen
Park . . . . .Allen Park MI
Oakwood Hospital and Medical
Center . . . . .Dearborn MI
Oakwood Hospital Annapolis
 Center . . . . .Wayne MI
Oakwood Hospital Merriman Center -
Westland . . . . .Westland MI
Oakwood Southshore Medical
Center . . . . .Trenton MI

Oasis Rehab Hospital
. . . . .New Orleans LA
Oasis Rehab Hospital of Lafayette
. . . . .New Orleans LA
Ocala Regional Medical Center
. . . . .Ocala FL
Ocean Beach Hospital . . .Ilwaco WA
Ocean Springs Hospital
. . . . .Ocean Springs MS
Ochiltree General Hospital
. . . . .Perryton TX
Ochsner Foundation Hospital
. . . . .New Orleans LA
Oconee Memorial Hospital
. . . . .Seneca SC
Oconee Regional Medical
Center . . . . .Milledgeville GA
Oconto Memorial Hospital
. . . . .Oconto WI
Odessa Memorial Hospital
. . . . .Odessa WA
Odessa Regional Hospital
. . . . .Odessa TX
Ogallala Community Hospital
. . . . .Ogallala NE
Ogden Regional Medical
Center . . . . .Ogden UT
Ohio County Hospital . . .Hartford KY
Ohio State University Medical
Center . . . . .Columbus OH
Ohio Valley General Hospita
. . . . .Mc Kees Rocks PA
Ohio Valley General Medical
Center . . . . .Wheeling WV
Ohsu Doernbecher Children's
Hospital . . . . .Portland OR
Ojai Valley Community Hospital
. . . . .Ojai CA
Okanogan-douglas District
 Hospital . . . . .Brewster WA
Okeene Municipal Hospital
. . . . .Okeene OK
Oklahoma Center For Orthopaedic
and Multi-Specialty
. . . . .Oklahoma City OK
Oklahoma Neurorestoration
Center . . . . .Broken Arrow OK
Oklahoma Spine Hospital
. . . . .Oklahoma City OK
Oklahoma University Medical Center -
Everett Tower . . . .Oklahoma City OK
Oklahoma University Medical Center -
Presbyterian Tower
. . . . .Oklahoma City OK
Okmulgee Hospital . . .Okmulgee OK
Okolona Community Hospital
. . . . .Okolona MS
Oktibbeha County Hospital
. . . . .Starkville MS
Olathe Medical Center . . . .Olathe KS
Olean General Hospital . . .Olean NY
Olmsted Hospital . . . . .Rochester MN

Olympic Memorial Hospital
. . . . .Port Angeles WA
Oneida City Hospital . . . . .Oneida NY
Oneida County Hospital . . . .Malad ID
Onslow Memorial Hospital
. . . . .Jacksonville NC
Ontonagon Memorial Hospital
. . . . .Ontonagon MI
Opelousas General Hospital
. . . . .Opelousas LA
Opportunities Inc - Chemical
Dependency Treatment Center
. . . . .Watonga OK
Orange City Municipal Hospital
. . . . .Orange City IA
Orange Coast Memorial Medical
Center . . . . .Fountain Valley CA
Orange Park Medical Center
. . . . .Orange Park FL
Orange Regional Medical Center-
Arden Hill . . . . .Goshen NY
Orange Regional Medical Center-
Horton Campus . . . . .Middletown NY
Oregon Health Services University
Hospital and Clinic . . . . .Portland OR
Oregon State Hospital . . . .Salem OR
Orem Community Hospital
. . . . .Orem UT
Orlando Regional - Saint Cloud
Hospital . . . . . . .Saint Cloud FL
Orlando Regional Medical Center
. . . . .Orlando FL
Oroville Hospital . . . . . .Oroville CA
Orthopaedic Hospital of Wisconsin
. . . . .Glendale WI
Orthopedic Hospital
. . . . .Los Angeles CA
Orthopedic Hospital of Oklahoma
. . . . .Tulsa OK
Orthopedic Specialty Hospital
. . . . .Salt Lake City UT
Ortonville Municipal Hospital
. . . . .Ortonville MN
Osawatomie State Hospital
Psychiatric . . . . . . .Osawatomie KS
Osborne County Memorial
 Hospital . . . . .Osborne KS
Osceola Community Hospital
. . . . .Sibley IA
Osceola Medical Center
. . . . .Osceola WI
Osceola Regional Medica
Center . . . . .Kissimmee FL
Osmond General Hospital
. . . . .Osmond NE
Osseo Medical Center/Nursing
 Home . . . . .Osseo WI
Ossining Correctional Facilities
Hospital . . . . .Ossining NY
Osteopathic Medical Center
of Texas . . . . .Fort Worth TX
Osu and Harding Behavioral
Healthcare . . . . . . .Worthington OH

Alphabetical Index

Osu Hospital - East . . .Columbus OH
Oswego Hospital . . . . . .Oswego NY
Oswego Medical Center
. . . . .Oswego KS
Othello Community Hospital
. . . . .Othello WA
Otis R Bowen Center For Human
Services . . . . .Warsaw IN
Otsego Memorial Hospital
. . . . .Gaylord MI
Ottawa County Hospital
. . . . .Minneapolis KS
Otto Kaiser Memorial Hospital
. . . . .Kenedy TX
Ottumwa Regional Health Center
. . . . .Ottumwa IA
Ouachita County Medical Center
. . . . .Camden AR
Our Children's House at Baylor
. . . . .Dallas TX
Our Community Hospital
. . . . .Scotland Neck NC
Our Lady of Bellefonte Hospital
. . . . .Ashland KY
Our Lady of Lourdes Medical
Center . . . . .Camden NJ
Our Lady of Lourdes Memorial
Hospital . . . . .Binghamton NY
Our Lady of Lourdes Regional
Medical Center . . . . . .Lafayette LA
Our Lady of Mercy Hospital -
Pelham Bay . . . . .Bronx NY
Our Lady of Mercy Medical Center
Flor D'urso . . . . .Bronx NY
Our Lady of Peace Hospital
. . . . .South Bend IN
Our Lady of The Lake Regional
Medical Center . . . .Baton Rouge LA
Our Lady of The Resurrection
Medical Center . . . . .Chicago IL
Our Lady of The Way Hospital
. . . . .Martin KY
Our Lady of Victory
. . . . .Lackawanna NY
Outer Banks Hospital
. . . . .Nags Head NC
Overlake Hospital Medical
Center . . . . .Bellevue WA
Overland Park Regional Medical
Center . . . . .Overland Park KS
Overlook Hospital . . . . . .Summit NJ
Owatonna Hospital . . .Owatonna MN
Owensboro Medical Health
System . . . . .Owensboro KY
Ozark Health Medical Center
. . . . .Clinton AR
Ozarks Medical Center
. . . . .West Plains MO
Pacific Alliance Medical Center
. . . . .Los Angeles CA
Pacific Communities Hospital
. . . . .Newport OR

Pacific Hospital of Long Beach
. . . . .Long Beach CA
Pacific Medical Center & Clinics
. . . . .Seattle WA
Pacifica Hospital of The Valley
. . . . .Sun Valley CA
Padre Behavioral Health System
. . . . .Corpus Christi TX
Page Hospital . . . . .Page AZ
Page Memorial Hospital . . .Luray VA
Palacios Community Medical
Center . . . . .Palacios TX
Palestine Regional Medical Center -
East . . . . .Palestine TX
Palestine Regional Rehab
Hospital . . . . .Palestine TX
Palisades Medical Center
. . . . .North Bergen NJ
Palm Beach Gardens Medical
Center . . . .Palm Beach Gardens FL
Palm Drive Hospital . .Sebastopol CA
Palm Springs General Hospital
. . . . .Hialeah FL
Palmer Lutheran Health Center
. . . . .West Union IA
Palmerton Hospital . . . .Palmerton PA
Palmetto Baptist Medical Center at
Columbia . . . . .Columbia SC
Palmetto Baptist Medical Center-
Easley . . . . .Easley SC
Palmetto General Hospital
. . . . .Hialeah FL
Palmetto Lowcountry Behavioral
Health System . . . . .Charleston SC
Palmetto Richland Hospital
. . . . .Columbia SC
Palms of Pasadena Hospital
. . . . .Saint Petersburg FL
Palms West Hospital
. . . . .Loxahatchee FL
Palmyra Medical Centers
. . . . .Albany GA
Palo Alto County Hospital
. . . . .Emmetsburg IA
Palo Pinto General Hospital
. . . . .Mineral Wells TX
Palo Verde Hospital . . . . .Tucson AZ
Palo Verde Hospital . . . . . .Blythe CA
Palomar Medical Center
. . . . .Escondido CA
Palos Community Hospital
. . . . .Palos Heights IL
Pampa Regional Medical Center
. . . . .Pampa TX
Pan American Communit
Hospital . . . . .El Paso TX
Pan American Hospital . . . .Miami FL
Pana Community Hospital . . .Pana IL
Paoli Memorial Hospital . . .Paoli PA
Paradise Valley Hospital .Phoenix AZ
Paradise Valley Hospital
. . . . .National City CA
Parc Place . . . . .Chandler AZ

Paris Community Hospital . . .Paris IL
Park Anaheim Healthcare
Center . . . . .Anaheim CA
Park Place Medical Center
. . . . .Port Arthur TX
Park Plaza Hospital . . . . .Houston TX
Park Ridge Hospital . . .Rochester NY
Park Ridge Hospital . . . .Fletcher NC
Park View Hospital . . . . .El Reno OK
Park View Specialty Hospital
Springfield . . . . .Springfield MA
Parkland Health and Hospital
System . . . . .Dallas TX
Parkland Health Center
. . . . .Farmington MO
Parkland Health Center -
Bonne Terre . . . . . .Bonne Terre MO
Parkland Medical Center . . .Derry NH
Parkridge Medical Center
. . . . .Chattanooga TN
Parkside Behavioral Healthcare
. . . . .Columbus OH
Parkside Hospital . . . . . . .Tulsa OK
Parkview Behavioral Health
. . . . .Fort Wayne IN
Parkview Community Hospital
. . . . .Riverside CA
Parkview Episcopal Medical
Center . . . . .Pueblo CO
Parkview Healthcare Center
. . . . .Anaheim CA
Parkview Hospital . . . .Fort Wayne IN
Parkview Hospital . . . .Brunswick ME
Parkview Hospital . . .Philadelphia PA
Parkview Hospital . . . . . .Wheeler TX
Parkview Huntington Hospital
. . . . .Huntington IN
Parkview Noble Hospital
. . . . .Kendallville IN
Parkview Regional Hospital
. . . . .Mexia TX
Parkview Whitley Hospital
. . . . .Columbia City IN
Parkway Hospital . . . .Forest Hills NY
Parkway Medical Center .Atlanta GA
Parkway Medical Center Hospital
. . . . .Decatur AL
Parkway Regional Hospital
. . . . .Fulton KY
Parkway Regional Medical
Center . . . . . .North Miami Beach FL
Parkwood Hospital
. . . . .Olive Branch MS
Parma Community General
Hospital . . . . .Parma OH
Parmer County Communit
Hospital . . . . .Friona TX
Parrish Medical Center . .Titusville FL
Parsons State Hospital and
Training . . . . .Parsons KS
Pascack Valley Hospital
. . . . .Westwood NJ

Alphabetical Index

Pasco Community Hospital . . . . .Dade City FL
Passaic Beth Israel Hospital . . . . .Passaic NJ
Passavant Area Hospital . . . . .Jacksonville IL
Pathway Treatment Center . . . . .Kalispell MT
Pathways of Tennessee .Jackson TN
Patients Hospital of Redding . . . . .Redding CA
Patrick B Harris Psychiatric Hospital . . . . .Anderson SC
Pattie A Clay Hospital .Richmond KY
Patton State Hospital . . . . .Patton CA
Paul B Hall Regional Medical Center . . . . .Paintsville KY
Paul Oliver Memorial Hospital . . . . .Frankfort MI
Paulding County Hospital . . . . .Paulding OH
Pauls Valley General Hospital . . . . .Pauls Valley OK
Pavia Hospital . . . . . . .Santurce PR
Pavilion Foundation . . .Champaign IL
Pavilion, The . . . . .Pensacola FL
Pawhuska Hospital . . .Pawhuska OK
Pawnee County Memoria Hospital . . . . .Pawnee City NE
Pawnee Municipal Hospital Authority . . . . .Pawnee OK
Payne Whitney Psychiatric Clinic . . . . .New York NY
Paynesville Healthcare Hospital . . . . .Paynesville MN
Payson Regional Medical Center . . . . .Payson AZ
Peace Harbor Hospital . .Florence OR
Peacehealth Saint John Medical Center . . . . .Longview WA
Peach Regional Medical Center . . . . .Fort Valley GA
Peachford Behavioral Health System . . . . .Atlanta GA
Peak Hospital . . . . .Santa Teresa NM
Pearl River County Hospital . . . . .Poplarville MS
Pecos County General Hospital .Iraan TX
Pecos County Memorial Hospital . . . . .Fort Stockton TX
Pekin Memorial Hospital . . . .Pekin IL
Pella Regional Health Center .Pella IA
Pembina County Memoria Hospital . . . . .Cavalier ND
Pembroke Hospital . . .Pembroke MA
Pemiscot Memorial Hospital .Hayti MO
Pender Community Hospital . . . . .Pender NE
Pender Memorial Hospital . . . . .Burgaw NC

Pendleton Memorial Methodist Hospital . . . . .New Orleans LA
Peninsula Behavioral Center . . . . .Hampton VA
Peninsula Health Care . .Louisville TN
Peninsula Hospital Center . . . . .Far Rockaway NY
Peninsula Regional Medical Center . . . . .Salisbury MD
Penisula Medical Center . . . . .Burlingame CA
Pennock Hospital . . . . .Hastings MI
Pennsylvania Hospital . . . . .Philadelphia PA
Pennsylvania State University - Milton S Hershey Medical Center . . . . .Hershey PA
Penobscot Bay Medical Center . . . . .Rockport ME
Penobscot Valley Hospital . . . . .Lincoln ME
Penrose Community Hospital . . . . .Colorado Springs CO
Penrose Saint Francis Health System . . . . . .Colorado Springs CO
Peoples Memorial Hospital . . . . .Independence IA
Perham Memorial Hospital . . . . .Perham MN
Perkins County Hospital . . .Grant NE
Permian General Hospital . . . . .Andrews TX
Perry Community Hospital . . . . .Linden TN
Perry County General Hospital . . . . .Richton MS
Perry County Memorial Hospital . . . . .Tell City IN
Perry County Memorial Hospital . . . . .Perryville MO
Perry General Hospital . . . .Perry GA
Perry Memorial Hospital . . . . .Princeton IL
Perry Memorial Hospital . . .Perry OK
Pershing General Hospital . . . . .Lovelock NV
Pershing Memorial Hospital . . . . .Brookfield MO
Person County Memorial Hospital . . . . .Roxboro NC
Petaluma Valley Hospital . . . . .Petaluma CA
Petersburg Medical Center . . . . .Petersburg AK
Peterson Hospital . . . . .Wheeling WV
Phelps County Regional Medical Center . . . . .Rolla MO
Phelps Memorial Health Center . . . . .Holdrege NE
Phelps Memorial Hospital . . . . .North Tarrytown NY
Phenix Regional Hospital . . . . .Columbus GA

Philhaven Hospital . . . . .Lebanon PA
Philhaven Hospital . . . . .Mount Gretna PA
Philipsburg Area Hospital . . . . .Philipsburg PA
Phillips County Hospital . . . . .Phillipsburg KS
Phillips County Medical Center-Maf . . . . .Malta MT
Phillips Eye Institute . . . . .Minneapolis MN
Phoebe Putney Memorial Hospital . . . . .Albany GA
Phoebe Worth Medical Center . . . . .Sylvester GA
Phoenix Baptist Hospital and Medical Center . . . .Phoenix AZ
Phoenix Childrens Hospital . . . . .Phoenix AZ
Phoenix Memorial Hospital . . . . .Phoenix AZ
Phoenixville Hospital University of Pa Health System . . . . . .Phoenixville PA
Phs Indian Health Service Hospital . . . . .Winterhaven CA
Phs Indian Hospital - Albuquerque . . . . .Albuquerque NM
Phs Indian Hospital - Belcourt . . . . .Belcourt ND
Phs Indian Hospital - Browning . . . . .Browning MT
Phs Indian Hospital - Cass Lake . . . . .Cass Lake MN
Phs Indian Hospital - Cherokee . . . . .Cherokee NC
Phs Indian Hospital - Clinton . . . . .Clinton OK
Phs Indian Hospital - Crow Agency . . . . .Crow Agency MT
Phs Indian Hospital - Eagle Butte . . . . .Eagle Butte SD
Phs Indian Hospital - Fort Defiance . . . . .Fort Defiance AZ
Phs Indian Hospital - Fort Yates . . . . .Fort Yates ND
Phs Indian Hospital - Fort Yuma . . . . .Yuma AZ
Phs Indian Hospital - Harlem . . . . .Harlem MT
Phs Indian Hospital - Lawton . . . . .Lawton OK
Phs Indian Hospital - Mescalero . . . . .Mescalero NM
Phs Indian Hospital - Parker . . . . .Parker AZ
Phs Indian Hospital - Pine Ridge . . . . .Pine Ridge SD
Phs Indian Hospital - Rapid City . . . . .Rapid City SD
Phs Indian Hospital - Red Lake . . . . .Red Lake MN
Phs Indian Hospital - Rosebud . . . . .Rosebud SD

Alphabetical Index

Phs Indian Hospital - San Carlos . . . . .San Carlos AZ
Phs Indian Hospital - Santa Fe . . . . .Santa Fe NM
Phs Indian Hospital - Sells . .Sells AZ
Phs Indian Hospital - Sisseton . . . . .Sisseton SD
Phs Indian Hospital - Wagner . . . . .Wagner SD
Phs Indian Hospital - Whiteriver . . . . .Whiteriver AZ
Phs Indian Hospital - Winnebago . . . . .Winnebago NE
Phs Indian Hospital - Zuni . . . . .Zuni NM
Phs Indian Hospital Acomita Canoncito Laquna . . . .San Fidel NM
Phs/Ihs Mount Edgecumbe Hospital . . . . .Sitka AK
Phs/Ihs Alaska Native Medical Center . . . . .Anchorage AK
Phs/Ihs Arctic Slope Native Assoc. and Samuel Simmonds Memorial Hospital . . . . .Barrow AK
Phs/Ihs Bristol Bay Area Health - Kanakanak Hospital . . .Dillingham AK
Phs/Ihs Carl Albert Indian Hospital . . . . .Ada OK
Phs/Ihs Chinle Comprehensive Health Care Facility . . . . . .Chinle AZ
Phs/Ihs Choctaw Nation Health Care Center . . . . .Talihina OK
Phs/Ihs Creek Nation Community Hospital . . . . .Okemah OK
Phs/Ihs Hopi Health Care Center . . . . .Polacca AZ
Phs/Ihs Hu Hu Kam Memorial Hospital . . . . .Sacaton AZ
Phs/Ihs Indian Health Center - Schurz . . . . .Schurz NV
Phs/Ihs Indian Hospital - Claremore . . . . .Claremore OK
Phs/Ihs Indian Hospital - Crownpoint . . . . . . .Crownpoint NM
Phs/Ihs Indian Medical Center - Gallup . . . . .Gallup NM
Phs/Ihs Northern Navajo Medical Center . . . . .Shiprock NM
Phs/Ihs Norton Sound Regional Hospital . . . . .Nome AK
Phs/Ihs Owyhee Community Hospital . . . . .Owyhee NV
Phs/Ihs Phoenix Indian Medical Center . . . . .Phoenix AZ
Phs/Ihs Tuba City Indian Medical Center . . . . .Tuba City AZ
Phs/Ihs W W Hastings Indian Hospital . . . . .Tahlequah OK
Phs/Ihs Yukon Kuskokwim Delta Regional Hospital . . . . . . .Bethel AK
Physicians Center . . . . .Bryan TX
Physicians Hospital of New Orleans . . . . .Alexandria LA

Physicians Hospital of Oklahoma . . . . .Oklahoma City OK
Physicians Surgical Specialty Hospital . . . . .Houma LA
Pickens County Medical Center . . . . .Carrollton AL
Piedmont Behavioral Health Center . . . . .Leesburg VA
Piedmont Geriatric Hospital . . . . .Burkeville VA
Piedmont Health Care System . . . . .Rock Hill SC
Piedmont Hospital . . . . .Atlanta GA
Piggott Community Hospital . . . . .Piggott AR
Pike Community Hospital . . . . .Waverly OH
Pike County Memorial Hospital . . . . .Murfreesboro AR
Pike County Memorial Hospital . . . . .Louisiana MO
Pikeville Methodist Hospital . . . . .Pikeville KY
Pilgrim Psychiatric Center . . . . .Brentwood NY
Pinckneyville Community Hospital . . . . .Pinckneyville IL
Pine Medical Center . .Sandstone MN
Pine Rest Christian Hospital . . . . .Grand Rapids MI
Pinecrest Rehabilitation Hospital . . . . .Delray Beach FL
Pineville Community Hospital . . . . .Pineville KY
Pinnacle Health - Polyclinic Hospital . . . . .Harrisburg PA
Pinnacle Health Hospital . . . . .Harrisburg PA
Pinnacle Pointe Hospital . . . . .Little Rock AR
Pioneer Community Hospital of Aberdeen . . . . .Aberdeen MS
Pioneer Medical Center Maf . . . . .Big Timber MT
Pioneer Memorial Hospital . . . . .Heppner OR
Pioneer Memorial Hospital . . . . .Prineville OR
Pioneer Memorial Hospital . . . . .Viborg SD
Pioneer Valley Hospital . . . . .West Valley City UT
Pioneers Hospital of Rio Blanco . . . . .Meeker CO
Pioneers Memorial Hospital . . . . .Brawley CA
Pipestone County Medical Center . . . . .Pipestone MN
Pitt County Memorial Hospital . . . . .Greenville NC
Pittsburgh Specialty Hospital . . . . .Calabasas CA

Placentia Linda Hospital . . . . .Placentia CA
Plains Memorial Hospital . . . . .Dimmitt TX
Plains Regional Medical Center Clovis . . . . .Clovis NM
Plainview Area Health System . . . . .Plainview NE
Plainville Rural Hospital . . . . .Plainville KS
Plantation General Hospital . . . . .Plantation FL
Plateau Medical Centers . . . . .Oak Hill WV
Platte Community Memorial Hospital . . . . .Platte SD
Platte County Memorial Hospital . . . . .Wheatland WY
Platte Valley Medical Center . . . . .Brighton CO
Plaza Medical Center Hospital Fort Worth . . . . .Fort Worth TX
Plaza Specialty Hospital . . . . .Houston TX
Pleasant Valley Hospital . . . . .Point Pleasant WV
Plum Creek Specialty Hospital . . . . .Amarillo TX
Plumas District Hospital . .Quincy CA
Pocahontas Community Hospital . . . . .Pocahontas IA
Pocahontas Memorial Hospital . . . . .Buckeye WV
Pocono Medical Center . . . . .East Stroudsburg PA
Pointe Coupee General Hospital . . . . .New Roads LA
Pointe Rtc . . . . . . .Santa Teresa NM
Polk Medical Center . .Cedartown GA
Polly Ryon Memorial Hospital . . . . .Richmond TX
Pomerado Hospital . . . . . .Poway CA
Pomerene Memorial Hospital . . . . .Millersburg OH
Pomona Valley Hospital Medical Center . . . . .Pomona CA
Pondera Medical Center . . . . .Conrad MT
Pontiac Correctional Center . . . . .Pontiac IL
Pontiac Osteopathic Hospital . . . . .Pontiac MI
Pontotoc Hospital . . . . .Pontotoc MS
Poplar Community Hospital . . . . .Poplar MT
Poplar Springs Hospital . . . . .Petersburg VA
Port Huron Hospital . . .Port Huron MI
Portage Health System . .Hancock MI
Porter Adventist Hospital . . . . .Denver CO
Porter Medical Center . . . . .Middlebury VT

Alphabetical Index

Porter Memorial Hospital . . . . .Valparaiso IN
Porterville Developmental Center . . . . .Porterville CA
Portland Adventist Medical Center . . . . .Portland OR
Portneuf Medical Center - East . . . . .Pocatello ID
Portneuf Medical Center - West . . . . .Pocatello ID
Portsmouth Regional Hospital . . . . .Portsmouth NH
Potomac Hospital . . .Woodbridge VA
Potomac Ridge Behavioral Health System . . . . .Rockville MD
Potomac Valley Hospital . . . . .Keyser WV
Pottstown Memorial Medical Center . . . . .Pottstown PA
Pottsville Hospital-Warne Clinic . . . . .Pottsville PA
Poudre Valley Hospital . . . . .Fort Collins CO
Powell County Memorial Hospital . . . . .Deer Lodge MT
Powell Hospital . . . . .Powell WY
Prague Municipal Hospital . . . . .Prague OK
Prairie Community Hospital .Terry MT
Prairie Du Chien Memorial Hospital . . . . . .Prairie Du Chien WI
Prairie Lakes Hospital and Care Center - Each . . . . . . .Watertown SD
Prairie View Mental Health Center .Newton KS
Pratt Regional Medical Center . . . . .Pratt KS
Prattville Baptist Medical Center . . . . .Prattville AL
Preferred Rehab Hospital . . . . .Baton Rouge LA
Prentice Women's Hospital .Chicago IL
Prentiss County Regional Hospital . . . . .Prentiss MS
Presbyterian - Saint Luke's Medical Center . . . . .Denver CO
Presbyterian Health Care System .Dallas TX
Presbyterian Hospital . . . . .Albuquerque NM
Presbyterian Hospital . . .Charlotte NC
Presbyterian Hospital Matthews . . . . .Matthews NC
Presbyterian Hospital of Allen . . . . .Allen TX
Presbyterian Hospital of Commerce . . . . .Commerce TX
Presbyterian Hospital of Greenville . . . . .Greenville TX
Presbyterian Hospital of Kaufman . . . . .Kaufman TX

Presbyterian Hospital of Plano .Plano TX
Presbyterian Hospital of Winnsboro . . . . .Winnsboro TX
Presbyterian Intercommunit Hospital . . . . .Whittier CA
Presbyterian-Denver Hospital . . . . .Denver CO
Presbyterian-Orthopaedic Hospital . . . . .Charlotte NC
Presbyterian-University of Pennsylvania Medical Center . . . . .Philadelphia PA
Presentation Medical Center .Rolla ND
Preston Memorial Hospital . . . . .Kingwood WV
Prevost Memorial Hospital . . . . .Donaldsonville LA
Primary Childrens Medical Center . . . . .Salt Lake City UT
Prince Georges Hospital Center . . . . .Cheverly MD
Prince William Hospital . . . . .Manassas VA
Princeton Community Hospital . . . . .Princeton WV
Proctor Community Hospital .Peoria IL
Professional Rehab Hospital . . . . .Ferriday LA
Progressive Hospital . .Las Vegas NV
Prosser Memorial Hospital . . . . .Prosser WA
Provena Covenant Medical Center Champaign-urbana . . . . . .Urbana IL
Provena Mercy Center . . . .Aurora IL
Provena Saint Joseph Medical Center . . . . .Joliet IL
Provena Saint Marys Hospital . . . . .Kankakee IL
Providence Alaska Medical Center . . . . .Anchorage AK
Providence Everett Medical Center . . . . .Everett WA
Providence Everett Medical Center-Colby . . . . .Everett WA
Providence Health Center . .Waco TX
Providence Holy Cross Medical Center . . . . .Mission Hills CA
Providence Hood River Memorial Hospital . . . . .Hood River OR
Providence Hospital . . . . . .Mobile AL
Providence Hospital . . . . .Washington DC
Providence Hospital . . . .Holyoke MA
Providence Hospital . . .Southfield MI
Providence Hospital . . .Columbia SC
Providence Hospital . . .Centralia WA
Providence Hospital Northeast . . . . .Columbia SC
Providence Kodiak Island Medical Center . . . . .Kodiak AK

Providence Medford Medical Center . . . . .Medford OR
Providence Medical Center . . . . .Kansas City KS
Providence Medical Center . . . . .Wayne NE
Providence Memorial Hospital . . . . .El Paso TX
Providence Milwaukie Hospital . . . . .Milwaukie OR
Providence Newberg Hospital . . . . .Newberg OR
Providence Portland Medical Center . . . . .Portland OR
Providence Saint Joseph Medical Center . . . . .Burbank CA
Providence Saint Peter Hospital . . . . .Olympia WA
Providence Saint Vincent Medical Center . . . . .Portland OR
Providence Seaside Hospital . . . . .Seaside OR
Providence Seward Medical Center . . . . .Seward AK
Providence Toppenish Hospital . . . . .Toppenish WA
Providence Yakima Medical Center . . . . .Yakima WA
Provident Hospital of Chicago . . . . .Chicago IL
Provo Canyon School . . . . .Orem UT
Prowers Medical Center . .Lamar CO
Psychiatric Hospital at Vanderbilt . . . . .Nashville TN
Psychiatric Institute of Washington . . . . . . .Washington DC
Psychiatric Services - Lac & Usc Medical Center . . . . .Los Angeles CA
Psychiatric Services - Lac and Usc Medical Center . . . . . .Rosemead CA
Puget Sound Hospital . . .Tacoma WA
Pulaski Community Hospital . . . . .Pulaski VA
Pulaski Memorial Hospital . . . . .Winamac IN
Pullman Memorial Hospital . . . . .Pullman WA
Pungo District Hospital . . . . .Belhaven NC
Punxsutawney Area Hospital . . . . .Punxsutawney PA
Purcell Municipal Hospital . . . . .Purcell OK
Pushmataha County-Town of Antlers Hospital Authority . . . . . .Antlers OK
Putnam County Hospital . . . . .Greencastle IN
Putnam County Memoria Hospital . . . . .Unionville MO
Putnam General Hospital . . . . .Eatonton GA
Putnam General Hospital . . . . .Hurricane WV

219

Alphabetical Index

Putnam Hospital Center . .Carmel NY
Putnam Medical Center . .Palatka FL
Queen of Angels/hollywood
Presbyterian Medical Center
. . . . .Los Angeles CA
Queen of Peace Hospital
. . . . .New Prague MN
Queen of The Valley Hospital
. . . . .Napa CA
Queens Childrens Psych Center
. . . . .Bellerose NY
Queens Hospital Center
. . . . .Jamaica NY
Queens Medical Center . .Honolulu HI
Quentin Mease Hospital
. . . . .Houston TX
Quillen Rehab Hospital
. . . . .Johnson City TN
Quincy and South Shore Mental
Health Center . . . . .Quincy MA
Quincy Hospital . . . . . . .Quincy MA
Quincy Valley Medical Center
. . . . .Quincy WA
Quitman County Hospital and NH
. . . . .Marks MS
R E Thomason General Hospital
. . . . .El Paso TX
R J Reynolds-Patrick Community
Hospital . . . . .Stuart VA
Rabun County Memorial Hospital
. . . . .Clayton GA
Rahway Memorial Hospital
. . . . .Rahway NJ
Rainbow Babies and Childrens
Hospital . . . . .Cleveland OH
Rainbow Mental Health Facility
. . . . .Kansas City KS
Raleigh Community Hospital
. . . . .Raleigh NC
Raleigh Community Hospital
. . . . .Nashville TN
Raleigh General Hospital-Beckley
Campus . . . . .Beckley WV
Ramapo Ridge Psychiatric
Hospital . . . . .Wyckoff NJ
Ramsay Youth Services . .Dothan AL
Rancho Los Amigos Medical
Center . . . . .Downey CA
Rancho Mirage Cardiology Medical
Center . . . . .Rancho Mirage CA
Rancho Springs Medical Center
. . . . .Murrieta CA
Rancocas Hospital . . . . .Riverside NJ
Randolph County Hospital
. . . . .Roanoke AL
Randolph County Medical Center
. . . . .Pocahontas AR
Randolph Hospital . . . .Asheboro NC
Rangely District Hospital
. . . . .Rangely CO
Ranken Jordan Pediatric Rehab
. . . . .Creve Coeur MO

Rankin County Hospital District
. . . . .Rankin TX
Rankin Medical Center . .Brandon MS
Ransom Memorial Hospital
. . . . .Ottawa KS
Rapid City Regional Hospital
. . . . .Rapid City SD
Rapides Regional Medica
Center . . . . .Alexandria LA
Rappahannock General Hospital
. . . . .Kilmarnock VA
Raritan Bay Medical Center
. . . . .Old Bridge NJ
Raritan Bay Medical Center
. . . . .Perth Amboy NJ
Raulerson Hospital . .Okeechobee FL
Ravenswood Hospital and Medical
Center . . . . .Chicago IL
Rawlins County Hospital and Health
Center . . . . .Atwood KS
Ray County Memorial Hospital
. . . . .Richmond MO
Raymond Blank Memorial Hospital
For Children . . . . .Des Moines IA
Raymond W Bliss Army Community
Hospital . . . . . . .Fort Huachuca AZ
Reading Hospital and Medical
Center . . . . .Reading PA
Reagan Memorial Hospital
. . . . .Big Lake TX
Rebsamen Regional Medical
Center . . . . .Jacksonville AR
Recovery Center at Gresham
. . . . .Gresham OR
Red Bay Hospital . . . . . .Red Bay AL
Red Bud Regional Hospital
. . . . .Red Bud IL
Red River Behavioral Health
Services . . . . .Wichita Falls TX
Redding Medical Center
. . . . .Redding CA
Redgate Recovery Center
. . . . .Long Beach CA
Redington Fairview Genera
Hospital . . . . .Skowhegan ME
Redlands Community Hospital
. . . . .Redlands CA
Redmond Regional Medical
Center . . . . .Rome GA
Redwood Falls Municipal Hospital
. . . . .Redwood Falls MN
Redwood Memorial Hospital
. . . . .Fortuna CA
Reedsburg Area Medical Center
. . . . .Reedsburg WI
Reeves County Hospital . . .Pecos TX
Refugio Memorial Hospital
. . . . .Refugio TX
Regency Hospital of Akron
. . . . .Barberton OH
Regency Hospital of Florence
. . . . .Florence SC

Regina Medical Center
. . . . .Hastings MN
Regional Health Services of
Howard County . . . . .Cresco IA
Regional Hospital For Resp and
Complex Care . . . . .Seattle WA
Regional Medical Center - Bayonet
Point . . . . .Hudson FL
Regional Medical Center at
Memphis . . . . .Memphis TN
Regional Medical Center of
Hopkins County . . . .Madisonville KY
Regional Medical Center of
Northeast Arkansas . . .Jonesboro AR
Regional Medical Center of
Northeast Iowa . . . . .Manchester IA
Regional Medical Center of
Orangeburg and Calhoun
. . . . .Orangeburg SC
Regional Medical Center of
San Jose . . . . .San Jose CA
Regional West Medical Center
. . . . .Scottsbluff NE
Regions Hospital . . . . .Saint Paul MN
Rehab Hospital of Acadiana
. . . . .Lafayette LA
Rehab Hospital of The Cape and
Islands . . . . .East Sandwich MA
Rehab Institute . . . . .Kansas City MO
Rehabilitation Hospital of
Connecticut . . . . .Hartford CT
Rehabilitation Hospital of
Fort Wayne . . . . . . .Fort Wayne IN
Rehabilitation Hospital
Indiana . . . . .Indianapolis IN
Rehabilitation Hospital of
Rhode Island . . . .North Smithfield RI
Rehabilitation Hospital of
The Pacific . . . . .Honolulu HI
Rehabilitation Hospital of
Tinton Falls . . . . . . .Tinton Falls NJ
Rehabilitation Institute . . . .Detroit MI
Rehabilitation Institute of
Chicago . . . . .Chicago IL
Rehabilitation Institute
of Saint Louis . . . . . .Saint Louis MO
Rehabilitation Institute of
West Florida . . . . .Pensacola FL
Rehoboth Mckinley Christian
Health Service . . . . . . .Gallup NM
Reid Hospital and Health Care
Services . . . . .Richmond IN
Renaissance Hospital and Medical
Centers . . . . .Detroit MI
Renaissance Womens Hospital of
Edmond . . . . .Edmond OK
Renfrew Center . . . . .Philadelphia PA
Renville County Hospital . .Olivia MN
Republic County Hospital
. . . . .Belleville KS
Research Belton Hospital
. . . . .Belton MO

Alphabetical Index

Research Medical Center
................Kansas City MO
Research Psychiatric Center
................Kansas City MO
Reston Hospital Center . . .Reston VA
Restorative Care Hospital
................Jackson MS
Resurrection Medical Center
................Chicago IL
Retreat Hospital ......Richmond VA
Rex Hospital ....Raleigh NC
Reynolds Army Community
Hospital ....Fort Sill OK
Reynolds County General Memorial
Hospital ....Ellington MO
Reynolds Memorial Hospital
................Glen Dale WV
Rhd Memorial Medical Center
................Dallas TX
Rhea Medical Center ....Dayton TN
Rhode Island Hospital
................Providence RI
Rice County District One Hospital
................Faribault MN
Rice Medical Center . .Eagle Lake TX
Rice Memorial Hospital . .Willmar MN
Richard H Hutchings Psychiatric
Center ....Syracuse NY
Richard H Young Hospital
................Kearney NE
Richard P. Stadter Psychiatric
Center ....Grand Forks ND
Richards Memorial Hospital
................Rockdale TX
Richardson Medical Center
................Rayville LA
Richardson Regional Medical
Center ....Richardson TX
Richardton Health Center
................Richardton ND
Richland Hospital . . .Richland Ctr WI
Richland Memorial Hospital
................Olney IL
Richland Parish Hospital Delhi
................Delhi LA
Richland Parish Rehabilitation
Hospital ....Rayville LA
Richmond Community Hospital
................Richmond VA
Richmond Eye and Ear Hospital
................Richmond VA
Richmond Memorial Hospital
................Rockingham NC
Richmond State Hospital
................Richmond IN
Richwood Area Community
Hospital ....Richmond WV
Riddle Memorial Hospital . .Media PA
Rideout Memorial Hospital
................Marysville CA
Ridge Behavioral Health System
................Lexington KY

Ridgecrest Regional Hospital
................Ridgecrest CA
Ridgeview Institute .....Smyrna GA
Ridgeview Medical Center
................Waconia MN
Ridgeview Psychiatric Hospital and
Center ....Oak Ridge TN
Riley Hospital For Children
................Indianapolis IN
Riley Memorial Hospital
................Meridian MS
Ringgold County Hospital
................Mount Ayr IA
Rio Grande Hospital . . .Del Norte CO
Rio Grande Regional Hospital
................Mc Allen TX
Rio Grande State Mental Health
Center ....Harlingen TX
Rio Vista Rehab Hospital
................El Paso TX
Ripley County Memorial
Hospital ....Doniphan MO
Ripon Medical Center .....Ripon WI
Rivendell Behavioral Health
................Benton AR
Rivendell Behavioral Health
Services ......Bowling Green KY
River Crest Hospital . .San Angelo TX
River Falls Area Hospital
................River Falls WI
River Hospital . . .Alexandria Bay NY
River North Hospital & Transitional
Health Service ....Many LA
River Oaks Child and Adolescent
Hospital ....Harahan LA
River Oaks Hospital ....Harahan LA
River Oaks Hospital ....Jackson MS
River Parishes Hospital
................La Place LA
River Park Hospital . .Mc Minnville TN
River Park Hospital . .Huntington WV
River Region Medical Center
................Vicksburg MS
River Region Medical Center -
West ....Vicksburg MS
River Valley Behavioral Health
................Owensboro KY
River West Medical Center
................Plaquemine LA
Riverbend Rehab Hospital
................Columbia LA
Riveredge Hospital . . .Forest Park IL
Riverland Medical Center Ferriday LA
Riverside Community Hospital
................Riverside CA
Riverside County Regional Medical
Center ....Moreno Valley CA
Riverside General Hospital
................Houston TX
Riverside Hospital . . .Washington DC
Riverside Hospital ....South Bend IN
Riverside Hospital ......Trenton MI

Riverside Medical Center
................Franklinton LA
Riverside Medical Center
................Waupaca WI
Riverside Medical Center
Hospital ....Kankakee IL
Riverside Mercy Hospital
................Toledo OH
Riverside Methodist Hospital
................Columbus OH
Riverside Psychiatric Institute
................Newport News VA
Riverside Regional Medical
Center ....Newport News VA
Riverside Rehab Institute
................Newport News VA
Riverside Tappahannock
Hospital ....Tappahannock VA
Riverside Walter Reed Hospital
................Gloucester VA
Riverton Memorial Hospital
................Riverton WY
Riverview Hospital . . .Noblesville IN
Riverview Hospital ....Crookston MN
Riverview Hospital Association
................Wisconsin Rapids WI
Riverview Hospital For Children
................Middletown CT
Riverview Medical Center
................Red Bank NJ
Riverview Regional Medical
Center ....Gadsden AL
Riverwood Health Care Center
................Aitkin MN
Rml Specialty Hospital . . .Hinsdale IL
Roane General Hospital
................Spencer WV
Roane Medical Center . .Harriman TN
Roanoke Chowan Hospital
................Ahoskie NC
Roanoke Memorial Rehab
Center ....Roanoke VA
Robert E. Bush Naval Hospital
................Twenty-Nine Palms CA
Robert F Kennedy Medical
Center ....Hawthorne CA
Robert H Ballard Rehab
Hospital ....San Bernardino CA
Robert Packer Hospital ....Sayre PA
Robert Wood Johnson University
Hospital ....New Brunswick NJ
Robinson Memorial Hospital
................Ravenna OH
Rochelle Community Hospital
................Rochelle IL
Rochester General Hospital
................Rochester NY
Rochester Methodist Hospital
................Rochester MN
Rochester Psychiatric Center
................Rochester NY
Rock County Hospital
................Bassett NE

Alphabetical Index

Rock County Mental Health Serv
...............Janesville WI
Rock Creek Center ......Lemont IL
Rockcastle Hospital
...............Mount Vernon KY
Rockdale Hospital .....Conyers GA
Rockefeller University Hospital
...............New York NY
Rockford Center ......Newark DE
Rockford Memorial Hospital
...............Rockford IL
Rockingham Memorial Hospital
...............Harrisonburg VA
Rockland Children's Psychiatric
Center ....Orangeburg NY
Rockland Psych Center
...............Orangeburg NY
Rockville General Hospital
...............Vernon CT
Roger C. Peace Rehab Hospital
...............Greenville SC
Roger Mills Memorial Hospital
...............Cheyenne OK
Roger Williams Hospital
...............Providence RI
Rogers City Rehabilitation
Hospital ....Rogers City MI
Rogers Memorial Hospital
...............Milwaukee WI
Rogers Memorial Hospital
...............Oconomowoc WI
Rogue Valley Medical Center
...............Medford OR
Rolling Hills Hospital ......Ada OK
Rolling Plains Memorial Hospital
...............Sweetwater TX
Rollins-Brook Community
Hospital ....Lampasas TX
Rome Hospital and Murphy Memorial
Hospital ....Rome NY
Roosevelt General Hospital
...............Portales NM
Roosevelt Memorial Medical
Center ....Culbertson MT
Roosevelt Warm Springs Institute For
Rehab ....Warm Springs GA
Roper Hospital North
...............Charleston SC
Rose Medical Center ....Denver CO
Roseau Area Hospital District
...............Roseau MN
Rosebud Health Care Center
...............Forsyth MT
Roseland Community Hospital
...............Chicago IL
Roswell Park Cancer Institute
...............Buffalo NY
Round Rock Medical Center
...............Round Rock TX
Roundup Memorial Hospital
...............Roundup MT
Rowan Regional Medical Center
...............Salisbury NC

Roxborough Memorial Hospital
...............Philadelphia PA
Roy Lester Schneider Hospital
...............Saint Thomas U
Royal Oaks Hospital ..Windsor MO
Ruby Valley Hospital ...Sheridan MT
Rumford Community Hospital
...............Rumford ME
Runnells Specialized Hospital-Union
County ....Berkeley Heights NJ
Rush County Healthcare Center
...............La Crosse KS
Rush Foundation Hospital
...............Meridian MS
Rush Memorial Hospital
...............Rushville IN
Rush North Shore Medical
Center ....Skokie IL
Rush-Copley Memorial Hospital
...............Aurora IL
Rush-Presbyterian-Saint Lukes
Medical Center ....Chicago IL
Rusk County Memorial Hospital
...............Ladysmith WI
Rusk Institute of Rehabilitation
Medicine ....New York NY
Rusk Rehabilitation Center
...............Columbia MO
Rusk State Hospital ......Rusk TX
Russell County Hospital
...............Russell Springs KY
Russell County Medical Center
...............Lebanon VA
Russell Hospital ...Alexander City AL
Russell Regional Hospital
...............Russell KS
Russellville Hospital ..Russellville AL
Rutherford Hospital
...............Rutherfordton NC
Rutland Regional Medical
Center ....Rutland VT
Rwj University Hospital a
Hamilton ....Hamilton NJ
Ryder Memorial Hospital
...............Humacao PR
Rye Psych Hospital Center ..Rye NY
Sabetha Community Hospital
...............Sabetha KS
Sabine County Hospital
...............Hemphill TX
Sabine Medical Center ....Many LA
Sac-Osage Hospital ....Osceola MO
Sacred Heart Hospital
...............Pensacola FL
Sacred Heart Hospital ....Chicago IL
Sacred Heart Hospital
...............Cumberland MD
Sacred Heart Hospital
...............Eau Claire WI
Sacred Heart Hospital
...............Tomahawk WI
Sacred Heart Medical Center
...............Eugene OR

Sacred Heart Medical Center
...............Spokane WA
Sacred Heart Rehab Institute
...............Milwaukee WI
Sacred Heart Saint Marys
Hospital ....Rhinelander WI
Sacret Heart Hospital ..Allentown PA
Saddleback Memorial Medical
Center ....Laguna Hills CA
Sagamore Children's Psychiatric
Centers .....Huntington Station NY
Sage Memorial Hospital ..Ganado AZ
Sage Rehab Institute
...............Baton Rouge LA
Saint Agnes Hospital ..Baltimore MD
Saint Agnes Hospital
...............Fond Du Lac WI
Saint Agnes Medical Center
...............Fresno CA
Saint Agnes Medical Center
...............Philadelphia PA
Saint Alexius Hospital
...............Saint Louis MO
Saint Alexius Hospital - Jefferson
Campus ....Saint Louis MO
Saint Alexius Medical Center
...............Hoffman Estates IL
Saint Alexius Medical Center
...............Bismarck ND
Saint Aloisius Medical Center
...............Harvey ND
Saint Alphonsus Regional Medical
Center ....Boise ID
Saint Andrews Health Center
...............Bottineau ND
Saint Andrews Hospital
...............Boothbay Hbr ME
Saint Anne General Hospital
...............Raceland LA
Saint Anne Mercy Hospital
...............Toledo OH
Saint Anne Rehab Hospital
...............Raceland LA
Saint Annes Hospital ..Fall River MA
Saint Anns Hospital of Columbus
...............Westerville OH
Saint Anthony Central Hospital
...............Denver CO
Saint Anthony Community
Hospital ....Warwick NY
Saint Anthony Health Center
...............Alton IL
Saint Anthony Hospital
...............Oklahoma City OK
Saint Anthony Hospital
...............Pendleton OR
Saint Anthony Medical Center
...............Rockford IL
Saint Anthony Medical Center
...............Crown Point IN
Saint Anthony Memorial Health
Centers ....Michigan City IN

Alphabetical Index

Saint Anthony North Hospital . . . . Westminster CO
Saint Anthony Regional Hospital . . . . Carroll IA
Saint Anthonys Hospital . . . . Morrilton AR
Saint Anthonys Hospital . . . . Saint Petersburg FL
Saint Anthonys Hospital . . Chicago IL
Saint Anthonys Medical Center . . . . Saint Louis MO
Saint Anthonys Memorial Hospital . . . . Effingham IL
Saint Barnabas Hospital . . . Bronx NY
Saint Barnabas Medical Center . . . . Livingston NJ
Saint Benedicts Family Medical Center . . . . Jerome ID
Saint Bernard Hospital . . . Chicago IL
Saint Bernardine Medical Center . . . . San Bernardino CA
Saint Bernards Behavioral Health . . . . Jonesboro AR
Saint Bernards Providence Hospital . . . . Milbank SD
Saint Bernards Regional Medical Center . . . . Jonesboro AR
Saint Catherine Health Center . . . . Katy TX
Saint Catherine Hospital . . . . East Chicago IN
Saint Catherine Hospital . . . . Garden City KS
Saint Catherine of Siena Medical Center . . . . Smithtown NY
Saint Catherine's Rehabilitation Hospital . . . . North Miami FL
Saint Catherines Hospital . . . . Kenosha WI
Saint Charles General Hospital . . . . New Orleans LA
Saint Charles Hospital . . . . Port Jefferson NY
Saint Charles Medical Center . . . . Bend OR
Saint Charles Mercy Hospital . . . . Oregon OH
Saint Charles Parish Hospital . . . . Luling LA
Saint Christophers Hospital For Children . . . . Philadelphia PA
Saint Clair Memorial Hospital . . . . Pittsburgh PA
Saint Clair Regional Hospital . . . . Pell City AL
Saint Claire Medical Center . . . . Morehead KY
Saint Clare Hospital . . Lakewood WA
Saint Clare Hospital and Health Services . . . . Baraboo WI
Saint Clare Medical Center . . . . Crawfordsville IN

Saint Clare's Hospital - Boonton Township . . . . . Boonton Township NJ
Saint Clares Hospital . . . . Alton IL
Saint Clares Hospital . . . . . Dover NJ
Saint Clares Hospital . . . . Schenectady NY
Saint Clares Hospital-Denville . . . . Denville NJ
Saint Clares Hospital-Sussex . . . . Sussex NJ
Saint Claude Medical Center . . . . New Orleans LA
Saint Cloud Hospital . . . . Saint Cloud MN
Saint Croix Valley Memorial Hospital . . . . . . Saint Croix Falls WI
Saint Davids Medical Center . . . . Austin TX
Saint Davids Pavilion . . . . . Austin TX
Saint Davids Rehabilitation Center . . . . Austin TX
Saint Dominic Jackson Memorial Hospital . . . . Jackson MS
Saint Dominics Hospital . . . . Manteca CA
Saint Edward Mercy Medical Center . . . . Fort Smith AR
Saint Elizabeth Ann Seton Hospital . . . . Evansville IN
Saint Elizabeth Ann Seton Specialty Care . . . . Carmel IN
Saint Elizabeth Community Health Center . . . . Lincoln NE
Saint Elizabeth Community Hospital . . . . Red Bluff CA
Saint Elizabeth Health Center . . . . Youngstown OH
Saint Elizabeth Health Services . . . . Baker City OR
Saint Elizabeth Hospital . . Belleville IL
Saint Elizabeth Hospital . . . . Gonzales LA
Saint Elizabeth Hospital . . . . Wabasha MN
Saint Elizabeth Hospital . . . . Appleton WI
Saint Elizabeth Hospital of Chicago . . . . Chicago IL
Saint Elizabeth Medical Center . . . . Lafayette IN
Saint Elizabeth Medical Center - North . . . . Covington KY
Saint Elizabeth Medical Center Grant County . . . . Williamstown KY
Saint Elizabeth Medical Center-South . . . . . . Edgewood KY
Saint Elizabeths Hospital . . . . Washington DC
Saint Elizabeths Hospital . . . . Brighton MA
Saint Elizabeths Hospital . . . Utica NY
Saint Eugene Medical Center . . . . Dillon SC

Saint Francis at Ellsworth . . . . Ellsworth KS
Saint Francis at Salina . . . . Salina KS
Saint Francis Behavioral Health Care . . . . Portland CT
Saint Francis Community Hospital . . . . Federal Way WA
Saint Francis Health Care System - Mt. Sinai Campus . . . . . . Hartford CT
Saint Francis Health Center . . . . Colorado Springs CO
Saint Francis Healthcare Center . . . . Green Springs OH
Saint Francis Hospital . . . . Wilmington DE
Saint Francis Hospital . . . . Columbus GA
Saint Francis Hospital . . Litchfield IL
Saint Francis Hospital . . Escanaba MI
Saint Francis Hospital . . Maryville MO
Saint Francis Hospital . . . . Mountain View MO
Saint Francis Hospital . . . . Poughkeepsie NY
Saint Francis Hospital . . . . Roslyn NY
Saint Francis Hospital . . . . . Tulsa OK
Saint Francis Hospital . . Memphis TN
Saint Francis Hospital . . . . Charleston WV
Saint Francis Hospital . . . . Milwaukee WI
Saint Francis Hospital - Cranberry . . . Cranberry Township PA
Saint Francis Hospital - The Turning Point . . . . Beacon NY
Saint Francis Hospital and Health Center . . . . Blue Island IL
Saint Francis Hospital and Health Center . . . . Mooresville IN
Saint Francis Hospital and Medical Center . . . . Hartford CT
Saint Francis Hospital and Medical Center . . . . Topeka KS
Saint Francis Hospital at Broken Arrow . . . . Broken Arrow OK
Saint Francis Hospital Center . . . . Beech Grove IN
Saint Francis Hospital Center - South . . . . Indianapolis IN
Saint Francis Hospital of Evanston . . . . Evanston IL
Saint Francis Hospital of New Castle . . . . . . New Castle PA
Saint Francis Medical Center . . . . Lynwood CA
Saint Francis Medical Center . . . . Honolulu HI
Saint Francis Medical Center . . . . Peoria IL
Saint Francis Medical Center . . . . Monroe LA
Saint Francis Medical Center . . . . Breckenridge MN

Alphabetical Index

Saint Francis Medical Center
. . . . .Cape Girardeau MO
Saint Francis Medical Center
. . . . .Grand Island NE
Saint Francis Medical Center
. . . . .Trenton NJ
Saint Francis Medical Center
. . . . .Pittsburgh PA
Saint Francis Medical Center-West
. . . . .Ewa Beach HI
Saint Francis Memorial Hospital
. . . . .San Francisco CA
Saint Francis Memorial Hospital
. . . . .West Point NE
Saint Francis Regional Medical
Center . . . . .Shakopee MN
Saint Francis Specialty Hospital
. . . . .Monroe LA
Saint Francis Women's & Family
Hospital . . . . .Greenville SC
Saint Gabriels Hospital
. . . . .Little Falls MN
Saint Helena Hospital
. . . . .Deer Park CA
Saint Helena Parish Hospital
. . . . .Greensburg LA
Saint James Community Hospital
. . . . .Butte MT
Saint James Health Services
. . . . .Saint James MN
Saint James Hospital . . . . .Pontiac IL
Saint James Hospital . . . .Newark NJ
Saint James Hospital and Health
Centers . . . . .Chicago Heights IL
Saint James Mercy Hospital
. . . . .Hornell NY
Saint James of Olympia Fields
Medical Center . . . .Olympia Fields IL
Saint James Parish Hospital
. . . . .Lutcher LA
Saint James Psychiatric Hospital
. . . . .Lutcher LA
Saint John Episcopal Hospital
. . . . .Far Rockaway NY
Saint John Health System Oakland
General . . . . . .Madison Heights MI
Saint John Hospital
. . . . .Leavenworth KS
Saint John Hospital and Medical
Center . . . . .Detroit MI
Saint John Macomb Hospital
Center . . . . .Warren MI
Saint John Medical Center
. . . . .Tulsa OK
Saint John North Shore Hospital
. . . . .Harrison Township MI
Saint John Northeast Community
Hospital . . . . .Detroit MI
Saint John River District Hospital
. . . . .East China MI
Saint John Sapulpa . . . . .Sapulpa OK
Saint John Vianney Hospital
. . . . .Downingtown PA

Saint John West Shore Hospital
. . . . .Westlake OH
Saint John's Health System
. . . . .Anderson IN
Saint John's Queens Hospital - Div
of Catholic Medical Center
. . . . .Elmhurst NY
Saint John's Rehabilitation
Hospital . . . . .Harahan LA
Saint Johns Detroit Riverview
Hospital . . . . .Detroit MI
Saint Johns Hospital . . .Springfield IL
Saint Johns Hospital . . .Jackson WY
Saint Johns Hospital Health
Center . . . . .Santa Monica CA
Saint Johns Lutheran Hospital
. . . . .Libby MT
Saint Johns Mercy Hospital
. . . . .Washington MO
Saint Johns Mercy Medical
Center . . . . .Creve Coeur MO
Saint Johns Northeast Community
Hospital . . . . .Maplewood MN
Saint Johns Pleasant Valley
Hospital . . . . .Camarillo CA
Saint Johns Regional Health
Center . . . . .Springfield MO
Saint Johns Regional Medical
Center . . . . .Oxnard CA
Saint Johns Regional Medical
Center . . . . .Joplin MO
Saint Johns Rehabilitation
Hospital . . . . .Lauderdale Lakes FL
Saint Johns Riverside Hospital
. . . . .Yonkers NY
Saint Joseph Community
Hospital . . . . .Mishawaka IN
Saint Joseph East . . . .Lexington KY
Saint Joseph Health Care
. . . . .Albuquerque NM
Saint Joseph Health Care - Northwest
Heights . . . . .Albuquerque NM
Saint Joseph Health Center
. . . . .Kansas City MO
Saint Joseph Health Center
. . . . .Saint Charles MO
Saint Joseph Health Services of
Rhode Island - Our Lady of Fatima
Hospital . . . . . . .North Providence RI
Saint Joseph Hospital . . . .Eureka CA
Saint Joseph Hospital . . .Orange CA
Saint Joseph Hospital . . .Augusta GA
Saint Joseph Hospital . . . . .Elgin IL
Saint Joseph Hospital . .Lexington KY
Saint Joseph Hospital . . .Bangor ME
Saint Joseph Hospital . .Kirkwood MO
Saint Joseph Hospital . . .Polson MT
Saint Joseph Hospital . . .Nashua NH
Saint Joseph Hospital
. . . . .Philadelphia PA
Saint Joseph Hospital
. . . . .Buckhannon WV

Saint Joseph Hospital and Health
Care Center . . . . .Chicago IL
Saint Joseph Hospital and Health
Center . . . . .Kokomo IN
Saint Joseph Hospital and Medical
Center . . . . .Tacoma WA
Saint Joseph Hospital For Specialty
Care . . . . .Providence RI
Saint Joseph Hospital West
. . . . .Lake Saint Louis MO
Saint Joseph Intercommunit
Hospital . . . . .Cheektowaga NY
Saint Joseph Medical Center
. . . . .Bloomington IL
Saint Joseph Medical Center
. . . . .Towson MD
Saint Joseph Medical Center
. . . . .Reading PA
Saint Joseph Medical Center of Fort
Wayne . . . . .Fort Wayne IN
Saint Joseph Memorial Hospital
. . . . .Murphysboro IL
Saint Joseph Mercy Hospital
. . . . .Ann Arbor MI
Saint Joseph Mercy Hospital
. . . . .Pontiac MI
Saint Joseph Mercy Livingston
Hospital . . . . .Howell MI
Saint Joseph Regional Health
Center . . . . .Bryan TX
Saint Joseph Regional Medical
Center . . . . .Lewiston ID
Saint Joseph Rehab Therapy
Services . . . . .Albuquerque NM
Saint Joseph West Mesa Hospital
. . . . .Albuquerque NM
Saint Joseph's Hospital
. . . . .Flushing NY
Saint Joseph's Mercy Hospital
East . . . . .Mount Clemens MI
Saint Joseph's Mercy Hospital
West . . . . .Clinton Township MI
Saint Joseph's Wayne Hospital
. . . . .Wayne NJ
Saint Josephs Behavioral Health
Center . . . . .Stockton CA
Saint Josephs Community Hospital
of West Bend . . . . . . .West Bend WI
Saint Josephs Health Center
. . . . .Warren OH
Saint Josephs Hospital . . .Tampa FL
Saint Josephs Hospital
. . . . .Savannah GA
Saint Josephs Hospital . . .Breese IL
Saint Josephs Hospital . .Highland IL
Saint Josephs Hospital
. . . . .Huntingburg IN
Saint Josephs Hospital
. . . . .Park Rapids MN
Saint Josephs Hospital
. . . . .Saint Paul MN
Saint Josephs Hospital . .Paterson NJ
Saint Josephs Hospital . . .Elmira NY

Alphabetical Index

Saint Josephs Hospital .Asheville NC
Saint Josephs Hospital . . . . .Bellingham WA
Saint Josephs Hospital . . . . .Chewelah WA
Saint Josephs Hospital . . . . .Parkersburg WV
Saint Josephs Hospital . . . . .Chippewa Falls WI
Saint Josephs Hospital . . . . .Marshfield WI
Saint Josephs Hospital . . . . .Milwaukee WI
Saint Josephs Hospital Health Center . . . . .Syracuse NY
Saint Josephs Hospital Medical Center . . . . .Phoenix AZ
Saint Josephs Hospital of Atlanta . . . . .Atlanta GA
Saint Josephs Hospital/Health Center . . . . .Dickinson ND
Saint Josephs Medical Center . . . . .Brainerd MN
Saint Josephs Medical Center . . . . .Yonkers NY
Saint Josephs Medical Center of Stockton . . . . .Stockton CA
Saint Josephs Memorial Hospital . . . . .Hillsboro WI
Saint Josephs Mercy Hospital . . . . .Centerville IA
Saint Josephs Mercy North . . . . .Romeo MI
Saint Josephs Regional Health Center . . . . .Hot Springs AR
Saint Josephs Regional Medical Center . . . . .Plymouth IN
Saint Josephs Regional Medical Center . . . . .South Bend IN
Saint Josephs Womens Hospital . . . . .Tampa FL
Saint Jude Childrens Research Hospital . . . . .Memphis TN
Saint Jude Medical Center . . . . .Fullerton CA
Saint Landry Extended Care Hospital . . . . .Opelousas LA
Saint Lawrence Psych Center . . . . .Ogdensburg NY
Saint Lawrence Rehabilitation Center . . . . .Lawrenceville NJ
Saint Louis Childrens Hospital . . . . .Saint Louis MO
Saint Louis Connect Care Medical Center . . . . .Saint Louis MO
Saint Louis Psych Rehab Hospital . . . . .Saint Louis MO
Saint Louis University Hospital . . . . .Saint Louis MO
Saint Louise Regional Medical Center . . . . .Gilroy CA

Saint Lucie Medical Center . . . . .Port Saint Lucie FL
Saint Luke Community Hospital . . . . .Ronan MT
Saint Luke Hospital . . . . . .Marion KS
Saint Luke Hospital East . . . . .Fort Thomas KY
Saint Luke Hospital West . . . . .Florence KY
Saint Luke Institute . . . . .Silver Spring MD
Saint Luke Medical Center . . . . .Santa Ana CA
Saint Luke's Hospital - Allentown Campus . . . . .Allentown PA
Saint Luke's Medical Center - Wood River . . . . .Ketchum ID
Saint Luke's Northland Hospital . . . . .Kansas City MO
Saint Luke's South Hospital . . . . .Overland Park KS
Saint Lukes - Roosevelt Hospital . . . . .New York NY
Saint Lukes Baptist Hospital . . . . .San Antonio TX
Saint Lukes Behavioral Health Center . . . . .Phoenix AZ
Saint Lukes Episcopal Hospital . . . . .Houston TX
Saint Lukes Hospital . . . . .San Francisco CA
Saint Lukes Hospital . . . . .Jacksonville FL
Saint Lukes Hospital . . . . .Cedar Rapids IA
Saint Lukes Hospital . . . . .New Bedford MA
Saint Lukes Hospital . . . . .Chesterfield MO
Saint Lukes Hospital . . Columbus NC
Saint Lukes Hospital . . . . .Crosby ND
Saint Lukes Hospital . . .Maumee OH
Saint Lukes Hospital . .Bluefield WV
Saint Lukes Hospital of Bethlehem . . . . .Bethlehem PA
Saint Lukes Hospital of Duluth . . . . .Duluth MN
Saint Lukes Hospital of Kansas City . . . . .Kansas City MO
Saint Lukes Hospital of Newburgh . . . . .Newburgh NY
Saint Lukes Medical Center . . . . .Phoenix AZ
Saint Lukes Medical Center . . . . .Milwaukee WI
Saint Lukes Memorial Hospital Center . . . . .Utica NY
Saint Lukes Miners Memorial Medical Center . . . . .Coaldale PA
Saint Lukes Northland Hospital . . . . .Smithville MO
Saint Lukes Quakertown Hospital . . . . .Quakertown PA

Saint Lukes Regional Medical Center . . . . .Boise ID
Saint Lukes Regional Medical Center . . . . .Sioux City IA
Saint Lukes Rehabilitation Institute . . . . .Spokane WA
Saint Lukes Roosevelt Hospital Center . . . . .New York NY
Saint Lukes Southshore . .Cudahy WI
Saint Margaret Mercy Healthcare Centers - North . . . . . .Hammond IN
Saint Margaret Mercy Healthcare Centers - South . . . . .Dyer IN
Saint Margarets Hospital . . . . .Spring Valley IL
Saint Marks Hospital . . . . .Salt Lake City UT
Saint Martin Hospital . . . . .Breaux Bridge LA
Saint Mary Corwin Medical Center . . . . .Pueblo CO
Saint Mary Medical Center . . . . .Long Beach CA
Saint Mary Medical Center . . . . .Galesburg IL
Saint Mary Medical Center . . . . .Hobart IN
Saint Mary Medical Center . . . . .Langhorne PA
Saint Mary Medical Center . . . . .Walla Walla WA
Saint Mary Mercy Hospital . . . . .Livonia MI
Saint Mary of Nazareth Hospital Center . . . . .Chicago IL
Saint Mary Regional Medical Center . . . . .Apple Valley CA
Saint Mary Rogers Memorial Hospital . . . . .Rogers AR
Saint Mary's Hospital . . . . .Leonardtown MD
Saint Mary's Hospital & Rehabilitation Center . . . . .Minneapolis MN
Saint Mary's Hospital - Behavioral Medicine . . . . .Milwaukee WI
Saint Mary's Medical Center . . . . .La Follette TN
Saint Marys Health Center . . . . .Jefferson City MO
Saint Marys Health Center . . . . .Richmond Heights MO
Saint Marys Health Services . . . . .Grand Rapids MI
Saint Marys Hospital . .Waterbury CT
Saint Marys Hospital . . . . .Cottonwood ID
Saint Marys Hospital . . . .Centralia IL
Saint Marys Hospital . . . . .Decatur IL
Saint Marys Hospital . . . . .Streator IL
Saint Marys Hospital . .Rochester MN
Saint Marys Hospital . . . . .Nebraska City NE
Saint Marys Hospital . . .Hoboken NJ

Alphabetical Index

Saint Marys Hospital . . . . .Orange NJ
Saint Marys Hospital . . . .Passaic NJ
Saint Marys Hospital
. . . . .Amsterdam NY
Saint Marys Hospital . .Brooklyn NY
Saint Marys Hospital . .Rochester NY
Saint Marys Hospital . . . . .Pierre SD
Saint Marys Hospital . . . . .Norton VA
Saint Marys Hospital
. . . . .Huntington WV
Saint Marys Hospital and Medical
Center . . . . .Grand Junction CO
Saint Marys Hospital For Children
. . . . .Bayside NY
Saint Marys Hospital Medical
Center . . . . .San Francisco CA
Saint Marys Hospital Medical
Center . . . . .Green Bay WI
Saint Marys Hospital Medical
Center . . . . .Madison WI
Saint Marys Hospital of Athens
. . . . .Athens GA
Saint Marys Hospital of Blue
Springs . . . . .Blue Springs MO
Saint Marys Hospital of East Saint
Louis . . . . .East Saint Louis IL
Saint Marys Hospital of Milwaukee
. . . . .Milwaukee WI
Saint Marys Hospital of Richmond
. . . . .Richmond VA
Saint Marys Hospital of Superior
. . . . .Superior WI
Saint Marys Hospital Ozaukee
. . . . .Mequon WI
Saint Marys Medical Center
. . . . .West Palm Beach FL
Saint Marys Medical Center
. . . . .Saginaw MI
Saint Marys Medical Center
. . . . .Duluth MN
Saint Marys Medical Center
. . . . .Knoxville TN
Saint Marys Medical Center of
Evansville . . . . .Evansville IN
Saint Marys Mercy Hospital
. . . . .Enid OK
Saint Marys Regional Health
Center . . . . .Detroit Lakes MN
Saint Marys Regional Medical
Center . . . . .Russellville AR
Saint Marys Regional Medical
Center . . . . .Lewiston ME
Saint Marys Regional Medical
Center . . . . .Reno NV
Saint Marys Warrick . . . .Boonville IN
Saint Michael Hospital
. . . . .Cleveland OH
Saint Michael Hospital
. . . . .Oklahoma City OK
Saint Michael Hospital
. . . . .Milwaukee WI
Saint Michaels Hospital
. . . . .Sauk Centre MN

Saint Michaels Hospital . .Tyndall SD
Saint Michaels Hospital
. . . . .Stevens Point WI
Saint Michaels Medical
Center . . . . .Newark NJ
Saint Nicholas Hospital
. . . . .Sheboygan WI
Saint Patrick Hospital
. . . . .Lake Charles LA
Saint Patrick Hospital . . .Missoula MT
Saint Patrick's Psychiatric
Hospital . . . . .Monroe LA
Saint Paul Medical Center
. . . . .Dallas TX
Saint Peter Chemical Dependency
Center . . . . .Lacey WA
Saint Peter Community
Hospital . . . . .Saint Peter MN
Saint Peter Regional Treatment
Center . . . . .Saint Peter MN
Saint Peters Community
Hospital . . . . .Helena MT
Saint Peters Hospital . . . .Albany NY
Saint Peters University
Hospital . . . . . . .New Brunswick NJ
Saint Petersburg General
Hospital . . . . . . .Saint Petersburg FL
Saint Ritas Medical Center
. . . . .Lima OH
Saint Rose Dominican Hospital -
Rose De Lima Campus
. . . . .Henderson NV
Saint Rose Dominican Hospital -
Siena Campus . . . . .Henderson NV
Saint Rose Hospital . . .Hayward CA
Saint Tammany Parish Hospital
. . . . .Covington LA
Saint Thomas Hospital . .Nashville TN
Saint Thomas More Hospital
. . . . .Canon City CO
Saint Vincent Carmel Hospital
. . . . .Carmel IN
Saint Vincent Charity Hospital
. . . . .Cleveland OH
Saint Vincent Children's Specialty
Hospital . . . . .Indianapolis IN
Saint Vincent Clay Hospital
. . . . .Brazil IN
Saint Vincent Doctors Hospital
. . . . .Little Rock AR
Saint Vincent Frankfort Hospital
. . . . .Frankfort IN
Saint Vincent General Hospital
District . . . . .Leadville CO
Saint Vincent Health Center . .Erie PA
Saint Vincent Hospital . .Santa Fe NM
Saint Vincent Hospital . .Harrison NY
Saint Vincent Hospital
. . . . .Green Bay WI
Saint Vincent Hospital and Health
Care Center . . . . .Indianapolis IN
Saint Vincent Hospital and Health
Center . . . . .Billings MT

Saint Vincent Hospital at Worcester
Medical Center . . . . . .Worcester MA
Saint Vincent Infirmary Medical
Center . . . . .Little Rock AR
Saint Vincent Jennings Community
Hospital . . . . .North Vernon IN
Saint Vincent Medical Center
. . . . .Los Angeles CA
Saint Vincent Medical Center -
Sherwood . . . . .Sherwood AR
Saint Vincent Memorial
Hospital . . . . .Taylorville IL
Saint Vincent Mercy Hospital
. . . . .Elwood IN
Saint Vincent Midtown Hospital
. . . . .New York NY
Saint Vincent North Rehabilitation
Hospital . . . . .Sherwood AR
Saint Vincent Randolph County
Hospital . . . . .Winchester IN
Saint Vincent Stress Center
. . . . .Indianapolis IN
Saint Vincent Williamsport
Hospital . . . . .Williamsport IN
Saint Vincent's Catholic Medical
Center - Bayley Seton Campus
. . . . .Staten Island NY
Saint Vincents Catholic Medical
Center . . . . .Staten Island NY
Saint Vincents Hospital
. . . . .Birmingham AL
Saint Vincents Hospital Medical
Center . . . . .New York NY
Saint Vincents Medical Center
. . . . .Bridgeport CT
Saint Vincents Medical Center
. . . . .Jacksonville FL
Saint Vincents Mercy Medical
Center . . . . .Toledo OH
Saints Memorial Medical Center
. . . . .Lowell MA
Sakakawea Medical Center
. . . . .Hazen ND
Salem Community Hospital
. . . . .Salem OH
Salem Hospital . . . . .Salem MA
Salem Hospital . . . . .Salem OR
Salem Hospital - Psychiatric
Medicine Center . . . . . . .Salem OR
Salem Hospital Rehab Center
. . . . .Salem OR
Salem Memorial Hospital District
. . . . .Salem MO
Salem Township Hospital . . .Salem IL
Salina Regional Health Care Center -
Penn Campus . . . . .Salina KS
Salina Regional Medical
Center . . . . .Salina KS
Salina Surgical Hospital . . .Salina KS
Salinas Valley Memorial
Hospital . . . . .Salinas CA
Saline Community Hospital
. . . . .Saline MI

Alphabetical Index

Saline Memorial Hospital . . . . .Benton AR
Salt Lake Regional Medical Center . . . . .Salt Lake City UT
Salt Lake Specialty Medical Center . . . . .West Valley City UT
Samaritan Behavioral Health . . . . .Scottsdale AZ
Samaritan Behavioral Health Center Scottsdale . . . . .Scottsdale AZ
Samaritan Hospital . . . . .Troy NY
Samaritan Hospital . .Moses Lake WA
Samaritan Hospital Lexington . . . . .Lexington KY
Samaritan Medical Center . . . . .Watertown NY
Samaritan Memorial Hospital . . . . .Macon MO
Samaritan Regional Health System . . . . .Ashland OH
Same Day Surgery Center . . . . .Rapid City SD
Sampson Regional Medical Center . . . . .Clinton NC
Samuel Mahelona Memorial Hospital . . . . .Kapaa HI
San Angelo Community Medical Center . . . . .San Angelo TX
San Antonio Community Hospital . . . . .Upland CA
San Antonio State Hospital . . . . .San Antonio TX
San Augustine Memorial Hospital . . . . . . .San Augustine TX
San Bernardino Community Hospital . . . . .San Bernardino CA
San Carlos General Hospital . . . . .Santurce PR
San Clemente Hospital and Medical Center . . . . .San Clemente CA
San Diego Choices . . .San Diego CA
San Diego County Psychiatric Hospital . . . . .San Diego CA
San Diego Hospice Acute Care Center . . . . .San Diego CA
San Diego Rehabilitation Institute . . . . .San Diego CA
San Dimas Community Hospital . . . . .San Dimas CA
San Francisco General Hospital . . . . .San Francisco CA
San Gabriel Valley Medical Center . . . . .San Gabriel CA
San Gorgonio Memorial Hospital . . . . .Banning CA
San Jacinto Methodist Hospital . . . . .Baytown TX
San Jacinto Methodist Hospital - Alexander . . . . .Baytown TX
San Joaquin Community Hospital . . . . .Bakersfield CA
San Joaquin General Hospital . . . . .French Camp CA

San Joaquin Valley Rehabilitation Hospital . . . . .Fresno CA
San Jose Medical Center . . . . .San Jose CA
San Juan Bautista Medical Center . . . . .Caguas PR
San Juan Capestrano Psychiatric Hospital . . . . .Rio Piedras PR
San Juan Hospital . . . .Monticello UT
San Juan Municipal Hospital . . . . .Rio Piedras PR
San Juan Regional Medical Center . . . . .Farmington NM
San Leandro Hospital . . . . .San Leandro CA
San Luis Valley Regional Medical Center . . . . .Alamosa CO
San Marcos Treatment Center . . . . .San Marcos TX
San Mateo County General Hospital . . . . .San Mateo CA
San Pablo Hospital . . . .Bayamon PR
San Pedro Hospital . . .San Pedro CA
San Ramon Regional Medical Center . . . . .San Ramon CA
San Vicente Hospital . . . . .Los Angeles CA
Sand Lake Hospital . . . . .Orlando FL
Sandhills Regional Medical Center . . . . .Hamlet NC
Sandypines . . . . .Tequesta FL
Sanpete Hospital . . . . .Mount Pleasant UT
Santa Barbara Cottage Hospital . . . . . . .Santa Barbara CA
Santa Barbara County Mental Health . . .Santa Barbara CA
Santa Clara Valley Medical Center . . . . .San Jose CA
Santa Monica - Ucla Medical Center . . . . .Santa Monica CA
Santa Paula Memorial Hospital . . . . .Santa Paula CA
Santa Rosa Clinic . . . . .Guayama PR
Santa Rosa Medical Center . . . . .Milton FL
Santa Rosa Memorial Hospital . . . . .Santa Rosa CA
Santa Teresa Community Hospital . . . . .San Jose CA
Santa Teresita Hospital . . .Duarte CA
Santa Ynez Valley Cottage Hospital . . . . .Solvang CA
Santiam Memorial Hospital . . . . .Stayton OR
Santo Asilo De Damas Hospital . . . . .Ponce PR
Sarah Bush Lincoln Health Center . . . . .Mattoon IL
Sarah D Culbertson Memorial Hospital . . . . .Rushville IL
Sarasota Memorial Bayside Center . . . . .Sarasota FL

Sarasota Memorial Hospital . . . . .Sarasota FL
Saratoga Hospital . . . . .Saratoga Springs NY
Sartori Memorial Hospital . . . . .Cedar Falls IA
Satanta District Hospital . .Satanta KS
Satilla Regional Medical Center . . . . .Waycross GA
Sauk Prairie Memorial Hospital . . . . .Prairie Du Sac WI
Saunders County Community Hospital . . . . .Wahoo NE
Savannas Hospital . . . . .Port Saint Lucie FL
Savoy Medical Center . . .Mamou LA
Sayre Memorial Hospital . .Sayre OK
Scci Hospital . . . . .Fargo ND
Scci Hospital - Aurora . . . .Aurora CO
Scci Hospital - Central Dakotas . . . . .Mandan ND
Scci Hospital - Detroit . . . . .Detroit MI
Scci Hospital - Easton . . . .Easton PA
Scci Hospital - El Paso . .El Paso TX
Scci Hospital - Harrisburg . . . . .Harrisburg PA
Scci Hospital - Lima . . . . . . .Lima OH
Scci Hospital - Mansfield . . . . .Mansfield OH
Scci Hospital - San Angelo . . . . .San Angelo TX
Scci Hospital at City Park Center . . . . .Aurora CO
Scci Hospital Houston Central . . . . .Houston TX
Scci Hospital of Amarillo . . . . .Amarillo TX
Scci Hospital of Kokomo . .Dallas TX
Scci Hospital of Victoria . .Victoria TX
Scenic Mountain Medical Center . . . . .Big Spring TX
Scheurer Hospital . . . . . .Pigeon MI
Schick-Shadel Hospital . .Seattle WA
Schleicher County Medical Center . . . . .Eldorado TX
Schneider Children's Hospital . . . . .New York NY
Schoolcraft Memorial Hospital . . . . .Manistique MI
Schumpert Medical Center . . . . .Shreveport LA
Schuyler Hospital . .Montour Falls NY
Schwab Rehabilitation Center . . . . .Chicago IL
Sci Laurel Highlands Prison . . . . .Somerset PA
Scotland County Memorial Hospital . . . . .Memphis MO
Scotland Landmann-Jungman Memorial Hospital . . . . .Scotland SD
Scotland Memorial Hospital . . . . .Laurinburg NC
Scott and White Hospital . .Temple TX

Alphabetical Index

Scott County Hospital . . Scott City KS
Scott County Hospital . . . . Oneida TN
Scott Memorial Hospital
. . . . Scottsburg IN
Scott Regional Hospital . . Morton MS
Scottish Rite Childrens Medical
Center . . . . Atlanta GA
Scottsdale Health Care-Osborn
. . . . Scottsdale AZ
Scottsdale Healthcare
. . . . Scottsdale AZ
Screven County Hospital
. . . . Sylvania GA
Scripps Green Hospital . . La Jolla CA
Scripps Memorial Hospital Chula
Vista . . . . Chula Vista CA
Scripps Memorial Hospital
Encinitas . . . . Encinitas CA
Scripps Memorial Hospital
La Jolla . . . . La Jolla CA
Scripps Mercy Hospital and Medical
Center . . . . San Diego CA
Seacoast Medical Center
. . . . Little River SC
Searcy Hospital . . Mount Vernon AL
Seattle Cancer Care Alliance
. . . . Seattle WA
Sebastian River Medical Center
. . . . Sebastian FL
Sebasticook Valley Hospital
. . . . Pittsfield ME
2nd Medical Group
. . . . . Barksdale Air Force Base LA
Sedan City Hospital . . . . . . Sedan KS
Sedgwick County Memorial
Hospital . . . . Julesburg CO
Seidle Memorial Hospital
. . . . Mechanicsburg PA
Seiling Municipal Hospital
Authority . . . . Seiling OK
Selby General Hospital . . Marietta OH
Select Specialty Hospital
. . . . Beech Grove IN
Select Specialty Hospital
. . . . Conroe TX
Select Specialty Hospital
Phoenix . . . . Phoenix AZ
Select Specialty Hospital
Akron . . . . Akron OH
Select Specialty Hospital -
Ann Arbor . . . . Ann Arbor MI
Select Specialty Hospital -
Atlanta . . . . Atlanta GA
Select Specialty Hospital -
Augusta . . . . Augusta GA
Select Specialty Hospital - Battle
Creek . . . . Battle Creek MI
Select Specialty Hospital -
Biloxi . . . . Biloxi MS
Select Specialty Hospital -
Birmingham . . . . Birmingham AL

Select Specialty Hospital -
Birmingham Princeton
. . . . Birmingham AL
Select Specialty Hospital -
Bloomington . . . . Bloomington IN
Select Specialty Hospital -
Camp Hill . . . . Camp Hill PA
Select Specialty Hospital -
Charleston . . . . Charleston WV
Select Specialty Hospital -
Cincinnati . . . . Cincinnati OH
Select Specialty Hospital -
Columbus . . . . Columbus OH
Select Specialty Hospital -
Columbus . . . . Columbus OH
Select Specialty Hospital -
Columbus/grant . . . . . Columbus OH
Select Specialty Hospital -
Columbus/riverside . . . Columbus OH
Select Specialty Hospital -
Dallas . . . . Dallas TX
Select Specialty Hospital - Denver
Denver CO
Select Specialty Hospital - Denver
South . . . . Denver CO
Select Specialty Hospital -
Durham . . . . Durham NC
Select Specialty Hospital -
Erie . . . . Erie PA
Select Specialty Hospital -
Evansville . . . . Evansville IN
Select Specialty Hospital -
Flint . . . . Flint MI
Select Specialty Hospital -
Fort Smith . . . . Fort Smith AR
Select Specialty Hospital -
Fort Wayne . . . . Fort Wayne IN
Select Specialty Hospital -
Greensburg . . . . Greensburg PA
Select Specialty Hospital -
Gulfport . . . . Gulfport MS
Select Specialty Hospital - Houston
Heights . . . . Houston TX
Select Specialty Hospital - Houston
Medical Center . . . . Houston TX
Select Specialty Hospital - Houston
West . . . . Houston TX
Select Specialty Hospital -
Indianapolis . . . . Indianapolis IN
Select Specialty Hospital -
Jackson . . . . Jackson MS
Select Specialty Hospital -
Johnstown . . . . Johnstown PA
Select Specialty Hospital - Kansas
City . . . . Shawnee Mission KS
Select Specialty Hospital -
Knoxville . . . . Knoxville TN
Select Specialty Hospital -
Lexington . . . . Lexington KY
Select Specialty Hospital -
Little Rock . . . . Little Rock AR
Select Specialty Hospital -
Macomb County . Mount Clemens MI

Select Specialty Hospital -
Memphis . . . . Memphis TN
Select Specialty Hospital
Mesa . . . . Mesa AZ
Select Specialty Hospital -
Miami . . . . Miami FL
Select Specialty Hospital -
Milwaukee . . . . West Allis WI
Select Specialty Hospital -
Milwaukee/Saint Lukes
. . . . Milwaukee WI
Select Specialty Hospital -
Nashville . . . . Nashville TN
Select Specialty Hospital - New
Orleans . . . . Metairie LA
Select Specialty Hospital - North
Dallas . . . . Carrollton TX
Select Specialty Hospital - North
Knoxville . . . . Knoxville TN
Select Specialty Hospital - Northwest
Detroit . . . . Detroit MI
Select Specialty Hospital - Northwest
Indiana . . . . Hammond IN
Select Specialty Hospital - Oklahoma
City . . . . Oklahoma City OK
Select Specialty Hospital - Oklahoma
City East . . . . . . Oklahoma City OK
Select Specialty Hospital -
Omaha . . . . Papillion NE
Select Specialty Hospital -
Philadelphia/aemc . . . Philadelphia PA
Select Specialty Hospital -
Pittsburgh . . . . Pittsburgh PA
Select Specialty Hospital -
Pontiac . . . . Pontiac MI
Select Specialty Hospital -
Saginaw . . . . Saginaw MI
Select Specialty Hospital -
Saint Louis . . . . Saint Louis MO
Select Specialty Hospital - San
Antonio . . . . San Antonio TX
Select Specialty Hospital -
Sioux Falls . . . . Sioux Falls SD
Select Specialty Hospital - South
Dallas . . . . De Soto TX
Select Specialty Hospital -
Topeka . . . . Topeka KS
Select Specialty Hospital -
Tri-city . . . . Bristol TN
Select Specialty Hospital -
Tulsa . . . . Tulsa OK
Select Specialty Hospital - Western
Michigan . . . . Muskegon MI
Select Specialty Hospital -
Wichita . . . . Wichita KS
Select Specialty Hospital -
Wilmington . . . . Wilmington DE
Select Specialty Hospital -
Wyandotte . . . . Wyandotte MI
Select Specialty Hospital -
York . . . . York PA
Select Specialty Hospital -
Youngstown . . . . Youngstown OH

Alphabetical Index

Select Specialty Hospital of Northwest Detroit . . . . .Detroit MI
Self Memorial Hospital . . . . .Greenwood SC
Selma District Hospital . . . .Selma CA
Seminole Medical Center-Hospital . . . . .Seminole OK
Sempercare Hospital - Akron . . . . .Akron OH
Sempercare Hospital of Lancaster . . . . .Lancaster PA
Sempercare Hospital of Little Rock . . . . .Little Rock AR
Sempercare Hospitals - Colorado Springs . . . . . .Colorado Springs CO
Sempervirens . . . . .Eureka CA
Seneca District Hospital . . . . .Chester CA
Senior Horizons . . . . . .Scottsdale AZ
Sentara Bayside Hospital . . . . .Virginia Beach VA
Sentara Careplex Hospital . . . . .Hampton VA
Sentara Leigh Hospital . . .Norfolk VA
Sentara Norfolk General Hospital .Norfolk VA
Sequoia Hospital . .Redwood City CA
Sequoyah Memorial Hospital .Sallisaw OK
Serenity Lane . . . . .Eugene OR
Seton Edgar B Davis Memorial Hospital . . . . .Luling TX
Seton Health - Saint Mary's Hospital . . . . .Troy NY
Seton Highland Lakes Medical Center . . . . .Burnet TX
Seton Medical Center . .Daly City CA
Seton Medical Center . . . . .Austin TX
Seton Medical Center Coastside . . . . .Moss Beach CA
Seton Northwest Hospital . .Austin TX
Seton Shoal Creek Hospital . . . . .Austin TX
Seven Rivers Community Hospital . . . . .Crystal River FL
7th Medical Group . . . . .Dyess Air Force Base TX
78th Medical Group . . . . .Robins Air Force Base GA
75th Medical Group . . . . .Hill Air Force Base UT
74th Medical Group .Wright-Patterson Air Force Base OH
72nd Medical Group . . . . .Tinker Air Force Base OK
Sevier Valley Hospital . . .Richfield UT
Sewickley Valley Hospital . . . . .Sewickley PA
Seymour Hospital . . . . . .Seymour TX
Shady Grove Adventist Hospital . . . . .Rockville MD
Shamokin Area Community Hospital . . . . .Coal Township PA

Shamrock General Hospital . . . . .Shamrock TX
Shands Agh Hospital . .Gainesville FL
Shands at Lake Shore Hospital . . . . .Lake City FL
Shands at Live Oak . . . .Live Oak FL
Shands at Starke . . . . .Starke FL
Shands Hospital at The University of Florida . . . . .Gainesville FL
Shands Jacksonville Medical Center . . . . .Jacksonville FL
Shands Jacksonville Medical Center . . . . .Jacksonville FL
Shands Rehab Hospital . . . . .Gainesville FL
Shannon Medical Center-Saint John Campus . . . . .San Angelo TX
Shannon West Texas Memorial Hospital . . . . .San Angelo TX
Share Medical Center . . . . . .Alva OK
Sharkey Isaquena Community Hospital . . . . .Rolling Fork MS
Sharon Hospital . . . . . . .Sharon CT
Sharon Regional Health System . . . . .Sharon PA
Sharp Chula Vista Medical Center . . . . .Chula Vista CA
Sharp Coronado Hospital and Health Center . . . . .Coronado CA
Sharp Mary Birch Hospital For Women . . . . .San Diego CA
Sharp Memorial Hospital . . . . .San Diego CA
Sharp-Mesa Vista Hospital . . . . .San Diego CA
Shasta County In-Patient Mental Health Services . . . . . .Redding CA
Shaughnessy-Kaplan Rehab Hospital Hospital . . . . . . .Salem MA
Shawano Medical Center . . . . .Shawano WI
Shawnee Mission Medical Center . . . . . .Shawnee Mission KS
Sheboygan Memorial Medical Center . . . . .Sheboygan WI
Sheehan Memorial Hospital . . . . .Buffalo NY
Shelby Baptist Medical Center . . . . .Alabaster AL
Shelby County Myrtue Memorial Hospital . . . . .Harlan IA
Shelby Hospital . . . . .Shelby OH
Shelby Memorial Hospital . . . . .Shelbyville IL
Shelby Regional Medical Center .Center TX
Sheltering Arms Hospital . . . . .Mechanicsville VA
Shenandoah County Memorial Hospital . . . . .Woodstock VA
Shenandoah Memorial Hospital . . . . .Shenandoah IA
Shepherd Hill Hospital . . .Newark OH

Shepherd Spinal Center . .Atlanta GA
Sheppard Enoch Pratt Hospital .Towson MD
Sheridan Community Hospital . . . . .Sheridan MI
Sheridan County Health Complex . . . . .Hoxie KS
Sheridan Memorial Hospital . . . . .Plentywood MT
Sherman Hospital . . . . .Elgin IL
Sherman Oaks Hospital and Health Center . . . . .Sherman Oaks CA
Shoals Hospital . . .Muscle Shoals AL
Shodair Childrens Hospital .Helena MT
Shore Memorial Hospital . . . . .Somers Point NJ
Shore Memorial Hospital . . . . .Nassawadox VA
Shore Rehabilitation Institute . . . . .Point Pleasant NJ
Shoreline Behavioral Center . . . . .Toms River NJ
Shoshone Medical Center . . . . .Kellogg ID
Shriners Burn Institute . . . . .Galveston TX
Shriners Hospital . . . . . . .Chicago IL
Shriners Hospital . . . . .Lexington KY
Shriners Hospital . . . .Shreveport LA
Shriners Hospital . . . .Springfield MA
Shriners Hospital . . .Minneapolis MN
Shriners Hospital . . . .Saint Louis MO
Shriners Hospital . . . . .Erie PA
Shriners Hospital . . . .Philadelphia PA
Shriners Hospital For Children . . . . .Los Angeles CA
Shriners Hospital For Children . . . . .Sacramento CA
Shriners Hospital For Children .Tampa FL
Shriners Hospital For Children . . . . .Honolulu HI
Shriners Hospital For Children . . . . .Cincinnati OH
Shriners Hospital For Children . . . . .Portland OR
Shriners Hospital For Children . . . . .Greenville SC
Shriners Hospital For Children . . . . .Houston TX
Shriners Hospital For Children . . . . .Salt Lake City UT
Shriners Hospitals For Children - Shriners Burns Hospital . .Boston MA
Shriners Hospitals For Children - Spokane . . . . .Spokane WA
Sibley Medical Center . .Arlington MN
Sibley Memorial Hospital . . . . .Washington DC
Sid Peterson Memorial Hospital . . . . .Kerrville TX
Sidney Health Center . . . .Sidney MT

Alphabetical Index

Sierra Kings District Hospital . . . . .Reedley CA
Sierra Medical Center . . .El Paso TX
Sierra Nevada Memorial Hospital . . . . .Grass Valley CA
Sierra Valley District Hospital . . . . .Loyalton CA
Sierra View District Hospital . . . . .Porterville CA
Sierra Vista Community Hospital . . . . .Sierra Vista AZ
Sierra Vista Hospital . . . . .Sacramento CA
Sierra Vista Hospital . . . . . . .Truth Or Consequences NM
Sierra Vista Regional Medical Center . . . . . .San Luis Obispo CA
Siloam Springs Memorial Hospital . . . . .Siloam Springs AR
Silver Cross Hospital . . . . . .Joliet IL
Silver Hill Hospital . .New Canaan CT
Silverton Hospital . . . . .Silverton OR
Simi Valley Hospital - South . . . . .Simi Valley CA
Simi Valley Hospital and Health Care Services . . . . .Simi Valley CA
Simpson General Hospital . . . . .Mendenhall MS
Sinai Hospital . . . . . . .Baltimore MD
Sinai-grace Hospital . . . . .Detroit MI
Singing River Hospital . . . . .Pascagoula MS
Sioux Falls Surgical Center Llp . . . . .Sioux Falls SD
Sioux Valley Behavioral Health System . . . . .Sioux Falls SD
Sioux Valley Health Services-Canby Campus . . . . .Canby MN
Sioux Valley Hospital . . . . .Sioux Falls SD
Sioux Valley Medical Center . . . . .Vermillion SD
Sioux Valley Memorial Hospital . . . . .Cherokee IA
Siouxland Surgery Center Ltd Partnership . . . . .Dakota Dunes SD
Siskin Hospital For Physical Rehab . . . . .Chattanooga TN
Sisters of Charity Hospital . . . . .Buffalo NY
Sistersville General Hospital . . . . .Sistersville WV
Sitka Community Hospital . .Sitka AK
6th Medical Group . . . . .Mac Dill Air Force Base FL
60th Medical Group - David Grant Medical Center . . . . .Travis Air Force Base CA
Skaggs Community Health Center . . . . .Branson MO
Skiff Medical Center . . . . .Newton IA
Sky Ridge Medical Center . . . . .Lone Tree CO

Skyline Hospital . . .White Salmon WA
Skyline Medical Center . . . . .Nashville TN
Sleepy Eye Municipal Hospital . . . . .Sleepy Eye MN
Slidell Memorial Hospital . . .Slidell LA
Sloan Kettering Cancer Center . . . . .New York NY
Smith County Memorial Hospital . . . . .Smith Center KS
Smith County Memorial Hospital . . . . .Carthage TN
Smith Northview Hospital . . . . .Valdosta GA
Smithville Regional Hospital . . . . .Smithville TX
Smyth County Community Hospital . . . . .Marion VA
Snoqualmie Valley Hospital . . . . .Snoqualmie WA
Snowden at Fredericksburg . . . . .Fredericksburg VA
Socorro General Hospital . . . . .Socorro NM
Solaris Health Systems . . .Edison NJ
Soldiers and Sailors Memorial Hospital . . . . .Penn Yan NY
Soldiers and Sailors Memorial Hospital . . . . .Wellsboro PA
Soldiers Home of Holyoke . . . . .Holyoke MA
Somerset Community Hospital . . . . .Somerset PA
Somerset Medical Center . . . . .Somerville NJ
Somerville Hospital . . .Somerville MA
Sonoma Developmental Center . . . . .Eldridge CA
Sonoma Valley Hospital . . . . .Sonoma CA
Sonora Behavioral Health . . . . .Tucson AZ
Sonora Community Hospital . . . . .Sonora CA
Sound Shore Medical Center . . . . .New Rochelle NY
South Austin Hospital . . . . .Austin TX
South Baldwin Regional Medical Center . . . . .Foley AL
South Barry County Memorial . . . . .Cassville MO
South Bay Hospital . . . . .Sun City Center FL
South Beach Psychiatric Center . . . . .Staten Island NY
South Big Horn County Hospital . . . . .Greybull WY
South Cameron Memorial Hospital . . . . .Cameron LA
South Carolina State Hospital . . . . .Columbia SC
South Central Kansas Regional Medical Center . . . .Arkansas City KS

South Central Regional Medical Center . . . . .Laurel MS
South Coast Hospital Group/Tobey Hospital . . . . .Wareham MA
South Coast Medical Center . . . . .Laguna Beach CA
South County Hospital . .Wakefield RI
South Dakota Human Services Center . . . . .Yankton SD
South Davis Community Hospital . . . . .Bountiful UT
South Florida Baptist Hospital . . . . .Plant City FL
South Florida Evaluation & Treatment Center . . . . .Miami FL
South Florida State Hospital . . . . .Pembroke Pines FL
South Fulton Medical Center . . . . .East Point GA
South Georgia Medical Center . . . . .Valdosta GA
South Haven Community Hospital . . . . .South Haven MI
South Hill Medical Center . . . . .Spokane WA
South Jersey Hospital - Bridgton . . . . .Bridgeton NJ
South Jersey Hospital - Elmer . . . . .Elmer NJ
South Jersey Hospital - Newcomb . . . . .Vineland NJ
South Lake Memorial Hospital . . . . .Clermont FL
South Lincoln Medical Center . . . . .Kemmerer WY
South Lyon Medical Center . . . . .Yerington NV
South Miami Hospital . . . . .Miami FL
South Mississippi Stat Hospital . . . . .Purvis MS
South Nassau Community Hospital . . . . .Oceanside NY
South Oaks Hospital . . .Amityville NY
South Peninsula Hospital . . . . .Homer AK
South Pointe Hospital . . . . .Warrensville Heights OH
South Seminole Community Hospital . . . . .Longwood FL
South Shore Hospital . . . .Chicago IL
South Shore Hospital . . . . .South Weymouth MA
South Shore Hospital and Medical Center . . . . .Miami Beach FL
South Suburban Hospital . . . . .Hazel Crest IL
South Sunflower County Hospital . . . . .Indianola MS
South Texas Hospital . .Harlingen TX
South Texas Regional Medical Center . . . . .Jourdanton TX
Southampton Hospital . . . . .Southampton NY

Alphabetical Index

Southampton Memorial Hospital . . . . Franklin VA
Southcrest Hospital . . . . . . Tulsa OK
Southeast Alabama Medical Center . . . . Dothan AL
Southeast Arizona Medical Center . . . . Douglas AZ
Southeast Baptist Hospital . . . . San Antonio TX
Southeast Colorado Hospital . . . . Springfield CO
Southeast Georgia Regional Medical Center . . . . Brunswick GA
Southeast Louisiana Hospital . . . . Mandeville LA
Southeast Missouri Hospital . . . . Cape Girardeau MO
Southeast Missouri Mental Health Center . . . . Farmington MO
Southeast Regional Medical Center . . . . Kentwood LA
Southeastern Ohio Regional Medical Center . . . . Cambridge OH
Southeastern Regional Medical Center . . . . Lumberton NC
Southern Chester County Medical Center . . . . West Grove PA
Southern Coos Hospital . . . . Bandon OR
Southern Hills Medical Center . . . . Nashville TN
Southern Indiana Rehabilitation Hospital . . . . New Albany IN
Southern Inyo Hospital . . . . Lone Pine CA
Southern Maine Medical Center . . . . Biddeford ME
Southern Maryland Hospital . . . . Clinton MD
Southern Nevada Adult Mental Health . . . . Las Vegas NV
Southern New Hampshire Medical Center . . . . Nashua NH
Southern Ocean County Hospital . . . . Manahawkin NJ
Southern Ohio Medical Center . . . . Portsmouth OH
Southern Regional Medical Center . . . . Riverdale GA
Southern Tennessee Medical Center . . . . Winchester TN
Southern Virginia Mental Health Institute . . . . Danville VA
Southern Winds Hospital-Westchester . . . . Hialeah FL
Southlake Center For Mental Health . . . . Merrillville IN
Southside Community Hospital . . . . Farmville VA
Southside Hospital . . . Bay Shore NY
Southside Regional Medical Center . . . . Petersburg VA
Southview Hospital . . . . . Dayton OH

Southwest Connecticut Mental Health System . . . . Bridgeport CT
Southwest Florida Regional Medical Center . . . . Fort Myers FL
Southwest General Health Center . . . . . Middleburg Heights OH
Southwest General Hospital . . . . San Antonio TX
Southwest Georgia Regional Medical Center . . . . Cuthbert GA
Southwest Health Center . . . . Cuba City WI
Southwest Health Center . . . . Platteville WI
Southwest Health System . . . . Cortez CO
Southwest Healthcare Services . . . . Bowman ND
Southwest Hospital and Medical Center . . . . Atlanta GA
Southwest Medical Center . . . . Liberal KS
Southwest Mental Health Center . . . . San Antonio TX
Southwest Mississippi Medical Center . . . . McComb MS
Southwest Regional Medical Center . . . . Little Rock AR
Southwest Regional Medical Complex . . . . Lubbock TX
Southwest Texas Methodist Hospital . . . . San Antonio TX
Southwest Washington Medical Center . . . . Vancouver WA
Southwestern Hospital . . . Lawton OK
Southwestern Memorial Hospital . . . . Weatherford OK
Southwestern Michigan Rehabilitation Hospital . . . . Battle Creek MI
Southwestern State Hospital . . . . Thomasville GA
Southwestern Vermont Medical Center . . . . Bennington VT
Southwestern Virginia Mental Health Institute . . . . Marion VA
Southwood Psychiatric Hospital . . . . Pittsburgh PA
Spalding Regional Hospital . . . . Griffin GA
Spalding Rehabilitation Hospital . . . . Aurora CO
Spanish Peaks Regional Health Center . . . . Walsenburg CO
Sparks Regional Medical Center . . . . Fort Smith AR
Sparrow Health System - Saint Lawrence Hospital . . . . . . Lansing MI
Sparta Community Hospital District . . . . Sparta IL
Spartanburg Hospital For Restorative Care . . . . Spartanburg SC
Spartanburg Regional Medical Center . . . . Spartanburg SC

Spaulding Rehab Hospital . . . . Boston MA
Speare Memorial Hospital . . . . Plymouth NH
Spearfish Surgery Center . . . . Spearfish SD
Speciality Hospital of Jacksonville . . . . Jacksonville FL
Speciality Hospital of Meridian . . . . Meridian MS
Specialty Hospital of Lorain . . . . Lorain OH
Specialty Hospital of Mahoning Valley . . . . Youngstown OH
Specialty Hospital of Mid America . . . . Overland Park KS
Specialty Hospital of New Orleans . . . . New Orleans LA
Specialty Hospital of Rome . . . . Rome GA
Spectrum Health - Blodgett Campus . . . . Grand Rapids MI
Spectrum Health - Kent Community . . . . Grand Rapids MI
Spectrum Health - Reed City Campus . . . . Reed City MI
Spectrum Health Care - Downtown . . . . Grand Rapids MI
Spencer Municipal Hospital . . . . Spencer IA
Spine Hospital of South Texas . . . . San Antonio TX
Spooner Health System and Nursing Home . . . . Spooner WI
Spring Branch Medical Center . . . . Houston TX
Spring Grove Hospital Center . . . . Catonsville MD
Spring Harbor Hospital . . . . South Portland ME
Spring Hill Regional Hospital . . . . Spring Hill FL
Spring Mountain Treatment Center . . . . Las Vegas NV
Spring Valley Hospital Medical Center . . . . Las Vegas NV
Springbrook Behavioral Healthcare . . . . Travelers Rest SC
Springbrook Hospital . Brooksville FL
Springfield Hospital . . Springfield PA
Springfield Hospital . . Springfield VT
Springfield Hospital Center . . . . Sykesville MD
Springfield Medical Center . . . . Springfield MN
Springhill Medical Center . . Mobile AL
Springhill Medical Center . . . . Springhill LA
Springs Memorial Hospital . . . . Lancaster SC
Spruce Pine Community Hospital . . . . Spruce Pine NC

Alphabetical Index

Ssm Rehabilitation Institute . . . . .Saint Louis MO
St Luke's Episcopal Hospital . . . . .Ponce PR
St Lukes Episcopal Hospital . . . . .Ponce PR
Stafford District Hospital #4 . . . . .Stafford KS
Stamford Hospital . . . . .Stamford CT
Stamford Memorial Hospital . . . . .Stamford TX
Standish Community Hospital . . . . .Standish MI
Stanford University Hospital . . . . .Stanford CA
Stanislaus Surgical Hospital . . . . .Modesto CA
Stanly Memorial Hospital . . . . .Albemarle NC
Stanton County Hospital . . . . .Johnson KS
Star Valley Hospital . . . . . .Afton WY
Starke Memorial Hospital . . .Knox IN
Starlite Village Hospital . . . . .Center Point TX
Starr County Memorial Hospital . . . . .Rio Grande City TX
State Correctional Institute at Camp Hill . . . . .Camp Hill PA
State Correctional Institute-Waymart . . . . .Waymart PA
State Correctional Institution Hospital . . . . .Pittsburgh PA
State Hospital North Idaho . . . . .Orofino ID
State Psychiatric Hospital . . . . .Iowa City IA
State Psychiatric Hospital . . . . .Concord NH
Staten Island University Hospital - Concord . . . . .Staten Island NY
Staten Island University Hospital-North . . . . .Staten Island NY
Staten Island University Hospital-South . . . . .Staten Island NY
Stateville Correctional Center . . . . .Joliet IL
Ste Genevieve County Memorial Hospital . . . . . .Sainte Genevieve MO
Steele Memorial Hospital . . . . .Salmon ID
Stephens County Hospital . . . . .Toccoa GA
Stephens Memorial Hospital . . . . .Norway ME
Stephens Memorial Hospital . . . . .Breckenridge TX
Sterling Medical Center . . . . .Waltham MA
Sterling Regional Medical Center . . . . .Sterling CO
Sterlington Rehab Hospital . . . . .Sterlington LA

Stevens County Hospital . . . . .Hugoton KS
Stevens Medical Center . .Morris MN
Stevens Memorial Hospital . . . . .Edmonds WA
Stewart Memorial Community Hospital . . . . .Lake City IA
Stewart Webster Hospital . . . . .Richland GA
Stillman Infirmary-Harvard University . . . . .Cambridge MA
Stillwater Community Hospital . . . . .Columbus MT
Stillwater Medical Center . . . . .Stillwater OK
Stokes-Reynolds Memorial Hospital . . . . .Danbury NC
Stone County Hospital . .Wiggins MS
Stone County Medical Center . . . . .Mountain View AR
Stone Pavilion . . . . .Chicago IL
Stonecrest Medical Center . . . . .Smyrna TN
Stones River Hospital . . . . .Woodbury TN
Stonewall Jackson Hospital . . . . .Lexington VA
Stonewall Jackson Memorial Hospital . . . . .Weston WV
Stonewall Memorial Hospital . . . . .Aspermont TX
Stony Lodge Hospital . . .Ossining NY
Stormont Vail Health Care . . . . .Topeka KS
Story County Hospital . . . .Nevada IA
Stoughton Hospital . . . .Stoughton WI
Straith Hospital For Special Surgery . . . . .Southfield MI
Straub Hospital . . . . . . .Honolulu HI
Streamwood Hospital . . . . .Streamwood IL
Stringfellow Memorial Hospital . . . . .Anniston AL
Strong Memorial Hospital . . . . .Rochester NY
Stroud Municipal Hospital . . . . .Stroud OK
Sturdy Memorial Hospital . . . . .Attleboro MA
Sturgis Community Health Care Center . . . . .Sturgis SD
Sturgis Hospital . . . . .Sturgis MI
Stuttgart Regional Medical Center . . . . .Stuttgart AR
Suburban General Hospital . . . . .Pittsburgh PA
Suburban Hospital Association . . . . .Bethesda MD
Suburban Medical Center . . . . .Paramount CA
Sullivan County Community Hospital . . . . .Sullivan IN

Sullivan County Memorial Hospital . . . . .Milan MO
Summa Health - Akron City Hospital . . . . .Akron OH
Summa Health - Saint Thomas Hospital . . . . .Akron OH
Summerlin Hospital Medical Center . . . . .Las Vegas NV
Summers County Appalachian Regional Hospital . . . . . . .Hinton WV
Summersville Memorial Hospital . . . . .Summersville WV
Summerville Medical Center . . . . .Summerville SC
Summit . . . . .Apopka FL
Summit Behavioral Healthcare . . . . .Cincinnati OH
Summit Hospital . . .Baton Rouge LA
Summit Hospital . . . . . . .Summit NJ
Summit Hospital of Southwest Louisiana . . . . .Sulphur LA
Summit Hospital of Northwest Louisiana . . . . .Bossier City LA
Summit Hospital of Southeast Arizona . . . . .Tucson AZ
Summit Medical Center . . . . .Oakland CA
Summit Medical Center . . . . .Hermitage TN
Summit Park Hospital . . .Pomona NY
Sumner County Hospital District #1 . . . . .Caldwell KS
Sumner Regional Medical Center . . . . .Wellington KS
Sumner Regional Medical Center . . . . .Gallatin TN
Sumter Regional Hospital . . . . .Americus GA
Sun Coast Hospital . . . . . . .Largo FL
Sunbury Community Hospital . . . . .Sunbury PA
Sunhealth Behavioral Health System . . . . .Boise ID
Sunhealth Boswell Memorial Hospital . . . . .Sun City AZ
Sunnyside Community Hospital . . . . .Sunnyside WA
Sunnyview Hospital Rehab Center . . . . .Schenectady NY
Sunrise Canyon Hospital . . . . .Lubbock TX
Sunrise Hospital and Medical Center . . . . .Las Vegas NV
Sunrise Regional . . . . . . .Miami FL
Suny Upstate Medical Center . . . . .Syracuse NY
Surgical and Diagnostic Center of Great Bend . . . . . . .Great Bend KS
Surgical Hospital of Oklahoma . . . . .Oklahoma City OK
Surprise Valley Community Hospital . . . . .Cedarville CA

Alphabetical Index

Susan B Allen Memorial Hospital . . . . El Dorado KS
Sussex Correctional Institution . . . . Georgetown DE
Sutter Amador Hospital . . Jackson CA
Sutter Auburn Faith Hospital . . . . Auburn CA
Sutter Center For Psychiatry . . . . Sacramento CA
Sutter Coast Hospital . . . . Crescent City CA
Sutter Davis Hospital . . . . . Davis CA
Sutter General Hospital . . . . Sacramento CA
Sutter Lakeside Hospital . . . . Lakeport CA
Sutter Maternity and Surger Center . . . . Santa Cruz CA
Sutter Medical Center of Santa Rosa . . . . Santa Rosa CA
Sutter Memorial Hospital . . . . Sacramento CA
Sutter Roseville Medical Center . . . . Roseville CA
Sutter Solano Medical Center . . . . Vallejo CA
Sutter Warrack Hospital . . . . Santa Rosa CA
Swain County Hospital . . . . Bryson City NC
Swedish American Hospital . . . . Rockford IL
Swedish and Providence Medical Center . . . . Seattle WA
Swedish Covenant Hospital . . . . Chicago IL
Swedish Medical Center . . . . Englewood CO
Swedish Medical Center . . Seattle WA
Swedish Medical Center-Ballard . . . . Seattle WA
Sweeny Community Hospital . . . . Sweeny TX
Sweetwater Hospital . . . . Sweetwater TN
Swift County-Benson Hospital . . . . Benson MN
Swisher Memorial Hospital . . Tulia TX
Sycamore Hospital/Medical Center . . . . Miamisburg OH
Sycamore Shoals Hospital . . . . Elizabethton TN
Sylvan Grove Hospital . . Jackson GA
Syringa General Hospital . . . . Grangeville ID
T J Samson Community Hospital . . . . Glasgow KY
T. C. Thompson Children's Hospital . . . . Chattanooga TN
Tacachale Dahlia Hospital Unit . . . . Gainesville FL
Tacoma General Hospital . . . . Tacoma WA

Tahlequah City Hospital . . . . Tahlequah OK
Tahoe Forest Hospital . . . Truckee CA
Tahoe Pacific Hospital . . . Sparks NV
Tahoe Pacific West . . . . . . Reno NV
Takoma Adventist Hospital . . . . Greeneville TN
Tallahassee Memorial Regional Medical Center . . . . . Tallahassee FL
Tallahatchie General Hospital . . . . Charleston MS
Tampa General Hospital . . . Tampa FL
Tanner Medical Center Villa Rica . . . . Villa Rica GA
Tanner Memorial Center . . . . Carrollton GA
Taunton State Hospital . . Taunton MA
Tawas Saint Joseph Hospital . . . . Tawas City MI
Taylor County Hospital . . . . Campbellsville KY
Taylor Hardin Secure Medical Facility . . . . Tuscaloosa AL
Taylor Hospital . . . . . Ridley Park PA
Taylor Manor Hospital . . . . Ellicott City MD
Taylor Regional Hospital . . . . Hawkinsville GA
Taylor Telfair Regional Hospital . . . . Mc Rae GA
Tazewell Community Hospital . . . . Tazewell VA
Teche Regional Medical Center . . . . Morgan City LA
Tehachapi Hospital . . . Tehachapi CA
Telecare/Solano Psychiatric Health Facility . . . . Fairfield CA
Tempe Saint Lukes Hospital . . . . Tempe AZ
Temple Community Hospital . . . . Los Angeles CA
Temple East - Northeastern Hospital . . . . Philadelphia PA
Temple East Neumann Medical Center . . . . Philadelphia PA
Temple Lower Bucks Hospital . . . . Bristol PA
Temple University Children's Medical Center . . . . Philadelphia PA
Temple University Hospital . . . . Philadelphia PA
Temple University Hospital - Episcopal . . . . Philadelphia PA
Ten Broeck Dupont . . . . Louisville KY
Ten Broeck Hospital . . Louisville KY
Ten Broeck River Hospital . . . . Jacksonville FL
Tennessee Christian Medical Center . . . . Madison TN
Tennessee Christian Medical Center . . . . Portland TN
Tennessee Neurorestoration Center . . . . Gallatin TN

10th Medical Group - Usaf Academy Hospital . . US Air Force Academy CO
Terre Haute Regional Hospital . . . . Terre Haute IN
Terrebonne General Medical Center . . . . Houma LA
Terrell State Hospital . . . . Terrell TX
Terrence Cardinal Cooke Health Care Center . . . . New York NY
Teton Medical Center Maf . . . . Choteau MT
Teton Valley Hospital . . . . Driggs ID
Tewksbury Hospital . . . Tewksbury MA
Texas Center For Infectious Disease . . . . San Antonio TX
Texas Childrens Hospital . . . . Houston TX
Texas County Memorial Hospital . . . . Houston MO
Texas Neuro Rehab Center . . . . Austin TX
Texas Orthopedic Hospital . . . . Houston TX
Texas Scottish Rite Hospital . . . . Dallas TX
Texoma Medical Center . . Denison TX
Texoma Medical Center . . . . Sherman TX
Texoma Medical Center Restorative Care . . . . Denison TX
Texsan Heart Hospital . . . . San Antonio TX
Thayer County Health Services . . . . Hebron NE
The Villages Regional Hospital . . . . The Villages FL
Theda Clark Memorial Hospital . . . . Neenah WI
Thibodaux Regional Health Centers . . . . Thibodaux LA
3rd Medical Group . . . . . . Elmendorf Air Force Base AK
30th Medical Group . . . . . Vandenberg Air Force Base CA
Thomas B Finan Center . . . . Cumberland MD
Thomas H Boyd Memorial Hospital . . . . Carrollton IL
Thomas Hospital . . . . . Fairhope AL
Thomas Jefferson University Hospital . . . . Philadelphia PA
Thomas Jefferson University Hospital . . . . Philadelphia PA
Thomas Memorial Hospital . . . . South Charleston WV
Thomasville Infirmary . . . . Thomasville AL
Thomasville Medical Center . . . . Thomasville NC
Thompson Health . . Canandaigua NY
Thoms Rehabilitation Hospital . . . . Asheville NC

Alphabetical Index

Thorek Hospital and Medical Center . . . . .Chicago IL
Three Gables Surgery Center . . . . .Proctorville OH
355th Medical Group . .Davis-Monthan Air Force Base AZ
305th Medical Group, Walson Airforce Clinic . . . . .Fort Dix NJ
347th Medical Group . . . . .Moody Air Force Base GA
319th Medical Group . . . . .Grand Forks Air Force Bas ND
375th Medical Group . . . . .Scott Air Force Base IL
377th Medical Group . . . . . . .Kirtland Air Force Base NM
366th Medical Group . .Mountain Home Air Force Base ID
325th Medical Group . . . . .Tyndall Air Force Base FL
Three Rivers Area Hospital . . . . .Three Rivers MI
Three Rivers Behavioral Health System . . . . . . .West Columbia SC
Three Rivers Community Hospital & Health Center - Washington . . . . .Grants Pass OR
Three Rivers Healthcare - North . . . . .Poplar Bluff MO
Three Rivers Healthcare - South . . . . .Poplar Bluff MO
Three Rivers Hospital . . .Waverly TN
Three Rivers Medical Center . . . . .Louisa KY
Throckmorton County Memorial Hospital . . . . .Throckmorton TX
Thunder Road Chemical Dependency Recovery Hospital . . . . .Oakland CA
Thunderbird Samaritan Hospital and Health Center . . . . .Glendale AZ
Tift Regional Hospital . . . . .Tifton GA
Tilden Community Hospital . . . . .Tilden NE
Tillamook County General Hospital . . . . .Tillamook OR
Timber Ridge Ranch . . . . .Benton AR
Timberlawn Mental Health System . . . . .Dallas TX
Timpanogos Regional Hospital . . . . .Orem UT
Tinley Park Mental Health Center . . . . .Tinley Park IL
Tioga Medical Center . . . . .Tioga ND
Tippah County Hospital . . .Ripley MS
Tipton County Memorial Hospital . . . . .Tipton IN
Titus County Memorial Hospital . . . . .Mount Pleasant TX
Titusville Hospital . . . . . .Titusville PA
Tod Hospital For Children . . . . .Youngstown OH
Toledo Children's Hospital . . . . .Toledo OH

Toledo Hospital . . . . .Toledo OH
Tomah Memorial Hospital . . . . .Tomah WI
Tomball Regional Hospital . . . . .Tomball TX
Tops Surgical Specialty Hospital . . . . .Houston TX
Torrance Memorial Medical Center . . . . .Torrance CA
Torrance State Hospital . . . . .Torrance PA
Torrington Community Hospital . . . . .Torrington WY
Touchette Regional Hospital . . . . .Centreville IL
Touro Infirmary . . . . .New Orleans LA
Touro Rehab Center . . . . .New Orleans LA
Town and Country Hospital . . . . .Tampa FL
Towner County Medical Center . . . . .Cando ND
Trace Regional Hospital and Swing Bed . . . . .Houston MS
Tracy Community Memorial Hospital . . . . .Tracy CA
Tracy Municipal Hospital . . .Tracy MN
Transylvania Community Hospital . . . . .Brevard NC
Trego County-Lemke Memorial Hospital . . . . .Wakeeney KS
Trenton Psychiatric Hospital . . . . .Trenton NJ
Tri City Medical Center . . . . .Oceanside CA
Tri City Regional Medical Center . . . . .Hawaiian Gardens CA
Tri County Baptist Hospital . . . . .La Grange KY
Tri County Hospital . . . . .Wadena MN
Tri County Hospital . . . . .Lexington NE
Tri County Memorial Hospital . . . . .Gowanda NY
Tri County Memorial Hospital . . . . .Whitehall WI
Tri Parish Rehab Hospital . . . . .Leesville LA
Tri State Memorial Hospital . . . . .Clarkston WA
Tri Valley Health System . . . . .Cambridge NE
Tri Ward General Hospital . . . . .Bernice LA
Tri-Lakes Medical Center . . . . .Batesville MS
Tri-Parish Rehab Hospital . . . . .Rosepine LA
Trident Medical Center . . . . .Charleston SC
Trigg County Hospital . . . . .Cadiz KY
Trigg Memorial Hospital . . . . .Tucumcari NM
Trillium Hospital . . . . .Jackson MI

Trinitas Hospital . . . . . . .Elizabeth NJ
Trinitas Hospital - Jersey Street . . . . .Elizabeth NJ
Trinitas Hospital - New Point . . . . .Elizabeth NJ
Trinity Community Hospital . . . . .Jasper FL
Trinity Community Medical Center of Brenham . . . . .Brenham TX
Trinity General Hospital . . . . .Weaverville CA
Trinity Health . . . . .Minot ND
Trinity Hospital . . . . .Chicago IL
Trinity Hospital . . . . .Erin TN
Trinity Medical Center . .Davenport IA
Trinity Medical Center . .Carrollton TX
Trinity Medical Center - Seventh Street Campus . . . . .Moline IL
Trinity Medical Center East . . . . .Steubenville OH
Trinity Medical Center West . . . . .Rock Island IL
Trinity Medical Center West . . . . .Steubenville OH
Trinity Regional Hospital . . . . .Fort Dodge IA
Trinity Springs East Pavilion . . . . .Fort Worth TX
Tripler Army Medical Center . . . . .Honolulu HI
Triumph Hospital - East Houston . . . . .Channelview TX
Triumph Hospital of North Houston . . . . .Houston TX
Trousdale Medical Center . . . . .Hartsville TN
Troy Community Hospital . . .Troy PA
Troy Regional Medical Center . . . . .Troy AL
Truman Medical Center . . . . .Kansas City MO
Truman Medical Center East . . . . .Kansas City MO
Trumbull Memorial Hospital . . . . .Warren OH
Tuality Community Hospital . . . . .Hillsboro OR
Tuality Forest Grove Hospital . . . . .Forest Grove OR
Tucson Heart Hospital . . .Tucson AZ
Tucson Medical Center . . .Tucson AZ
Tuffs-New England Medical Center . . . . .Boston MA
Tulane Medical Center . . . . .New Orleans LA
Tulare District Hospital . . . .Tulare CA
Tulsa Regional Medical Center . . . . .Tulsa OK
Tuolumne General Hospital . . . . .Sonora CA
Tuomey Health Care System . . . . .Sumter SC
Turning Point Hospital . . .Moultrie GA

Alphabetical Index

Tustin Hospital and Medical Center . . . . .Tustin CA
Twelve Oaks . . . . .Houston TX
Twelve Oaks Medical Center . . . . .Houston TX
20th Medical Group . . . . .Shaw Air Force Base SC
28th Medical Group . . . . . . .Ellsworth Air Force Base SD
27th Medical Group . . . . .Cannon Air Force Base NM
Twin Cities Community Hospital . . . . .Templeton CA
Twin Cities Hospital . . . . .Niceville FL
Twin City Hospital . . . . .Dennison OH
Twin County Regional Hospital . . . . .Galax VA
Twin Falls Clinic Hospital . . . . .Twin Falls ID
Twin Rivers Regional Medical Center . . . . .Kennett MO
Twin Valley Psych System-Columbus Campus . . .Columbus OH
Twin Valley Psych System-Dayton Campus . . . . .Dayton OH
Twins Lakes Regional Medical Center . . . . .Leitchfield KY
Two Rivers Psychiatric Hospital . . . . .Kansas City MO
Tyler County Hospital . .Woodville TX
Tyler Health Care Center . . .Tyler MN
Tyler Holmes Memorial Hospital . . . . .Winona MS
Tyler Memorial Hospital . . . . .Tunkhannock PA
Tyrone Hospital . . . . .Tyrone PA
U.S. Army Aeromedical Center . . . . .Fort Rucker AL
U.S. Coast Guard Academy Clinic . . . . .New London CT
U.S. Medical Center For Federal Prisoners . . . . .Springfield MO
Uab Medical West . . . .Bessemer AL
Uhhs Memorial Hospital of Geneva . . . . .Geneva OH
Uintah Basin Medical Center . . . . .Roosevelt UT
Ukiah Valley Medical Center/Hospital . . . . .Ukiah CA
Underwood Memorial Hospital . . . . .Woodbury NJ
Uni-Med Medical Center . . .Minot ND
Unicoi County Memorial Hospital . . . . .Erwin TN
Unicol Hospital Services . . .Miami FL
Unicol Hospital Services . . . . .North Miami FL
Unicol Hospital Services . . . . .Pembroke Pines FL
Union City Memorial Hospital . . . . .Union City PA
Union Community Health Center . . . . .Bronx NY

Union County General Hospital . . . . .Clayton NM
Union County Hospital . . . . . .Anna IL
Union General Hospital . . . . .Blairsville GA
Union General Hospital . . . . .Farmerville LA
Union Hospital . . . . . .Terre Haute IN
Union Hospital . . . . .Lynn MA
Union Hospital . . . . .Union NJ
Union Hospital . . . . . . .Mayville ND
Union Hospital . . . . .Dover OH
Union Hospital-Cecil County . . . . .Elkton MD
Union Memorial Hospital . . . . .Baltimore MD
Union Regional Medical Center . . . . .Monroe NC
Uniontown Hospital . . .Uniontown PA
United Community Hospital . . . . .Grove City PA
United General Hospital . . . . .Sedro Woolley WA
United Health Services-Wilson Memorial Hospital . .Johnson City NY
United Hospital Center . . . . .Clarksburg WV
United Hospital District . . . . .Blue Earth MN
United Hospital Medical Center . . . . .Port Chester NY
United Hospitals . . . .Saint Paul MN
United Medical Center . . . . .Cheyenne WY
United Memorial Hospital . . . . .Greenville MI
United Memorial Medical Center - Bank Street . . . . .Batavia NY
United Memorial Medical Center - North Street . . . . .Batavia NY
United Regional Health Care System . . . . .Wichita Falls TX
United Regional Health Care System . . . . .Wichita Falls TX
United Samaritans Medical Center - Logan . . . . .Danville IL
United Samaritans Medical Center-Sager . . . . .Danville IL
Unity Health Center - North . . . . .Shawnee OK
Unity Health Center - South . . . . .Shawnee OK
Unity Hospital . . . . .Muscatine IA
Unity Hospital . . . . .Fridley MN
Unity Hospital . . . . .Grafton ND
University Behavioral Center Crossroads Hospital . . . . .Orlando FL
University Community Hospital . . . . .Tampa FL
University Community Hospital at Carrollwood . . . . .Tampa FL
University Community Medical Center . . . . .San Diego CA

University District Hospital . . . . .Rio Piedras PR
University Health Services . . . . .Amherst MA
University Health Services, Tang Center . . . . .Berkeley CA
University Health System . . . . .San Antonio TX
University Hospital . . . . .Augusta GA
University Hospital . . . .Lexington MS
University Hospital . .Stony Brook NY
University Hospital . . . .Cincinnati OH
University Hospital - Laurelwood . . . . .Willoughby OH
University Hospital - Richmond Heights . . . . .Richmond Heights OH
University Hospital and Medical Center . . . . .Tamarac FL
University Hospital Health System Geauga Regional Hospital . . . . .Chardon OH
University Hospital of Arkansas . . . . .Little Rock AR
University Hospital of Brooklyn . . . . .Brooklyn NY
University Hospital-Bedford Medical Center . . . . .Bedford OH
University Hospitals-Cleveland . . . . .Cleveland OH
University Medical Center . . . . .Tucson AZ
University Medical Center . . . . .Fresno CA
University Medical Center . . . . .Lafayette LA
University Medical Center . . . . .Minneapolis MN
University Medical Center . . . . .Lebanon TN
University Medical Center . . . . .Lubbock TX
University Medical Center of Southern Nevada . . .Las Vegas NV
University of Alabama Hospital . . . . .Birmingham AL
University of California - Davis Medical Center . . . . .Sacramento CA
University of California - San Diego Medical Center . . . . . .San Diego CA
University of California - Los Angeles Medical Center . . . . .Los Angeles CA
University of California - Thornton Hospital . . . . .La Jolla CA
University of California Irvine Medical Center . . . . .Orange CA
University of California Los Angeles (Ucla) Neuropsychiatric Hospital Clinic . . . . .Los Angeles CA
University of California Medical Center - San Francisco . . . . .San Francisco CA
University of Chicago Hospitals . . . . .Chicago IL

235

Alphabetical Index

University of Colorado Hospital and Health Science . . . . .Denver CO
University of Connecticut Health Center and John Dempsey Hospital . . . . .Farmington CT
University of Illinois Hospital .Chicago IL
University of Iowa Hospital and Clinic . . . . .Iowa City IA
University of Kansas Medical Center . . . . .Kansas City KS
University of Kentucky - Chandler Hospital . . . . .Lexington KY
University of Louisville Hospital . . . . .Louisville KY
University of Maryland Medical System . . . . .Baltimore MD
University of Massachusetts Memorial Health Care Center - University Campus . . . . .Worcester MA
University of Massachusetts Memorial Health Care . . . . .Worcester MA
University of Massachusetts Memorial Medical Center - Hahnemann Campus . . . . .Worcester MA
University of Medicine & Dentistry of NJ - University Behavioral Healthcare . . . . .Piscataway NJ
University of Medicine-Dentistry of New Jersey Hospital . . . . .Newark NJ
University of Miami Hospital and Clinics . . . . .Miami FL
University of Michigan Health System . . . . .Ann Arbor MI
University of Mississippi Medical Center . . . . .Jackson MS
University of Missouri Hospital and Clinics . . . . .Columbia MO
University of Nebraska Medical Center . . . . .Omaha NE
University of New Mexico Children's Psychiatric Hospital . . . . .Albuquerque NM
University of New Mexico Hospital . . . . .Albuquerque NM
University of New Mexico Mental Health . . . . .Albuquerque NM
University of North Carolina Hospital . . . . .Chapel Hill NC
University of Pennsylvania Hospital . . . . .Philadelphia PA
University of South Alabama Children's and Women's . .Mobile AL
University of South Alabama Knollwood Park Hospital . .Mobile AL
University of South Alabama Medical Center . . . . .Mobile AL
University of Southern California (Usc) Kenneth Norris Jr Cancer Hospital . . . . .Los Angeles CA
University of Southern California (Usc) University Hospital . . . . .Los Angeles CA

University of Tennessee - Bowld Hospital . . . . .Memphis TN
University of Tennessee Medical Center/hospital . . . . . .Knoxville TN
University of Texas Health Center .Tyler TX
University of Texas Medical Branch Galveston . . . . .Galveston TX
University of Tx M D Anderson Cancer Center . . . . .Houston TX
University of Utah Hospital . . . . .Salt Lake City UT
University of Utah Neuropsychiatric Institute . . . . .Salt Lake City UT
University of Virginia Hospital . . . . .Charlottesville VA
University of Washington Medical Center . . . . .Seattle WA
University of Wisconsin Hospitals/Clinics Authority . . . . .Madison WI
University Pavilion Hospital . . . . .Tamarac FL
University Pediatric Hospital . . . . .San Juan PR
University Specialty Hospital . . . . .Baltimore MD
Upland Hills Health . . .Dodgeville WI
Upmc - Bedford Memorial Hospital . . . . .Everett PA
Upmc - Braddock Hospital . . . . .Braddock PA
Upmc - Horizon Hospital . . . . .Greenville PA
Upmc - Oil City . . . . .Oil City PA
Upmc - Passavant Hospital . . . . .Pittsburgh PA
Upmc - Presbyterian . . .Pittsburgh PA
Upmc - Saint Margaret . . . . .Pittsburgh PA
Upmc - South Side . . . .Pittsburgh PA
Upmc Eye and Ear Hospital of Pittsburgh . . . . .Pittsburgh PA
Upmc Mckeesport Hospital . . . . .Mc Keesport PA
Upmc Montefiore Hospital . . . . .Pittsburgh PA
Upmc Northwest . . . . . .Franklin PA
Upmc Rehabilitation Hospital . . . . .Pittsburgh PA
Upmc Shadyside Hospital . . . . .Pittsburgh PA
Upper Chesapeake Medical Center . . . . .Bel Air MD
Upper Connecticut Valley Hospital . . . . .Colebrook NH
Upper Shore Community Mental Health Center . . . . .Chestertown MD
Upper Valley Medical Center .Troy OH
Upson Regional Medical Center . . . . .Thomaston GA

Upstate Carolina Medical Center . . . . .Gaffney SC
Utah State Hospital-Psychiatric . . . . .Provo UT
Utah Valley Regional Medical Center . . . . .Provo UT
Uva/Healthsouth Rehabilitation Hospital . . . . .Charlottesville VA
Uvalde Memorial Hospital . . . . .Uvalde TX
Va Healthcare System - Central Alabama East . . . . . . .Tuskegee AL
Va Department of Veterans Affairs . . . . .Rocky Hill CT
Va Healthcare Center - Eugene J. Towbin . . . . .North Little Rock AR
Va Healthcare System - Brooklyn . . . . .Brooklyn NY
Va Healthcare System - Greater Los Angeles . . . . .Los Angeles CA
Va Healthcare System - Alaska . . . . .Anchorage AK
Va Healthcare System - Albuquerque . . . . .Albuquerque NM
Va Healthcare System - Amarillo . . . . .Amarillo TX
Va Healthcare System - Ann Arbor . . . . .Ann Arbor MI
Va Healthcare System - Batavia . . . . .Batavia NY
Va Healthcare System - Black Hills at Hot Springs . . . . .Hot Springs SD
Va Healthcare System - Buffalo . . . . .Buffalo NY
Va Healthcare System - Castle Point . . . . .Castle Point NY
Va Healthcare System - Central Alabama West . . . . .Montgomery AL
Va Healthcare System - Central California . . . . .Fresno CA
Va Healthcare System - Chicago at Lakeside . . . . .Chicago IL
Va Healthcare System - Chicago at Westside . . . . .Chicago IL
Va Healthcare System - Connecticut at Newington . . . . .Newington CT
Va Healthcare System - Connecticut at West Haven . . . . .West Haven CT
Va Healthcare System - Danville . . . . .Danville IL
Va Healthcare System - East Orange . . . . .East Orange NJ
Va Healthcare System - El Paso . . . . .El Paso TX
Va Healthcare System - Fort Wayne . . . . .Fort Wayne IN
Va Healthcare System - Knoxville . . . . .Knoxville IA
Va Healthcare System - Lyons . . . . .Lyons NJ
Va Healthcare System - Marion . . . . .Marion IN

Alphabetical Index

Va Healthcare System - Montana ....Fort Harrison MT
Va Healthcare System - New York ....New York NY
Va Healthcare System - Northern Arizona ....Prescott AZ
Va Healthcare System - Northern California ....Martinez CA
Va Healthcare System - Palo Alto ....Palo Alto CA
Va Healthcare System - Pittsburgh at Delafield ....Pittsburgh PA
Va Healthcare System - Pittsburgh at Highland ....Pittsburgh PA
Va Healthcare System - Pittsburgh at University ....Pittsburgh PA
Va Healthcare System - Puget Sound ....Seattle WA
Va Healthcare System - Reno ....Reno NV
Va Healthcare System - Roseburg ....Roseburg OR
Va Healthcare System - Salt Lake City ....Salt Lake City UT
Va Healthcare System - Sam Rayburn ....Bonham TX
Va Healthcare System - San Antonio ....San Antonio TX
Va Healthcare System - San Diego ....San Diego CA
Va Healthcare System - Southern Arizona ....Tucson AZ
Va Healthcare System - Southern Nevada ....Las Vegas NV
Va Healthcare System - Southern Oregon Rehab Center ....White City OR
Va Hospital - Edith Nourse Rogers ....Bedford MA
Va Medical Center - Atlanta ....Decatur GA
Va Medical Center - Carl T Hayden ....Phoenix AZ
Va Medical Center - Aleda E. Lutz ....Saginaw MI
Va Medical Center - Alexandria ....Pineville LA
Va Medical Center - Alvin C York ....Murfreesboro TN
Va Medical Center - Asheville ....Asheville NC
Va Medical Center - Augusta ....Augusta GA
Va Medical Center - Baltimore ....Baltimore MD
Va Medical Center - Bath ...Bath NY
Va Medical Center - Battle Creek ....Battle Creek MI
Va Medical Center - Bay Pines ....Bay Pines FL
Va Medical Center - Beckley ....Beckley WV

Va Medical Center - Bill Hefner ....Salisbury NC
Va Medical Center - Biloxi/Gulfport ....Biloxi MS
Va Medical Center - Birmingham ....Birmingham AL
Va Medical Center - Boise ..Boise ID
Va Medical Center - Boston at Brockton ....Brockton MA
Va Medical Center - Bronx ....Bronx NY
Va Medical Center - Butler ....Butler PA
Va Medical Center - Canandaigua ....Canandaigua NY
Va Medical Center - Carl Vinson ....Dublin GA
Va Medical Center - Cheyenne ....Cheyenne WY
Va Medical Center - Chillicothe ....Chillicothe OH
Va Medical Center - Cincinnati ....Cincinnati OH
Va Medical Center - Clement Zablocki ....Milwaukee WI
Va Medical Center - Coatesville ....Coatesville PA
Va Medical Center - Colmery O'Neil ....Topeka KS
Va Medical Center - Dallas ....Dallas TX
Va Medical Center - Dayton ....Dayton OH
Va Medical Center - Denver ....Denver CO
Va Medical Center - Des Moines ....Des Moines IA
Va Medical Center - Durham ....Durham NC
Va Medical Center - Dwight D. Eisenhower ......Leavenworth KS
Va Medical Center - Edward Hines Jr. ....Hines IL
Va Medical Center - Erie ....Erie PA
Va Medical Center - Fargo ....Fargo ND
Va Medical Center - Fayetteville ....Fayetteville AR
Va Medical Center - Fayetteville ....Fayetteville NC
Va Medical Center - Fort Meade ....Fort Meade SD
Va Medical Center - G. V. Montgomery ....Jackson MS
Va Medical Center - Gainesville ....Gainesville FL
Va Medical Center - Grand Island ....Grand Island NE
Va Medical Center - Grand Junction ....Grand Junction CO
Va Medical Center - Hampton ....Hampton VA

Va Medical Center - Harry S Truman ....Columbia MO
Va Medical Center - Houston ....Houston TX
Va Medical Center - Hunter Holmes Mcguire ....Richmond VA
Va Medical Center - Huntington ....Huntington WV
Va Medical Center - Iowa City ....Iowa City IA
Va Medical Center - Iron Mountain ....Iron Mountain MI
Va Medical Center - J.M. Wainwright ....Walla Walla WA
Va Medical Center - James A Haley ....Tampa FL
Va Medical Center - James E. Van Zandt ....Altoona PA
Va Medical Center - Jerry L. Pettis ....Loma Linda CA
Va Medical Center - John D. Dingell ....Detroit MI
Va Medical Center - John J. Pershing ....Poplar Bluff MO
Va Medical Center - John L. McClellan Memorial Hospital .Little Rock AR
Va Medical Center - Kansas City ....Kansas City MO
Va Medical Center - Lake City ....Lake City FL
Va Medical Center - Lebanon ....Lebanon PA
Va Medical Center - Lexington ....Lexington KY
Va Medical Center - Livermore ....Livermore CA
Va Medical Center - Long Beach ....Long Beach CA
Va Medical Center - Louis A Johnson ....Clarksburg WV
Va Medical Center - Louis Stokes ....Cleveland OH
Va Medical Center - Louisville ....Louisville KY
Va Medical Center - Manchester ....Manchester NH
Va Medical Center - Marion ....Marion IL
Va Medical Center - Martinsburg ....Martinsburg WV
Va Medical Center - Memphis ....Memphis TN
Va Medical Center - Menlo Park ....Menlo Park CA
Va Medical Center - Miami ....Miami FL
Va Medical Center - Minneapolis ....Minneapolis MN
Va Medical Center - Mountain Home ....Mountain Home TN
Va Medical Center - Muskogee ....Muskogee OK

Alphabetical Index

Va Medical Center - Nashville ....Nashville TN
Va Medical Center - New Orleans ....New Orleans LA
Va Medical Center - North Chicago ....North Chicago IL
Va Medical Center - Northampton ....Leeds MA
Va Medical Center - Northport ....Northport NY
Va Medical Center - Oklahoma City ....Oklahoma City OK
Va Medical Center - Olin E. Teague ....Temple TX
Va Medical Center - Omaha ....Omaha NE
Va Medical Center - Overton Brooks ....Shreveport LA
Va Medical Center - Perry Point ....Perry Point MD
Va Medical Center - Philadelphia ....Philadelphia PA
Va Medical Center - Portland ....Portland OR
Va Medical Center - Providence ....Providence RI
Va Medical Center - Ralph H Johnson ....Charleston SC
Va Medical Center - Richard L. Roudebush ....Indianapolis IN
Va Medical Center - Sacramento at Mather ....Sacramento CA
Va Medical Center - Saint Cloud ....Saint Cloud MN
Va Medical Center - Saint Louis ....Saint Louis MO
Va Medical Center - Salem ....Salem VA
Va Medical Center - Samuel S. Stratton ....Albany NY
Va Medical Center - San Francisco ....San Francisco CA
Va Medical Center - Sheridan ....Sheridan WY
Va Medical Center - Sioux Falls ....Sioux Falls SD
Va Medical Center - Spark Matsunaga ....Honolulu HI
Va Medical Center - Spokane ....Spokane WA
Va Medical Center - Syracuse ....Syracuse NY
Va Medical Center - Togus ....Togus ME
Va Medical Center - Tomah ....Tomah WI
Va Medical Center - Tuscaloosa ....Tuscaloosa AL
Va Medical Center - Waco ..Waco TX
Va Medical Center - Washington DC ....Washington DC
Va Medical Center - West Palm Beach ....West Palm Beach FL

Va Medical Center - West Roxbury ....West Roxbury MA
Va Medical Center - West Texas ....Big Spring TX
Va Medical Center - White River Junction ....White River Junction VT
Va Medical Center - Wichita ....Wichita KS
Va Medical Center - Wilkes Barre ....Wilkes-Barre PA
Va Medical Center - William S Middleton Memorial .....Madison WI
Va Medical Center - Wilmington ....Wilmington DE
Va Medical Center - Wm Jennings Bryan Dorn ....Columbia SC
Va Medical Center at Jamaica Plain ....Boston MA
Va Rehabilitation and Extended Care - Martinez ....Martinez CA
Va Rehabilitation and Extended Care Center ....Baltimore MD
Vaca Valley Hospital ...Vacaville CA
Vail Valley Medical Center ...Vail CO
Val Verde Regional Medical Center ....Del Rio TX
Valdese General Hospital ....Valdese NC
Valdez Community Hospital ....Valdez AK
Valle Vista Hospital ...Greenwood IN
Valley Baptist Medical Center ....Harlingen TX
Valley Behavioral Health System ....Chattanooga TN
Valley Care Medical Center ....Pleasanton CA
Valley Community Hospital ....Dallas OR
Valley County Hospital ......Ord NE
Valley Forge Medical Center and Hospital ....Norristown PA
Valley General Hospital ..Monroe WA
Valley Hospital ....Palmer AK
Valley Hospital .....Ridgewood NJ
Valley Hospital and Medical Center ....Spokane WA
Valley Hospital Medical Center ....Las Vegas NV
Valley Lutheran Hospital ...Mesa AZ
Valley Medical Center ...Renton WA
Valley Memorial Hospital ....Livermore CA
Valley Plaza Doctors Hospital ....Perris CA
Valley Presbyterian Hospital ....Van Nuys CA
Valley Regional Hospital ....Claremont NH
Valley Regional Medical Center ....Brownsville TX
Valley View Hospital ....Glenwood Springs CO

Valley View Medical Center ....Cedar City UT
Valley View Regional Hospital ....Ada OK
Valley View/Aurora Medical Centers of Sheboygan County ..Plymouth WI
Valley West Community Hospital ....Sandwich IL
Van Buren County Memorial Hospital ....Keosauqua IA
Van Mater Healthsouth ..Rockford IL
Van Wert County Hospital ....Van Wert OH
Vanderbilt Stallworth Rehab Hospital Lp ....Nashville TN
Vanderbilt University Medical Center ....Nashville TN
Vassar Brothers Hospital ....Poughkeepsie NY
Vaughan Regional Medical Center ....Selma AL
Vcu Health Systems ...Richmond VA
Ventura County Medical Center ....Ventura CA
Verde Valley Medical Center ....Cottonwood AZ
Verdugo Hills Hospital ..Glendale CA
Vermilion Hospital .....Lafayette LA
Vermilion Rehab Hospital ....Abbeville LA
Vermont State Hospital ....Waterbury VT
Vernon Memorial Hospital ....Viroqua WI
Vernon State Hospital ....Vernon TX
Veterans Memorial Hospital ....Waukon IA
Veterans Memorial Hospital of Meigs Co ....Gallipolis OH
Via Christi Oklahoma Regional Medical Center ......Ponca City OK
Via Christi Region Medical-Saint Joseph ....Wichita KS
Via Christi Regional Medical-Saint Francis ....Wichita KS
Via Christi Rehabilitation Center ....Wichita KS
Via Christi Riverside Medical Center ....Wichita KS
Victor Valley Community Hospital ....Victorville CA
Victoria Warm Springs Rehab Hospital ....Victoria TX
Victory Medical Center ...Stanley WI
Victory Memorial Hospital ....Brooklyn NY
Villa Fairmont Mental Health Rehabilitation Center ....San Leandro CA
Villa Feliciana Medical Complex ....Jackson LA
Ville Platte Medical Center ....Ville Platte LA

Alphabetical Index

Virginia Baptist Hospital . . . . .Lynchburg VA
Virginia Beach General Hospital . . . . .Virginia Beach VA
Virginia Beach Psychiatric Center . . . . .Virginia Beach VA
Virginia Gay Hospital . . . . . .Vinton IA
Virginia Hospital Center - Arlington . . . . .Arlington VA
Virginia Mason Medical Center . . . . .Seattle WA
Virginia Regional Medical Center . . . . .Virginia MN
Virtua Memorial Hospital-Burlington County . . . . .Mount Holly NJ
Virtua West Jersey Hospital-Voorhees . . . . .Voorhees NJ
Virtue Street Medical Pavilion . . . . .Chalmette LA
Vista Del Mar Hospital . . .Ventura CA
Vista Health . . . . .Fayetteville AR
Vista Health Saint Therese Medical Center . . . . .Waukegan IL
Vista Health Victory Memorial Hospital . . . . .Waukegan IL
Vista Medical Center . .Pasadena TX
Voorhees Pediatric Rehabilitation Hospital . . . . .Marlton NJ
W J Mangold Memorial Hospital . . . . .Lockney TX
W. J. Barge Memorial Hospital . . . . .Greenville SC
Wabash County Hospital . . . . .Wabash IN
Wabash General Hospital District . . . . .Mount Carmel IL
Wabash Valley Hospital Mental Health . . . . .West Lafayette IN
Waccamaw Community Hospital . . . . .Murrells Inlet SC
Wadley Regional Medical Center . . . . .Texarkana TX
Wadsworth Rittman Hospital . . . . .Wadsworth OH
Wagner Community Memorial Hospital . . . . .Wagner SD
Wagoner Community Hospital . . . . .Wagoner OK
Wahiawa General Hospital . . . . .Wahiawa HI
Wahoe Rehabilitation Hospital . . . . .Reno NV
Wake County Alcoholism Treatment Center . . . . .Raleigh NC
Wake Forest University - Baptist Behavioral Health Center . . . . .Winston-Salem NC
Wake Medical Center . . .Raleigh NC
Wakemed Zebulon/Wendell . . . . .Zebulon NC
Waldo County General Hospital . . . . .Belfast ME

Walker Baptist Medical Center . . . . .Jasper AL
Walla Walla General Hospital . . . . .Walla Walla WA
Wallace Thomson Hospital . . . . .Union SC
Wallowa Memorial Hospital . . . . .Enterprise OR
Walls Regional Hospital . . . . .Cleburne TX
Walter B Jones Alcohol and Drug Abuse . . . . .Greenville NC
Walter Knox Memorial Hospital . . . . .Emmett ID
Walter P Carter Center . . . . .Baltimore MD
Walter Reed Army Medical Center . . . . .Washington DC
Walter Reuther Hospital . . . . .Westland MI
Walthall County General Hospital . . . . .Tylertown MS
Walton Medical Center . .Monroe GA
Walton Rehabilitation Hospital . . . . .Augusta GA
Wamego City Hospital . .Wamego KS
Ward Memorial Hospital . . . . .Monahans TX
Warm Springs and Baptist Rehab Network . . . . .San Antonio TX
Warm Springs Specialty Hospital . . . . .Gonzales TX
Warminster Hospital . .Warminster PA
Warren G. Magnuson Clinical Center . . . . .Bethesda MD
Warren General Hospital . .Warren PA
Warren Hospital . . . . .Phillipsburg NJ
Warren Memorial Hospital . . . . .Friend NE
Warren Memorial Hospital . . . . .Front Royal VA
Warren State Hospital . . . . .North Warren PA
Warren State Hospital . . . .Warren PA
Warwick Behavioral Health . . . . .East New Market MD
Waseca Medical Center . . . . .Waseca MN
Washakie County Memorial Hospital . . . . .Worland WY
Washington Adventist Hospital . . . . .Takoma Park MD
Washington County Hospital . . . . .Nashville IL
Washington County Hospital . . . . .Washington IA
Washington County Hospital . . . . .Washington KS
Washington County Hospital . . . . .Hagerstown MD
Washington County Hospital . . . . .Plymouth NC

Washington County Infirmary and Nursing Home . . . . .Chatom AL
Washington County Memorial Hospital . . . . .Salem IN
Washington County Memorial Hospital . . . . .Potosi MO
Washington County Regional Medical Center . . . . .Sandersville GA
Washington Hospital . . . .Fremont CA
Washington Hospital . . . . .Washington PA
Washington Hospital Center . . . . .Washington DC
Washington Regional Medical Center . . . . .Fayetteville AR
Washington Saint Tammany Regional Medical Center . . . . . .Bogalusa LA
Washington State Penitentiary Hospital . . . . .Walla Walla WA
Washoe Medical Center . . .Reno NV
Washoe Village Acute Rehabilitation Hospital . . . . .Reno NV
Watauga Medical Center . .Boone NC
Waterbury Hospital Health Center . . . . .Waterbury CT
Watertown Memorial Hospital . . . . .Watertown WI
Watonga Municipal Hospital . . . . .Watonga OK
Watsonville Community Hospital . . . . .Watsonville CA
Waukesha County Mental Health Center . . . . .Waukesha WI
Waukesha Memorial Hospital . . . . .Waukesha WI
Waupun Memorial Hospital . . . . .Waupun WI
Wausau Hospital . . . . . . .Wausau WI
Waverly Municipal Hospital . . . . .Waverly IA
Wayne County Hospital . .Corydon IA
Wayne County Hospital . . . . .Monticello KY
Wayne General Hospital . . . . .Waynesboro MS
Wayne Hospital . . . . . .Greenville OH
Wayne Medical Center . . . . .Waynesboro TN
Wayne Memorial Hospital . .Jesup GA
Wayne Memorial Hospital . . . . .Goldsboro NC
Wayne Memorial Hospital . . . . .Honesdale PA
Waynesboro Hospital . . . . .Waynesboro PA
Webster County Community Hospital . . . . .Red Cloud NE
Webster County Memorial Hospital . . . . .Webster Springs WV
Webster General Hospital . . . . .Eupora MS
Wedowee Hospital . . . .Wedowee AL

Alphabetical Index

Weed Army Usa Meddac Community Hospital . . . . .Fort Irwin CA
Weeks Memorial Hospital-Swing . . . . .Lancaster NH
Weiner Memorial Medical Center . . . . .Marshall MN
Weirton Medical Center . .Weirton WV
Weisbrod Memorial County Hospital . . . . .Eads CO
Weiser Memorial Hospital . .Weiser ID
Welch Emergency Hospital . . . . .Welch WV
Wellington Regional Medical Center . . . . . .West Palm Beach FL
Wellmont Hawkins County Memorial Hospital . . . . .Rogersville TN
Wellmont Holston Valley Medical Center . . . . .Kingsport TN
Wells Community Hospital .Bluffton IN
Wellspring Foundation . . . . .Bethlehem CT
Wellstar Cobb Hospital . . .Austell GA
Wellstar Douglas Hospital . . . . .Douglasville GA
Wellstar Kennestone Hospital . . . . .Marietta GA
Wellstar Paulding Hospital . . . . .Dallas GA
Wellstar Windy Hill Hospital . . . . .Marietta GA
Welmont Lonesome Pine Hospital . . . . . . .Big Stone Gap VA
Wenatchee Valley Hospital . . . . .Wenatchee WA
Wentworth-Douglass Hospital . . . . .Dover NH
Wernersville State Hospital . . . . .Wernersville PA
Wesley Long Community Hospital . . . . .Greensboro NC
Wesley Medical Center . . .Wichita KS
Wesley Medical Center . . . . .Hattiesburg MS
Wesley Rehabilitation Hospital . . . . .Wichita KS
Wesley Woods Geriatric Hospital . . . . .Atlanta GA
West Allis Memorial Hospital . . . . .West Allis WI
West Anaheim Medical Center . . . . .Anaheim CA
West Boca Medical Center . . . . .Boca Raton FL
West Branch Regional Medical Center . . . . . . .West Branch MI
West Calcasieu Cameron Hospital . . . . .Sulphur LA
West Carroll Memorial Hospital . . . . .Oak Grove LA
West Central Community Hospital . . . . .Clinton IN

West Central Georgia Regional Hospital . . . . .Columbus GA
West Feliciana Parish Hospital . . . . .Saint Francisville LA
West Florida Community Care Center . . . . .Milton FL
West Florida Regional Medical Center . . . . .Pensacola FL
West Gables Rehabilitation Hospital . . . . .Miami FL
West Georgia Medical Center . . . . .La Grange GA
West Hills Hospital . . . . . . .Reno NV
West Hills Hospital & Medical Center . . . . .West Hills CA
West Holt Medical Center . . . . .Atkinson NE
West Houston Medical Center . . . . .Houston TX
West Hudson Hospital . . . .Kearny NJ
West Jefferson Medical Center . . . . .Marrero LA
West Jersey Hospital - Marlton . . . . .Marlton NJ
West Jersey Hospital-Berlin . . . . .Berlin NJ
West Jersey Hospital-Camden . . . . .Camden NJ
West Marion Community Hospital . . . . .Ocala FL
West Oaks Hospital . . . .Houston TX
West Park Hospital District . . . . .Cody WY
West River Regional Medical Center . . . . .Hettinger ND
West Seattle Psychiatric Hospital . . . . .Seattle WA
West Shore Hospital . . . .Manistee MI
West Suburban Hospital Medical Center . . . . .Oak Park IL
West Valley Medical Center . . . . .Caldwell ID
West Virginia Rehab Hospital . . . . .Institute WV
West Virginia University Hospital . . . . .Morgantown WV
Westborough State Hospital Daniels Building . . . . .Westborough MA
Westbrook Health Center . . . . .Westbrook MN
Westchester General Hospital . . . . .Miami FL
Westchester Medical Center . . . . .Valhalla NY
Westerly Hospital . . . . . .Westerly RI
Western Arizona Regional Medical Center . . . . .Bullhead City AZ
Western Baptist Hospital . . . . .Paducah KY
Western Maryland Hospital Center . . . . .Hagerstown MD
Western Massachusetts Hospital . . . . .Westfield MA

Western Medical Center . . . . .Santa Ana CA
Western Medical Center Hospital Anaheim . . . . .Anaheim CA
Western Mental Health Institute . . . . .Bolivar TN
Western Missouri Medical Center . . . . .Warrensburg MO
Western Missouri Mhc . . . . .Kansas City MO
Western New York Children's Psychiatric Center . . . . . .Buffalo NY
Western Pennsylvania Hospital . . . . .Pittsburgh PA
Western Plains Regional Hospital . . . . .Dodge City KS
Western Psychiatric Institute . . . . .Pittsburgh PA
Western Reserve Care System . . . . .Youngstown OH
Western State Hospital . . . . .Hopkinsville KY
Western State Hospital . .Staunton VA
Western State Hospital . .Tacoma WA
Western State Psychiatric Center . . . . .Fort Supply OK
Western State Psychiatric Center . . . . .Woodard OK
Western Wake Medical Center . . . . .Cary NC
Westfield Memorial Hospital . . . . .Westfield NY
Westlake Community Hospital . . . . .Melrose Park IL
Westlake Regional Hospital . . . . .Columbia KY
Westmoreland Regional Hospital . . . . .Greensburg PA
Weston County Health Services . . . . .Newcastle WY
Westpark Surgery Center . . . . .Mc Kinney TX
Westside Regional Medical Center . . . . .Plantation FL
Westview Hospital . . .Indianapolis IN
Westwood Lodge Hospital . . . . .Westwood MA
Wetumka General Hospital . . . . .Wetumka OK
Wetzel County Hospital . . . . .New Martinsville WV
Wheatland Memorial Hospital . . . . .Harlowton MT
Wheaton Community Hospital . . . . .Wheaton MN
Wheeler County Hospital . . . . .Glenwood GA
Wheeling Hospital . . . .Wheeling WV
Whidbey General Hospital . . . . .Coupeville WA
Whidden Memorial Hospital . . . . .Everett MA

Alphabetical Index

White Community Hospital ....Aurora MN
White County Community Hospital ....Sparta TN
White County Medical Center ....Searcy AR
White County Medical Center ....Carmi IL
White County Memorial Hospital ....Monticello IN
White Memorial Medical Center ....Los Angeles CA
White Mountain Community Hospital ....Springerville AZ
White Plains Hospital Medical Center ....White Plains NY
White River Medical Center ....Batesville AR
Whitesburg Appalachian Regional Hospital ....Whitesburg KY
Whitfield Medical Surgical Hospital ....Whitfield MS
Whiting Forensic Division-Valley Hospital ....Middletown CT
Whitman Hospital and Medical Center ....Colfax WA
Whitten Center Hospital ..Clinton SC
Whittier Hospital Medical Center ....Whittier CA
Whittier Rehab Hospital - Westborough .....Westborough MA
Whittier Rehabilitation Hospital ....Haverhill MA
Wichita County Hospital ....Leoti KS
Wichita County Hospital Long Term Care ....Leoti KS
Wichita Specialty Hospital ....Wichita KS
Wichita Valley Rehab Hospital ....Wichita Falls TX
Wickenburg Regional Hospital ....Wickenburg AZ
Wide Horizon .....Wheat Ridge CO
Wilbarger General Hospital ....Vernon TX
Wilcox Memorial Hospital ...Lihue HI
Wild Rose Community Memorial Hospital ....Wild Rose WI
Wildwood Lifestyle Center and Hospital ....Wildwood GA
Wilkes Barre General Hospital ....Wilkes-Barre PA
Wilkes Regional Medical Center ....North Wilkesboro NC
Willamette Falls Hospital ....Oregon City OR
Willamette Valley Medical Center ....McMinnville OR
Willapa Harbor Hospital ....South Bend WA
William B Kessler Memorial Hospital ....Hammonton NJ

William B. Ririe Hospital ....East Ely NV
William Beaumont Army Medical Center ....El Paso TX
William Beaumont Hospital ....Royal Oak MI
William Beaumont Hospital - Troy ....Troy MI
William N Wishard Memorial Hospital ....Indianapolis IN
William Newton Memorial Hospital ....Winfield KS
William R Sharpe Hospital at Weston ....Weston WV
William S Hall Psychiatric Institute ....Columbia SC
William W Backus Hospital ....Norwich CT
Williamsburg Community Hospital ....Williamsburg VA
Williamsburg Regional Hospital ....Kingstree SC
Williamson Appalachian Regional Hospital ......South Williamson KY
Williamson Medical Center ....Franklin TN
Williamson Memorial Hospital ....Williamson WV
Williamsport Hospital ....Williamsport PA
Willingway Hospital ...Statesboro GA
Willis Knighton Bossier Health Center ....Bossier City LA
Willis Knighton Medical Center ....Shreveport LA
Willmar Regional Treatment Center ....Willmar MN
Willoughs Healthcare System at Naples ....Naples FL
Willow Creek Women's Hospital ....Johnson AR
Willow Crest Hospital .....Miami OK
Willow Springs Center ....Reno NV
Wills Eye Hospital ...Philadelphia PA
Wills Memorial Hospital ....Washington GA
Wilmington Hospital ..Wilmington DE
Wilmington Treatment Center ....Wilmington NC
Wilson County Hospital ....Neodesha KS
Wilson Medical Center ....Darlington SC
Wilson Memorial Hospital ....Wilson NC
Wilson Memorial Hospital ....Sidney OH
Wilson Memorial Hospital ....Floresville TX
Wilson N Jones Medical Center - North ....Sherman TX
Wilson N Jones Memorial Hospital ....Sherman TX

Winchester Hospital ..Winchester MA
Winchester Medical Center ....Winchester VA
Windber Medical Center ....Windber PA
Windham Community Memorial Hospital and Hatch Hospital ....Willimantic CT
Windmoor Healthcare of Clearwater ....Clearwater FL
Windom Area Hospital ..Windom MN
Windsor Hospital ..Chagrin Falls OH
Windwood Hospital .....Rome GA
Wing Memorial Hospital ..Palmer MA
Winkler County Memorial Hospital ....Kermit TX
Winn Army Community Hospital ....Fort Stewart GA
Winn Parish Medical Center ....Winnfield LA
Winnebago Mental Health Institute ....Winnebago WI
Winner Regional Healthcare Center ....Winner SD
Winneshiek County Memorial Hospital ....Decorah IA
Winnie Community Hospital ....Winnie TX
Winona Health ....Winona MN
Winona Memorial Hospital ....Indianapolis IN
Winslow Memorial Hospital ....Winslow AZ
Winston Medical Center ....Louisville MS
Winter Haven Hospital ....Winter Haven FL
Winter Park Memorial Hospital ....Winter Park FL
Winthrop University Hospital ....Mineola NY
Wiregrass Medical Center ....Geneva AL
Wirth Regional Hospital ....Oakland City IN
Wise Regional Health System ....Decatur TX
Wishek Community Hospital ....Wishek ND
Witham Memorial Hospital ....Lebanon IN
Womack Army Medical Center ....Fort Bragg NC
Womans Hospital ...Baton Rouge LA
Womans Hospital of Texas ....Houston TX
Women and Childrens Hospital ....Lake Charles LA
Women and Infants Hospital of Rhode Island ....Providence RI
Women's and Children's Hospital - Lac ....Los Angeles CA
Women's Hospital .....Newburgh IN

241

Alphabetical Index

Women's Hospital at River Oaks ... Flowood MS

Womens and Childrens Hospital ... Lafayette LA

Womens Christian Association Hospital ... Jamestown NY

Womens East Pavilion ... Chattanooga TN

Womens Hospital of Greensboro ... Greensboro NC

Womens Hospital-Indianapolis ... Indianapolis IN

Wood County Hospital ... Bowling Green OH

Woodbridge Development Center ... Woodbridge NJ

Woodhull Medical/mental Health Center ... Brooklyn NY

Woodland Community Hospital ... Cullman AL

Woodland Health Care ... Woodland CA

Woodland Heights Medical Center ... Lufkin TX

Woodland Park Hospital ... Portland OR

Woodlawn Hospital .... Rochester IN

Woodridge Hospital .Johnson City TN

Woodrow Wilson Rehabilitation Center ... Fishersville VA

Woods Memorial Hospital ... Etowah TN

Woodside Hospital .... Leesburg VA

Woodson Children's Psychiatric Unit ... Saint Joseph MO

Woodward Hospital and Health Center ... Woodward OK

Woodward Resource Center ... Woodward IA

Woodwinds Health Campus ... Woodbury MN

Wooster Community Hospital ... Wooster OH

Worcester State Hospital ... Worcester MA

Worthington Regional Hospital ... Worthington MN

Wrangell General Hospital ... Wrangell AK

Wray Community District Hospital ... Wray CO

Wright Medical Center .... Clarion IA

Wright Memorial Hospital ... Trenton MO

Wuesthoff Memorial Hospital ... Rockledge FL

Wyandot Memorial Hospital ... Upper Sandusky OH

Wyckoff Heights Hospital ... Brooklyn NY

Wyoming Behavioral Institute ... Casper WY

Wyoming County Community Hospital ... Warsaw NY

Wyoming Medical Center ... Casper WY

Wyoming State Hospital ... Evanston WY

Wythe County Community Hospital ... Wytheville VA

Yakima Valley Memorial Hospital ... Yakima WA

Yale Psychiatric Institute ... New Haven CT

Yale-New Haven Hospital ... New Haven CT

Yalobusha General Hospital ... Water Valley MS

Yampa Valley Medical Center ... Steamboat Springs CO

Yancey Community Medical Center ... Burnsville NC

Yavapai Regional Medical Center ... Prescott AZ

Yoakum Community Hospital ... Yoakum TX

Yoakum County Hospital ... Denver City TX

Yonkers General Hospital ... Yonkers NY

York General Hospital ..... York NE

York Hospital ... York ME

York Hospital ... York PA

Youville Hospital .... Cambridge MA

Yuma District Hospital .... Yuma CO

Yuma Regional Medical Center ... Yuma AZ

Zale Lipshy University Hospital ... Dallas TX

Zeeland Community Hospital ... Zeeland MI

Zumbrota Hospital .... Zumbrota MN

Health Information Toll-Free Numbers

ADOPTION

Bethany Christian Services
(800) 238-4269
24-hour crisis hotline
National Adoption Center
(800) 862-3678
9:00 a.m.–5:00 p.m.

AGING

American Health Assistance Foundation
(800) 437-2423
9:00 a.m.–5:00 p.m.
Eldercare Locator
(800) 677-1116
9:00 a.m.–8 p.m.
National Institute on Aging Information Center
(800) 222-2225
(800) 222-4225 (TTY)
8:30 a.m.–5:00 p.m.

AIDS/HIV

AIDS Clinical Trials
Information Service
(800) 874-2572
9:00 a.m.–7:00 p.m.
CDC National Prevention Information Network (NPIN)
(800) 458-5231
(800) 243-7012 (TTY)
(888) 282-7681 (Fax)
9:00 a.m.–6:00 p.m., Monday–Friday

CDC National STD/AIDS Hotline
(800) 227-8922 English (STD)
(800) 342-2437 English (AIDS)
(800) 344-7432 (Spanish)
(800) 243-7889 (TTY)
English: 24 hours/7 days a week; Spanish: 8 a.m.–2 a.m., 7 days a week (eastern time); TTY: 10:00 a.m.–10:00 p.m., Monday–Friday (eastern time)

HIV/AIDS Treatment Information Service
(800) HIV-0440
9:00 a.m.–7:00 p.m. All calls are confidential.

Project Inform National HIV/AIDS Treatment Hotline
(800) 822-7422
9:00 a.m.–5:00 p.m., Monday-Friday (Pacific time)
10:00 a.m.–4:00 p.m., Saturday (Pacific time)

Health Information Toll-Free Numbers

ALCOHOL ABUSE

See also Drug Abuse
ADCARE Hospital Helpline
(800) 252-6465
24 hours

Al-Anon Family Group Headquarters
(888) 425-2666
8:00 a.m.–6:00 p.m., Monday–Friday

Alcohol and Drug Helpline
(800) 821-4357
24 hours

American Council on Alcoholism
(800) 527-5344
9:00 a.m.–5:00 p.m., Monday–Friday

Calix Society
(800) 398-0524
9:00 a.m.–12:00 p.m. (answering machine at other times)

Children of Alcoholics Foundation
(800) 359-2623
24 hours

National Clearinghouse for Alcohol and Drug Information
(800) 729-6686
(800) 487-4889 (TTY/TDD)
8:30 a.m.–6:00 p.m.

National Council on Alcoholism and Drug Dependence, Inc.
(800) 622-2255
9:00 a.m.–5:00 p.m. (eastern time)

ALLERGY/ASTHMA

See LUNG DISEASE/ASTHMA/ALLERGY
The Food Allergy and Anaphylaxis Network
(800) 929-4040
9:00 a.m.–5:00 p.m.

National Jewish Medical and Research Center
(800) 222-5864 (LUNG LINE)
(800) 552-5864 (LUNG FACTS)
8:00 a.m.–5:00 p.m. (mountain time)
LUNG FACTS, a companion to LUNG LINE, is a 24-hour, 7-days-a-week automated information service.

Health Information Toll-Free Numbers

ALZHEIMER'S DISEASE

See also AGING

Alzheimer's Association
(800) 272-3900
The information and referral line is available 24 hours; operators staff the line 8 a.m.–5 p.m. (central time). Leave message after hours.

Alzheimer's Disease Education and Referral Center
(800) 438-4380
8:30 a.m.–5:00 p.m.

ARTHRITIS

American Juvenile Arthritis Organization
(800) 283-7800
9:00 a.m.–5:00 p.m., Monday–Friday (eastern time)

Arthritis Foundation: Arthritis Answers Information Hotline
(800) 283-7800
9:00 a.m.–5:00 p.m., Monday–Friday (eastern time)

Lyme Disease Foundation, Inc.
(800) 886-5963
9:00 a.m.–5:00 p.m., Monday–Friday (eastern time)

National Institute of Arthritis and Musculoskeletal and Skin Diseases Information Clearinghouse
(877) 226-4267
8:30 a.m.–5:00 p.m. (eastern time)

AUDIOVISUALS

See LIBRARY SERVICES

AUTISM

See CHILD DEVELOPMENT/PARENTING

AUTOIMMUNE DISEASES

American Autoimmune Related Diseases Association, Inc.
(800) 598-4668
9:30 a.m.–5:00 p.m, Monday–Friday
National Institute of Arthritis and Musculoskeletal and Skin Diseases Information Clearinghouse
(877) 226-4267
8:30 a.m.–5:00 p.m. (eastern time)

BONE MARROW

See CANCER

Health Information Toll-Free Numbers

BONE DISEASE

Osteoporosis and Related Bone Diseases National Resource Center
(800) 624-2663

BRAIN TUMORS

American Brain Tumor Association
(800) 886-2282
9:00 a.m.–5:00 p.m., Monday–Friday (central time)

The Brain Tumor Society
(800) 770-TBTS
8:30 a.m.–5:30 p.m. (eastern time)

National Brain Tumor Foundation
(800) 934-CURE
9:00 a.m.–5:00 p.m. (Pacific time)

CANCER

ACS, National Cancer Information Center
(800) 227-2345 (Voice/TDD/TT)
American Cancer Society Reach to Recovery Program
(800) 227-2345
24 Hours, 7 days a week
Cancer Hope Network
(877) HOPENET
9:00 a.m.–5:30 p.m.

Candlelighters Childhood Cancer Foundation
(800) 366-2223
10:00 a.m.–4:00 p.m.

Kidney Cancer Association
(800) 850-9132
9:00 a.m.–5:30 p.m. (central time)

National Alliance of Breast Cancer Organizations
(888) 806-2226

National Bone Marrow Transplant Link
(800) 546-5268

National Cancer Institute Information Service
(800) 422-6237
9:00 a.m.–4:30 p.m.

National Marrow Donor Program®
(800) 627-7692
Professional staff answer questions from 8:00 a.m.–6:00 p.m. (central time); recorded message at all other times.

Susan G. Komen Breast Cancer Foundation
(800) 462-9273
9:00 a.m.–4:30 p.m. (central time)

Health Information Toll-Free Numbers

Us Too! International
(800) 808-7866
9:00 a.m.–5:00 p.m., Monday–Friday (central time)

Y-ME National Breast Cancer Organization
(800) 221-2141 (English)
(800) 986-9505 (Spanish)
9:00 a.m.–5:00 p.m. (central time)
24-hour hotline

CEREBRAL PALSY

See RARE DISEASES/DISORDERS

CHEMICAL PRODUCTS/PESTICIDES

See also HOUSING
National Pesticide Information Center
(800) 858-7378 TDD capability
6:30 a.m.–4:30 p.m., 7 days a week (Pacific time)
Voice mail provided for off-hours calls.

CHILD ABUSE/MISSING CHILDREN/MENTAL HEALTH

Child Find of America, Inc.
(800) 426-5678 (I–AM–LOST)
(800) 292-9688 (Parental abduction)
9:00 a.m.–5:00 p.m.

CHILDHELP USA®
National Child Abuse Hotline
(800) 4-A-CHILD
(800) 2-A-CHILD (TDD)

Covenant House Nineline
(800) 999-9999

Girls and Boys Town National Hotline
(800) 448-3000
(800) 448-1833 (TDD)
Spanish-speaking operators available; TDD capability.

National Center for Missing and Exploited Children
(800) 843-5678
(800) 826-7653 (TDD)
Ability to serve callers in over 140 languages.

National Childwatch
(800) 222-1464
8:00 a.m.–4:30 p.m.

National Clearinghouse on Child Abuse and Neglect Information
(800) 394-3366

Health Information Toll-Free Numbers

National Runaway Switchboard
(800) 621-4000
(800) 621-0394 (TDD)
Has access to AT&T Language Line

National Youth Crisis Hotline
(800) 448-4663

CHILD DEVELOPMENT/PARENTING

MAGIC Foundation for Children's Growth, The
(800) 362-4423
9:00 a.m.–5:00 p.m. (central time)

National Association for the Education of Young Children
(800) 424-2460
9:00 a.m.–5:00 p.m. (eastern time)

National Institute of Child Health and Human Development (NICHD) Information Resource Center
(800) 370-2943
(800) 505-2742 "Back to Sleep" Campaign
8:30 a.m.–5:00 p.m., Monday–Friday (eastern time)

National Lekotek Center
(800) 366-7529
(800) 573-4446 (Voice and TTY)
9:00 a.m.–5:00 p.m. (central time)

National Organization on Fetal Alcohol Syndrome
(800) 666-6327 Voice Mail 24 hours/7 days a week; all answered

SIDS Information Line
(800) 505-2742
8:00 a.m.–8:00 p.m.

Starlight Children's Foundation
(800) 274-7827
9:00 a.m.–5:00 p.m. (Pacific time)

Zero to Three: National Center for Infants, Toddlers and Families
(800) 899-4301
9:00 a.m.–5:00 p.m.

CHRONIC FATIGUE SYMDROME

See RARE DISEASES/DISORDERS

Health Information Toll-Free Numbers

CRISIS INTERVENTION

All operate 24 hours, 7 days a week.

A–WAY–OUT
(800) 292–9688

Provides unique crisis mediation program for parents contemplating abduction of their children, or who have already abducted their children and want to use Child Find Volunteer Family Mediators to resolve their custody dispute.

CHILDHELP USA®
National Child Abuse Hotline
(800) 4-A-CHILD
(800) 2-A-CHILD (TDD)

Provides multilingual crisis intervention and professional counseling on child abuse and domestic violence issues. Gives referrals to local agencies offering counseling and other services related to child abuse, adult survivor issues, and domestic violence. Provides literature on child abuse in English and Spanish.

Covenant House Nineline
(800) 999-9999

Crisis line for youth, teens, and families. Locally based referrals throughout the United States. Help for youth and parents regarding drugs, abuse, homelessness, runaway children, and message relays.

Girls and Boys Town National Hotline
(800) 448-3000
(800) 448-1833 (TTD)

Provides short-term intervention and counseling and refers callers to local community resources. Counsels on parent-child conflicts, family issues, suicide, pregnancy, runaway youth, physical and sexual abuse, and other issues that impact children and families. Spanish-speaking operators are available. TDD capability.

National Center for Missing and Exploited Children
(800) 843-5678
(800) 826-7653 (TDD)

Operates a hotline for reporting missing children and sightings of missing children. Offers assistance and training to law enforcement agents. Takes reports of sexually exploited children. Serves as the National Child Porn TipLine. Provides books and other publications on prevention and issues related to missing and sexually exploited children. Ability to serve callers in over 140 languages.

National Runaway Switchboard
(800) 621-4000
(800) 621-0394 (TDD)

Provides crisis intervention and travel assistance information to runaways. Gives referrals to shelters nationwide. Also relays messages to, or sets up conference calls with, parents at the request of the child. Has access to AT&T Language Line.

Health Information Toll-Free Numbers

National Youth Crisis Hotline
(800) 448-4663

Provides counseling and referrals to local drug treatment centers, shelters, and counseling services. Responds to youth dealing with pregnancy, molestation, suicide, and child abuse.

Rape, Abuse, and Incest National (RAIN) Network
(800) 656-4673

Connects caller to the nearest counseling center that provides counseling for rape, abuse, and incest victims.

CYSTIC FIBROSIS

See RARE DISEASES/DISORDERS

DIABETES/DIGESTIVE DISEASES

American Association of Diabetes Educators
(800) 832-6874
24 hours a day

American Diabetes Association
(800) 342-2383
(800) ADA-ORDER (Fax, Order Fulfillment)
8:30 a.m.–5:00 p.m.

Crohn's and Colitis Foundation of America, Inc.
(800) 932-2423
(800) 343-3637 (Warehouse)
9:00 a.m.–5:00 p.m. Recording after hours.
Warehouse is open 8:00 a.m.–5:00 p.m.

Juvenile Diabetes Foundation International Hotline
(800) 223-1138
9:00 a.m.–5:00 p.m.

National Center for Chronic Disease Prevention and Health Promotion, CDC
(877) CDC-DIAB
(877) 232-3422
8:00 a.m.–5:00 p.m.

DISABLING CONDITIONS/DISABILITIES ACCESS

ADA Technical Assistance Hotline
(800) 466-4232
9:00 a.m.–5:00 p.m. (Pacific time)

Americans with Disabilities Act Hotline
(800) 514-0301
(800) 514-0308 (TTY)
ADA specialists available 10 a.m.–6:00 p.m. on Monday, Tuesday, Wednesday, and Friday and 1:00 p.m.–6:00 p.m. on Thursday.

Health Information Toll-Free Numbers

Children's Craniofacial Association
(800) 535-3643
9:00 a.m.–5:00 p.m., Monday–Friday (central time)

Easter Seal Society
(800) 221-6827
8:30 a.m.–5:00 p.m. (central time)

FACES: The National Craniofacial Association
(800) 332-2373
9:00 a.m.–5:00 p.m.

Families of Spinal Muscular Atrophy
(800) 886-1762
7:00 a.m.–3:00 p.m. (central time)

Job Accommodation Network
(800) 232-9675 (Voice/TTY)
(800) 526-7234 (Voice/TTY)
Services available in English, Spanish, and French.
8:00 a.m.–8:00 p.m., Monday–Thursday; 8:00 a.m.–7:00 p.m., Friday (eastern time)

National Information Center for Children and Youth with Disabilities
(800) 695-0285 (Voice/TTY)
9:30 a.m.–6:30 p.m., or leave recorded message after hours.

National Rehabilitation Information Center (NARIC)
(800) 346-2742 (Voice/TDD)
9:00 a.m.–5:00 p.m., Monday–Friday (eastern time)

Scoliosis Association
(800) 800-0669
9:00 a.m.–5:00 p.m.

DOWN SYNDROME

See RARE DISEASES/DISORDERS

DRINKING WATER SAFETY

Safe Drinking Water Hotline
(800) 426-4791
Information provided in English and Spanish.
9:00 a.m.–5:30 p.m., weekdays, except Federal holidays.

Water Quality Association
(800) 749-0234 (Consumer Information)

DRUG ABUSE

See also ALCOHOL ABUSE and SUBSTANCE ABUSE
Drug-Free Workplace Helpline
(800) 967-5752
9:00 a.m.–5:30 p.m., Monday–Friday (eastern time)

Health Information Toll-Free Numbers

Drug Help
(800) 662-HELP

Housing and Urban Development Drug Information and Strategy Clearinghouse
(800) 955-2232
9:00 a.m.–6:00 p.m.

National Parents Resource Institute for Drug Education Surveys
(800) 279-6361
8:30 a.m.–4:30 p.m.

DWARFISM

Human Growth Foundation
(800) 451-6434
9:00 a.m.–5:00 p.m.

DYSLEXIA

See LEARNING DISORDERS

ENDOMETRIOSIS

See WOMEN

ENVIRONMENT

Indoor Air Quality Information Clearinghouse
(800) 438-4318
9:00 a.m.–5:00 p.m., Monday–Friday (eastern time)

U.S. Environmental Protection Agency, Environmental Justice Hotline
(800) 962-6215
8:00 a.m.–5:30 p.m., Monday–Friday (eastern time)

EPILEPSY

See RARE DISEASES/DISORDERS

ESSENTIAL TREMOR

International Essential Tremor Foundation
(888) 387-3667

ETHICS

Joseph and Rose Kennedy Institute of Ethics, National Reference Center for Bioethics Literature
(800) 633-3849
9:00 a.m.–5:00 p.m., Monday, Wednesday, Thursday, Friday (academic year only); 9:00 a.m.–8:00 p.m., Tuesday; 10:00 a.m.–3:00 p.m., Saturday, except summers and holidays. 9:00 a.m.–5:00 p.m. during the summer.

Health Information Toll-Free Numbers

FIRE PREVENTION

National Fire Protection Association
(800) 344-3555 (Customer Service)
7:30 a.m.–8 p.m.

FITNESS

Aerobics and Fitness Foundation of America
(800) 446-2322 (For Professionals)
(800) 968-7263 (Consumer Hotline)
7:00 a.m.–6:00 p.m.

American Council on Exercise
(800) 825-3636

American Running Association
(800) 776-2732
9:00 a.m.–5:00 p.m.

Consumer Fitness Hotline
(800) 529-8227 (Recording)
8:00 a.m.–5:00 p.m. (Pacific time)

National Institute of Diabetes and Digestive and Kidney Diseases (NIDDK)
The Weight Control Information Network
(877) 946-4627

TOPS Club, Inc.
(800) 932-8677
8:00 a.m.–4:30 p.m., Monday–Friday (central time); Recorded message after hours and on weekends.

YMCA of the USA
(800) 872-9622
8:30 a.m.–5:00 p.m. (central time)

FOOD SAFETY

Center for Food Safety
(888) SAFEFOOD
12:00 p.m.-4:00 p.m.

GAY, LESBIAN, BISEXUAL, TRANSGENDER HEALTH

Foster Care Helpline
(866) 542-8336 x350
6:00 a.m.–2:30 p.m., Monday–Friday (Pacific time); Messages may be left 24 hours.

Gay, Lesbian, Bisexual, and Transgender Helpline
(888) 340-4528
3:00 p.m.–8:00 p.m., Monday–Friday; 2:00 p.m.–7:00 p.m., Saturday (Pacific time)

Gay & Lesbian National Hotline
(888) 843-4564
7:00 p.m.–9:00 p.m., Monday–Friday, 9:00 a.m.–2:00 p.m., Saturday, (Pacific time)
Gay and Lesbian Victims' Assistance Hotline

Health Information Toll-Free Numbers

(800) 259-1536
24 hour hotline

The Peer Listening Line
(800) 399-7337
8:00 p.m.–1:00 a.m., Monday–Friday (Pacific time)

The Trevor Helpline
(800) 850-8078
24-hour confidential hotline

Youth Legal Information Line
(800) 528-3257
9:00 a.m.–5:00 p.m., Monday–Friday (Pacific time)

GENERAL HEALTH

Agency for Healthcare Research and Quality Clearinghouse
(800) 358-9295
8:00 a.m.–5:00 p.m.

Air Lifeline
(877) AIR-LIFE
7:30 a.m.–4:30 p.m. (Pacific time)

American Chiropractic Association
(800) 986-4636
8:30 a.m.–5:30 p.m.

American Osteopathic Association
(800) 621-1773
8:30 a.m.–4:30 p.m. (central time)

American Podiatric Medical Association, Inc.
(800) 366-8227 (Recording)

Health Resources and Services Administration (HRSA) Information Center
(888) 275-4772

MedicAlert Foundation
(800) 432-5378

Mercy Medical Airlift/National Patient Travel Center
(800) 296-1217
9:00 a.m.–5:00 p.m. (eastern time)

National Center for Complementary and Alternative Medicine Clearinghouse
(888) 644-6226 (Voice, TTY, and faxback)
8:30 a.m.–5:00 p.m., Monday–Friday (eastern time)

National Health Information Center
(800) 336-4797
9:00 a.m.–5:30 p.m., Monday–Friday (eastern time)

Health Information Toll-Free Numbers

National Health Service Corps
(800) 221-9393 Scholarships/Loan Repayment & Job Opportunities in underserved areas
8:30 a.m.–5:00 p.m. (eastern time)

National Hispanic Family Health Helpline
(866) SU-FAMILIA (783-2645)
9:00 a.m.–6:00 p.m., Monday–Friday (eastern time)

Office for Civil Rights
(800) 368-1019 (Recording)
(800) 527-7697 (TDD)

U.S. Food and Drug Administration
(888) 463-6332
(800) 332-1088 (MedWatch)
(800) 532-4440 (Consumer Inquiries)

Well Spouse Foundation
(800) 838-0879
9:00 a.m.–5:00 p.m.
24-hour recording – leave message

GENETIC DISEASES

Genetic and Rare Diseases Information Center
(888) 205-2311
(888) 205-3223 (TTY)
12:00 p.m.–6:00 p.m., Monday–Friday (eastern time)

HEADACHE/HEAD INJURY

American Council for Headache Education
(800) 255-2243
8:00 a.m.–5:00 p.m., Monday–Friday (eastern time)

Brain Injury Association, Inc.
(800) 444-6443 (Family Helpline)
9:00 a.m.–5:00 p.m.

National Headache Foundation
(888) 643-5552
9:00 a.m.–5:00 p.m. (central time)

HEARING AND SPEECH

American Society for Deaf Children
(800) 942-2732

American Speech-Language-Hearing Association
(800) 638-8255
8:30 a.m.–5:00 p.m. (eastern time)

Health Information Toll-Free Numbers

DB-LINK
(National Information Clearinghouse on Children Who Are Deaf-Blind)
(800) 438-9376
(800) 854-7013 (TTY)
9:00 a.m.–5:00 p.m. (eastern time)

Dial A Hearing Screening Test (Occupational Hearing Services)
(800) 222-3277 (Voice/TTY)
9:00 a.m.–5:00 p.m., Monday–Friday (eastern time)

The Ear Foundation at Baptist Hospital
(800) 545-4327
8:30 a.m.–4:30 p.m. (central time), or leave recorded message after hours.

Hear Now
(800) 648-4327 (Voice/TDD)
9:00 a.m.–4:00 p.m. (mountain time)

John Tracy Clinic
(800) 522-4582 (Voice/TDD)
8:00 a.m.–4:00 p.m., Monday–Friday (Pacific time)
Leave recorded message after hours.

International Hearing Society
(800) 521-5247 (Recording)
10:00 a.m.–4:00 p.m.

National Family Association for Deaf-Blind
(800) 255-0411, x 224
8:45 a.m.–4:30 p.m., Monday–Friday (eastern time)

National Institute on Deafness and Other Communication Disorders Information Clearinghouse
(800) 241-1044
(800) 241-1055 (TTY)
8:30 a.m.–5:00 p.m., Monday–Friday (eastern time)

Vestibular Disorders Association
(800) 837-8428
24-hour answering machine

HEART DISEASE

American Heart Association
(800) 242-8721
6:00 a.m.–12:00 p.m.

Heart Information Service
(800) 292-2221
7:00 a.m.–6:00 p.m. (central time), or leave a recorded message after hours.

National Heart, Lung, and Blood Institute Health Information Center
(800) 575-9355 (High Blood Pressure and Cholesterol Information Hotline)

24-hour recording of information on high blood pressure and high blood cholesterol in English and Spanish.
HISTIOCYTOSIS

Health Information Toll-Free Numbers

See RARE DISEASES/DISORDERS

HOMELESSNESS

National Resource Center on Homelessness and Mental Illness
(800) 444-7415
8:30 a.m.–5:00 p.m.

HORMONAL DISORDERS

Thyroid Foundation of America, Inc.
(800) 832-8321
8:30 a.m.–4:00 p.m.
The Thyroid Society for Education and Research
(800) 849-7643
8:00 a.m.–4:00 p.m. (Central)

HOSPITAL/HOSPICE CARE

Children's Hospice International
(800) 242-4453
9:00 a.m.–5:30 p.m., Monday–Friday (eastern time)

Hill-Burton Free Medical Care Program
(800) 638-0742
(800) 492-0359 (in MD)
9:30 a.m.–5:30 p.m., or leave a recorded message after hours.

National Association of Hospital Hospitality Houses, Inc.
(800) 542-9730
8:30 a.m.–5:00 p.m., Monday–Friday (eastern time)

National Hospice Organization
(800) 658-8898
9:00 a.m.–5:00 p.m.

Shriners Hospital Referral Line
(800) 237-5055
8:00 a.m.–5:00 p.m. (central time)

HOUSING

See also CHEMICAL PRODUCTS/PESTICIDES and LEAD
Housing and Urban Development User
(800) 245-2691
(800) 483-2209 (TDD)
8:30 a.m.–5:15 p.m.

HUNTINGTON'S DISEASE

See RARE DISEASES/DISORDERS

Health Information Toll-Free Numbers

IMMUNIZATION

CDC Immunization Hotline
(800) 232-7468 (24-hour recording)
8:00 a.m.–11:00 p.m.

IMPOTENCE

Impotence Information Center
(800) 843-4315
8:30 a.m.–5:00 p.m., Monday–Friday (central time), or leave a recorded message after hours.

INSURANCE/MEDICARE/MEDICAID

DHHS Inspector General's Hotline
(800) 447-8477
8:00 a.m.–5:00 p.m.

Insure Kids Now! Health Resources and Services Administration
(877) 543-7669
8:00 a.m.–5:00 p.m., Monday–Friday (eastern time)

Medicare Issues Hotline
(800) 633-4227
(800) 820-1202 (TDD/TTY)
8:00 a.m.–8:00 p.m. (central time)

Pension Benefit Guaranty Corporation
(800) 400-7242
8:00 a.m.–5:00 p.m.

Social Security Administration
(800) 772-1213
7:00 a.m.–7:00 p.m.

JUSTICE

National Criminal Justice Reference Service (NCJRS)
(800) 851-3420
8:30 a.m.–7:00 p.m. Leave recorded message after hours.

KIDNEY DISEASE

See UROLOGICAL DISORDERS

LEAD

See also HOUSING
National Lead Information Center
(800) 532-3394 (Hotline)
(800) 877-8339 (TDD)
(800) 424-5323 (Clearinghouse)
8:30 a.m.–6:00 p.m.

Health Information Toll-Free Numbers

LEARNING DISORDERS

Children and Adults with Attention Deficit Disorders (C.H.A.D.D.)
(800) 233-4050
8:00 a.m.–5:30 p.m., Monday–Friday

The Orton Dyslexia Society
(800) 222-3123 (Recording and mail box)

LIBRARY SERVICES

Captioned Media Program, The National Association for the Deaf
(800) 237-6213
(800) 237-6819 (TTY)
(800) 538-5636 (Fax)
8:30 a.m.–5:00 p.m., Monday–Friday (eastern time)

National Library of Medicine, National Institutes of Health
(888) 346-3656

National Library Service for the Blind and Physically Handicapped
(800) 424-8567
8:00 a.m.–4:30 p.m.

Recording for the Blind and Dyslexic
(800) 221-4792
8:30 a.m.–4:30 p.m.

LIVER DISEASES

American Liver Foundation
(800) 223-0179
9:00 a.m.–5:00 p.m.

Hepatitis Foundation International
(800) 891-0707
9:00 a.m.–5:00 p.m., Monday–Friday (eastern time)

LUNG DISEASE/ASTHMA/ALLERGY

American Lung Association
(800) 586-4872
(800) 528-2971 (Living Bank)
8:30 a.m.–4:30 p.m.

Asthma and Allergy Foundation of America
(800) 7-ASTHMA (727-8462)
7:00 a.m.–Midnight. Provides recording when not in operation.

Asthma Information Line
(800) 822-2762

Health Information Toll-Free Numbers

National Jewish Medical and Research Center
(800) 222-5864 (LUNG LINE)
(800) 552-5864 (LUNG FACTS)
8:00 a.m.–5:00 p.m., Monday–Friday (mountain time)
LUNG FACTS, a companion to LUNG LINE, is a 24-hour, 7-days-a-week automated information service.

MATERNAL AND INFANT HEALTH

Genetic Alliance
(800) 336-4363
9:00 a.m.–5:00 p.m. (eastern time)

La Leche League International
(800) La Leche (525-3243)
9:00 a.m.–3:00 p.m. (central time)

National Fragile X Foundation
(800) 688-8765
9:00 a.m.–5:00 p.m. (Pacific time)

National Life Center/Pregnancy Hotline
(800) 848-5683

Prenatal Care Hotline
(800) 311-2229 (English)
(800) 504-7081 (Spanish)
8:30 a.m.–5:00 p.m.

MEDICARE/MEDICAID

See INSURANCE/MEDICARE/MEDICAID

MENTAL HEALTH

See also CHILD ABUSE/MISSING CHILDREN/MENTAL HEALTH
American Academy of Child & Adolescent Psychiatry
(800) 333-7636
8:30 a.m.–5:00 p.m., Monday–Friday (eastern time)

The ARC of the United States
(800) 433-5255
8:30 a.m.–5:30 p.m.

National Alliance for the Mentally Ill
(800) 950-6264 Helpline

National Council on Problem Gambling
(800) 522-4700

National Foundation for Depressive Illness
(800) 239-1265 (Recording)

National Gaucher Foundation
(800) 925-8885
9:00 a.m.–5:00 p.m., Monday–Friday (eastern time)
National Hopeline Network

Health Information Toll-Free Numbers

(800) SUICIDE (784-2433)
24 hours

National Mental Health Association
(800) 969-6642
(800) 433-5959 (TTY)
9:00 a.m.–5:00 p.m., (eastern time)

SAMHSA's National Mental Health Information Center
(800) 789-2647
8:30 a.m.–5:00 p.m., Monday–Friday (eastern time)

MINORITY HEALTH

Office of Minority Health Resource Center
(800) 444-6472
8:30 a.m.—5:00 p.m.

NUTRITION

American Dietetic Association's Consumer Nutrition Hotline
(800) 366-1655
9:00 a.m.–4:00 p.m. (central time)
TDD available.

American Institute for Cancer Research
(800) 843-8114
9:00 a.m.–5:00 p.m., Monday–Friday (eastern time)

National Dairy Council
(800) 426-8271
(800) 974-6455 (Fax)
8:00 a.m.–5:00 p.m. (central time)

ORAL HEALTH

American Dental Association
(800) 947-4746
(800) 621-8099 (Public Information)
7:00 a.m.–5:00 p.m. (central time)

ORGAN DONATION

See also VISION and UROLOGICAL DISORDERS
The Living Bank
(800) 528-2971
7:30 a.m.–4:30 p.m. (central time)

National Marrow Donor Program®
(800) 627-7692

United Network for Organ Sharing
(888) TXINFO1
24 hours

PARALYSIS AND SPINAL CORD INJURY

Health Information Toll-Free Numbers

See also STROKE
Christopher Reeve Paralysis Association
(800) 225-0292
9:00 a.m.–5:00 p.m.

National Rehabilitation Information Center (NARIC)
(800) 346-2742 (Voice/TDD)
9:00 a.m.–5:00 p.m., Monday–Friday (eastern time)

National Stroke Association
(800) 787-6537
9:00 a.m.–5:00 p.m.

Paralyzed Veterans of America
(800) 424-8200
(800) 232-1782 Healthcare Hotline
(800) 416-7622 (TDD)
9:00 a.m.–5:00 p.m., Monday–Friday (eastern time)

PARKINSON'S DISEASE

American Parkinson's Disease Association
(800) 223-2732
9:00 a.m.–5:00 p.m.
Leave recorded message after hours.

National Parkinson Foundation, Inc.
(800) 327-4545
8:00 a.m.–5:00 p.m., Monday–Friday (eastern time); recorded messages at all other times.

Parkinson's Disease Foundation
(800) 457-6676
9:00 a.m.–5:00 p.m., Monday-Friday

PESTICIDES

See CHEMICAL PRODUCTS/PESTICIDES

PRACTITIONER REPORTING

USP Practitioners Reporting Network
(800) 487-7776
(800) 233-7767 (Medication error)
Recording operates 24 hours a day; staff available 9:00 a.m.–4:30 p.m., Monday–Friday. Medication error telephone number records information 24 hours a day.

PREGNANCY/MISCARRIAGE

Bradley Method of Natural Childbirth
(800) 422-4784
9:00 a.m.–5:00 p.m. (Pacific time).
Leave recorded message after hours.

Health Information Toll-Free Numbers

DES Action USA
(800) 337-9288
9:00 a.m.–4:00 p.m. (Pacific time)

International Childbirth Education Association
(800) 624-4934 (Book Center orders)
8:00 a.m.–4:30 p.m. (central time)
Summers: 8:00 a.m.–1:00 p.m., Fridays

Lamaze International
(800) 368-4404
9:00 a.m.–5:00 p.m., Monday–Friday (eastern time)

Liberty Godparent Home
(800) 542-4453
8:00 a.m.–4:30 p.m.
24-hour hotline
National Abortion Federation
(800) 772-9100
9:00 a.m.–7:00 p.m.

PROFESSIONALS

ADA Information Center/National Center for Disability Services
(800) 949-4232
8:30 a.m.–5:00 p.m.

The Alliance for Aging Research
(800) 639-2421
9:00 a.m.–5:00 p.m., 24-hour voice mail

American Academy of Allergy, Asthma and Immunology
(800) 822-2762 (central time)

American Academy of Ophthalmology
(800) 222-3937
8:00 a.m.–4:00 p.m. (Pacific time)

American Alliance for Health, Recreation, Physical Education, and Dance
(800) 213-7198
8:00 a.m.–4:30 p.m. (eastern time)

American Association for Health Education
(800) 213-7198
8:00 a.m.–4:30 p.m. (eastern time)

American Association of Critical Care Nurses
(800) 899-2226
7:30 a.m.–4:30 p.m. (Pacific time)

American Council for the Blind
(800) 424-8666
9:00 a.m.–5:00 p.m.

Health Information Toll-Free Numbers

American Counseling Association
(800) 347-6647
8:00 a.m.–6:00 p.m.

American Nurses Association
(800) 274-4ANA
9:00 a.m.–5:00 p.m.

American Occupational Therapy Association
(800) 729-2682
(800) 377-8555 (TDD)
(800) 701-7735 (Fax-on-Request)

American School Food Service Association
(800) 877-8822
8:30 a.m.–5:30 p.m., Monday–Friday (eastern time)

Aplastic Anemia and MDS International Foundation, Inc.
(800) 747-2820
9:00 a.m.–5:00 p.m., Monday–Friday (eastern time)

Arthritis National Research Foundation
(800) 588-2873
8:30 a.m.–5:00 p.m. (Pacific time)

Association for Applied Psychophysiology and Biofeedback
(800) 477-8892
8:00 a.m.–5:00 p.m. (mountain time)

Association of American Physicians and Surgeons
(800) 635-1196
8:00 a.m.–6:00 p.m. (mountain time)

Association of Operating Room Nurses
(800) 755-2676
8:00 a.m.–4:30 p.m. (mountain time)

Center for Substance Abuse Treatment, SAMHSA
(800) 662-4357

College of American Pathologists
(800) 323-4040
8:30 a.m.–5:00 p.m. (central time)

Dystonia Medical Research Foundation
(800) 377-3978
9:00 a.m.–5:00 p.m., Monday–Friday (central time)

Federal Emergency Management Agency
(800) 879-6076
8:00 a.m.–4:30 p.m.

Federal Information Center, GSA
(800) 688-9889
(800) 326-2996 (TTY)
9:00 a.m.–8:00 p.m.

Health Information Toll-Free Numbers

For Kids Sake, Inc.
(800) 898-4543
9:00 a.m.–5:00 p.m. (central time)

Glaucoma Research Foundation
(800) 826-6693
9:00 a.m.–5:00 p.m. (Pacific time)

Immune Deficiency Foundation
(800) 296-4433
9:00 a.m.–5:00 p.m.

International Childbirth Education Association
(800) 624-4934
8:30 a.m.–4:30 p.m. (central time)

International Chiropractors Association
(800) 423-4690
9:00 a.m.–5:30 p.m.

Leukemia & Lymphoma Society, The
(800) 955-4572
9:00 a.m.–6:00 p.m., Monday–Friday (eastern time)

Lighthouse International Center for Education, Information, and Resource Services
(800) 829-0500
9:00 a.m.–8 p.m., Monday–Friday (eastern time)

Medical Institute for Sexual Health
(800) 892–9484 (publication orders only)
8:15 a.m.-5:00 p.m. (central time)

National Center for HIV, STD, and TB Prevention, Centers for Disease Control and Prevention
(888) CDC-FACT (232-3228)

National Child Care Information Center, ACF
(800) 616-2242
(800) 516-2242 (TTY)
(800) 716-2242 (Fax)
8:30 a.m.–5:30 p.m., Wednesdays, 8:30 a.m.-8:00 p.m.

National Clearinghouse of Rehabilitation Training Materials
(800) 223-5219
8:00 a.m.–5:00 p.m. (central time)

National Institute for Occupational Safety and Health (NIOSH), CDC
(800) 356-4674
8:00 a.m.–4:00 p.m. (eastern time)

National Jewish Medical and Research Center
(800) 222-5864
8:00 a.m.–5:00 p.m. (mountain time)

Health Information Toll-Free Numbers

National Pediculosis Association
(800) 446-4672
8:30 a.m.–4:30 p.m., 24-hour voice mail

National Prevention Information Network
(800) 458-5231
9:00 a.m.–6:00 p.m.

National Resource Center on Domestic Violence
(800) 537-2238
(800) 553-2508 (TTY)
8:00 a.m.–5:00 p.m., 24-hour voice mail

National Technical Information Service
(800) 553-6847
8:00 a.m.–6:00 p.m.
Office of National Drug Control Policy
(800) 666-3332
8:30 a.m.–5 :15 p.m.

Prevent Child Abuse America
(800) 556-2722 (Recording)

Research to Prevent Blindness
(800) 621-0026
9:00 a.m.–5:00 p.m.

RADIATION

National Association of Radiation Survivors
(800) 798-5102
9:00 a.m.–5:00 p.m. (Pacific time)

*RARE DISEASES/DISORDERS**

*A rare disorder is defined as a disorder that affects less than 1 percent of the population at any given time.
American Behcet's Disease Association
(800) 723-4238
9:00 a.m.–5:00 p.m. (Pacific time)

American Cleft Palate-Craniofacial Association/Cleft Palate Foundation
(800) 242-5338 (Parent Hotline Only)

American Leprosy Missions (Hansen's Disease)
(800) 543-3135
8:00 a.m.–5:00 p.m., Monday–Friday (eastern time)

American SIDS Institute
(800) 232-7437
9:00 a.m.–5:00 p.m. (eastern time); Leave recorded message after hours (staff on call 24 hours, 7 days a week).

Health Information Toll-Free Numbers

Amyotrophic Lateral Sclerosis Association (ALS, Lou Gehrig's Disease)
(800) 782-4747
7:30 a.m.–4:00 p.m. (Pacific time)
Leave a recorded message after hours.

Batten's Disease Support and Research Association
(800) 448-4570
8:00 a.m.–5:00 p.m. 24-hour recording

Charcot-Marie-Tooth Association
(800) 606-2682
9:00 a.m.–5:00 p.m., Monday–Friday (eastern time)

CFIDS Association of America, The
(800) 442-3437

Cooley's Anemia Foundation
(800) 522-7222
9:00 a.m.–5:00 p.m.

Cornelia de Lange Syndrome Foundation, Inc.
(800) 223-8355
(800) 753-2357 (U.S. and Canada)
8:00 a.m.–5:00 p.m. (eastern time)
Leave a recorded message after hours.

Cystic Fibrosis Foundation
(800) 344-4823
8:30 a.m.–5:30 p.m.

Epilepsy Foundation
(800) 332-4050 (National Epilepsy Library)
(800) 332-1000
(800) 213-5821 (Publications)
9:30 a.m.–5:00 p.m., Monday–Friday (eastern time)

Epilepsy Information Service
(800) 642-0500 (voice mail after hours)
8:00 a.m.–5:00 p.m.

Fibromyalgia Network
(800) 853-2929
8:00 a.m.–4:00 p.m., Monday–Thursday (mountain time)

Genetic and Rare Diseases Information Center
(888) 205-2311
(888) 205-3223 (TTY)
12:00 p.m.–6:00 p.m., Monday–Friday (eastern time)

Histiocytosis Association of America
(800) 548-2758
9:00 a.m.–4:30 p.m., Monday–Friday (eastern time)
Voice mail after hours.

Health Information Toll-Free Numbers

Huntington's Disease Society of America, Inc.
(800) 345-4372
9:00 a.m.–5:00 p.m., Monday–Friday (eastern time)

International Rett Syndrome Association
(800) 818-7388
9:00 a.m.–5:00 p.m., Monday–Friday (eastern time)

Lupus Foundation of America
(800) 558-0121 (English)
(800) 558-0231 (Spanish)

Les Turner Amyotrophic Lateral Sclerosis Foundation, Ltd.
(888) ALS-1107
8:00 a.m.–5:00 p.m. (central time)

Multiple Sclerosis Association of America
(800) 532-7667
9:00 a.m.–5:00 p.m., Monday–Thursday

Multiple Sclerosis Foundation
(800) 441-7055
8:30 a.m.–7:00 p.m., Monday–Friday (eastern time)

Muscular Dystrophy Association
(800) 572-1717
9:00 a.m.–5:00 p.m. (mountain time)

Myasthenia Gravis Foundation
(800) 541-5454
8:45 a.m.–4:45 p.m. (central time)

National Down Syndrome Congress
(800) 232-6372
9:00 a.m.–5:30 p.m. Recording after hours.

National Down Syndrome Society Hotline
(800) 221-4602
9:00 a.m.–5:00 p.m.

National Hansen's Disease Programs
(800) 642-2477
8:00 a.m.–4:30 p.m. (central time)

National Hemophilia Foundation
(888) 463-6643
9:00 a.m.–5:00 p.m.
Summer: 9 a.m.–5:30 p.m., Monday-Thursday, 9:00 a.m.–3:00 p.m., Friday

National Institute of Arthritis and Musculoskeletal and Skin Diseases Information Clearinghouse
(877) 226-4267
8:30 a.m.–5:00 p.m. (eastern time)

Health Information Toll-Free Numbers

National Jewish Medical and Research Center
(800) 222-5864 (LUNG LINE)
(800) 552-5864 (LUNG FACTS)
8:00 a.m.–5:00 p.m. (mountain time)
LUNG FACTS, a companion to LUNG LINE, is a 24-hour, 7-days-a-week automated information service.

National Lymphedema Network
(800) 541-3259
8:00 a.m.–5:00 p.m. (Pacific time)
Leave recorded message.

National Marfan Foundation
(800) 8-MARFAN
8:00 a.m.–4:00 p.m.

National Multiple Sclerosis Society
(800) 344-4867
9:00 a.m.–5:00 p.m.

National Neurofibromatosis Foundation
(800) 323-7938
9:00 a.m.–5:00 p.m.
National Organization for Albinism and Hypopigmentation
(800) 473-2310
24-hour Voicemail

National Organization for Rare Disorders
(800) 999-6673
9:00 a.m.–5:00 p.m.
Leave recorded message after hours.

National Reye's Syndrome Foundation
(800) 233-7393
8:00 a.m.–5:00 p.m., Monday–Friday (eastern time)
Leave recorded message after hours.

National Sjogren's Syndrome Association
(800) 395-6772
9:00 a.m.–3:00 p.m.

National Spasmodic Torticollis Association
(800) 487-8385
9:00 a.m.–5:00 p.m., Monday–Friday (Pacific time)

National Tuberous Sclerosis Association
(800) 225-6872
8:30 a.m.–5:00 p.m.

Neurofibromatosis, Inc.
(800) 942-6825
24-hour message line

Office of Orphan Products Development, Food and Drug Administration
(800) 300-7469
8:30 a.m.–4:30 p.m., Monday–Friday (eastern time)
Osteogenesis Imperfecta Foundation, Inc.

Health Information Toll-Free Numbers

(800) 981-2663
9:00 a.m.–5:00 p.m., Monday–Friday (eastern time)

Paget Foundation for Paget's Disease of Bone and Related Disorders, The
(800) 237-2438
9:00 a.m.–5:00 p.m.

Prader-Willi Syndrome Association
(800) 926-4797
9:00 a.m.–7:00 p.m.

Restless Legs Syndrome Foundation
(877) 463-6757

Scleroderma Foundation
(800) 722-4673
8:30 a.m.–5:00 p.m. (eastern time)

Sickle Cell Disease Association of America, Inc.
(800) 421-8453
8:30 a.m.–5:00 p.m. (Pacific time)
Recording after hours.

SIDS Alliance
(800) 221-7437
9:00 a.m.–5:00 p.m. (eastern time)

Sjogren's Syndrome Foundation, Inc.
(800) 475-6473 (voice mail only)
9:00 a.m.–5:00 p.m.

Spina Bifida Association of America
(800) 621-3141
9:00 a.m.–5:00 p.m.

Spondylitis Association of America
(800) 777-8189
8:00 a.m.–5:00 p.m. (Pacific time)
Leave recorded message after hours.

Sturge-Weber Foundation
(800) 627-5482
9:00 a.m.–3:00 p.m.

Support Organization for Trisomy 18, 13 and Related Disorders
(800) 716-7638
Leave recorded message.

Tourette Syndrome Association, Inc.
(800) 237-0717
9:00 a.m.–5:00 p.m.

Treacher Collins Foundation
(800) 823-2055

Health Information Toll-Free Numbers

Turner Syndrome Society of the United States
(800) 365-9944
9:00 a.m.–5:00 p.m., Monday–Friday (central time)

United Cerebral Palsy Association
(800) 872-5827
8:00 a.m.–5:30 p.m.

United Leukodystrophy Foundation
(800) 728-5483
8:30 a.m.–5:00 p.m., 7 days (central time)

Wegener's Granulomatosis Association
(800) 277-9474
8:30 a.m.–5:00 p.m., Monday–Friday (central time)

Wilson's Disease Association
(800) 399-0266 (voice mail)

REHABILITATION

See also DISABLING CONDITIONS and PARALYSIS AND SPINAL CORD INJURY
ABLEDATA
(800) 227-0216
8:00 a.m.–5:30 p.m., Monday–Friday, except Federal holidays (eastern time)

National Institute for Rehabilitation Engineering
(800) 736-2216
9:00 a.m.–5:00 p.m. (eastern time)

Phoenix Society for Burn Survivors
(800) 888-2876
9:00 a.m.–5:00 p.m.

United Ostomy Association
(800) 826-0826
6:30 a.m.–4:30 p.m., Monday–Thursday
6:30 a.m.–3:30 p.m., Friday (Pacific time)

RESTLESS LEGS SYNDROME

See RARE DISORDERS

SAFETY

See also CHEMICAL PRODUCTS/PESTICIDES
Clearinghouse for Occupational Safety and Health Information, National Institute for Occupational Safety and Health
(800) 356-4674
9:00 a.m.–4:00 p.m. (eastern time)

Danny Foundation, The
(800) 833-2669
8:30 a.m.–5:00 p.m. (Pacific time)

Health Information Toll-Free Numbers

National Childwatch
(800) 222-1464
7:00 a.m.–4:30 p.m.

National Highway Traffic Safety Administration Auto Safety Hotline
(800) 424-9393 (Recording)
(800) 424-9153 (TTY)
8:00 a.m.–10 p.m.

National Program for Playground Safety
(800) 554-7529
8:00 a.m.–5:00 p.m., (central time)

National Safety Council
(800) 621-7615
(800) 767-7236 (National Radon Hotline)
8:30 a.m.–4:45 p.m.

Office of Navigation Safety and Waterway Services, U.S. Coast Guard Customer Infoline
(800) 368-5647
(800) 689-0816 (TDD/TTY)
8:00 a.m.–4:00 p.m.

Safe Sitter
(800) 255-4089
8:30 a.m.–5:00 p.m., Monday–Friday (eastern time)

U.S. Consumer Product Safety Commission Hotline
(800) 638-2772
(800) 638-8270 (TDD)
24-hour messages

SEXUAL EDUCATION

Planned Parenthood Federation of America, Inc.
(800) 669-0156
(800) 230-7526 (Recording)
9:00 a.m.–5:00 p.m.

SEXUALLY TRANSMITTED DISEASES

See also AIDS/HIV
CDC National STD/AIDS Hotline
(800) 227-8922 English (STD)
(800) 342-2437 English (AIDS)
(800) 344-7432 (Spanish)
(800) 243-7889 (TTY)

English: 24 hours/7 days a week; Spanish: 8:00 a.m.–2:00 a.m., 7 days a week (eastern time); TTY:
10:00 a.m.–10:00 p.m., Monday–Friday (eastern time)

National Herpes Resource Center
(800) 230-6039
9:00 a.m.–7:00 p.m., Monday–Friday (eastern time)

Health Information Toll-Free Numbers

SKIN DISEASE

Foundation for Ichthyosis and Related Skin Types, Inc.
(800) 545-3286
9:00 a.m.–5:00 p.m. (eastern time)

National Institute of Arthritis and Musculoskeletal and Skin Diseases Information Clearinghouse
(877) 226-4267
8:30 a.m.–5:00 p.m., Monday–Friday (eastern time)

National Psoriasis Foundation
(800) 723-9166
8:00 a.m.–5:00 p.m. (Pacific time)

SPINAL CORD INJURY

See PARALYSIS AND SPINAL CORD INJURY

SMOKING

Office on Smoking and Health
(800) 232-1311 (Recording)

STROKE

See also PARALYSIS AND SPINAL CORD INJURY
American Heart Association Stroke Connection
(800) 553-6321
7:30 a.m.–7:00 p.m. (central time), Monday–Friday

National Institute of Neurological Disorders and Stroke
(800) 352-9424
8:30 a.m.–5:00 p.m., Monday–Friday (eastern time)

STUTTERING

National Center for Stuttering
(800) 221-2483
10:00 a.m.–5:00 p.m.

Stuttering Foundation of America, The
(800) 992-9392
9:00 a.m.–5:00 p.m. (eastern time)

SUBSTANCE ABUSE

See also ALCOHOL ABUSE and DRUG ABUSE
National Inhalant Prevention Coalition
(800) 269-4237 (Recording)
8:00 a.m.–7:00 p.m. (central time)

SUDDEN INFANT DEATH SYNDROME

See RARE DISORDERS

SURGERY/FACIAL PLASTIC SURGERY

Health Information Toll-Free Numbers

American Society for Dermatologic Surgery, Inc.
(800) 441-2737 (Recording)
8:30 a.m.–5:00 p.m. (central time)

American Society of Plastic and Reconstructive Surgeons, Inc.
(800) 635-0635
8:00 a.m.–5:00 p.m. (central time)
Leave recorded message after hours.

Facial Plastic Surgery Information Service
(800) 332-3223
8:30 a.m.–5:30 p.m., Monday–Friday

SUICIDE PREVENTION HOTLINES

National Hopeline Network
(800) SUICIDE (784-2433)
24 hours

The Trevor Helpline
(800) 850-8078

The Trevor Helpline is a national toll-free suicide hotline for gay and questioning youth. It's open 24 hours a day, seven days a week, 365 days a year. Teens with nowhere to turn can call and talk to trained counselors, find local resources and take important steps on their way to becoming healthy adults.

TRAUMA

American Trauma Society (ATS)
(800) 556-7890
8:30 a.m.–4:30 p.m.

UROLOGICAL DISORDERS

American Association of Kidney Patients
(800) 749-2257
8:30 a.m.–5:00 p.m., Monday–Friday

American Foundation for Urologic Disease
(800) 242-2383 (Recording)
8:30 a.m.–5:00 p.m.

American Kidney Fund
(800) 638-8299
9:00 a.m.–5:00 p.m.

Health Care Services (National Kidney Foundation)
(800) 622-9010
8:30 a.m.–5:30 p.m.

Incontinence Information Center
(800) 843-4315
8:30 a.m.–5:00 p.m. (central time), or leave recorded message after hours
National Association for Continence
(800) 252-3337

Health Information Toll-Free Numbers

8:00 a.m.–5:00 p.m., Monday–Friday (eastern time)

PKD Foundation
(800) 753-2873
8:00 a.m.–5:00 p.m. (central time)
Prostate Information Center
(800) 543-9632
8:30 a.m.–5:00 p.m. (central time), or leave recorded message after hours

The Simon Foundation for Continence
(800) 237-4666 (24 hours)

VENEREAL DISEASES

See SEXUALLY TRANSMITTED DISEASES

VETERANS

National Veterans Services Fund, Inc.
(800) 521-0198
9:00 a.m.–4:00 p.m., Monday–Friday

Persian Gulf Veterans Information Helpline
(800) 749-8387
8:00 a.m.–4:00 p.m. (central time)

VISION

See also LIBRARY SERVICES and HEARING AND SPEECH
American Council of the Blind
(800) 424-8666
9:00 a.m.–5:00 p.m., Monday–Friday
2:00 p.m.–5:00 p.m. (to reach a staff person)

Better Vision Institute
(800) 424-8422
8:30 a.m.–5:00 p.m.

Blind Children's Center
(800) 222-3566
(800) 222-3567 (International calls)
8:00 a.m.–4:00 p.m. (Pacific time)

Braille Institute
(800) 272-4553
8:30 a.m.–5:00 p.m., Monday–Friday (Pacific time)

Foundation Fighting Blindness, The
(800) 683-5555
(800) 683-5551 (TDD)
9:00 a.m.–4:00 p.m., Monday–Friday (eastern time)

Health Information Toll-Free Numbers

Glaucoma Research Foundation
(800) 826-6693
9:00 a.m.–5:00 p.m. (Pacific time)

Guide Dog Foundation for the Blind, Inc.
(800) 548-4337
8:00 a.m.–5:00 p.m.

Guide Dogs for the Blind
(800) 295-4050
8:00 a.m.–5:00 p.m., Monday–Friday (Pacific time)

Lighthouse International Center for Education, Information, and Resource Services
(800) 829-0500
9:00 a.m.–8:00 p.m., Monday–Friday (eastern time)

Louisiana Center for the Blind
(800) 234-4166
8:00 a.m.–5:00 p.m. (central time)

National Alliance of Blind Students
(800) 424-8666
9:00 a.m.–5:00 p.m.

National Association for Parents of Children with Visual Impairments
(800) 562-6265 (Recording)
9:00 a.m.–5:00 p.m.

National Eye Care Project Helpline
(800) 222-3937
24 hours, 7 days a week

National Eye Research Foundation
(800) 621-2258
8:30 a.m.–5:00 p.m. (central time)
Leave recorded message after hours.

National Family Association for Deaf-Blind
(800) 255-0411, x224
8:45 a.m.–4:30 p.m., Monday–Friday (eastern time)

National Information Clearinghouse on Children Who Are Deaf-Blind (DB-LINK)
(800) 438-9376
(800) 854-7013 (TTY)
9:00 a.m.–5:00 p.m. (eastern time)

Prevent Blindness Center for Sight
(800) 331-2020
9:00 a.m.–5:00 p.m. (central time)

VIOLENCE

Gay and Lesbian Victims' Assistance Hotline
(800) 259-1536
24 hour hotline

Health Information Toll-Free Numbers

National Domestic Violence Hotline
(800) 799-7233
(800) 787-3224 (TDD)
National Organization for Victim Assistance
(800) 879-6682
24 hours

Rape, Abuse, and Incest National Network
(800) 656-4673

WOMEN

Endometriosis Association
(800) 992-3636 (Recording)

National Osteoporosis Foundation
(800) 223-9994
24 hours

National Women's Health Information Center
(800) 994-9662
(888) 220-5446 (TDD)
9:00 a.m.–6:00 p.m.

PMS Access
(800) 222-4767 (Recording)
7:30 a.m.–5:30 p.m. (central time)

Women's Health America Group
(800) 558-7046 (Recording)
8:30 a.m.–5:30 p.m. (central time)

Women's Sports Foundation
(800) 227-3988
9:00 a.m.–5:00 p.m.

TOLL-FREE NUMBERS FOR HEALTH INFORMATION · DIAL 1-800
(unless 877/888 is specified)

ACS, National Cancer Information Center, 227-2345 (Voice /TDD/TT)
ADA Information Center/National Center for Disability Services, 949-4232
ADA Technical Assistance Hotline, 466-4232
ADCARE Hospital Helpline, 252-6465
Aerobics and Fitness Foundation of America, 968-7263 (Consumers); 446-2322 (Professionals)
Agency for Healthcare Research and Quality Clearinghouse, 358-9295
AIDS Clinical Trials Information Service, 874-2572
Air Lifeline, (877) 247-5433
Al-Anon Family Group Headquarters, 425-2666
Alcohol and Drug Helpline, 821-4357
Alliance for Aging Research, The, 639-2421
Alzheimer's Association, 272-3900
Alzheimer's Disease Education and Referral Center, 438-4380
American Academy of Allergy, Asthma and Immunology, 822-2762

Health Information Toll-Free Numbers

American Academy of Child & Adolescent Psychiatry, 333-7636
American Academy of Ophthalmology, 222-3937
American Alliance for Health, Recreation, Physical Education and Dance, 213-7198
American Association for Health Education, 213-7198
American Association of Critical Care Nurses, 899-2226
American Association of Diabetes Educators, 832-6874
American Association of Kidney Patients, 749-2257
American Autoimmune Related Diseases Association, Inc., 598-4668
American Behcet's Disease Association, 723-4238
American Brain Tumor Association, 886-2282
American Chiropractic Association, 986-4636
American Cleft Palate-Craniofacial Association/Cleft Palate Foundation, 242-5338
American Council for Headache Education, 255-2243
American Council of the Blind, 424-8666
American Council on Alcoholism, 527-5344
American Council on Exercise, 825-3636
American Counseling Association, 347-6647
American Dental Association, 947-4746; 621-8099 (Public Information)
American Diabetes Association, 342-3472; 232-6733 (Fax Order Fulfillment)
American Dietetic Association's Consumer Nutrition Hotline, 366-1655
American Foundation for Urologic Disease, 242-2383
American Health Assistance Foundation, 437-2423
American Heart Association, 242-8721
American Heart Association Stroke Connection, 553-6321
American Institute for Cancer Research, 843-8114
American Juvenile Arthritis Organization, 283-7800
American Kidney Fund, 638-8299
American Leprosy Missions (Hansen's Disease), 543-3135
American Liver Foundation, 223-0179
American Lung Association, 586-4872; 528-2971 (Living Bank)
American Nurses Association, 274-4262
American Occupational Therapy Association, 729-2682; 377-8555 (TDD)
American Osteopathic Association, 621-1773
American Parkinson's Disease Association, 223-2732
American Podiatric Medical Association, Inc., 366-8227
American Running Association, 776-2732
American School Food Service Association, 877-8822
American SIDS Institute, 232-7437
American Society for Deaf Children, 942-2732
American Society for Dermatologic Surgery, Inc., 441-2737
American Society of Plastic and Reconstructive Surgeons, Inc. 635-0635
American Speech-Language-Hearing Association, 638-8255
American Trauma Society, 556-7890
Americans with Disabilities Act Hotline, 514-0301; 514-0383 (TTY)
Amyotrophic Lateral Sclerosis Association, 782-4747
Aplastic Anemia and MDS International Foundation, Inc., 747-2820
ARC of the United States, The, 433-5255
Arthritis Foundation: Arthritis Answers Information Hotline, 283-7800
Arthritis National Research Foundation, 588-2873
Association for Applied Psychophysiology and Biofeedback, 477-8892
Association of American Physicians and Surgeons, 635-1196
Association of Operating Room Nurses, 755-2676
Asthma and Allergy Foundation of America, 727-8462
Asthma Information Line, 822-2762
A-WAY-OUT, 292-9688

Health Information Toll-Free Numbers

Batten's Disease Support and Research Association, 448-4570
Bethany Christian Services, 238-4269
Better Vision Institute, 424-8422
Blind Children's Center, 222-3566
Bradley Method of Natural Childbirth, 422-4784
Braille Institute, 272-4553
Brain Injury Association, 444-6443
Brain Tumor Society, The, 770-TBTS
Calix Society, 398-0524
Cancer Hope Network, (877) 467-3638
Candlelighters Childhood Cancer Foundation, 366-2223
Captioned Media Program, National Association for the Deaf, The, 237-6213; 237-6819 (TTY); 538-5636 (Fax)
CDC Immunization Hotline, 232-7468
CDC National Prevention Information Network (NPIN), 458-5231; 243-7012 (TTY); (888) 282-7681 (Fax)
CDC National STD/AIDS Hotline, 227-8922 (STD/English); 342-2437 (AIDS/English); 344-7432 (Spanish); 243-7889 (TTY)
Center for Food Safety, (888) 723-3366
Center for Substance Abuse Treatment, SAMHSA, 662-4357
CFIDS Association of American, 442-3437
Charcot-Marie-Tooth Association, 606-2682
Child Find of America, Inc., 426-5678; 292-9688
CHILDHELP USA® Child Abuse Hotline, 4-A-24453; 2-A-24453 (TDD)
Children and Adults with Attention Deficit Disorder, 233-4050
Children of Alcoholics Foundation, 359-3623
Children's Craniofacial Association, 535-3643
Children's Hospice International, 242-4453
Christopher Reeve Paralysis Association, 225-0292
Clearinghouse for Occupational Safety and Health Information, 356-4674
College of American Pathologists, 323-4040
Consumer Fitness Hotline, 529-8227
Cooley's Anemia Foundation, 522-7222
Cornelia de Lange Syndrome Foundation, 223-8355; 753-2357
Covenant House Nineline, 999-9999
Crohn's and Colitis Foundation of America, Inc., 932-2423
Cystic Fibrosis Foundation, 344-4823
Danny Foundation, The, 833-2669
DB-Link, 438-9376; 854-7013 (TTY)
DES Action USA, DES-9288
DHHS Inspector General's Hotline, 447-8477
Dial A Hearing Screening Test, 222-3277 (Voice)
Drug-Free Workplace Helpline, WORKPLACE (967-5752)
Drug Help, 662-4357
Dystonia Medical Research Foundation, 377-3978
Ear Foundation at Baptist Hospital, The, 545-4327
Easter Seal Society, 221-6827
Eldercare Locator, 677-1116
Endometriosis Association, 992-3636
Epilepsy Foundation, 332-1000; 332-4050 (Library); 213-5821 (Publications)
Epilepsy Information Service, 642-0500
FACES: The National Craniofacial Association, 332-2373
Facial Plastic Surgery Information Service, 332-3223
Families of Spinal Muscular Atrophy, 886-1762
Federal Emergency Management Agency, 879-6076
Federal Information Center, GSA, 688-9889; 326-2996 (TTY)
Fibromyalgia Network, 853-2929

Health Information Toll-Free Numbers

Food Allergy and Anaphylaxis Network, The, 929-4040
For Kids Sake, Inc., 898-4543
Foster Care Helpline, (866) 542-8336 x350
Foundation Fighting Blindness, The, 683-5555; 683-5551 (TDD)
Foundation for Ichthyosis and Related Skin Types, Inc., 545-3286
Gay and Lesbian Victims' Assistance Hotline, 259-1536
Gay, Lesbian, Bisexual, and Transgender Helpline, (888) 340-4528
Gay & Lesbian National Hotline, (888) 843-4564
Genetic Alliance, 336-4363
Genetic and Rare Diseases Information Center, (888) 205-2311; (888) 205-3223 (TTY)
Girls and Boys Town National Hotline, 448-3000; 448-1833 (TDD)
Glaucoma Research Foundation, 826-6693
Guide Dog Foundation for the Blind, Inc., 548-4337
Guide Dogs for the Blind, 295-4050
Health Care Services (National Kidney Foundation), 622-9010
Health Resources and Services Administration Information Center, (888) 275-4772
Hear Now, 648-4327 (Voice/TDD)
Heart Information Service, 292-2221
Hepatitis Foundation International, 891-0707
Hill-Burton Free Medical Care Program, 638-0742; 492-0359 (in MD)
Histiocytosis Association of America, 548-2758
HIV/AIDS Treatment Information Service, 448-0440
Housing and Urban Development Drug Information and Strategy Clearinghouse, 955-2232
Housing and Urban Development User, 245-2691; 483-2209 (TDD)
Human Growth Foundation, 451-6434
Huntington's Disease Society of America, 345-4372
Immune Deficiency Foundation, 296-4433
Impotence Information Center, 843-4315
Incontinence Information Center, 843-4315
Indoor Air Quality Information Clearinghouse, 438-4318
Insure Kids Now, Health Resources and Services Administration, (877) 543-7669
International Childbirth Education Association, 624-4934 (orders only)
International Chiropractors Association, 423-4690
International Essential Tremor Foundation, (888) 387-3667
International Hearing Society, 521-5247
International Rett Syndrome Association, 818-7388
Job Accommodation Network, 232-9675 (Voice/TTY); 526-7234 (Voice/TTY)
John Tracy Clinic, 522-4582 (Voice/TDD)
Joseph and Rose Kennedy Institute of Ethics, 633-3849
Juvenile Diabetes Foundation International Hotline, 223-1138
Kidney Cancer Association, 850-9132
La Leche League International, 525-3243
Lamaze International, 368-4404
Les Turner Amyotrophic Lateral Sclerosis Foundation, Ltd., (888) 257-1107
Leukemia & Lymphoma Society, 955-4572
Liberty Godparent Home, 542-4453
Lighthouse International Center for Education, Information, and Resource Services 829-0500
Living Bank, The, 528-2971
Louisiana Center for the Blind, 234-4166
Lupus Foundation of America, 558-0121 (English); 558-0231 (Spanish)
Lyme Disease Foundation, Inc., 886-5963
MAGIC Foundation for Children's Growth, The, 362-4423
Medical Institute for Sexual Health, 892-9484
MedicAlert Foundation, 432-5378
Medicare Issues Hotline, 633-4227; 820-1202 (TDD/TTY)
Mercy Medical Airlift/National Patient Travel Center, 296-1217

Health Information Toll-Free Numbers

Multiple Sclerosis Association of America, 532-7667
Multiple Sclerosis Foundation, 441-7055
Muscular Dystrophy Association, 572-1717
Myasthenia Gravis Foundation, 541-5454
National Abortion Federation, 772-9100
National Adoption Center, 862-3678
National Alliance for the Mentally Ill, 950-6264
National Alliance of Blind Students, 424-8666
National Alliance of Breast Cancer Organizations, (888) 806-2226
National Association for Continence, 252-3337
National Association for Parents of Children with Visual Impairments, 562-6265
National Association for the Education of Young Children, 424-2460
National Association of Hospital Hospitality Houses, Inc., 542-9730
National Association of Radiation Survivors, 798-5102
National Bone Marrow Transplant Link, 546-5268
National Brain Tumor Foundation, 934-2873
National Cancer Institute Information Service, 422-6237
National Center for Chronic Disease Prevention and Health Promotion, (877) 232-3422
National Center for Complementary and Alternative Medicine Clearinghouse, (888) 644-6226 (Voice and TTY); (800) 531-1794 (Fax-back)
National Center for HIV, STD, and TB Prevention, CDC, (888) 232-3228
National Center for Missing and Exploited Children, 843-5678; 826-7653 (TDD)
National Center for Stuttering, 221-2483
National Child Care Information Center, 616-2242; 516-2242 (TTY); 716-2242 (Fax)
National Childwatch, 222-1464
National Clearinghouse for Alcohol and Drug Information, 729-6686; 487-4889 (TTY/TDD)
National Clearinghouse of Rehabilitation Training Materials, 223-5219
National Clearinghouse on Child Abuse and Neglect Information, 394-3366
National Council on Alcoholism and Drug Dependence, Inc., 622-2255
National Council on Problem Gambling, 522-4700
National Criminal Justice Reference Service, 851-3420
National Dairy Council, 426-8271; 974-6455 (Fax)
National Domestic Violence Hotline, 799-SAFE; 787-3224 (TDD)
National Down Syndrome Congress, 232-6372
National Down Syndrome Society Hotline, 221-4602
National Eye Care Project Helpline, 222-3937
National Eye Research Foundation, 621-2258
National Family Association for Deaf-Blind, 255-0411, x 224
National Fire Protection Association, 344-3555
National Foundation for Depressive Illness, 239-1265
National Fragile X Foundation, 688-8765
National Gaucher Foundation, 925-8885
National Hansen's Disease Programs, 642-2477
National Headache Foundation, (888) 643-5552
National Health Information Center, 336-4797
National Health Service Corps, 221-9393 (Scholarships/Loan Repayment & Job Opportunities in underserved areas)
National Heart, Lung, and Blood Institute Health Information Center, 575-9355 (High Blood Pressure and Cholesterol Information Hotline)
National Hemophilia Foundation, (888) 463-6643
National Herpes Resource Center, 230-6039
National Highway Traffic Safety Administration Auto Safety Hotline, 424-9393; 424-9153 (TTY)
National Hispanic Family Health Helpline, (866) 783-2645
National Hopeline Network, 784-2433
National Hospice Organization, 658-8898
National Information Center for Children and Youth With Disabilities, 695-0285 (Voice/TT)

Health Information Toll-Free Numbers

National Information Clearinghouse on Children Who Are Deaf-Blind, 438-9367; 854-7013 (TTY)
National Prevention Information Network, 458-5231
National Inhalant Prevention Coalition, 269-4237
National Institute for Rehabilitation Engineering, 736-2216
National Institute of Arthritis and Musculoskeletal and Skin Diseases Information Clearinghouse, (877) 226-4267
National Institute of Neurological Disorders and Stroke, 352-9424
National Institute on Aging Information Center, 222-2225; 222-4225 (TTY)
National Institute on Deafness and Other Communication Disorders Information Clearinghouse, 241-1044; 241-1055 (TT)
National Jewish Medical and Research Center, 552-5864 (LUNG FACTS); 222-5864 (LUNG LINE)
National Lead Information Hotline, 532-3394 (Hotline); 424--5323 (Clearinghouse); 877-8339 (TDD)
National Leigh's Disease Foundation, 819-2551
National Lekotek Center, 366-PLAY; 573-4446 (Voice and TTY)
National Library of Medicine, (888) 346-3656
National Library Service for the Blind and Physically Handicapped, 424-8567
National Life Center/Pregnancy Hotline, 848-5683
National Lymphedema Network, 541-3259
National Marfan Foundation, 862-7326
National Marrow Donor Program®, 627-7692
National Mental Health Association, 969-6642
National Multiple Sclerosis Society, 344-4867
National Neurofibromatosis Foundation, 323--7938
National Organization for Albinism and Hypopigmentation, 473--2310
National Organization for Rare Disorders, 999-6673
National Organization for Victim Assistance, 879-6682
National Organization on Fetal Alcohol Syndrome, 666-6327
National Parents Resource Institute for Drug Education Surveys, 279-6361; 853-7867 (Taped Drug Information)
National Parkinson Foundation, Inc., 327-4545
National Pediculosis Association, 446-4672
National Pesticide Information Center, 858-7378
National Program for Playground Safety, 554-7529
National Psoriasis Foundation, 723-9166
National Rehabilitation Information Center, 346-2742 (Voice/TDD)
National Resource Center on Domestic Violence, 537-2238
National Resource Center on Homelessness and Mental Illness, 444-7415
National Reye's Syndrome Foundation, 233-7393
National Runaway Switchboard, 621-4000; 621-0394 (TDD)
National Safety Council, 621-7615
National Sjogren's Syndrome Association, 395-6772
National Spasmodic Torticollis Association, 487-8385
National Spinal Cord Injury Association, 962-9629
National Stroke Association, 787-6537
National Technical Information Service, 553-6847
National Tuberous Sclerosis Association, 225-6872
National Veterans Services Fund, 521-0198
National Women's Health Information Center, 994-9662
National Youth Crisis Hotline, 448-4663
Neurofibromatosis, Inc., 942-6825
Office for Civil Rights, 368-1019; 527-7697 (TDD)
Office of Minority Health Resource Center, 444-6472
Office of National Drug Control Policy, 666-3332
Office of Navigation Safety and Waterway Services, U.S. Coast Guard Customer InfoLine, 368-5647, 689-0816 (TDD/TT)
Office of Orphan Products Development, Food and Drug Administration, 300-7469

Health Information Toll-Free Numbers

Office on Smoking and Health, 232-1311
Orton Dyslexia Society, The, 222-3123
Osteogenesis Imperfecta Foundation, 981-2663
Osteoporosis and Related Bone Diseases National Resource Center, 624-2663
Paget Foundation for Paget's Disease of Bone and Related Disorders, 237-2438
Paralyzed Veterans of America, 424-8200; 232-1782; 416-7622 (TDD)
Parkinson's Disease Foundation, 457-6676
Peer Listening Line, 399-7337
Pension Benefit Guaranty Corporation, 400-7242
Persian Gulf Veterans Information Helpline, 749-8387
Phoenix Society for Burn Survivors, 888-2876
Planned Parenthood Federation of America, 230-7526; 669-0156
PMS Access, 222-4767
PKD Foundation, 753-2873
Prader-Willi Syndrome Association, 926-4797
Prenatal Care Hotline, 311-2229
Prevent Blindness Center for Sight, 331-2020
Prevent Child Abuse America, 556-2722
Prostate Information Center, 543-9632
Project Inform HIV/AIDS Treatment Hotline, 822-7422
Rape, Abuse, and Incest National Network, 656-4673
Reach to Recovery Program, 227-2345
Recording for the Blind and Dyslexic, 221-4792
Research to Prevent Blindness, 621-0026
Restless Legs Syndrome Foundation, (877) 463-6757
Safe Drinking Water Hotline, 426-4791
Safe Sitter, 255-4089
SAMHSA's National Mental Health Information Center, 789-2647
Scleroderma Foundation, 722-4673
Scoliosis Association, 800-0669
Shriners Hospital Referral Line, 237-5055
Sickle Cell Disease Association of America, Inc., 421-8453
SIDS Alliance, 221-7437
SIDS Information Line, 505-2742
Simon Foundation for Continence, The, 237-4666
Sjogren's Syndrome Foundation, Inc., 475-6473
Social Security Administration, 772-1213
Spina Bifida Association of America, 621-3141
Spondylitis Association of America, 777-8189
Starlight Children's Foundation, 274-7827
Sturge-Weber Foundation, 627-5482
Stuttering Foundation of America, 992-9392
Support Organization for Trisomy 18, 13 and Related Disorders, 716-7638
Susan G. Komen Breast Cancer Foundation, 462-9273
Thyroid Foundation of America, Inc., 832-8321
Thyroid Society for Education and Research, The, 849-7643
TOPS Club, Inc., 932-8677
Tourette Syndrome Association, Inc., 237-0717
Treacher Collins Foundation, TCF-2055
Trevor Helpline, 850-8078
Turner Syndrome Society of the United States, 365-9944
United Cerebral Palsy Association, 872-5827
United Leukodystrophy Foundation, 728-5483
United Network for Organ Sharing, (888) 894-6361
United Ostomy Association, 826-0826
U.S. Consumer Product Safety Commission Hotline, 638-2772; 638-8270 (TDD)

Health Information Toll-Free Numbers

U.S. Environmental Protection Agency, 962-6215
U.S. Food and Drug Administration, 332-1088 (Medwatch); 532-4440 (Consumer Inquiries)
USP Practitioners Reporting Network, 487-7776; 233-7767 (Medication Error)
Us Too! International, 808-7866
Youth Legal Information Line, 528-3257
Vestibular Disorders Association, 837-8428
Vietnam Veterans Agent Orange Victims, 521-0198
Water Quality Association, 749-0234 (Consumer Information)
Wegener's Granulomatosis Association, Inc., 277-9474
Weight Control Information Network (WIN), The, (877) 946-4627
Well Spouse Foundation, 838-0879
Wilson's Disease Association, 399-0266
Women's Health America Group, 558-7046
Women's Sports Foundation, 227-3988
YMCA of the USA, 872-9622
Y-ME National Organization for Breast Cancer Information Support Program, 221-2141 (English), 986-9505 (Spanish)
Zero to Three: National Center for Infants, Toddlers and Families, 899-4301

"Source: 2003 Toll-Free Numbers for Health Information, National Health Information Center,
Office of Disease Prevention and Health Promotion, U.S. Department of Health and Human Services, Washington, DC."

HOSPITAL TELEPHONE DIRECTORY
2004 Edition

Please send _____ copy (ies) of the HOSPITAL TELEPHONE DIRECTORY at $104.00 each.
Shipping and Handling $7.00. Add sales tax where applicable.

☐ Check enclosed – Amount $ _____   Date _____

Name _____   Title _____

Institution/Company _____   Dept. _____

Address _____

City/State/Zip _____   Phone _____

Make check payable to: **UNICOL, Inc.**
Mail to: 655 N.W. 128th Street / P.O. Box 1690   Miami, FL 33168
Call: (305) 769-1808   •   Fax: (305) 769-1817   •   Web: unicol-publishing.com

- -

HOSPITAL TELEPHONE DIRECTORY
2004 Edition

Please send _____ copy (ies) of the HOSPITAL TELEPHONE DIRECTORY at $104.00 each.
Shipping and Handling $7.00. Add sales tax where applicable.

☐ Check enclosed – Amount $ _____   Date _____

Name _____   Title _____

Institution/Company _____   Dept. _____

Address _____

City/State/Zip _____   Phone _____

Make check payable to: **UNICOL, Inc.**
Mail to: 655 N.W. 128th Street / P.O. Box 1690   Miami, FL 33168
Call: (305) 769-1808   •   Fax: (305) 769-1817   •   Web: unicol-publishing.com

- -

HOSPITAL TELEPHONE DIRECTORY
2004 Edition

Please send _____ copy (ies) of the HOSPITAL TELEPHONE DIRECTORY at $104.00 each.
Shipping and Handling $7.00. Add sales tax where applicable.

☐ Check enclosed – Amount $ _____   Date _____

Name _____   Title _____

Institution/Company _____   Dept. _____

Address _____

City/State/Zip _____   Phone _____

Make check payable to: **UNICOL, Inc.**
Mail to: 655 N.W. 128th Street / P.O. Box 1690   Miami, FL 33168
Call: (305) 769-1808   •   Fax: (305) 769-1817   •   Web: unicol-publishing.com

Printed in the United States
16863LVS00001B/169-238